Readings in
CyberEthics

Second Edition

Edited by

Richard A. Spinello
Boston College

Herman T. Tavani
Rivier College

JONES AND BARTLETT PUBLISHERS
Sudbury, Massachusetts
BOSTON   TORONTO   LONDON   SINGAPORE

World Headquarters

Jones and Bartlett
  Publishers
40 Tall Pine Drive
Sudbury, MA 01776
978-443-5000
info@jbpub.com
www.jbpub.com

Jones and Bartlett
  Publishers Canada
2406 Nikanna Road
Mississauga, ON L5C 2W6
CANADA

Jones and Bartlett
  Publishers International
Barb House, Barb Mews
London W6 7PA
UK

Cover images © Photodisc and AbleStock

Library of Congress Cataloging-in-Publication Data

Readings in cyberethics / [edited by] Richard A. Spinello, Herman T.
Tavani.— 2nd ed.
    p. cm.
Includes bibliographical references.
  ISBN 0-7637-2410-6 (paperback)
  1. Computer networks—Moral and ethical aspects. I. Spinello, Richard
A. II. Tavani, Herman T.
  TK5105.5.R3722 2004
  175—dc22

                                    2003021673

Acquisitions Editor: Stephen Solomon
Production Manager: Amy Rose
Marketing Manager: Matthew Bennett
Editorial Assistant: Caroline Senay
Production Assistant: Tracey Chapman
Cover Design: Kristin E. Ohlin
Text Design: Anne Spencer
Composition: Dartmouth Publishing, Inc.
Printing and Binding: Malloy, Inc.
Cover Printing: Malloy, Inc.

Printed in the United States of America

08 07 06 05 04   10 9 8 7 6 5 4 3 2 1

For Michael, Marie, Michael, and Nicholas — R.A.S.

For my sisters: Marie, Joanne, Clare, Dolores, Sharon,
and Susan — H.T.T.

Preface to the Second Edition

The impetus for putting together this revised edition of the *Reader* is the rapid changes that continue to reshape the technical, social, legal, and moral landscape of cyberspace. For example, we have seen the diffusion of peer-to-peer architectures that make it easier to download digital music and movies. This has provoked the ire of the entertainment industry, which has retaliated by filing lawsuits against individuals accused of illegally distributing music over the Internet. Similarly, new systems such as facial recognition software are now being deployed to increase security, but those technologies run the risk of encroaching upon privacy rights. At the same time, there have been extraordinary legal developments—new laws like the Children's Internet Protection Act (CIPA) and various court decisions—defining new constraints for Web surfers and content distributors. The substance and pace of this change strongly suggest the need for this Second Edition.

In addition, as the field of information technology ethics continues to mature there is new scholarship that deserves a broad audience. Obviously, we cannot include all of this noteworthy new work, but we do include what we feel are the most significant contributions to this field that have been written within the last several years.

The second edition of *Readings in CyberEthics* includes fifty readings, sixteen of which are new to this edition. It also includes revisions to some of the cases included in the (forty-four) readings that comprised the first edition. Among the most notable changes in this edition are the following:

Chapter One: Two new readings have been added—"The Foundationalist Debate in Computer Ethics," and "Common Morality and Computing"—in order to provide more background material on ethical theory, especially as it applies to computers and information technology.

Chapter Two: Included in this chapter are a summary of the Children's Internet Protection Act and excerpts from the 2003 Supreme Court ruling that upheld the constitutionality of this controversial law; expanded and updated treatment of ISP liability issues in a new reading entitled, "Agents of Harm or Agents of Grace: The Legal and Ethical Aspects of Identifying Harm and Assigning Responsibility in a Networked World."

Chapter Three: A revised version of the DeCSS case, that covers the arguments and results of the appeal (*Universal* v. *Corley*, 2001); a new case study on the legality and ethical propriety of peer-to-peer networks such as KaZaA; expanded coverage of the open source software phenomenon with an essay called "Ethical Issues in Open Source Software."

Chapter Five: We have added three new timely readings on cyberterrorism, cyberstalking, and the use of facial recognition systems (a controversial form of biometric technology) in public places.

Chapter Six: We have substantially reorganized the material on professional and ethical responsibility, and have included seven new readings. Three of these focus on raising the level of ethical awareness among computer professionals: "Life Cycles of Computer and CyberEthics," "Unintentional Power in the Design of Computing Systems," and "The Wheel." We also include new essays concerned with risk assessment and the challenge of developing safe and reliable computer systems. Another key topic considered in this new material is the question of whether controversial research and development in fields such as nanocomputing should be allowed to continue in its present form, or should be regulated by some professional or governmental agency.

We have also expanded the discussion questions included in the introduction to each chapter and we continue to encourage readers to make ample use of the website that accompanies this book, along with its companion, *Cyberethics: Morality and Law in Cyberspace*. We will continue to update this Web site, www.jbpub.com/cyberethics, so that more current resources and articles are available to users of these books.

Acknowledgments

Once again, we express our gratitude to the contributors who graciously agreed to have their articles and essays included in this edition of the *Reader*. We also wish to thank Stephen Solomon, Amy Rose, Tracey Chapman, and others at Jones and Bartlett for their helpful support in getting the second edition of this volume to print.

R. A. *Spinello*
H. T. *Tavani*

Preface

In comparison to other areas of applied ethics, the field of computer ethics is just beginning to mature. During the past decade, new books, journals, and conferences have proliferated. There have been discussions and disagreements about computer ethics methodologies. At the same time, university curriculums now offer a wide variety of courses such as "Ethical Issues and Information Technology," "Information Ethics," and "The Internet and Society." One can even find more specialized seminars on topics such as Internet privacy. Related courses on cyberlaw and public policy are also becoming standard fare in law schools and schools of business or government.

The content of this relatively new field of applied ethics is quite dynamic, changing rapidly to reflect the impact of the Internet and the Web on our social, political, and legal institutions. As the Internet insinuates itself into the culture at large, arguably a new set of issues has emerged that were not extant ten years ago. Napster, open source code, spam, black holes, PICS, cookies, website hacking, weblining, framing and caching— these are just some of the terms that conjure up a new breed of ethical and social problems that must be carefully considered by moralists and policy makers. In many of these situations there are "policy vacuums," as Professor James Moor describes them, and ethical analysis is necessary in order to legitimize new policies, laws, or norms that will address these problems fairly and carefully.

Although we do not necessarily consider Internet ethics as a separate field of study from computer ethics, the focus among many scholars working in this field is clearly shifting to the novel challenges posed by living in an online world of ubiquitous networked communications. There are more serious and insidious threats to privacy, an understandable clamoring for some type of content controls to constrain purveyors of pornography, concerns about "cybersmears" from anonymous sources, and genuine confusion about the scope of intellectual property ownership.

Of course, the generic issues of privacy, speech, and intellectual property are certainly not new and have been amply covered in computer ethics texts for the past two decades. But the Internet has given them a new twist and steered current debates about computer ethics in new directions. Hence when we refer to Internet ethics we do not intend to imply or presume that this is a separate field of study from computer ethics. Rather, it is computer ethics with a narrower focus, because it excludes topics (such as software quality and reliability) that do not pertain to the Internet or the complications of living and working in a networked environment. We do, however, include a chapter on professional ethics that indirectly discusses some of these issues as they pertain to professional responsibility and professional codes of conduct.

Readings in CyberEthics has been compiled as a resource for those interested in doing research or teaching in this area of computer ethics that concentrates on the moral implications of the increasing ubiquity of the Internet. Can a measure of privacy be preserved on the Web? Does the Internet mean the end of copyright protection as we know it? Can government surveillance of criminals and civil liberties coexist in cyberspace? Is there a right to anonymous speech on the Internet? These are just some of the many vexing questions that surface here.

This book is a companion volume to *Cyberethics: Morality and Law in Cyberspace*, (Sudbury, MA: Jones and Bartlett, 2000), which is a short narrative about the salient social and moral issues triggered by the explosive growth of the Internet. The aim of this reader is to cover in more depth the topics and issues introduced in the *Cyberethics* book. It includes forty-four selections that deal with a number of cutting edge topics from different and often conflicting perspectives. The readings are organized to take the reader from a discussion on theoretical ethical issues and regulatory challenges to a treatment of four fundamental, interrelated issues of "cyberethics": *speech, property, privacy, and security.*

The readings will provide a more comprehensive coverage of these major topics, which have been introduced and concisely presented in *Cyberethics.* For example, the various readings on privacy will allow students to follow up on some of the key themes raised in the privacy chapter of *Cyberethics,* and to explore issues such as data mining, "cookie" technology, or workplace surveillance in much more depth. And the readings on intellectual property raise important philosophical questions about the legitimacy and scope of copyright protection. Other readings in this section will differ in focus as they consider topics such as the impact of the recent legislation on the fair use provision of the copyright law. Our final chapter includes readings that discuss important issues of professional responsibility and conduct for those employed in the computer and information professions.

These readings, which all have a publisher's date of 1996 or later, have been assembled from leading journals and periodicals, such as *Computers and Society, Communications of the ACM, Ethics and Information Technology,* and *The Information Society.* In our view, several of the selections, written by many of the leading scholars and teachers in computer and information ethics, will become classics in their respective fields. Each reading has been chosen for its timeliness, richness, and incisiveness, and because it reflects in some way the vibrancy and direction of these areas of study.

The readings have also been selected to offer a balanced overview of controversial issues. Thus, they present opposing viewpoints on matters ranging from the suitability of filtering pornographic speech to the advisability and risks of preserving anonymous speech in cyberspace. All of the readings present contemporary issues that are attuned to the realities of the complex commercial and social environment of the Internet. Our objective is to present conflicting and clashing opinions on many topics, which will enable students and other readers to engage in their own careful appraisals of the issues and to make their own enlightened and well-informed decisions.

While most of the selections have been authored by ethicists and philosophers active in this field, several contributions come from computer scientists and social scientists. Other contributions come from scholars in the legal profession and address the legal dimension of certain issues, such as intellectual property. These readings also raise broader concerns such as whether or not litigation and centralized regulation is the best way to control new technologies. Will judicial intervention or new regulations stymie innovation on the Net, or will it bring a necessary order and civility to interactions there? We include these readings because we believe it is critical to consider from a moral viewpoint how policy should be made in terms of changes to the structure of the Internet.

We envision several different audiences for this book. It is primarily a textbook for undergraduate and graduate courses or a supplementary text for specialized ethics seminars. It can stand on its own, or it can be used with the *Cyberethics* text that has already been published. In either case, it is most suitable for an entire course devoted to the topic of "Internet Ethics." It would also work quite well in the following areas: computer ethics courses; information ethics courses; business ethics courses; "technology and society" courses; information management, MIS, or computer science courses that contain an ethics module. The book could also be used in executive education courses in corporate or university settings that deal with ethics and policy issues on the Internet.

Moreover, the readings are interesting and provocative enough to merit the attention of general readers outside the academic environment. There are many thoughtful people who appreciate the complexity and significance of these issues. We hope that they, too, can get a deeper understanding of "cyberethics" by perusing the essays in this book.

Finally, we want to point out that a comprehensive website (www.jbpub.com/cyberethics) augments this text. It contains numerous links to additional readings and to other websites. The website also includes sample syllabi for courses organized around these readings, as well as some suggestions for "white paper" topics or other projects. This is an invaluable resource for students and others interested in exploring the issues presented in the book in even greater depth. Also, we will rely on this website as a vehicle for keeping up with this field and for keeping this book current, by providing background information on important new developments.

The *Reader* and the website are meant to be used together in order to enhance the academic experience of studying cyberspace ethics; one complements the other. It is our hope that both those who use this book in the classroom and the general reader will access this website for its supplementary material and its other supportive features.

Acknowledgments

We wish to thank the contributors who so graciously agreed to have their articles or essays included in this modest volume. Their enthusiasm and support for this project has inspired our efforts. If this book is a success, it is primarily because of the high quality and thoroughness of their work.

We also thank our respective institutions, Boston College and Rivier College, for their assistance. Special thanks to the Carroll School of Management of Boston College for its modest financial support. And thanks to our students who are the real reason behind this book.

We have also benefited from the opportunity to share insights with our colleagues at annual conferences such as Computer Ethics Philosophical Enquiry (CEPE) and ETHICOMP. Our interactions during these events have broadened and refined our understanding of the issues covered in this text. Several of the articles included in this reader were originally presented at these conferences.

Two papers in the intellectual property chapter were originally presented at The Fourth Annual Ethics and Technology Conference held at Boston College in 1999. This conference is an annual event, and is a joint effort of Boston College, Loyola University/Chicago, and Santa Clara University. We are grateful to the organizers for facilitating the publication of these papers and for their work in promoting research in this area.

Thanks to Michael Stranz and Amy Rose as well as to many others at Jones and Bartlett for their keen interest in this project and their helpful support in the difficult task of assembling all of this material into a uniform whole. And finally we also owe a great personal debt to our spouses—Susan and Joanne—for their forbearance and patience during the many days spent working on this book. They give this work meaning and purpose.

R. A. *Spinello*
H. T. *Tavani*

Contents

Contributors

Alison Adam is a Reader in the Information Systems Institute at the University of Salford, UK.

James Boyle is Professor of Law at Duke University Law School, USA.

Philip Brey is Associate Professor and Vice Chair of the Department of Philosophy at the University of Twente, The Netherlands.

Johannes J. Britz is Visiting Professor in the School of Information Studies at the University of Wisconsin–Milwaukee, USA, and Professor in the School of Information Technology, University of Pretoria, South Africa.

Elizabeth A. Buchanan is Assistant Professor and Co-Director, Center for Information Policy Research, School of Information Studies, University of Wisconsin–Milwaukee, USA.

Terrell Ward Bynum is Professor of Philosophy and Director of the Research Center on Computing & Society at Southern Connecticut State University, USA.

L. Jean Camp is Associate Professor at Harvard University's Kennedy School of Government, USA.

Jacques N. Catudal is Associate Professor of Philosophy and Vice Provost of Academic Affairs at Drexel University, USA.

Dorothy E. Denning is a professor in the Department of Defense Analysis at the Naval Postgraduate School, USA.

Dag Elgesem is Associate Professor, Section for Humanistic Informatics, University of Bergen, Norway.

Richard G. Epstein is Professor of Computer Science at West Chester University, USA.

Luciano Floridi is Associate Professor of Logic and Epistemology at the University of Bari, Italy, and Markle Foundation Research Fellow at the University of Oxford, UK.

Joseph S. Fulda, C.S.E., Ph.D. is a contributing editor *of Ideas on Liberty*, an associate editor of *Sexuality & Culture*, and writes the "AI Watch" column for *Computers and Society*.

Bernard Gert is Stone Professor of Intellectual and Moral Philosophy at Dartmouth College, USA.

Abby A. Goodrum is Assistant Professor in the College of Information Science and Technology at Drexel University, USA.

Don Gotterbarn is Professor of Computer Science at East Tennessee State University and Director of the Software Engineering Ethics Research Institute, USA.

Frances S. Grodzinsky is Professor of Computer Science and Information Technology at Sacred Heart University in Fairfield, Connecticut, USA.

Chuck Huff is Professor of Psychology at St. Olaf College in Northfield, Minnesota, USA.

Lucas D. Introna is a Reader in the Center for the Study of Technology and Organisation, Lancaster University, UK.

Deborah G. Johnson is Olsson Professor of Applied Ethics in the Department of Technology, Culture and Communication at the University of Virginia, USA.

Larry Lessig is Professor of Law at Stanford University Law School, USA.

Tomas A. Lipinski is Associate Professor and Co-Director of the Center for Information Policy Research, School of Information Studies, University of Wisconsin–Milwaukee, USA.

Mark Manion is Director of the Program in Philosophy at Drexel University, USA.

Michael C. McFarland, S.J. is the President of Holy Cross College in Worcester, Massachusetts, USA.

Keith Miller is Professor of Computer Science at the University of Illinois at Springfield, USA.

James H. Moor is Professor of Philosophy at Dartmouth College, USA.

Helen Nissenbaum is Associate Professor of Culture and Communication and Computer Science, and a Senior Fellow of the Information Law Institute, New York University, USA.

David G. Post is Professor of Law at Temple University Law School in Philadelphia, and a Senior Fellow at the Tech Center at George Mason University Law School in Arlington, Virginia, USA.

Eric Raymond, author of many technical books and articles, is the Technical Director of Chester County Interlink, Pennsylvania, USA.

Richard S. Rosenberg is Professor of Computer Science at the University of British Columbia, Canada.

J.W. Sanders is a Fellow of Lady Margaret Hall and University Lecturer in Computation at the University of Oxford, UK.

John W. Snapper is Professor of Philosophy at the Illinois Institute of Technology, USA.

Jeroen van den Hoven is Professor of Philosophy and Information Technology at the Department of Philosophy of Erasmus University of Rotterdam, The Netherlands.

Irma van der Ploeg (Ph.D.) is a researcher at the Center for the Philosophy of Information and Communication Technologies, located at the Faculty of Philosophy, Erasmus University of Rotterdam, The Netherlands.

Anton H. Vedder is an Associate Professor of Law and Ethics at the Faculty of Law at Tilburg University, The Netherlands.

Shelly Warwick is an Assistant Professor at the Graduate School of Library and Information Studies, Queens College, City University of New York, USA.

John Weckert is Principal Research Fellow at the Centre for Applied Philosophy and Public Ethics, and Associate Professor of Information Technology, at Charles Sturt University in Australia.

Marty J. Wolf teaches computer ethics and bioinformatics at Bemidji State University, Minnesota, USA.

About the Editors

Richard A. Spinello (Ph.D., Fordham University) is an Associate Research Professor in the Carroll School of Management at Boston College. Prior to joining the faculty of Boston College he worked as a programmer, consultant, and marketing manager in the software industry. He is Co-Executive Director of the International Society for Ethics and Information Technology (INSEIT). He has written and edited five books on computer ethics, including his most recent work, *Regulating Cyberspace: The Policies and Technologies of Control*. He has also written numerous articles and scholarly papers on ethics and management.

Herman T. Tavani (Ph.D., Temple University) is Chair of the Philosophy Department and Director of the Liberal Studies Program at Rivier College, Nashua, NH. He is Co-Executive Director of the International Society for Ethics and Information Technology (INSEIT) and Secretary/Treasurer of the Association for Computing's Special Interest Group on Computers and Society (ACM SIGCAS). The author of numerous publications in computer ethics, including his recent book *Ethics and Technology: Ethical Issues in an Age of Information and Communication Technology*, he is Book Review Editor of the journal *Ethics and Information Technology*, Bibliography Editor of *Computers and Society Magazine*, and Editor of the *INSEIT Newsletter*.

Introduction to Chapter 1: Cybertechnology, Ethical Concepts, and Methodological Frameworks: An Introduction to Cyberethics

What exactly is *cyberethics?* How did the field develop? What issues define this relatively new field, and what kind of methodology should be used in this area of applied ethics? Is a new system of ethics needed for the cyber era? These questions, among others, are addressed in the readings in Chapter 1.

Cyberethics can be defined as the field of applied ethics that examines moral, legal, and social issues in the development and use of cybertechnology. *Cybertechnology,* in turn, refers to a broad spectrum of technologies that range from stand-alone computers to the cluster of networked computing, information, and communication technologies.[1] Until recently, many have used the expression "computer ethics" to refer to the field that we call cyberethics. Note, however, that "computer ethics" can easily suggest the study of ethical issues that are associated primarily with computing machines or with the computing profession. Because the readings in this volume examine a much wider range of ethical issues, we believe that the term "cyberethics" better captures these issues. Other expressions that also have been used to refer to this relatively new field of applied ethics are "Internet ethics" and "information ethics." The cyberethics issues that we examine in this text are broader in scope than the set of issues likely to be considered under the heading "Internet ethics." And because cyberethics issues are concerned with ethical aspects of information as they relate specifically to networked computing and communications devices, "information ethics" is too general a heading. Hence, our preference for using the term *cyberethics* to describe the range of issues we examine in this book of readings! At times, however, the expression "computer ethics" and the term "cyberethics" are used interchangeably in this chapter as well as in other sections of this book.

---

[1] The definitions of "cyberethics" and "cybertechnology" used here are extracted from Tavani (2004). See also the definition of "cyberethics" in Spinello (2003).

The Computer Ethics/Cyberethics Evolution

The first three readings are contributed by three "pioneers" in the field of cyberethics: Terrell Bynum, Deborah Johnson, and James Moor. Collectively, these readings cover a wide range of topics, which include: (1) a description of how the field of cyberethics emerged and has subsequently evolved; (2) a consideration of whether cybertechnology has raised any special moral issues; and (3) a proposal for a methodological framework to carry out cyberethics research.

In the opening reading, "Ethics and the Information Revolution," Terrell Bynum traces the development of the field of cyberethics[2] from its informal and humble origin in the 1940s and 1950s to the present. Beginning with a discussion of some insights by Norbert Weiner (who coined the term "cybernetics" in the late 1940s), Bynum provides a fairly comprehensive overview of some of the important contributions made by key figures in the field. His paper also identifies and briefly describes some of the central topics and themes that define this field of applied ethics. Bynum concludes his essay with a brief description of two very different hypotheses about the field's future.

Has cybertechnology introduced any unique moral issues? This question continues to be debated in the cyberethics literature. At one end of the spectrum are those who believe that, essentially, there is nothing new or special about ethical issues associated with computers and cybertechnology. Proponents of this view claim, for example, that privacy violations are privacy violations and that crime is crime, regardless of the arena in which they occur. At the other extreme are philosophers who, like Walter Maner (1996), hold that computer use has generated some unique ethical issues that would not exist without cybertechnology. Maner argues that because we are unable to find "satisfactory non-computer analogies" for certain moral issues involving computers, at least some computer ethics issues are unique. Deborah Johnson (2001) has taken what could be viewed as a middle ground in this debate. Using a genus-species analogy, she suggests that ethical issues raised by computer technology can best be understood as a "new species" of (existing) generic moral problems.

In our second reading, entitled "Ethics On-Line," Deborah Johnson argues that, with respect to ethical considerations, Internet technology has three special features worth considering. First, the *scope* of the Internet is global and interactive; second, the Internet enables users to interact and communicate with *anonymity;* and third, Internet technology makes the *reproducibility* of information possible in ways that were not previously. Although she believes that these features may make a "moral difference"

---

[2] Bynum uses the expression "global information ethics" to refer to the field that we call cyberethics. (See also Bynum and Rogerson, 1996.)

in that they make behavior in an electronic network morally different from off-line behavior, Johnson does not claim that the Internet has necessarily introduced any unique ethical issues. Elsewhere, Johnson (2001) suggests that one's perspective on this debate is often influenced by one's starting point. She notes that if one starts from the vantage point of technology, for example, one is drawn to the uniqueness of many of the features of computers. On the other hand, starting from the perspective of ethics causes one to focus on human behavior and human values rather than on the specific details and nuances of computer technology itself.[3]

James Moor, in the chapter's third reading, expands on some points introduced in his seminal article "What Is Computer Ethics?" (1985). In that work, Moor argued that computer technology, unlike previous technologies, is "logically malleable" because it can be molded to perform a variety of functions. Consider that most technologies are designed to perform some particular function or task. For example, microwave ovens were designed specifically to cook, reheat, and defrost food, and videocassette recorders (VCRs) were designed to record and play video programs. As such, microwave ovens cannot be used to record and view video programs, and VCRs cannot be used to cook, reheat, or defrost food. But a computer, based on the instructions given by its user, can perform a range of diverse tasks. A computer can be instructed, via different software applications, to function as a video game, a word processor, a spreadsheet, a medium to send and receive email messages, an interface to Web sites, and so forth. Moor points out that because computers are so malleable, they can create "new possibilities for human action."

Moor goes on to note that these new possibilities for action, which would appear to be limitless, can also generate certain voids or what he calls "vacuums." In effect, two different kinds of vacuums can arise: (a) vacuums regarding laws and social policies that are needed to guide us in the new choices for action made possible by computers, which Moor calls "policy vacuums;" and (b) vacuums involving conceptual frameworks needed to understand and articulate obscure aspects of certain normative issues that emerge, which he calls "conceptual muddles." Moor claims that even after the conceptual muddles are resolved and the emergent ethical issues have become more clearly understood and articulated, we sometimes discover that none of our existing laws and social policies apply. Consequently we often need to revise existing social policies or create new policies, and then we need to justify the revised or the newly created social policies. According to Moor's analysis, then, an adequate computer ethics methodology consists of four steps:

---

[3] For extended discussions of issues that are associated with and that underlie the uniqueness debate in computer ethics, see Himma (2003) and Tavani (2002).

(i)   identify any policy vacuums that arise;

(ii) clarify any conceptual muddles that also arise;

(iii) revise existing social policies or, if necessary, formulate new policies; and

(iv) justify the revised or the newly formulated social policies.

As noted previously, the third reading in Chapter 1, Moor's "Reason, Relativity, and Responsibility in Computer Ethics," expands upon many of the ideas introduced in his classic (1985) article. In his later work, Moor argues that a separate field of computer ethics is needed because ordinary ethics, or what he calls "routine ethics," cannot sufficiently deal with many of the ethical issues generated by computing technology. Moor argues that routine ethics is inadequate because it underestimates the kinds of challenges that at least some computer ethics problems pose for our traditional conceptual frameworks. He also rejects ethical relativism—the view that there are no universal standards of morality—as an alternative strategy, arguing that it is inadequate because it underestimates the significance that certain universal core human values play in morality. He then shows how "limited relativity" and rational standards can coexist in computer ethics. In this essay, Moor also introduces the notion of "informational enrichment," which he illustrates through examples that include money, war, privacy, and copyright.

For many philosophers working in computer ethics, Moor's approach has become the "standard" methodology for this relatively new field of applied ethics. Recently, however, some researchers have suggested ways in which that methodology may be revised. The fourth, fifth, and sixth readings—by Philip Brey ("Disclosive Computer Ethics"), Alison Adam ("Gender and Computer Ethics"), and Luciano Floridi and J. W. Sanders ("The Foundationalist Debate in Computer Ethics"), respectively—include three different arguments for why the standard methodology should be modified or expanded.

Cyberethics Methodology

In a critique of what he describes as "mainstream computer ethics," Brey argues for an alternative methodology that he calls "disclosive computer ethics." An important aspect of this methodological framework is that it aims at "disclosing" non-obvious features embedded in computer systems, that can have moral implications. To carry out this task, Brey argues that computer ethics research should be both interdisciplinary and multi-level. It should be multi-level, he claims, because computer ethics research must distinguish among three levels: a disclosure level, a theoretical level, and an application level. Brey believes that philosophers and both computer and social scientists need to collaborate in the interdisciplinary research process. At the disclosure level, computer scientists have the technical expertise needed to identify and thus to "disclose" embedded features in computer systems that are morally "opaque" or nontransparent. Philosophers are needed to analyze conceptual aspects of these newly disclosed features at the theoretical level to determine if the set of standard (existing) ethical theories can be used successfully or if a revised (or possibly even a new) theory is needed. (At this stage, researchers can also test to see whether any policy vacuums and conceptual vacuums have emerged.) Finally, at the application level, social scientists, philosophers, and computer scientists need to work collaboratively in applying ethical theory to the particular issues and practices that have been disclosed.

Whereas Brey focuses on the need to disclose embedded normative features in cybertechnology, which can also introduce new biases and reinforce existing ones, Alison Adam believes that an adequate computer ethics methodology must also explicitly take into account gender-related biases. She considers how feminist ethics can be combined with empirical studies, which emphasize observation and interviewing, to move computer ethics research to a level where the implications of computing for gender issues are more easily recognized. Discovering these implications can, she further notes, affect our attitudes toward traditional computer ethics issues such as privacy and power. And this, in turn, can affect the kind of social policies we frame in response to these and other related computer ethics issues. Both Adam and Brey suggest that their alternative methodological schemes will not only help to eliminate certain kinds of biases affecting cyberethics research, but that their frameworks also can influence the way that we identify ethical issues and formulate social policies involving cybertechnology.

In the sixth reading, Luciano Floridi and J. W. Sanders propose yet another methodological framework, called "Information Ethics" or "IE," to counter a certain bias in cyberethics research. IE builds on an earlier framework introduced by Floridi (1999), where he argues that ethics research in computing is biased toward privileging certain kinds of entities—viz., those entities that reside in what he calls the "biosphere." Because of this bias, Floridi believes that the standard model for computer ethics research fails to consider the ethical significance of entities that exist in the realm of the "infosphere."

In one sense, IE can be viewed as an extension of the methodology used by environmental ethics researchers. Many researchers in this field have pointed out that traditional ethical analysis has tended to be "anthropocentric" in that it grants moral consideration only to humans. Some environmental ethicists have argued that the sphere of moral consideration needs to be extended to include all biological entities that make up the biosphere, including our ecosystem itself (or what Floridi and Sanders call the "ecosphere"). According to Floridi and Sanders, however, the argument advanced by these environmental ethicists does not go far enough. Floridi and Sanders claim that the environmentalist's methodology is still biased because it is "biocentric." Instead, they argue for a methodological framework that extends moral consideration to include what they call "information entities" (which reside in the "infosphere"). Specifically, they argue that at least some non-biological entities also deserve moral consideration. And because the conventional methodological framework used in computer ethics fails to consider the moral status of information entities, Floridi and Sanders conclude that the field's standard methodology is not sufficiently robust. Hence, their claim for the need for their IE methodological scheme.

Some may find the IE methodological framework advocated by Floridi and Sanders to be controversial, perhaps even radical. However, recent developments in artificial intelligence, including the emergence of "artificial electronic agents" and "softbots," have caused some computer ethicists to seriously consider whether "autonomous artificial agents" and other kinds of "information entities" that appear to exhibit behavior that is both rational and autonomous should receive moral consideration.

Ethical Theory

As noted earlier in our brief discussion of Moor's influential article on computer ethics (published in 1985), we must *justify* the new and revised social policies that we frame in response to "policy vacuums." To justify social policies, philosophers have typically appealed to one or more standard ethical theories. Ethical theories based on criteria of *consequences* or *duty* generally receive the most attention in the philosophical literature. Utilitarianism, one form of consequentialist ethical theory, proceeds on the notion that we can determine whether or not a particular social policy is morally acceptable simply by assessing the consequences that would likely result from implementing that policy. Generally speaking, utilitarians are interested in advancing only those social policies that produce the greatest good (social utility) for the greatest number of individuals. Deontological (duty-based) ethical theories, on the other hand, reject the view that consequences can be used as the appropriate criterion to determine whether a particular social policy is morally acceptable. Deontologists point out that a policy may yield desirable consequences for the greatest number of people and still be a morally unacceptable policy.

For deontologists, a policy is morally acceptable only if everyone affected by that policy is respected as an individual and is given equal consideration. In this scheme, it is not morally permissible for some individuals to be used as a means to some further end (e.g., an end in which the majority of individuals are affected favorably at the expense of the minority); rather, each individual is considered to be an *end-in-him-/herself*. Deontologists argue that we have a moral duty to ensure that each individual is treated accordingly.

Some critics of utilitarianism argue that because utilitarians are so preoccupied with promoting happiness for the majority, they ignore the importance of justice and fairness for each individual. Conversely, deontologists are often accused of ignoring the importance of happiness and overall social utility, because they focus exclusively on the primacy of notions such as duty, autonomy, rights, and respect for each individual. Presumably, an ideal solution would be to frame a more comprehensive ethical theory that combined the strengths of both utilititarianism and deontologism, while avoiding their respective weaknesses. However, philosophers have not had an easy time in synthesizing these theories in a way that is both coherent and logically consistent.

Some have questioned whether we can successfully apply *any* of our standard ethical theories—including utilitarianism and deontologism—to cyberethics issues. Recall that earlier in our introduction to Chapter 1, we briefly considered whether some cyberethics issues might be unique ethical issues. There we also saw that philosophers like Walter Maner (1996) believe that new ethical issues have indeed emerged from the use of computers. If Maner and others are correct, does it follow that we also need a new ethical theory to handle the new ethical issues generated by computers and cybertechnology? Or can existing ethical theories be applied to them? Even if new ethical issues have been generated by cybertechnology, we can still question if a new ethical theory is required to handle them. Floridi and Sanders, in the sixth reading of this chapter, argue that because at least some computer ethics issues are "sufficiently novel," and because these issues stretch and strain our existing conceptual and theoretical framework for ethics, traditional theories are inadequate for computer ethics. The authors also believe that their methodological framework of Information Ethics (described previously) provides an adequate ethical framework for understanding the "novel" ethical issues generated by cybertechnology.

Bernard Gert, in the chapter's seventh reading (entitled "Common Morality and Computing"), would agree with Floridi and Sanders in their claim that standard ethical theories such as utilitarianism and deontologism are inadequate, but with different reasoning. For Gert, the key problem is not that standard ethical theories do not apply to moral issues involving computers and cybertechnology per se. Rather, these kinds of ethical theories are inadequate models for understanding and analyzing everyday moral issues or what some philosophers call "ordinary ethics." Gert suggests that the accounts of morality provided by utilitarian and deontological theories are both artificial and simplistic; he proposes that our system of ordinary moral rules, which he calls common morality, should be used as an alternative to those theories. He defines common morality as "the *moral system* that most people use, usually not consciously, in deciding how to act when confronting moral problems and in making moral judgments." Gert suggests that the common moral system, which he also describes as "public and informal," has rules that are already known, at least implicitly, by everyone. He elaborates on these and other aspects of the moral system in his book *Morality* (1998).[4]

It is important to reiterate that Gert does not argue that issues raised by computers and cybertechnology necessitate his account of morality. Rather, he argues that this account of a moral system is essential to understand and analyze moral issues in general. In his essay in Chapter 1, however, Gert shows how his system of common morality can be applied to a specific issue in computer ethics. He argues that the rules that comprise our system of common morality can help us to get a clearer answer to that problem than can be gained by the application of traditional ethical theories like utilitarianism and deontologism. Specifically, Gert states that common morality provides a clearer answer to the question of whether it would ever be morally permissible to make an unauthorized copy of a proprietary software program for a friend.

In our final reading in Chapter 1, James Moor takes a different tack from both Gert and Floridi and Sanders by proposing a scheme that incorporates key features of utilitarianism and deontologism into one comprehensive moral theory. Moor's ethical theory has also been influenced, in part, by certain aspects of Gert's notion of a common moral system. For example, like Gert, Moor believes that there are common moral values; Moor calls these values "core values." In other ways, however, Moor's theory is very different from Gert's notion of common morality because it attempts to integrate aspects of traditional ethical theories into a single unified ethical theory.

---

[4] For an excellent summary and analysis of Gert's moral system, as well as an account of how Gert's system can be applied to issues involving computers, see Triplett (2002). Triplett argues that Gert's account of morality avoids the dogmatism found in many absolutist theories, while avoiding the kind of relativism rampant in our popular culture.

As we saw in our discussion of Moor's essay entitled "Reason, Relativity, and Responsibility in Computer Ethics" (included as the third reading of Chapter 1), Moor argued that "routine ethics," which includes routine ethical theories, is an inadequate framework to understand and analyze many of the issues that computer technology generates. In the chapter's closing reading, "Just Consequentialism and Computing," he proposes an ethical theory that emphasizes the *consequences* of social policies within the constraints of *justice*. Hence, his decision to call this theory "Just Consequentialism."

The application of Moor's just consequentialist theory requires two stages: (i) a deliberation stage, and (ii) a selection stage. When deliberating about social policies, Moor claims that we must consider only "just policies." We can determine which policies will qualify as just policies by applying what he calls the "impartiality test." To satisfy this condition, policies must: (a) cause no "unjustified harms" to individuals and groups; and (b) support justice, individual rights, etc. From the set of just policies, we will want to select the "best policy." This is done at the selection stage, Moor notes, by additionally ranking those policies in terms of their perceived benefits and justifiable harms. At that stage, we must then carefully weigh the relative good consequences in the set of just policies, which were generated at the deliberation stage.

Moor concedes that there may not always be universal agreement on which social policy is the best policy, since reasonable people can and will disagree. But, like Gert, Moor believes that by appealing to certain "core values," which are common in all moral systems, we can at least agree on which policies are unjust; and we eliminate those unjust social policies *before* moving on to the *selection stage*. To show how his theory can be applied to certain policy vacuums in the context of cybertechnology, Moor considers a scenario involving the installation of defective computer chips.

Moor's essay on "Just Consequentialism and Computing" concludes our first chapter. However, we should not infer that all of the important questions pertaining to the role that ethical theory plays in the analysis of cyberethics issues have been answered. Much more can be said about the importance of ethical theory in cyberethics; however, we encourage readers who are interested in additional information on this topic to consult the References and Suggested Further Readings included at the end of this introduction.

We also encourage readers to use the various conceptual tools provided in the readings in Chapter 1 when analyzing specific moral problems in computing raised in the subsequent chapters. In approaching moral problems related to speech, property, privacy, and security in cyberspace—i.e., issues discussed in the readings included in Chapters 2 through 5, respectively—readers may find it useful to re-read certain articles in Chapter 1; they can analyze those problems through the lens of theoretical and methodological frameworks. Readings in Chapter 1 can also aid in one's analysis of ethical issues affecting computer professionals, which are discussed in the readings included in Chapter 6.

Discussion Questions

1. Identify and briefly describe the significance of the "historical milestones" in Terrell Bynum's account of the development of the field of computer ethics. Who were some of the key figures responsible for developing this field of applied ethics? What does Bynum mean by the phrase"Global Information Ethics"?

2. According to Deborah Johnson, what are three "special features" of on-line communication (as opposed to off-line communication), and what is their significance for on-line ethics? Can you think of any ethical issues involving Internet technology that are actually *unique* ethical issues? If so, how are those issues unique?

3. What exactly does James Moor mean by expressions such as "logically malleable," "conceptual muddle," "policy vacuum," and "informational enrichment"? Why, according to Moor, are both "routine ethics " and "cultural relativism" inadequate for doing computer ethics?

4. What does Philip Brey mean by the expression "disclosive computer ethics"? How is it different from what he calls "mainstream computer ethics"? Why does Brey believe that an adequate computer ethics methodology must be multi-level and interdisciplinary?

5. Why does Alison Adam believe that the methodology used in computer ethics needs to be "gender informed"? How can such a methodology give us a different perspective on traditional computer ethics issues such as privacy and power?

6. What do Luciano Floridi and J. W. Sanders mean by the expression "Information Ethics"? In what key ways do Floridi and Sanders believe that IE is an improved methodological scheme over conventional computer ethics methodology?

7. What does Bernard Gert mean by "common morality"? How can that notion of a moral system be applied to ethical issues in computing?

8. What are some of the essential differences between consequence-based (utilitarian) and duty-based (deontological) ethical theories? How does James Moor's theory of "just consequentialism" incorporate aspects of utilitarian and deontological ethical theories?

References

Bynum, Terrell W. and Simon Rogerson (1996). "Global Information Ethics: Introduction and Overview," *Science and Engineering Ethics,* Vol. 2, No. 2, pp. 131–136.

Floridi, Luciano (1999). "Information Ethics: On the Philosophical Foundation of Computer Ethics," *Ethics and Information Technology,* Vol. 1, No. 1, pp. 37–56.

Gert, Bernard (1998). *Morality: Its Nature and Justification.* New York: Oxford University Press.

Himma, Kenneth E. (2003). "The Relationship Between the Uniqueness of Computer Ethics and Its Independence as a Discipline in Applied Ethics." *Proceedings of the Sixth Annual Conference on Ethics and Technology.* Chestnut Hill, MA: Boston College Press, pp. 128–142.

Johnson, Deborah G. (2001). *Computer Ethics.* 3rd ed. Upper Saddle River, New Jersey: Prentice Hall.

Maner, Walter (1996). "Unique Ethical Problems in Information Technology," *Science and Engineering* Ethics, Vol. 2, No. 2, pp. 137–154.

Moor, James H. (1985). "What Is Computer Ethics?" *Metaphilosophy,* Vol. 16, No. 4, pp. 266–275.

Spinello, Richard A. (2003). *CyberEthics: Morality and Law in Cyberspace.* 2nd ed., Sudbury, MA: Jones and Bartlett Publishers.

Tavani, Herman T. (2002). "The Uniqueness Debate in Computer Ethics: What Exactly Is at Issue, and Why Does it Matter?" *Ethics and Information Technology,* Vol. 4, No. 1, pp. 37–54.

Tavani, Herman T. (2004). *Ethics and Technology: Ethical Issues in an Age of Information and Communication Technology.* Hoboken, NJ: John Wiley and Sons.

Triplett, Timm (2002). "Bernard Gert's *Morality* and Its Application to Computer Ethics," *Ethics and Information Technology,* Vol. 4, No. 1, pp. 79–92.

Suggestions for Further Readings

Adam, Alison and Jacqueline Ofori-Amanfo (2000). "Does Gender Matter in Computer Ethics?" *Ethics and Information Technology,* Vol. 2, No. 1, pp. 37–47.

Baase, Sara (2003). *A Gift of Fire: Social, Legal, and Ethical Issues in Computing.* 2nd ed. Upper Saddle River, NJ: Prentice Hall.

Baird, Robert M., Reagan Ramsower, and Stuart E. Rosenbaum, eds. (2000). *Cyberethics: Social and Moral Issues in the Computer Age.* Amherst, NY: Prometheus Books.

Bynum, Terrell W. (1999). "The Development of Computer Ethics as a Philosophical Field of Study," *Australian Journal of Professional and Applied Ethics,* Vol. 1, No. 1, pp. 1–29.

De George, Richard T. (2003). *Ethics of Information Technology and Business.* Blackwell Publishers.

Edgar, Stacey L. (2003). *Morality and Machines: Perspectives on Computer Ethics.* 2nd ed., Sudbury, MA: Jones and Bartlett Publishers.

Ermann, M. David, Mary B. Williams, and Michele S. Schauf, eds. (1997). *Computers, Ethics, and Society.* 2nd. ed. New York: Oxford University Press.

Floridi, Luciano (2002). "On the Intrinsic Value of Information Objects and the Infosphere," *Ethics and Information Technology,* Vol. 4, No. 4, pp. 287–304.

Friedman, Batya, ed. (1997). *Human Values and the Design of Computer Technology.* Cambridge University Press.

Halbert, Terry and Elaine Ignulli (2002). *Cyberethics.* Belmont, CA: Thompson Southwestern Learning.

Hester, D. Micah and Paul J. Ford, eds. (2001). *Computers and Ethics in the Cyberage.* Upper Saddle River, NJ: Prentice Hall.

Johnson, Deborah G. and Helen Nissenbaum, eds. (1995). *Computing, Ethics and Social Values.* Englewood Cliffs, New Jersey: Prentice Hall.

Langford, Duncan ed. (2000). *Internet Ethics.* London: MacMillan/New York: St. Martin's Press.

Moor, James H. and Terrell Ward Bynum, eds. (2002). *Cyberphilosophy: The Intersection of Computing and Philosophy.* Malden, MA: Blackwell Publishers.

Rosenberg, Richard S. (1997). *The Social Impact of Computing.* 2nd ed. San Diego, CA: Academic Press.

Rudinow, Joel and Anthony Graybosch, eds. (2002). *Ethics and Values in the Information Age.* Belmont, CA: Wadsworth.

Spinello, Richard A. (2003). *Case Studies in Computer and Information Ethics.* 2nd ed. Englewood Cliffs, NJ: Prentice Hall.

Tavani, Herman T. (2001). "The State of Computer Ethics as a Philosophical Field of Enquiry," *Ethics and Information Technology,*" Vol. 3, No. 2, pp. 97–108.

van den Hoven, Jeroen (1997). "Computer Ethics and Moral Methodology," *Metaphilosophy,* Vol. 28, No. 3, 234–248.

Weckert, John and Douglas Adeney (1998). *Computer and Information Ethics*. Westport, CT: Greenwood Press.

Woodbury, Marsha Cook (2002). *Computer and Information Ethics.* Champaign, IL: Stipes Publishing.

Ethics and the Information Revolution[1]

Terrell Ward Bynum

The Information Revolution

Powerful technologies have profound social consequences. Consider for example the impacts of farming, printing, and industrialization upon the world. Information and communication technology (ICT) is no exception. As Simon Rogerson and the present writer have noted,

> Computing technology is the most powerful and most flexible technology ever devised. For this reason, computing is changing everything—where and how we work, where and how we learn, shop, eat, vote, receive medical care, spend free time, make war, make friends, make love [Rogerson and Bynum, June 9, 1995].

The growing information revolution, therefore, is not "merely technological"—it is *fundamentally social and ethical*. The reason why information technology is so powerful is well explained by James Moor in his classic article "What Is Computer Ethics?" [Moor, 1985]. The computer, he says, is almost a "universal tool"—because it is "logically malleable," it can be shaped and molded to perform nearly any task.

Information Technology and Human Values

Millions of tasks are now routinely performed by computers. Indeed, ICT has become so flexible and inexpensive that it has seeped into life almost unnoticed in household appliances, banks and shops, automobiles and airplanes, schools and medical clinics, to mention only a few examples. In industrialized nations of the world, the information revolution already (in the year 2000) has significantly changed many aspects of life, such as banking and commerce, work and employment, medical care, national defense, transportation, and entertainment. Indeed ICT has begun to profoundly affect (in both good and bad ways) community life, family life, human relationships, education, freedom, democracy, and so on.

This essay originally appeared in *Ethics in the Age of Information Technology*, Linkoping University, Sweden, 2000, pp. 32–55. Copyright © 2000 by Terrell Ward Bynum. Reprinted by permission.

The remainder of the industrialized world has quickly followed the example of the United States into the "Information Age." Will the less-industrialized parts of the globe join the revolution as well? Perhaps there will be significant delays. Andrzej Kocikowski [Kocikowski, 1996] has noted, for example, that economic and social factors in many countries make it difficult at present for ICT to be introduced on a wide scale. For this reason, the Information Revolution might proceed slowly, at best, in places like Eastern Europe, Africa, and Latin America.

On the other hand, Krystyna Gorniak-Kocikowska [1996] has pointed out that "Computers do not know borders. Computer networks, unlike other mass media, have a truly global character." And Jacek Sojka [1996] has commented that

> Access to cyberspace is much easier than to the world's business and management techniques. Because of information technology there are no peripheries. Even the more distant developing countries can fully participate in cyberspace and look forward to new opportunities offered by global networks [Sojka, 192]...
>
> ...the net constitutes the only realm of freedom in many non-democratic countries. Also the opportunities which the Internet offers to commerce guarantee its freedom: no country could afford losing this competitive advantage [Sojka, 198].

For these reasons, as well as the rapidly decreasing cost of ICT, the Information Revolution may affect all parts of the earth more quickly than people now believe. It is therefore imperative that, around the globe, public policy makers, leaders of business and industry, teachers, social thinkers, computer professionals, and private citizens take an interest in the social and ethical impacts of information and communication technology.

To study and analyze the ethical impacts of ICT, a new academic field—currently called "Computer Ethics"—has emerged. University modules, conferences, workshops, professional organizations, curriculum materials, books, articles, journals, and research centers have been created—both in the USA and other industrialized nations.[2] And this rapidly developing field of Computer Ethics is quickly being transformed into the much broader and more significant research area of "Global Information Ethics" as discussed below.

Computer Ethics: Some Historical Milestones

Some important milestones in the history of Computer Ethics include the following:

1940s and 1950s:

Computer Ethics as a field of study was founded by MIT professor Norbert Wiener during World War Two (early 1940s) while helping to develop an antiaircraft cannon capable of shooting down fast warplanes. The engineering challenge of this project caused Wiener and some colleagues to create a new field of research that Wiener called "cybernetics"—the science of information feedback systems. The concepts of cybernetics, when combined with digital computers under development at that time, led Wiener to draw some remarkably insightful ethical conclusions about the technology that we now call ICT. He perceptively foresaw revolutionary social and ethical consequences. In 1948, for example, in his book *Cybernetics: or Control and Communication in the Animal and the Machine*, he said the following:

> *It has long been clear to me that the modern ultra-rapid computing machine was in principle an ideal central nervous system to an apparatus for automatic control; and that its input and output need not be in the form of numbers or diagrams but might very well be, respectively, the readings of artificial sense organs, such as photoelectric cells or thermometers, and the performance of motors or solenoids. . . . we are already in a position to construct artificial machines of almost any degree of elaborateness of performance. Long before Nagasaki and the public awareness of the atomic bomb, it had occurred to me that we were here in the presence of another social potentiality of unheard-of importance for good and for evil. (pp. 27–28)*

In 1950 Wiener published his monumental computer ethics book, *The Human Use of Human Beings,* which not only established him as the founder of Computer Ethics, but—far more importantly—laid down a comprehensive computer ethics foundation that remains today (half a century later!) a powerful basis for computer ethics research and analysis. (However, he did not use the name "Computer Ethics," which came into common use more than two decades later.)

Wiener's book included (1) an account of the purpose of a human life, (2) four principles of justice, (3) a powerful method for doing applied ethics, (4) discussions of the fundamental questions of Computer Ethics, and (5) examples of key computer ethics topics. [Wiener 1950/1954, see also Bynum 1999].

Wiener's foundation of Computer Ethics was far ahead of its time, and it was virtually ignored for decades. In his view, the integration of computer technology into society will eventually constitute the remaking of society—the "second industrial revolution." It will require a multi-faceted process taking decades of effort, and it will radically change everything. A project so vast will necessarily include a wide diversity of tasks and challenges. Workers must adjust to radical changes in the workplace; governments must establish new laws and regulations; industry and businesses must create new policies and practices; professional organizations must develop new codes of conduct for their members; sociologists and psychologists must study and understand new social and psychological phenomena; and philosophers must rethink and redefine old social and ethical concepts.

1960s:
In the mid 1960s, Donn Parker of SRI International in Menlo Park, California began to examine unethical and illegal uses of computers by computer professionals. "It seemed," Parker said, "that when people entered the computer center they left their

ethics at the door."[3] He collected examples of computer crime and other unethical computerized activities. He published "Rules of Ethics in Information Processing" in *Communications of the ACM* in 1968, and he headed the development of the first Code of Professional Conduct for the Association for Computing Machinery (eventually adopted by the ACM in 1973). Over the next two decades, Parker went on to produce books, articles, speeches, and workshops[4] that re-launched the field of Computer Ethics, giving it momentum and importance that continues to grow today. Parker is, in this sense, the second founder of Computer Ethics after Norbert Wiener.

1970s:

During the late 1960s, Joseph Weizenbaum, a computer scientist at MIT in Boston, created a computer program that he called ELIZA. In his first experiment with ELIZA, he scripted it to provide a crude imitation of "a Rogerian psychotherapist engaged in an initial interview with a patient." Weizenbaum was shocked at the reactions people had to his simple computer program: Some practicing psychiatrists saw it as evidence that computers would soon be performing automated psychotherapy, and even computer scholars at MIT became emotionally involved with the computer, sharing their intimate thoughts with it. Weizenbaum was extremely concerned that an "information processing model" of human beings was reinforcing an already growing tendency among scientists, and even the general public, to see humans as mere machines. In the early 1970s, Weizenbaum undertook a book-writing project to defend the view that humans are much more than information processors. The project resulted in Weizenbaum's book, *Computer Power and Human Reason* [Weizenbaum, 1976], which is now considered a classic in Computer Ethics. Weizenbaum's book, plus the courses he offered at MIT and the many speeches he gave around the country in the 1970s, inspired many thinkers and projects in Computer Ethics. He stands with Norbert Wiener and Donn Parker as a key person in the formative history of the subject.

In the mid 1970s, Walter Maner (then of Old Dominion University in Virginia; now at Bowling Green State University in Ohio) began to use the term "Computer Ethics" to refer to *that field of applied professional ethics dealing with ethical problems aggravated, transformed, or created by computer technology.* Maner offered an experimental course on the subject at Old Dominion University. During the late 1970s (and indeed into the mid 1980s), he generated much interest in university-level Computer Ethics courses by offering a variety of workshops and lectures at computer science conferences and philosophy conferences across America. In 1978 he also self-published and disseminated his *Starter Kit in Computer Ethics* [Maner, 1980], which contained curriculum materials and pedagogical advice for university teachers to develop Computer Ethics courses. The *Starter Kit* included suggested course descriptions for university catalogs, a rationale for offering such a course in the university curriculum, a list of course objectives, some teaching tips and discussions of topics like privacy and confidentiality, computer crime, computer decisions, technological dependence, and professional codes of ethics. Maner's trailblazing course, plus his *Starter Kit* and the many conference workshops he conducted, had a significant impact upon the teaching of Computer Ethics across America. Many university courses were put in place because of him, and several important scholars were attracted into the field.

1980s:

By the 1980s, a number of social and ethical consequences of information technology were becoming public issues in America and Europe: issues like computer-enabled crime, disasters caused by computer failures, invasions of privacy via computer databases, and major law suits regarding software ownership. Because of the work of Parker, Weizenbaum, Maner, and others, the foundation had been laid for Computer Ethics as an academic discipline. The time was right, therefore, for an explosion of activities in Computer Ethics.

In the mid-80s, James Moor of Dartmouth College published his article "What Is Computer Ethics?" in *Computers and Ethics,* a special issue of the journal *Metaphilosophy* [Moor, 1985].

In addition, Deborah Johnson of Rensselaer Polytechnic Institute published *Computer Ethics* [Johnson, 1985], the first textbook—and for more than a decade, the *defining* textbook—in the field. There were also relevant books published in psychology and sociology: For example, Sherry Turkle of MIT wrote *The Second Self* [Turkle, 1984], a book on the impact of computing on the human psyche, and Judith Perrolle produced *Computers and Social Change: Information, Property and Power* [Perrolle, 1987], a sociological approach to computing and human values.

In 1978, the present author (Terrell Ward Bynum) was attracted to the field of Computer Ethics by Walter Maner. In the early 80s, Bynum assisted Maner in publishing his *Starter Kit in Computer Ethics* at a time when most philosophers and computer scientists considered the field to be unimportant [Maner, 1996]. Bynum, like Maner before him, also developed and taught university courses on university campuses, and conducted workshops at a number of conferences in the USA. In 1985, as Editor of *Metaphilosophy*, Bynum put together a special issue devoted to Computer Ethics; in 1987, he created the Research Center on Computing & Society at Southern Connecticut State University. In 1988 Bynum began planning (with Maner) the first international conference on Computer Ethics (eventually held in 1991), which ultimately attracted participants from seven countries and 32 US states. The conference included philosophers, computer professionals, sociologists, psychologists, lawyers, business leaders, news reporters, and government officials. It generated a set of monographs, video programs, and curriculum materials that are now being used on hundreds of university campuses around the world [van Speybroeck, July 1994].

1990s:

By the mid 1990s, interest in Computer Ethics as a field of research had spread to Europe and Australia. This important development was significantly aided by the pioneering work of Simon Rogerson of De Montfort University (UK), who established the Centre for Computing and Social Responsibility and initiated, with the present writer, a series of influential international conferences: the ETHICOMP conferences. In Rogerson's view, there is need in the 1990s for a "second generation" of Computer Ethics developments:

The mid-1990s has heralded the beginning of a second generation of Computer Ethics. The time has come to build upon and elaborate the conceptual foundation whilst, in parallel, developing the frameworks within which practical action can occur, thus reducing the probability of unforeseen effects of information technology application [Rogerson, Spring 1996, 2; Rogerson and Bynum, 1997].

Redefining the Field of Computer Ethics

In the 1940s and early 1950s, the field that is now called "Computer Ethics" was given a solid foundation by Norbert Wiener, whose seminal works, unhappily, were essentially ignored for decades. The field is now in the process of being recreated and redefined, and it is so new that those developing it are still struggling to delineate its essence and boundaries. Let us briefly consider five different attempts to define the field:

Walter Maner

When he coined the term "Computer Ethics" in the mid-70s, Maner defined the discipline as one that examines "ethical problems aggravated, transformed, or created by computer technology." Some old ethical problems, he said, are made worse by computers, while others are wholly new because of information technology. By analogy with the more developed field of medical ethics, Maner focused attention upon applications of traditional ethical theories used by philosophers doing "applied ethics"—especially analyses using the utilitarian ethics of the English philosophers Jeremy Bentham and John Stuart Mill, or the rationalist ethics of the German philosopher Immanual Kant.

Deborah Johnson

In her book, *Computer Ethics*, Johnson [1985] defined the field as one that studies the way in which computers "pose new versions of standard moral problems and moral dilemmas, exacerbating the old problems, and forcing us to apply ordinary moral norms in uncharted realms" [Johnson, 1]. Like Maner before her, Johnson employed the "applied philosophy" approach of using procedures and concepts from utilitarianism and Kantianism. But, unlike Maner, she did not believe that computers create wholly new moral problems. Rather, she thought that computers gave a "new twist" to ethical issues that were already well known.

James Moor

Moor's definition of Computer Ethics in his article "What Is Computer Ethics?" [Moor, 1985] is much broader and more wide-ranging than that of Maner or Johnson. It is independent of any specific philosopher's theory, and it is compatible with a wide variety of methodological approaches to ethical problem-solving. Over the past decade, Moor's definition has been the most influential one. He defines Computer

Ethics as a field concerned with "policy vacuums" and "conceptual muddles" regarding the social and ethical use of information technology:

> A typical problem in Computer Ethics arises because there is a policy vacuum about how computer technology should be used. Computers provide us with new capabilities and these in turn give us new choices for action. Often, either no policies for conduct in these situations exist or existing policies seem inadequate. A central task of Computer Ethics is to determine what we should do in such cases, that is, formulate policies to guide our actions.... One difficulty is that along with a policy vacuum there is often a conceptual vacuum. Although a problem in Computer Ethics may seem clear initially, a little reflection reveals a conceptual muddle. What is needed in such cases is an analysis that provides a coherent conceptual framework within which to formulate a policy for action [Moor, 1985, 266].

Moor says that computer technology is genuinely revolutionary because it is "logically malleable":

> Computers are logically malleable in that they can be shaped and molded to do any activity that can be characterized in terms of inputs, outputs and connecting logical operations.... Because logic applies everywhere, the potential applications of computer technology appear limitless. The computer is the nearest thing we have to a universal tool. Indeed, the limits of computers are largely the limits of our own creativity [Moor, 1985, 269].

According to Moor, the computer revolution will occur in two stages. The first stage is that of "technological introduction" in which computer technology is developed and refined. This already occurred in America during the first forty years after the Second World War. The second stage—one that the industrialized world has only recently entered—is that of "technological permeation" in which technology gets integrated into everyday human activities and into social institutions, changing the very meaning of fundamental concepts, such as "money," "education," "work," and "fair elections."

Terrell Ward Bynum

Moor's way of defining the field of Computer Ethics is very powerful and suggestive. It is broad enough to be compatible with a wide range of philosophical theories and methodologies, and it is rooted in a very perceptive understanding of how technological revolutions proceed. Currently it is the best available definition of the field.

Nevertheless, there is yet another way of defining Computer Ethics that is also very helpful—and also compatible with a wide variety of theories and approaches. Indeed, this "other way" is an elaboration of an additional suggestion in Moor's 1985 paper [page 266, paragraph 2]. According to this definition (adapted from Moor and developed by the present author in 1989) Computer Ethics *identifies and analyzes the impacts of information technology on social and human values like health, wealth, work, opportunity, freedom, democracy, knowledge, privacy, security, self-fulfillment, etc.* This very broad view of Computer Ethics embraces applied ethics, sociology of computing, technology assessment, computer law, and related fields, and it employs concepts, theories, and methodologies from those and any other relevant disciplines [Bynum, 1993].

This conception of Computer Ethics is motivated by the belief that—eventually—information technology will profoundly affect everything that human beings hold dear.

Donald Gotterbarn

In the 1990s, Donald Gotterbarn has been a strong advocate for a different approach to defining the field of Computer Ethics. In Gotterbarn's view, Computer Ethics should be viewed as a branch of *professional ethics,* which is concerned primarily with standards of practice and codes of conduct of computing professionals:

> *There is little attention paid to the domain of professional ethics— the values that guide the day-to-day activities of computing professionals in their role as professionals. By computing professional I mean anyone involved in the design and development of computer artifacts... The ethical decisions made during the development of these artifacts have a direct relationship to many of the issues discussed under the broader concept of computer ethics [Gotterbarn, 1991].*

With this more narrow definition of Computer Ethics in mind, Gotterbarn has been involved in a number of related activities, such as co-authoring the latest version of the ACM Code of Ethics and Professional Conduct and working to establish licensing standards for software engineers [Anderson, Johnson, Gotterbarn, and Perrolle, 1993; Gotterbarn, 1992].

Sample Topics in Computer Ethics

No matter which re-definition of Computer Ethics one chooses, the best way to understand what the field is like is to examine some example sub-areas of current interest. Consider the following four:

Computers in the Workplace

As a "universal" tool that can, in principle, perform almost any task, computers obviously pose a threat to jobs. Although they occasionally need repair, computers don't require sleep, they don't get tired, they don't go home ill or take time off for rest and relaxation. At the same time, computers are often far more efficient than humans in performing many tasks. Therefore, economic incentives to replace humans with computerized devices are very high. Indeed, in the industrialized world many workers already have been replaced by computerized devices—bank tellers, auto workers, telephone operators, typists, graphic artists, security guards, assembly-line workers, and on and on. In addition, even professionals like medical doctors, lawyers, teachers, accountants, and psychologists are finding that computers can perform many of their traditional professional duties quite effectively.

The outlook, however, is not all bad. Consider, for example, the fact that the computer industry already has generated a wide variety of new jobs: hardware engineers, software engineers, systems analysts, information technology teachers, computer sales clerks, and so on. Thus it appears that, in the short run, computer-generated unemployment will be an important social problem; but in the long run, information technology will create many more jobs than it eliminates.

Even when a job is not eliminated by computers, it can be radically altered. For example, airline pilots still sit at the controls of commercial airplanes; but during much of a flight the pilot simply watches as a computer flies the plane. Similarly, those who prepare food in restaurants or make products in factories may still have jobs; but often they simply push buttons and watch as computerized devices actually perform the needed tasks. In this way, it is possible for computers to cause "de-skilling"of workers, turning them into passive observers and button pushers. Again, however, the picture is not all bad because computers have also generated new jobs that require new sophisticated skills to perform—for example, "computer assisted drafting" and "keyhole" surgery.

Another workplace issue concerns health and safety. As Forester and Morrison point out [Forester and Morrison, 140–72, Chapter 8], when information technology is introduced into a workplace, it is important to consider likely impacts upon health and job satisfaction of workers who will use it. It is possible, for example, that such workers will feel stressed trying to keep up with high-speed computerized devices—or they may be injured by repeating the same physical movement over and over—or their health may be threatened by radiation emanating from computer monitors.

These are just a few of the social and ethical issues that arise when information technology is introduced into the workplace.

Computer Security
In this era of computer "viruses" and international spying by "hackers" who are thousands of miles away, it is clear that computer security is a topic of concern in the field of Computer Ethics. The problem is not so much the *physical* security of the hardware (protecting it from theft, fire, flood, etc.), but rather *logical* security, which Spafford, Heaphy, and Ferbrache [Spafford, et al, 1989] divide into five aspects:

1. Privacy and confidentiality of data
2. Integrity—assuring that data and programs are not modified without proper authority

3. Unimpaired service

4. Consistency—ensuring that the data and behavior we see today will be the same tomorrow

5. Controlling access to resources

Malicious software, or "programmed threats," provide a significant challenge to computer security. These include "viruses," which cannot run on their own, but rather are inserted into other computer programs; "worms," which can move from machine to machine across networks, and may have parts of themselves running on different machines; "Trojan horses," which appear to be one sort of program, but actually are doing damage behind the scenes; "logic bombs," which check for particular conditions and then execute when those conditions arise; and "bacteria" or "rabbits," which multiply rapidly and fill up the computer's memory.

Computer crimes, such as embezzlement or planting of logic bombs, are normally committed by trusted personnel who have permission to use the computer system. Computer security, therefore, must also be concerned with the actions of trusted computer users.

Another major risk to computer security is the so-called "hacker" who breaks into someone's computer system without permission. Some hackers intentionally steal data or commit vandalism, while others merely "explore" the system to see how it works and what files it contains. These "explorers" often claim to be benevolent defenders of freedom and fighters against rip-offs by major corporations or spying by government agents. These self-appointed vigilantes of cyberspace say they do no harm, and claim to be helpful to society by exposing security risks. However every act of hacking is harmful, because any known successful penetration of a computer system requires the owner to thoroughly check for damaged or lost data and programs. Even if the hacker did indeed make no changes, the computer's owner must run through a thorough investigation of the compromised system [Spafford, 1992].

Software Ownership

One of the more controversial areas of Computer Ethics concerns software ownership. Some people, like Richard Stallman who started the Free Software Foundation, believe that software ownership should not be allowed at all. He claims that all information should be free, and all programs should be available for copying, studying, and modifying by anyone who wishes to do so [Stallman, 1993]. Others argue that software companies or programmers would not invest weeks and months of work and significant funds in the development of software if they could not get the investment back in the form of license fees or sales [Johnson, 1992, 1–8].

Today's software industry is a multibillion dollar part of the economy, and software companies claim to lose billions of dollars per year through illegal copying ("software piracy"). Many people think that software should be ownable, but "casual copying" of personally owned programs for one's friends should also be permitted. The software industry claims that millions of dollars in sales are lost because of such copying. Ownership is a complex matter, since there are several different aspects of software that can be owned and three different types of ownership: copyrights, trade secrets, and patents. One can own the following aspects of a program:

1. The "source code," which is written by the programmer(s) in a high-level computer language like Pascal or C++.
2. The "object code," which is a machine-language translation of the source code.
3. The "algorithm," which is the sequence of machine commands that the source code and object code represent.
4. The "look and feel" of a program, which is the way the program appears on the screen and interfaces with users.

A very controversial issue today is owning a patent on a computer algorithm. A patent provides an exclusive monopoly on the use of the patented item, so the owner of an algorithm can deny others use of the mathematical formulas that are part of the algorithm. Mathematicians and scientists are outraged, claiming that algorithm patents effectively remove parts of mathematics from the public domain, and thereby threaten to cripple science. In addition, running a preliminary "patent search" to make sure that your "new" program does not violate anyone's software patent is a costly and time consuming process. As a result, only very large companies with big budgets can afford to run such a search. This effectively eliminates many small software companies, stifling competition, and decreasing the variety of programs available to the society [The League for Programming Freedom, 1992, 54–66].

Professional Responsibility
Computer professionals have specialized knowledge and often have positions with authority and respect in the community. For this reason, they are able to have a significant impact upon the world, including many of the things that people value. *Along with such power to change the world comes the duty to exercise that power responsibly.*

Computer professionals find themselves in a variety of professional relationships with other people, including:

employer—employee

client—professional

professional—professional

society—professional

These relationships involve a diversity of interests, and sometimes these interests can come into conflict with each other. Responsible computer professionals, therefore, will be aware of possible conflicts of interest and try to avoid them [Johnson, 1994, 37–57, Chapter 3].

Professional organizations in the USA, like the Association for Computing Machinery (ACM) and the Institute of Electrical and Electronic Engineers (IEEE), have established codes of ethics, curriculum guidelines, and accreditation requirements to help computer professionals understand and manage ethical responsibilities. For example, in 1991, a Joint Curriculum Task Force of the ACM and IEEE adopted a set of guidelines

("Curriculum 1991") for college programs in computer science. The guidelines say that a significant component of Computer Ethics (in the broad sense) should be included in undergraduate education in computer science [Turner, June 1991, 69–84].

In addition, both the ACM and IEEE have adopted Codes of Ethics for their members [Johnson, 1994, 165–73, 177]. The most recent ACM Code (1992), for example, includes "general moral imperatives," such as "avoid harm to others" and "be honest and trustworthy." Also included are "more specific professional responsibilities" like "acquire and maintain professional competence" and "know and respect existing laws pertaining to professional work." The IEEE Code of Ethics (1990) includes such principles as "avoid real or perceived conflicts of interest whenever possible" and "be honest and realistic in stating claims or estimates based on available data."

The Accreditation Board for Engineering Technologies (ABET) has long required an ethics component in the computer engineering curriculum. In 1991, the Computer Sciences Accreditation Commission/Computer Sciences Accreditation Board (CSAC/CSAB) also adopted the requirement that a significant component of Computer Ethics be included in any computer sciences degree granting program that is nationally accredited [Conry, 1992].

It is clear that professional organizations in computer science recognize and insist upon standards of professional responsibility for their members.

Global Information Ethics

The above paragraphs provide a brief description of Computer Ethics—some of its history, some attempts to define it, and some sample areas of study. But that is the past. Computer Ethics today is rapidly evolving into a broader and even more important field, which might reasonably be called "Global Information Ethics." Global networks like the Internet and especially the World Wide Web are connecting people all over the earth. As Krystyna Gorniak-Kocikowska perceptively notes in her important paper, "The Computer Revolution and the Problem of Global Ethics" [Gorniak-Kocikowska, 1996, 186–88], for the first time in history, efforts to develop mutually agreed standards of conduct, and efforts to advance and defend human values, are being made in a truly global context. So, for the first time in the history of the earth, ethics and values will be debated and transformed in a context that is not limited to a particular geographic region, or constrained by a specific religion or culture. This may very well be one of the most important social developments in history. Consider just a few of the global issues:

Global Laws

If computer users in the United States, for example, wish to protect their freedom of speech on the Internet, whose laws apply? Over one hundred countries are already interconnected by the Internet, so the United States Constitution (with its First Amendment protection for freedom of speech) is just a "local law" on the Internet—it does not apply to the rest of the world. How can issues like freedom of speech, control of "pornography," protection of intellectual property, invasions of privacy, and many others to be governed by law when well over a hundred countries are involved? If a citizen in a European country, for example, has Internet dealings with someone in a far-away land, and the government of that land considers those dealing to be illegal, can the European be tried by the courts in the far-away country?

Global Cyberbusiness

The world is very close to having technology that can provide electronic privacy and security on the Internet sufficient to safely conduct international business transactions. Once this technology is in place, there will be a rapid expansion of global Cyberbusiness. Nations with a technological infrastructure already in place will enjoy rapid economic growth, while the rest of the world lags behind. What will be the political and economic fallout from rapid growth of global Cyberbusiness? Will accepted business practices in one part of the world be perceived as "cheating" or "fraud" in other parts of the world? Will a few wealthy nations widen the already big gap between rich and poor? Will political and even military confrontations emerge?

Global Education

If inexpensive access to the global information net is provided to rich and poor alike—to poverty-stricken people in ghettos, to poor nations in the "third world," etc.—for the first time in history, nearly everyone on earth will have access to daily news from a free press; to texts, documents, and art works from great libraries and museums of the world; to political, religious, and social practices of peoples everywhere. What will be the impact of this sudden and profound "global education" upon political dictatorships, isolated communities, coherent cultures, religious practices, etc.? If great universities of the world begin to offer degrees and knowledge via Internet courses and modules, will "lesser" universities be damaged or even forced out of business?

Information Rich and Information Poor

The gap between rich and poor nations, and even between rich and poor citizens in industrialized countries, is already disturbingly wide. As educational opportunities, business and employment opportunities, medical services, and many other necessities of life move more and more into Cyberspace, will the gaps between rich and poor become even worse?

The Future of Computer Ethics?

Given the explosive growth of Computer Ethics during the past two decades, the field appears to have a very robust and significant future. How can it be, then, that two important thinkers—Krystyna Gorniak-Kocikowska and Deborah Johnson—have recently argued that Computer Ethics will *disappear* as a branch of applied ethics?

The Gorniak Hypothesis—In 1995, Gorniak-Kocikowska predicted that Computer Ethics, which is currently considered just a branch of applied ethics, will eventually evolve into something much more. [See Gorniak-Kocikowska, 1996] It will evolve, she said, into a system of global ethics applicable in every culture on earth:

> Just as the major ethical theories of Bentham and Kant were devel-
> oped in response to the printing press revolution, so a new ethical the-
> ory is likely to emerge from computer ethics in response to the computer
> revolution. The newly emerging field of information ethics, therefore,
> is much more important than even its founders and advocates believe.
> (p. 177)
>
>   . . .
>
>   The very nature of the Computer Revolution indicates that the eth-
> ic of the future will have a global character. It will be global in a spa-
> tial sense, since it will encompass the entire Globe. It will also be global
> in the sense that it will address the totality of human actions and rela-
> tions. (p.179)
>
>   . . .
>
>   ...the rules of computer ethics, no matter how well thought through,
> will be ineffective unless respected by the vast majority of or maybe
> even all computer users. This means that in the future, the rules of
> computer ethics should be respected by the majority (or all) of the
> human inhabitants of the Earth . . . . In other words, computer ethics
> will become universal, it will be a global ethic. (p.187)

According to the Gorniak hypothesis, "local" ethical theories like Europe's Benthamite and Kantian systems and the ethical systems of other cultures in Asia, Africa, the Pacific Islands, etc., will eventually be superceded by a global ethics evolving from today's Computer Ethics. "Computer" ethics, then, will become the "ordinary" ethics of the information age.

The Johnson Hypothesis—In her 1999 ETHICOMP paper [Johnson 1999], Deborah Johnson expressed a view that, upon first sight, may seem to be the same as Gorniak's:

> I offer you a picture of computer ethics in which computer ethics as
> such disappears. . . . We will be able to say both that computer ethics
> has become ordinary ethics and that ordinary ethics has become com-
> puter ethics. (pp. 17–18)

But a closer look at the Johnson hypothesis reveals that it is very different. On Gorniak's view, the computer revolution will eventually lead to a new ethical system, global and cross-cultural in nature. The new "ethics for the information age," according to Gorniak, will supplant parochial theories like Bentham's and Kant's— theories based on relatively isolated cultures in Europe, Asia, Africa, and other "local" regions of the globe.

Johnson's hypothesis, in reality, is essentially the opposite of Gorniak's. It is another way of stating Johnson's often-defended view that Computer Ethics concerns "new species of generic moral problems." It assumes that Computer Ethics, rather than replacing theories like Bentham's and Kant's, will continue to presuppose them.

Current ethical theories and principles, according to Johnson, will remain the bedrock foundation of ethical thinking and analysis, and the computer revolution will *not* lead to a revolution in ethics.

At the dawn of the 21st century, then, Computer Ethics thinkers have offered the world two very different views of the likely ethical relevance of computer technology. The Wiener-Maner-Gorniak point of view sees computer technology as *ethically revolutionary*, requiring human beings to re-examine the foundations of ethics and the very definition of a human life. The more conservative Johnson perspective is that Western ethics will remain unaffected—that computer ethics issues are simply the same old ethics questions with a new twist—and consequently Computer Ethics as a distinct branch of philosophy will ultimately disappear.

Notes

1. This is an expanded version of a Polish-language article in Kocikowski, Andrzej, Terrell Ward Bynum, and Krystyna Gorniak-Kocikowska, Wprowadzenie do etyki informatycznej, Humaniora Press, Poland, (1997). A previous English-language version also appeared in Terrell Ward Bynum and James H. Moor, eds, *The Digital Phoenix: How Computers are Changing Philosophy*, Blackwell, 1998.

2. For example, in 1995 the "Global Consortium on Computing and Social Values" was formed from three research centers, including one in England and one in Poland: The Research Center on Computing & Society, Southern Connecticut State University, USA, founded in 1987; the Centre for Computing and Social Responsibility, De Montfort University, UK, founded in 1995; and the Center for Business and Computer Ethics, Adam Mickiewicz University, Poland, also founded in 1995. These three research centers—through their publications, international conferences, research projects, World Wide Web pages, and international advisory boards—have stimulated cooperation and research among scholars around the globe.

3. Comments by Donn Parker [Fodor and Bynum, 1992].

4. See, for example, Donn Parker's publications: Parker, Donn. (1968) "Rules of Ethics in Information Processing," *Communications of the ACM*, Vol. 11. 198–201; Parker, Donn, Susan Nycum, and Stephen S. Oura. (1973) *Computer Abuse: Final Report Prepared for the National Science Foundation.* Stanford Research Institute; Parker, Donn. (1976) *Crime By Computer*, Charles Scribner's Sons; Parker, Donn. (1979) *Ethical Conflicts in Computer Science and Technology.* AFIPS Press; Parker, Donn. (1979) *Computer Crime: Criminal Justice Resource Manual.* U.S. Government Printing Office. (Second Edition 1989); Parker, Donn. (1982) "Ethical Dilemmas in Computer Technology," Hoffman, W. and J. Moore, eds. *Ethics and the Management of Computer Technology.* Oelgeschlager, Gunn, and Hain; Parker, Donn. (Summer 1988) "Ethics for Information Systems Personnel," *Journal of Information Systems Management*, 44–48; Parker, Donn, S. Swope, and B. N. Baker. (1990) *Ethical Conflicts in Information & Computer Science, Technology & Business*, QED Information Sciences.

References

Anderson, Ronald, Deborah Johnson, Donald Gotterbarn, and Judith Perrolle. (February 1993) "Using the New ACM Code of Ethics in Decision Making," *Communications of the ACM,* Vol. 36, 98–107.

Bynum, Terrell Ward. (1993) "Computer Ethics in the Computer Science Curriculum," Bynum, Terrell Ward, Walter Maner and John L. Fodor, eds. (1993) *Teaching Computer Ethics.* Research Center on Computing & Society.

Bynum, Terrell Ward. (1999) "The Foundation of Computer Ethics," a keynote address at the AICEC99 Conference, Melbourne, Australia, July 1999.

Conry, Susan. (1992) "Interview on Computer Science Accreditation," Bynum, Terrell Ward and John L. Fodor, creators, *Computer Ethics in the Computer Science Curriculum* (a video program). New Haven, CT: Educational Media Resources.

Fodor, John L. and Terrell Ward Bynum, creators. (1992) *What Is Computer Ethics?* (a video program). Educational Media Resources, Inc.

Forester, Tom and Perry Morrison. (1990) *Computer Ethics: Cautionary Tales and Ethical Dilemmas in Computing.* Cambridge, MA: MIT Press.

Gorniak-Kocikowska, Krystyna. (1996) "The Computer Revolution and the Problem of Global Ethics" in Bynum and Rogerson. (1996) *Global Information Ethics*, Opragen Publications, 177–90.

Gotterbarn, Donald. (1991) "Computer Ethics: Responsibility Regained," *National Forum: The Phi Beta Kappa Journal.* Vol. 71, 26–31.

Gotterbarn, Donald. (1992) "You Don't Have the Right to Do It Wrong," *CIO.*

Johnson, Deborah G. (1985) *Computer Ethics*. Prentice Hall, 2nd Edition, 1994.

Johnson, Deborah G. (1992) "Proprietary Rights in Computer Software: Individual and Policy Issues," Bynum, Terrell Ward, Walter Maner and John L. Fodor, eds. (1992) *Software Ownership and Intellectual Property Rights.* Research Center on Computing & Society.

Johnson, Deborah G. (1999) "Computer Ethics in the 21st Century," a keynote address at the ETHICOMP99 Conference, Rome, Italy, October 1999.

Kocikowski, Andrzej. (1996) "Geography and Computer Ethics: An Eastern European Perspective," Bynum, Terrell Ward and Simon Rogerson, eds. (1996) *Global Information Ethics*, Opragen Publications, 201–10. (April 1996) *Science and Engineering Ethics.*

The League for Programming Freedom. (1992) "Against Software Patents," Bynum, Terrell Ward, Walter Maner and John L. Fodor, eds. (1992) *Software Ownership and Intellectual Property Rights*, Research Center on Computing & Society.

Maner, Walter. (1980) *Starter Kit in Computer Ethics*, Helvetia Press (published in cooperation with the National Information and Resource Center for Teaching Philosophy).

Maner, Walter. (1996) "Unique Ethical Problems in Information Technology," Bynum and Rogerson. (1996) 137–52.

Moor, James H. (1985) "What Is Computer Ethics?" Bynum, Terrell Ward, ed. (1985) *Computers and Ethics.* Blackwell, 266–75. (October 1985) *Metaphilosophy.*

Perrolle, Judith A. (1987) *Computers and Social Change: Information, Property, and Power.* Wadsworth.

Rogerson, Simon. (Spring 1996) "The Ethics of Computing: The First and Second Generations," *The UK Business Ethics Network News*.

Rogerson, Simon and Terrell Ward Bynum, eds. (1997) *Information Ethics: A Reader*, Blackwell. This anthology contains articles from ETHICOMP95 and ETHICOMP96.

Rogerson, Simon and Terrell Ward Bynum. (June 9, 1995) "Cyberspace: The Ethical Frontier," *Times Higher Education Supplement*, The London Times.

Sojka, Jacek. (1996) "Business Ethics and Computer Ethics: The View from Poland" in Bynum and Rogerson. (1996) *Global Information Ethics*, Opragen Publications, 191–200.

Spafford, Eugene, et al. (1989) *Computer Viruses: Dealing with Electronic Vandalism and Programmed Threats.* ADAPSO.

Spafford, Eugene. (1992) "Are Computer Hacker Break-Ins Ethical?" *Journal of Systems and Software*, January 1992, Vol. 17, 41–47.

Stallman, Richard. (1992) "Why Software Should Be Free," Bynum, Terrell Ward, Walter Maner and John L. Fodor, eds. (1992) *Software Ownership and Intellectual Property Rights*, Research Center on Computing & Society, 35–52.

Turkle, Sherry. (1984) *The Second Self: Computers and the Human Spirit.* Simon & Schuster.

Turner, A. Joseph. (June 1991) "Summary of the ACM/IEEE-CS Joint Curriculum Task Force Report: Computing Curricula, 1991," *Communications of the ACM*, Vol. 34, No. 6., 69–84.

van Speybroeck, James. (July 1994) "Review of *Starter Kit on Teaching Computer Ethics,*" by Bynum, Terrell Ward, Walter Maner and John L. Fodor, eds. *Computing Reviews*, 357–8.

Weizenbaum, Joseph. (1976) *Computer Power and Human Reason: From Judgment to Calculation*, Freeman.

Wiener, Norbert. (1948) *Cybernetics: or Control and Communication in the Animal and the Machine*, Technology Press.

Wiener, Norbert. (1950/1954) *The Human Use of Human Beings: Cybernetics and Society*, Houghton Mifflin, 1950. (Second Edition Revised, Doubleday Anchor, 1954.)

Ethics On-Line

Deborah G. Johnson

As a nation, we are in the process of making fundamental decisions about the future of our system of on-line communication. The public discussion taking place is revealed in the visions of the future that are being put forth. We have Vice President Al Gore using the metaphor of *electronic superhighways of the future* and seeing a national and global information infrastructure as the means by which the U.S. will emerge triumphant in global economic competition [7]. We have John Barlow, Mitch Kapor, and the Electronic Frontier Foundation using a highly gendered metaphor of the new frontier, cyberspace, in which thugs, overzealous sheriffs, and the *pioneers of the 21st Century* are fighting it out [1, 11]. We have visions of a new form of democracy emerging on-line as political alliances are formed and social movements gather force without mediation from mass media.[1] We have visions of this evolving technology bringing into our homes the ultimate in entertainment choice together with the efficiency of being able to carry on all of our daily inter-actions with keystrokes and screens, e.g., shopping, working, job searching, bank-ing [5]. The visions sometimes include the possibility of escape into Disney-like, virtual worlds [2]. These are all highly value-laden and interest-laden visions com-peting for our attention. While they are all possible, none of them is inevitable. Rather they work as self-fulling prophecies; the vision we embrace will shape what we make of on-line communication.

On-line communication has been evolving and growing at an unprecedented pace, and there is every indication that the demand for it will continue. Its evolu-tion, however, has not been without problems and the most disturbing of these prob-lems involves human behavior. Disturbing and disruptive behavior ranges from unauthorized access, theft of electronic property [14], launching of destructive

---

This essay originally appeared in *Communications of the ACM* 40: 1 (January) 1997: 60–69. Copyright © 1997 by the Association for Computing Machinery. Reprinted by permission.

[1] One documented example of this is the protest against Lotus Development Corporation's product, Lotus Marketplace: Households. The product was a CD-ROM direct mail marketing database containing information on 120 million Americans. The announcement of the product began a discussion in several on-line forums, and discussions multiplied and gathered momentum as information, letters of protest, and statements were forwarded from group to group. Thousands of individuals took action by writing to Lotus and requesting that their names be removed from the database. Much of this was done via e-mail directly to the Lotus Corporation [8, 17].

worms and viruses [3], racism, defamation [4], harassment, to a recent incident involving a form of rape on-line [6]. Our responses to this behavior will shape the future of on-line communication and will determine to what extent and in what ways the promise of electronic networking technology is realized in the future.

Thus far, our primary responses to behavioral problems on-line have been legal and technological. As problems have been identified and defined, laws have been extended or created, and law enforcement has entered this new domain [3]. We have new technologies for virus detection and for encryption and decryption of information. Our knowledge of how to secure our systems and detect or trace transactions has improved.

These approaches alone, however, will never be adequate to control behavior on-line. Our only hope is for individuals to internalize norms of behavior. That is how most behavior is controlled off-line. Individuals implicitly understand that certain behavior is unacceptable, undesirable, or inappropriate, and they act accordingly. To achieve this on-line, it is important that we discuss the character of on-line behavior, and reveal its underlying meaning and the reasons for declaring it acceptable or unacceptable, desirable or undesirable, right or wrong, legal or illegal. Users must become aware of the meaning and consequences of their actions on-line.

The issues and problems in electronic networks are the problems of the world around them. The problems have to do with who we are and what we do *off-line*. The problems are the problems of modern, highly industrialized, democratic societies. Computer technology did not come into being in a vacuum. It was created and shaped in response to pushes and pulls in our way of life, our culture, politics, and social institutions.

The ethical issues surrounding computers are a new species of generic moral problems [9]. This is as true when it comes to on-line communication as any other area of computing. The generic problems involve privacy, property, drawing the line between individual freedom and (public and private) authority, treating one another with respect, ascribing responsibility, and so on. When activities are mediated or implemented by computers, they have new features. The issues have a new twist that make them unusual, even though the core issue is not. For example, before computers, we never had to think through property rights in terms of lines of code—strings of linguistic symbols—that could be implemented by a machine, but throughout history new discoveries have repeatedly challenged traditional notions of property. We have never confronted a threat to privacy of the kind or scale that computers make possible, but other technologies, e.g., cameras and telephones, have threatened privacy in the past. It is the same when it comes to electronic networks. Activities in networks have special features, though the activities themselves do not fall into new categories of human behavior. We send messages, exchange information, use language, play, work, and so on. With computer networks we have new versions of activities that take place off-line, and new species of problems that have arisen before.

In this paper I identify three special features of on-line communication, and I briefly discuss the moral implications of each. I focus in on anonymity and uncover its benefits and dangers. I argue that we need not eliminate anonymity from all forms of on-line communication, but we should restrict it. I conclude by identifying three principles that should shape social behavior on-line.

Special Characteristics of Communication in Networks

Communication in computer networks has several characteristics making it different from face-to-face communication and other forms of technology-mediated communication, such as telephone, fax, and mass media. These features may make a moral difference in the sense that they may make behavior in an electronic network morally different than comparable behavior off-line.

Scope

Individuals communicating in electronic networks have a much broader reach than they do off-line. A message sent by one individual can reach vast numbers of individuals around the world, and may do so very quickly. The combination of factors—number of individuals reached, speed, and availability to individuals—make the scope special. The speed/immediacy of on-line communication is not unusual in itself for it is available in face-to-face and telephone communication. The vastness of the reach, also, is not unusual in itself in that radio, television, and telephone have this reach. With radio and television, however, communication is one way and with telephone communication, it is typically restricted to only one or a few individuals at a given time. Interactivity is, also, not unusual itself since it is a given in face-to-face communication. It seems to be the combination of vastness of reach, immediacy, and availability to individuals for interactivity that makes for something unusual here. I use *scope* to refer to all three of these factors together.

We might think of scope as *power*. An action—a communication or transfer of information—in a network can have much greater power than an action in ordinary space. When I say something to someone standing next to me or publish an article in a journal, my action has a certain reach that is a function of the physical world. In a network, the impact of a comparable act is magnified many times over. I post an idea on an electronic bulletin board, and it reaches thousands of people around the world in a very short period of time; moreover, it may exist, in the sense of being available to others, virtually forever. Similarly, off-line, I write some computer code, and my action brings about some changes in the way my computer works; on-line, I write some computer code (say, a worm), send it out, and it brings down systems across the world.

One way that scope or power has moral implications is that we generally expect those engaged in powerful activities to take greater care. We restrict who can use powerful technologies, for example, by licensing their use. We license automobile drivers, pilots, those who perform surgery, and we regulate many types of businesses that involve dangerous industrial processes. We expect and require those who are using more powerful, especially dangerous, technologies to take precautions and exercise greater care than those who are using less powerful technologies, e.g., a megaphone, a camera. Indeed, we often hold individuals legally liable for the effects of their actions when they use powerful technologies recklessly.

Anonymity

In networks, individuals can communicate without identity, using pseudonyms and taking on different personas. Moreover, someone may *grab* someone else's words and alter them, or may *grab* someone else's identity and distribute words as if they were the words of the other. In face-to-face, telephone, and media communication, individuals can wear disguises and lie about who they are and what they want; voices can be altered through the telephone; and reporters can fabricate video material; FBI agents can go undercover. The distinction is that off-line anonymity requires effort on the part of the individual seeking anonymity whereas on-line anonymity is often the natural state; at least, it is in those environments where an individual is given a generic user ID. The individual must make an effort in order to establish his or her real identify. In this sense, anonymity may be said to be *favored* in on-line communication.[2] Furthermore, the ultimate test of identity off-line is seeing the person face-to-face. The fact that this test is not available on-line also seems to favor anonymity.[3]

Anonymity creates problems of integrity. The anonymity disconnects the words from the person. It is possible for my words to be taken by someone and distributed as their words; for my words to be taken, altered, and then distributed as my words; and for words to be created entirely by someone else, and attributed to me. Again, comparable disconnections can and do happen in ordinary space, but they require quite different physical behaviors.

The moral significance of these characteristics will be explored later. For the moment, it is important to note that trust in the information we use in decision making and trust in the individuals with whom we have relationships seems crucial to our way of being. Yet, trust is difficult to develop in an environment in which one can not be sure of the identities of persons with whom one is communicating. It is difficult to develop a reliable history of experiences with specific persons.

Reproducibility

Information can be reproduced on-line without loss of value and in such a way that the originator or holder of the information would not notice. Of course, in the ordinary world, information can be reproduced via copying machines and cameras. In electronic networks, however, there is no loss of value in the process of reproduction. A copied program or copied data set is perfectly usable, and the reproduction can be such that there is no evidence that copying has been done; that is, the person who created or owns the information has no reason to believe it has been copied. The difference here is the difference between taking a painting—the painter or owner no longer has the painting and can see that it is gone—and copying a data set—the creator or owner still has the data set and may have no indication that a copy was made.

---

[2] It would be a mistake to claim that anonymity is an intrinsic feature of the technology for the technology could be physically designed to diminish the possibility of anonymity.

[3] Screen-image-to-screen-image contact is available and is likely to improve in quality over time, but it is unlikely that this will ever be as credible as seeing a person face-to-face since screen-image-to-screen-image contact may lead to virtual-image-to-virtual-image contact.

Another aspect of reproducibility is that activities in an electronic network can be recorded and observed. In ordinary space, I utter a sentence to a friend, my friend hears, understands, and the words are gone (or, at most, locked in the memories of my friend and me). Not so in most forms of on-line communication. The words are there until someone or some event deletes them. Depending on where I have sent them, they may be available to others who can copy and send them to others, ad infinitum, or they may be available to those who manage and monitor the technology, or they may be available to snoopers.

Reproducibility is related to both scope and anonymity. Reproducibility creates the possibility of permanence or, at least, endurance of information. This adds to the increased scope of actions in networks; that is, actions endure in computer networks. The problem of integrity of information that arises from anonymity (the disconnection between words and person) also arises from the reproducibility of the information. One can anonymously grab words and attribute or alter them because of their reproducibility.

Reproducibility has moral implications because it goes counter to our traditional notions of property and personal privacy. Our notions of property are associated with the idea of control; an owner can control the use of her property. Our notions of privacy are based on a physical world in which actions are performed and then they are gone; they are irretrievable. (Tape recorders and cameras have also changed this.) In the case of electronic networks, the medium in which an action occurs makes reproduction and observation easier than in ordinary space. Though it depends on how the system is set up, effort is generally necessary to delete an action in a computer network, whereas, in ordinary space, effort is necessary to record it. So, reproducibility, like anonymity, seems to be favored in computer networks.

In summary, these three special features of communication in networks lead, either directly or indirectly, to problems on-line.[4] The breadth of **scope** means that individuals can do a wide variety of things to one another on-line that would be impossible or extremely difficult to do off-line. Individuals can do things to one another on-line that would require physical closeness and a different set of physical behaviors off-line. They can snoop, steal, harass, defame, and sabotage on-line; they can affect thousands of individuals who are vastly, geographically distant. **Anonymity** leads to serious problems for the integrity of information and com-

---

[4] While it is tempting to think of these characteristics as *intrinsic* features of communication in computer networks, and, therefore, as unchangeable features, this temptation should be resisted. In ordinary space, it may seem at first glance that privacy is favored because of our bodies and brains. No one can see what I am thinking; I can pull someone away from a crowd and whisper in their ear. But it is not just our bodies and brains that make for privacy in ordinary space. Social, cultural, and political practices create and support the privacy of ordinary space. We build structures with walls, pass laws specifying that criminal justice agencies cannot wiretap without cause, expect that our neighbors will not set up telescopes aimed at our windows. The same can be said about the special features of computer networks. Networking technology has been designed to embody certain characteristics. Reproducibility, for example, is a function of the design and could be designed away. (If we design network hardware with the Clipper chip, to ensure the possibility of decryption, then we will have designed in reproducibility [13].)

munication. **Reproducibility** also threatens the integrity of information, and it means that acts of communication and/or information have endurance. Reproducibility also facilitates surveillance.

Anonymity

A wide variety of forums now exist for informal interactions on-line—different kinds of bulletin-boards, discussion groups, e-mail, role playing games, and so on. All three of the characteristics discussed above are likely to be addressed and impacted as electronic networks evolve. Each offers benefits and creates dangers. The benefits and dangers seem to come together. The scope of network communications, for example, brings people together, makes the world seem smaller, opens up opportunities for increased exchange of ideas and information, and at the same time, brings greater danger of harm—harm on a grander scale. Reproducibility creates the possibility of massive amounts of information being available to many more individuals than ever before, at very little cost, with great convenience, and so on. At the same time, reproducibility also means greater opportunity for theft and sabotage of information. For the remainder of this paper, the benefits and dangers of anonymity will be addressed. The anonymity available on-line is likely to figure prominently in the future development of networked communication systems, both as a feature to be preserved and as a feature to be controlled. Clarity on its value and disvalue will insure that we take advantage of its benefits and minimize its dangers.

Anonymity does not seem to be bad in itself. In fact, it can be beneficial in certain contexts, such as contexts in which race, gender, or physical appearance get in the way of fair treatment. In these contexts, anonymity serves as an equalizer. In on-line education, for example, biases are removed from student-to-student interactions as well as from the teacher's evaluations of students. Anonymity may, also, facilitate participation in certain activities. Individuals who might not otherwise participate in discussions with, say, other rape victims or battered wives or ex-criminals may be more willing to take part under the shroud of anonymity. Participation may provide individuals with valuable information or much needed emotional release. Even in less sensitive contexts, individuals may be more likely to say what they think when they have a degree of anonymity; in formal situations such as in the workplace, individuals may think more creatively and provide better feedback to authorities when they have the shroud of anonymity.

Anonymity is, nevertheless, problematic in networks, and this seems to be so for at least three related reasons:

1. Off-line as well as on-line, anonymity is problematic because it **makes the process of identifying and catching criminals more difficult.** Here anonymity is still not bad in itself, but bad because of an effect that it has. Tracking down those

who snoop, steal, and sabotage, as well as those who harass or libel others is made more difficult.

2. The second problem with anonymity is related directly to one of its advantages mentioned above. Anonymity creates a shroud under which people are not afraid to say what they think. This is good when it facilitates discussions that are likely to help discussants deal with their feelings, find comfort from those who have had similar experiences, or acquire useful information. On the other hand, anonymity is not so good when it **frees individuals to behave in undesirable and harmful ways** [12, 15, 18]. Those who might not snoop, steal, harass, make racist comments, or confront others with pornography off-line may be more likely to do so under the shroud of anonymity on-line. Being observed and identified by others seems to serve as a form of social control on undesirable behavior, one that is not present on-line.

3. Anonymity **contributes to the lack of integrity of on-line information**. We are inundated with information off-line and on-line, and forced, thereby, to make choices about what to rely upon, i.e., what information to give weight to, when we form opinions and make decisions. One of the ways we do this is by developing a history of experiences with various sources of information. Over the course of time, based on our experiences, we come to trust some sources more than others, or to trust certain sources for certain purposes. This is true in both personal relationships and our relationships with the media. The best example is the way in which individuals typically deal with the wide variety of news sources—newspapers, magazines, and individual reporters. Experiences with each help one to make judgements about which to rely upon and when.

This way of dealing with massive amounts of information is not, however, available in an environment in which the identities of the sources of information are uncertain. The same person may be contributing information under multiple identities; the same identity may be used by multiple individuals. In effect, you don't know the sources of the information you receive; you can't develop a history of experiences with a source. The fact that words can be stolen and altered also contributes to this problem.

Diminished Trust

These three problems with anonymity contribute to a general situation of **diminished trust**. One cannot put one's trust in information and individuals on-line for a variety of reasons: one does not know, at least, in the ordinary sense of *know*, the individuals with whom one is communicating; the system of communication is vulnerable to sabotage; individuals are more likely to behave in undesirable ways due to their anonymity, so you can't be sure how you will be treated; and so on.

The problem of diminished trust comes into focus when we consider the case in which women in an on-line discussion group on women's issues discovered that a participant whom they believed to be an older single woman confined to a wheelchair was in reality a male psychiatrist in his thirties [16]. The women who had participated in the forum were shocked and upset when they found out that a person with whom they had shared their intimate thoughts was not who they thought she was. We might view this simply as a case of deception, but that would miss an important component. Participants in the discussion group had come to place their trust in a persona based on a history of experiences (communications) with that persona. They felt, I presume, betrayed when they discovered the participant's true identity.

Now, some might say the women who participated in the forum were wrong to put any trust in an on-line persona. They were naive to assume that anyone on-line is who they claim to be. This response is disturbing for it suggests that we must give up trust altogether when it comes to on-line communication. It may well be smart, at this point in time, to presume very little and to be very cautious. However, it would be a shame if we came to accept diminished trust as a given in on-line communication. There is no reason to believe that conditions necessary for more trust could not be created.

Trust seems to be built on the development of expectations that continue to be met. Individuals feel deceived and betrayed when they have expectations that are not met. I expect that my friend will not tell anyone what I have said. I expect when I enter a discussion with colleagues that what I say will be treated with respect. I expect that my friends will not lie to me. And so on. My trust is betrayed when individuals fail to fulfill these expectations.

How expectations are created is an extremely complicated matter. Quite often they are embodied in cultural patterns and institutional structures and transmitted implicitly. Other times they are formally created and meticulously reinforced. Other times they are quite informal. They are generally diverse; that is, individuals have varying expectations about the same situation.

Variety and Consent

What seems most important in promoting trust is that there is some sort of match between what individuals expect and what actually happens. In this regard, what seems most important for computer networks is that individuals are informed about what to expect when they enter an on-line environment and that the environment is what it purports to be.

We can have a wide variety of forms of on-line communication with a high level of trust if the rules are known or explained to individuals before they enter an environment. We can have environments in which there is a high degree of anonymity, environments in which an operator goes to great lengths to check and verify the identity (and even the credentials) of someone before they are allowed to participate, and environments in between these two extremes. We can have filtered and unfiltered discussions, discussions filtered by diverse criteria. The important thing is, as already indicated, that individuals know what they are getting into before they enter.

This approach will not, by any means, solve all the problems of social behavior on-line. Indeed, many forms of on-line discussion are already taking place, and it is already clear that one of the persistent problems is how to deal with individuals who refuse, for whatever reason, to play by *the rules*. The important and difficult issue for any individual or group of individuals setting up an informal discussion arena on-line involves deciding how open or closed the forum should be, and how to deal with those who refuse to behave according to the rules.

The primary principle that ought to be followed now is that the rules are specified *up front*, that is, before an individual begins using a system [10]. Variety can prevail as long as those who communicate on-line understand that the rules of various modes of electronic exchange vary. The metaphor of different rooms works well here. What the rules are depends on where you go. Some rooms are private, some public. Some have narrow purposes and familiar cultures. Others are broad and may have strange cultures. But wherever you go, you are either informed immediately or can find out easily what the rules are and what the consequences of violation of the rules will be.

Conclusion

Law and technology will never be enough to solve behavioral problems on-line. Individuals will have to internalize norms of behavior for their on-line interactions. After identifying three special features of on-line communication as compared with off-line communication, I have argued for anonymity having benefits and dangers. My analysis suggests that we need not insist that individuals always be anonymous or always reveal their identity. Rather, I have argued for instituting a principle whereby the rules of all forums are explicit and the consequences for violation are specified. Individuals can then choose which forums they want to join and will know what to expect as they participate.

The ethical issues that arise on-line are not so different from ethical issues off-line. Hence, it should not surprise us if the most defensible norms for behavior on-line are identical to norms of behavior off-line. On-line ethics would seem to call for the following of three general rules.

1. Know the rules of the forums in which you communicate and follow them.
2. Respect the privacy and property rights of others. When in doubt, assume the user wants privacy and ownership.
3. Respect the individuals with whom you communicate and those who are affected by your communication; that is, do not deceive, defame, or harass.

Acknowledgments
This paper is a shortened version of a paper prepared for a project on the Legal, Ethical, and Technological Aspects of Computer and Network Use and Abuse undertaken by the Directorate for Science and Policy Programs of the American Association for the Advancement of Science. The project had the sponsorship of the AAAS-ABA National Conference of Lawyers and Scientists and funding from the National Science Foundation. The paper was greatly improved by critical comments from the advisory committee for this project and from participants in a workshop in December, 1993 at the National Academy of Sciences Beckman Center in Irvine, California. I received additional suggestions from the reviewers and editors of this special issue of CACM. I am particularly grateful to Chuck Huff for pointing me to the relevant social science literature and to Peter Neumann for his editing.

References
1. Barlow, J. P. Coming into the country. *Communications of the ACM* 34, 3 (March, 1991), 19–21.
2. Benedikt, M., Ed. *Cyberspace: First Steps*. The MIT Press, Cambridge, MA, 1991.
3. Branscomb, A. W. Rogue Computer Programs and Computer Rogues: Tailoring the Punishment to Fit the Crime. *Rutgers Computer & Technology Law Journal* 16 (1990), 1–61.
4. Charles, R. Computer Bulletin Boards and Defamation: Who Should Be Liable? Under What Standard? *The Journal of Law and Technology* 2 (1987): 121–150.
5. Chapman, G. and Rotenberg, M. A National Information Infrastructure: A Public Interest Opportunity. *The CPSR Newsletter* 11, 2 (Summer, 1993), 1.
6. Dibbell, J. A Rape in Cyberspace. *The Village Voice* 38 (December 21 1993), 36–42.
7. Gore, A. Infrastructure for the Global Village. *Scientific American* (1991), 108–111.
8. Gurak, L. J. *The Rhetorical Dynamics of A Community Protest in Cyberspace: The Case of Lotus Marketplace*, dissertation, Rensselaer Polytechnic Institute, 1994.
9. Johnson, D. G. *Computer Ethics*. Prentice Hall, Englewood Cliffs, NJ., 1985, 1994.
10. Johnson, D. G. The Public-Private Status of Transactions in Computer Networks, *The Information Web,* edited by C. Gould, Westview Press, Boulder, CO, 1989.
11. Kapor, M. Civil Liberties in Cyberspace. *Scientific American* (1991), 116–120.
12. Kiesler, S., Siegel, J. and McGuire, T. W. Social Psychological Aspects of Computer-Mediated Communication. *American Psychologist* 39 10 (1984), 1123–1134.
13. Levy, S. Battle of the Clipper Chip. *New York Times Magazine* (June 12, 1994), 44.
14. Spafford, E. H. Are Computer Hacker Break-Ins Ethical? In *Computers, Ethics, and Social Values* edited by D. G. Johnson and H. Nissenbaum, Prentice Hall, Englewood Cliffs, NJ, 1995.
15. Sproull, L. and Kiesler, S. Reducing Social Context Cues: Electronic Mail in Organizational Communication. *Management Science* 32, 11 (November, 1986), 1492–1512.
16. Stone, A. R. Will the Real Body Please Stand Up? in *Cyberspace: First Steps*, edited by Michael Benedikt, MIT Press, Cambridge, MA, 1991, 81–118.
17. Winner, L. A Victory for Computer Populism. *Technology Review* (May/June, 1991), 66.
18. Zimbardo, P. G. The Human Choice: Individuation, Reason, and Order versus Deindividuation, Impulse, and Chaos in *Nebraska Symposium on Motivation* edited by Arnold, W. J., and Levine, D., University of Nebraska Press, Lincoln, Nebraska, 1969.

Reason, Relativity, and Responsibility in Computer Ethics[1]

James H. Moor

Searching for Ethics in the Global Village

As computing becomes more prevalent, computer ethics becomes more difficult and more important. As Terry Bynum and Simon Rogerson put it,

> We are entering a generation marked by globalization and ubiqui-tous computing. The second generation of computer ethics, therefore, must be an era of 'global information ethics.' The stakes are much higher, and consequently considerations and applications of Information Ethics must be broader, more profound and above all effec-tive in helping to realize a democratic and empowering technology rather than an enslaving or debilitating one. [1996, p. 135]

I heartily concur with the concern that Bynum and Rogerson express about the global impact of computing. The number and kinds of applications of computing increase dramatically each year and the impact of computing is felt around the plan-et. The ubiquitous use of electronic mail, electronic funds transfer, reservation sys-tems, the world wide web, etc. places millions of the inhabitants of the planet in a global electronic village. Communication and actions at a distance have never been easier. We are definitely in a computer revolution. We are beyond the intro-duction stage of the revolution in which computers are curiosities of limited pow-er used only by a few. Now entire populations of developed countries are in the

This essay originally appeared in *Computers and Society*, Vol. 28, No. 1 (March) 1998: 14–21. Copyright © 1998 by James H. Moor. Reprinted by permission.

[1] An earlier version of this paper was presented as a keynote address at Ethicomp96 in Madrid, Spain. It served as the basis for the presentation, "How Can Ethical Theory Be Applied to Information Technology," delivered at FINE99 in Kyoto, Japan, March, 1999.

permeation stage of the revolution in which computers are rapidly moving to every aspect of daily life.

The computer revolution has a life of its own. Recently, in northern California, about one sixth of the phone calls didn't connect because of excessive use of the internet. People are surging to gain access to computer technology. They see it as not only a part of their daily lives but a necessary venue for routine communication and commercial transactions. In fact, the surge has become so great that America On-Line, a prominent internet server, offered its customers refunds because the demand for connection overwhelmed the company's own computer technology after the company gave unlimited access to its customers for a flat fee. The widespread desire to be wired should make us reflect on what awaits as the computer revolution explodes around the world. The digital genie is out of the bottle on a world-wide scale.

The prospects of a global village in which everyone on the planet is connected to everyone else with regard to computing power and communication is breathtaking. What is difficult to comprehend is what impact this will have on human life. Surely some of the effects will be quite positive and others quite negative. The question is to what extent can we bring ethics to bear on the computer revolution in order to guide us to a better world or at least prevent us from falling into a worse world. With the newly acquired advantages of computer technology, few would want to put the genie completely back into the bottle. And yet given the nature of the revolutionary beast, I am not sure it is possible to completely control it, though we certainly can modify its evolution. Aspects of the computer revolution will continue to spring up in unpredictable ways—in some cases causing us considerable grief. Therefore, it is extremely important to be alert to what is happening. Because the computer revolution has the potential of having major effects on how we lead our lives, the paramount issue of how we should control computing and the flow of information needs to be addressed on an ongoing basis in order to shape the technology to serve us to our mutual benefit. We must remain vigilant and proactive so that we don't pillage the global village.

Although almost everyone would agree that computing is having a significant, if not a revolutionary, impact on the world, and that ethical issues about applications of this surging technology should be raised, there is disagreement about the nature of computer ethics. Let me describe two positions with which I disagree. Both of these positions are popular, but I believe both of them mislead us about the real nature of computer ethics and undercut potential for progress in the field. The first view I will call the "Routine Ethics" position. According to the Routine Ethics position, ethical problems in computing are regarded as no different from ethical problems in any field. There is nothing special about them. We apply established customs, laws, and norms and assess the situations straightforwardly. Sometimes people steal cars and sometimes people steal computers. What's the difference? The second view is usually called "Cultural Relativism." On this view, local customs and laws determine what is right and wrong, but, because computing technology, like the world wide web, crosses cultural boundaries, the problems of computer ethics are intractable. Free speech is permitted in the United States but not in China. How can we justify a standard for or against free speech on the world wide web? Routine Ethics makes computer ethics trivial and Cultural Relativism makes it impossible.

I believe that both the views of Routine Ethics and Cultural Relativism are incorrect particularly when used to characterize computer ethics. The former underestimates the changes that occur in our conceptual framework and the latter underestimates the stability of our core human values. The problems of computer ethics, at least in some cases, are special and exert pressure on our understanding. And yet our fundamental values, based on our common human nature, give us an opportunity for rational discussion even among cultures with different customs. The purpose of this paper is to explain how it is possible to have both reason and relativity in computer ethics. Only with such an understanding is global responsibility in computer ethics possible.

Logical Malleability and Informational Enrichment

Computers are *logically malleable*. This is the feature that makes computers so revolutionary. They are logically malleable in that they can be manipulated to do any activity that can be characterized in terms of inputs, outputs, and connecting logical operations. Computers can be manipulated syntactically and semantically. Syntactically, a computer's performance can be changed through alterations in its program. And semantically the states of a computer may represent anything one chooses, from the sales of a stock market to the trajectory of a spacecraft. Computers are general purpose machines like no others. That is why they are now found in almost every aspect of our lives and that is why a computer revolution is taking place.

Computers are also *informationally enriching*. Because of their logical malleability, computers are put to many uses in diverse activities. Once in place, computers can be modified to enhance capabilities and improve overall performance even further. Often, computerized activities become informationalized, i.e., the processing of information becomes a crucial ingredient in performing and understanding the activities themselves. When this happens both the activities and the conceptions of the activities become informationally enriched.

The process of informational enrichment is gradual and is more manifest in some activities than in others. What is striking is how often and the extent to which it does occur. In a typical scenario, a computer is introduced merely as a tool to perform a job or to assist in an activity. Gradually the computer becomes an essential part of the methodology of doing the job or performing the activity. To do it properly is to use a computer. Over time the job or activity is viewed increasingly as an informational phenomenon so that information processing is taken as a salient or even defining feature.

Consider some examples of informational enrichment. At one time in the United States money was backed by gold. There was an exchange of paper bills, but the bills were merely coupons that could, at least in principle, be redeemed for gold or perhaps silver. For sometime the United States remained on the gold standard so that paper bills were markers for money. Monetary transactions were grounded in gold. Then the gold standard was dropped and the paper bills became the money. To have money was to have the paper presumably backed by good faith and trust in the government. Now paper has been augmented with credit cards and debit cards that can be read by computers. Of course, these cards are not the real money because one can always exchange the credits for paper money. But, it is likely that the use of paper money will decrease and the electronic tokens on the cards or in a bank's computer will become the money. Some cards now have chips embedded in them so that they can be loaded with electronic money which is then transferred as information to a merchant at the point of sale. We are headed for a cashless society. Monetary transactions are increasingly grounded in information. Money may come to be conceived as an elaborate computable function among people. In the computer age the concept of money is becoming informationally enriched.

As another example of informational enrichment consider the evolving nature of warfare. Traditionally, in warfare different sides send people into battle who fight with each other at close quarters until one side has killed or captured so many that the other side surrenders. Of course, information has always been important in warfare, but now, given advances in computing, the importance of information is overwhelming. The battlefield is rapidly becoming computerized. The stealth bomber used by the United States during the Gulf War was the result of computerized engineering. Computers designed the shape of the aircraft so that it would be nearly invisible to radar. The aircraft's design deprived Iraq of information. The Gulf War was about information and the lack of it. Bombs were dropped and guided by lasers and computers. Missiles were launched from ships and sought their targets by reading the terrain using computer guidance systems. The first objective of the armed forces under General H. Norman Schwarzkopf's command was to eliminate the ability of Iraq to communicate among its own forces or to use its aircraft detection systems. Schwarzkopf remarked after the war that it was the first time an enemy was brought to his knees by denial of information. As war becomes increasingly computerized, it may be less necessary or desirable to send men and women into the battlefield. Wars ultimately will be about the destruction of information or the introduction of misleading information. One side surrenders when it is not able to obtain and control certain kinds of information. This may not be a bad result. Better that data die, than people. Perhaps the "gun standard" will fade away just as the gold standard did. In any event, as warfare becomes increasingly computerized, our concept of war becomes informationally enriched. The information processing model is seizing the high ground.

Informational enrichment can also affect ethical and legal practices and concepts. Consider the concept of privacy as it has evolved in the United States as an example [Moor, 1990]. Privacy is not explicitly mentioned in the Declaration of Independence or in the Constitution of the United States though there are portions of these documents that implicitly support a notion of privacy as protection from governmental intrusion, particularly the physical invasion of people's houses. The notion of privacy has been an evolving concept in the United States. For instance, in the 1960s and 70s the legal concept of privacy was expanded to include protection against government interference in personal decisions about contraception and abortion. Today, the concept of privacy includes these earlier elements but increasingly focuses on informational privacy. This shift in emphasis has been brought about because of the development of the computer and its use in collecting large databases of personal information.

The computer, originally viewed by many as little more than an electronic filing cabinet, rapidly revealed its potential. Once data is entered into a computer it can be sorted, searched, and accessed in extraordinarily easy ways that paper files cannot be—at least in practical amounts of time. The activity of storing and retrieving information has been enhanced to the extent that all of us now have a legitimate basis for concern about the improper use and release of personal information through computers. The computerization of credit histories and medical records for use in normal business provides an ongoing possibility for misuse and abuse. Because of the widespread application of computer technology, our concern about privacy today goes far beyond the original concern about the physical intrusion of governmental forces into our houses. Now concerns about privacy are increasingly about the improper access, use, and manipulation of personal information by the government and many others who have access to computerized records. The original concept of privacy in the United States has become informationally enriched in the computer age.

Even concepts that begin as informational concepts can be informationally enriched. As an example consider the legal concept of copyright. Legislation protecting the products of authors and inventors is authorized by the Constitution of the United States. Early copyright laws were passed to protect literary works and patent laws were passed to protect inventions. Copyright laws in the U.S. have been amended over the years to extend the length of protection to authors and to protect a wider and wider range of materials including music and photographs. But until the computer age, the underlying conception of copyright was always the protection of items that could be read and understood by humans. For example, in the early part of the Twentieth Century an attempt to protect piano rolls by copyright was denied on the grounds that piano rolls were not in human-readable form.

In the 1960s programmers began to submit copies of printouts of their programs for copyright protection. The printouts were in human-readable form. But what programmers wanted to protect was not the printouts of programs but the programs as they existed on computers. However, the programs, as they existed on computers, were not in human-readable form. If the human readable printouts were to count as surrogates to protect the machine versions of programs, copyright law had to be stretched. Moreover, if machine readable programs were protectable by copyright, then it would seem that programs as instantiated on computer chips might be protectable by copyright as well. Copyright protection was so extended. Through the development of computing, the concept of copyright has become informationally enriched. Copyright extends not only to computer languages, but computer languages in forms readable only by machines. Indeed, what is copyrightable today sometimes looks more like an invention than a literary work.

I have used the concepts of money, war, privacy, and copyright as examples of informational enrichment. There are many more. It is difficult to think of an activity now being done extensively by computers that has not been informationally enriched. In some cases this enrichment is so salient that our concepts shift somewhat. They too become informationally enriched. In the computer age we live in a different world.

The Special Nature of Computer Ethics

I maintain that computer ethics is a special field of ethical research and application. Let me begin by describing computer ethics and then making a case for its special nature.

> *Computer ethics has two parts: (i) the analysis of the nature and social impact of computer technology and (ii) the corresponding formulation and justification of policies for the ethical use of such technology. I use the phrase "computer technology" because I take the subject matter of the field broadly to include computers and associated technology including software, hardware, and networks. [Moor, 1985]*

We need thoughtful analyses of situations in which computers have an impact, and we need to formulate and justify policies for using them ethically. Although we need to analyze before we can formulate and justify a policy, the process of discovery often comes in the reverse order. We know that computing technology is being employed in a given situation, but we are puzzled by how it should be used. There is a *policy vacuum*. For example, should a supervisor be allowed to read a subordinate's e-mail? Or should the government be allowed to censor information on the internet? Initially, there may be no clear policies on such matters. They never arose before. There are policy vacuums in such situations. Sometimes it may be simply a matter of establishing some policy but often one must analyze the situation further. Is e-mail in the workplace more like correspondence on company stationary in company files or more like private and personal phone conversations? Is the internet more like a passive magazine or more like an active television? One often finds oneself in a *conceptual muddle*. The issues are not trivial matters of semantics. If someone's health status is discovered through e-mail or an impressionable child is exposed to distressing material on the internet, the consequences may be significant. Obtaining a clear conception of the situation on which to formulate ethical policies is the logical first step in analysis, although chronologically one's uncertainty about the appropriate policy may precede and motivate the search for conceptual clarification. Given a tentative understanding of the situation, one can propose and evaluate possible policies for proper conduct. The evaluation of a policy will usually require a close examination and perhaps refinement of one's values. Such policy evaluation may lead one back for further conceptual clarification and then further policy formulation and evaluation. Eventually, some clear understanding and justifiable policy should emerge. Of course, with the discovery of new consequences and the application of new technology to the situation, the cycle of conceptual clarification and policy formulation and evaluation may have to be repeated on an ongoing basis.

Because computers are logically malleable, they will continue to be applied in unpredictable and novel ways generating numerous policy vacuums for the foreseeable future. Moreover, because computerized situations often become informationally enriched, we will continue to find ourselves in conceptual muddles about how precisely to understand these situations. This is not to say that we can't achieve conceptual clarity and that we can't formulate and justify reasonable policies. Rather it is to point out that the task of computer ethics is, if not Sisyphian, at least ongoing and formidable. No other field of ethics has these features to the degree that computer ethics does. Computer ethics is not simply ethics rotely applied to computing. Typically problems in computer ethics require more than straightforward application of ethical principles to situations. Considerable interpretation is required before appropriate policies can be formulated and justified. Of course, to say that computer ethics is a special field of ethics does not mean that every ethical problem involving computers is unique or difficult to understand. Stealing a computer may be a simple case of theft. A straightforward application of an ethical principle is appropriate. In such a situation there are no policy vacuums and no conceptual muddles. And to say that computer ethics is a special field of ethics does not mean that other fields of applied ethics do not have some instances of policy vacuums and conceptual confusion. Medical technology raises questions about what policy to follow for brain dead patients and conceptual questions about what counts as life. What is special about computer ethics is that it has a continually large number of evolving situations that are difficult to conceptualize clearly and find justified ethical policies. Doing computer ethics is not impossible, but doing it typically involves much more than rote application of existing norms.

I have argued that computer ethics is special but is the subject matter *unique?* The answer depends upon what one means by "the subject matter." If by "the subject matter" one means "computing technology" then computer ethics is unique, for computing technology possesses unique properties [Maner, 1996]. I believe their most important property is logical malleability, which explains the ongoing wave of revolution and generation of ethical problems. If by "the subject matter" one has in mind the occurrence of some novel ethical issues, then computer ethics is not unique because other fields of ethics sometimes consider novel situations that require revisions of conceptual frameworks and new policy formulation. If by "the subject matter" one means "the overall range, depth and novelty of ethical issues generated by a technology," then computer ethics is unique. No other technology, as revolutionary as it may be for a given area, has and will have the scope, depth, and novelty of impact that computing technology has and will have. There is no mystery why computer ethics has a prominence that toaster ethics, locomotive ethics, and sewing machine ethics do not.

In summary, what is unique about computer ethics is computing technology itself and what makes computer ethics different as a field of ethics is the scope, depth, and novelty of ethical situations for which conceptual revisions and policy adjustments are required. Deborah Johnson, in her excellent introduction to computer ethics, avoids taking sides on the issue of the uniqueness of computer ethics and suggests that ethical issues surrounding computers are *"new species of old moral issues."* Johnson goes on to say,

> *The metaphor of species and genus encompasses the element of truth on each side of the debate in that a new species has some unique characteristics making it different from any other species, but at the same*

time, the species has generic or fundamental characteristics that are
common to all members of the genus. [1994, p. 10]

Perhaps, the ambiguity in the question about the uniqueness of computer ethics suggests this middle ground approach. But I believe that Johnson's characterization of a problem of computer ethics as just another species of a fixed ethical genus is somewhat misleading because the conceptual uncertainty generated by some problems in computer ethics affects not only our understanding of the particular situation but also the ethical and legal categories that apply to it. As I have suggested, ethical and legal categories, such as privacy and copyright, can shift in meaning as they become informationally enriched. The novelty of the species sometimes infects the genus. Whether or not one regards computer ethics as unique, computer ethics is definitely a demanding field of ethics that requires more than routine application of principles.

Reasons within Relative Frameworks

I have been arguing against understanding computer ethics in terms of Routine Ethics because the application of computing technology regularly produces policy vacuums and informational enrichment that promotes conceptual shifts, if not outright conceptual muddles. Computer ethics is not rote. But, the rejection of Routine Ethics leaves many uncomfortable. If ethics is not routine, how can it be done at all? Retreating to a position of Cultural Relativism will not solve the problem. According to Cultural Relativism, ethical issues must be decided situationally on the basis of local customs and laws. Two problems immediately confront us with such a position with regard to computer ethics. First, because computing activity is globally interactive, appealing to local customs and laws will not in general provide us with an answer to what we should do when customs and laws conflict. On the world wide web, information flows without regard to particular customs. Which customs should we apply in regulating it? To pick the customs of any one culture seems arbitrary. Do we pick the customs of the culture in which it appears on the computer screen or the customs of the culture from which it originates or the customs of the cultures through which it passes? Second, all of the difficulties with Routine Ethics continue to apply. A policy vacuum may occur for every culture. A computing situation may be so novel that there are no customs or laws established anywhere to cope with it. Initially, an appeal to Cultural Relativism may seem like a sophisticated and plausible attempt to escape the parochial limits of Routine Ethics, but on closer inspection it has the limitations of Routine Ethics and more.

The shortcomings and difficulties with Routine Ethics and Cultural Relativism may make one cautious about doing applied ethics at all. If people differ in their ethical judgments, how can disagreements be avoided or resolved? It is for this reason, I think, that computer scientists and others are sometimes reluctant to teach computer ethics. Ethical issues seem to be too elusive and vague. But a safe retreat to a realm of pure facts where everything is black or white, true or false, without any consideration of values is never possible. Every science, including computer science, rests on value judgments. If, for example, truth is not taken as an important value by scientists, the enterprise of science cannot begin.

My position is that all interesting human enterprises, including computing, are conducted within frameworks of values. Moreover, these frameworks can be rationally criticized and adjusted. Sometimes they are criticized externally from the vantage point of other frameworks and sometimes they are critiqued internally. Some value frameworks, such as those in an emerging science like computer science, undergo rapid evolution. Other value frameworks are more stable. Value frameworks provide us with the sorts of reasons we consider relevant when justifying particular value judgments. Human values are relative, but not simply in the shallow sense of Cultural Relativism. Our most basic values are relative to our humanity, which provides us with a shared framework in which to conduct reasoned arguments about what we ought to do.

My intent is not to search for a way to eliminate value disputes altogether, which I do not think is possible, but to show how some reasoned discussion about value issues is possible even when customs may be absent or in conflict. To say that values are relative means that they are not absolute; it does not mean they are random or uncommon or uncriticizable. Perhaps, reflecting about reasoning with relative values is like thinking about swimming for the first time. It seems impossible. Why doesn't one sink to the bottom? How can one move if the water moves when pushed? Why doesn't one drown? But, swimming without drowning is possible and so is reasoning with relative values. In fact, not only is it possible; we do it all the time. Given the relativity of values, is there any hope for rational discussion in computer ethics? Absolutely!

My presentation will be in two steps. First, I will discuss the ubiquity of nonethical values and emphasize their use in every aspect of human activity—we cannot escape value decision-making even if we wanted to do so. I will use computer science itself as an example, though any interesting human enterprise could serve as an illustration. And second, I will discuss the use of values in making ethical decisions. My position is that an accommodation between reasoned argument and relativity of values is possible. We can acknowledge the difference in values among people and among cultures and still engage in rational discussions about the best policies for using computer technology.

Let me begin with emphasizing the ubiquity of values in our lives. In every reasonably complex human activity, decisions are made that require value choices at least implicitly. Cooks make value decisions about what constitutes a good meal. Business people make value decisions about good investments. Lawyers make decisions about good jurors. All of these endeavors utilize facts, but the facts are always in the escort of values. Each discipline has its own cluster of values that members of the discipline use in making decisions. Even scientists, who pride themselves in establishing facts, must utilize values at least implicitly. In order to gather the facts, scientists must know what counts as good evidence, what counts as good methodology, and what counts as good explanation. Values permeate our lives. I am not speaking here primarily of ethical values. Rather these are the values of daily activities that make our activities purposeful. Values are so much a part of what we do that we often don't reflect on the fact that values are at work when we make ordinary decisions. Value judgments cannot be escaped by any of us in work or play. Values saturate our decision making and are necessary for the flourishing of the activities of life.

Even if one agrees that non-ethical values cannot be escaped in doing ordinary activities, there is still the concern that the relativity of values makes it impossible to have reasoned disputes. After all, cooks, business people, lawyers, and scientists disagree among themselves. To examine the problem of relativity of values, let's use the activity of computer science as an example. In doing computer science, like other sophisticated human activities, one must make decisions and these decisions utilize, often implicitly, sets of non-ethical values. These are the values of the discipline. For instance, a computer scientist knows what makes a computer program a good program. Here I am using "good" primarily in a non-ethical sense. A good computer program is one that works, that has been thoroughly tested, that doesn't have bugs, that is well-structured, that is well-documented, that runs efficiently, that is easy to maintain, and that has a friendly interface. All of the properties of a good program reflect values. They are the features that make one computer program *better* than another. Moreover, this set of related values, which constitutes a set of standards within computer science, is widely shared among computer scientists. Given these standards, rational discussions can be conducted about how to improve a particular computer program. Moreover, policies regarding good programming techniques can be reasonably justified relative to the set of standards. For instance, one might argue for a policy of using object-oriented programming on the grounds that it leads to fewer bugs and computer code that is easier to maintain.

Computer scientists, like everyone else, can have disagreements, including disagreements about the standards. But disagreements that might appear to be about values are sometimes merely disagreements about facts. If there is a disagreement about the justification of the policy to use object-oriented programming, the real disagreement may be about whether or not object-oriented programming really leads to fewer bugs and code that is easier to maintain. Such a dispute might be put to an empirical test. In this situation it is not a dispute about the importance of bug-free, easily maintainable code, but about how well object-oriented programming achieves these valued goals. Thus, disputes that initially may strike us as irreconcilable disputes about values may really be disputes about the facts of the matter subject to empirical adjudication.

Naturally, computer scientists can also disagree about the values that make up a good computer program as well. Some may rank documentation as essential and others may take it to be a less important optional feature. Depending upon the ranking of the different values, different judgments can be made regarding which programs are better than others and which policies about constructing computer programs are the most important. What I want to emphasize, however, is the degree of consensus that exists among computer scientists about what constitutes a good computer program. The specific rankings may differ somewhat from person to person but a pattern of agreement emerges about the types of programs that are the best. No computer scientist regards ineffective, untested, buggy, unstructured, undocumented, inefficient, unmaintainable code with an unfriendly interface as a good program. It just doesn't happen. In a sense, the shared standards define the field and determine who is qualified and indeed who is in the field at all. If one prefers to produce buggy, "spaghetti code" programs, one is not doing serious computer science at all.

Discussions of the relativity of values sometimes engage in the *Many/Any Fallacy*. This fallacy occurs when one reasons from the fact that many alternatives are acceptable to the claim that any alternative is acceptable. There are many acceptable ways for a travel agent to route someone between Boston and Madrid. It doesn't follow that any way of sending someone between these cities is acceptable. Traveling through the center of the Earth and going via the North Star are not included. Many different computer programs may be good but not just any computer program is good.

To summarize, non-ethical values play a role in our decision making in all interesting human activities, including computer science. No escape to a safe realm of pure facts, even in science, is ever possible. The standards of value of a discipline may be widely shared, implicit, and go unnoticed, but they are always there. Moreover, every discipline has sufficient agreement upon what the standards are to conduct its business. Without some consensus on what is valuable, progress in a discipline is impossible.

Core Values

Given that some consensus about values within communities with shared preferences exists, is there any basis for consensus about values among communities? Ethical judgments are made beyond the narrow bounds of special interest communities. Given differences among communities, let alone differences among cultures, how is it possible to ground ethical judgments? Ethical judgments about computing technology may seem even more dubious. Because computing technology generates policy vacuums, i.e., creates situations in which there are no established policies based on custom, law, or religion, we are confronted with the difficult task of justifying ethical policies about novel applications of computing technology even within one community.

To address these challenges we must begin by asking whether we share any values as human beings. What do we have in common? I believe that there is a set of core values that are shared by most, if not all, humans. They are familiar to all of us. Life and happiness are two of the most obvious such values. At the very least people want to avoid death and pain for themselves. Of course, in some situations people give up their lives and suffer pain to accomplish certain objectives. But, generally speaking people do not intentionally hurt and kill themselves for no reason. There is a prima facie value on life and happiness for humans. Other core values (or core goods) for humans include ability, freedom, knowledge, resources, and security. These values are articulated in different ways in different cultures but all cultures place importance on these values to some extent. Obviously, some cultures may distribute these goods unequally among their members, but no culture disregards these values completely. No culture or individual human could continue to exist and disregard the core values entirely. Humans need nourishment and cultures need to raise their young to survive. These kinds of activities require at least some ability, freedom, knowledge, resources, and security. The fact that humans share some basic values is not surprising. These values provide some evolutionary advantages. Individuals and cultures that completely neglect the core goods will not exist for very long.

The core values provide standards with which to evaluate the rationality of our actions and policies. They give us reasons to favor some courses of action over others. They provide a framework of values for judging the activities of others as well. As we become acquainted with other cultures, differences often strike us. The members of other cultures eat different meals, wear different clothing, and live in different shelters. But at a more abstract level people are remarkably alike. Initially, we may find the habits of others to be strange, silly, or bizarre, but after investigation we don't find them to be unintelligible. Activities that may appear at first to be random or purposeless are in fact ordered and purposeful. This doesn't make the practices of others uncriticizable, any more than our own are uncriticizable, but it does make them understandable.

Discussions of relativism in ethics often include examples of the Many/Any Fallacy. Many different customs exist, and, so it is argued, any custom may exist. Not so. Some possible practices are ruled out and other practices (in some form or other) are required if a culture is to exist. Core human values are articulated in a multitude of delightful ways but they also constrain the realm of possibilities. Again, "relative" doesn't mean "random."

To say that we share the core values is only a first step in the argument toward grounding ethical judgments. The most evil villain and the most corrupt society will exhibit core human values on an individual basis. Possessing core human values is a sign of being rational but is not a sufficient condition for being ethical. To adopt the *ethical point of view* one must respect others and their core values. All things being equal, people do not want to suffer death, pain, disability, interference, deception, loss of resources, or intrusion.

If we respect the core values of everyone, then we have some standards by which to evaluate actions and policies. The core values provide a framework for analysis in computer ethics. By using the core value framework, some policies for applying computer technology can be judged to be better than others. Let's consider a set of *possible* policies for the activities of a web browser as an example.

Possible Policies for a Web Site

1. Destroy information on the user's hard disk by leaving a time bomb on the user's hard disk.
2. Remove information from the user's hard disk without the user's knowledge.
3. Leave a "cookie" (information about the user's preferences) on the user's hard disk without informing the user.
4. Leave a "cookie" on the user's hard disk and inform the user.
5. Do not leave or take any permanent information from the user's hard disk.
6. Give the user the information and ability to accept or decline cookies.

If we respect others and their core values, i.e., take the ethical point of view, then these policies can be ranked at least roughly. Policies 1 and 2 are clearly unacceptable. Nobody contacts a web site wishing or expecting to have his or her hard disk erased or information stolen. The information found on a hard disk is a resource of the user that requires respect and protection. Policy 3 is better than 1 or 2. People may benefit from having their preferences recorded so that the web site can tailor its responses more effectively the next time it is visited. Yet, information is being left on the user's hard disk without their knowledge. Some deception may be involved. Policy 4 is better than 3 in that the user is informed about the activity. Policy 6 is better still in that the user has both the knowledge and the ability to allow or refuse the cookies. Given these advantages, Policy 6 is better than 5 though 5 would be a perfectly acceptable policy in that no harm is being caused to the user.

This analysis of the comparative strengths and weaknesses of these policies could be elaborated but enough has been said to make several points. People may not agree on exactly how to rank these policies. Some may believe that the theft of information is worse than its destruction and so Policy 2 is worse than Policy 1. Some may believe that Policy 6 creates some risks because of possible misunderstandings about what is being placed on a hard disk and so Policy 5 is better than Policy 6. But nobody would argue from an ethical point of view that Policy 1 or 2 is acceptable. Most would agree that some of the other policies are acceptable and that some are better than others. Moreover, even when there is disagreement about the rankings, the disagreements may have as much to do with factual matters as with value differences. As a matter of fact, does the loss of information cause more damage than its destruction, and as a matter of fact do misunderstandings about what is or is not left on a hard disk occur? Apparent value differences may be open to empirical resolution.

The situation is parallel to the evaluation of computer programs. Computer scientists have substantial agreement that some computer programs are terrible and some are very good. There are disagreements about the rankings of some in the middle. Often reasons can be given about why some are better than others. Similarly, some policies for using computers are ethically not acceptable whereas others clearly are. People may have different rankings, but these rankings, assuming an ethical point of view, will have significant positive correlation. Moreover, people can give reasons why some policies are better than others. The core values provide a set of standards by which we can evaluate different policies. They tell us what to look for when making our assessments about the benefits and harms of different policies. They give us the reasons for preferring one policy over another. They suggest ways to modify policies to make them better.

Responsibility, Resolution, and Residue

There are many levels of relativity in value judgments. Some of our values are relative to our being human. If we were angels or creatures from another dimension, our core values might be different. And then, of course, different cultures articulate the core human values differently. And different individuals within a culture may differ in their assessments of values. Indeed, some values of one individual may change over time. I have been arguing that such relativity is compatible with a rational discussion of ethical issues and resolution of at least some ethical disputes. We are after all human beings, not angels or creatures from another dimension. We share core values. This provides us with a set of standards with which to assess policies even in situations in which no previous policies exist and with which to assess other value frameworks when disagreements occur.

Ethical responsibility begins by taking the ethical point of view. We must respect others and their core values. If we can avoid policies that result in significant harm to others, that would be a good beginning toward responsible ethical conduct. Some policies are so obviously harmful that they are readily rejected by our core value standards. Selling computer software that is known to malfunction in a way that is likely to result in death is an obvious example. Other policies easily meet our standards. Building computer interfaces that facilitate use by the disabled is a clear example. And of course, some policies for managing computer technology will be disputed. However, some of the ethical policies under dispute may be subject to further rational discussion and resolution. The major resolution technique, which I have been emphasizing, is the empirical investigation of the actual consequences of proposed policies. For instance, some people might propose a limitation on free speech on the internet on the grounds that such freedom would lead to an unstable society or to severe psychological damage of some citizens. Advocates of free speech might appeal to its usefulness in transmitting knowledge and its effectiveness in calling attention to the flaws of government. To some extent these are empirical claims that can be confirmed or disconfirmed, which in turn may suggest compromises and modifications of policies.

Another resolution technique is to assume an impartial position when evaluating policies. Imagine yourself as an outsider not being benefited or harmed by a policy. Is it a fair policy? Is it a policy that you would advocate if you were suddenly placed in a position in which you were affected by the policy. It may be tempting to be the seller of defective software, but nobody wants to be a buyer of defective software. And finally, analogies are sometimes useful in resolving disagreements. If a computing professional would not approve of her stockbroker withholding information from her about the volatility of stock she is considering buying, it would seem by analogy she should share information with a client about the instability of a computer program that the client is considering purchasing.

All of these techniques for resolution can help form a consensus about acceptable policies. But when the resolution techniques have gone as far as they can, some residue of disagreement may remain. Even in these situations, alternative policies may be available that all parties can accept. But, a residue of ethical difference is not to be feared. Disputes occur in every human endeavor and yet progress is made. Computer ethics is no different in this regard. The chief threat to computer ethics is not the possibility that a residue of disagreements about which policies are best will remain after debates on the issues are completed, but a failure to debate the ethical issues of computing technology at all. If we naively regard the issues of computer ethics as routine or, even worse, as unsolvable, then we are in the greatest danger of being harmed by computer technology. Responsibility requires us to adopt the ethical point of view and to engage in ongoing conceptu-al analysis and policy formulation and justification with regard to this ever-evolving technology. Because the computer revolution now engulfs the entire world, it is crucial that the issues of computer ethics be addressed on a global level. The glob-al village needs to conduct a global conversation about the social and ethical impact of computing and what should be done about it. Fortunately, computing may help us to conduct exactly that conversation.[2]

References

Bynum, Terrell, and Simon Rogerson. [1996] "Introduction and Overview: Global Information Ethics." *Science and Engineering Ethics,* 2 (2):131–136.

Johnson, Deborah. [1994] *Computer Ethics*. 2nd ed. Englewood Cliffs, New Jersey: Prentice Hall, Inc.

Maner, Walter. [1996] "Unique Ethical Problems in Information Technology." *Science and Engineering Ethics,* 2 (2):137–154.

Moor, James. [1985] "What is Computer Ethics?" *Metaphilosophy,* 16 (4):266–275.

Moor, James. [1990] "Ethics of Privacy Protection." *Library Trends,* 39 (1 & 2):69–82.

---

[2] Thanks to Deborah Johnson and Keith Miller for helpful suggestions about this paper.

Disclosive Computer Ethics

Philip Brey

This essay provides a critique of mainstream computer ethics and argues for the importance of a complementary approach called disclosive computer ethics, which is concerned with the moral deciphering of embedded values and norms in computer systems, applications, and practices. Also, four key values are proposed as starting points for disclosive studies in computer ethics: justice, autonomy, democracy, and privacy. Finally, it is argued that research in disclosive computer ethics should be multi-level and interdisciplinary, distinguishing between a disclosure level, a theoretical level, and an application level.

Limitations of Mainstream Computer Ethics

The aim of this essay is to outline a particular approach to computer ethics called *disclosive computer ethics*. Although already increasingly influential within computer ethics, disclosive computer ethics still deviates from mainstream approaches in computer ethics. *Mainstream computer ethics* is a name that will be used in this essay for those approches that currently make up the mainstream in computer ethics. These are approaches that follow what I will call the *standard model of applied ethics*. In this section, I will sketch the standard model of applied ethics, illustrate how mainstream computer ethics fits this model, and then go on to outline limitations of this model that are overcome by disclosive computer ethics. My aim is not to present disclosive computer ethics as a rival approach, but rather as an approach that is complementary to mainstream computer ethics. The remaining sections of the essay will be devoted to an outline and defense of disclosive computer ethics as an approach within computer ethics.

Mainstream computer ethics, I will argue, takes as its point of departure a particular model of applied ethics that may be called the standard model, because it is used in the vast majority of work in applied ethics. Studies in applied ethics that adopt the standard model aim to clarify and evaluate morally controversial practices through an application and defense of moral principles. Research within this model usually proceeds in three steps. First, an individual or collective practice is outlined that has been the topic of moral controversy. A biomedical ethicist, for

This essay originally appeared in *Computers and Society*, Vol. 30, No. 4 (December) 2000: 10–16. Copyright © 2000 by Philip Brey. Reprinted by permission.

example, may write about euthanasia, cloning, informed consent, or late-term abortion. Likewise, environmental ethicists may focus on wetlands development, the use of nuclear energy, or emission of greenhouse gases. Next, an attempt is usually made to clarify and situate the practice, through conceptual analysis and fact-finding. For example, an ethical study of late-term abortion may analyze the concept of personhood, distinguish different stages in the development of the fetus, and describe existing procedures and techniques for late-term abortions. Third, moral principles are outlined, along with moral judgments or intuitions, and applied to the topic. This is a deliberative process, with arguments for and against particular principles or their applicability to the case. The outcome is a moral evaluation of the practice that is investigated.

The standard model of applied ethics is adopted in most of the literature in computer ethics. In mainstream computer ethics, a typical study begins by identifying a morally controversial practice, like software theft, hacking, electronic monitoring, or Internet pornography. Next, the practice is described and analyzed in descriptive terms, and finally, moral principles and judgments are applied to it and moral deliberation takes place, resulting in a moral evaluation, and optionally, a set of policy recommendations.

In the context of this essay, three features of mainstream computer ethics are particularly noteworthy. First, mainstream computer ethics focuses on *existing* moral controversies. That is, its focus is on issues that are recognized by many as being morally problematic. Second, its focus is on *practices*, i.e., the individual or collective behavior of persons. It aims to evaluate and devise policies for these practices. And third, its focus usually is on the *use* of computer technology, as opposed to, for example, its design or advertisement. As Moor summed it up in his influential essay "What is computer ethics?" (1985), "A typical problem in computer ethics arises because there is a policy vacuum about how computer technology should be used." (p. 266).

Here, a first limitation of mainstream computer ethics may be identified. Mainstream computer ethics limits itself to the analysis of morally controversial practices for which a policy vacuum currently exists. But what about computer-related practices that are not (yet) morally controversial, but that nevertheless have moral import? Surely, one would not want such practices to be ignored. Let us call a practice that has moral import but that is not generally recognized as morally controversial *a (morally) nontransparent* or *opaque* practice. Clearly, some of the research effort in computer ethics should be devoted to identifying and studying morally nontransparent practices. I take this to be part of the *critical* function of computer ethics.

Computer-related practices may be morally opaque for two reasons: because they are unknown or because they have a false appearance of moral neutrality. Many computer-related practices are simply unfamiliar or unknown to most people, because they are not visible for the average computer user and are not widely discussed in the media, and these practices consequently fail to be identified as morally controversial. Most Internet users, for example, are unfamiliar with the ways in which their browsing behavior is monitored on-line. Even though on-line monitoring is not an issue for most Internet users to concern themselves with, I claim that it is part of the critical function of computer ethics to identify, analyze, morally evaluate, and devise policy guidelines for on-line monitoring.

The second way in which moral nontransparency may arise is when a practice is familiar in its basic form, but is not recognized as having the moral implications that it in fact has. The hardware, software, techniques, and procedures used in computing practice often have the appearance of *moral neutrality* when in fact they are not morally neutral. For example, search engines used on the Internet seem to have the innocuous taks of helping users to quickly find relevant information. However, as Introna and Nissenbaum (2000) have argued, the particular search algorithms used in search engines are far from neutral, and are often discriminatory in giving the highest rankings to sites that are large, popular, and designed by knowledge-able computer professionals. In this way these search algorithms threaten the idea of the Web as a public space in which everyone has an equal opportunity to let one's voice be heard.

The above remarks about the moral non-neutrality of many technologies and techniques point to a second limitation of mainstream computer ethics. Mainstream computer ethics focuses on the morality of practices, particularly on the use of computer technology. What is often marginalized in the discussion, or left out entirely, is the moral role of the technology that is being used. That is, the design features of computer systems and software are often taken as a given in computer ethics. The technology is taken as a neutral tool with which both moral and immoral actions can be performed, and the focus is on these actions. In philosophical and empirical studies of technology, however, it is by now accepted that technologies are not neutral, and that they often play an active part in shaping their environments. A colloary of this view is that technological artifacts may themselves become the object of moral scrutiny, independently from, and prior to, particular ways of using them.

The notion that technology can have moral properties is an extension of the notion that it can have political properties (e.g., Winner 1980; Sclove 1995; Feenberg, 1999). As Winner (1980) has argued, technological artifacts and systems function much like laws, by constraining behavior and serving as frameworks for public order. Richard Sclove has made the same point by identifying technical artifacts as elements of social structure. Sclove defines the social structure of a society as its "background features that help define or regulate patterns of human interaction. Familiar examples include laws, dominant political and economic institutions, and systems of cultural belief." (1995, p. 11). He argues that technologies should also be included in this list, because they have the same kinds of structural effects as these other elements of social structure.

Technologies are, for example, capable of coercing individuals to behave in certain ways, may provide opportunities and constraints, may affect cultural belief systems, and may require certain background conditions for them to function properly.[1] Many such structural effects of technology may be analyzed from a moral point of view. Feenberg, finally, has explained that the political properties of technical artifacts often become opaque because the artifact is accepted in society as apolitical: It is understood in terms of a *technical code*, which is a neutral specification of

---

[1] Extended discussion and examples of these properties of technologies are found in Winner (1980), Sclove (1995), Pfaffenberger (1992), and Akrich (1992).

its technical properties and functions that obscures the nonneutral social and political properties of the artifact (Feenberg, 1999).

The notion that technologies are themselves worthy objects of moral analysis is perhaps especially true for computer technology. This is because computer systems have become, because of their information processing abilities, important determinants in many human decision-making processes, behaviors, and social relations. Computer systems often function less as background technologies and more as active constitutents in the shaping of society. This active role of computer systems warrants special attention in computer ethics to their design features, as an object of moral analysis, largely independently of their use. To conclude, mainstream computer ethics has two important, interrelated limitations: it tends to focus too narrowly on publicly recognized moral dilemmas, and it tends to downplay computer technology itself as an object of moral analysis.

Hidden Morality and Disclosive Computer Ethics

Disclosive computer ethics is the name I propose for a family of recent approaches in computer ethics that are centrally concerned with the moral deciphering of computer technology. This work distinguishes itself from mainstream computer ethics on exactly the two points mentioned: it tends to be concerned with the uncovering of moral issues and features in computing that had not until then gained much recognition, and its focus tends to be on the design features of computer technology. Disclosive studies in computer ethics are hence studies concerned with disclosing and evaluating embedded normativity in computer systems, applications, and practices. Its major contribution to computer ethics is not so much found in the development or application of ethical theory, but rather in the description of computer technology and related practices in a way that reveals their moral importance.

Existing work in computer ethics that takes a disclosive approach covers moral issues such as privacy, democracy, distributive justice, and autonomy, and covers the full spectrum of information and communication technologies. Friedman and Nissenbaum (1997), for example, is a study of bias in computer systems. Such biases are usually not recognized, but Friedman and Nissenbaum try to reveal the existence of bias by describing computer systems with bias and by bringing into view the possible unjust consequences of such systems (see also Brey, 1998). Examples of biased computer systems or programs are educational programs that have much more appeal to boys than to girls, thus displaying a gender bias, loan approval software that gives negative recommendations for loans to individuals with ethnic surnames, databases for matching organ donors with potential transplant recipients that systematically favor individuals retrieved and displayed on initial screens over individuals displayed on later screens.

Similarly, Brey (1999; 1998) is concerned with the consequences of the design of computer systems for the autonomy of users. Computer systems may undermine the autonomy of users by being designed to facilitate monitoring by others, or by imposing their own operational logic on the user, thus limiting creativity and choice, or by making users dependent on systems operators or others for maintenance or access to systems functions. Most of the space in these two papers is devoted to revealing the potential impacts of computer designs on the autonomy of users, and much less attention is paid to theorizing and applying moral principles of autonomy.

Other examples of disclosive studies in computer ethics are Nissenbaum (1997), who reveals the moral importance of practices of registering public information, Blanchette (1998), who reveals the importance of trust relations in cryptographic protocols and payment mechanisms, Introna and Nissenbaum (2000), who decipher the hidden politics of search engines, Agre and Mailloux (1997), who reveal the implications for privacy of Intelligent Vehicle-Highway Systems that collect vast amounts of data on individuals' travel patterns, Tavani (1999), who analyzes the implications of data mining for privacy, and Johnson (1997), who analyzes anti-democratic tendencies inherent within the structure and organization of the Internet.

Admittedly, the description of technologies and practices so as to reveal their moral importance presupposes that one can already discern what is and what is not morally important, and hence that relevant moral values have already been formulated before analysis comes off the ground. However, this does not mean that one must already be equipped with moral theories before disclosive analysis can take place. The (potential) moral importance of designs or practices is already sufficiently established if it is shown that these designs or practices yield, for example, an unequal distribution of power or of goods, that they diminish privacy or freedom (according to common-sense notions of these terms), that they negatively affect social relations or statuses, or that they touch on other important moral values that are widely shared in society. Therefore, disclosive analysis can remain largely pretheoretical, and a more precise moral evaluation can wait until after disclosive analysis.

Thus, a disclosive study in computer ethics may take the form of a two-stage process. In the first stage of analysis, some technology (X) is analyzed from the point of view of a relevant moral value (Y) (where Y is, e.g., privacy, justice, freedom, etc.), which is only given a loose, common-sense definition. This analysis may yield a tentative conclusion that certain features of X tend to undermine (or perhaps sustain) Y in particular ways. For example, it may be found that search engines in use on the Internet tend to undermine informational privacy, where informational privacy is defined loosely as the control that individuals have over the disclosure of information about their person. This analysis may prompt a second stage in which theories of informational privacy are applied and perhaps further developed so as to arrive at a more specific normative evaluation of the privacy-aspects of search engines, which can also be used to arrive at policy guidelines regarding their design, use, and regulation.

Of course, it is also possible to do disclosive analysis in a more theory-driven way. In the above example, one would then start with a moral theory of informational privacy that would contain specific moral principles, and then analyze the manner in which search engines uphold or fail to uphold these principles. Optionally, this analysis could again result in a set of policy recommendations regarding the privacy-aspects of search engines.

Pretheoretical and theory-driven approaches are both acceptable varieties of disclosive computer ethics. There are, however, at least two reasons why a theory-driven variety may ultimately be less preferable. First, a theory-driven approach

tends to makes the acceptance of a disclosive analysis dependent on the acceptance of a particular moral theory. For example, a study that shows that existing
search engines violate a particular conception of informational privacy found in
theory T may not convince someone that search engines raise issues for informational privacy if that person rejects T. That person might have been convinced
by an analysis that had started with a loose definition of informational privacy,
and proceeded to show that search engines pose a problem for informational privacy according to this loose definition. Second, a theory-driven approach will
already contain preconceptions about the technology or practice that is under
scrutiny, because it already employs a highly theoretical vocabulary in the analysis of observable phenomena, which may include empirical presuppositions. It may
therefore come to observations that are as based in part on preconceptions, at points
where more neutral descriptions may be preferable. In conclusion, there are good
reasons not to choose a theory-driven approach in disclosive computer ethics if
given the choice.

It may be objected that the stated opposition between a pretheoretical and a
theory-driven approach is untenable. It is questionable whether there can be a
theory-neutral and uncontroversial common-sense definition of moral values like
freedom, privacy, and justice. Any articulation of such values necessarily invokes
theoretical assumptions. For example, a common-sense definition of freedom as
the ability to act without coercion or interference by others makes the questionable theoretical assumption that freedom is to be defined negatively in terms of
the absence of constraints on action. It implicitly rejects positive conceptions of
freedom (Berlin, 1969) in which freedom depends on self-mastery, or the ability to
make autonomous decisions for which one is willing to bear responsibility and that
one can explain by reference to one's own ideas and purposes.

This objection has some validity: Alleged common-sense definitions of moral
values are always theory-laden and never account for everyone's moral intuitions
regarding these values. Still, it would be prudent to maintain a distinction between
a pretheoretical and a theory-driven approach, and to prefer the former, for two
reasons. First, even if alleged "common-sense" definitions of moral values are theory-laden, there is still a vast difference between a theory-laden definition and a
full-blown moral theory of that value, such as a theory of freedom or justice. Such
a theory necessarily contains many more theoretical assumptions than a mere definition, and therefore leads to analyses that are much more theory-laden.

Second, value definitions in disclosive analysis need only function as operational
tools for the identification of features of computer systems and practices that are
potentially morally controversial. They are like fishing nets: They may bring up items
that one was looking for as well as items that are of no interest. For example, to
start off a disclosive analysis, a feature of a computer system may initially be identified as (potentially) unjust when it systematically favors the interests of some user
groups over those of others. A disclosive analysis will then bring to light many features of computer systems that are (potentially) unjust according to this definition.
A subsequent theoretical analysis can decide which of these features are indeed
unjust. It can then be decided, for example, that only some of these are: Those features that go as far as to effect an unequal distribution of primary social goods

according to Rawls's theory of justice (Rawls, 1971). The point of disclosive analysis is hence to make potentially morally controversial computer features and practices visible; whether these are also really morally wrong, and if so, how wrong they are, can be decided later in a theoretical analysis.

Key Values as Departure Points for Analysis

Disclosive computer ethics hence uncovers and morally evaluates values and norms embedded in the design and application of computer systems. For it to qualify as computer ethics, the values and norms in question must be *moral* values and norms. Many values and norms are nonmoral, including values like efficiency and profit or norms that prescribe the correct usage of words or the right kind of batteries to use in an applicance. Although any distinction between moral and nonmoral values and norms is bound to be controversial, moral norms and values are usually recognized as pertaining to the rightness or wrongness, or goodness or badness, of actions and those who perform them, and correspondingly, to the praiseworthiness or blameworthiness of these actions and persons, and often point back to more fundamental values that are thought to jointly make up human conceptions of the Good.

I will proceed to propose four fundamental values that may constitute a point of departure for future studies in disclosive computer ethics. These values deserve special attention because they are amongst those values that are held in the highest esteem in Western democracies, and because previous studies in disclosive computer ethics have shown that morally opaque computer-related practices often threaten or support these values. All four of these values are widely agreed to be important by both the average citizen in Western democracies, as well as by politicians, legal specialists, and intellectuals; they are amongst those values that receive most attention in ethics, law, and political theory, and specific policies and laws exist to promote them (e.g., privacy is promoted by numerous privacy laws and policies across the world). Moreover, these values are often considered to be fundamental: They do not reduce to more fundamental values, and they are themselves foundational to other values.

There are perhaps other values that also have this status (e.g., sustainability), but these are not affected as much (positively or negatively) by computer technology. Freedom, justice, democracy, and privacy are all very much at stake in the present information society, and often they are eroded or promoted in ways that are unclear, because they are affected by computer-related practices that remain morally opaque. For this reason, then, these four values arguably have a special status in disclosive computer ethics. In what follows, I will propose relatively informal, though necessarily controversial, definitions of these concepts and then outline different issues in computer ethics in which they have been shown to play a role.

1. Justice

The notion of justice is usually understood as implying that individuals should not be advantaged or disadvantaged unfairly or undeservedly. This implies, amongst other things, that society should not promote the unfair distribution of social goods. In particular, society should not promote the unfair distribution of very basic social goods, such as rights and liberties, powers and opportunities, income and wealth, and the social bases of self-respect, as these are essential for individuals to carrying out their life plans. Following Rawls (1971), ethicists often call such social goods *primary* social goods. So there is a shared agreement of society that the distribution of primary social goods in society should not unfairly disadvantage some members. Disagreements exist mostly just on particular distribution models of primary social goods.

Disclosive studies of computer systems and justice are studies of ways in which these systems, or particular applications of them, affect unequal distribution of (primary) social goods for which no immediate justification exists. These studies will normally focus on particular social goods, such as powers, freedoms, job opportunities, or social statuses, and relate these to specific types of computer systems and applications, and different social groups. To these analyses, explicit theories of distributive justice may then be applied to argue whether resulting inequalities are indeed unjust and to make policy recommendations.

2. Autonomy (and freedom)

Whereas the notion of freedom is probably familiar to a larger segment of society than the notion of autonomy, the latter notion is arguably more fundamental. Individual autonomy is commonly taken to mean that individuals have a number of rights to individual freedoms, such as the right to freedom of speech, to religion, to peaceful assembly, and to privacy. Freedom rights such as these are fundamental because they ensure that human beings are able to draw out their own life plans that reflect, as much as possible, values and needs of their own, instead of those of the government or of other citizens. In other words, freedom rights protect goods that are fundamental for carrying out one's own life plan. If one has no privacy, if one cannot practice one's religion, or if one cannot speak freely, one lacks some of the most basic goods that are prerequisite to carrying out one's life plan.

The ideal of individual autonomy has long been defended as fundamental to human flourishing and self-development (e.g., Dworkin, 1988; Hill, 1991). Individual autonomy is often defined as self-governance, that is, the ability to construct one's own goals and values, and to have the freedom to make choices and plans and act in ways that are believed by one to help achieve these goals and promote these values. Individual autonomy is often defended as important because such self-governance is required for self-realization, that is, it is a freedom one must have in order to create a life that is experienced by oneself as meaningful and fulfilling. As Dworkin has pointed out, moreover, individual autonomy may be a requirement for a conception of human beings as equals. If some human beings are not autonomous, they cannot give equal input into moral principles that are aimed to reflect individual preferences, and hence they cannot function as equals in moral life (1988: 30–31).

Disclosive studies of computer systems and autonomy are studies of ways in which these systems or uses of them affect the autonomy or freedom of their users and possible third parties. This includes studies of how computer systems may constrain their users and may help install dependencies (on computer systems themselves, system operators, managers, etc.). It also includes studies of constraints on freedom of information that consider the freedom of individuals to acquire, possess, or distribute certain sorts of information. Also, studies of computer systems and autonomy need not be limited to individual autonomy. Autonomy of organizations and nation states, also called independence or sovereignty, is also a widely shared moral goal, and implications of computer technology for sovereignty is therefore also a worthy topic of investigation.

3. Democracy

Although different conceptions of democracy exist, the idea is widely shared that democracy is rule by "the people," and implies that a democratic society or organization has procedures for political decision-making in which every member has the opportunity to exert influence so as to have his or her interests taken into account. This implies that political power is not concentrated in the hands of individuals or organizations that cannot be held accountable by the public but is instead distributed to a greater or lesser degree over all members of society.

Although the value of democracy relates to the values of justice and autonomy, it is generally held to be a separate value, and therefore separate disclosive studies of computer systems and democracy are warranted (cf. Sclove, 1995). These are studies designed to investigate whether particular computer technologies or applications effect redistributions of political power in societies or organizations such that a loss or gain in democratic content is implied. Particularly important is the question of who has control over information and communication processes in societies and organizations, as ownership of and control over information has become an important source of political power in society.

4. Privacy

Privacy is often taken to be an aspect of autonomy. Yet, because of its importance in relation to computer technology, it merits to be treated separately. Privacy is the freedom granted to individuals to control their exposure to others. A customary distinction is that between *relational* and *informational* privacy. Relational privacy is the control over one's person and one's personal environment, and concerns the freedom to be left alone without observation or interference by others. Informational privacy is one's control over personal information, in the form of text, pictures, recordings, etc. Disclosive studies of computer systems and privacy analyze the implications of computer systems and applications for relational and informational privacy.

Evidently, the above four values do not exhaust the set of moral values that may be taken as the point of departure of disclosive studies in computer ethics. Other values may also be taken as departure points, including values on which no societal consensus exists (e.g., specific religious or cultural values). It may be worth investigating, in particular, to what extent computer technology affects general aspects of the quality of life or quality of society (Brey, 1997).

If disclosive studies of computer technology are to qualify as studies in ethics, then it is necessary that analysis be explicitly centered around moral values like the ones discussed above. A mere investigation of the way in which computer technology affects distributions of wealth and power is not in itself a study in ethics, even if it is motivated by an interest in moral issues, as an explicit normative thematization is lacking. However, such studies may constitute useful inputs for research in computer ethics in which normative issues *are* explicitly thematized.

The Need for Multi-Level Interdisciplinary Research

Disclosive computer ethics requires an approach that is multi-level and interdisciplinary. It is multi-level in that research is to take place at various stages or levels. Three such levels can be discerned. First, there is the *disclosure level*, which is the initial level at which disclosive computer ethics research takes place. At this level, some type of computer system or software is analyzed from the point of view of a relevant moral value like privacy or justice.

Second, there is the *theoretical level*, which is the level at which moral theory is developed and refined. As Jim Moor (1985) has pointed out, the changing settings and practices that emerge with new computer technology may yield new values, as well as require the reconsideration of old values. There may also be new moral dilemmas because of conflicting values that suddenly clash when brought together in new settings and practices. It may then be found that existing moral theory has not adequately theorized these values and value conflicts. Privacy, for example, is now recognized by many computer ethicists as requiring more attention than it has previously received in moral theory. In part this is due to reconceptualizations of the private and public sphere brought about by the use of computer technology, which has resulted in inadequacies in existing moral theory about privacy. It is therefore fitting for computer ethicists to contribute to the development of moral theory about privacy. In general, it is part of the task of computer ethics to *further develop and modify existing moral theory* when existing theory is insufficient or inadequate in light of new demands generated by new practices involving computer technology.

Third, there is the *application level*, in which, in varying degrees of specificity and concreteness, moral theory is applied to analyses that are the outcome of research at the disclosure level. For example, the question of what amount of protection should be granted to software developers against the copying of their programs may be answered by applying consequentialist or natural law theories of property, and the question of what actions governments should take in helping citizens have access to computers may be answered by applying Rawls's principles of justice.[2] The application level is where moral deliberation takes place. Usually this involves the joint consideration of moral theory, moral judgments or intuitions, and background facts or theories, rather than a slavish application of preexisting moral rules.

Whereas computer ethics research at the theoretical level only requires philosophical expertise and may be carried out by philosophers, this is not so for research at the disclosure and application levels. Research at the disclosure level often requires considerable knowledge of the technological aspects of the system or practice that is studied, and often also requires expertise in social science for the analysis of the way in which the functioning of systems is dependent on human actions, rules, and institutions. So ideally, research at the disclosure level is a cooperative venture between computer scientists, social scientists, and philosophers. If not, it should at least be carried out by researchers with an adequate interdisciplinary background.

---

[2] See for further discussion van den Hoven (1997), who discusses models for applying moral theory in applied ethics.

Research at the application level may be argued to be a philosopher's job again, as applying moral theory (e.g., weighing moral principles against considered moral judgments) seems to make an appeal to mostly philosophical skills (van den Hoven, 1997). However, even if bringing moral theory in agreement with moral judgments, empirical facts, scientific claims, and other relevant sources of information is an activity that mostly appeals to philosophical skills, the information that must be processed in this task largely of a nonphilosophical kind. Philosophers engaged in this activity must therefore have a solid grasp of the social, legal, and technical aspects of the technology or practice on which they are to pass moral judgments, or should opt to work with experts in these areas.

Conclusion

Disclosive computer ethics constitutes a much needed approach in computer ethics that deviates from traditional approaches in applied ethics, which usually focus on morally controversial practices and neglect embedded normativity in technological systems and practices, and still often concentrate on formulating and applying moral theory. As has been argued, disclosive computer ethics should preferably not be theory-driven, should be multi-level and interdisciplinary, and should focus on four key values: justice, autonomy, democracy, and privacy. The proposed disclosive method may well be generalized to other areas of applied ethics in which technology plays an important role.

References

Agre, P. and Mailloux, C. (1997) Social Choice about Privacy: Intelligent Vehicle-Highway Systems in the United States, in *Human Values and the Design of Computer Technology* (ed. B. Friedman), Cambridge University Press, Cambridge.

Akrich, M. (1992) The Description of Technical Objects, in *Shaping Technology/Building Society: Studies in Sociotechnical Change* (eds. W. Bijker and J. Law), MIT Press, Cambridge, MA.

Berlin, I. (1969) *Four Essays on Liberty*. Oxford University Press, Oxford.

Blanchette, J. (1998) On the Social Discourse of Cryptology. Paper presented at *CEPE98*, London School of Economics and Political Science, 14–15 December.

Brey, P. (1997) New Media and the Quality of Life, *Technè, Society for Philosophy and Technology Quarterly* 3:1, 1–23.

Brey, P. (1998) The Politics of Computer Systems and the Ethics of Design, in *Computer Ethics: Philosophical Enquiry* (ed. J. van den Hoven), Rotterdam University Press, Rotterdam.

Brey, P. (1999) Worker Autonomy and the Drama of Digital Networks in Organizations, *Journal of Business Ethics* 22:1, 15–25.

Dworkin, G. (1988) *The Theory and Practice of Autonomy*, Cambridge University Press, Cambridge.

Feenberg, A. (1999) *Questioning Technology*. Routledge, London and New York.

Friedman, B. and Nissenbaum, H. (1997) Bias in Computer Systems, in *Human Values and the Design of Computer Technology* (ed. B. Friedman), Cambridge University Press, Cambridge.

Hill, T. (1991) *Autonomy and Self-Respect*. Cambridge University Press, Cambridge.

Hoven, J. van den (1997) Computer Ethics and Moral Methodology. *Metaphilosophy* **28**: 3, 234–248.

Introna, L. and Nissenbaum, H. (2000) The Public Good Vision of the Internet and The Politics of Search Engines, *Preferred Placement. Knowledge Politics on the Web* (ed. R. Rogers), Jan van Eyck Akademie Editions, Maastricht.

Johnson, D. (1997) Is the Global Information Infrastructure a Democratic Technology? *Computers & Society* 27: 20–26.

Moor, J. (1985) What is Computer Ethics? *Metaphilosophy*, **16**, 266–275.

Nissenbaum, H. (1998) Can We Protect Privacy in Public? in *Computer Ethics: Philosophical Enquiry* (ed. J. van den Hoven), Rotterdam University Press, Rotterdam.

Pfaffenberger, B. (1992) Technological Dramas, *Science, Technology, and Human Values* **17**: 282–312.

Rawls, J. (1971) *A Theory of Justice*, Harvard University Press, Cambridge, MA.

Sclove, R. (1995) *Democracy and Technology,* Guilford Press, New York.

Tavani, H. (1999) Informational Privacy, Data Mining, and the Internet, *Ethics and Information Technology* **1**, 137–145.

Winner, L. (1980) Do Artifacts Have Politics? *Daedalus* **109**: 121–136.

Gender and Computer Ethics

Alison Adam

This paper reviews the relatively small body of work in computer ethics that looks at the question of whether gender makes any difference to ethical decisions. There are two strands of writing on gender and computer ethics. The first focuses on problems of women's access to computer technology; the second concentrates on whether there are differences between men and women's ethical decision making in relation to information and computing technologies (ICTs). I criticize the latter area, arguing that such studies survey student audiences, that they emphasize the result of an ethical decision over the process of arriving at the decision, that they are problematic in relation to research methodology, and that they are undertheorized. Given that traditional ethical theories largely ignore gender, I offer a gender based ethics in terms of feminist ethics as the best place to look for theoretical substance. The paper concludes by considering how feminist ethics can be combined with empirical studies that emphasize observation and interviewing in order to move gender and computer ethics onward from statistical studies of men's and women's ethical decisions toward more substantially theorized studies of areas in computer ethics that have gender implications, such as privacy and power.

Introduction

The topic of gender has been somewhat neglected in computer ethics writing to date. Nevertheless there is a small body of work that takes seriously the point of view that gender has some bearing on computer ethics problems. This paper critically reviews that research to argue that current directions in gender and computer ethics research are somewhat problematic and could benefit from a better balance between statistically based empirical research and a more substantial theoretical understanding of gender and computer ethics. In this paper I characterize two strands of writing on gender and computer ethics. The first focuses on problems of women's access to computer technology; the second concentrates on whether there are differences between men and women's ethical decision-making in relation to information and computing technologies (ICTs). I engage with the latter area of research arguing that there

This essay originally appeared in *Computers and Society*, Vol. 30, No. 4 (December) 2000: 17–24. Copyright © 2000 by Alison Adam. Reprinted by permission.

are problems in confining surveys to a student audience, that such studies privilege the result of an ethical decision over the process of arriving at the decision, that they often fall prey to the qualitative/quantitative debate bedeviling much work on ICTs and information systems, and that they are frequently undertheorized.

Although computer ethics research must always maintain a balance between empirical research and theory, gender and computer ethics research is long overdue for more substantial theorizing. Given that traditional ethical theories largely ignore gender, I offer a gender based ethics in terms of feminist ethics as the best place to look for theoretical substance. Feminist ethics has witnessed a tremendous growth in interest within feminist philosophy and so holds much explanatory potential, not just for gender and computer ethics problems, but as an alternative ethics for computer ethics, in general, to rank alongside more traditional approaches from utilitarianism, Kantian ethics, or virtue ethics. After briefly describing the possibilities inherent in feminist ethics, the paper concludes by considering how it can be combined with empirical studies that emphasize observation and interviewing in order to move gender and ethics onward from statistical studies of men's and women's ethical decisions toward more substantially theorized studies of areas in computer ethics that have gender implications, such as privacy and power, which are, as yet largely unexplored.

Gender and Computer Ethics—Barriers and Pipelines

In this and the following section, I explore the two main strands of current research in gender and computer ethics. The first strand can be viewed as a spillover from information systems and computing research on barriers and "pipelines" (Camp, 1997), which tends to see the gender and ICT problem as one of women's access to ICTs and their continuing low representation in computing all the way through the educational process through to the world of work. Until recently such research found voice more substantially in the research areas of work, education, psychology (Brosnan, 1998), and on the fringes of computing disciplines (e.g., see Lovegrove and Segal, 1991; Lander and Adam,1997; Grundy, 1996). However papers in this general mold are beginning to appear in ethics journals and computer ethics conferences suggesting that authors are starting to cast the women and computing access/exclusion problem as an explicitly ethical problem, although this is not how the area has been traditionally seen in the past (e.g., see Rogerson and Stack, 1997; Panteli and Stack, 1998; Turner, 1998; Panteli et al., 1999; Turner, 1999).

I do not wish to elaborate an extensive commentary on this first strand of research on gender and computer ethics. However, I note that studies that discuss the low numbers of women in computing have been criticized in the past for adopting a traditional, liberal position that characterizes the gender and computing problem in terms of educating, socializing, and persuading women rather than challenging the subject matter and deeper structures of the subject (Henwood, 1993). Apart from anything else, the liberal argument, in leaving the organization of computing unchallenged, does little to alleviate women's position in relation to computing education and work; campaigns to attract women based on such a position do not work. In noting that an unanalyzed liberalism is a trap for the unwary, I do not want to imply that the gender and computer ethics work I cite above suffers from it. Interestingly, because such work is beginning to view itself as ethics research, it sidesteps some of the criticisms of liberalism. Although the woman and computing problem is not new, it is still there. Numbers of women through all levels of computing remain low, meaning that women are still being excluded from employment in well-paid and interesting careers for whatever reason, and so it is a problem still to be solved. Casting this more as an ethical problem than an access problem starts to make the issue look less like a question of why women are not, apparently, taking up the opportunities being offered to them, and more like an ethical and political problem of exclusion. In other words, it moves the onus for change away from women, and their apparent failure to take up challenges, toward the computer industry's failure to examine and change its exclusionary practices. Apart from anything else, this work serves to act as an important reminder of how little has changed for women in the computing industry in the last twenty or so years.

Gender and Computer Ethics—Men's and Women's Moral Decision Making

The other strand of research on gender and computer ethics focuses on concerns more central to computer ethics as a whole, namely the question of whether there are detectable differences between men's and women's ethical decision making in relation to computer ethics (Mason and Mudrack, 1996; MacDonald and Pak, 1996; Khazanchi, 1995; Kreie and Cronan, 1998; Bissett and Shipton, 1999; Escribano et al., 1999). Broadly speaking, the research methodology used in these studies can be characterized as follows. A population of subjects (in these studies always a student population) is surveyed by questionnaire and is asked to rate responses either in relation to a set of questions or a set of artificial scenarios. Responses are usually Yes/No or rated against a Likert scale. The results are then analyzed quantitatively (some using little more than percentages, but mostly using more sophisticated statistical methods); this may involve splitting out various ethical variables and rating subjects' responses against them. The analysis is then turned back from quantitative measures into qualitative conclusions that are, in some cases, that women are more ethical than men in relation to computer ethics problems, in other cases that there is no discernable difference. Interestingly, none of the studies found that men were more ethical than women. Sometimes these results are related, theoretically, to Gilligan's (1982) "In a Different Voice" (Bissett and Shipton, 1999; Mason and Mudrack, 1996; McDonald and Pak, 1996), which is the best known work in feminist ethics, but others make no use of feminist or gender-based ethics in terms of explanation (Kreie and Cronan, 1998). The following paragraphs describe these studies in more detail.

Much decision making in relation to computer technologies takes place within the workplace, therefore gender studies within business ethics and information systems are relevant even if ICTs, as such, are not the main focus. Hence the first three studies briefly outlined here are concerned with more general business ethics decision making in relation to gender. In style and substance they are very similar to the computer ethics studies I describe in more detail below. I include these to sharpen my characterization of the style of research methodology being used, to illustrate that results regarding the importance of gender in ethical decision making are quite inconclusive, and finally to strengthen my critique of this methodology, which follows later in the paper.

Mason and Mudrack's (1996) questionnaire study of undergraduate and graduate business students in a classroom setting tested gender socialization and occupational socialization theories against a set of ethical variables. Gender socialization theory suggests differences in ethics variables regardless of the employment position of subjects, while occupational socialization theory implies that employees are similar in outlook and gender differences will not figure in ethical decision making. So the first theory argues for an ethics split along gendered lines, while the second argues that occupational experiences tended to override socialized gender positions, suggesting that men and women are likely to have similar ethical preferences in the workplace. Responses were rated against Froelich and Kottke's (1991) standard ethics measure as the authors recognize the idiosyncrasy of measures often used in business ethics research. Results were analyzed using standard statistical measures. Their results fitted neither theory. "Although no significant gender differences emerged in individuals lacking full time employment, significant differences existed between employed women and men, with women appearing 'more ethical'." (Mason and Mudrack, 1996, 599). The authors commented on the fact they were using students as subjects, albeit students in employment, and noted that this could make their study results more homogeneous than with a more general population.

McDonald and Pak's (1996) research amongst business managers and MBA students (via postal and directly distributed questionnaires) in Canada, Malaysia, New Zealand, and Hong Kong studied cultural and organizational differences as well as gender differences in ethical decision making. They focused on the decision making process and noted that there has been relatively little research on the cognitive processes involved. Based on the literature on ethical frameworks, they arrived at a framework containing a set of their own ethical elements including self interest, utilitarianism, duty, justice, religious convictions, etc. A set of ethical scenarios were devised to explore these elements and subjects were invited to agree or disagree with the scenarios on a five point Likert scale. The results were analyzed statistically and were opposite to Mason and Mudrack's (1996) findings in that they found no major difference between male and female business managers in considering ethical business decisions. However a breakdown by country indicated more distinct differences in ethical frameworks used in each cultural location.

Reiss and Mitra's (1998) study of ethical beliefs amongst college students once more used a questionnaire with a Likert scale where students were asked to rate various actions on a five point scale from very acceptable to very unacceptable. These authors (Reiss and Mitra, 1998, 1983) noted that previous studies tend to split equally amongst those that find women more ethical and those that find no difference. Apparently no study finds men to be more ethical than women in relation to business ethics. The authors analyzed their results statistically to find partial support for the hypothesis that men tended to find behaviors of a dubious ethical nature more acceptable than did women.

Focusing more specifically on computer ethics, I discuss the studies of Khazanchi (1996) and Kreie and Cronan (1998), respectively. Khazanchi's aim was to understand whether gender differences influence the degree to which individuals recognize unethical conduct in the use and development of information technology. To this end, a sample of undergraduate and graduate business students was surveyed against a set of seven ethical scenarios and were asked to rate these as to degree of unethicalness. These scenarios reflected categories comprising the ethical responsibilities of IS professionals regarding disclosure, social responsibility, integrity, conflict of interest, accountability, protection of privacy, and personal conduct and were derived from Parker's (1980) earlier research. Subjects were asked to rate the unethical acts in each scenario against a 7-point Likert scale where 1= "absolutely not unethical" and 7= "absolutely unethical" with no labels for the intermediate range. Khanzanchi then derived an aggregate score of unethicalness and correlated this against gender. Despite concerns as to the external validity of using students in the survey, he found that the women of his survey consistently outperformed the men in identifying unethical actions across all his scenarios. "The present study shows the ability to recognize (and ultimately resist) unethical actions involving IS dilemmas rests in part on the nature of the ethical dilemma and differences in gender of the adjudicator. The findings provide an insight into gender differences in the ethical judgment of future leaders and managers in the management information systems discipline." (Khazanchi, 1996, 744).

Bissett and Shipton's (1999) questionnaire survey of IT professionals studying part-time used a set of scenarios with respondents rating whether they would undertake similar behaviour on a scale of "always" to "never." They found a small positive correlation between female gender and a tendency to consider the feelings of others. By contrast, Escribano, Pena, and Extremera's (1999) survey of university students involved Yes/No responses to a number of questions. They found the women in their survey far more interested in the ethical aspects of information technologies than were the men, despite the fact that they used such technologies much less than the male respondents.

Probably the most prominent of recent studies of gender and computer ethics is Kreie and Cronan's (1998) research. These researchers explored men's and women's moral decision making in relation to a set of computer ethics cases. The examples were, by and large, not blatantly criminal, but were designed to reflect the situations we are often presented with in the workplace where extensive computer systems and networks are pervasive, e.g., viewing sensitive data, making an electronic copy, etc. The main research method in the study involved asking respondents to rate their responses against a set of influential environmental factors such as societal, individual, professional, and legal belief systems. In addition, there are so-called "personal values." The authors proposed these factors as those that influence ethical decision making. Once again a student population was surveyed and asked to rate whether the behavior described in a given scenario was acceptable or unacceptable.

Following the survey it appears that some discussions with students helped explain judgments about the various scenarios. Respondents were also asked about

their moral obligation to take corrective action and whether knowledge of negative consequences, e.g., a fine or reprimand, would affect what a person should or
should not do. For each scenario the respondents were asked which set of values
(e.g., personal values, societal, environmental, etc.) influenced their decision most.
The authors' conclusion was that most people were strongly influenced by their
personal values. Kreie and Cronan (1998, 76) conclude: "Men and women were distinctly different in their assessment of what is ethical and unethical behavior. For
all scenarios, men were less likely to consider a behavior as unethical. Moreover,
their judgement was most often influenced by their personal values and one environmental cue—whether the action was legal. Women were more conservative in
their judgements and considered more environmental cues, as well as their own
personal values." Kreie and Cronan (ibid.) make suggestions as to the policy implications of these results: "From the manager's viewpoint, men may be influenced
more effectively through statements of what is legal (or not). Women might be effectively influenced by passive deterrents (policy statements and awareness training
of unacceptable ethical behaviour.)"

Critique of Gender and Computer Ethics Studies

I have described a number of empirical studies of gender and business ethics and
gender and computer ethics. I now wish to comment on a number of aspects of
these studies and argue that these aspects are problematic. These are described
under the following sub-headings: student population, quantitative vs. qualitative
research methodology, ethical decisions vs. ethical processes and how to get at the
latter, and lack of appropriate theory.

Student Population

In every one of the studies detailed above, a student population was surveyed. As
university teachers it seems we are unable to resist the temptation to utilize that
most captive of audiences, our students! (Adam and Ofori-Amanfo, 2000). Although
it is clear that in some of the studies the students also worked or had work experience, this is still problematic. This is not just because, as Mason and Mudrack (1996)
note, this may give a certain homogeneity to the results obtained. More importantly
there is a hidden power relationship variable between student and teacher that none
of these studies has made explicit. A student and teacher do not stand in the same
relationship as a researcher and a member of the public, for example. This points
out the need to be much more aware of power relationships in computer ethics,
an area that has hitherto received little attention (Adam and Ofori-Amanfo, 2000).

Quantitative vs. Qualitative Research Methodology

All the studies detailed above were similar in approach in that they all employed
questionnaire surveys, either with a binary or 5-point or 7-point Likert scale, which
could then be analyzed quantitatively for statistical significance. I am aware that
a number of the studies I discuss are from one journal (Journal of Business Ethics)
and that journals often have a preferred style, albeit often a tacit one. That apart,
it is interesting that authors are prepared to use statistically-based questionnaire

approaches so uncritically. There are a number of problems with such an approach. Only the Bissett and Shipton (1999) paper points to the problem of whether what people say they do is the same as what they do in a real-life situation. This may be even more of a problem than usual in the present set of studies as respondents are explicitly asked whether they would behave in some potentially immoral or even illegal way. In other words, respondents are not being asked to choose between categories that are anything like neutral. It is naturally tempting to cast oneself as more moral in the questionnaire than one might be in real life.

This is clearly a well trodden path in all social research; nevertheless it cannot be ignored and points to the need for consideration of the appropriateness of other research methods.

There is also the question of what responses on a numerical scale actually mean and whether subjects can reliably attach meaning to the individual intervals in a 7-point scale. Is 1= "absolutely not unethical" the same as "absolutely ethical" or not and does it differ from 2="not quite so absolutely unethical"?

It is interesting that none of the authors in these studies proposed interviewing or ethnographic techniques such as participant observation (e.g., see Forsythe 1993a, 1993b). Participant observation requires an often lengthy period amongst the culture under study. The observer becomes part of and participates in the culture (e.g., in Jordan's (1978) study of birth in four different cultures, as a woman with a free pair of hands she was called upon to help deliver a baby!). But, at the same time, the observer must retain a degree of strangeness from the culture under study otherwise he/she will begin to take for granted aspects of that culture that need to be analyzed and made explicit. For computer ethics, the promise of participant observation lies in the potential to witness ethical reasoning as it happens. This may reveal it to be a process with a much more complex and less clear-cut structure and that may not even result in a decision at all, when compared with the instant Yes/No decisions prompted by questionnaires.

One cannot help but note that interviewing and participant observation are not only much more time consuming techniques but also that their results are much less amenable to rendering into numerical form. Questionnaires can be made to yield numbers that can then be fed into the statistical mill no matter what the validity of the original qualitative assumptions on which they were based. The generalizability from small numbers (some studies report less than two hundred respondents) can also be questioned.

In performing a quantitative analysis of qualitative elements, the studies described above appear to be falling prey to the common assumption prevalent in computing that has been criticized elsewhere, namely that objective factors are available and that these can somehow be factored out and used, like the factors in a mathematical expression (Adam, 1998). Indeed in the Kreie and Cronan (1998) study there is the additional assumption that even if such factors do have some reality as discrete factors, we can reliably separate our beliefs and rate them against things such as social, psychological, or religious beliefs. Can we do this in such a way that each belief system can be identified in an individual's response and can be treated separately? Apart from questioning the validity of such a factoring process, I argue that it allows authors to hide behind the apparent authority of their statistics, obviating the will to develop a more thoroughgoing, conceptual, theoretical analysis. In other words, numbers cannot replace theoretical, conceptual explanations.

The qualitative/quantitative conundrum, to which the above discussion suggests gender and computer ethics empirical studies are rapidly falling prey, is part of a larger debate between qualitative and quantitative research methodologies. This discussion applies not just to work in gender and computer ethics, although it is starkly visible in the studies I outline above, but is more generally a part of research in information systems and business. Oakley (2000) points out that this has been a long-running issue in the social sciences. She argues that it is not nearly as clear-cut as it appears as it is impossible to be completely qualitative, e.g., we talk of "some," "more," "less." Similarly it is impossible to be completely quantitative as our quantities are quantities of some quality. Despite this, the debate has assumed an unwelcome polarity, a kind of "paradigm war" (Oakley 2000, 31). Inevitably one side tends to dominate, and in many parts of the social sciences, good research is thought of in terms of quantitative research.

Somewhat belatedly the qualitative/quantitative debate has filtered into business and management and into information systems research where the two camps are seen as "hard" and "soft," roughly translating into quantitative and qualitative, and where the hard or quantitative enjoys a hegemony (Fitzgerald and Howcroft, 1998). There are also certain tacit geographical mappings with quantitative techniques favored in North America and qualitative approaches more popular in Scandinavia and Europe. With the pressure on academics world-wide to publish, it is small wonder that readily achieved statistical surveys should predominate in gender and computer ethics research as elsewhere.

All the studies reviewed above used statistical analyses. As to the reliability of ethical data gathered by questionnaire, we need to be wary of conclusions based on results from such methods. Given these considerations, there are strong reasons to believe that empirical ethical studies are not at a sufficiently mature research stage to use statistical methods with certainty. There are alternatives. Gilligan's (1982) study of moral reasoning focuses on a conceptual analysis. This involved interviewing respondents about fictitious ethical scenarios. Analyzing both boys' and girls' responses, she was able to map these both against Kohlberg's standard account of ethical maturity and against an alternative theoretical stance of care ethics. At the stage of empirical enquiry currently obtained in computer ethics, I argue that a more conceptual approach provides the best way forward in the short term.

Ethical Decisions vs. Ethical Processes

All these considerations imply that empirical research in this area has not yet got to grips with understanding the process of making an ethical decision. If we were to focus on the process rather than the decision, this would make the decision seem less important *per se*, as quite different approaches can arrive at the same decision through different routes. This aspect is well known to computer ethics researchers, as in Johnson's (1994) description of act utilitarianism as being similar to ethical relativism. Looking at processes rather than decisions would also mean that we would have to be much more sophisticated about our theorizing, as I shall suggest below, and stop treating gender as a unitary, unanalyzed variable. Apart from any other reason, this tends toward essentialism, i.e., the assumption that men and women have essential, fixed characteristics.

Questionnaire techniques focus too sharply on the decision made rather than how the decision was achieved, except insofar as these techniques account for decisions by the kind of factoring process I describe above. It is no easy matter to find ways of getting at the process of ethical decision making. None of the studies related above is substantially reflective on the adequacies of their data gathering methods in this respect. Yet my arguments imply that, in the longer term, if we wish to gather data about real ethical decision making in the field, we must turn to more anthropologically inspired methods, in particular, forms of ethnography and participant observation where the observer participates and becomes part of the culture. Such an approach is likely to yield much richer accounts of the ethical decision process than can be gained by questionnaire type surveys.

Lack of Theory

The arguments of the last three sections taken together suggest that existing work on empirical research on gender and computer ethics is undertheorized. Part of the problem is that the field is far more fragmented than I have made it appear in this review. By and large, the studies I discuss here do not appear to "know" about one another. There is little sense of a tradition where one study builds on another; wheels are continually reinvented. A second aspect of the weak theoretical base of this research is displayed in the way that, for some of the papers reviewed, the authors end up making often unwarranted generalizations that do not appear to follow from their research, by way of conclusion. For instance, Kreie and Cronan (1998) conclude from their study that women are more conservative in their ethical judgment than men and that they might be best with passive deterrents toward unethical behavior, while men might require more substantial ethical deterrents. It is hard to see why women's apparent tendency toward more ethical behavior should make them more conservative. This does not follow from the research issues here but starts to look like a stereotypical judgment about an expectation of men's more "laddish" behavior against a well-behaved female stereotype. It is just such a stereotypical judgment that feminist ethics seeks to argue against. Similarly Khazanchi's (1996) conclusion is that women are better able to recognize "and ultimately resist" unethical behavior. However, it is not clear why the ability to resist unethical behavior should go alongside the ability to recognize it. One is reminded of the old saying often attached to cookie jars as a deterrent: "I can resist everything except temptation." Once again this conclusion smacks of gender stereotypes of women's "good" behavior.

But the most significant aspect of the undertheorizing problem relates to the way that this research makes so little reference to the, by now, quite substantial body of research on feminist ethics that could be used to help explain results. We can take Gilligan's (1982) "In A Different Voice" as a kind of minimum level of reference to feminist ethics. Of the research reviewed above, only McDonald and Pak (1996), Mason and Mudrack (1996), and Bissett and Shipton (1999) refer to it and, indeed, it is the only work of feminist ethics referenced in any of the studies.

Surprisingly, Kreie and Cronan (1998) make no reference either to Gilligan nor to any other part to the large body of writing in feminist ethics that might have helped them explain their results. Indeed they make no attempt to explain *why* their research apparently reveals differences between men and women. This is all the more surprising given that Gilligan's work is very widely known over a number of domains, unlike other work in feminist ethics. Importantly, had Kreie and Cronan (1998) understood the debate surrounding Gilligan's work, which also centered around an empirical study, they would have been able to apply not only her arguments but also the criticism of her arguments to good effect on their own study. On the latter point, Larrabee (1993) notes that one of the criticisms of Gilligan's research was that she asked her respondents to work through a number of artificial case studies rather than observing them making real, live ethical decisions. As I have argued above, this is difficult research to undertake and it requires a time-consuming observational approach rather than a survey.

A similar criticism of Kreie and Cronan (1998) applies. Asking respondents to approve or disapprove of a scenario where software is copied illegally is likely to invoke disapproval in subjects. We all like to be seen as good software citizens. However, like driving slightly above the speed limit, small scale software copying is rife and this study just does not get at subjects' moral decision making in real scenarios where they may be faced with the decision of whether or not to copy some desirable and readily available piece of software. This is very like the argument in Nissenbaum's (1995) "Should I Copy My Neighbor's Software?" On the face of it, taking the viewpoint of standard ethical positions, the answer appears to be "no." But following Nissenbaum's detailed arguments shows that the answer is not nearly so clear cut when one probes the reasons in more detail. The binary approval/disapproval in Kreie and Cronan (1998) or scales of approval and disapproval invoked by Likert scale studies evoke too sharp a Yes/No response. Indeed there are hints that the researchers found the responses too clear cut in the Kreie and Cronan (1998) study where the authors go back and interview groups of students as to how they arrived at decisions. In other words, these authors find themselves obliged to go back in order to probe the processes behind the decisions.

A Plea for Feminist Ethics

The last section made the case that research on gender and computer ethics is currently undertheorized. I would like to argue that there are strong reasons to suggest that feminist ethics can be used to offer fruitful readings of gender and computer ethics problems.

We need to begin the process of exploring the alternative ethics that feminism can offer computer ethics. This can be used to understand how collectivist approaches to ethics can offer alternative readings of traditional computer ethics problems such as hacking, privacy, and on-line harassment. For instance, a feminist reading of privacy suggests strongly that privacy issues are not the same for men and for women (DeCew, 1997). Furthermore we need to understand the gender implications of new potentially privacy-threatening technologies, e.g., cookies, data mining, and biometrics. All these have yet to receive a reading from the point of view of feminist ethics. It may well be the case that women have different responses to men in regard to computer privacy as DeCew (1997) suggests that women and men have different views and expectations of privacy in general.

Secondly, feminist ethics brings a direct consideration of questions of power that are so often absent in traditional ethical theories. Utilitarianism argues for the greatest good for the greatest number. But who is to decide whether one good is better than another? We do not all have an equal say. Tong (1993) argues that it is powerful groups, usually white professional men, who are the decision makers in contemporary cost-benefit analyses. Questions of power are often disguised, but they are crucial to the ethical decision-making process. For instance, it was noted above that in the empirical studies discussed, there is a disguised power relation between the university teachers undertaking the surveys and the students who take part. This suggests that a study of problems relating to Internet pornography and cyberstalking in terms of gender ethics might prove instructive. Issues of power must be rendered visible to make these and other areas understandable.

Finally, given that theories of feminist ethics rest on the hypothesis that women's moral decision making is different from men's in important ways, we need to understand the implications of this for computer ethics. In particular, we need to examine empirical evidence for a different ethical point of view amongst women insofar as it relates to the problems of computer ethics. So far this has barely been attempted in current gender and computer ethics studies (but see Adam and Ofori-Amanfo, 2000).

Categorical claims that gender either definitely does or definitely does not make a material difference to moral reasoning relating to the use of computers somehow misses the point. More important is the question of whether or not the more collectivist "ethic of care" approach to ethics advocated in feminist approaches to ethics can offer alternative and perhaps better ways to tackle computer ethics problems.

Feminist ethics has two major roles. The first is to challenge the traditional ethical canon; the second is to develop theoretical ideas derived, in part, from the challenge to mainstream ethics to develop a new ethics with which to make normative judgments on ethical problems from a wide range of domains.

Jaggar (1991) has described the rise of feminist ethics, particularly within North American academic feminism, and its search for possible models. Feminist ethical discussion in the 1960s and 1970s focused on grass-roots issues such as sexualities and domestic labor, in other words more pragmatic equal opportunity type issues. This strand of research merged with theoretical critiques of traditional ethical theory from about the 1970s onwards. Further research focused on the question of whether there is a distinctively feminine moral experience. Gilligan's much quoted book, "In a Different Voice," was enormously influential in developing an empirical demonstration against Lawrence Kohlberg's views that women's moral development is somehow inferior to men's. It is interesting to note that, in the gender and computer ethics studies described above, not one found men's ethical decision making to be more moral than women's, while several found women's to be more moral than men's. These empirical findings would be extremely difficult to explain under the Kohlberg model.

Gilligan argued instead that women often construct moral dilemmas as conflicts of responsibilities rather than rights and that, in resolving such conflicts, they seek to repair and strengthen networks of relationships. This demonstrates feminist ethics' commitment to responsibility rather than rights, the collective social group rather than the individual, and an ethic based on caring rather than the supposedly impartial individual reason of the Kantian moral agent. Indeed the concept of an "ethic of care" has emerged as a strong theme, if not the strongest theme, in feminist ethics. Jaggar (1991) has termed it "a minor academic industry." Other writers who have developed further the concept of an ethic of care include Ruddick (1989) in her book, "Maternal Thinking," and more recently the extended analyses of Bowden (1997), Tronto (1993), and Walker (1998).

Considerable debate continues to surround Gilligan's work. Although she was criticized and subsequently revised her position, her work has made an enormous impact in the academy beyond the disciplines of ethics and psychology. This is why it is surprising to see it discussed in so few of the gender and computer ethics studies. When it was first published, its ideas were very radical. On the one hand, she does claim that women's moral development is different than men's, but on the other she argues that traditional scholarship on ethical development is not neutral but is designed to favor a masculine, individualistic, rationalistic, justice and rights-based approach to ethics over a feminine, communitarian care-based approach. I have argued above that there is some evidence that gender and computer ethics studies are making stereotypical judgments of women's "goodness" that do not follow from the research. Whether or not one agrees with her, she has put firmly on the agenda the possibility that, in moral terms, women speak in a different voice.

Conclusion

In this paper I have characterized two strands of gender and computer ethics research. The first casts women's exclusion from the computing industry as an ethical problem. Although this type of research has sometimes been criticized for its tendency toward liberalism, I argue that it is broadly beneficial to be reminded that the well-known problem of women's low numbers in computing has not gone away. More pertinently I have focused on empirical survey studies of men's and women's ethical decision making in relation to business ethics and computer ethics. Existing studies are seen to be problematic on several counts. They survey student populations, thus obscuring questions of power differentials between researcher and student; they accept uncritically that quantitative survey analyses of conceptual questions are meaningful; they focus on decisions made rather than the process of making decisions; and they are under-theorized.

Part of the problem lies in the way that there is, as yet, no real tradition of gender and computer ethics research that builds upon past empirical and theoretical research. To begin to build such a tradition, two related things are needed. First of all we need to explore alternatives to the survey technique currently employed in so many empirical studies; in particular, I argue that we can expect to be more successful in uncovering the processes of ethical reasoning using observational and interviewing strategies. Secondly we need to combine more thoroughgoing empirical studies with theorizing from the burgeoning literature of feminist ethics to offer alternative readings of issues such as power and privacy. Only then can we begin to see what feminist ethics can offer computer ethics.

References

Adam, A. (1998) *Artificial knowing: Gender and the thinking machine*. Routledge, London and New York.

Adam, A. and Ofori-Amanfo, J. (2000) Does gender matter in computer ethics? *Ethics and Information Technology*, **2**(1), 37–47.

Bissett, A. and Shipton, G. (1999) An investigation into gender differences in the ethical attitudes of IT professionals, ETHICOMP99, Rome, October, 1999.

Bowden, P. (1997) *Caring: Gender-sensitive ethics*. Routledge, London and New York.

Brosnan, M. J. (1998) *Technophobia: The psychological impact of information technology*. Routledge, London and New York.

Camp, T. (1997) The incredible shrinking pipeline, *Communications of the ACM*, **40**(10), 103–10.

DeCew, J. W. (1997) *In pursuit of privacy: Law, ethics and the rise of technology*. Cornell University Press, Ithaca and London.

Escribano, J J., Pena, R., and Extremera, J. (1999) Differences between men and women in terms of usage and assessment of information technologies, ETHICOMP99, Rome, October, 1999.

Fitzgerald, B. and Howcroft, D. (1998) Towards dissolution of the IS research debate: From polarisation to polarity, *Journal of Information Technology*, **13**, 313–26.

Forsythe, D. (1993a) Engineering knowledge: The construction of knowledge in artificial intelligence, *Social Studies of Science*, **23**, 445–77.

Forsythe, D. (1993b) The construction of work in artificial intelligence, *Science Technology and Human Values*, **18**(4), 460–79.

Froelich, K. S. and Kotte, J. L. (1991) Measuring individual beliefs about organizational ethics. *Educational and Psychological Measurement*, **51**, 377–83.

Gilligan, C. (1982) *In a different voice: Psychological theory and women's development*. Harvard University Press, Cambridge, MA.

Grundy, F. (1996) *Women and computers*. Intellect Books, Exeter, UK.

Henwood, F. (1993) Establishing gender perspectives on information technology: Problems, issues and opportunities, in *Gendered by design? Information technology and office systems* (eds. E. Green, J. Owen and D. Pain), Taylor and Francis, London, 31–49.

Jaggar, A. (1991) *Feminist ethics: Projects, problems, prospects*, in *Feminist ethics* (ed. C. Card), University Press of Kansas, Lawrence, Kansas, 78–104.

Johnson, D. G. (1994) *Computer ethics*. Prentice Hall, Englewood Cliffs, NJ, 2nd edition.

Jordan, B. (1978) Birth in four cultures.

Khazanchi, D. (1995) Unethical behavior in information systems: The gender factor, *Journal of Business Ethics*, **14**, 741–9.

Kreie, J. and Cronan, T. P. (1998) How men and women view ethics, *Communications of the ACM*, **41**(9), 70–6.

Lander, R. and Adam, A., eds. (1997) *Women in computing*. Intellect Books, Exeter, UK.

Larrabee, M. J. (1993) ed. *An ethic of care,* Routledge, New York and London.

Lovegrove, G. and Segal, B., eds. (1991) *Women into computing; selected papers,* 1998–1990. Springer-Verlag, London and Berlin.

Mason, E. S. and Mudrack, P.E. (1996) Gender and ethical orientation: A test of gender and occupational socialization theories. *Journal of Business Ethics*, **15**, 599–604.

McDonald, G. and Pak, P.C. (1996) It's all fair in love, war and business: Cognitive philosophies in ethical decision making, *Journal of Business Ethics*, **15**, 973–96.

Nissenbaum, H. (1995) Should I copy my neighbor's software? in *Computers, ethics and social values* (eds. D. G. Johnson and H. Nissenbaum), Prentice Hall, Upper Saddle River, NJ, 200–13.

Oakley, A. (2000) *Experiments in knowing: Gender and method in the social sciences,* Polity Press, Cambridge, UK.

Panteli, A., Stack, J., Ramsay, H. (1999) Gender and professional ethics in the IT industry, *Journal of Business Ethics*, **22(1)**, 51–61.

Panteli, N. and Stack, J. (1998) Women and computing: The ethical responsibility of the IT industry, ETHICOMP98, Rotterdam, March, 1998.

Parker, D. B. (1980) *Ethical conflicts in computer science and technology*. AFIPS Press, Arlington, VA.

Reiss, M. C. and Mitra, K. (1998) The effects of individual difference factors on the acceptability of ethical and unethical workplace behaviors. *Journal of Business Ethics*, **17,** 1581–93.

Rogerson, S. and Stack, J. (1997) Women in IT, The IMIS's column on computer ethics. Available at http://www.ccsr.cms.dmu.ac.uk/resources/general/ethicol/Ecv7no6.html as of 28th Feb., 2000.

Ruddick, S. (1989) *Maternal thinking: Toward a politics of peace.* Beacon, Boston, MA.

Tong, R. (1993) *Feminine and feminist ethics.* Wadsworth, Belmont, CA.

Tronto, J. (1993) *Moral boundaries: A political argument for an ethic of care.* Routledge, New York and London.

Turner, E. (1998) The case for responsibility of the computing industry to promote equal presentation of women and men in advertising campaigns, ETHICOMP98, Rotterdam, March, 1998.

Turner, E. (1999) Gender and ethnicity of computing, perceptions of the future generation, ETHICOMP99, Rome, October, 1999.

Walker, M. U. (1998) *Moral understandings: A feminist study in ethics.* Routledge, New York and London.

The Foundationalist Debate in Computer Ethics*

L. Floridi and J. W. Sanders

This paper provides a critical analysis of the debate on the foundations of Computer Ethics (CE). Starting from a discussion of Moor's classic interpretation of the need for CE caused by a policy and conceptual vacuum, five positions in the literature are identified and discussed. According to the "no resolution approach," CE can have no foundation. The "professional approach" argues that CE is only a professional ethics. For the "radical approach" CE deals with absolutely unique issues, in need of a unique approach. The "conservative approach" sees CE as a specific applied ethics, which discusses new species of traditional moral issues. Finally, the "innovative approach" defends the view that theoretical CE can expand the metaethical discourse with a substantially new perspective. In the course of the analysis, it is argued that, although CE issues are not uncontroversially unique, they are sufficiently novel to render inadequate the adoption of standard macroethics—such as Utilitarianism and Deontologism—as the foundation of CE, and hence to prompt the search for a robust ethical theory. Information Ethics (IE) is proposed for that theory, as the satisfactory foundation for CE. IE is characterised as a biologically unbiased extension of environmental ethics, based on the concepts of information object/ infosphere/entropy rather than life/ecosystem/pain. In light of the discussion provided in this paper, it is suggested that CE is worthy of independent, philosophical study because it requires its own application-specific knowledge and is capable of supporting a methodological foundation, IE.[1]

---

* This essay appears for the first time in *Readings in CyberEthics* (2nd ed). Copyright © 2003 by Luciano Floridi and J.W. Sanders. Printed by permission.

* This paper is a revised version of "Computer Ethics: Mapping the Foundationalist Debate," *Ethics and Information Technology* 2002 (4.1), 1–9. We are grateful to Kluwer for permission to reproduce parts of the original text.

[1] The following list of abbreviations are used throughout this paper: CA = conservative approach; CE = computer ethics; IA = innovative approach; ICT = information and communication technologies; IE = information ethics; NA = no resolution approach; PA = professional approach; PE = pop ethics; RA = radical approach.

1. Introduction

Computer Ethics (CE) stems from practical concerns arising in connection with the impact of Information and Communication Technologies (ICT) on contemporary society. The so-called digital revolution has caused new and largely unanticipated problems, thus outpacing ethical, theoretical and legal developments.[2] In order to fill this policy and conceptual vacuum (Moor 1985), CE carries out an extended and intensive study of individual cases, amounting very often to real-world issues rather than mere mental experiments, usually in terms of reasoning by analogy. The result has been inconsistencies, inadequacies, and a frustrating lack of general principles.

CE's aim is to reach decisions based on principled choices and defensible ethical criteria, and hence to provide more generalised conclusions in terms of conceptual evaluations, moral insights, normative guidelines, educational programs, legal advice, industrial standards, and so forth, which may apply to whole classes of comparable cases. So, at least since the seventies,[3] CE focus has moved from problem analysis—primarily aimed at sensitising public opinion, professionals, and politicians—to tactical solutions, resulting, for example, in the evolution of professional codes of conduct, technical standards, usage regulations, and new legislation.

The constant risk of the bottom-up procedure just described has remained the spreading of ad hoc or casuistic approaches to ethical problems. Prompted partly by this difficulty, partly by a natural process of self-conscious maturation as an independent discipline, CE has further combined tactical solutions with more strategic and global analyses. The foundationalist debate is an essential part of this top-down development. It is characterised by a metatheoretical reflection on the nature and justification of CE and of its tasks, and by the discussion of CE's relations with the broader context of metaethical theories.

Can CE amount to a coherent and cohesive discipline, rather than a more or less heterogeneous and random collection of ICT-related ethical problems, applied analyses, and practical solutions? If so, what is its conceptual rationale? And how does it compare with other ethical theories? Five approaches to the foundation of CE that have emerged in the literature can be explained as resulting from different answers to those questions. In the following pages they are referred to as the No Resolution Approach (NA), the Professional Approach (PA), the Radical Approach (RA), the Conservative Approach (CA), and the Innovative Approach (IA). The order in this list is both historical and logical. In the rest of this article it is argued that

- NA provides a minimalist starting point, methodologically useful, which prompts the development of the other four approaches;

- PA represents a valuable professional approach to CE, which leads to the adoption of a theoretical position when metaethical issues are in question;

- RA stresses the novelty of CE;

- CA connects CE to other standard ethics; and

---

[2] See Bynum 1998, Bynum 2000 and Johnson 1999 and 2001 for an overview.

[3] Bynum 2000 reconstructs the history of earlier works in CE.

- IA, relying on the previous approaches, succeeds in providing a satisfactory answer to the foundationalist question, by presenting Information Ethics (IE) as the theoretical foundation of CE.

2. The "No Resolution Approach": Computer Ethics is not a real discipline

The expression "no resolution view" (or approach) is introduced in Gotterbarn 1991:

The "no resolution view" has been reinforced by some recent works. For example, Donn Parker (1981) uses a voting methodology to decide what is ethical in computing. [...] He says, this work was not guided by a concept of computer ethics nor was there an attempt to discover ethical principles. [...] Not only was there an absence of a concept of computer ethics, but the primary direction was an emphasis on proscribed activities. [...] Parker used the diversity of opinions expressed about these scenarios to argue that there was no such thing as computer ethics. And a fortiori, that it could not be taught in a computer science curriculum.

According to the "no resolution approach" (NA), CE problems represent unsolvable dilemma and CE is itself a pointless exercise, having no conceptual foundation.

NA is convincingly criticised in Gotterbarn (1991 and 1992), which analyses Parker (1981, 1982, and 1990). Empirically, the evolution of CE has proved NA to be unnecessarily pessimistic. CE problems are successfully solved, CE-related legislation is approved and enacted, professional standards and codes have been promoted, and so forth. It is understandable, perhaps, that the view arose at a time when both public and professionals were being alerted to wide-ranging unethical uses of ICT. The reason that Parker did not infer an almost opposite conclusion (i.e., that CE is essential) from the "emphasis on proscribed activities" is presumably his voting methodology. It is dangerous to infer, from inconsistent replies to a question, that it has no answer. The same reasoning might lead one to believe, after asking a representative sample of supporters, that neither side would win the test at Lord's.[4]

NA's emphasis on the wide variety of proscribed activities is characteristic. Bynum (1992) has described such an approach as "pop ethics" (PE). PE is characterised by usually unsystematic and heterogeneous collections of dramatic stories, discussed in order "to raise questions of unethicality rather than ethicality" (Parker 1981). Its goal is largely negative—namely "to sensitise people to the fact that computer technology has social and ethical consequences" (Bynum 1992)—and it is not neutral. That is why it played a useful role at the beginning of the development of CE, at around the time when "hacker" became used disparagingly, for example. It is comparable to early work done in business ethics: it points to whatever goes wrong but fails to promote a relevant, beneficial, professional ethos.

Gotterbarn comments:

> "Pop" ethics might have had a place when computing was a remote and esoteric discipline, but I believe that in the current environment this approach is dangerous to the preservation and enhancement of values. This model of computer ethics does not forward any of the pedagogical objectives for teaching ethics [prescribed by PA]. (Gotterbarn 1992)

---

[4] Lord's is one of England's test-match grounds and the headquarters of cricket's governing body. It is named after Thomas Lord (1757–1832).

Nonetheless, PE offers a few advantages. First, some sensitisation to ethical problems is an important preliminary to CE. There is little point in providing a solution to someone unaware of the problem, particularly when the solution is not simple. Second, the variety of concerns (professional, legal, moral, social, political, etc.) is vital to CE and must be appreciated from the start. For this purpose a variety of case studies helps. For instance, Epstein (1997) provides an example of PE found by many lecturers to be useful as preliminary reading for a course in CE. The objection to PE is that it goes no further than cataloguing examples, and that it is frequently used to support NA. Third, methodologically, NA provides a useful point of reference, because it represents an ideal lowest bound for the foundationalist debate, comparable to the role played by relativism in metaethics. In terms of logical analysis, any other approach can be seen as starting from the assumption that NA should be avoided, if possible. Positions can then be ranked depending on their distance from NA, whilst failure to defend any successful alternative confirms NA as the only negative conclusion.

3. The Professional Approach: Computer Ethics Is a Pedagogical Methodology

The first positive reaction to the policy vacuum has been an appeal to the social responsibility of computer professionals. This has meant, among other things, developing a professional-ethics approach (PA) to CE, which has stressed pedagogical need (for an overview see Gotterbarn 1991, 1992). According to PA, CE should:

> introduce the students to the responsibilities of their profession, articulate the standards and methods used to resolve non-technical ethics questions about their profession, develop some proactive skills to reduce the likelihood of future ethical problems, [...] indoctrinate the students to a particular set of values [...] and teach the laws related to a particular profession to avoid malpractice suits. (Gotterbarn 1992)

PA argues that there is no deep theoretical difference between CE and other professional ethics, like business ethics, medical ethics, or engineering ethics, only a variety of pedagogical contexts (Gotterbarn 1991 and 1992). And since CE courses have the goal of creating ethically-minded professionals not ethicists, it is not necessary, and it may actually be better not to have philosophers teaching them. After all,

> philosophers are no more educated in morality than their colleagues in the dairy barn; they are trained in moral theory, which bears about the same relation to the moral life that fluid mechanics bears to milking a cow. (Robert K. Fullinwider, cited in Gotterbarn 1992)

This argument is not uncommon in academe. Mathematics courses, for example, are taken by many faculties, from Engineering to Economics. But should the lectures be given by mathematicians, who are presumably masters of the material, or lecturers from the application area, who may appreciate better its particular application? Apart from political and financial arguments, the latter view is often seen as reinforcing a sense of "subject" in the application domain, whilst the less applied view of the former may be seen as broadening an established subject with new applications.

The arguments concerning the lecturing of Applied Ethics appear similar. It may perhaps be argued that at university level, such courses ought to enable participants to solve new problems as they arise (what are the fundamentals?), whilst in specialised professional institutions such courses are typically under pressure to be more prescriptive:

> *In applied professional ethics courses, our aim is not the acquaintance with complex ethical theories, rather it is recognizing role responsibility and awareness of the nature of the profession. (Gotterbarn, 1992)*

PA has a number of major advantages. It stresses the vital importance of CE education, taking seriously issues like technical standards and requirements, professional guidelines, specific legislation or regulations, levels of excellence and so forth. It thus exposes the risky and untenable nature of NA and places PE in perspective, revealing it insufficient by itself. PA defends the value and importance of a constructive PE, by developing a "proactive" professional ethics (standards, obligations, responsibilities, expectations, etc.), favourable to value-supporting and welfare-enhancing (development and uses of) ICT products (Bynum 1992; Gotterbarn 1992). Furthermore, PA defends a realistic pedagogical attitude, pragmatically useful to sensitise and instruct students and professionals. Its ultimate aim is to ensure that:

> *ethical values, rules and judgements [are] applied in a computing context based on professional standards and a concern for the user of the computing artefact. (Gotterbarn 1991)*

One of the primary results of PA has been the elaboration and adoption of usage regulations and codes of conduct in ICT contexts (libraries, universities, offices, etc.), within industry and in professional associations and organisations, as well as the promotion of certification of computer professionals. PA addresses mainly ICT practitioners, especially those involved in software development, where technical standards and specific legislation provide a reliable, if minimal, frame of reference. As we shall see, PA's goals are pedagogical not metaethical. Unfortunately, sometimes this is forgotten and PA is presented as the only correct way to understand the whole field itself, as if CE could be reduced to a professional ethics in a strict sense:

> *The only way to make sense of "Computer Ethics" is to narrow its focus to those actions that are within the horizon of control of the individual moral computer professional (Gotterbarn 1991, see also Gotterbarn 1992; Gotterbarn 2001 presents a less radical view).*

This strong view has further led to radically anti-philosophical positions (Langford 1995 is a good example, although he seems to have modified his position recently).

A strong PA is far too restrictive, for at least three reasons. First, strong PA disregards the significant fact that, contrary to other purely professional issues, CE problems—e.g., privacy, accuracy, security, reliability, intellectual property, and access—permeate all aspects of contemporary life. Although strong PA can rightly argue that moral problems somehow involving ICT (e.g., theft using a computer) should not be vaguely confused with distinctively CE problems (e.g., software copyright issues), this restriction does not yet justify the reduction of all palpably CE problems to just professional issues. To be coherent, strong PA could reply that any citizen of an information society should be treated, to various degrees, as an ICT professional, to whom some corresponding professional guidelines should apply. But this would mean merely accepting the fact that CE cannot be reduced to a specific professional ethics without the latter losing its perspicuous meaning. Strong PA becomes undefeatable but empty.

Second, interpreting PA as providing a conceptual foundation for CE is to commit a mistake of levels. It is like attempting to define arithmetic on the basis only of what is taught in an introductory course. Without a theoretical approach, PA is mere para-CE, to use an apt expression coined by Keith Miller and adopted by Bynum (1992) in analogy with paramedic, to describe a middle level between pop CE and theoretical CE. Theoretical CE underpins PA and requires a different approach from it.

Finally, understanding CE as just a professional ethics, not in need of any further conceptual foundation, means running the risk of being at best critical but naive, and at worst dogmatic and conservative. On the one hand, focusing on case-based analyses and analogical reasoning, a critical PA will painfully and slowly attempt to re-discover inductively and bottom-up ethical distinctions, clarifications, theories and so forth already available and discussed in specialised literature. On the other hand, an uncritical PA will tend to treat ethical problems and solutions as misleadingly simple, non-conflicting, self-evident, and uncontroversial, a matter of mere indoctrination, as exemplified in "The 10 Commandments of Computer Ethics" approach. Deferring to some contingent "normal ethics" currently accepted within the agent's society, to adapt a Kuhnian expression, is itself a very significant ethical decision, at least because, when normal ethics is methodologically coherent, it often limits itself to providing negative prescriptions, since lists of "don'ts" are easier to implement, and much less questionable, than positive recommendations. Moral standards, values, and choices are always legitimised by ethical positions and arguments, at least implicitly. Applying normal ethics may then be sufficient in everyday life; but it is only the first step toward a mature approach that can uncover, evaluate, criticise, and modify at least some of the accepted presuppositions working in CE, and thus hope to improve them. PA may be seen, pragmatically, as an historical first step toward a more mature CE.

4. Theoretical Computer Ethics and the Uniqueness Debate

Any applied or professional ethics must necessarily make room for critical theorising, even if it does not have to consider it one of its own tasks. PA at its best distinguishes between pedagogical problems and metatheoretical research, descriptive and normative questions, practical and theoretical issues, commonsensical applications and conceptual criticisms of some normal ethics.

Among the fundamental questions that PA does not mean (and should not be expected) to address are: why does ICT raise moral issues? Are CE issues unique (in the sense of requiring their own theoretical investigations, not entirely derivative from standard ethics)? Or are they simply moral issues that happen to involve ICT? What kind of ethics is CE? What justifies a certain methodology in CE, e.g., reasoning by analogy and case-based analysis? What is CE rationale? What is the contribution of CE to the ethical discourse? PA programmatically avoids entering into such investigations and coherently leaves them to theoretical CE.

Theoretical CE can therefore be introduced as the logical stage following pop CE, NA, and PA. Historically, it has developed along two lines, which can be usefully reconstructed through the "uniqueness debate." This has aimed to determine whether the moral issues confronting CE are unique, and hence whether CE should be developed as an independent field of research with a specific area of application and an autonomous, theoretical foundation.

The uniqueness debate arises from two different interpretations of the policy vacuum problem, one more radical, the other more conservative (Floridi 1999b is a collection of papers, Bynum 2000 and Tavani 2002 provide two informative reviews). Let us see them separately.

5. The Radical Approach: Computer Ethics as a Unique Discipline

According to the radical approach (RA), the presence of a policy and conceptual vacuum indicates that CE deals with absolutely unique issues, in need of a completely new approach (Mason 1986, Maner 1996, 1999). Thus, RA argues that

> [Computer Ethics] must exist as a field worthy of study in its own right and not because it can provide a useful means to certain socially noble ends. To exist and to endure as a separate field, there must be a unique domain for computer ethics distinct from the domain for moral education, distinct even from the domains of other kinds of professional and applied ethics. Like James Moor, I believe computers are special technology and raise special ethical issues, hence that computer ethics deserves special status. (Maner 1999)

In terms of logical analysis, RA presents several advantages. It counteracts the risk run by NA of under-evaluating CE problems. Taking seriously their gravity and unprecedented novelty, RA improves on the various pop versions of CE, including PA, by stressing the methodological necessity of providing the field with a robust and autonomous theoretical rationale, if it wishes to deal with ICT-related moral issues successfully. Nevertheless, RA is confronted by at least four problems.

First, to establish that CE is a unique field, the argument quoted above (Maner 1999) requires the explicit and uncontroversial identification of some unique area of study.[5] Yet, RA seems unable to show the absolute uniqueness of any CE problem. None of the cases provided by Maner 1996 and 1999 is uncontroversially unique, for example. That is to be expected. It would be very surprising if any significant moral issue

---

[5] To be precise the argument appears to be of the form "uniqueness only if special domain" and "special domain" therefore "uniqueness." This is a classic fallacy. The argument can be rectified if "only if" is replaced by "if"; that is, in the original words, if "there must be" is replaced by "it suffices that there be," which at least renders the argument valid, if less plausible.

were to belong fully and exclusively only to a limited conceptual region, without inter-acting with the rest of the ethical context. It does not happen in any other special context—consider, for example, business ethics, medical ethics, and environmental ethics—and it remains to be shown why it should happen even in principle in CE.

Second, in reply to the difficulty just seen, one may argue that CE problems could be made, or become, or discovered to be increasingly specific, until they justify the position defended by RA. Yet, insofar as the reply is safe it is also uninteresting because empirically unfalsifiable. It certainly keeps the burden of proof on the RA side. And this is not the only problem. For suppose that a domain of unique ethi-cal issues in CE were available in principle. The basic line of reasoning would still be unacceptable. The "uniqueness" of a certain topic is not simply inherited as a property by the discipline that studies it.[6] On the one hand, specific moral prob-lems—e.g., abortion, or the profit motive—may still require only some evolution-ary adaptation of old macroethical solutions—that is, theoretical, field-independent, applicable ethics—to e.g., medical or business ethics. On the other hand, specific disciplines such as environmental ethics, are not necessarily so because they are involved with unique problems, for they may share their subjects—e.g., the value of life or the concept of welfare—with other disciplines, the difference resting, for example, in their methodologies, aims, or perspectives.

The other two problems encountered by RA are methodological. Given the inter-relatedness of ethical issues and the untenability of the inference "unique topic→ unique discipline," it is not surprising that RA is forced to leave unspecified what a mature CE could amount to in detail, as a unique discipline. Finally, by overstressing the uniqueness of CE, RA runs the risk of isolating the latter from the more gen-eral context of metaethical theories. This would mean missing the opportunity to enrich the ethical discourse.

6. The Conservative Approach: Computer Ethics as Applied Ethics

Some of the problems just seen are neatly avoided by the conservative approach (CA). CA defends two theses:

a) classic macroethics—especially Consequentialism, Deontologism, Virtue Ethics, and Contractualism—are sufficient to cope with the policy vacuum. These theories might need to be adapted, enriched, and extended, but they have most of, if not all, the conceptual resources required to deal with CE questions successful-ly and satisfactorily;

b) certain ethical issues are transformed by the use of ICT, but they represent only new species of traditional moral issues, to which already available metaeth-ical theories need to, and can successfully, be applied. They are not and cannot be a source of a new, macroethical theory.

From (a) and (b) it follows that CE is a microethics, that is, a practical, field-depend-ent, applied and professional ethics.

To explain both theses, Johnson (1999) introduces an evolutionary metaphor (see also Naresh 1999 for a similar approach):

---

[6] As an example, consider a set of objects with four legs: it clearly does not have the property of having four legs.

Extending the idea that computer technology creates new possibilities, in a seminal article, Moor (1985) suggested that we think of the ethical questions surrounding computer and information technology as policy vacuums. Computer and information technology creates innumerable opportunities. This means that we are confronted with choices about whether and how to pursue these opportunities, and we find a vacuum of policies on how to make these choices. [...] I propose that we think of the ethical issues surrounding computer and information technology as new species of traditional moral issues. On this account, the idea is that computer-ethical issues can be classified into traditional ethical categories. They always involve familiar moral ideas such as personal privacy, harm, taking responsibility for the consequences of one's action, putting people at risk, and so on. On the other hand, the presence of computer technology often means that the issues arise with a new twist, a new feature, a new possibility. The new feature makes it difficult to draw on traditional moral concepts and norms. [...] The genus-species account emphasizes the idea that the ethical issues surrounding computer technology are first and foremost ethical. This is the best way to understand computer-ethical issues because ethical issues are always about human beings.

Since CA presents CE as an interface between ICT-related moral problems and standard macroethics, it enjoys all the advantages associated with a strong theoretical position. CA rejects NA. It accepts pop CE's recommendation: CE problems are important and significant, so much so that, for CA, they deserve to be approached both pragmatically and theoretically. It is compatible with, and indeed reinforces PA, since, for CA, CE is an ethics for the citizen of the information society, not just for the ICT professional. Being based on a macroethic perspective, CA can both promote a constructive attitude, like PA, and hope to adopt an evaluative stance, thus avoiding a naive or uncritical reliance on some contingent normal ethics. Finally, CA avoids RA's untenable equation and corresponding "isolationism," because the development of an evolutionary rather than a revolutionary interpretation of CE problems allows it to integrate them well within the broader context of the ethical discourse. Is then the CA position devoid of difficulties? Not yet, for CA is still faced by four shortcomings.

First, thesis (a) is weaker and hence less controversial than (b), but it is still controversial. It is at least questionable whether standard macroethics do indeed have all or even most of the necessary resources to deal with CE problems satisfactorily, without reducing these problems to their (of the macroethics) own conceptual frames, thus erasing their true novelty (Floridi [1999a] provides arguments against (a)). It may be argued that precisely the fact that CE problems were unpredicted and are perceived as radically new challenges the possibility of merely adapting old ethical theories to the new context.

Second, CA is metatheoretically underdetermined. The evolutionary metaphor incorporates the tension between a radical and a traditional approach but does not resolve it. New species of moral problems could be so revolutionarily different from their ancestors—the digital instrumentation of the world can create such entirely new moral issues, unique to CE and that do not surface in other areas—to require a "unique" approach, as suggested by RA. Or they may represent just minor and marginal changes, perfectly disregardable for any theoretical purpose, as the conservative approach wishes to argue. The trouble is that CA, left with the tension now hidden in the evolutionary perspective, implicitly opts for the conservative solution, and treats CE as an applied ethics, but then it does not and cannot indicate which macroethics should be applied. At best, this leads to the adoption of some standard macroethics to deal with CE problems, e.g., Consequentialism, and, when the choice is not arbitrary, this further justifies the claim that, in terms of ethical theorising, there is not much to be learned philosophically from this applied field. If new ICT-related moral problems have any theoretical value, either by themselves or because embedded in original contexts, this is only insofar as they provide further evidence for the discussion of well-established macroethical doctrines. In this way, CA approaches NA: there are no CE specific problems, only ethical problems involving ICT. At worst, CA's lack of commitment leads to a muddle of syncretic and eclectic positions, often acritical and overlooking the theoretical complexity of the problems involved. CA's lack of an explicit metaethical commitment generates a logical regress: having accepted CE as a microethics, one then needs a metatheoretical analysis to evaluate which macroethics is most suitable to deal with CE problems. This logical regress tends to be solved by appealing either to some common-sensical view or to pedagogical needs. The former solution leads back to the assumption of some contingent, normal ethics as providing CE rationale (to use a simplified example: I do CE by using Habermas' dialogue ethics because this is what my society approves as normal ethics). It thus undermines the critical and normative advantage that CA hopes to have over other approaches. The latter solution (to use another simplified example: I do CE by using Virtue Ethics because this is what my students find more intuitive), apart from being equally arbitrary, represents the kind of unnecessary intrusion of philosophy into professional matters so rightly criticised in PA literature. Software engineers should not be required to read the Nicomachean Ethics.

Third, CA is methodologically poor. This is a consequence of the first problem. Lacking a clear macroethical commitment, CA cannot provide an explicit methodology either. It then ends by relying on common-sense, case-based analysis and analogical reasonings, which are usually insufficient means to understand what CA itself acknowledges to be new and complex issues in CE.

Fourth, CA is metaethically unidirectional. Arguing for (b), CA rejects a priori and without explicit arguments the possibility, envisaged by RA, that CE problems might enrich the ethical discourse by promoting a new macroethical perspective. It addresses the question "what can ethics do for CE?" but fails to ask the conceptually more interesting question "is there anything that CE can do for ethics?" Thus, it runs the risk of missing what is intrinsically new in CE, not at the level of problems and concepts, but at the level of contribution to metaethics. A mere extension of standard macroethics does not enable one to uncover new possibilities.[7]

---

[7] Gorniak-Kocikowska (1996), for example, argues that computer ethics is the most important theoretical development in ethics since the Enlightenment.

7. The Innovative Approach: Information Ethics as the Foundation of Computer Ethics

There is a third possible approach to theoretical CE, which is neither conservative nor radical, but innovative (IA).[8] IA builds on CA's advantages, but it avoids its shortcomings by rejecting the conservative restriction made explicit in (b).

According to IA, CE problems, the corresponding policy and conceptual vacuum, the uniqueness debate and the difficulties encountered by RA and CA in developing a cohesive metaethical approach strongly suggest that the monopoly exercised by standard macroethics in theoretical CE is unjustified. ICT, by transforming in a profound way the context in which moral issues arise, not only adds interesting new dimensions to old problems, but leads us to rethink, methodologically, the very grounds on which our ethical positions are based. Although the novelty of CE is not so dramatic as to require the development of an utterly new, separate, and unrelated discipline, it certainly shows the limits of traditional approaches to the ethical discourse, and encourages a fruitful modification in the metatheoretical perspective. Rather than allowing standard macroethics to occupy the territory of CE arbitrarily, as happens with CA, or exiling CE in an impossibly isolated and independent position, as proposed by RA, IA argues that theoretical CE should be promoted to the level of another macroethics because it does have something distinctive and substantial to say on moral problems, and hence can enrich the metaethical discourse with a new and interesting approach of unquestionable philosophical value.

In previous works, we have defined this macroethical perspective *Information Ethics* (Floridi 1999a and 2003; Floridi and Sanders 1999 and 2001). Information Ethics (IE), understood as the theoretical foundation of applied CE, is a non-standard, environmental macroethics, patient-oriented and ontocentric, based on the concepts of informational object/infosphere/entropy rather than living organism/ecosystem/pain. The definition requires some elucidations.

The interpretation of what is the primary object of the ethical discourse is a matter of philosophical orientation. Some macroethical positions (e.g., Virtue Ethics) concentrate their attention on the moral nature and development of the agent. They are properly described as agent-oriented, "subjective" ethics. Since the agent is usually assumed to be a *single person,* they tend to be individualistic and anthropocentric. Some other positions (e.g., Consequentialism, Contractualism, and Deontologism) concentrate their attention on the moral nature and value of the (single and human) agent's actions. They are "relational" and action-oriented theories, intrinsically social in nature. Agent-oriented, intra-subjective theories and action-oriented, inter-subjective theories can be defined as "standard" or "classic," without necessarily associating any positive evaluation with either of these two adjectives. Standard macroethics tend to take only a relative interest in the "patient," the third element in a moral relation, which is on the receiving end of the action, and endures its effects. Ontic power, however, brings with it new moral responsibilities. One can respect only what one no longer fears, yet knowledge is a process of increasing emancipation from reality and, in a world in which humanity can influence, control, or manipulate practically every aspect of reality, philosophical attention is finally drawn to the importance of moral concerns that are not immediately agent/action-oriented and anthropocentric. Medical Ethics, Bioethics, and Environmental Ethics are among the best known examples of this non-standard

---

[8] Bynum (1998) and (2000) outline the need for an innovative approach to CE.

approach. They attempt to develop a patient-oriented ethics in which the "patient" may be not only a human being, but also any form of life. Indeed, Land Ethics extends the concept of patient to any component of the environment, thus coming close to the object-oriented approach defended by IE (Rowlands 2000).

Capturing what is a pre-theoretical but very common intuition, non-standard ethics hold the broad view that any form of life has some essential proprieties or moral interests that deserve and demand to be respected, even if not absolutely but minimally, that is, in a possibly overridable sense. They argue that the nature and well-being of the patient constitute (at least in part) its moral standing, and that the patient makes important claims on the interacting agent, which in principle ought to contribute to the guidance of the agent's ethical decisions and the constraining of the agent's moral behaviour. Non-standard macroethics place the "receiver" of the action at the centre of the ethical discourse, and displace its "source" to its periphery. In so doing, they help to widen further the anthropocentric view of who or what may qualify in principle as a focus of moral concern.

The development of ethical theories just sketched provides a useful explanation as well as a further, metatheoretical, justification of IE. The various difficulties encountered by other approaches to CE can be reconnected to the fact that, far from being a classic, agent/action-oriented ethics, as it may deceptively seem at first sight, CE is primarily an ethics of being rather than conduct or becoming, and hence qualifies as non-standard. The fundamental difference, which sets IE apart from all other members of the same class of non-standard theories, is ontological. In IE, informational objects as such, rather than just living systems in general, are raised to the role of universal patients of any action (see Floridi 2003 for a full defence of this view).

Biocentric ethics usually ground their analyses of the moral standing of bio-entities and ecological systems on the intrinsic worthiness of life and the intrinsically negative value of suffering. IE suggests that there is something even more elemental than life, namely being, understood as information; and something more fundamental than pain, namely entropy. According to IE, one should also evaluate the duty of any moral agent in terms of contribution to the growth of the infosphere, and any process, action, or event that negatively affects the whole infosphere, not just an informational object, as an increase in its level of entropy and hence an instance of evil. Without information there is no moral action, but in IE information moves from being a necessary, epistemic prerequisite for any morally responsible action to being its primary object, by adopting an informational ontology in which human beings as well as animals, plants, and artifacts are interpreted as informational entities.

The crucial importance of the radical change in ontological perspective cannot be overestimated. Typical non-standard ethics can reach their high level of universalisation of the ethical discourse only thanks to their biocentric nature. However, this also means that even Bioethics and Environmental Ethics fail to achieve a level of complete impartiality, because they are still biased against what is inanimate, lifeless, intangible, or abstract (even Land Ethics is biased against technology and artifacts, for example). From their perspective, only what is intuitively alive deserves to be considered as a proper centre of moral claims, no matter how minimal, so a whole universe escapes their attention. Now this is precisely the fundamental limit overcome by IE, which further lowers the minimal condition that needs to be satisfied, in order to qualify as a centre of moral concern, to the common factor shared by any entity, namely its informational state. And since any form of being is in any case also a coherent body of information, to say that IE is info-centric is tantamount to interpreting it, correctly, as an ontocentric theory.

8. Conclusion

The ethical question asked by IE is: "What is good for an informational entity and the infosphere in general?" The answer is provided by a minimalist theory of deserts: any informational entity is recognised to be the centre of some basic ethical claims, which deserve recognition and should help to regulate the implementation of any information process involving it. Approval or disapproval of any information process is then based on how the latter affects the essence of the informational entities it involves and, more generally, the whole infosphere, i.e., on how successful or unsuccessful it is in respecting the ethical claims attributable to the informational entities involved, and hence in improving or impoverishing the infosphere. IE brings to ultimate completion the process of enlarging the concept of what may count as a centre of minimal moral concern, which now includes every informational entity. This is why it can present itself as a non-standard, patient-oriented and ontocentric macroethics.

It may be objected that, as the theoretical foundation of CE, IE places the latter at a level of metaphysical abstraction too philosophical to make it of any direct utility for immediate needs. Yet, this is the inevitable price to be paid for any attempt to provide CE with an autonomous rationale. One must polarise theory and practice to strengthen both. IE is not immediately useful to solve specific CE problems, but it provides the conceptual grounds that can guide problem-solving procedures in CE.[9] Through IE, CE can develop its own methodological foundation, and hence support autonomous theoretical analyses of domain-specific issues, including pressing practical problems, which in turn can be used to test its methodology. IE's position, like that of any other macroethics, is not devoid of problems. But it can interact with other metaethical theories and it contributes an important new perspective: a process or action may be morally good or bad irrespective of its consequences, motives, universality, or virtuous nature, but depending on how it affects the infosphere. This is a major advantage. Without IE's contribution our understanding of moral facts in general, not just of CE problems in particular, would be less complete. The foundationalist debate in CE has lead to the shaping of a new ethical view.

References

Bynum T. W. (ed.) 1985, *Computers and Ethics* (Oxford: Blackwell, published as the October 1985 issue of *Metaphilosophy*).

Bynum T. W. 1992, "Human Values and the Computer Science Curriculum", http://www.southernct.edu/organizations/rccs/resources/teaching/teaching_mono/bynum/bynum_human_values.html

---

[9] On IE as the ecological ethics of the new information environment, see Floridi 2001 and 2002.

Bynum T. W. 1998, "Global Information Ethics and the Information Revolution" in Bynum and Moor 1998, 274–289.

Bynum T. W. and Moor J. H. (eds.) 1998, *The Digital Phoenix: How Computers are Changing Philosophy* (Oxford: Blackwell).

Bynum T. W. 2000, "A Very Short History of Computer Ethics," *APA Newsletters on Philosophy and Computers,* Spring, 99.2:163–165 (See also http://www.southernct.edu/organizations/rccs/resources/research/introduction/bynum_shrt_hist.html.)

Epstein R. 1997, *The Case of the Killer Robot* (New York: John Wiley and Sons).

Floridi L. 1999a, "Information Ethics: On the Philosophical Foundation of Computer Ethics" *Ethics and Information Technology* 1 (1) 37–56, preprint available at http://www.wolfson.ox.ac.uk/floridi/papers.htm

Floridi L. (ed.) 1999b, *Etica & Politica,* special issue on *Computer Ethics,* 2, http://www.univ.trieste.it/~dipfilo/ etica_e_politica/1999_2/homepage.html.

Floridi L. 2001, "Ethics in the Infosphere," *The Philosophers' Magazine* 6 (2001), pp. 18–19.

Floridi L. 2002, "Information Ethics: An Environmental Approach to the Digital Divide," *Philosophy in the Contemporary World* 2002 (9.1), 39–45, preprint available at http://www.wolfson.ox.ac.uk/floridi/papers.htm

Floridi L. 2003, "On the Intrinsic Value of Information Objects and the Infosphere," *Ethics and Information Technology* 2003 (4.4), 287–304, preprint available at http://www.wolfson.ox.ac.uk/floridi/papers.htm

Floridi L. and Sanders J. 1999, "Entropy as Evil in Information Ethics," in Floridi 1999b, http://www.univ.trieste.it/~dipfilo/ etica_e_politica/1999_2/homepage.html

Floridi L. and Sanders J. 2001, "Artificial Evil and the Foundation of Computer Ethics," *Ethics and Information Technology* 2001 (3.1), 55–66; and also Etica & Politica 2000 (2.2), http://www.univ.trieste.it/~dipfilo/etica_e_politica/2000_2/index.html

Forester, T. and Morrison P. 1990 *Computer Ethics: Cautionary Tales and Ethical Dilemmas in Computing* (Cambridge, Mass: MIT Press, 2nd ed. 1994).

Gorniak-Kocikowska K. 1996, "The Computer Revolution and the Problem of Global Ethics," *Science and Engineering Ethics* 2.2, 177–90.

Gotterbarn D. W. 1991, "Computer Ethics: Responsibility Regained," first published in the National Forum, rep. in *Business Legal and Ethical Issues,* Australian Computer Society August 1993 and in Johnson and Nissenbaum 1995, http://www-cs.etsu-tn.edu/gotterbarn/artpp1.htm

Gotterbarn D. W. 1992, "The Use and Abuse of Computer Ethics," special ethics issue of *The Journal of Systems and Software,* 17.1, http://www.southernct.edu/organizations/rccs/resources/teaching/teaching_mono/gotter-barn02/gotterbarn02_intro.html

Gotterbarn D. W. 2001, "Software Engineering Ethics," *Encyclopedia of Software Engineering,* 2nd ed., J. Marciniak (ed.) (New York: Wiley-Interscience).

Johnson D. G. 1999, "Sorting Out the Uniqueness of Computer-Ethical Issues," in Floridi 1999b, http://www.univ.trieste.it/~dipfilo/ etica_e_politica/1999_2/homepage.html.

Johnson D. G. and Nissenbaum H. (eds.) 1995, *Computers, Ethics, and Social Values* (Englewood Cliffs, NJ: Prentice Hall).

Johnson D. G. 2001, *Computer Ethics,* 3rd ed. (Upper Saddle River, New Jersey: Prentice Hall).

Langford D. 1995, Practical Computer Ethics (London: McGraw-Hill).

Maner W. 1996, "Unique Ethical Problems in Information Technology," *Science and Engineering Ethics,* 2.2, 137–54. Revised version in Maner (1999).

Maner W. 1999, "Is Computer Ethics Unique?", in Floridi 1999b, http://www.univ.trieste.it/~dipfilo/etica_e_politica/1999_2/homepage.html.

Mason R. 1986, "Four Ethical Issues of the Information Age," *MIS Quarterly* 10.1, 5–12.

Moor J. H. 1985, "What is Computer Ethics?" Metaphilosophy 16 (4): 266–275, http://www.south-ernct.edu/organizations/rccs/resources/teaching/teaching_mono/moor/moor_definition.html

Naresh S. 1999, "Ethical Norms for the Information Society," in *Proceedings of the First Session of UNESCO's COMEST,* Oslo, April 1999, pp. 169–177 (Paris: UNESCO).

Parker D. B. 1981, *Ethical Conflicts in Computer Science and Technology* (Arlington, VA: AFIPS Press).

Parker D. B. 1982, "Ethical Dilemmas in Computer Technology," in *Ethics and the Management of Computer Technology,* W. M. Hoffman and J. M. Moore (eds.) (Cambridge, MA: Oelgeschlager, Gunn & Hain).

Parker D. B. 1990, *Ethical Conflicts in Information and Computer Science, Technology, and Business* (Wellesley, MA: QED Information Sciences).

Rowlands M. 2000, The Environmental Crisis–*Understanding the Value of Nature* (New York: St. Martin's Press).

Tavani H. T. 2000, "Computer Ethics: Current Perspectives and Resources," *APA Newsletters on Philosophy and Computers,* Spring, 99.2: 166–170. (See also http://www.apa.udel.edu/apa/publications/newsletters/v99n2/computers/feature-tavani.asp.)

Tavani H. T. 2002, "The Uniqueness Debate in Computer Ethics: What Exactly Is at Issue, and Why Does it Matter?", *Ethics and Information Technology* 4.1, 37–54.

Common Morality and Computing

Bernard Gert

Introduction

We are aware that many people believe there is no substantial agreement on moral matters. We are also aware that there is even less agreement on the adequacy of any account of morality. We believe that these views are due to the understandable, but misleading, concentration on controversial moral issues without realizing that such controversial matters form only a very small part of those matters about which people make moral decisions and judgements. Indeed, most moral matters are so uncontroversial that people do not even make any conscious decision concerning them. The uncontroversial nature of these matters is shown by everyone's lack of hesitancy in making negative moral judgements about those who harm others simply for their own personal interests. It is shown by the same lack of hesitancy in making moral judgements condemning unjustified deception, breaking of promises, cheating, disobeying the law, and not doing one's duty.

We believe that an explicit, clear, and comprehensive account of morality would help to make clear the uncontroversial nature of many moral decisions. We also believe that such an account would help in understanding, and sometimes even resolving, some of the controversial moral problems that are arising in the field of computing. Our account provides a common framework on which all of the disputing parties can agree, for this account does not settle most controversial issues. By clarifying the causes of disagreement and allowing that more than one alternative may be morally acceptable, it provides a better chance to manage that disagreement in a productive way. Thus we think that making the common moral system explicit may actually have some practical benefits.[1]

Those who deny the possibility of a comprehensive account of morality may actually be denying that any systematic account of morality provides an answer to every moral problem. But we have already acknowledged that the common moral system does not provide a unique solution to every moral problem. Common morality does provide a unique answer in many cases, however, most of these cases are

This essay originally appeared in *Ethics and Information Technology*, **1**: 57–64, 1999. Copyright © 1999 by Kluwer Academic Publishers. Reprinted by permission.

[1] A more extended account of morality, and of the moral theory that justifies it is contained in Bernard Gert, *Morality: Its Nature and Justification*, Oxford University Press, 1998.

not interesting. Only in a very few situations does an explicit account of morality settle what initially seemed to be a controversial matter, e.g., whether one should violate the law and make copies of software programs for one's friends.[2] Although most controversial cases do not have unique answers, even in these cases an explicit account of morality is often quite useful, for it shows that there are significant limits to legitimate moral disagreement. That there is no agreement on the right answer does not mean that there is no agreement that most of the proposed answers are wrong. The moral system provides a method for distinguishing between morally acceptable answers and morally unacceptable answers; that there is not always agreement on the best solution does not mean that there is not general agreement on the boundaries of what is morally acceptable. The fact that moral disagreement on some issues is compatible with complete agreement on many other issues seems to be almost universally overlooked. Most philosophers seem to hold that if equally informed impartial rational persons can disagree on some moral matters, they can disagree on all of them. Thus most philosophers hold either that there is a unique right answer to every moral question or that there is no unique right answer to any moral question. The unexciting but correct view is that some moral questions have unique right answers and some do not. There is far more moral agreement than there is moral disagreement, but the areas of moral disagreement are much more interesting to discuss and so are discussed far more often.

Common Morality

Common morality is the moral system that people use, usually not consciously, in deciding how to act when confronting moral problems and in making their moral judgements. Although most moral decisions are not made by explicitly employing any account of morality, we hope to provide a framework of common morality that will accomplish three tasks: 1) make clear that there is agreement on the overwhelming majority of cases; 2) make clear the sources of moral disagreement and explain why there may sometimes be no unique best solution; and 3) make clear that new and perplexing problems can be described in a way that shows their similarity to more familiar moral matters. We also hope this account of morality will be used to teach those entering the computing industry that the moral framework that is used in computing is the same moral framework that they have always used.

Most moral theories, e.g., consequentialist or deontological, no matter how complex they are themselves, unfortunately present an overly simple account of common morality.[3] Indeed, many philosophers regard their moral theories as generating a new and improved morality, rather than as describing and justifying common morality. Many even seem to value simplicity more than agreement with common moral judgements. Reacting to this oversimplification of morality, many

---

[2] See Helen Nissenbaum, Should I Copy my Neighbor's Software? In Deborah G. Johnson and Helen Nissenbaum, editors, *Computers, Ethics, & Social Values*. Prentice Hall, Englewood, New Jersey, pp. 201–213, 1995.

[3] That is why Helen Nissenbaum (op. cit.) finds it so easy to show that the standard consequentialist and moral rights theories that she reconstructs do not provide adequate arguments showing that it is unjustified to violate a morally acceptable law by copying software programs for one's friends.

in applied ethics, claim to be antimoral theory. They quite rightly regard these overly simple accounts of morality as worse than useless. Unfortunately, they seem to accept the false claim that common morality must be simple. The anti-theory view sometimes leads people to accept the incorrect and destructive view that all moral reasoning is ad hoc or completely relative to the situation or to the people making the decisions or judgements.

Morality is primarily a guide for action, not an account of what counts as the best state of affairs. The danger in viewing morality as being concerned with the best state of affairs is that what is regarded as the best state of affairs can sometimes be brought about only in a morally unacceptable way, e.g., deception. Of course, whether one's behavior is morally unacceptable may be determined by the end to be achieved, e.g., preventing serious harm to people often justifies deception. The following is a definition of morality that captures what most people mean by that term. *Morality is an informal public system applying to all rational persons, governing behavior that affects others, and includes what are commonly known as the moral rules, ideals, and virtues and has the lessening of evil or harm as its goal.*

A public system is a system that has the following two characteristics. (1) All persons to whom it applies (i.e., those whose behavior is to be guided and judged by that system), understand it (i.e., know what behavior the system prohibits, requires, encourages, and allows). (2) It is not irrational for any of these persons to accept being guided and judged by that system. The clearest example of a public system is a game. A game has an inherent goal and a set of rules that form a system that is understood by all of the players; and it is not irrational for all players to use the goal and the rules of the game to guide their own behavior and to judge the behavior of other players by them. Although a game is a public system, it applies only to those playing the game; if they do not want to gain the goal of the game, they do not need to play it, i.e., abide by its rules. Morality is a public system that applies to all moral agents; it applies to all rational persons simply in virtue of their being responsible for their actions. This may explain Kant's claim that the demands of morality are categorical, not hypothetical.

In order for all rational persons to know what morality requires, prohibits, allows, and encourages, knowledge of the moral system cannot involve any beliefs that are not held by all rational persons. Thus, no facts discovered by modern science can be necessary, for none of these facts are known by all moral agents. The same is true of all religious beliefs, for no particular religious belief is held by all rational persons. Only those beliefs that it would be irrational for any moral agent not to hold, are essential for knowledge of morality. We call such beliefs *rationally required* beliefs. Beliefs that it would be irrational for any moral agent to hold, we call *rationally prohibited* beliefs. Beliefs that are neither rational required nor rationally prohibited, we call *rationally allowed* beliefs.

Rationally required beliefs include general factual beliefs such as: people are vulnerable, they can be harmed by other people; and people are fallible, they have limited knowledge. Having these beliefs is necessary in order to be a moral agent. On the other hand, *rationally allowed* beliefs, such as scientific or religious beliefs, cannot be necessary to be a moral agent, even though some rationally allowed beliefs, e.g., beliefs about the facts of the particular case may be necessary for making particular moral decisions or judgments. There are also rationally required personal beliefs, e.g., beliefs that one is also vulnerable and fallible. However, personal beliefs about one's race, gender, religion, abilities, etc., are not rationally required, because not all moral agents share these same beliefs about themselves, and so these beliefs cannot be used to develop the moral system.

Although all those who are held responsible for their actions know what morality requires, etc. morality is not a simple system. A useful analogy is the grammatical system used by all competent speakers of a language. Almost no competent speaker can explicitly describe this system, yet they all know it in the sense that they make use of it when speaking and in interpreting the speech of others. If presented with an explicit account of the grammatical system, competent speakers have the final word on its accuracy. It would be a mistake to accept any description of a grammatical system that rules out speaking in a way that they know is commonly regarded as acceptable or allows speaking in a way that they know is commonly regarded as completely unacceptable.

Morality is an informal public system, i.e., a public system that has no authoritative judges or procedures for determining a unique correct answer. A formal system such as law, or a formal public system, such as a game of a professional sport, has procedures for arriving at a unique correct answer within that system. But when people get together to play a game of cards, or backyard basketball, they are involved in an informal public system. For the game even to get started, there must be overwhelming agreement on how the game is to be played, but disagreements can arise that have no agreed upon way to be resolved. These disagreements are either resolved in an ad hoc fashion, e.g., flipping a coin or asking a passerby, or are not resolved at all, e.g., the game is disbanded. But generally these games continue with no serious problems.

Morality, like all informal public systems, presupposes overwhelming agreement on most matters that are likely to arise. However, like all informal public systems, it has no established procedures or authorities that can resolve every moral disagreement. There is no equivalent in morality to the United States Supreme court in deciding legal disputes, or the Pope in deciding some religious matters for Roman Catholics. When morality does not provide a unique right answer and a decision has to be made, the decision is often made in an ad hoc fashion, e.g., people may ask a friend for advice. If the moral disagreement is about some important social issue, e.g., abortion, the problem is transferred from the moral system to the political or legal system.

Abortion is an unresolvable moral question because it involves the scope of morality, that is, it concerns who is impartially protected by the moral rules. Although everyone agrees that all moral agents are protected by the moral rules, there is no agreement on what other beings are protected, e.g., potential moral agents. Since it has to be decided whether or not abortions are to be allowed and under what circumstances, the question is transferred to the legal and political system. The question is resolved on a practical level, but the moral question is not resolved, as is shown by the continuing intense moral debate on the matter. But almost everyone, including those who are opposed to abortion, agrees that it is not morally justified to cause harm, that is, to kill or injure doctors and others involved in providing abortions. Thus, despite what anti-abortion groups claim about the immorality of abortion, most of them seem to recognize that rational impartial persons can disagree about the moral acceptability of abortion and so it is not justified for individuals to harm others in attempting to prevent abortions.

In addition to differences concerning the scope of morality, another source of unresolvable disagreement in moral judgement is due to differences in the rankings of harms, including differences in how one ranks probabilities of harms. Disagreements on the proper speed limit is a disagreement about whether the certain deprivation of some freedom to millions, viz., the freedom to drive between 55 miles an hour and 70 miles an hour, is justified by the high probability that some lives will be saved. Everyone agrees that there should be some speed limits on most roads, but there is disagreement as to what that speed limit should be. Most of this disagreement, like most moral disagreement, is due to a disagreement about the facts, e.g., how many fewer accidents, injuries, and deaths would there be if the speed limit were ten miles less? But even if people agreed on the facts, they still might disagree, e.g., about whether saving ten lives justifies reducing the speed limit by ten miles per hour. Similarly, everyone agrees that there should be laws restricting the copying of software, but there are factual disagreements about the effects of different laws and there may be unresolvable disagreements concerning the rankings of the harms and benefits involved and hence on the details of what those restrictions should be.

The Moral Rules

In this paper, I shall concentrate on the moral rules and their place in the moral system. The existence of a common morality is shown by the widespread agreement on what counts as a moral rule, i.e., a rule whose violation is immoral unless one has an adequate justification. Everyone agrees that harming people, i.e., killing them, causing them pain or disability, and depriving them of freedom or pleasure, is immoral unless one has an adequate justification. Similarly, everyone agrees that violating those norms that are essential to the successful functioning of all societies, i.e., deceiving, breaking a promise, cheating, breaking the law, and neglecting one's duties, also needs justification in order not to be immoral. No one has any real doubts about any of this.

For cultural and aesthetic reasons, I prefer to formulate the moral rules in a way that results in there being ten rules, but as indicated above, one could formulate the rules so that there are only two rules, 'Do not cause harm.' and 'Do not violate the norms necessary for society.' But if one chooses to have only these two rules, it would be necessary to list the different kinds of harms, in order to make clear that rational persons can disagree in their ranking of these harms. It would also be necessary to explicitly identify the universally justified norms, i.e., those that are necessary for a society to function, and distinguish them from norms that are not so justified. Nonetheless, there are contexts in which it may be appropriate to list only two moral rules, or perhaps only one, e.g., 'Do not cause harm or increase the probability of harm being suffered.' Although having only one or two rules can be advantageous in certain contexts, I shall list ten rules that would be supported by all impartial rational persons who used only rationally required beliefs. I call these rules the justified moral rules.

The justified moral rules:

1. Do not kill.
2. Do not cause pain.
3. Do not disable.
4. Do not deprive of freedom.
5. Do not deprive of pleasure.
6. Do not deceive.
7. Keep your promises.
8. Do not cheat.
9. Obey the law.
10. Do your duty.[4]

As indicated above, these rules are not absolute; they all have justified exceptions, and most moral problems involve determining which exceptions are justified. Although there is some disagreement about the scope of these rules, e.g., whether animals or embryos are protected by them, this kind of disagreement has no place in computer ethics until computers develop sufficiently that they can be regarded as persons with interests. But doubt about whether harming animals or intelligent computers needs to be justified should not lead to any doubt that harming moral agents, i.e., adults like us, needs justification. People also disagree about what counts as an adequate moral justification for some particular violation of a rule, e.g., deceiving or breaking the law, and on some features of an adequate justification, but everyone agrees that what counts as an adequate justification for one person must be an adequate justification for anyone else in the same situation, i.e., when all of the morally relevant features of the two situations are the same. This is part of what is meant by saying that morality requires impartiality.

In order to capture both the fact that the moral rules must be obeyed impartially and the possibility of disagreement concerning what actions count as justified violations, it is necessary to make explicit the attitude that all impartial rational persons take toward the rules. I call this the moral attitude, for it expresses the morally correct attitude toward the moral rules,

> *Everyone is always to obey a moral rule except when a fully informed rational person can publicly allow violating it. If all fully informed rational persons publicly allow the violation, it is strongly justified. If fully informed rational persons disagree about whether to publicly allow the violation, it is weakly justified.*

---

[4] In this formulation, the term "duty" is being used in its everyday sense to refer to what is required by one's role in society, primarily one's job, not as philosophers customarily use it, which is to say, simply as a synonym for "what one morally ought to do."

To "publicly allow" a violation is to claim that one would allow that kind of violation to be part of the 'informal public system' that is common morality. In less technical terms, to publicly allow a violation is to claim that one would be willing for everyone to know that kind of violation was allowed. What counts as the same kind of violation is determined by the morally relevant features of the violation. If two violations have all of the same morally relevant features, then they are the same kind of violation.

When deciding whether or not an impartial rational person can advocate that a violation of a moral rule be publicly allowed, the kind of violation must be described using only morally relevant features. Since the morally relevant features are part of the moral system, they must be understood by all moral agents. This means that any description of the violation must be such that it can be reformulated in a way that all moral agents can understand it. Limiting the way in which a violation must be described makes it easier for people to discover that their decision or judgment is biased by some consideration that is not morally relevant. All of the morally relevant features that we have discovered so far are answers to the following questions. It is quite likely that other morally relevant features will be discovered, but we think that we have discovered the major features. Of course, in any actual situation, it is the particular facts of the situation that determine the answers to these questions, but all of these answers can be given in a way that can be understood by all moral agents.

1. What moral rules would be violated?
2. What harms would be (a) avoided (not caused), (b) prevented, and (c) caused? (This means foreseeable harms and includes probabilities as well as kind and extent.)
3. What are the relevant beliefs and desires of the people toward whom the rule is being violated?
4. Does one have a relationship with the person(s) toward whom the rule is being violated such that one sometimes has a duty to violate moral rules with regard to the person(s) without their consent?
5. What benefits would be caused? (This means foreseeable benefits and also includes probabilities, as well as kind and extent).
6. Is an unjustified or weakly justified violation of a moral rule being prevented?
7. Is an unjustified or weakly justified violation of a moral rule being punished?
8. Are there any alternative actions that would be preferable?
9. Is the violation being done intentionally or only knowingly?
10. Is it an emergency situation that no person is likely to plan to be in?

When considering the harms being avoided (not caused), prevented, and caused, and the benefits being promoted, one must consider not only the kind of benefits or harms involved, one must also consider their seriousness, duration, and probability. If more than one person is affected, one must consider not only how many people will be affected, but also the distribution of the harms and benefits. Anyone who claims to be acting or judging as an impartial rational person who holds that one of the two violations be publicly allowed must hold that the other also be publicly allowed. This simply follows from morality requiring impartiality when considering a violation of a moral rule.

Consideration of a Particular Case

We can now examine the seemingly controversial case mentioned on page one, 'whether one should violate the law and make copies of software programs for one's friends.' It might be rational to favour allowing a person to illegally copy software for a friend. It might even be rational to favour allowing everyone to know that they can illegally copy software for a friend. But in order to have the kind of impartiality required by morality, one can not limit the subject matter of the law to a particular law one dislikes. This would be like people saying that it is justified to violate the law prohibiting smoking by minors, but not justified to violate the law prohibiting drinking by minors. Or that it is justified to violate the law prohibiting one's favourite illegal drug, but not justified to violate the law prohibiting other illegal drugs. In order to justify illegally copying software, one has to hold either that the law is clearly an unjust one, or that it is morally justifiable to break morally acceptable laws with which one disagrees for the benefit of oneself or one's friends. A seemingly controversial case is one in which the law is morally unacceptable, in the sense that no fully informed impartial rational person would favour that law over other alternatives, but the law is not unjust in any clear or straightforward sense.

No one holds that it is morally justifiable to break morally acceptable laws concerning computing with which one disagrees for the benefit of oneself or one's friends. Present copying laws are not clearly unjust, so that it seems that the only way to justify violating the law prohibiting copying software is to show that the law is morally unacceptable. However, if some fully informed impartial rational persons would publicly allow the restrictions imposed by the present law, that is, if they would be willing for everyone to know that such restrictions are allowed, then the law is morally acceptable and it is not morally justified to violate that law under normal circumstances. Similarly, if the speed limit that is adopted for certain roads in one state, is such that some fully informed, impartial rational persons would favor such a law, then under normal circumstances, it is not morally justified to exceed that speed limit. One can only justifiably violate a morally acceptable law in circumstances where one would be willing to publicly allow any morally acceptable law to be violated. To publicly allow a violation of a rule is to propose that this kind of violation be allowed by the public system that is morality. That is why the impartiality required by morality does not allow one to break a law when one cannot describe the situation by means of the morally relevant features that all moral agents can understand.

This means that one cannot justifiably pick some special class of morally acceptable laws, e.g., speeding laws, and claim that one would favour everyone knowing that they are allowed to violate those particular morally acceptable laws. In order to justify the violation of a morally acceptable law, one must be able to describe the circumstances in terms of morally relevant features that everyone can understand. It is not justifiable to violate a law simply because one believes, even justifiably believes, some other law would be better. To publicly allow violations in such circumstances, that is, to favour everyone knowing that they are allowed to violate the law in such circumstances, would lead to anarchy and no impartial rational person would publicly allow it.

Only the requirement that the violation be publicly allowed, which requires that it be formulated in terms of the morally relevant features that all rational persons can understand, guarantees the kind of impartially required by morality.When one is impartial in the way required by morality, it is clear that, except to prevent serious harms, one is not justified in breaking a morally acceptable law. In the situation described by Helen Nissenbaum, it is clear that serious harms are not being prevented, rather one is simply doing a favour for a friend.

Even if the law is not a morally acceptable one, e.g., if there are better laws, that is, laws that all fully informed impartial rational persons would prefer to the present law, it is still not clear that it is justifiable to violate the law.[5] It would have to be obvious that the present law is morally unacceptable before it would be clear that it is justifiable to violate it.Whether some other law would be a better law than the present law is a difficult question, and I do not know enough about the law to claim that there might not be several better laws. It might be that a more liberal copying law would be preferable to the restrictive one now in place, but that is certainly not obvious. If, as is most likely, fully informed, impartial rational persons disagree, and some favour the present law, it should be clear to all that it is not morally justifiable to violate the law simply to benefit a friend.

Two people, both fully informed, impartial and rational, who agree that two actions count as the same kind of violation, need not always agree on whether or not to advocate that this kind of violation be publicly allowed. They may rank the benefits and harms involved differently or they may differ in their estimate of the consequences of publicly allowing this kind of violation. But sometimes this disagreement may be due to one of them having too narrow a description of the kind of violation in question. For example, two persons may agree that one particular act of illegally copying a software program to benefit a friend will have no significant harmful consequences. However, they may disagree about the consequences of publicly allowing that kind of violation, one holding that everyone knowing that this kind of violation is allowed will result in a very significant harm to software companies, and the other holding that it will result in only an insignificant harm, which will be more than justified by the benefits gained by one's friends from such copying. Thus it may seem that there is an unresolvable moral disagreement.

However, 'illegally copying a software program' does not describe the act solely in terms of the morally relevant features. It brings in one's biases with regard to software; it allows one not to be impartial without even realizing it. Especially when one also brings in other irrelevant factors, such as, that the benefit of the illegal act is not oneself, but one's friend; as if whether it is oneself or a friend who benefits from the illegal act is a morally relevant feature. Doing something for a friend may be a good motive, but motives do not determine the morality of an action. If they did then all genuinely paternalistic deception by doctors would be morally acceptable. As discussed early, it seems that the proper description of the act is "violating a morally acceptable law to gain some benefit." Described in this way, no impartial rational person would publicly allow the act, hence it is an unjustified violation.

This consideration of this particular case, which at first seems controversial, shows the usefulness of a clear, comprehensive, and precise formulation of the moral system. Note that, unlike the discussion of what would be the best law concerning the copying of software, the discussion of whether it is justifiable to illegally copy software does not require an intimate knowledge of the nature of software,

---

[5] See Le Droit de Nature. *Le Pouvoir et le Droit: Hobbes et les fondements de la Loi*, Textes r´eunis par by Louis Roux etFrançois Triçaud, Publications de l'Universit´e de Saint-´Etienne,pp. 27 –48, 1992. That paper explains and supports Hobbes's argument that it is better for every person to obey a law rather than follow their own rule, even if each of the rules that a personwants to follow is such that it if it were the law it would be a better law than the present law.

and the relations between the producers and users of software. If some impartial rational person could favour such a law, it is clear that it is unjustifiable to violate that law in order to do a favour for a friend. However, most morally problematic cases, e.g., those that involve the making of laws or policies concerning copying software, their ownership, etc. are very unlikely to have such clear answers. Nor is it likely that one will be able to provide even plausible answers without an intimate knowledge of the nature of software, and the relations between the producers and users of software. Induction on the basis of a single example is always very risky.

Alternative Moral Theories

It may clarify our account of the justified moral system to compare it with the views put forward by many contemporary followers of Immanuel Kant (1724 –1804) and John Stuart Mill (1806-1873). These views are close to the two views that Nissenbaum uses when trying to show that the moral arguments prohibiting the copying of software do not work. It may not be fair to Kant and Mill to compare their views with our account of the moral system sketched in this paper, for Kant and Mill have far more to say than we will be able to present in this paper. However, neither Kant norMill nor their contemporary followers discuss the morally relevant features and so they provide no plausible account of how one determines whether two violations count as violations of the same kind for the purpose of moral decision making. Further, neither view has an account of impartiality nor does either recognize that morality is an informal public system.

On a Kantian deontological system one should never act in any way that one cannot will to be a universal law. If it would be impossible for everyone always to do a specific kind of action, then everyone is prohibited from doing that same kind of action. For example, what makes it morally prohibited to make lying promises is that if everyone always made lying promises, it would impossible for there to be a practice of promising. On the common moral system, one is prohibited from doing a kind of action only if, given the morally relevant facts, no impartial rational person would publicly allow that kind of action. A Kantian system seems to rule out ever making lying promises, whereas the moral system allows the making of lying promises in some circumstances, e.g., when making the lying promise is necessary to prevent a harm sufficiently great that it is rational to estimate that less overall harm would be suffered even if everyone knew that such lying promises were allowed in these kinds of circumstances.

On a consequentialist system one not only may, but should, violate any common moral rule if the foreseeable consequences of that particular violation, (including the effects on future obedience to the rule), are better than the consequences of not violating the rule.[6] A consequentialist system is concerned only with the foreseeable consequences of the particular violation, not with the foreseeable consequences of that kind of violation being publicly allowed.[7] Nissenbaum correctly uses this feature of consequentialism to show that the claim that copying is immoral is not supported. On the moral system, however, it is precisely the foreseeable consequences of that kind of violation being publicly allowed that are decisive in determining

---

[6] By a consequentialist system we mean an act consequentialist system, for rule consequentialism, regarded as a system for guiding behavior, is a deontological system. Rules are an essential feature of the system, not merely a useful device for calculating the consequences of the particular act.

[7] Some consequentialists claim that their systems use actual consequences, not merely foreseeable ones, but this has such counter intuitive results that it cannot be taken seriously.

whether or not it is morally allowed. The consequences of the particular violation are important only in determining the kind of violation. A consequentialist system favors breaking a morally acceptable law if it were extremely unlikely that one would get caught, no harm would result from that particular violation of the law, and you or your friend would benefit from the violation.

According to Classical Utilitarianism (Bentham and Mill), the only relevant consequences are pleasure and pain. Later consequentialists allow for the relevance of other consequences, e.g., death and disability. They claim that the act which is morally best is that which produces the greatest balance of benefits over harms. It is, paradoxically, the kind of moral theory usually held by people who claim that they have no moral theory. Their view is often expressed in phrases like the following: 'It is all right to do anything as long as no one gets hurt,' 'It is the actual consequences that count, not some silly rules,' or 'What is important is that things turn out for the best, not how one goes about making that happen.' On the moral system, it is not the consequences of the particular violation that are decisive in determining its justifiability, but rather the consequences of such a violation being publicly allowed.

As we have described the common moral system, it is dependent on certain features of human nature, viz., that people are vulnerable and fallible, and it also regards rationality as involving the avoidance of harms. Kant thinks of morality as completely independent of human nature and he has a very different account of rationality. Thus morality differs from a Kantian system and resembles a consequentialist system in that it has a purpose, and consequences are explicitly taken into consideration. It resembles a Kantian system and differs from an act consequentialist system in that morality is a public system in which rules are essential.

The Kantian system requires all of one's actions to be tested for impartiality by the categorical imperative, and consequentialist systems require one to regard the interests of everyone impartially. Common morality does not require impartiality with respect to all of one's actions, nor that one regard the interests of everyone impartially; it requires impartiality only when considering the violation of a moral rule. Indeed, it is humanly impossible to regard the interests of everyone impartially, even when concerned only with moral agents. Impartiality with respect to the moral ideals (Kant's imperfect duties) is also humanly impossible. That all the moral rules are, or can be taken as, prohibitions, is what makes it humanly possible for them to be followed impartially. The public nature of morality and the limited knowledge of rational persons help to explain why impartial obedience to the moral rules is required to achieve the point of morality, which is lessening the suffering of harm. Morality also differs from the systems of both Kant and Mill in that it does not require all moral questions to have unique answers, but explicitly allows for a limited area of disagreement among equally informed impartial rational persons.

References

Bernard Gert. *MORALITY: Its Nature and Justification,* Oxford University Press, 408 pp., 1998.

Bernard Gert. *Le Droit de Nature. Le Pouvoir et le Droit: Hobbes et les fondements de la Loi.* Textes réunis par Louis Roux et François Triçaud. Publications de l'Université de Saint-Étienne, pp. 27–48, 1992.

Helen Nissenbaum. Should I Copy my Neighbor's Software? Deborah G. Johnson and Helen Nissenbaum, editors, *Computers, Ethics, & Social Values.* Prentice Hall, Englewood, New Jersey, pp. 201–213, 1995.

Just Consequentialism and Computing

James H. Moor

Computer and information ethics, as well as other fields of applied ethics, need ethical theories that coherently unify deontological and consequentialist aspects of ethical analysis. The proposed theory of just consequentialism emphasizes consequences of policies within the constraints of justice. This makes just consequentialism a practical and theoretically sound approach to ethical problems of computer and information ethics.

Introduction

The malleability of computers allows them to be used in novel and unexpected ways, ways for which we frequently do not have formulated policies for controlling their use.[1] Advancing computer technology produces policy vacuums in its wake. And even when relevant policies do exist, they are often ambiguous or inadequate as they were designed for times with a less versatile technology than computing. A basic job of computer ethics is to identify these policy needs, clarify related conceptual confusions, formulate appropriate new policies, and ethically justify them.

Policies are rules of conduct ranging from formal laws to informal, implicit guidelines for action. Policies recommend kinds of actions that are sometimes contingent upon different situations. "Turn off your computer when you are finished" is a policy, though probably one without much ethical significance. "Don't steal computer chips" is another policy with more obvious ethical content. Even when policies are the policies of others, they can help us to regulate our lives. We know what to expect and can react accordingly. If a restaurant has the policy of using caller ID to capture the numbers of incoming phone calls, then, if we don't want to have our phone number known by the restaurant, we can block the caller ID system or use another restaurant. In this discussion our concern is with those computing policies that make an ethical difference and how to evaluate them properly.

This essay originally appeared in *Ethics and Information Technology,* **1**: 65–69, 1999. Copyright © 1999 by Kluwer Academic Publishers. Reprinted by permission.

[1] James H. Moor. What Is Computer Ethics? *Metaphilosophy,* 16(4), pp. 266–275, 1985.

Viewing issues in the ethics of computing in terms of policies is important. Policies have the right level of generality to consider in assessing the morality of conduct. Every action can be considered as an instance of a policy—in this kind of situation such and such action is allowed or required or forbidden. Understanding actions as exemplars of more general normative prescriptions promotes responsibility and more careful reflection on conduct. The word "policy" is intended to suggest both that there can be justified exemptions (policies are not absolute rules) and a level of obligation (policies are not mere suggestions).

We want our policies for computing to be ethical, but what should we look for when constructing ethical computing policies? When we turn to traditional ethical theories for help, we discover a strong rivalry exists between the leading contenders—consequentialist theories that emphasize the consequences of actions and deontological theories that stress rights and duties. Indeed, consequentialist theories and deontological theories are often presented as hopelessly incompatible. Philosophers perhaps take some pernicious delight in being gadflies and stirring things up, sometimes to revel in the conflicts among ethical theories. But the absence of resolution among the ethical theories leaves many with a somewhat jaundiced estimate of the value of ethical theory altogether. Applied ethicists, searching for practical guidance, find themselves immersed in ad hoc analyses of ethical problems and selecting solutions from an inconsistent pile of principles.

I believe that ethics needs more unifying theories that call upon the various strengths of the traditional approaches to ethics. One is reminded of the story of the elephant in which each observer obtaining evidence from only part of the elephant gives a description of the creature that diverges dramatically from the descriptions by others. Of course, there is an overall description of the elephant that makes sense of the individual, apparently incompatible, descriptions. Similarly, the elephant of ethical theory has been described by conflicting descriptions. Our job is to try to discover, if possible, an overall description of the elephant that will make sense of these apparently incompatible descriptions. This paper takes a few steps in that direction.

Consequentialism Constrained by Justice

The ethical evaluation of a given policy requires the evaluation of the consequences of that policy and often the consequences of the policy compared with the consequences of other possible policies. If our actions involving computers had no harmful consequences, policies would not be needed. However, conventional consequentialism has well-known shortcomings. Among other objections, consequentialism seems to be insensitive to issues of justice. I believe there may be a unifying ethical theory that allows us to take into account the consequences of policies, while at the same time making sure that these policies are constrained by principles of justice.

When considering consequences we evaluate the benefits and harms. Human beings have a common nature. At the core, humans have similar kinds of values, i.e., what kinds of things they consider to be goods (benefits) and what kinds of things they consider to be evils (harms). In general the core goods include life, happiness, and autonomy and the core evils include death, unhappiness, and lack of autonomy. By "happiness" I mean simply "pleasure and the absence of pain." The notion of autonomy here needs some explanation as the term is used by others in different ways. Obviously, humans do not share all their goals in common. But no matter what goals humans seek, they need ability, security, knowledge, freedom, opportunity, and resources in order to accomplish their projects. These are the kinds of goods that permit each of us to do whatever we want to. For brevity I will call this set of goods the "goods of autonomy" or simply "autonomy." The goods of autonomy are just the goods we would ask for in order to complete our projects.[2] For a given individual, the goods of autonomy are not necessarily any less valuable than happiness or even life. Some people will give up happiness for knowledge and some will give up life without freedom. Individuals will rank the core values differently and even the same individual may rank the core values differently during her lifetime. But for good evolutionary reasons all rational human beings put high positive value on life, happiness, and autonomy at least for themselves and those for whom they care. If they did not, they would not survive very long.

Of course, humans are not necessarily concerned about the lives, happiness, and autonomy of others, but they are concerned about their own. To be ethical one must not inflict unjustified harm (death, suffering, or decreased autonomy) on others. To take the ethical point of view is to be concerned for others at least to the extent that one tries to avoid harming them. The fact that humans value and disvalue the same kinds of things suggests that, contrary to the claims of some kinds of relativism, there may be common standards by which humans of different cultures can evaluate actions and policies.[3]

The combined notions of human life, happiness, and autonomy may not be far from what Aristotle meant by "human flourishing." Thus, from an ethical point of view we seek computing policies that at least protect, if not promote, human flourishing. Another way to make this point is to regard the core goods as marking fundamental human rights—at least as negative human rights. Humans ought to have their lives, happiness, and autonomy protected. And this principle of justice—the protection of fundamental human rights—should guide us in shaping ethical policies for using computer technology. When humans are using computer technology to harm other humans, there is a burden of justification on those doing the harming.

We have the beginning of a unifying ethical theory. When evaluating policies for computing, we need to evaluate the consequences of the proposed policies. We know what the core goods and evils are. And we want to protect human rights. Nobody should be harmed. The theory so far does constrain consequentialism by considerations of justice, but perhaps too well. Realistically, harmful consequences cannot always be avoided and sometimes it seems justified to cause harm to

---

[2] "ASK FOR" is a good way to remember the goods of autonomy: [A]bility, [S]ecurity. [K]nowledge, [F]reedom, [O]pportunity, [R]esources.

[3] James H. Moor. "Reason, Relativity, and Responsibility in Computer Ethics." *Computers and Society*, 28(1), pp. 14–21, 1998.

others, e.g., in giving punishment or defending oneself. Is there an approach to justice that will allow us to resolve conflicts of action or policy when causing harm seems unavoidable or even reasonable?

Bernard Gert provides us with a notion of moral impartiality that offers a good insight to justice that is useful in resolving these conflicts.[4] His moral theory inspires and informs the following analysis, though I will not do justice to his account of justice.

Justice requires an impartiality toward the kinds of policies we allow. Therefore, it is unjust for someone to use a kind of policy that he would not allow others to use. Consider the policy of a company knowingly and secretly installing defective computer chips in its products for sale. This policy of installing defective chips in products is an instance of a more general kind of policy that permits the manufacture and deceptive selling of resources that may significantly harm people. No rational person would accept this kind of public policy, for that would have to allow others to follow the same policy putting oneself at an unacceptable level of risk.

Now consider another example of a policy. A person who intrudes into my house uninvited will be electronically monitored and reported electronically to the police. Such a policy will result in causing harm to an intruder. Is it justified? Violating my security is a harm to me; it violates my privacy and puts me at risk. If we take an impartial point of view, then the policy stated more abstractly becomes people are allowed to harm (within limits) other people who are unjustly harming them. A rational, impartial person could accept such a policy in that others could be allowed to follow it as well. Others following such a policy will not harm you unless you harm them first.

This impartiality test can be used to evaluate whether or not exceptions to existing policies are justified. Suppose an airline has a policy of flying its planes on time and allowing computer systems to do the flying. This permits efficient and timely service on which its customers count. Now suppose the airline suddenly discovers a bug in their software that may endanger its planes and its passengers. Clearly the airline should request that human pilots fly its planes already in the air and ground the rest until the software problem is located and removed. Passengers will be harmed by delays and lost opportunities to fly but any rational, impartial person would allow such an exception to this policy if it meant avoiding significant risk of death. Such an exception can be made part of the policy and publicly advocated.

Gert applies his account of impartiality to potential violations of moral rules. This is a two-step procedure in which one abstracts the essential features of the situation using morally relevant features and then asks whether the resulting rule so modified could be publicly allowed, i.e., what consequences would follow if everyone knew about this kind of violation and could do it. I have done an analogous operation on the above examples by abstracting the policy and then asking what would be the consequences if such policies were publicly allowed.

---

[4] Gert, Bernard. *Morality: Its Nature and Justification.* Oxford, Oxford University Press, 1998.

Gert refers to his view of impartiality as "the blindfold of justice." The blindfold removes all knowledge of who will benefit or will be harmed by one's choices. This is similar to John Rawls' veil of ignorance [5] except that Gert allows those who are blindfolded to assign different weights to the benefits and harms. As a result there is room for disagreement that is not permitted in Rawls' account. Not all rational, impartial people will agree on every judgment. However, some judgments will be shared by all rational, impartial people.

If the blindfold of justice is applied to computing policies, some policies will be regarded as unjust by all rational, impartial people, some policies will be regarded as just by all rational, impartial people, and some will be in dispute. This approach is good enough to provide just constraints on consequentialism. We first require that all computing policies pass the impartiality test. Clearly, our computing policies should not be among those that every rational, impartial person would regard as unjust. Then we can further select policies by looking at their beneficial consequences. We are not ethically required to select policies with the best possible outcomes, but we can assess the merits of various policies using consequentialist considerations and we may select very good ones from those that are just.

The Good as the Enemy of the Just

We should develop computing policies in such a way that they are above all just. Then we can make the policies as good as reasonably possible. Our first priority should be to avoid unjustifiable harming of others by protecting their rights and then to increase benefits.

It may be tempting in some situations to focus on the strikingly good consequences of a policy while ignoring injustice. The potential good in a given situation is so good that it seems to justify being unjust. Suppose a company wants to market a set of CDs with extensive personal information about people in a country.[6] The good from a marketing point of view is staggering. Every marketer would be able to know considerable personal details about the citizens of a country and send out relevant marketing materials to those who need it. The good that looks so good in the short run may be overwhelmed by harm in the long run. The conventional consequentialist would point out that harm is done initially to people's autonomy and should not be overlooked. Because people's privacy is invaded, their security is reduced. With release of the CDs, people would become vulnerable to misuses of the information such as losing employment or losing insurance privileges. The just consequentialist has a further concern. Even if we stipulate that no such long term harm will occur through the release of this information, there is still collateral damage. If releasing these CDs filled with personal information is allowable, then similar activities are allowable in similar situations. In other words, by our impartiality principle, anyone else can inflict similar harms and put people at similar risks if the good from doing so seems substantial. Given the fallibility of humans, no rational, impartial person would be willing to take this risk.

---

[5] John Rawls. *A Theory of Justice*, Cambridge, Massachusetts, Harvard University Press, 1971.

[6] In 1990, Lotus Corporation was planning to sell software with a database of 120 million Americans including names, addresses, incomes, buying habits, and other personal data. Lotus aborted the idea due to public outrage.

Consider another example. The current copyright law protects software. Suppose someone decides to give a copy of her word processing software illegally to another person, a lowly graduate student.[7] There is potentially lost revenue to the software manufacturer but suppose that the graduate student receiving the software is living on limited means and would not be able to buy the software anyway. The student is someone who would benefit greatly from having the software if she had it. Why not illegally copy software in such cases? The foreseeable good is tempting. The conventional consequentialist may agree or more cautiously respond that the graduate student or the dispenser of illegal software may be discovered, which would lead to unanticipated harm. For example, the university protecting itself from lawsuits may have a rule that a doctoral dissertation discovered to be written on illegal software is not acceptable. The just consequentialist would point out in addition that there is collateral damage. If someone can violate the law in this case to benefit a friend, then by the impartiality principle, others can do so as well. Not only may other software be copied illegally to help friends, but other laws seem equally open to violation on the presumption that some people are being helped. Given the fallibility of humans, no rational, impartial person would want to take this risk.

This analysis is based upon the assumption that the copyright law itself is just. The law has been properly enacted and does not unjustifiably violate anyone's fundamental human rights. The copyright law does seem to be just in this way. However, this leaves open the question of whether the copyright law could be better. We might in fact want to allow greater fair use in the copying of software and enact better laws.

Sometimes it is said, "The ends do not justify the means." In one sense this statement is clearly false. If the ends don't justify the means, what would? If we take the ends to be our core goods, then they are satisfactory ends for the purposes of justification. In another sense this claim may mean "The ends do not justify any means that harm people." This is also false. One has to look at a situation impartially and ask what kinds of policies for conduct should apply. Sometimes harming some people somewhat to avoid much greater harm to them or others is completely justified. Or the claim might mean "The ends do not justify using unjust means." This is the interpretation of the claim that is true. This is precisely what happens when the good becomes the enemy of the just. Good ends somehow blind us to the injustice of the means.

We want good computing policies that promote human flourishing, consequences are important, but only as long as the policies themselves remain just. Unjust policies will in the long run, both directly and indirectly, undermine the benefits of these policies no matter how good they are.

Computing in Uncharted Waters

Setting ethical policies for computing might be compared to setting a course while sailing. A sailor may chart a course to her destination by dead reckoning; carefully laying out the course in a straight line on a chart. But sometimes there are no

---

[7] Compare Nissenbaum (1995) and Gert (1999).

charts, and, even if there are, experienced sailors know how difficult it is to keep the course true. Winds, currents, and tides are constantly changing. Sailors do not continually steer on course and trim their sails precisely. Midcourse adjustments are necessary and proper and should be expected. Similarly, setting ethical policies for computing is something of an approximation. Nobody can accurately predict the many changing factors in computing situations. Given the logical malleability of computing, many new opportunities and unexpected developments will arise. Human reactions to these new possibilities are equally difficult to predict. Midcourse adjustments in computing policy are necessary and proper and should be expected.

Sailors take danger bearings to avoid dangerous objects such as a reef. Certain courses should not be taken. This leaves open many other courses as good options, and reasonable sailors may disagree about which is best. Some may prefer to get to the destination in the shortest time, others may want to see a scenic island, and still others may wish to set a course to improve a suntan. Similarly, in setting computing policy there are policies we want to avoid. We do not want our policies to violate fundamental human rights unjustly. But given that our policies are just, many good policy options may be available, though people may have legitimate disagreements about which is best.

References

Bernard Gert. *Morality: Its Nature and Justification*. Oxford, Oxford University Press, 1998.

Bernard Gert. Common Morality and Computing. *Ethics and Information Technology* 1 (1): 57–64, 1999.

James H. Moor. What Is Computer Ethics? *Metaphilosophy* 16 (4): 266–275, 1985.

James H. Moor. Reason, Relativity, and Responsibility in Computer Ethics. *Computers & Society* 28 (1): 14–21, 1998.

Helen Nissenbaum. Should I Copy My Neighbor's Software? Deborah G. Johnson and Helen Nissenbaum, editors, *Computers, Ethics, and Social Values*, Englewood, New Jersey, Prentice Hall, pp. 201–213, 1995.

John Rawls. *A Theory of Justice*. Cambridge, Massachusetts, Harvard University Press, 1971.

Introduction to Chapter 2: Regulating the Net: Free Expression and Content Controls

The Internet has greatly expanded the opportunity for ordinary citizens to exercise their free speech rights. Through this democratic forum anyone can become a "town crier," propagating news stories, advertising commercial products, or spreading gossip. The Web also functions as a virtual public library, providing a rich source of material for educators, students, and professionals. Anyone who uses the Net or frequents web sites appreciates that Internet speech is extraordinary in its breadth and diversity.

But not all forms of speech are welcome in cyberspace. There is concern about pornography, hate speech, defamation, spam, and other forms of anti-social expression. In the United States, pornography is viewed as a particularly insidious problem, while European countries like Germany and France are more concerned about hate speech. Many worry that children will be exposed to too much harmful material on the Net, but there is no consensus on how to deal with this problem. The issue is compounded because of the current architecture of the Internet, which makes it difficult to identify and deny minors access. As Lessig (1999) discussed, architecture is the key for understanding why law has been so impotent in dealing with problematic forms of Internet speech: "Relative anonymity, decentralized distribution, multiple points of access, no necessary tie to geography, no simple system to identify content, tools of encryption—all these features and consequences of the Internet protocol make it difficult to control speech in cyberspace."

Nonetheless, the United States government sought to deal with the pervasive problem of Internet pornography with a piece of legislation called the Communications Decency Act of 1996 (CDA). This ill-fated law criminalized the "knowing" transmission of "obscene or indecent" material over the Net to anyone under the age of eighteen. Shortly after the CDA was signed into law, the ACLU and several other groups filed a lawsuit, claiming that the CDA violated the First Amendment. One year after its passage, the Supreme Court struck down the law because it interfered with the First Amendment rights of adults to access pornographic sites. According to the majority opinion in *Reno v. ACLU* (1997), the Act "suppresses a large amount of speech that adults have a constitutional right to receive and to address to one another." Moreover, the law's reference to "indecent" material is unconstitutionally vague. In a dramatic statement in support of the ACLU's position the Supreme Court claimed that "any content-based regulation of the Internet, no matter how benign the purpose, could burn the global village to roast the pig" (*Reno v. ACLU*, 1997).

But in October, 1998 Congress tried again, passing the more precisely written Child Online Protection Act (COPA), which was also immediately challenged by the ACLU. The Act required web site operators to restrict access to any material deemed to be "harmful to minors." Such material had to be obscene or meet three requirements (for example, the material "depicts, describes, or represents, in a manner patently offensive with respect to minors, an actual or simulated sexual act or sexual conduct. . . or lewd exhibition of the genitals. . . "). However, the Supreme Court found that like its predecessor, the CDA, COPA was still unconstitutional.

In the wake of these judicial decisions those concerned with Internet pornography have looked to other means of content control such as code-based solutions like filtering technologies. Filters are programs that screen Internet content and block access to unacceptable web sites. Families, for example, can purchase filters that deny children access to any site considered by the author of the filtering program to be a purveyor of indecent or obscene sexual material.

In the stream of content distribution, filters can be invoked at any level. Downstream, in the home, private filters may be a reasonable solution for concerned parents to shield their children from pornographic material. But many argue that filtering upstream at the institutional, Internet Service Provider (ISP), or state level is an ineffectual and repressive solution; they contend that too many legitimate voices will often get fenced out in the process. Filters on the Net impede the free flow of information and thereby undermine the Net's power as a democratizing medium. According to Shapiro (1999), the result of too much filtering and personalization "in the aggregate is that the speech of certain individuals—especially marginal speakers—may well be lost in cyberspace."

Despite earlier setbacks, Congress once again determined that it needed to take action against cyberporn. As a result, the Children's Internet Protection Act (CIPA) was passed in 2000. The government sought to use private surrogates, that is, libraries and schools, to regulate speech available to minors. According to CIPA, these institutions will be denied subsidies for Internet access unless they install filters to block out pornographic material.

This protracted and ongoing cyberporn controversy underscores the volatile nature of the debate concerning the scope of free speech rights in cyberspace. While libertarians argue for unfettered speech on this medium, moderate voices in this debate identify a more nuanced challenge: to preserve a democratic vision of the Internet while ensuring that the proper limitations are put in place to deal with truly dangerous or disruptive forms of speech. They remind us that despite the broad scope of First Amendment protection for free speech, limits exist on what people can say or publish in any forum, including the Internet. Defining those precise boundaries, of course, has always been a great moral and legal challenge, but that does not mean that the effort should be abandoned.

The readings in this chapter grapple with these questions and provide different perspectives on controversial free speech issues. When does speech become truly dangerous? Can speech on the Net be regulated through conventional legal means or through common law principles? What is the relationship of code (e.g., filtering systems) to law? What are the dangers of heavily relying on filters and other methods of content control? How should we handle other problematic forms of expression like spam and defamation? Also, what is the role of third parties, such as Internet Service Providers, in all of this? If injury is caused when their customers post libelous or hateful remarks on the Internet, should those ISPs incur some liability?

The initial article of this chapter, "Is the Global Information Infrastructure a Democratic Technology?" by Deborah Johnson, approaches the free speech issue from a broad perspective. Johnson notes that cyberspace or the Global Information Infrastructure (GII) is often perceived to be a democratic technology because it promotes opportunities for speech. In her article, Johnson carefully considers the merits of this position; she states that to say that the GII is democratic is to assert that this technology has a value embedded in it. She reviews several models to help us understand the meaning of an "embedded value," so that the notion can be intelligibly applied to the GII.

Professor Larry Lessig, in the chapter's second reading, "The Laws of Cyberspace," discusses the regulation of cyberspace behavior and indecency on the Net. Lessig focuses extensively on the unique nature of the Internet and the implications for Internet governance. In this article and in his book, *Code and Other Laws of Cyberspace* (1999), Lessig argues that there are four constraints on behavior that apply in both real and virtual space: laws, the marketplace, norms, and code. The most significant of these is code, because the code or architectures of the Internet tend to make it less regulable, i.e., there is less that government can do. Lessig is worried, however, that in its zeal to curb indecent speech and deal with other forms of purportedly deviant behavior, the government will seek to change the code of cyberspace from an architecture of freedom to one of control.

The third selection, "Of Black Holes and Decentralized Law-Making in Cyberspace," focuses on a proper remedy for spam (unsolicited commercial e-mail). The problem of spam is intensifying—in 2004 the average user will receive almost 3,000 unsolicited commercial messages a year and by 2007 spam is likely to amount to 60% of every user's e-mail (Agoc, 2003). Because spam "shifts costs from the advertiser to several other parties including the recipients of the ad, the Internet Service Providers, and even to other users of the Internet who are indirectly inconvenienced by this practice," (Spinello, 1999) spam is considered an unethical abuse of the system.

In this article, David Post describes a way to block spam—the Realtime Blackhole List (RBL). The nonprofit organization Mail Abuse Prevention System (MAPS) manages the RBL. This list contains Internet Protocol addresses determined by MAPS to be spammers. When a complaint gets lodged against them, and that complaint is verified by MAPS, spammers end up on this list. Those blacklisted will have their e-mail bounced by ISPs and other organizations that subscribe to this list. In addition, ISPs that encourage spammers can end up as Listed ISPs; other ISPs may choose to configure their system so that their customers cannot exchange e-mail with clients of Listed ISPs.

Post carefully considers whether the RBL is a socially and politically acceptable way to deal with the problem of spam. When do private speech restrictions such as this one begin to have a negative impact on our First Amendment rights? Is this the most prudent way to make Internet policy or should there be federal laws to handle spam? Lessig disagrees with the informal approach to policy making implicit in the creation and adoption of RBL. But Post believes that Lessig and others should not so quickly dismiss this decentralized and "semi-chaotic" method for constructing policies in cyberspace. He cites the "jurisdictional conundrum" of cyberspace as one reason why centralized controls may be less effective in dealing with spam in this unique realm.

With the next selection, "Fahrenheit 451.2: Is Cyberspace Burning?", we turn from spam to the problem of cyberporn. This special report, prepared by the ACLU, presents a libertarian perspective on free speech. It warns readers of a threat far more subtle than heavy-handed government censorship in cyberspace: the deployment of "private" filtering and blocking mechanisms. In this essay, the authors argue against the use of these conventional technologies to curtail speech even when the efforts are aimed at minors. These technologies represent some of the architectures of control that Lessig had in mind. The ACLU is deeply concerned about those who seek to control unfettered online content for ideological reasons. They delineate reasons why self-rating and third party rating schemes are misguided, and make the case that blocking software should not be used by libraries.

Professor Rosenberg echoes similar themes in the fifth essay of the chapter entitled "Filtering the Internet in the USA: Free Speech Denied?" This article supports some of the key conclusions reached in "Fahrenheit 451.2." It discusses the significant problems of filters and content-based blocking programs in libraries and schools, including their lack of transparency. According to Rosenberg, "The commitment of librarians to the basic principle of free and open access to information, whether in hard copy or electronic form, must be supported by the population at large."

The Rosenberg article is followed by excerpts from the Supreme Court's 6-3 decision to overturn a lower court ruling and uphold the controversial Children's Internet Protection Act (U.S. v. American Library Association). We include substantial excerpts from the majority opinion written by Chief Justice Rehnquist and a dissenting opinion written by Justice Stevens. By juxtaposing these conflicting views, readers can evaluate the benefits and shortcomings involved in using filtering systems to suppress speech.

This general theme of censorship and content control is continued with a slightly different focus in Jacques Catudal's article, "Censorship, the Internet, and the Child Pornography Law of 1996: A Critique." Catudal argues that this Act is too broad in its proscriptions and thereby violates the First Amendment. He offers an amended version of the law that protects against harmful practices without violating the rights of adults. In April 2002, the U.S. Supreme Court struck down the congressional ban on virtual child pornography.

The final essay, "Agents of Harm or Agents of Grace: The Legal and Ethical Aspects of Identifying Harm and Assigning Responsibility in a Networked World," looks at online defamation and the difficulties of assigning responsibility in cyberspace. To what degree, if any, should Internet Service Providers be held accountable for preventing or limiting the damage of defamatory statements made by individual users? On the one hand, mandating ISP liability could have an unwanted chilling effect on free expression in cyberspace; on the other hand, failure to require

ISPs to take adequate measures to curtail libel is not conducive to civil discourse or to the protection of private reputation. To some extent, the scope of ISP liability depends on how we conceive the ISP's role—is it a publisher like *The New York Times,* a distributor like a bookstore, or something else entirely?

In their thorough treatment of this topic, Lipinski, Buchanan, and Britz also consider jurisdictional issues in cyberspace and whether the global scope of the Net can be reconciled with the desire for local control. An Australian court's ruling in the *Gutnick* v. *Dow Jones* & *Co.* (2002) case raises the question of how organizations can manage the risk of doing business in cyberspace when local statutes have global reach.

Discussion Questions

1. Does cyberspace have unique features that justify greater or lesser speech protections for pornography? How can children best be protected from the large volume of pornography available on the Web?

2. Do you agree with the libertarian philosophy regarding First Amendment issues that is articulated in the Fahrenheit 451.2 article? Explain your answer.

3. Consider the problem of libel and defamation in cyberspace. Does the opportunity to be a "town crier" and reach a large audience by way of the Internet preclude strong legal protection for private individuals?

4. Do you agree with the Supreme Court's controversial decision in the CIPA case? What is the basis for your decision?

5. Should virtual child pornography be denied First Amendment protection? Explain your reasoning.

6. Summarize the main themes of Professor Post's article on black holes. Do you agree with his conclusions? Do you side with Lessig or Post?

References

Agoc, C. (2003). "Losing the War on Spam," *Wired,* September, p. 50.

Lessig, Larry (1999). *Code and Other Laws of Cyberspace,* New York: Basic Books.

Reno v. *ACLU* (1997). 521 U.S. 844.

Shapiro, Andrew (1999). *The Control Revolution.* New York: Century Foundation Books.

Spinello, Richard (1999). "Ethical Reflections on the Problem of Spam," *Ethics and Information Technology,* Vol 1, No.3, pp. 185–191.

Suggestions for Further Reading

Electronic Privacy Information Center, *Filters and Freedom.* Washington, D.C.: Electronic Privacy Information Center, 1999.

Fried, Charles (2000). "Perfect Freedom or Perfect Control," 114 *Harvard Law Review 606.*

Godwin, Michael (1998). *CyberRights.* New York: Random House.

Lessig, Larry (1999). *Code and Other Laws of Cyberspace,* New York: Basic Books [See especially Chapters 1–5, and Chapter 12 on free speech].

Reno v. *American Civil Liberties Union* (1997) 96 U.S. 511.

Spinello, Richard (2003). "Free Speech in Cyberspace." Chapter 3 in *CyberEthics: Morality and Law in Cyberspace,* 2nd ed. Sudbury, MA: Jones and Bartlett.

Tavani, Herman (2004). "Regulating Commerce and Speech in Cyberspace. " Chapter 9 in *Ethics & Technology: Ethical Issues in an Age of Information and Communication Technology.* Hoboken, NJ: John Wiley and Sons.

Weckert, John (2000). "What is So Bad about Internet Content Regulation?" *Ethics and Information Technology.* Vol. 2, No. 2. pp. 105–111.

Is the Global Information Infrastructure a Democratic Technology?[1]

Deborah G. Johnson

Introduction

The global information infrastructure (hereafter the GII) is often claimed to be a democratic technology. It is said to create electronic democracy, to facilitate or enhance democratic processes.[2] The aim of this paper is to explore what these claims might mean and to suggest approaches to the GII that will be fruitful for evaluating such claims. The undertaking will shed light on the social, and particularly value, implications of the GII. The task necessarily involves three fundamental questions: What is the GII? What is democracy? What does it mean to say that a technology carries a value?

To say that the GII is democratic is to say that this technology has a value embedded in it, that it contains or favors or facilitates democracy. Democracy is a value in the sense that when individuals make claims about the Internet or the GII being democratic, they are claiming that there is a strong link between the technology and patterns of behavior associated with democracy and considered desirable. Hence, to understand whether the GII is democratic, we must first understand what it could mean to say that values are embedded in a technology. This is the task I undertake in the first sections of this paper. Later I turn to democracy and the GII.

I have paid little attention to defining or even describing the GII. A characterization of this technology is difficult in part because it is continuously evolving. Broadly, I understand the GII to be the coming together of computer/information

This essay originally appeared in *Computers and Society*, Vol. 27, No. 3 (September) 1997: 20–26. Copyright © 2000 by Deborah G. Johnson. Reprinted by permission.

[1] An earlier version of this paper was presented at the conference on Computer Ethics held at Linkoping University, Linkoping, Sweden, June 9, 1997.

[2] See for example: Howard Rheingold, "The Great Equalizer," *Whole Earth Review*, Summer 1991, pp. 5–11; Rick Henderson, "Cyberdemocracy," *Reason*, 1995, April, pp. 43–46; Mark Poster, "CyberDemocracy: Internet and the Public Sphere"; A. Calabrese and M. Borchert, "Prospects for electronic democracy in the United States: rethinking communication and social policy," *Media, Culture & Society*, 1996, Vol. 18: 249–268.

technology with telecommunications. It originated with the Internet, but that name now seems inappropriate since the technology has evolved (e.g., it now includes the World Wide Web) and because uses, ownership, and maintenance conditions have radically changed from those of the Internet. The system is now used for such a wide variety of activities that they are too numerous to delineate.

The infrastructures in which many aspects of our lives used to take place—work, shopping, banking, and entertainment—are being recreated, and transformed in the GII. The new medium has characteristics different from the physical, geographic world in which our bodies live, and these special characteristics affect social values. For example, property, privacy, and responsibility are being re-thought because of the extent to which anonymity and reproducibility are possible in the new medium.[3] Hence, the question of this paper—Is the global information infrastructure a democratic technology?—sheds light on the quite different, but related, question whether democracy, as it has traditionally been understood, can be realized in a world that does not depend on physical, geographic space.

Technology and Values

Up until twenty years ago or less, the literature on science and technology was filled with claims about their value-neutrality. Many scholars believed that technologies did not embody values, and emphasized that values come into play, if at all, only when technologies are used. Perhaps the best or most familiar example of this is the claim about guns, i.e., "guns don't kill, people do," as if a gun were a neutral tool. Computers, as well, were thought to be neutral tools that acquire values only when used for particular purposes.

The claim that technology is value-neutral rested in part on the alliance between science and technology, with several ideas about science shaping ideas about technology. The presumption about science was that it is objective and that it progresses in a natural sequence or evolution. The unfolding of our knowledge was thought to be dictated by nature, not by society. New discoveries were thought to proceed and progress in a natural order. The same would be said about technology. It was understood to have a natural order of development that was thought to be somewhat independent (though perhaps less so than science) of social forces.

These presumptions have now been rejected (or at least substantially modified and qualified) by most scholars in the field of science and technologies studies (STS). It is now well-accepted among STS scholars that technology (as well as science) is value-laden; that is, that the directions and content of science are socially influenced; that technologies are developed in a social context that pushes and pulls and shapes its development. Even those who resist these claims, insofar as they apply to scientific method, recognize that when it comes to topic choice and funding, science is shaped by social forces.

Two tenets now form the foundation of science and technology studies: that technology shapes social patterns, and that technology is shaped by its social context.

---

[3] In an earlier paper, "Ethics On line" (*Communications of the ACM*, 1997), I identify scope, anonymity, and reproducibility as special features of communication in the GII, features with important ethical implications.

Bijker (1995) aptly and concisely describes the unfolding of these two trends in STS studies. He characterizes the scholarship of the last 50 years as moving like a pendulum from one of these tenets to the other with smaller and smaller swings over time until the two work closely together.

> "Before the 1940s the social sciences did not pay much attention to the study of the detailed development of technical artifacts and society. ...[4] The pendulum started to swing, and especially historians, some economists, and, later, philosophers and sociologists discovered technology. The swing went too far, however, and technology was viewed as an autonomous factor to which society had to bow. Technology was all important. With the rise of social shaping models, the pendulum swung back from this technological determinist conception. But again the swing went a little too far. The impact theme almost disappeared from view and technology seemed merely a social construct that could not appear in an obdurate, transformations-resisting, and society shaping form. Recently the pendulum started to swing back again to redress this imbalance. Technology recaptured some of its obduracy without completely losing its socially shaped character. The swings are smaller now. Perhaps we should say that the pendulum is not moving anymore in a flat plane but moves in Foucaultian circles." (p. 254)

For the purposes of this paper, it is important to note that the *social* encompasses *values* (though the two are neither synonymous, nor identical). Values are one aspect of the social. Hence, Bijker's articulation of the two tenets of STS includes the claims that: (1) values shape technologies and (2) technologies shape values.

By implication, then, we should expect the GII to carry values with it, i.e., to shape, enhance or diminish, afford or constrain values, and we should expect that the GII has been shaped by social values. Still, these claims are too abstract to point us to where or how to look at the GII. We need to understand more concretely what it could mean to say that a technology is value-laden or that values are embedded in technologies.

In this paper, I focus primarily on one of the two tenets, that technologies shape values. Thus, I ask what values are embedded in the GII. I touch only briefly on values that shaped the development of the GII.

Values Embedded in Technologies

What, then, does it mean to say that values are embedded in technology? Winner (1986) addressed this matter head on in his famous article, "Do Artifacts Have Politics?" He distinguishes two views. The first is the view that values are inherent to technology. Winner writes,

---

[4] Bijker cites Mumford and Ogburn as two exceptions.

"According to this view, the adoption of a given technical system unavoidably brings with it conditions for human relationships that have a distinctive political cast—for example, centralized or decentralized, egalitarian or inegalitarian, repressive or liberating. ... [C]ertain kinds of technology do not allow such flexibility, ... to choose them is to choose unalterably a particular form of political life." (p. 29)

In contrast, Winner identifies a second view according to which "a given kind of technology is strongly compatible with, but does not strictly require, social and political relationships of a particular stripe." (p. 32)

Winner goes on to mention solar energy as an example of a technology that has been said to be more compatible with a democratic, egalitarian society than, say, petroleum-based energy systems or nuclear power, but nothing about solar energy requires democracy.

Winner sets us on the right path, though we need to be clear on the distinctions he is making. The first distinction is that between intractable properties and flexible properties. These are *properties of the technology* The second distinction has to do with *the relationship between the properties of the technology and the social relationships necessitated by the properties* Some technologies require patterns or types of social relationships and social organization; others are compatible with alternative types of social relationships and social organization. Winner is particularly concerned with patterns of power and authority in these social relationships.

To summarize his view, then, he claims that: (1) technologies embody values insofar as they have properties that are linked to social relationships, in particular relationships involving power and authority; and, (2) technologies may do this in one of two ways, either (a) by having intractable properties that require particular types of social relationships and authority, or (b) by having flexible properties compatible with diverse patterns of social organization and authority. In the latter case, the pattern of social relationships surrounding a technology is determined, presumably, by something other than the technology (e.g., prevailing social patterns at the time of the technology's introduction).

In terms of democracy, then, a technology may have: (a) intractable properties that require democratic patterns of authority; (b) intractable properties that require non-democratic (or anti-democratic) patterns of authority; or (c) flexible properties that are compatible with either pattern of authority.

If we use these distinctions to ask questions about the GII, they point, in particular, to patterns of social relationships surrounding the GII. Many who claim that the GII is democratic seem to have in mind that it facilitates "unmediated" communication connections between individuals. Even if we accept, for the moment, the claim that such communication is "unmediated, " we still have to ask whether this property—unmediated communication—is intractable or flexible. Is communication in the GII inherently unmediated, or is the GII compatible with both mediated or unmediated communication? It might be argued that the GII is "intractably" democratic because telecommunications lines (which are a hard, not a flexible property of the GII) connect every individual to every other individual in the world. Of course, every individual in the world is not yet connected to every other individual in the world because millions of individuals do not have access to telecommunications lines, let alone computers. Still, the argument could be made that the technology makes such connections possible in principle, and, therefore, that the technology embodies a pattern of social relationships connecting all individuals to all others. This account makes some sense of the claim that the GII is democratic.

However, the conclusion is much too quickly drawn, for several reasons. For one, it is significant that telecommunications lines do not yet go to every individual. The fact that some individuals are not connected suggests that the GII can be undemocratic in its hard (physical) structure; that is, the technology is compatible with inclusion *or exclusion*. It appears to be compatible both with every individual being connected to every other individual and with use by a subgroup (an elite) that is facilitated in promoting its interests and capable of excluding others from access or use. Limiting access to a subgroup can be achieved either via hardware (wires) or software. That is, even if physical wires were to connect every individual to every other individual, the technology allows information to be routed in selective and exclusionary ways (as payment for service or for information is making clear).

The characterization of the technology as facilitating "unmediated" communication is misleading. Communications scholars have referred to exchanges via this technology as "computer-mediated" communication (CMC), explicitly recognizing that communication is mediated in the new medium. The issue then becomes understanding how "computer mediation" may affect communication. Our concern is whether computer mediation promotes or diminishes democracy. The literature on electronic democracy suggests that the mere fact that the technology provides forums for individuals to discuss political issues makes the technology democratic. Once again, however, this conclusion is drawn too quickly. In order to conclude that discussions on the GII are democratic or that they enhance democratic processes depends much more on who is talking to whom, what they are talking about, and what procedural rules are in place.

In any case, the idea that the GII is democratic because it connects every individual to every other individual and allows individuals to engage in political discussion puts the emphasis on the users of the technology. It focuses attention on what the technology facilitates. Winner's analysis points, however, not so much to the users of technology as to the social relationships required to produce and maintain a technology. Winner's analysis suggests that we ask about the types of social relationships required to manage and maintain the system. These relationships are, of course, complex and evolving, especially as the technology expands on a global scale. As well, ownership and management has been changing in the U.S. from a publicly funded, decentralized, cooperative system to a private, more centralized, commercial system. While all complex systems, especially those of a global scale, require cooperation, it would be naive to suppose that the management and maintenance of such a system does not require hierarchical relationships and centralized control, i.e., undemocratic relationships.

Winner's account is useful in bringing to the fore both the distinction between intractable and flexible properties and the focus on social relationships necessary for maintenance and management of a technology. Nevertheless, there are other possible meanings to the claim that technologies are value-laden, and it is important to distinguish several more of these before continuing. Discussions of the value-ladeness of technology are often muddled and suggestive and I have tried below to sort out some of the possible meanings of the claim that technology is value-laden.

1. The Moral/Metaphysical Meaning of Embedded Values

On this type of account, values pervade the invention and production of a technology, and these values are put into technology in such a way that they cannot be separated from it. The invention and production of the technology may, therefore, be tainted because of the practices, institutions, and people involved in its creation, even though these no longer exist. For example, a structure built by slaves, knowledge created by Nazi scientists, projects done by the military, are all tainted by the character of the activities by which they were created.

On this account, there is an inseparability, an inalterable link, between a technology and the institutions, practices, and actors that produced it. The inalterable link here is metaphysical in the sense that the carryover is in the very existence (being) of the thing, even though it may not be in any physical feature of it. The link is moral in the sense that what carries over from the history of the technology's development is a moral quality. The history of a technology's production involved moral values and those values persist in the technology's being. Most importantly, since the technology's history contains moral values that carry over in its being, those who use the technology become implicated in that history.

2. The Support Meaning of Embedded Values

This account is similar to the preceding in the sense that it also affirms an inseparability between the technology and its invention and/or production, but on this account, the institutions, actors, and practices are current (ongoing) and the inseparability has to do with support. Those who use or purchase the technology, in effect, support or endorse or promote the values that create it. The technology is value-laden in the sense that using it supports the values that produced it. For example, when one uses plastic water bottles, one supports petroleum-dependence and, therefore, imperialistic governments. Values are embedded in the technology in the sense that the act of purchasing and/or using the technology implicitly involves support for institutions, actors, and practices that themselves embody values.

3. The Material Meaning of Embedded Values

On a third type of account, the values embedded in a technology no longer reside in the institutions and practices that produced it; the technology is, in some sense, separable from its origins. On this type of account, the material object carries values in its design (Gorenstein, 1996). Its design may be the result of activities that put values into it, but we need not know about or think about those activities to confront the values in the technology. Values are in the physical or material being of the thing. They inhere in it and can be read from it. There seem to be at least two different versions of this account.

a. On one version, material objects embody values in the sense that they convey values (ideas) in their design, and we can read (see, experience, be influenced by) these values by viewing or interacting with the object. For example, a plastic water bottle may be designed in a way that makes it comfortable to hold with one hand. It may be small enough to put in a jacket pocket or it may have a small piece that allows it to be hooked onto a belt. Just by looking at the bottle, a person can tell that it is meant to be held, put in a pocket, or used in moving about—walking or running. Similarly, a pitcher with a handle and spout carries the idea of fluid being contained, lifted with the hand, and poured. A gun carries the idea of being held in a hand, aimed, and sending projectiles at high speeds. Perhaps it doesn't contain killing per se, but it contains the idea of a hard, fast-moving projectile directed at an object or in a specific direction. On this version of the material account, the design of a technology conveys ideas about the technology's relationship to the human body or to a task, and in this sense it contains values. The values are activities, tasks, or functions facilitated by the thing.

b. Winner's account seems to be a somewhat different version of a material account. His idea seems to be that the design requires or is compatible with certain types of social relationships, especially relationships of power and authority. The use of the technology requires (or, when put together with other social conditions, leads to) certain patterns of social life and social behavior. Here it is not just that there is an idea in the design, not just that certain tasks or activities are facilitated, but rather that the technology (in the case of intractable properties) can only be used by adopting particular social patterns. Those social patterns come with (are carried by) the technology, and they embody values.

These two versions of material accounts cannot be distinguished too sharply; one seems to meld into the other. Winner's account is material in the sense that the connection of the technology to social relationships is in the technology's material being or design. In his description of the Long Island bridges built so that public buses could not go under (thus insuring that the poor, lower classes couldn't go to beaches where the wealthy went to swim), class difference—a value—is in the height of the bridge. So, the physical design of a technology contains values in the sense that it facilitates tasks, activities, purposes (version a), and some of these activities lead to particular social relationships, relationships of power and authority (version b).

4. The Expressive Meaning of Embedded Values

On a fourth type of account, technologies have social meaning, and, therefore, values. The values in the technology can only be understood by understanding the social context of the technology. This social context may refer to the use of the technology but it may also have little to do with explicit purpose or use. Sclove's idea that technologies have polypotency is helpful here (Sclove, 1995).

> "In other words, technologies exhibit superfluous efficacy or "polypotency" in their functions, effects, and meanings. ... For example, when a man uses an ordinary hammer to pound nails, he also learns about the texture and structural properties of materials, he exercises and develops his muscles, he improves his hand-eye coordination, and he generates

noise, all while stressing and wearing the hammer itself. As his com-
petence at hammering grows, he feels his self-respect affirmed and
approved. At another level, his activity resonates with half-conscious
memories of primeval myths about Vulcan and Thor. He is also reminded
of the blacksmith and the mythology of the American frontier. He thinks
of a judge's gavel, the hammer as a symbol of justice, and a song pop-
ularized by the folksinging trio Peter, Paul, and Mary.... So, is the nail
entering the board necessarily the most important feature of the activ-
ity called "hammering"? Hammers, like all technologies, are polypotent
in their social functions, effects, and meanings." (pp.20–21)

On this account of the value-ladeness of technology, we may buy and use things because of their symbolic meaning in our culture, not only because of their focal function. We don't buy cars capable of going 120 miles per hour because of this function for we rarely, if ever, have the opportunity, let alone need, to drive at such a speed. Rather we buy them because of their meaning in our culture—macho, sexy, successful. Statistics and computer-generated data add authority and the appearance of being up-to-date to a presentation (even if they don't convey any other significant information).

This type of account of values embedded in a technology is similar to the material account in that on both types of account, values are thought to be amenable to being read off the technology. On the expressive meaning account, however, values are dependent on social context so that one cannot understand the values expressed in a technology unless one understands its social context.

Now, these four types of accounts are not mutually exclusive. They can apply simultaneously to the same technology. They should be kept distinct primarily because they point to very different ways in which values may be embedded in technologies and, therefore, they recommend quite different directions of analysis of technology.

Values Embedded in the Global Information Infrastructure

How do these accounts help to understand values embedded in the GII? Do any of them point to the GII being democratic?

1. The Moral/Metaphysical Meaning of Embedded Values

Moral/metaphysical accounts generally come into play when something noteworthy has occurred in the development of a technology. It may be something good, as in the case of Tang's origins in NASA's project to send humans to the moon, or it may be something horrible, as in the case of the Volkswagon bug being conceived in Nazi Germany. In either case, the technology is thought to carry the values of its noteworthy history. When it comes to the GII, then, we have to examine its origins, that is, the institutions, practices, and people involved in its development, to see what moral values it carries.

While a full examination will not be undertaken here, it is interesting to note conflicting values in the historical roots of the GII. The GII is an evolution of the

Internet, and the Internet had its origins in the U.S. military. It would seem, then, that those who think military endeavors are immoral might find the GII tainted by its origins. This association, however, is rarely expressed in social commentary on the GII, and certainly not in the context of the technology's democratic qualities.

On the other hand, the GII's more recent roots are generally understood to be in academe and the culture of hackers. In the early history of computers, hackers were not criminals, but computer enthusiasts. The culture of hackers is described as a culture of sharing and openness, an environment in which individuals would spend long hours helping each other figure out how to do things with computers, improving on each others programs with no interest in who owned what or what credit would be assigned to whom. An examination of this period in the GII's history might reveal values associated with democracy such as sharing, openness, bonds between individuals, and decentralized activity (Levy, 1984).

A linking of the GII with the culture of hackers may be at work in the thinking of those who claim the GII is democratic; however, it is difficult to imagine the link being affirmed as moral or metaphysical. That is, there may be an association, but not one that would lead to a strong case for the GII being democratic.

2. The Support Meaning of Embedded Values

On the support account, we should look not to the history of the GII, but to the institutions, practices, and people who currently produce and maintain it. We should ask what values are found there and whether these values are worthy of our support and endorsement. Since we are interested in democracy, such an analysis must focus on whether these institutions and practices are democratic. This is a complex undertaking given that the GII is now a global system. The institutions, practices, and people who produce and maintain it are in many different countries working in diverse conditions. Moreover, the system is still evolving. The U.S., for example, is in the midst of radical change as its portion of the system evolves from being publicly funded and available to a limited range of users, to a commercial system, privately owned and marketed broadly.

On this account of values embedded in a technology, the important point is to know what values one is supporting when one buys or uses a technology. The idea that users might be supporting democratic or undemocratic institutions when they use the GII is an idea that has not been addressed in discussions of the GII or its social impact. Indeed, a focus on the institutions, practices, and people who produce and maintain the system is likely to reveal quite undemocratic features of the technology, as will become clear later on.

3. The Material Meaning of Embedded Values

The material meaning of embedded values points in the direction of values embedded in the material design of the GII. This type of analysis was sketched out earlier when the web of hard wires connecting every individual to every other individual and the decentralized way in which information is routed were suggested to be hard features of the technology that embodied democracy. Both of these features do seem to be at the heart of claims about the democratic character of the technology. (In stark contrast would be a centralized system in which every bit of information moving through the system would have to pass through a central site from which it would be routed to its destination.)

However, the earlier discussion revealed these ideas to be premature. The GII is compatible with hard wires connecting everyone and with decentralized routing, but it is also compatible with limited access and centralized routing. Even if we move the argument to focus on individual autonomy and the idea that the GII allows individuals to control who they are connected to and what information they access, it is important to remember that this is a flexible property of the technology, not an intractable feature. The technology is also compatible with the invisible shaping of an individual's apparently autonomous control; it is compatible with centralized control, surveillance, and censorship. As an example of individual autonomous control being invisibly controlled, imagine search engines that display information in an order that is based on (gives priority to) how much has been paid to the developers of the search engine.

4. The Expressive Meaning of Embedded Values

Finally, the fourth account of embedded values points in the direction of an analysis of the cultural meaning of the GII. The social context in which the GII has been developed is complex and changing. Using Sclove's notion of polypotency would allow us to see a diverse set of values in the cultural meaning of the GII. Perhaps its most potent meaning is that it is "the future." The GII symbolizes the direction in which the world is headed. It symbolizes a future in which individuals are working, doing business, and being entertained on a global scale. The message of the technology (or at least the advertising and reporting about it) is that it is a high-speed train into the future and those who do not get on board now will be left behind forever.

The GII also expresses other social meanings, and the topic of this paper is itself evidence of the fact that its cultural meaning has been linked to democracy.

Democracy As the Starting Place: Power and Insularity

The preceding analysis suggests a number of fruitful directions for further research into the values embedded in the GII, research that would further our understanding of its democratic and undemocratic tendencies. The preceding preliminary analysis points in the direction of the technology having both democratic and undemocratic tendencies.

Yet another approach to this issue would be to deconstruct the notion of democracy, teasing out its elements and meanings, and then use these as the basis for an analysis. "Democracy" is used in a variety of different ways to refer to a variety of features of democratic societies. Anthony Arblaster (1987) recognizes this diversity and seeks to ferret out the kernel of meaning in definitions of democracy. He writes,

> "At the root of all definitions of democracy, however refined and complex, lies the idea of popular power, of a situation in which power, and perhaps authority too, rests with the people. That power or authority is usually thought of as being political, and it often therefore takes the form of an idea of popular sovereignty—the people as the ultimate political authority." [p. 8]

Popular sovereignty is the overarching idea at the root of many ideas associated with democracy, including the following: elections and representative government, participation (in government and other institutions), power in the hands of many rather than a few, joint deliberation, cultivation of active habits, equality, individual freedom, and individual rights.

Several of these elements came into play in the preceding discussion of the GII's democratic character. However, an approach that starts from the meaning of democracy would lead to additional, fruitful analysis. In particular, two elements point in the direction of anti-democratic tendencies of the GII: the idea of democracy as power in the hands of the many and the idea of democracy as involving joint deliberation.

Power to the Many

Tightly connected to Arblaster's idea of popular sovereignty is the idea of a government or society in which individual citizens have significant power. In other words, in a democracy (as opposed to a dictatorship or aristocracy or oligarchy) individuals have a say in the rules, laws, and policies (or representatives) by which they must live. This idea seems to be at work in the thinking of those who claim the GII is democratic. The reasoning would seem to go as follows: Democracy means power in the hands of the many; information is power; the GII puts information in the hands of the many; therefore, the GII is democratic.

The generally unexamined kingpin in this set of claims is the claim that "information is power." This phrase has been used over and over in public discussion and advertising of the GII. But, what does it mean to say that information is power? There are two radically different meanings. On the first interpretation "information is power" means that information *goes to* individuals and these individuals (the receivers of information) are, thereby, empowered. For example, I find out that my senator accepted a bribe; I am empowered to vote more intelligently. Or, I find useful information on the World Wide Web about a rare disease that I have; I am empowered in understanding and personally treating my illness.

The second meaning of "information is power" is that information is *sent by* some individual(s), and this individual (the sender of information) is, thereby, empowered. For example, those who write for the *New York Times* or those who advertise have power. They have the power to influence, shape, mold, and, in some sense, control those who receive information.

Those who think of the GII as democratic seem to have in mind the first meaning of "information is power." Putting information in the hands of individuals is perceived to be democratic because it empowers individuals. And, there are many examples of this type of empowerment taking place as a result of the GII. The GII creates enormous opportunities for access to information. Nevertheless, the second meaning of "information is power" is also at work in the GII and this is much less recognized. The assumption is made (based on the first meaning of "information is power") that more information is better, and the more the information, the better. What falls by the wayside is that individuals (as well as businesses and government) do not simply need information, they need *accurate, reliable, and relevant* information. The GII has created the availability of quantities of information well beyond the capabilities of most individuals to comprehend. This situation necessitates filtering and credentialing of information; yet little attention has been given to how this should or will happen in the GII. Authentication of information is being addressed by encryption technologies, but this by no means addresses the integrity of content. Those who send information and those who filter information will have enormous power (just as television stations do now). They will have the power to influence, shape, and ultimately control—on a global scale.

To make this point is not to deny that the GII can and will empower individuals—some individuals; rather it is to point to a countervailing tendency. The systems by which information is filtered on the GII are still evolving, and so it is unclear which tendency will dominate, which will be favored and how. It is important, however, to be aware of the potential downside. Those who filter information for us will have enormous power over us. Admittedly, the information we receive now is filtered, so that the threat is not of a new kind; nevertheless, the GII creates the capacity for this power to be more highly concentrated. Those who filter and package information for us in the GII will hold enormous power over us.

Joint Deliberation

An important feature of democracy tightly linked to popular sovereignty is the idea of joint deliberation. The idea of democracy is not merely the idea of individuals casting votes and thereby expressing their desires (as one does in the marketplace). Popular sovereignty has meant the populous getting together as a group or in subgroups for debate and discussion of issues they face jointly. In joint deliberation, individuals put their ideas on the table and listen to the responses of others. Ideas are submitted to critique. The process insures a degree of reflection. Better ideas emerge out of the combat of ideas. Ideas are formed in the process of discussion; individuals grow and learn; their active capacities are stimulated. And, bonds are developed between people as they jointly confront difficult issues.

While those who claim the GII is democratic have had in mind that the GII facilitates this joint deliberation by providing on-line forums for discussion, with the convenience of staying at home, there is, again, a countertrend that is not often recognized. The countertrend is a tendency toward, for lack of a better term, insularity. Individuals choose which forums they will participate in, what news they will read, who they will send and receive messages from, and so on. There is the possibility (if not likelihood) that individuals will choose like-minded people to chat with and news slanted in the direction of their already-formed biases; they will seek information on interests they already have. This is freedom and I can hardly argue against it. Nevertheless, there is the possibility that individuals will become even more isolated from diverse perspectives and people than they are now. Why deal with those with whom you have disagreements? Why deal with your difficult and "different" neighbors when you can simply avoid them? Why expose yourself to news perspectives that suggest something wrong with the views you presently hold? In the past, shared geographic space has necessitated contact and joint deliberation. It has compelled diverse people to figure out how to live together. That necessity becomes weaker and weaker when the infrastructure of so many activities is global.

The GII has one fairly obvious bias; it is a global system. While it does not compel anyone to interact globally, it facilitates global interaction (communication). The more time individuals spend communicating with people on-line, the less time they spend communicating off-line, or more to the point, the more individuals interact with others who are geographically distant, the less time they spend with those who are geographically close. This is typically seen as a good thing because it exposes individuals to diversity—individuals from other countries. The degree of diversity is, in fact, quite limited—to those who can afford to own computers, to those who know English, etc. However, it also means that individuals do not have to deal with others who occupy the homes and offices next door, i.e., those who are geographically close.

The tendency toward insularity is facilitated further by marketing strategies based on analysis of transactional data. One's personal tastes, hobbies, habits, needs, and desires can be inferred from one's activities in the GII. These are already being studied in efforts to provide consumers with what they want even before they want it. Individuals are facilitated in becoming more and more what they already are.

The GII raises a new version of an old and interesting issue having to do with the role of geographic space in democracy. In the new version, we ask whether democracy can be based on something other than shared space. Indeed, the global reach of the GII, together with its powerful role as an information system, lead one to wonder if national boundaries and national identities can endure. National boundaries are weakened when citizens are using a global communication system because information shapes attitudes, beliefs, and allegiances. It would seem that national boundaries will become weaker and weaker as individuals spend more time interacting with others who are geographically distant. Indeed, individuals may come to identify more with their information providers than their nation-states.

While democratic theorists have dealt with the varying geographic scale of nation-states, we now have the possibility of strong alliances among people based on something other than geographic location. Can democracy prevail in such an environment? The common space that people occupy has, historically, been the commonality that has drawn them into political communities. If we are less dependent on physical, geographic space, then what will bind us together?

References

Arblaster, A. (1987) *Democracy*. Minneapolis, University of Minnesota Press.

Bijker, W. (1995) "Sociohistorical Technology Studies" in *Handbook of Science and Technology Studies* edited by S. Jasanoff, G.E. Markle, J. C. Petersen and T. Pinch, Sage Publications.

Gorenstein, S. (1996) Introduction: Material Culture, *Knowledge and Society*, Volume 10, pp. 1–18.

Johnson, D. (1997) Ethics On line, *Communications of the ACM*, January, 1997, pp. 60–66.

Levy, S. (1984) *Hackers: Heroes of the Computer Revolution*. New York, Anchor/Doubleday.

Sclove, R. E. (1995) *Democracy and Technology*. New York, The Guilford Press.

Winner, L. (1986) "Do Artifacts Have Politics?" in *The Whale and the Reactor*. Chicago, The University of Chicago Press.

The Laws of Cyberspace

Larry Lessig

Before the revolution, the Tsar in Russia had a system of internal passports. The people hated this system. These passports marked the estate from which you came, and this marking determined the places you could go, with whom you could associate, what you could be. The passports were badges that granted access, or barred access. They controlled what in the Russian state Russians could come to know.

The Bolsheviks promised to change all this. They promised to abolish the internal passports. And soon upon their rise to power, they did just that. Russians were again free to travel where they wished. Where they could go was not determined by some document that they were required to carry with them. The abolition of the internal passport symbolized freedom for the Russian people—a democratization of citizenship in Russia.

This freedom, however, was not to last. A decade and a half later, faced with the prospect of starving peasants flooding the cities looking for food, Stalin brought back the system of internal passports. Peasants were again tied to their rural land (a restriction that remained throughout the 1970s). Russians were once again restricted by what their passport permitted. Once again, to gain access to Russia, Russians had to show something about who they were.

Behavior in the real world—this world, the world in which I am now speaking—is regulated by four sorts of constraints. Law is just one of those four constraints. Law regulates by sanctions imposed ex post—fail to pay your taxes and you are likely to go to jail; steal my car and you are also likely to go to jail. Law is the prominent of regulators. But it is just one of four.

Social norms are a second. They also regulate. Social norms—understandings or expectations about how I ought to behave, enforced not through some centralized norm enforcer, but rather through the understandings and expectations of just about everyone within a particular community—direct and constrain my behavior in a far wider array of contexts than any law. Norms say what clothes I will wear:

---

a suit, not a dress; they tell you to sit quietly, and politely, for at least 40 minutes while I speak; they organize how we will interact after this talk is over. Norms guide behavior; in this sense, they function as a second regulatory constraint.

The market is a third constraint. It regulates by price. The market limits the amount that I can spend on clothes, or the amount I can make from public speeches; it says I can command less for my writing than Madonna, or less for my singing than Pavarotti. Through the device of price, the market sets my opportunities, and through this range of opportunities, it regulates.

And finally, there is the constraint of what some might call nature, but which I want to call "architecture." This is the constraint of the world as I find it, even if this world as I find it is a world that others have made. That I cannot see through that wall is a constraint on my ability to know what is happening on the other side of the room. That there is no access-ramp to a library constrains the access of one bound to a wheelchair. These constraints, in the sense I mean here, regulate.

To understand a *regulation* then we must understand the sum of these four constraints operating together. Any one alone cannot represent the effect of the four together.

This is the age of the cyber-libertarian. It is a time when a certain hype about cyberspace has caught on. The hype goes like this: Cyberspace is unavoidable, and yet cyberspace is unregulable. No nation can live without it, yet no nation will be able to control behavior in it. Cyberspace is that place where individuals are, inherently, free from the control of real space sovereigns. It is, in the words of James Boyle, the great techno-"gotcha"—nations of the world, you can't live without it, but nations of the world, when you've got it, you won't live long with it.

My aim today is a different view about cyberspace. My aim is to attack this hype. For in my view, the world we are entering is not a world of perpetual freedom; or more precisely, the world we are entering is not a world where freedom is assured. Cyberspace has the potential to be the most fully and extensively regulated space that we have ever known—anywhere, at any time in our history. It has the potential to be the antithesis of a space of freedom. And unless we understand this potential, unless we see how this might be, we are likely to sleep through this transition from freedom into control. For that, in my view, is the transition we are seeing just now.

Now I want to make this argument by using the two introductions that I began with today—the story about Bolshevik Russia, and the idea about regulation. For they together will suggest where cyberspace is going, and more importantly, just how we can expect cyberspace to get there.

First the idea: Just as in real space, behavior in cyberspace is regulated by four sorts of constraints. Law is just one of those constraints. For the hype notwithstanding, there is law just now in cyberspace—copyright law, or defamation law, or sexual harassment law, all of which constrain behavior in cyberspace in the same way that they constrain behavior in real space.

There are also, perhaps quite surprisingly, norms in cyberspace—rules that govern behavior, and expose individuals to sanction from others. They too function in cyberspace as norms function in real space, threatening punishments ex post by a community.

And so too with the market. The market constrains in cyberspace, just as in real space. Change the price of access, the constraints on access differ. Change the structure of pricing access, and the regulation of marginal access shifts dramatically as well.

But for our purposes, the most significant of these four constraints on behavior in cyberspace is the analog to what I called *architecture* in real space: This I will call *code*. By code, I simply mean the software and hardware that constitutes cyberspace as it is—the set of protocols, the set of rules, implemented or codified, in the software of cyberspace itself, which determine how people interact, or exist, in this space. This code, like architecture in real space, sets the terms upon which I enter, or exist in cyberspace. It, like architecture, is not optional. I don't choose whether to obey the structures that it establishes—hackers might choose, but hackers are special. For the rest of us, life in cyberspace is subject to the code, just as life in real space is subject to the architectures of real space.

The substance of the constraints of code in cyberspace vary. But how they are experienced does not vary. In some places, one must enter a password before one gains access; in other places, one can enter whether identified or not. In some places, the transactions that one engages produce traces that link the transactions back to the individual; in other places, this link is achieved only if the individual chooses. In some places, one can select to speak a language that only the recipient can hear (through encryption); in other places, encryption is not an option.

The differences are constituted by the code of these different places. The code or software or architecture or protocols of these spaces set these features. They are features selected by code writers; they constrain some behavior by making other behavior possible. And in this sense, they, like architecture in real space, regulate behavior in cyberspace.

Code and market and norms and law together *regulate* in cyberspace as architecture and market and norms and law regulate in real space. And my claim is that as with real space regulation, we should consider how these four constraints operate together.

An example—a contrast between a regulation in real space and the same regulation in cyberspace—will make the point more clearly. Think about the concern in my country (some might call it obsession) with the regulation of indecency on the net.

This concern took off in the United States early in 1995. Its source was an extraordinary rise in ordinary users of the net, and therefore a rise in use by kids, and an even more extraordinary rise in the availability of what many call "porn" on the net. An extremely controversial (and fundamentally flawed) study published in the Georgetown University Law Review reported the net awash in porn. *Time* and *Newsweek* both ran cover story articles about its availability. And senators and congressmen were bombarded with demands to do something to regulate "cybersmut."

No doubt the fury at the time was great. But one might ask, why this fury was so great about porn in *cyberspace*. Certainly, more porn exists in real space than in cyberspace. So why the fury about access to porn in a place to which most kids don't have access?

To understand the why, think for a second about the same problem as it exists in real space. What regulates the distribution of porn in real space?

First: In America, laws in real space regulate the distribution of porn to kids—laws requiring sellers of porn to check the age of buyers, or laws requiring that sellers locate in a section of the city likely to be far from kids. But laws are not the most significant of the constraints on the distribution of porn to kids.

More important than laws are norms. Norms constrain adults not to sell porn to kids. Even among porn distributors this restriction is relatively effective.

And not just social norms. The market too constrains, for porn costs money, and kids have no money.

But the most important real space constraint is what I've called *architecture*. For all of these other regulations in real space depend on this constraint of architecture. Laws and norms and market can discriminate against kids in real space, since it is hard in real space to hide that you are a kid. Of course, a kid can don a mustache, and put on stilts, and try to enter a porn shop to buy porn. But for the most part, disguises will fail. For the most part, it will be too hard to hide that he is a kid. Thus, for the most part, constraints based on being a kid are constraints that can be effective.

Cyberspace is different. Even if we assume that the same laws apply to cyberspace as to real space, and even if we assume that the constraints of norms and the market are carried over as well, even so, there remains a critical difference between the two spaces. For while in real space it is hard to hide that you are a kid, in cyberspace, hiding who you are, or more precisely, hiding features about who you are, is the simplest thing in the world. The default in cyberspace is anonymity. And because it is so easy to hide who one is, it is practically impossible for the laws and norms to apply in cyberspace. For these laws to apply, one has to know that it is a kid one is dealing with. But the architecture of the space simply doesn't provide this information.

Now the important point is to see the difference and to identify its source. The difference is a difference in what I want to call the *regulability* of cyberspace—the ability of governments to regulate behavior there. As it is just now, cyberspace is a less *regulable* space than real space. There is less that government can do. The source of this difference in regulability is a difference in the architecture of the space—a difference in the code that constitutes cyberspace as it is. Its architecture, my claim is, renders it essentially unregulable.

Or so it did in 1995, and in 1996, when the U.S. Congress eventually got around to passing its attempt to deal with this problem—the Communications Decency Act. I'm going to talk a bit about what happened to that statute, but I first want to mark this period, and set it off from where we are today. It was the architecture of cyberspace in 1995 and 1996 that made it essentially unregulable.

Let's call that architecture Net95—as in 1995—and here are its features: So long as one had access to Net95, one could roam without identifying who one was. Net95 was Bolshevik Russia. One's identity, or features, were invisible to the net then, so one could enter and explore without credentials—without an internal passport. Access was open and universal, not conditioned upon credentials. It was, in a narrow sense of the term, an extraordinary democratic moment. Users were fundamentally equal. Essentially free.

It was against this background—against the background of the net as it was—Net95—that the Supreme Court then considered the Communications Decency Act. Two lower courts had struck the statute as a violation of the right to freedom of speech. And millions watched as the court considered arguments on the case—watched in cyberspace, as the arguments were reported, and debated, and critiqued.

And in June, last year, the Court affirmed the decision of the lower courts, holding the statute unconstitutional. Just why it was unconstitutional isn't so important for our purposes here. What is important is the rhetoric that leads the court to its conclusion.

For the decision hung crucially on claims about the architecture of the net as it was—on the architecture, that is, of Net95. Given that architecture, the court concluded, any regulation that attempted to zone kids from porn would be a regulation that was too burdensome on speakers and listeners. As the net was, regulation would be too burdensome.

But what was significant was that the court spoke as if this architecture of the net as it was—Net95—was the only architecture that the net could have. It spoke as if it had discovered the nature of the net, and was therefore deciding the nature of any possible regulation of the net.

But the problem with all this, of course, is that the net has no nature. There is no single architecture that is essential to the net's design. Net95 is a set of features, or protocols, that constituted the net at one period of time. But nothing requires that these features, or protocols, always constitute the net as it always will be. And indeed, nothing in what we've seen in the last 2 years should lead us to think that it will.

An example may make the point more simply. Before I was a professor at Harvard, I taught at the University of Chicago. If one wanted to gain access to the net at the university of Chicago, one simply connected one's machine to jacks located throughout the university. Any machine could be connected to those jacks, and once connected, any machine would then have full access to the internet. Access was anonymous, and complete, and free.

The reason for this freedom was a decision by the administration. For the Provost of the University of Chicago is Geof Stone, a former dean of the University of Chicago Law School, and a prominent free speech scholar. When the University was designing its net, the technicians asked the provost whether anonymous communication should be permitted. The provost, citing a principle that the rules regulating speech at the university would be as protective of free speech as the first amendment, said yes: One would have the right to communicate at the university anonymously, because the first amendment to the constitution would guarantee the same right vis-à-vis the government. From that policy decision flowed the architectural design of the University of Chicago's net.

At Harvard, the rules are different. One cannot connect one's machine to the net at Harvard unless one's machine is registered—licensed, approved, verified. Only members of the university community can register their machine. Once registered, all interactions with the network are potentially monitored, and identified to a particular machine. Indeed, anonymous speech on this net is not permitted—

against the rule. Access can be controlled based on who someone is; interactions can be traced based on what someone did.

The reason for this design is also due to the decision of an administrator—though this time an administrator less focused on the protections of the first amendment. Controlling access is the ideal at Harvard; facilitating access was the ideal at Chicago; technologies that make control possible were therefore chosen at Harvard; technologies that facilitate access chosen at Chicago.

Now this difference between the two networks is quite common today. The network at the University of Chicago is the architecture of the internet in 1995. It is, again, Net95. But the architecture at Harvard is not an internet architecture. It is rather an intranet architecture. The difference is simply this—that within an intranet, identity is sufficiently established such that access can be controlled, and usage monitored. The underlying protocols are still TCP/IP—meaning the fundamental or underlying protocols of the internet. But layered on top of this fundamental protocol is a set of protocols facilitating control. The Harvard network is the internet plus, where the plus means the power to control.

These two architectures reflect two philosophies about access. They reflect two sets of principles, or values, about how speech should be controlled. They parallel, I want to argue, the difference between political regimes of freedom, and political regimes of control. They track the difference in ideology between West and East Germany; between the United States and the former Soviet Republic; between the Republic of China and Mainland China. They stand for a difference between control and freedom—and they manifest this difference through the architecture or design of code. These architectures enable political values. They are in this sense political.

Now I don't offer this example to criticize Harvard. Harvard is a private institution; it is free, in a free society, to allocate its resources however it wishes. My point instead is simply to get you to see how architectures are many, and therefore how the choice of one is political. And how, at the level of a nation, architecture is inherently political. In the world of cyberspace, the selection of an architecture is as important as the choice of a constitution. For in a fundamental sense, the code of cyberspace is its constitution. It sets the terms upon which people get access; it sets the rules, it controls their behavior. In this sense, it is its own sovereignty; an alternative sovereignty, competing with real space sovereigns, in the regulation of behavior by real space citizens.

But the United States Supreme Court treated the question of architecture as if the architecture of this space were given. It spoke as if there were only one design for cyberspace—the design it had.

In this, the Supreme Court is not alone. For in my view, the single greatest error of theorists of cyberspace—of pundits, and especially lawyers thinking about regulation in this space—is this error of the Supreme Court. It is the error of naturalism as applied to cyberspace. It is the error of thinking that the architecture as we have it is an architecture that we will always have; that the space will guarantee us liberty, or freedom; that it will of necessity disable governments that want control.

This view is profoundly mistaken. Profoundly mistaken because while we celebrate the "inherent" freedom of the net, the architecture of the net is changing from under us. The architecture is shifting from an architecture of freedom to an architecture of control. It is shifting already without government's intervention, though government is quickly coming to see just how it might intervene to speed it up. And where government is now intervening, it is intervening in a way designed to change this very same architecture—to change it into an architecture of control, to make it, as I've said, more *regulable*. While pundits promise perpetual freedom built into the very architecture of the net itself, technicians and politicians are working together to change that architecture, to move it away from this architecture of freedom.

As theorists of this space, we must come to understand this change. We must recognize the political consequences of this change. And we must take responsibility for these consequences. For the trajectory of the change is unmistakable, and the fruit of this trajectory, poison.

As constitutionalists, we must then confront a fundamentally constitutional question: If there is a choice between architectures of control and architectures of freedom, then how do we decide these constitutional questions? If architectures are many, then does the constitution itself guide us in the selection of such architectures?

In my view, constitutional values do implicate the architecture of this space. In my view, constitutional values should guide us in our design of this space. And in my view, constitutional values should limit the types of regulability that this architecture permits.

But my view is absent in thinking about government's role in cyberspace. Indeed, my nation—for many years the symbol of freedom in a world where such freedom was rare—has become a leader in pushing the architecture of the internet from an architecture of freedom to an architecture of control. From an architecture, that is, that embraced the traditions of freedom expressed in our constitutional past, to an architecture that is fundamentally an anathema to those traditions.

But how? How can the government make these changes? How could the government effect this control? Many can't see how government could effect this control. So in the few minutes remaining in my talk today, I want show you how. I want to sketch for you a path from where we are to where I fear we are going. I want you to see how these changes are possible and how government can help make them permanent.

Return then with me to the idea that began this essay—the point about the different modalities of constraint—and notice something important about that idea that we have not so far remarked. I said at the start that we should think of law as just one of four modalities of constraint; that we should think of it as just one part of the structure of constraint that might be said to regulate.

One might take that to be an argument about law's insignificance. If so many forces other than law regulate, this might suggest that law itself can do relatively little.

But notice what should be obvious. In the model I have described, law is regulating by direct regulation—regulating an individual through the threat of punishment. But law regulates in other ways as well. It regulates indirectly as well as directly. And it regulates indirectly when it regulates these other modalities of constraint, so that they regulate differently. It can, that is, regulate norms, so norms regulate differently; it can regulate the market, so that the market regulates dif-

ferently; and it can regulate architecture, so that architecture regulates differently. In each case, the government can co-opt the other structures, so that they constrain to the government's end.

The same indirection is possible in cyberspace. But here, I suggest, the indirection will be even more significant. For here the government can not only regulate
indirectly to advance a particular substantive end of the government, but more significantly, the government can regulate to change the very *regulability* of the space.
The government, that is, can regulate the architectures of cyberspace, so that behavior in cyberspace becomes more regulable—indeed, to an architecture potentially
more regulable than anything we have known in the history of modern government.

Two examples will make the point—one an example of the government regulating to a particular substantive end, and the second, following from the first, an
example of the government regulating to increase regulability.

The first is the regulation of encryption. The government's concern with encryption has been with the technology's use in protecting privacy—its ability to hide
the content of communications from the eyes of an eavesdropping third party,
whether that third party is the government or a nosy neighbor. For much of the
history of the technology, the American government has heavily regulated the
technology. For a time it threatened to ban its use; it has consistently banned its
export (as if only Americans understand higher order mathematics), and for a period it hoped to flood the market with a standard encryption technology that would
leave a backdoor open for the government to enter.

The most recent proposals are the most significant. Last November, the FBI proposed a law that would require manufacturers to assure that any encryption system have built within it either a key recovery ability or an equivalent back door, so
that government agents could, if they need, get access to the content of such communications.

This is government's regulation of code, indirectly to regulate behavior. It is indirect regulation in the sense that I described before, and from a constitutional perspective—it is brilliant. Not brilliant because its ends are good; brilliant because
the American constitution, at least, offers very little control over government regulation like this. The American constitution offers little protections against the government's regulation of business, and given the interests of business, such
regulations are likely to be effective.

My second example follows from the first. For a second use of encryption is identification—as well as hiding what someone says, encryption, through digital certificates, can be used to authenticate who sent it. With the ability to authenticate who
someone is, the government could tell where someone comes from, or how old they
are. And with this ability—through certifying IDs—passports on the information
superhighway—governments could far more easily regulate behavior on this highway. It would recreate the power to control behavior—recreate the power to regulate.

Note what both regulations would achieve. Since the US is the largest market
for internet products, no product could hope to succeed unless it were successful
in the United States. Thus standards successfully imposed in the US becomes standards for the world. And these standards in particular would first facilitate regulation, and second, assure that communications on the internet could be broken

into by any government that followed the procedures outlined in the bill. But the standards that those governments would have to meet are not the standards of the US constitution. They are whatever standard local government happens to have—whether that government be the government of Mainland China or Switzerland.

The effect is that the United States government would be exporting an architecture that facilitates control, and control not just by other democratic governments, but by any government, however repressive. And by this, the US would move itself from a symbol of freedom, to a peddler of control. Having won the cold war, we would be pushing the techniques of our cold war enemies.

How should we respond? How should you—as sovereigns independent of the influence of any foreign government—and we, as liberal constitutionalists, respond? How should we respond to moves by a dominant political and economic power to influence the architecture of the dominant architecture of regulation by code—the internet?

Sovereigns must come to see this: That the code of cyberspace is itself a kind of sovereign. It is a competing sovereign. The code is itself a force that imposes its own rules on people who are there, but the people who are there are also the people who are here—citizens of the Republic of China, citizens of France, citizens of every nation in the world. The code regulates them, yet they are by right subject to the regulation of local sovereigns. The code thus competes with the regulatory power of local sovereigns. It competes with the political choices made by local sovereigns. And in this competition, as the net becomes a dominant place for business and social life, it will displace the regulations of local sovereigns. You as sovereigns were afraid of the competing influence of nations. Yet a new nation is now wired into your telephones, and its influence over your citizens is growing.

You, as sovereigns, will come to recognize this competition. And you should come to recognize and question the special role that the United States is playing in this competition. By virtue of the distribution of resources controlling the architecture of the net, the United States has a unique power over influencing the development of that architecture. It is as if the law of nature were being written, with the United States at the author's side. This power creates an important responsibility for the United States—and you must assure that it exercises its power responsibly.

The problem for constitutionalists—those concerned to preserve social and political liberties in this new space—is more difficult.

For return to the story that began this talk—the world of internal passports. One way to understand the story I've told today about cyberspace is in line with this story about the Tsar's Russia. The birth of the net was the revolution itself; life under Net95 was life in Bolshevik Russia (the good parts at least, where internal passports were eliminated); the Net as it is becoming is Stalin's Russia, where internal passports will again be required.

Now there's a cheat to that story—a rhetorical cheat that tends to obscure an important fact about real space life. For we all live in the world of internal passports. In the United States, in many places, one cannot live without a car and one can't drive a car without a license. A license is an internal passport: It says who you are, where you come from, how old you are, whether you've recently been convicted of a crime; it links your identity to a database that will reveal whether you've been arrested (whether convicted or not) or whether any warrants for your arrest in any jurisdiction in the nation are outstanding. The license is the internal passport of the modern American state. And no doubt its ability to control or identify is far better than the Tsar's Russia.

But in the United States—at least for those who don't appear to be immigrants, or a disfavored minority—the burden of these passports is slight. The will to regulate, to monitor, to track, is not strong enough in the United States to support any systematic effort to use these passports to control behavior. And the will is not strong enough because the cost of such control is so great. There are not checkpoints at each corner; one isn't required to register when moving through a city; one can walk around relatively anonymously most of the time. Technologies of control are possible, but in the main far too costly. And this costliness is, in large part, the source of great freedom. It is inefficiency in real space technologies of control that yield real space liberty.

But what if the cost of control drops dramatically. What if an architecture emerges that permits constant monitoring, an architecture that facilitates the constant tracking of behavior and movement? What if an architecture emerged that would costlessly collect data about individuals, about their behavior, about who they wanted to become? And what if the architecture could do that invisibly, without interfering with an individual's daily life at all?

This architecture is the world that the net is becoming. This is the picture of control it is growing into. As in real space, we will have passports in cyberspace. As in real space, these passports can be used to track our behavior. But in cyberspace, unlike real space, this monitoring, this tracking, this control of behavior, will all be much less expensive. This control will occur in the background, effectively and invisibly.

Now to describe this change is not to say whether it is for the good or bad. Indeed, I suggest that as constitutionalists, we must acknowledge a fundamental ambiguity in our present political judgments about liberty and control. I suggest that our peoples are divided in their reaction to this picture of a system of control at once perfect, and yet invisible. Many would say of this system—wonderful. All the better to trap the guilty, with little burden on the innocent. But there are many as well who would say of this system—awful. That while professing our ideals of liberty and freedom from government, we would have established a system of control far more effective than any in history before.

So the response to all this is not necessarily to give up the technologies of control. The response is not to insist that Net95 be the perpetual architecture of the net. The response instead is to find a way to *translate* what is salient and important about present day liberties and constitutional democracy into this architecture of the net. The point is to be critical of the power of this sovereign—this emerging sovereign—as we are properly critical of the power of any sovereign.

What are these limits: As government takes control or influences the architecture of the code of the net, at a minimum, we must assure that government does not get a monopoly on these technologies of control. We must assure that the sorts of checks that we build into any constitutional democracy get built into regulation by this constitution—the code. We must assure that the constraints of any constitutional democracy—the limits on efficiency constituted by Bills of Rights, and systems of checks and balances—get built into regulation by code. These limits are the "bugs" in the code of a constitutional democracy—and as John Perry Barlow says, we must build these bugs into the code of cyberspace. We must build them in so that they, by their inefficiency, might recreate some of the protections we have long known.

Cyberspace is regulated—by laws, but not just by law. The code of cyberspace is one of these laws. We must come to see how this code is an emerging sovereign—omnipresent, omnipotent, gentle, efficient, growing—and that we must develop against this sovereign the limits that we have developed against real space sovereigns. Sovereigns will always say—real space as well as cyberspace—that limits, and inefficiencies—bugs—are not necessary. But things move too quickly for such confidence. My fear is not just that against this sovereign, we have not yet developed a language of liberty. Nor that we haven't the time to develop such language. But my fear is that we sustain the will—the will of free societies for the past two centuries— to architect constitutions to protect freedom, efficiencies notwithstanding.

Of Black Holes and Decentralized Law-Making in Cyberspace

David G. Post[1]

There is, within the (rapidly-growing) community of people who spend their time thinking about law and policy in cyberspace, a rather interesting debate taking place. Though it is not always characterized in these terms, it reflects a conflict between competing visions of "order" and "disorder" in social systems. This is by no means a "new" debate, but it takes on a new shape in the rather special conditions of cyberspace—or so, at least, I hope to suggest in what follows.

The Incident

Last January, Professor Tom Field of the Franklin Pierce Law Center (FPLC) posted the following message to the Cyberprof listserve:[2]

"To all:

Assuming that this message isn't screened out by [the server at the University of Texas that hosts the Cyberprof discussion group], you might be interested in a 'small' problem FPLC faces. A few weeks ago, someone 'bounced' some spam off our server. It somehow corrupted our email system, and [now] I am beginning to get messages like this:

The message that you sent was undeliverable to the following: ipww@ljx.com

Transcript of session follows:

MAIL FROM: tfield@fplc.edu refused; see http://maps.vix.com/rbl/

I hope it never happens to you. Meanwhile, any ideas about how to deal with it?"[3]

This essay was originally presented at the Yale Information Society Project Conference *on Private Censorship/Perfect Choice*, 1999. Copyright © 1999 by David G. Post. Reprinted with permission.

The Explanation

There were, as it turned out, lots of ideas about how to deal with it—but that is getting ahead of myself. First, the facts, as best one can make them out here. Professor Field ("tfield@fplc.edu") had sent an e-mail message to an address at ljx.com. But the ljx.com e-mail server had refused to deliver the message to the intended recipient ("Mail From: tfield@fplc.edu refused") and returned it "undelivered" to Professor Field. What had happened? Why had it done so?

The explanation is provided—elliptically, to be sure—by the hyperlink reference ("see http://maps.vix.com/rbl/") in the message that Professor Field had received. If you do indeed "see http://maps.vix.com/rbl/," you are taken to the home page of something called the Mail Abuse Prevention System (MAPS). MAPS, the primary focus of this tale, is a California non-profit limited liability company.[4] It coordinates a kind of group boycott by Internet Service Providers (ISPs) for the purpose of reducing the flow of what is commonly called "spam"—unsolicited bulk e-mail. It operates, roughly, as follows.[5] The managers of MAPS create and maintain what they call the "Realtime Blackhole List" (RBL), which consists of a long list of Internet addresses.[6] They place on the RBL any Internet address from which, to their knowledge, spam has originated.[7] They also place on the RBL the address of any network that allows "open-mail relay"[8] or provides "spam support services."[9]

MAPS makes the RBL list available to ISPs and other network administrators on a subscription basis.[10] ISPs that subscribe to the RBL can, if they choose, set their mail handlers to delete all e-mail originating from, and/or going to, an address appearing on the list. That is, when an RBL-subscribing ISP receives a request to transmit e-mail to or from a subscriber, it checks the sender's numeric Internet address against the list of blackholed Internet addresses; if it finds a match, it deletes the message. The blackholed address thus, in a sense, disappears from the Internet as far as the subscribing ISP (and its customers) are concerned.

Apparently, Professor Field's network—fplc.edu—had been placed on the RBL—"blackholed"—and ljx.com, the home server of the intended recipient of Professor Field's e-mail, was an RBL subscriber. When the ljx.com mail server received Professor Field's message, it recognized the e-mail as originating from a blackholed address and deleted it, helpfully sending back the message, reproduced above, to Professor Field to inform him what was going on.

The Question

What are we to make of things like the RBL? Here we have a problem—the proliferation of unsolicited mass e-mailing operations—that is, we might agree, a serious, or at least a non-trivial, one. At just the moment that e-mail has become an indispensable form of communication, of incalculable commercial and non-commercial importance for a substantial and ever-growing segment of the world community, its value is being undermined by a barrage of unwanted and unsolicited communications.[11] But is the RBL a reasonable means of addressing this problem?

To what extent can we, and should we, rely on things like the RBL to devise a "solution" (however we might define a solution) to that problem?

The Debate

The question is, I think, both an interesting and an important one. Legal scholars have recently discovered—or re-discovered—the important role played by informal systems of decentralized, consensus-based social control in shaping human social behavior.[12] It is becoming increasingly clear that systems of rules and sanctions created and administered without reliance on State "authority," and outside of any formal State-managed process—"norms"—are powerful determinants of behavior in many contexts. And what is the RBL if not a textbook example of an informal, decentralized, norm-creation process? The MAPS operators propose a norm, a description of behavior that they consider, for whatever reason, unacceptable—allowing open mail relay systems, for example, or providing "spam support services."[13] They offer to serve as your agent—or, more accurately, as the agent for your network administrator or ISP—in identifying those who are violating this norm. They offer to keep you informed of those identifications (via the RBL). They propose to sanction norm-violators. The sanction they have in mind is the Ur-Sanction of informal social control processes: shunning. Those who choose to apply the sanction simply turn their backs on offenders, ceasing all (electronic) communication with them. MAPS helpfully provides you with the means to accomplish this sanction—software that will configure your system to delete e-mail to or from blackholed addresses.[14]

This is not, as it were, your father's norm-creation process; it has some unusual features missing from real-space norm-creation processes.[15] But it is norm-creation; whether or not it can helpfully be described as "bottom-up,"[16] it is surely both "informal" and "decentralized." Neither the decision to join (or not join) the group shunning exercise (i.e., to subscribe to the RBL in the first place), nor the shunning sanction imposed on violators of the norm, relies on access to (formal) State-supported enforcement devices or State-imposed legal sanctions,[17] and the decision whether to join that exercise is in the hands of a (relatively large) number of independently-acting agents.[18]

Conditions in cyberspace do seem to create, in Professor Elkin-Koren's words, "new opportunities for voluntary normative regimes" of this kind.[19] Not surprisingly, conflicts between formal and informal, centralized and decentralized, rule-making processes are at the heart of many of the important and challenging cyberspace policy debates. The extraordinary current turmoil in the domain name allocation system is one illustration. The story has been told in detail elsewhere.[20] Briefly, in the beginning—before the Internet became such a Big Deal—responsibility for operating the machines, and the databases on those machines, which correctly route Internet messages, fell to the Internet Assigned Number Authority (IANA), an imposing-sounding entity that, in reality, consisted of a small number of dedicated volunteers in southern California. As the Internet began its explosive growth, IANA's ability to maintain the system became increasingly overloaded; beginning in 1993, responsibility for maintaining these databases—at least, for three of the increasingly popular "generic top-level" domains—*.com, *.net, *.org, and the like—was handed over to a private firm, Network Solutions, Inc., under a con-tract—styled a "Cooperative Agreement"—funded by the U.S. government (first through the National Science Foundation, later through the Commerce Department's National Telecommunications and Information Administration).

When that cooperative agreement was due to expire in 1998, the Commerce Department had a decision to make. It could simply walk away from the relationship on the stated expiration date, which is ordinarily what happens when cooperative agree-ments (or any government contracts) expire. It rejected that option, however, taking the position that it would be "irresponsible to withdraw from its existing management role [in the domain name system] without taking steps to ensure the stability of the Internet."[21] The Internet naming system, it concluded, needed a "more formal and robust management structure," and it called for the creation of a new, not-for-profit corpora-tion formed by the "Internet stakeholders" themselves to manage the domain name system.[22] Shortly thereafter, control of this system was placed in the hands of a sin-gle institution—now known as ICANN, the Internet Corporation for Assigned Names and Numbers—which would have overall responsibility for setting the rules under which the domain name system would henceforth operate. Putting aside whatever one might think of this decision (or the manner in which ICANN has fulfilled its responsibilities [23]), the decision to centralize authority over this system in a single, government-author-ized entity will inevitably have deep implications for the Internet as a whole. The debate over the normative implications of these informal processes has become a live-ly one indeed. In one corner are commentators, myself included, who find these sys-tems normatively attractive, on both "legitimacy and "efficiency" grounds.[24] Legitimacy justifications rest on the view that informal private ordering schemes like the RBL are a "superior alternative to centralized government models in that [they are] the most consistent with autonomy and freedom."[25] By these lights, MAPS is normatively attrac-tive inasmuch as it constrains individuals' behavior only to the extent, and precisely to the extent, that others share MAPS' views on the definition of wrongdoing, the choice of appropriate sanction, the identity of the wrongdoers, etc; the MAPS opera-tors can persuade, cajole, and beg the thousands of ISPs to subscribe to the RBL, but they cannot force them to do so in any meaningful sense of that term. Efficiency jus-tifications rest on the extraordinary power of decentralized systems to generate, by means of repeated trial-and-error and the pull-and-tug of competing rules and count-er-rules, solutions to complex problems that can be found no other way.[26]

Others disagree, both with particular reference to institutions like the RBL[27] and in general,[28] arguing both that the efficiency benefits of these cyberspace norm-creation processes are overblown and that such processes systematically exclude "public values" from being incorporated into the norms they generate.

It is a rich debate that will, I suspect, be one of the enduring legacies of the study of the law of cyberspace. I want to put aside, for purposes of this essay, the many difficult, even profound, substantive questions raised in this debate, in order to focus a little attention instead on the meta-debate, on questions about the ways in which the substantive questions themselves can be explored and evaluated. We like to think, at least at a conceptual level, that we conduct this debate by placing decen-tralized rule-making processes (like the RBL) on the table, dissecting their features, and comparing them, on whatever normative or descriptive criteria we choose, with alternative processes. But there are serious impediments to our ability to do that, impediments that skew the inquiry into the virtues (or lack thereof) of decentralized processes. Let me try to explain the sorts of things I have in mind.

First, I would suggest that we understand little—far less than we need to—about the processes of self-ordering and informal coordination. The rise of the Internet itself shows us, I think, how little we know about the ways that decentralized, trial-and-error, consensual processes can build stable structures of literally unimaginable complexity and power. If cyberspace did not exist, we would all probably agree that it could not exist. How, after all, would we go about building something as ridiculously complex as a single interconnected global communications network? Who would we place in charge of such a project? How would we solve the seemingly impossible coordination problem facing anyone trying to construct that global network—constructing, and getting large numbers of people to adopt, what amounts to a single global language?[29]

Of course, we did, somehow, solve it, without any "authority" in charge of bringing it into being, in a remarkably short period of time, and to the surprise of virtually everyone.[30] A decentralized process of developing consensus among larger and larger numbers of geographically-dispersed individuals somehow managed to get us here. Emergent institutions like the Internet Engineering Task Force[31] (whose motto, "We reject Kings, Presidents, and voting; we seek rough consensus and working code," aptly captures its decentralized orientation), the World Wide Web Consortium,[32] the Internet Assigned Numbering Authority,[33] and the like—institutions with no authority whatsoever to act on anyone's behalf, no fixed address or membership, no formal legal existence—somehow got hundreds of millions of individuals across the globe to agree on a common syntax for their electronic conversations. The protocols of the global network, like the natural languages they so closely resemble, emerged from a process that was at its core unplanned and undirected. Though we can certainly point ex post to many individuals and institutions who played particularly important roles in its emergence, ex ante there was no one we could have pointed to as charged with "creating" the set of rules we now know as the Internet, any more than we can point to any one individual or institution charged with creating the set of rules for English syntax.

Could it have been built any other way? My instinct is that it could not have, that only an "authority-free" process of this kind could have constructed this system, that no one with the authority to build the Internet could have done so.[34] If I'm right, this is of considerable importance to the normative debate, for it obliterates the distinction between the normative and the descriptive aspects of the debate; if we were trying, circa 1965, to find the "best" way of constructing the protocols for the Internet, we would not lay alternative centralized and decentralized decision-making models side-by-side for comparison, for there would be no centralized model to examine that could accomplish the task. But this is, I admit, just instinct; I do not know of any analytic vocabulary or framework within which I could make that argument. Even if my instinct is correct, how would we have known that in 1965? How would we know it now?

Second, and relatedly, I believe that conditions in cyberspace make it difficult to specify the alternative processes with which decentralized processes are to be compared as part of this policy calculus. No one, of course, suggests that decentralized processes like the one of which the RBL is a part constitute rule-making Nirvana. The relevant normative question is always whether processes of this kind are better—however one chooses to define "better"—than available alternatives.[35]

We need, in other words, to be debating whether the process of which RBL is a part is better than—than what? As I look over the contributions to this debate I'm not always sure I can fill in that blank. Some of this is mere rhetorical device; it is always tempting to seize the rhetorical high ground by demonstrating the substantial distance between an opponent's position and perfection itself.[36] But there is a deeper problem here. Cyberspace is particularly, and genuinely, tricky on this score. What are the alternative rule-making processes or institutions that should be placed on the analytic table alongside the RBL? The problems posed by the borderless features of this new medium for traditional rule-making institutions, faced with the problem of mapping territorially-based legal regimes onto a medium in which physical location is of little significance, have long since passed into cliche; but that doesn't mean that they are not real problems. Whose rules regarding spam should we be comparing to MAPS'? The Virginia legislature's?[37] The United States Congress'?[38] The International Telecommunications Union's? UNESCO's? ICANN's?

The task of identifying the alternative rule-makers for purposes of normative comparison is made even more difficult than this because cyberspace, having emerged from decentralized disorder—from the primordial ooze of the Internet Engineering Task Force—may well create conditions that favor the growth of powerful centralizing forces.[39] The State of Virginia will soon discover that its anti-spam statute has little effect on the amount of spam that its citizens receive, because while spam originating anywhere on the network can easily make its way into Virginia, spam originating elsewhere—i.e., outside of Virginia's borders—is largely immune to Virginia's control.[40] The same will be true in regard to a federal anti-spam statute (if such a statute is enacted), just on a grander scale. We can already write the headline: "Use of Offshore E-Mail Servers Hinders Enforcement of Federal Spam Statute; Government Calls for International Cooperation to Solve 'Serious Problem.'" We will, inevitably (and, since we're on Internet Time, sooner than we think), hear calls for "international harmonization" of spam regulation, replicating the pattern currently spreading across the cyberspace legal spectrum. How can we factor this into the normative comparisons we are trying to make?

Third and finally, if all this weren't confusing enough, decentralized processes are fundamentally, and irreducibly, unpredictable. No one can say ex ante what kind of anti-spam rules will emerge from the RBL process, or how the domain name allocation system would today be operating had the Commerce Department chosen to step aside in 1998, because that information does not exist unless and until the process itself generates it. No one can say whether MAPS' initiative will, or will not, cause open-mail relay systems to disappear, because that depends upon the response of thousands of individual system administrators; no one can say whether alternative and as yet untried and perhaps unthought-of means of deterring spammers will prove more popular than MAPS; no one can say how spammers will react to the absence of open-mail relay (or to these other alternatives) or how the anti-spammers will react to those reactions, etc.

Because we cannot see, or imagine, where the RBL might take us—the rule(s) of spamming that the RBL and its variants could produce—we cannot lay these rules side-by-side with their centralized alternatives for purposes of analysis, deliberation, and debate. Our analytic table contains only, as it were, the bad news: the inherently disordered and aggravating messiness of decentralized processes, mail that doesn't reach its intended destination, disruptions of service, and the like.

It all makes for an apparently simple policy choice: order versus chaos. During all of the discussions—which can only be described as "frenzied"—leading up to the decision to grant ICANN the authority to manage the domain name system, I was continually struck by the impossibility of discussing rationally the course of action whereby the government would just walk away from the entire thing. The Commerce Department set forth a number of principles to guide its decision; the domain name system should "support competition and consumer choice," "reflect, as far as possible, the bottom-up governance that has characterized development of the Internet to date," and "reflect the diversity of [the Internet's] users and their needs" by "ensur[ing] international input in decision making."[41] But one principle was primus inter pares: "The U.S. government should end its role in the Internet number and name address systems in a responsible manner. This means, above all else, ensuring the stability of the Internet. The Internet functions well today, but its current technical management is probably not viable over the long term. We should not wait for it to break down before acting. Yet, we should not move so quickly, or depart so radically from the existing structures, that we disrupt the functioning of the Internet. The introduction of a new system should not disrupt current operations, or create competing root systems." [42]

The decentralized process that built the Internet protocols and the domain name system cannot, ex ante, "ensur[e] the stability of the Internet." If that is indeed the goal, that option is off the table. Because there is no way to answer the question "What kind of domain name system would we have today had the Commerce Department stepped aside in 1998?", that course of action could not be taken seriously.

My fear is that this leads to a policy-making catastrophe of significant proportions. A "stable" Internet is one locked in place, incapable of generating innovative responses to the very problems that it is itself bringing into existence. The very existence of the Internet should caution us against dismissing too quickly the notion that there are some problems that are best solved by these messy, disordered, semi-chaotic, unplanned, decentralized systems, and that the costs that necessarily accompany such unplanned disorder may sometimes be worth bearing.[43] But which problems? How can we know?

Endnotes

1. Associate Professor, Temple University School of Law; Postd@erols.com. An earlier version of this paper was originally presented at the Yale Information Society Project Conference on "Private Censorship/Perfect Choice," April 9, 1999. Thanks to Bill Scheinler for research assistance, and to the Temple Law School summer research grant fund for support in completing this paper.

2. Cyberprof is a listserve discussion group moderated by Professor Mark Lemley of the University of California-Berkeley.

3. E-mail from Tom Field to Cyberprof discussion group, Jan. 28, 1999 (thanks to Professor Field for his permission to quote the message here) (copy on file with the author).

4. See Robert McMillan, What Will Stop Spam? (last modified Nov. 20, 1999) <http://www.sunworld.com/sunworldonline/swol-12-1997/swol-12-vixie.html>. See generally, Mail Abuse Prevention System (visited Nov. 19, 1999) <http://mail-abuse.org>; Maps Realtime Blackhole List (visited Nov. 19, 1999) <http://maps.vix.com/rbl>.

5. See generally, supra note 4.

6. The RBL currently has approximately 1,400 entries. E-mail from Nick Nicholas, Executive Director, Mail Abuse Prevention System (Oct. 6, 1999) (on file with author). Most of these entries consist of only a single numeric Internet address; some, however, consist of the address of what is commonly called a "Class C" network, which itself contains 255 individual addresses. See Paul Vixie, MAPS RBL Candidacy (visited Nov. 19, 1999) <http://maps.vix. com/rbl/candidacy.html>.

7. Removal from the list requires a showing by the blackholed address, or the appropriate network administrator, that the spammer is no longer at the address in question and/or that a stronger "Terms of Use" agreement has been put in place for the network on which the spammer was located.

8. "Open-mail relay" refers to a practice whereby Internet mail servers process and transmit e-mail messages in circumstances in which neither the sender nor the recipient is an authenticated local user; that is, it allows "strangers" to access its mail handling facilities. Spammers, apparently, utilize open-mail relay sites to "launder" their e-mail; by using an open relay, their e-mail will appear to have originated from a source other than the true source, thereby making it difficult to trace or filter the messages. See Better Network Security Through Peer Pressure: Stopping Smurf and Spam (visited May 31, 1999) <http://securityportal.com/coverstory19990531.html>; Paul Hoffman, Allowing Relaying in SMTP: A Series of Surveys (visited Nov. 19, 1999) <http://www.imc.org/ube-relay.html>; Chip Rosenthal, MAPS TSI: Anti-relay: What is Third-Party Mail Relay? (visited July 31, 1999) <http://maps.vix.com/tsi/ar-what.html>; Vixie, supra note 6.

9. MAPS includes in this category such activities as hosting web pages that are listed as destination addresses in bulk e-mail, or providing e-mail forwarders or auto-responders that can be used by bulk e-mailers. See Vixie, supra note 6.

10. There is currently no charge to subscribe to the RBL. See Nick Nicholas & Chip Rosenthal, MAPS RBL Participants (visited Nov. 19, 1999) <http://maps.vix.com/rbl/participants. html>. The RBL currently has over 180 registered subscribers who receive full, frequently updated copies of the RBL for storage and use on their own routers and servers. These subscribers are required to execute a license agreement with MAPS, the terms of which are not publicly available. Id. In addition, there are "several thousand" other users who either receive the RBL via "EBGP4 Multi-Hop," a protocol used by routers on the Internet, or through direct queries on specific numeric Internet address to MAPS' RBL servers. Id.

11. Some have suggested—plausibly—that the explosion of mass e-mail is undermining the viability and even the existence of many open discussion forums (in particular, many Usenet newsgroups)—one of the Internet's earliest and most remarkable innovations. See Paul K. Ohm, Comment, On Regulating the Internet: Usenet, A Case Study, 46 *UCLA L. Rev.* 1941, 1951 (1999)

(noting that spam causes a dramatic decrease in Usenet's "signal-to-noise" ratio and is therefore considered a "major threat" to [Usenet's] continued popularity).

12. It is probably fair to point to Robert Ellickson's *Order Without Law: How Neighbors Settle Disputes* as the start of the rejuvenation of the study of norms within legal scholarship. The Symposium on Law, Economics, and Norms, 144 *U. Pa. L. Rev.* 1643 (1996), maps out much of the recent terrain.

13. MAPS provides an extensive rationale for its proposed norms. See Our Rationale for the MAPS RBL (last modified July 12, 1999) <http://maps.vix.com/rbl/rationale.html>.

14. The RBL has apparently become popular enough that many of the vendors of the most popular mail server configuration software provide support for RBL implementation in their products. See Paul Vixie, MAPS RBL Usage (visited Jan. 5, 2000) <http://maps.vix. com/rbl/usage.html>.

15. The implementation in software of this particular norm is surely an unusual feature of this process that has no clear analogue in real-space norm-creation schemes. Enforcement of norms by code is, as Professor Lessig has demonstrated, a large, and a most fundamental change. See Lawrence Lessig, *Code and Other Laws of Cyberspace* (1999). Cyberspace, in Lessig's words,

> ". . . demands a new understanding of how regulation works and of what regulates life there. It compels us to look beyond the traditional lawyer's scope—beyond laws, regulations, and norms. . . . In cyberspace we must understand how code regulates—how the software and hardware that make cyberspace what it is regulate cyberspace as it is. As William Mitchell puts it, this code is cyberspace's 'law.' Code is law."

16. Margaret Radin and R. Polk Wagner criticize what they describe as a "false dichotomy" between characterizations of "top-down" and "bottom-up" ordering. See Margaret Radin & R. Polk Wagner, "The Myth of Private Ordering: Rediscovering Legal Realism in Cyberspace," 73 *Chi.- Kent L. Rev.* 1127 (1998). Any rule-making regime, they suggest, "can be characterized as either [top-down or bottom-up], depending upon how you look at it." The point is an important one; rule-making processes are always top-down when seen from one level of the hierarchy of social institutions and bottom-up when seen from a different level. MAPS's decision-making process is top-down from the perspective of, say, the MAPS webmaster, who receives from " higher up" a list of sites to put on, or take off, the RBL each morning. This top-down process is simultane- ously a component of a bottom-up process from the perspective of someone looking at the responses of the Internet community as a whole to the proliferation of commercial e-mail. This is a feature of all networks (including social networks) consisting of embedded hierarchies; any element in the network is simultaneously at the top of some hierarchy(ies) and at the bottom of others. See David G. Post & Michael B. Eisen, "How Long is the Coastline of the Law? Thoughts on the Fractal Nature of Legal Systems," 29 *J.L.S.* 545 (2000) (describing this "dizzying" charac- teristic of embedded hierarchies as a consequence of their fractal structure).

17. You are not, in other words, subject to any sanction enforced through the formal State-created processes if you choose to join, or not to join, the MAPS exercise. If for any reason you do not approve of MAPS' particular definition of unacceptable behavior, their choice of sanction, the means they have chosen to implement that sanction, or their method of detecting violators sub- ject to the sanction, you can ignore them (or, if you'd like, to propose your own). MAPS can persuade, cajole, and beg the thousands of ISPs out there to join the group of RBL subscribers, but it cannot use State-sanctioned force to get them to do so.

18. Professor Elkin-Koren defines "decentralized" norm-creation processes as those in which the "power to create and shape . . . rules is not concentrated in the hands of any individual group, or institution [and which is] spread among various social agents." Niva Elkin-Koren, "Copyrights in Cyberspace—Rights Without Laws?", 73 *Chi.-Kent L. Rev.* 1155, 1161 (1998). As of June, 1999, there were over 6,000 ISPs in the United States alone offering Internet connectivity, see Jason Oxman, The FCC and the Unregulation of the Internet, FCC Office of Plans and Policy Working Paper No. 31 (last modified July 1999) <http://www. fcc.gov/Bureaus/OPP/working_papers/oppwp31.pdf>, and countless other network administrators in a position to subscribe (or not) to the RBL.

19. Elkin-Koren, supra note 18, at 1161–62 (Cyberspace "significantly reduces the costs of communicating and collecting information regarding individuals' preferences. It also facilitates fast and cost-effective information processing that allows real-time feedback on public preferences and choices. Cyberspace, thus, opens up opportunities for effective participation of individuals in defining the rules.").

20. See A. Michael Froomkin, "Of Governments and Governance," 14 *Berkeley Tech. L.J.* 617 (1999); Milton L. Mueller, Internet Domain Names: Privatization, Competition, and Freedom of Expression, Cato Briefing Paper No. 33 (last modified October 16, 1997) <http://www. cato.org/pubs/briefs/bp-033.html>; Jon Weinberg, "Testimony of Jon Weinberg, Professor of Law, Wayne State University before the U.S. House of Representatives Commerce Committee, Subcommittee on Oversight and Investigations, "Domain Name System Privatization: Is ICANN Out of Control?" (last modified July 22, 1999) <http://www.law.wayne.edu/weinberg/testimony.pdf>. The Department of Commerce's "White Paper," Management of Internet Names and Addresses (visited January 24, 2000) <http://www.ntia.doc.gov/ntiahome/domainname/6_5_98dns.htm>, has a comprehensive summary of the history of domain name and number administration on the Internet.

21. See Department of Commerce, supra note 20.

22. Id.

23. My own views have been set forth at length elsewhere. See David G. Post, Governing Cyberspace: Where is James Madison When We Need Him?(last modified June 6, 1999) <http://www.icannwatch.org/archives/essays/930604982.shtml>; David G. Post, Elusive Consensus (last modified July 21, 1999)<http://www.icannwatch.org/archives/ essays/932565188.shtml>; David G. Post, ICANN and Independent Review (last modified Aug. 1999) <http://www.icannwatch.org/reviewpanel/index.shtml>; David G. Post, Cyberspace's Constitutional Moment, *The American Lawyer,* Nov. 1998, at 117.

24. See, e.g., Tom W. Bell, "Fair Use v. Fared Use: The Impact of Automated Rights Management on Copyright's Fair Use Doctrine", *76 N.C. L. Rev.* 557 (1998); Llewellyn Joseph Gibbons, "No Regulation, Government Regulation, or Self-Regulation: Social Enforcement or Social Contracting for Governance in Cyberspace," 6 *Cornell J. L. & Pub. Pol'y* 475 (1997); I. Trotter Hardy, "The Proper Legal Regime for 'Cyberspace'", 55 *U. Pitt. L. Rev.* 993, 995–96 (1994); Maureen A. O'Rourke, "Copyright Preemption After the ProCD Case: A Market-Based Approach," 12 *Berkeley Tech. L. J.* 53, 80 (1997); David Post & David R. Johnson, "And How Shall the Net Be Governed? A Meditation on the Relative Virtues of Decentralized, Emergent Law," in *Coordinating the Internet* , (Brian Kahin & James Keller eds., 1997); David G. Post & David R. Johnson, "Chaos Prevailing on Every Continent: Towards a New Theory of

Decentralized Decision-Making in Complex Systems," 73 *Chi.-Kent. L. Rev.* 1055 (1998); David R. Johnson & David G. Post, "The New Civic Virtue of the Internet: Lessons from a Model of Complex Systems for the Governance of Cyberspace," in *The Emerging Internet* (1998 Annual Review of the Institute for Information Studies) (C. Firestone ed., 1998). The distinction between the "legitimacy" and "efficiency" justifications for decentralized Internet rule-making comes from Elkin-Koren, supra note 18, at 1166–79.

25. Elkin-Koren, supra note 18, at 1172.

26. Decentralized decision-making processes, in the language of complexity theory, are powerful algorithms for finding "high points on the fitness landscape" (i.e., solutions to problems defined over complex, interdependent spaces). See Post, "Chaos Prevailing on Every Continent," supra note 24, at 1081–86. The problem-solving power of decentralized systems is well-documented and reasonably non-controversial in mathematical, physical, and biological systems, underlying phenomena as diverse as parallel processing algorithms in computational mathematics and natural selection in the design of living things. See id. at 1083–1093.

27. Professor Lessig has written, in discussing the "spam wars," that ". . . these battles [between spammers and anti-spammers] will not go away. The power of the vigilantes will no doubt increase, as they hold out the ever-more-appealing promise of a world without spam. But the conflicts with these vigilantes will increase as well. Network service providers will struggle with antispam activists even as activists struggle with spam.

    "There's something wrong with this picture. This policy question will fundamentally affect the architecture of e-mail. The ideal solution would involve a mix of rules about spam and code to implement the rules. . . . Certainly, spam is an issue. But the real problem is that vigilantes and network service providers are deciding fundamental policy questions about how the Net will work—each group from its own perspective. This is policy-making by the 'invisible hand.' It's not that policy is not being made, but that those making the policy are unaccountable. . . . Is this how network policy should be made? The answer is obvious, even if the solution is not." Lawrence Lessig, The Spam Wars (last modified Dec. 31, 1998) <http://www.thestandard.com/articles/display/0,1449,3006,00.html> (emphasis added). This view—not only that we should not rely on the interplay [a misnomer, perhaps] between spammers and anti-spammers to make "network policy," but that it is "obvious" that we should not do so—seems to be widely shared. In the course of the most enlightening discussion of these questions on the Cyberprof listserve, see supra note 2, skepticism about bottom-up processes in general, and certainly about the RBL, was widespread. Cyberprof Listserve (selected postings Jan. 29–30, 1999) (copies on file with author). For example:

    "These private blacklists—however virtuous the maintainers might be—are a perfect example, in my humble opinion, of where bottom up doesn't work. The externality from this boycott is huge. Yet there is no body that can reckon that externality. "[My company] fell victim to [the RBL] during last summer. Given the nature of our proprietary architecture, making the fixes they wanted wasn't an option. While they eventually were forced to acknowledge this, we were blackholed for an unacceptable period of time while we tried to make them understand why we couldn't comply. The lack of formal process on their end seriously hampered our ability to get them to understand. Many of our customers had major problems arise during that time period because they couldn't use our service to get mail out to users on ISP who subscribed to the Vixie list.

"The average RBL'd site with an open mail relay is like a neighbor who allows members of the public open access to his yard, whence they deposit all sorts of trash into *my* yard. . . . Why can't I allow access to my yard without fear that some members of the public will abuse it to litter both mine and my neighbors' yards? Moreover, I wonder how many generations of locks and lock pickers we have yet to endure. Something is amiss in this let-it-all-hang-out picture."

Professor Field himself, it might be noted, shared this skepticism:

"I regard email as a tool, not a career. I appreciate that some are otherwise inclined, but neither I nor many other people are interested in its history and arcana. My point was and remains: Public policy should not require them to delve deeply to send a simple message and avoid what amounts to vandalism and vigilante responses thereto."

See also John Swartz, Anti-Spam Service or McCarthyism? Internet Group Puts Some ISPs on a Blacklist (last modified May 10, 1999) <http://www.sfgate.com/cgi-bin/article.cgi? file=/chronicle/archive/1999/05/10/BU76824.DTL> (describing MAPS' activities as a sort of "Cyber-McCarthyism").

28. Three of the contributions to the recent symposium on "The Internet and Legal Theory" focused on the deficiencies of informal Internet rule-making systems. See Elkin-Koren, supra note 18; Mark. A. Lemley, "The Law and Economics of Internet Norms", 73 *Chi.-Kent L. Rev.* 1257 (1998); Margaret Radin & R. Polk Wagner, supra note 16. See also Lawrence Lessig, *Code and Other Laws of Cyberspace* (1999).

29. The Internet is, at bottom, that language, the set of grammatical rules (the "Internet protocols" and related transmission and communication standards) that allow machines to exchange information with one another. Lawrence Lessig, Open Code and Open Societies: Values of Internet Governance (last modified May 11, 1999) <http://cyber.law.harvard. edu/works/lessig/kent.pdf>, at 11; David G. Post, What Larry Doesn't Get: A Libertarian Response to Lessig's "Code and Other Laws of Cyberspace," *Stan. L. Rev.* (forthcoming).

30. See "The Death of Distance," *The Economist*, Sept. 30, 1995, at 35, for what is probably the best general description of the striking inability of politicians, social theorists, and even some very savvy players within the computer industry itself to predict ex ante the emergence and growth of this medium.

31. Internet Engineering Task Force (visited Nov. 18, 1999) <http://www.ietf.org>.

32. World Wide Web Consortium (visited Nov. 18, 1999) <http://www.w3.org>.

33. Internet Assigned Number Authority (visited Nov. 18, 1999) <http://www.iana.org>.

34. The failure of the "official" standard-setting bodies—the International Organization for Standardization (ISO) and the International Telegraph and Telephone Consultative Committee (CCITT) (now the International Telecommunications Union (ITU))—to gain acceptance for their OSI internet working protocols is a nice case in point. See Katie Hafner & Michael Lyon, Where Wizards Stay Up Late: The Origins of the Internet, 246–251 (1996) (describing the battle between the OSI protocols and the ultimately-triumphant-and-dare-I-call-it-bottom-up TCP/IP protocols); Peter Salus, Protocol Wars: Is OSI Finally Dead?, 6 Connexions 16 (1995); see also John Lamouth, Understanding OSI (last modified Nov. 11, 1997) <http://www.salford.ac.uk/iti/books/osi/osi.html>; OSI (last modified May 16, 1998)

<http://webopedia.internet.com/Standards/Networking_Standards/OSI.html>. But one data point does not a theory make.

35. See Elkin-Koren, supra note 18, at 1188 ("private ordering should not be examined in the abstract, but rather in comparison to its alternatives"); Lemley, supra note 28, at 1261 (noting, by implication, the difficulties of analyzing questions of "comparative institutional governance").

36. This is a common enough technique to have its own name: the "Nirvana Fallacy." See, e.g., Harold Demsetz, "Information and Efficiency: Another Viewpoint," 12 *J. L. & Econ.* 1 (1969).

37. The John Marshall Law School maintains a useful database of state efforts to curb unsolicited bulk e-mail. See (last modified Mar. 5, 1999) <http://www.jmls.edu/cyber/statutes/email/state.html>. In 1998, for example, Virginia amended its computer trespass statute to provide that it is unlawful to "[f]alsify or forge electronic mail transmission information or other routing information in any manner in connection with the transmission of unsolicited bulk electronic mail through or into the computer network of an electronic mail service provider or its subscribers." VA. Code Ann. §18.2–152.4 (Michie 1999).

38. Numerous bills to regulate or proscribe certain types of e-mail were introduced in the 106th Congress alone, including: the Unsolicited Mail Act of 1999, H.R. 3113, 106th Cong. (1999); the Can Spam Act, H.R. 2162, 106th Cong. (1999); the E-Mail User Protection Act, H.R. 1910, 106th Cong. (1999); the Inbox Privacy Act of 1999, S. 759, 106th Cong. (1999); and the Telemarketing Fraud and Seniors Protection Act, S. 699, 106th Cong. (1999) and its House counterpart, the Protection Against Scams on Seniors Act of 1999, H.R. 612, 106th Cong. (1999).

39. See Lawrence Lessig, *Code and Other Laws of Cyberspace* 206 (1999):

"Just as there was a push toward convergence on a simple set of network protocols, there will be a push toward convergence on a uniform set of rules to govern network transactions. This set of rules will include not the law of trademark that many nations have, but a unified system of trademark, enforced by a single committee [citation omitted]; not a diverse set of policies governing privacy, but a single set of rules, implicit in the architecture of Internet protocols; not a range of contract law policies, implemented in different ways according to the values of different states, but a single, implicit set of rules decided through click-wrap agreements and enforced where the agreement says."

See also David G. Post, "Governing Cyberspace," 43 *Wayne L. Rev.* 155, 163–64 (1997).

40. That is, I realize, a somewhat controversial claim. See A. Michael Froomkin, "The Internet as a Source of Regulatory Arbitrage," in *Borders in Cyberspace: Information Policy and the Global Information Infrastructure* (Brian Kahin & Charles Nesson eds., 1997) (available at <http://www.law.miami.edu/~froomkin/articles/arbitr.htm>); Jack L. Goldsmith, "Against Cyberanarchy," 65 *U. Chi. L. Rev.* 1199 (1998). Doctrinal impediments to Virginia's assertion of extraterritorial jurisdiction over out-of-boundary spammers includes the Commerce Clause, see American Library Ass'n v. Pataki, 969 F. Supp. 160 (S.D.N.Y. 1997), and limitations on Virginia's "jurisdiction to prescribe" extraterritorially and limitations on the Virginia courts' ability to exercise personal jurisdiction over persons and entities residing elsewhere; even Professor Goldsmith, the most forceful critic of the notion that there are such impediments, agrees that in both the domestic and international arenas the "enforceable scope" of any jurisdiction's laws is "relatively narrow," extending "only to individual users or system operators with presence or assets in the enforcement jurisdiction." Jack L. Goldsmith, "Against Cyberanarchy," 65 *U. Chi. L. Rev.* 1199, 1220 (1998).

41. Department of Commerce, supra note 20.

42. Id.

43. Virginia Postrel captures an important dimension of this battle between those of different faiths regarding these matters in her discussion of the difference between "dynamists" and "stasists." See Virginia I. Postrel, *The Future and Its Enemies: The Growing Conflict over Creativity, Enterprise, and Progress* (1998).

Fahrenheit 451.2: Is Cyberspace Burning?

How Rating and Blocking Proposals May Torch Free Speech on the Internet

Executive Summary

In the landmark case Reno v. ACLU, the Supreme Court overturned the Communications Decency Act, declaring that the Internet deserves the same high level of free speech protection afforded to books and other printed matter.

But today, all that we have achieved may now be lost, if not in the bright flames of censorship, then in the dense smoke of the many ratings and blocking schemes promoted by some of the very people who fought for freedom.

The ACLU and others in the cyber-liberties community were genuinely alarmed by the tenor of a recent White House summit meeting on Internet censorship at which industry leaders pledged to create a variety of schemes to regulate and block controversial online speech.

But it was not any one proposal or announcement that caused our alarm; rather, it was the failure to examine the longer-term implications for the Internet of rating and blocking schemes.

The White House meeting was clearly the first step away from the principle that protection of the electronic word is analogous to protection of the printed word. Despite the Supreme Court's strong rejection of a broadcast analogy for the Internet, government and industry leaders alike are now inching toward the dangerous and incorrect position that the Internet is like television, and should be rated and censored accordingly.

Is Cyberspace burning? Not yet, perhaps. But where there's smoke, there's fire.

"Any content-based regulation of the Internet, no matter how benign the purpose, could burn the global village to roast the pig."

U.S. Supreme Court majority decision, *Reno v. ACLU* (June 26, 1997)

Introduction

In his chilling (and prescient) novel about censorship, Fahrenheit 451, author Ray Bradbury describes a futuristic society where books are outlawed. "Fahrenheit 451" is, of course, the temperature at which books burn.

In Bradbury's novel—and in the physical world—people censor the printed word by burning books. But in the virtual world, one can just as easily censor controversial speech by banishing it to the farthest corners of cyberspace using rating and blocking programs. Today, will Fahrenheit version 451.2—a new kind of virtual censorship—be the temperature at which cyberspace goes up in smoke?

The first flames of Internet censorship appeared two years ago, with the introduction of the Federal Communications Decency Act (CDA), outlawing "indecent" online speech. But in the landmark case Reno v. ACLU, the Supreme Court overturned the CDA, declaring that the Internet is entitled to the highest level of free speech protection. In other words, the Court said that online speech deserved the protection afforded to books and other printed matter.

Today, all that we have achieved may now be lost, if not in the bright flames of censorship then in the dense smoke of the many ratings and blocking schemes promoted by some of the very people who fought for freedom. And in the end, we may find that the censors have indeed succeeded in "burning down the house to roast the pig."

Is Cyberspace Burning?

The ashes of the CDA were barely smoldering when the White House called a summit meeting to encourage Internet users to self-rate their speech and to urge industry leaders to develop and deploy the tools for blocking "inappropriate" speech. The meeting was "voluntary," of course: the White House claimed it wasn't holding anyone's feet to the fire.

The ACLU and others in the cyber-liberties community were genuinely alarmed by the tenor of the White House summit and the unabashed enthusiasm for technological fixes that will make it easier to block or render invisible controversial speech. (Note: see appendix for detailed explanations of the various technologies.)

Industry leaders responded to the White House call with a barrage of announcements:

- Netscape announced plans to join Microsoft—together the two giants have 90% or more of the web browser market—in adopting PICS (Platform for Internet Content Selection), the rating standard that establishes a consistent way to rate and block online content

- IBM announced it was making a $100,000 grant to RSAC (Recreational Software Advisory Council) to encourage the use of its RSACi rating system. Microsoft

Explorer already employs the RSACi ratings system, Compuserve encourages its use, and it is fast becoming the de facto industry standard rating system

- Four of the major search engines—the services that allow users to conduct searches of the Internet for relevant sites—announced a plan to cooperate in the promotion of "self-regulation" of the Internet. The president of one, Lycos, was quoted in a news account as having "thrown down the gauntlet" to the other three, challenging them to agree to exclude unrated sites from search results

- Following the announcement of proposed legislation by Sen. Patty Murray (D Wash.), which would impose civil and ultimately criminal penalties on those who mis-rate a site, the makers of the blocking program Safe Surf proposed similar legislation, the "Online Cooperative Publishing Act."

But it was not any one proposal or announcement that caused our alarm; rather, it was the failure to examine the longer-term implications for the Internet of rating and blocking schemes.

What may be the result? The Internet will become bland and homogenized. The major commercial sites will still be readily available; they will have the resources and inclination to self-rate, and third-party rating services will be inclined to give them acceptable ratings. People who disseminate quirky and idiosyncratic speech, create individual home pages, or post to controversial news groups will be among the first Internet users blocked by filters and made invisible by the search engines. Controversial speech will still exist, but will only be visible to those with the tools and know-how to penetrate the dense smokescreen of industry "self-regulation."

As bad as this very real prospect is, it can get worse. Faced with the reality that, although harder to reach, sex, hate speech, and other controversial matter is still available on the Internet, how long will it be before governments begin to make use of an Internet already configured to accommodate massive censorship? If you look at these various proposals in a larger context, a very plausible scenario emerges. It is a scenario, which in some respects, has already been set in motion:

- First, the use of PICS becomes universal; providing a uniform method for content rating.

- Next, one or two rating systems dominate the market and become the de facto standard for the Internet.

- PICS and the dominant rating(s) system are built into Internet software as an automatic default.

- Unrated speech on the Internet is effectively blocked by these defaults.

- Search engines refuse to report on the existence of unrated or "unacceptably" rated sites.

- Governments frustrated by "indecency" still on the Internet make self-rating mandatory and mis-rating a crime.

The scenario is, for now, theoretical—but inevitable. It is clear that any scheme that allows access to unrated speech will fall afoul of the government-coerced push for a "family friendly" Internet. We are moving inexorably toward a system that blocks speech simply because it is unrated and makes criminals of those who mis-rate.

The White House meeting was clearly the first step in that direction and away from the principle that protection of the electronic word is analogous to protection of the printed word. Despite the Supreme Court's strong rejection of a broadcast analogy for the Internet, government and industry leaders alike are now inching toward the dangerous and incorrect position that the Internet is like television, and should be berated and censored accordingly.

Is Cyberspace burning? Not yet, perhaps. But where there's smoke, there's fire.

Free Speech Online: A Victory Under Siege

On June 26, 1997, the Supreme Court held in Reno v. ACLU that the Communications Decency Act, which would have made it a crime to communicate anything "indecent" on the Internet, violated the First Amendment. It was the nature of the Internet itself, and the quality of speech on the Internet, that led the Court to declare that the Internet is entitled to the same broad free speech protections given to books, magazines, and casual conversation.

The ACLU argued, and the Supreme Court agreed, that the CDA was unconstitutional because, although aimed at protecting minors, it effectively banned speech among adults. Similarly, many of the rating and blocking proposals, though designed to limit minors' access, will inevitably restrict the ability of adults to communicate on the Internet. In addition, such proposals will restrict the rights of older minors to gain access to material that clearly has value for them.

Rethinking the Rush to Rate

This paper examines the free speech implications of the various proposals for Internet blocking and rating. Individually, each of the proposals poses some threat to open and robust speech on the Internet; some pose a considerably greater threat than others.

Even more ominous is the fact that the various schemes for rating and blocking, taken together, could create a black cloud of private "voluntary" censorship that is every bit as threatening as the CDA itself to what the Supreme Court called "the most participatory form of mass speech yet developed."

We call on industry leaders, Internet users, policy makers, and parents groups to engage in a genuine debate about the free speech ramifications of the rating and blocking schemes being proposed.

To open the door to a meaningful discussion, we offer the following recommendations and principles:

Recommendations and Principles

- Internet users know best. The primary responsibility for determining what speech to access should remain with the individual Internet user; parents should take primary responsibility for determining what their children should access.

- Default setting on free speech. Industry should not develop products that require speakers to rate their own speech or be blocked by default.
- Buyers beware. The producers of user-based software programs should make their lists of blocked speech available to consumers. The industry should develop products that provide maximum user control.
- No government coercion or censorship. The First Amendment prevents the government from imposing, or from coercing industry into imposing, a mandatory Internet ratings scheme.
- Libraries are free speech zones. The First Amendment prevents the government, including public libraries, from mandating the use of user-based blocking software.

Six Reasons Why Self-Rating Schemes Are Wrong for the Internet

To begin with, the notion that citizens should "self-rate" their speech is contrary to the entire history of free speech in America. A proposal that we rate our online speech is no less offensive to the First Amendment than a proposal that publishers of books and magazines rate each and every article or story, or a proposal that everyone engaged in a street corner conversation rate his or her comments. But that is exactly what will happen to books, magazines, and any kind of speech that appears online under a self-rating scheme.

In order to illustrate the very practical consequences of these schemes, consider the following six reasons, and their accompanying examples, illustrating why the ACLU is against self-rating:

Reason #1: Self-Rating Schemes Will Cause Controversial Speech to Be Censored.
Kiyoshi Kuromiya, founder and sole operator of Critical Path AIDS Project, has a web site that includes safer sex information written in street language with explicit diagrams, in order to reach the widest possible audience. Kuromiya doesn't want to apply the rating "crude" or "explicit" to his speech, but if he doesn't, his site will be blocked as an unrated site. If he does rate, his speech will be lumped in with "pornography" and blocked from view. Under either choice, Kuromiya has been effectively blocked from reaching a large portion of his intended audience—teenage Internet users—as well as adults.

As this example shows, the consequences of rating are far from neutral. The ratings themselves are all pejorative by definition, and they result in certain speech being blocked.

The White House has compared Internet ratings to "food labels"—but that analogy is simply wrong. Food labels provide objective, scientifically verifiable information to help the consumer make choices about what to buy, e.g., the percentage of fat in a food product like milk. Internet ratings are subjective value judgments that result in certain speech being blocked to many viewers. Further, food labels are placed on products that are readily available to consumers—unlike Internet labels, which would place certain kinds of speech out of reach of Internet users.

What is most critical to this issue is that speech like Kuromiya's is entitled to the highest degree of Constitutional protection. This is why ratings requirements have never been imposed on those who speak via the printed word. Kuromiya could distribute the same material in print form on any street corner or in any bookstore without worrying about having to rate it. In fact, a number of Supreme Court cases have established that the First Amendment does not allow government to compel speakers to say something they don't want to say—and that includes pejorative ratings. There is simply no justification for treating the Internet any differently.

Reason #2: Self-Rating Is Burdensome, Unwieldy, and Costly.

Art on the Net is a large, non-profit web site that hosts online "studios" where hundreds of artists display their work. The vast majority of the artwork has no sexual content, although there's an occasional Rubenesque painting. The ratings systems don't make sense when applied to art. Yet Art on the Net would still have to review and apply a rating to the more than 26,000 pages on its site, which would require time and staff that they just don't have. Or, they would have to require the artists themselves to self-rate, an option they find objectionable. If they decline to rate, they will be blocked as an unrated site even though most Internet users would hardly object to the art reaching minors, let alone adults.

As the Supreme Court noted in Reno v. ACLU, one of the virtues of the Internet is that it provides "relatively unlimited, low-cost capacity for communication of all kinds." In striking down the CDA, the Court held that imposing age-verification costs on Internet speakers would be "prohibitively expensive for noncommercial—as well as some commercial—speakers." Similarly, the burdensome requirement of self-rating thousands of pages of information would effectively shut most noncommercial speakers out of the Internet marketplace.

The technology of embedding the rating is also far from trivial. In a winning ACLU case that challenged a New York state online censorship statute, ALA v. Pataki, one long-time Internet expert testified that he tried to embed an RSACi label in his online newsletter site but finally gave up after several hours.

In addition, the ratings systems are simply unequipped to deal with the diversity of content now available on the Internet. There is perhaps nothing as subjective as a viewer's reaction to art. As history has shown again and again, one woman's masterpiece is another woman's pornography. How can ratings such as "explicit" or "crude" be used to categorize art? Even ratings systems that try to take artistic value into account will be inherently subjective, especially when applied by artists themselves, who will naturally consider their own work to have merit.

The variety of news-related sites on the Web will be equally difficult to rate. Should explicit war footage be labeled "violent" and blocked from view to teenagers? If a long news article has one curse word, is the curse word rated individually, or is the entire story rated and then blocked?

Even those who propose that "legitimate" news organizations should not be required to rate their sites stumble over the question of who will decide what is legitimate news.

Reason #3: Conversation Can't Be Rated.

You are in a chat room or a discussion group—one of the thousands of conversational areas of the Net. A victim of sexual abuse has posted a plea for help, and you want to respond. You've heard about a variety of ratings systems, but you've never used one. You read the RSACi web page, but you can't figure out how to rate the discussion of sex and violence in your response. Aware of the penalties for mislabeling, you decide not to send your message after all. The burdens of self-rating really hit home when applied to the vibrant, conversational areas of the Internet. Most Internet users don't run web pages, but millions of people around the world send messages, short and long, every day, to chat rooms, news groups, and mailing lists. A rating requirement for these areas of the Internet would be analogous to requiring all of us to rate our telephone or street corner or dinner party or water cooler conversations.

The only other way to rate these areas of cyberspace would be to rate entire chatrooms or news groups rather than individual messages. But most discussion groups aren't controlled by a specific person, so who would be responsible for rating them? In addition, discussion groups that contain some objectionable material would likely also have a wide variety of speech totally appropriate and valuable for minors, but the entire forum would be blocked from view for everyone.

Reason #4: Self-Rating Will Create "Fortress America" on the Internet.

You are a native of Papua, New Guinea, and as an anthropologist you have published several papers about your native culture. You create a web site and post electronic versions of your papers, in order to share them with colleagues and other interested people around the world. You haven't heard about the move in America to rate Internet content. You don't know it, but since your site is unrated, none of your colleagues in America will be able to access it.

People from all corners of the globe—people who might otherwise never connect because of their vast geographical differences—can now communicate on the Internet both easily and cheaply. One of the most dangerous aspects of ratings systems is their potential to build borders around American- and foreign-created speech. It is important to remember that today, nearly half of all Internet speech originates from outside the United States.

Even if powerful American industry leaders coerced other countries into adopting American ratings systems, how would these ratings make any sense to a New Guinean? Imagine that one of the anthropology papers explicitly describes a ritual in which teenage boys engage in self-mutilation as part of a rite of passage in achieving manhood. Would you look at it through the eyes of an American and rate it "torture," or would you rate it "appropriate for minors" for the New Guinea audience?

Reason #5: Self-Ratings Will Only Encourage, Not Prevent, Government Regulation.

The webmaster for Betty's Smut Shack, a web site that sells sexually explicit photos, learns that many people won't get to his site if he either rates his site "sexually explicit" or fails to rate at all. He rates his entire web site "okay for minors." A powerful Congressman from the Midwest learns that the site is now available to minors. He is outraged, and quickly introduces a bill imposing criminal penalties for mis-rated sites.

Without a penalty system for mis-rating, the entire concept of a self-ratings system breaks down. The Supreme Court that decided Reno v. ACLU would probably agree that the statute theorized above would violate the First Amendment, but as we saw with the CDA, that won't necessarily prevent lawmakers from passing it.

In fact, as noted earlier, a senator from Washington state—home of industry giant Microsoft, among others—has already proposed a law that creates criminal penalties for mis-rating. Not to be outdone, the filtering software company Safe Surf has proposed the introduction of a virtually identical federal law, including a provision that allows parents to sue speakers for damages if they "negligently" mis-rate their speech.

The example above shows that, despite all good intentions, the application of ratings systems is likely to lead to heavy-handed government censorship. Moreover, the targets of that censorship are likely to be just the sort of relatively powerless and controversial speakers, like the groups Critical Path AIDS Project, Stop Prisoner Rape, Planned Parenthood, Human Rights Watch, and various gay and lesbian organizations, which we represented in Reno v. ACLU.

Reason #6: Self-Ratings Schemes Will Turn the Internet into a Homogenized Medium Dominated by Commercial Speakers.

Huge entertainment conglomerates, such as the Disney Corporation or Time Warner, consult their platoons of lawyers who advise that their web sites must be rated to reach the widest possible audience. They then hire and train staff to rate all of their web pages. Everybody in the world will have access to their speech.

There is no question that there may be some speakers on the Internet for whom the ratings systems will impose only minimal burdens: the large, powerful corporate speakers with the money to hire legal counsel and staff to apply the necessary ratings. The commercial side of the Net continues to grow, but so far the democratic nature of the Internet has put commercial speakers on equal footing with all of the other non-commercial and individual speakers.

Today, it is just as easy to find the Critical Path AIDS web site as it is to find the Disney site. Both speakers are able to reach a worldwide audience. But mandatory Internet self-rating could easily turn the most participatory communications medium the world has yet seen into a bland, homogenized, medium dominated by powerful American corporate speakers.

Is Third-Party Rating the Answer?

Third-party ratings systems, designed to work in tandem with PICS labeling, have been held out by some as the answer to the free speech problems posed by self-rating schemes. On the plus side, some argue, ratings by an independent third party could minimize the burden of self-rating on speakers and could reduce the inaccuracy and mis-rating problems of self-rating. In fact, one of the touted strengths of the original PICS proposal was that a variety of third-party ratings systems would develop and users could pick and choose from the system that best fit their values. But third party ratings systems still pose serious free speech concerns.

First, a multiplicity of ratings systems has not yet emerged on the market, probably due to the difficulty of any one company or organization trying to rate over a million web sites, with hundreds of new sites—not to mention discussion groups and chat rooms—springing up daily.

Second, under third-party rating systems, unrated sites still may be blocked.

When choosing which sites to rate first, it is likely that third-party raters will rate the most popular web sites first, marginalizing individual and non-commercial sites. And like the self-rating systems, third-party ratings will apply subjective and value-laden ratings that could result in valuable material being blocked to adults and older minors. In addition, available third-party rating systems have no notification procedure, so speakers have no way of knowing whether their speech has received a negative rating.

The fewer the third-party ratings products available, the greater the potential for arbitrary censorship. Powerful industry forces may lead one product to dominate the marketplace. If, for example, virtually all households use Microsoft Internet Explorer and Netscape, and the browsers, in turn, use RSACi as their system, RSACi could become the default censorship system for the Internet. In addition, federal and state governments could pass laws mandating use of a particular ratings system in schools or libraries. Either of these scenarios could devastate the diversity of the Internet marketplace.

Pro-censorship groups have argued that a third-party rating system for the Internet is no different from the voluntary Motion Picture Association of America ratings for movies that we've all lived with for years. But there is an important distinction: only a finite number of movies are produced in a given year. In contrast, the amount of content on the Internet is infinite. Movies are a static, definable product created by a small number of producers; speech on the Internet is seamless, interactive, and conversational. MPAA ratings also don't come with automatic blocking mechanisms.

The Problems with User-Based Blocking Software in the Home

With the explosive growth of the Internet, and in the wake of the recent censorship battles, the marketplace has responded with a wide variety of user-based blocking programs. Each company touts the speed and efficiency of its staff members in blocking speech that they have determined is inappropriate for minors. The programs also often block speech based on keywords. (This can result in sites such as www.middlesex.gov or www.SuperBowlXXX.com being blocked because they contain the keywords "sex" and "XXX.")

In Reno v. ACLU, the ACLU successfully argued that the CDA violated the First Amendment because it was not the least restrictive means of addressing the government's asserted interest in protecting children from inappropriate material. In supporting this argument, we suggested that a less restrictive alternative was the availability of user-based blocking programs, e.g., Net Nanny, that parents could use in the home if they wished to limit their child's Internet access.

While user-based blocking programs present troubling free speech concerns, we still believe today that they are far preferable to any statute that imposes criminal penalties on online speech. In contrast, many of the new ratings schemes pose far greater free speech concerns than do user-based software programs.

Each user installs the program on her home computer and turns the blocking mechanism on or off at will. The programs do not generally block sites that they haven't rated, which means that they are not 100 percent effective.

Unlike the third-party ratings or self-rating schemes, these products usually do not work in concert with browsers and search engines, so the home user rather than an outside company sets the defaults. (However, it should be noted that this "standalone" feature could theoretically work against free speech principles, since here, too, it would be relatively easy to draft a law mandating the use of the products, under threat of criminal penalties.)

While the use of these products avoids some of the larger control issues with ratings systems, the blocking programs are far from problem-free. A number of products have been shown to block access to a wide variety of information that many would consider appropriate for minors. For example, some block access to safer sex information, although the Supreme Court has held that teenagers have the right to obtain access to such information even without their parent's consent. Other products block access to information of interest to the gay and lesbian community. Some products even block speech simply because it criticizes their product.

Some products allow home users to add or subtract particular sites from a list of blocked sites. For example, a parent can decide to allow access to "playboy.com" by removing it from the blocked sites list, and can deny access to "powerrangers.com" by adding it to the list. However most products consider their lists of blocked speech to be proprietary information that they will not disclose.

Despite these problems, the use of blocking programs has been enthusiastically and uncritically endorsed by government and industry leaders alike. At the recent White House summit, Vice President Gore, along with industry and non-profit groups, announced the creation of www.netparents.org, a site that provides direct links to a variety of blocking programs.

The ACLU urges the producers of all of these products to put real power in users' hands and provide full disclosure of their list of blocked speech and the criteria for blocking.

In addition, the ACLU urges the industry to develop products that provide maximum user control. For example, all users should be able to adjust the products to account for the varying maturity level of minors, and to adjust the list of blocked sites to reflect their own values.

It should go without saying that under no set of circumstances can governments constitutionally require anyone—whether individual users or Internet Service Providers—to run user-based blocking programs when accessing or providing access to the Internet.

Why Blocking Software Should Not Be Used by Public Libraries

The "never-ending, worldwide conversation" of the Internet, as one lower court judge called it, is a conversation in which all citizens should be entitled to participate—whether they access the Internet from the library or from the home. Just as government cannot require home users or Internet Service Providers (ISPs) to use blocking programs or self-rating programs, libraries should not require patrons to use blocking software when accessing the Internet at the library. The ACLU, like the American Library Association (ALA), opposes the use of blocking software in public libraries.

Libraries have traditionally promoted free speech values by providing free books and information resources to people regardless of their age or income. Today, more than 20 percent of libraries in the United States offer free access to the Internet, and that number is growing daily. Libraries are critical to realizing the dream of universal access to the Internet, a dream that would be drastically altered if they were forced to become Internet censors.

In a recent announcement stating its policy, the ALA said:

> Libraries are places of inclusion rather than exclusion. Current blocking/filtering software prevents not only access to what some may consider "objectionable" material, but also blocks information protected by the First Amendment. The result is that legal and useful material will inevitably be blocked.

Librarians have never been in the business of determining what their patrons should read or see, and the fact that the material is now found on the Internet is no different. By installing inaccurate and unreliable blocking programs on library Internet terminals, public libraries—which are almost always governmental entities—would inevitably censor speech that patrons are constitutionally entitled to access.

It has been suggested that a library's decision to install blocking software is like other legitimate selection decisions that libraries routinely make when they add particular books to their collections. But in fact, blocking programs take selection decisions totally out of the hands of the librarian and place them in the hands of a company with no experience in library science. As the ALA noted, "(F)ilters can impose the producer's viewpoint on the community."

Because, as noted above, most filtering programs don't provide a list of the sites they block, libraries won't even know what resources are blocked. In addition, Internet speakers won't know which libraries have blocked access to their speech and won't be able to protest.

Installing blocking software in libraries to prevent adults as well as minors from accessing legally protected material raises severe First Amendment questions. Indeed, that principle—that governments can't block adult access to speech in the name of protecting children—was one of the key reasons for the Supreme Court's decision in Reno v. ACLU.

If adults are allowed full access, but minors are forced to use blocking programs, constitutional problems remain. Minors, especially older minors, have a constitutional right to access many of the resources that have been shown to be blocked by user-based blocking programs.

One of the virtues of the Internet is that it allows an isolated gay teenager in Des Moines, Iowa to talk to other teenagers around the globe who are also struggling with issues relating to their sexuality. It allows teens to find out how to avoid

AIDS and other sexually transmitted diseases even if they are too embarrassed to ask an adult in person or even too embarrassed to check out a book.

When the ACLU made this argument in Reno v. ACLU, it was considered controversial, even among our allies. But the Supreme Court agreed that minors have rights too. Library blocking proposals that allow minors full access to the Internet only with parental permission are unacceptable.

Libraries can and should take other actions that are more protective of online free speech principles. First, libraries can publicize and provide links to particular sites that have been recommended for children. Second, to avoid unwanted viewing by passersby (and to protect the confidentiality of users), libraries can install Internet access terminals in ways that minimize public view. Third, libraries can impose "content-neutral" time limits on Internet use.

Conclusion

The ACLU has always favored providing Internet users, especially parents, with more information. We welcomed, for example, the American Library Association's announcement at the White House summit of The Librarian's Guide to Cyberspace for Parents and Kids, a "comprehensive brochure and Web site combining Internet terminology, safety tips, site selection advice, and more than 50 of the most educational and entertaining sites available for children on the Internet."

In Reno v. ACLU, we noted that Federal and state governments are already vigorously enforcing existing obscenity, child pornography, and child solicitation laws on the Internet. In addition, Internet users must affirmatively seek out speech on the Internet; no one is caught by surprise.

In fact, many speakers on the Net provide preliminary information about the nature of their speech. The ACLU's site on America Online, for example, has a message on its home page announcing that the site is a "free speech zone." Many sites offering commercial transactions on the Net contain warnings concerning the security of Net information. Sites containing sexually explicit material often begin with a statement describing the adult nature of the material. Chat rooms and newsgroups have names that describe the subject being discussed. Even individual e-mail messages contain a subject line.

The preliminary information available on the Internet has several important components that distinguish it from all the ratings systems discussed above: (1) it is created and provided by the speaker; (2) it helps the user decide whether to read any further; (3) speakers who choose not to provide such information are not penalized; (4) it does not result in the automatic blocking of speech by an entity other than the speaker or reader before the speech has ever been viewed. Thus, the very nature of the Internet reveals why more speech is always a better solution than censorship for dealing with speech that someone may find objectionable.

It is not too late for the Internet community to slowly and carefully examine these proposals and to reject those that will transform the Internet from a true marketplace of ideas into just another mainstream, lifeless medium with content no more exciting or diverse than that of television.

Civil libertarians, human rights organizations, librarians and Internet users, speakers and providers all joined together to defeat the CDA. We achieved a stunning victory, establishing a legal framework that affords the Internet the highest constitutional protection. We put a quick end to a fire that was all but visible and threatening. The fire next time may be more difficult to detect—and extinguish.

Appendix: Internet Ratings Systems—How Do They Work?

The Technology: PICS, Browsers, Search Engines, and Ratings

The rating and blocking proposals discussed below all rely on a few key components of current Internet technology. While none of this technology will by itself censor speech, some of it may well enable censorship to occur.

PICS: The Platform for Internet Content Selection (PICS) is a rating standard that establishes a consistent way to rate and block online content. PICS was created by a large consortium of Internet industry leaders, and became operational last year. In theory, PICS does not incorporate or endorse any particular rating system—the technology is an empty vessel into which different rating systems can be poured. In reality, only three Third-party rating systems have been developed for PICS—SafeSurf, Net Shepherd, and the de facto industry standard RSACi.[1]

Browsers: Browsers are the software tool that Internet users need in order to access information on the World Wide Web. Two products, Microsoft's Internet Explorer and Netscape, currently control 90% of the browser market. Microsoft's Internet Explorer is now compatible with PICS. That is, Internet Explorer can now be configured to block speech that has been rated with PICS-compatible ratings. Netscape has announced that it will soon offer the same capability. When the blocking feature on the browser is activated, speech with negative ratings is blocked. In addition, because a vast majority of Internet sites remain unrated, the blocking feature can be configured to block all unrated sites.

Search Engines: Search engines are software programs that allow Internet users to conduct searches for content on a particular subject using a string of words or phrases. The search result typically provides a list of links to sites on the relevant topic. Four of the major search engines have announced a plan to cooperate in the move toward Internet ratings. For example, they may decide not to list sites that have negative ratings or that are unrated.

Ratings Systems: There are a few PICS-compatible ratings systems already in use. Two self-rating systems include RSACi and Safe Surf. RSACi, developed by the same group that rates video games, attempts to rate certain kinds of speech, like sex and violence, according to objective criteria describing the content. For example, it rates levels of violence from "harmless conflict; some damage to objects" to "creatures injured or killed." Levels of sexual content are rated from "passionate kissing" to "clothed sexual touching" to "explicit sexual activity; sex crimes." The context in which the material is presented is not considered under the RSACi system; for example, it doesn't distinguish educational materials from other materials.

Safe Surf applies a complicated ratings system on a variety of types of speech, from profanity to gambling. The ratings are more contextual, but they are also more subjective and value-laden. For example, Safe Surf rates sexual content from "artistic" to "erotic" to "explicit and crude pornographic."

Net Shepherd, a third-party rating system that has rated 300,000 sites, rates only for "maturity" and "quality."

Notes

1. While PICS could be put to legitimate use with adequate free speech safeguards, there is a very real fear that governments, especially authoritarian governments, will use the technology to impose severe content controls.

Credits

The principal authors of this white paper are Ann Beeson and Chris Hansen of the ACLU Legal Department and ACLU Associate Director Barry Steinhardt. Additional editorial contributions were provided by Marjorie Heins of the Legal Department, and Emily Whitfield of the Public Education Department. This report was prepared by the ACLU Public Education Department: Loren Siegel, Director; Rozella Floranz Kennedy, Editorial Manager; Ronald Cianfaglione, Designer.

Filtering the Internet in the USA: Free Speech Denied?

Richard S. Rosenberg

1. Introduction

Much of the motivation for filtering and blocking programs arises from the efforts in the U.S. to defeat the Communications Decency Act of 1996 (CDA) by showing that programs existed, or would soon exist, to control access at the local level, removing the need to place the burden on Internet Service Providers (ISPs). In some sense, this was a bargain made with the devil because those opposed to the CDA expected that filtering programs would largely be used in the privacy of one's home, not in public institutions such as libraries, schools, and community centres. This latter use imposes restrictions on the general public (library patrons) that do not apply to families that choose to purchase and use such programs in their homes. In public places, they violate individual choice by substituting software whose criteria of access are largely a mystery and are subject to a number of pressure groups with their own agendas. If filtering programs are to be used, and the current discussion in the U.S. Congress strongly suggests that their use will be made mandatory, then at the very least, the filtering criteria—keywords, local or remote lists—must be accessible to library patrons; otherwise, the process is simply a form of censorship. Since libraries are the only source of Internet access for many people, they should not limit that access by arbitrary means. In what follows, we will describe filtering programs and some examples of known problems associated with their use, both in Canada and the United States. The current debate will be characterized and criticized as well. Finally, some conclusions will be offered, in the light of the foregoing presentation.

This essay originally appeared in the *Proceedings of the Fourth ETHICOMP Conference*, Luiss Guido Carli University, Rome, Italy, 1999. Copyright © 1999 by Richard S. Rosenberg. Reprinted with permission.

2. Background

2.1 Definitions

Filtering or blocking software can be taken to be a mechanism used to

- restrict access to Internet content, based on an internal database of the product, or;
- restrict access to Internet content through a database maintained external to the product itself, or;
- restrict access to Internet content to certain ratings assigned to host sites by a third party, or;
- restrict access to Internet content by scanning content, based on a keyword, phrase, or text string or;
- restrict access to Internet content based on the source of the information.

[Statement on Library Use of Filtering Software, 1997].

Thus, access criteria are preset by the product manufacturer and can be altered by the regular downloading of updates or even altered, for certain of the filters, by the active user. Not surprisingly, most users, especially busy parents, are likely to use the default criteria and therefore have minimal awareness of which sites and newsgroups are not accessible. Since blocking and filtering programs are commonly available, the focus of this paper will be on their use; however, also of importance, and potentially more dangerous, are rating programs, analogous to systems in place for movies and television. Two systems—RSACi (Recreational Software Advisory Council on the Internet) and PICS (Platform for Internet Content Selection)—are intended to first encourage, and later require, Web sites and Newsgroups to rate themselves along a number of dimensions, for example, RSACi includes violence, nudity, sex, and language. Browsers and search engines could then be programmed to return or access sites and newsgroups that satisfy a preset profile. The dangers associated with self-rating schemes will be discussed later in this paper.

2.2 Examples of Problems with Blocking and Filtering Programs

"We'd rather block more than less." Brian Melbourn, director of product development for Solid Oak Software, makers of CyberSitter. [Berlin and Kantor, 1996]

The basic concern is that the features for blocking or restricting access are determined on the basis of criteria unavailable to the user. Thus, when a Web search is undertaken, what is **not** returned is a product of the inadequacies of the search query, the search engine style, and the filtering software. Censorship is a constant companion. The National Coalition Against Censorship [Censorship's Tools Du Jour, 1998] characterizes the problems associated with such programs as follows:

- Oversimplification. How to distinguish "good" sex (or violence) from "bad"?

- Overbreadth. Ratings and filters often ignore context and, thus, inevitably exclude material that users might want to have, along with material they might not want.

- Feasibility. The Internet is many times vaster [than television], and the task of describing its contents is virtually unimaginable.

- Subjectivity. Any rating system that classifies or describes content is dependent on the subjectivity of the rater. Even if all participants voluntarily agreed to self-rate, which is highly unlikely, different raters would describe or rate the same content differently.

- Full disclosure. Few Internet filters disclose what you lose by using them. The makers of these products claim that information is proprietary and its disclosure would provide a roadmap to objectionable material.

- Security. Filters and ratings give a false sense of security by suggesting that all parents need to do to protect children is to block disturbing ideas and images.

The current American political and social climate exhibits a measure of confusion that epitomizes a frantic attempt to solve perceived problems in a largely unprincipled manner. Some religious and politically conservative groups urge the government to take action to protect their children from Internet dangers, while rejecting almost all other federal interventions. This segment of society has certainly set the agenda for regulation and control with the result that filtering and blocking have become the preferred method to deal with sexually explicit and other possibly controversial Internet content.

3. Mainstream Loudoun, et. al. v. Board of Trustees of the Loudoun County Library

A number of libraries in the U.S. have had to respond to the concerns of parents that their children are not safe in public libraries because the children can visit Web sites that contain possibly sexually explicit material. One such library, in Loudoun County, Virginia, installed the filtering program X-Stop on all of its nine computers connected to the Internet in late 1997. Soon after, a group of citizens filed a lawsuit against the Board of Trustees, charging that their first Amendment rights had been compromised because X-Stop prevented access to many sites (see the list given above) that had no legal cause to be so restricted. In November 1998, Judge Leonie Brinkema delivered her opinion in the U.S. District Court, Eastern District of Virginia. The Conclusion to this opinion follows [Mainstream Loudoun, et. al. v. Board of Trustees of the Loudoun County Library, 1998]:

> Although defendant is under no obligation to provide Internet access to its patrons, it has chosen to do so and is therefore restricted by the First Amendment in the limitations it is allowed to place on patron access. Defendant has asserted a broad right to censor the expressive activity of the receipt and communication of information through the Internet with a Policy that (1) is

not necessary to further any compelling government interest; (2) is not nar-
rowly tailored; (3) restricts the access of adult patrons to protected material
just because the material is unfit for minors; (4) provides inadequate stan-
dards for restricting access; and (5) provides inadequate procedural safe-
guards to ensure prompt judicial review. Such a Policy offends the guarantee
of free speech in the First Amendment and is, therefore, unconstitutional.

Thus, on constitutional grounds, libraries must not restrict access to protected speech. It may be possible for other libraries to avoid a similar fate by designating a limited number of computers for the exclusive use of children in their Internet activities. Such computers, it could be argued, require the use of filtering and blocking programs to protect children, although some librarians would also resist this compromise as a violation of their commitment to open and free inquiry. In this regard the next section briefly reviews opinions and statements of professional librarians in North America.

4. Librarians and Filtering Programs

4.1 Canadian Library Association (CLA)

On November 8, 1997, the CLA issued a statement on Internet access in support of its existing position on intellectual freedom. Although the use of filtering and blocking programs is not explicitly mentioned, the following two relevant points are included as the CLA encourages libraries:

• to incorporate Internet use principles into overall policies on access to library resources, including time, place, and manner restrictions on Internet use, and user behaviour policies, [and]

• to educate their publics about intellectual freedom principles and the role of libraries in facilitating access to resources in various forms of media including the Internet [.]

[CLA Statement on Internet Access, 1997]

4.2 American Library Association (ALA) and Other Library Associations

Immediately following the U.S. Supreme Court's decision affirming that sections of the Communications Decency Act were unconstitutional, the ALA's Intellectual Freedom Committee issued a statement about the use of filtering software in libraries. It should be recalled that the Justices were impressed by the development of this technology to provide control by parents in their homes. There is little argument about actions taken to filter the Internet in the privacy of one's home, although one might hope that an informed public would use the software sparingly. The debate turns on the use of filtering software in public places such as libraries, schools, and community centres. First Amendment protection and local versus federal control come into play. Not surprisingly, the ALA's statement [Statement on Library Use of Filtering Software, 1997] included such an admonition as,

Uphold the First Amendment by establishing and implementing written guidelines and policies on Internet use in your library in keeping with your library's overall policies on access to library materials.

These sentiments are echoed in the recommendations of other national and international library associations. For example, the International Federation of Library Associations and Institutions, "calls upon libraries and library staff to adhere to the principles of intellectual freedom, uninhibited access to information and freedom of expression and to recognize the privacy of library user" [Statement on Libraries and Intellectual Freedom, 1999]. The U.S. National Commission on Libraries and Information Science (NCLIS) adopted the following resolution in December 1998: "The U.S. National Commission on Libraries and Information Science feels strongly that the governing body of every school and public library, in order to meet its trustee responsibilities, should establish, formally approve, and periodically review a written acceptable use policy statement on Internet access" [Kids and the Internet: The Promise and the Perils, 1999]. NCLIS also recommends a number of potential solutions for dealing with a number of recognized "perils" and "policy Issues," such as the following:

- Separate terminals can be provided for adults and children, or multiple profiles can be installed on terminals, so that children are not allowed the same access as older people.

- Libraries can provide Internet training, education, and other awareness programs to parents and teachers that alert them to both the promise and the perils of the Internet and describe how they can help children have a safe and rewarding experience online.

- Internet access terminals can be configured with software that can be turned on or off and restricts access to designated web sites or specific Internet functions.

Thus, although the use of blocking and filtering software, if not by category, is recommended, it is in the context of education, and the provision of designated computers for children, not in the spirit of restriction and limitation.

5. Discussion and Analysis

Space precludes a detailed analysis, but a few points must be made. The commitment of librarians to the basic principle of free and open access to information, whether in hard copy or in electronic form, must be supported by the population at large. For public agencies such as schools and libraries to restrict access to the Internet by means of filtering or blocking programs is a dangerous activity that severely compromises First Amendment protection in the U.S. What must be confronted, however, is the deeply held concern by many that their children will encounter "dangerous" material on the Internet, whether by choice or accidentally. One of the issues is to what degree children have First Amendment rights; unfortunately, no more can be said here. Another is the danger of self-rating systems as applied to movies, television, and Web sites or newsgroups. Why a danger? Let me state as emphatically as I can—self-rating is destructive of art, quality, and self-respect. The concern with causing offense or with disturbing established social mores tends to so limit expression that mediocrity becomes the fashion of the day. A convincing example is the Comics Code forced upon the industry by a concern with excessive violence, sex, and immorality some thirty years ago. Here are a few choice selections:

- Policemen, judges, government officials, and respected institutions shall never be presented in such a way as to create disrespect for established authority.
- In every instance good shall triumph over evil and the criminal punished for his misdeeds.
- Ridicule or attack on any religious or racial group is never permissible.
- Passion or romantic interest shall never be treated in such a way as to stimulate the lower and baser emotions.

[Standards of the Comics Code Authority, 1971]

6. Conclusions

If filtering software is going to be used, in spite of all the foregoing arguments against its use, then David Jones, the president of Electronic Frontier Canada, [Jones, 1998] strongly suggests that the following conditions be included:

a. The specific criteria for censoring web sites must be approved by the Library Board, and made available to the public on request.
b. The implementation of this censorship must be in the control of the library staff, and not some outside company, which could not be held accountable to this Board or to the community.
c. The black list of censored web sites, together with the reason for blocking access to each site, should not be a secret. It should be made available to the public on request.
d. There should be a procedure for members of the public to ask library staff to reconsider classifications of web sites, both to have some removed from the black list, and also to have some new ones added.

After several failed attempts to enact legislation requiring schools and libraries to implement filtering and blocking software, the U.S. Congress, "pass [ed] the Consequences for Juvenile Offenders Act, which includes an amendment to require schools and libraries to install technology to screen out material 'harmful' to minors as a condition of receiving a federal Net access subsidy, known as the e-rate" [Macavinta, 1999]. The motivation for this legislation was the terrible murders of school children by school children in Littleton, Colorado earlier this year. Violence and sex on the Internet were quickly identified by many as a primary cause and hence the relatively easy passage in the House, 287–139. How will "harmful" be defined? A previous failed attempt to legislate foundered on the word "indecent." At the same time, legislators found it impossible to restrict access to guns, a more probable factor in the Littleton tragedy than free speech. If filtering is the answer, what exactly is the question?

Acknowledgments

Grateful appreciation is given to David Jones, president of Electronic Frontier Canada, Sheryl Adam, and other dedicated librarians, and of course, the National Sciences and Engineering Research Council for its support of this research project.

References

Berlin, E. and Kantor, A. (1996), The Surfboard: Who Will Watch the Watchmen? Internet World Online. Accessed from the Web page with URL: <http://www.internetworld.com/current/watchmen.html> on October 5, 1996.

Censorship in a Box: Why Blocking Software is Wrong for Public Libraries (1998), American Civil Liberties Union, June 17. Available at the Web Page with URL: < http://www.aclu.org/issues/cyber/box.html>.

Jones, David (1998), Speaking Notes for a presentation to the Board of Directors for the Burlington Public Library [Burlington, Ontario]. Available at the Web page with URL: <http://insight.mcmaster.ca/org/efc/pages/pr/bpl.djones.21may98.html>.

Kids and the Internet: The Promise and the Perils (1998), U.S. National Commission on Libraries and Information Science. Available at the Web page with URL: < http://www.nclis.gov/info/kid_inter.pdf>.

Mainstream Loudoun, et. al. v. Board of Trustees of the Loudoun County Library (1998), U.S. District Court, Eastern District of Virginia, Case No. 97-2049-A., November 23. Available at the Web Page with URL: <http://www.techlawjournal.com/courts/loudon/81123op.htm>.

Macavinta, C. (1999), House passes Net filtering bill. CNET News.com, June 18. Available at the Web page with URL: <http://www.news.com/News/Item/0,4,38018,00.html>.

Sites Censored by Censorship Software, (1997), Peacefire. Accessed from the Web page with URL: <http://www.peacefire.org/censorware/censored sites.shtml> on February 25, 1999.

Standards of the Comics Code Authority, (1971), In Daniels, L. Comix, *A History of Comic Books in America,* Outerbridge and Deinstfrey: New York. Accessed from the Web page with URL: < http://www.mit.edu/activities/safe/labeling/comics-code-1954> on June 14, 1999.

Statement on Libraries and Intellectual Freedom, (1999), The International Federation of Library Associations and Institutions, March 24. Available at the Web page with URL: < http://ifla.org/V/press/pr990326.htm>.

Statement on Library Use of Filtering Software, (1997), American Library Association/Freedom of Information Committee, July 1. Available at the Web page with URL: <http://www.ala.org/alaorg/oif/filt_stm.html>.

U. S. Supreme Court, ACLU v. Reno. (1997).

United States v. American Library Association, Inc.

Case Background

This case arose from a challenge to a federal law known as the Children's Internet Protection Act (CIPA). CIPA requires public libraries and schools to install anti-pornography filters as a condition for receiving government subsidies. Two forms of federal assistance are available. The E-rate program, established by the Telecommunications Act of 1996, allows libraries to purchase Internet access at a discount. For the year ending June, 2002 libraries in the U.S. received discounts totaling $58.5 million. Also, the Library Services and Technology Act (LSTA) provides funds to libraries to purchase telecommunications technologies and computer systems. According to CIPA, libraries cannot receive these funds unless they have "a policy of Internet safety for minors that includes the operation of a technology protection measure" that protects children and adults from obscenity and child pornography and that protects children from "visual depictions" that are "harmful to minors."

In April 2001, a group of libraries and library associations (including Multnomah County Public Library in Oregon, the Santa Cruz Public Library Joint Powers Authority, and the Connecticut Library Association) initiated a lawsuit against the government, claiming that CIPA was unconstitutional. This suit, *Multnomah Public Library et al. v. U.S.* was filed in the United States District Court for the Eastern District of Pennsylvania. The plaintiffs also included several Internet authors and publishers who alleged that their speech would be blocked by this law.

The plaintiffs argued that filters were imprecise and "blunt" instruments, inadvertently blocking out Web pages that did not contain pornographic material. In addition to overblocking, the lawsuit argues, filtering mechanisms will not be able to block offensive Web sites that should be blocked. Technology protection measures cannot block access to *all* the material that is obscene, child pornographic, or harmful to minors as those categories are defined by CIPA [§1721 (c)].

The lawsuit stated several other reasons for opposition to CIPA. For example, the law applies to adults as well as to children. Filters can be circumvented for an adult (and in some cases also for minors) only if that individual can demonstrate the need to access a certain Web site for a "bona fide research purpose." Libraries argue that it may not be practical to temporarily disable a blocking program. CIPA therefore forces libraries to make available for adults a level of speech that is suitable for children.

This reading is an excerpt from the Supreme Court case, *United States et al. v. American Library Association, Inc. et al.*, 123 S. ct 2293, decided June 23, 2003. It has been prepared by the editors and appears for the first time in *Readings in CyberEthics, Second Edition.*

In general, the plaintiffs in this lawsuit reject CIPA because it "distorts" the traditional role of the library, which is to provide open and unfettered access to the broadest range of content. Hence, in their view this constitutionally flawed legislation interferes with rights of information providers and it subverts the library's primary mission as a purveyor of information resources.

In the summer of 2002, a federal judicial panel of the U.S. District Court for the Third Circuit struck down the law. The court concluded that sections of this law were "invalid under the First Amendment." According to Judge Becker,

> *In providing even filtered Internet access, public libraries create a public forum open to any speaker around the world to communicate with library patrons via the Internet on a virtually unlimited number of topics. Where the state provides access to a "vast democratic forum," open to any member of the public to speak on subjects "as diverse as human thought," the state's decision selectively to exclude from the forum speech whose content the state disfavors is subject to strict scrutiny. . . .Under strict scrutiny, a public library's use of filtering software is permissible only if it is narrowly tailored to further a compelling government interest and no less restrictive alternative would serve that interest. . . .Under these circumstances we are constrained to conclude that the library plaintiffs must prevail in their contention that C.I.P.A. requires them to violate the First Amendment rights of their patrons, and accordingly is facially invalid* (Multnomah v. U.S., 2002).

The Government appealed the case to the Supreme Court, and in late June, 2003, that court vacated the District Court's ruling and upheld CIPA. In its 6-3 decision the Supreme Court concluded that limitations imposed by CIPA on Internet access were equivalent to limitations on access to books that librarians choose to acquire or not acquire. It is worth noting that all nine justices agreed that there was no constitutional problem with restricting the access of children to pornographic material. There was also consensus that filters are "blunt" or imprecise instruments for accomplishing this objective, since they sometimes block sites that adults have a right to see. For example, obscene material is not protected by the First Amendment, so access should be denied to both adults and children. However, filters cannot easily identify and block obscene material without blocking other material that is acceptable for adults. According to Greenhouse (2003), the real question "was the extent to which this 'overblocking' infringes the First Amendment rights of adult library users."

Below are excerpts from Chief Justice Rehnquist's opinion for four of the six justices who voted in the majority. Also included is an excerpt from the dissenting opinion of Justice Stevens.

Excerpts from Supreme Court Decision, U.S. v. ALA

Chief Justice Rehnquist announced the judgment of the Court and delivered an opinion, in which Justice O'Connor, Justice Scalia, and Justice Thomas joined. (Justices Kennedy and Breyer concurred but wrote separate opinions).

After a trial, the District Court ruled that CIPA was facially uncon-stitutional and enjoined the relevant agencies and officials from with-holding federal assistance for failure to comply with CIPA. The District Court held that Congress had exceeded its authority under the Spending Clause, U.S. Const., Art. I, §8, cl. 1, because, in the court's view, "any public library that complies with CIPA's conditions will nec-essarily violate the First Amendment." 201 F. Supp. 2d, at 453. The court acknowledged that "generally the First Amendment subjects libraries' content-based decisions about which print materials to acquire for their collections to only rational [basis] review." But it dis-tinguished libraries' decisions to make certain Internet material inac-cessible. "The central difference," the court stated, "is that by providing patrons with even filtered Internet access, the library permits patrons to receive speech on a virtually unlimited number of topics, from a virtually unlimited number of speakers, without attempting to restrict patrons' access to speech that the library, in the exercise of its pro-fessional judgment, determines to be particularly valuable." Reasoning that "the provision of Internet access within a public library ... is for use by the public ... for expressive activity," the court analyzed such access as a "designated public forum." The District Court also likened Internet access in libraries to "traditional public [areas] ... such as sidewalks and parks" because it "promotes First Amendment values in an analogous manner."

Based on both of these grounds, the court held that the filtering software contemplated by CIPA was a content-based restriction on access to a public forum, and was therefore subject to strict scrutiny. Applying this standard, the District Court held that, although the Government has a compelling interest "in preventing the dissemina-tion of obscenity, child pornography, or, in the case of minors, mate-rial harmful to minors," the use of software filters is not narrowly tailored to further those interests. We noted probable jurisdiction, 537 U.S. 1017 (2002), and now reverse.

Congress has wide latitude to attach conditions to the receipt of federal assistance in order to further its policy objectives. South Dakota v. Dole, 483 U.S. 203 , 206 (1987). But Congress may not "induce" the recipient "to engage in activities that would themselves be unconstitutional." To determine whether libraries would violate the First Amendment by employing the filtering software that CIPA requires, we must first examine the role of libraries in our society.

Public libraries pursue the worthy missions of facilitating learning and cultural enrichment. Appellee ALA's Library Bill of Rights states that libraries should provide "[b]ooks and other ... resources ... for the interest, information, and enlightenment of all people of the community the library serves." 201 F. Supp. 2d, at 420 (internal quotation marks omitted). To fulfill their traditional missions, public libraries must have broad discretion to decide what material to provide to their patrons. Although they seek to provide a wide array of information, their goal has never been to provide "universal coverage." Instead, public libraries seek to provide materials "that would be of the greatest direct benefit or interest to the community." To this end, libraries collect only those materials deemed to have "requisite and appropriate quality." See W. Katz, Collection Development: The Selection of Materials for Libraries 6 (1980) ("The librarian's responsibility ... is to separate out the gold from the garbage, not to preserve everything"); F. Drury, Book Selection xi (1930) ("[I]t is the aim of the selector to give the public, not everything it wants, but the best that it will read or use to advantage"); App. 636 (Rebuttal Expert Report of Donald G. Davis, Jr.) ("A hypothetical collection of everything that has been produced is not only of dubious value, but actually detrimental to users trying to find what they want to find and really need").

We have held in two analogous contexts that the government has broad discretion to make content-based judgments in deciding what private speech to make available to the public. In Arkansas Ed. Television Comm'n v. Forbes, 523 U.S. 666 (1998), we held that public forum principles do not generally apply to a public television station's editorial judgments regarding the private speech it presents to its viewers. "[B]road rights of access for outside speakers would be antithetical, as a general rule, to the discretion that stations and their editorial staff must exercise to fulfill their journalistic purpose and statutory obligations." Id., at 673. Recognizing a broad right of public access "would [also] risk implicating the courts in judgments that should be left to the exercise of journalistic discretion." Id., at 674.

Similarly, in National Endowment for Arts v. Finley, 524 U.S. 569 (1998), we upheld an art funding program that required the National Endowment for the Arts (NEA) to use content-based criteria in making funding decisions. We explained that "[a]ny content-based considerations that may be taken into account in the grant-making process are a consequence of the nature of arts funding." Id., at 585. In particular, "[t]he very assumption of the NEA is that grants will be awarded according to the 'artistic worth of competing applicants,' and absolute neutrality is simply inconceivable." Ibid.. We expressly declined to apply forum analysis, reasoning that it would conflict with "NEA's mandate ... to make esthetic judgments, and the inherently content-based 'excellence' threshold for NEA support." Id., at 586.

The principles underlying Forbes and Finley also apply to a public library's exercise of judgment in selecting the material it provides to its patrons. Just as forum analysis and heightened judicial scrutiny are incompatible with the role of public television stations and the role of the NEA, they are also incompatible with the discretion that public libraries must have to fulfill their traditional missions. Public library staffs necessarily consider content in making collection decisions and enjoy broad discretion in making them.

The public forum principles on which the District Court relied, are out of place in the context of this case. Internet access in public libraries is neither a "traditional" nor a "designated" public forum. See Cornelius v. NAACP Legal Defense & Ed. Fund, Inc., 473 U.S. 788 (1985) (describing types of forums). First, this resource–which did not exist until quite recently–has not "immemorially been held in trust for the use of the public and, time out of mind, ... been used for purposes of assembly, communication of thoughts between citizens, and discussing public questions." International Soc. for Krishna Consciousness, Inc. v. Lee, 505 U.S. 672 (1992). We have "rejected the view that traditional public forum status extends beyond its historic confines." Forbes, supra, at 678. The doctrines surrounding traditional public forums may not be extended to situations where such history is lacking.

Nor does Internet access in a public library satisfy our definition of a "designated public forum." To create such a forum, the government must make an affirmative choice to open up its property for use as a public forum. Cornelius, supra, at 802—803; Perry Ed. Assn. v. Perry Local Educators' Assn., 460 U.S. 37, 45 (1983). "The government does not create a public forum by inaction or by permitting limited discourse, but only by intentionally opening a non-traditional forum for public discourse." Cornelius, supra, at 802. The District Court likened public libraries' Internet terminals to the forum at issue in Rosenberger v. Rector and Visitors of Univ. of Va., 515 U.S. 819 (1995). 201 F. Supp. 2d, at 465. In Rosenberger, we considered the

"Student Activity Fund" established by the University of Virginia that subsidized all manner of student publications except those based on religion. We held that the fund had created a limited public forum by giving public money to student groups who wished to publish, and therefore could not discriminate on the basis of viewpoint.

The situation here is very different. A public library does not acquire Internet terminals in order to create a public forum for Web publishers to express themselves, any more than it collects books in order to provide a public forum for the authors of books to speak. It provides Internet access, not to "encourage a diversity of views from private speakers," (Rosenberger) but for the same reasons it offers other library resources: to facilitate research, learning, and recreational pursuits by furnishing materials of requisite and appropriate quality. See Cornelius noting, in upholding limits on participation in the Combined Federal Campaign (CFC), that "[t]he Government did not create the CFC for purposes of providing a forum for expressive activity"). As Congress recognized, "[t]he Internet is simply another method for making information available in a school or library." S. Rep. No. 106—141, p. 7 (1999). It is "no more than a technological extension of the book stack."

The District Court disagreed because, whereas a library reviews and affirmatively chooses to acquire every book in its collection, it does not review every Web site that it makes available. 201 F. Supp. 2d. Based on this distinction, the court reasoned that a public library enjoys less discretion in deciding which Internet materials to make available than in making book selections. We do not find this distinction constitutionally relevant. A library's failure to make quality-based judgments about all the material it furnishes from the Web does not somehow taint the judgments it does make. A library's need to exercise judgment in making collection decisions depends on its traditional role in identifying suitable and worthwhile material; it is no less entitled to play that role when it collects material from the Internet than when it collects material from any other source. Most libraries already exclude pornography from their print collections because they deem it inappropriate for inclusion. We do not subject these decisions to heightened scrutiny; it would make little sense to treat libraries' judgments to block online pornography any differently, when these judgments are made for just the same reason.

Moreover, because of the vast quantity of material on the Internet and the rapid pace at which it changes, libraries cannot possibly segregate, item by item, all the Internet material that is appropriate for inclusion from all that is not. While a library could limit its Internet collection to just those sites it found worthwhile, it could do so only at the cost of excluding an enormous amount of valuable information that it lacks the capacity to review. Given that tradeoff, it is entirely reasonable for public libraries to reject that approach and instead exclude certain categories of content, without making individualized judgments that everything they do make available has requisite and appropriate quality.

Like the District Court, the dissents fault the tendency of filtering software to "overblock"–that is, to erroneously block access to constitutionally protected speech that falls outside the categories that software users intend to block. [See opinion (below) of Justice Stevens.] Due to the software's limitations, "[m]any erroneously blocked [Web] pages contain content that is completely innocuous for both adults and minors, and that no rational person could conclude matches the filtering companies' category definitions, such as 'pornography' or 'sex.'" 201 F. Supp. 2d, at 449. Assuming that such erroneous blocking presents constitutional difficulties, any such concerns are dispelled by the ease with which patrons may have the filtering software disabled. When a patron encounters a blocked site, he need only ask a librarian to unblock it or (at least in the case of adults) disable the filter. As the District Court found, libraries have the capacity to permanently unblock any erroneously blocked site, and the Solicitor General stated at oral argument that a "library may ... eliminate the filtering with respect to specific sites ... at the request of a patron." Tr. of Oral Arg. 4. With respect to adults, CIPA also expressly authorizes library officials to "disable" a filter altogether "to enable access for bona fide research or other lawful purposes." The Solicitor General confirmed that a "librarian can, in response to a request from a patron, unblock the filtering mechanism altogether," Tr. of Oral Arg. 11, and further explained that a patron would not "have to explain ... why he was asking a site to be unblocked or the filtering to be disabled." The District Court viewed unblocking and disabling as inadequate because some patrons may be too embarrassed to request them. But the Constitution does not guarantee the right to acquire information at a public library without any risk of embarrassment.

Appellees urge us to affirm the District Court's judgment on the alternative ground that CIPA imposes an unconstitutional condition on the receipt of federal assistance. Under this doctrine, "the government 'may not deny a benefit to a person on a basis that infringes his constitutionally protected ... freedom of speech' even if he has no entitlement to that benefit." Board of Comm'rs, Wabaunsee Cty. v. Umbehr, 518 U.S. 668, 674 (1996). Appellees argue that CIPA imposes an unconstitutional condition on libraries that receive E-rate and LSTA subsidies by requiring them, as a condition on their receipt of federal funds, to surrender their First Amendment right to provide the public with access to constitutionally protected speech. The Government counters that this claim fails because Government entities do not have First Amendment rights. See Columbia Broadcasting System, Inc. v. Democratic National Committee, 412 U.S. 94, 139 (1973) (Stewart, J., concurring) ("The First Amendment protects the press from governmental interference; it confers no analogous protection on the government"); id., at 139, n. 7 ("The purpose of the First Amendment is to protect private expression" (quoting T. Emerson, The System of Freedom of Expression 700 (1970)).

We need not decide this question because, even assuming that appellees may assert an "unconstitutional conditions" claim, this claim would fail on the merits. Within broad limits, "when the Government appropriates public funds to establish a program it is entitled to define the limits of that program." Rust v. Sullivan, 500 U.S. 173, 194 (1991). In Rust, Congress had appropriated federal funding for family planning services and forbidden the use of such funds in programs that provided abortion counseling. Recipients of these funds challenged this restriction, arguing that it impermissibly conditioned the receipt of a benefit on the relinquishment of their constitutional right to engage in abortion counseling. We rejected that claim, recognizing that "the Government [was] not denying a benefit to anyone, but [was] instead simply insisting that public funds be spent for the purposes for which they were authorized." Ibid.

The same is true here. The E-rate and LSTA programs were intended to help public libraries fulfill their traditional role of obtaining material of requisite and appropriate quality for educational and informational purposes. Congress may certainly insist that these "public funds be spent for the purposes for which they were authorized." Ibid. Especially because public libraries have traditionally excluded pornographic material from their other collections, Congress could reasonably impose a parallel limitation on its Internet assistance programs. As the use of filtering software helps to carry out these programs, it is a permissible condition under Rust.

Justice Stevens asserts the premise that "[a] federal statute penalizing a library for failing to install filtering software on every one of its Internet-accessible computers would unquestionably violate [the First] Amendment." But–assuming again that public libraries have First Amendment rights–CIPA does not "penalize" libraries that choose not to install such software, or deny them the right to provide their patrons with unfiltered Internet access. Rather, CIPA simply reflects Congress' decision not to subsidize their doing so. To the extent that libraries wish to offer unfiltered access, they are free to do so without federal assistance. "A refusal to fund protected activity, without more, cannot be equated with the imposition of a 'penalty' on that activity." Rust, supra, at 193 (quoting Harris v. McRae, 448 U.S. 297, 317 (1980)).

Appellees mistakenly contend, in reliance on Legal Services Corporation v. Velazquez, 531 U.S. 533 (2001), that CIPA's filtering conditions "[d]istor[t] the [u]sual [f]unctioning of [p]ublic [l]ibraries." Brief for Appellees ALA et al. 40 (citing Velazquez, supra, at 543). In Velazquez, the Court concluded that a Government program of furnishing legal aid to the indigent differed from the program in Rust "[i]n th[e] vital respect" that the role of lawyers who represent clients in welfare disputes is to advocate against the Government, and there was thus an assumption that counsel would be free of state control. The Court concluded that the restriction on advocacy in such welfare disputes would distort the usual functioning of the legal profession and the federal and state courts before which the lawyers appeared. Public libraries, by contrast, have no comparable role that pits them against the Government, and there is no comparable assumption that they must be free of any conditions that their benefactors might attach to the use of donated funds or other assistance.

Because public libraries' use of Internet filtering software does not violate their patrons' First Amendment rights, CIPA does not induce libraries to violate the Constitution, and is a valid exercise of Congress' spending power. Nor does CIPA impose an unconstitutional condition on public libraries. Therefore, the judgment of the District Court for the Eastern District of Pennsylvania is reversed.

Justice Stevens, dissenting.

To fulfill their traditional missions, public libraries must have broad discretion to decide what material to provide their patrons. Accordingly, I agree with the plurality that it is neither inappropriate nor unconstitutional for a local library to experiment with filtering software as a means of curtailing children's access to Internet Web sites displaying sexually explicit images. I also agree with the plurality that the 7% of public libraries that decided to use such software on all of their Internet terminals in 2000 did not act unlawfully. Whether it is constitutional for the Congress of the United States to impose that requirement on the other 93%, however, raises a vastly *different question. Rather than allowing local decision makers to tailor their responses to local problems, the Children's Internet Protection Act (CIPA) operates as a blunt nationwide restraint on adult access to "an enormous amount of valuable information" that individual librarians cannot possibly review. Most of that information is constitutionally protected speech. In my view, this restraint is unconstitutional.*

I

The unchallenged findings of fact made by the District Court reveal fundamental defects in the filtering software that is now available or that will be available in the foreseeable future. Because the software relies on key words or phrases to block undesirable sites, it does not have the capacity to exclude a precisely defined category of images. As the District Court explained:

"[T]he search engines that software companies use for harvesting are able to search text only, not images. This is of critical importance, because CIPA, by its own terms, covers only 'visual depictions.' <u>20 U.S.C. § 9134</u> (f)(1)(A)(i); <u>47 U.S.C. § 254</u> (h)(5)(B)(i). Image recognition technology is immature, ineffective, and unlikely to improve substantially in the near future. None of the filtering software companies deposed in this case employs image recognition technology when harvesting or categorizing URLs. Due to the reliance on automated text analysis and the absence of image recognition technology, a Web page with sexually explicit images and no text cannot be harvested using a search engine. This problem is complicated by the fact that Web site publishers may use image files rather than text to represent words, i.e., they may use a file that computers understand to be a picture, like a photograph of a printed word, rather than regular text, making automated review of their textual content impossible. For example, if the Playboy Web site displays its name using a logo rather than regular text, a search engine would not see or recognize the Playboy name in that logo." 201 F. Supp. 2d 401 (ED Pa. 2002).

Given the quantity and ever-changing character of Web sites offering free sexually explicit material, it is inevitable that a substantial amount of such material will never be blocked. Because of this "underblocking," the statute will provide parents with a false sense of security without really solving the problem that motivated its enactment. Conversely, the software's reliance on words to identify undesirable sites necessarily results in the blocking of thousands of pages that "contain content that is completely innocuous for both adults and minors, and that no rational person could conclude matches the fil-tering companies' category definitions, such as 'pornography' or 'sex.' In my judgment, a statutory blunderbuss that mandates this vast amount of "overblocking" abridges the freedom of speech protected by the First Amendment.

The effect of the overblocking is the functional equivalent of a host of individual decisions excluding hundreds of thousands of individual constitutionally protected messages from Internet terminals located in public libraries throughout the Nation. Neither the interest in suppressing unlawful speech nor the interest in protecting children from access to harmful materials justifies this overly broad restriction on adult access to protected speech. "The Government may not suppress lawful speech as the means to suppress unlawful speech." Ashcroft v. Free Speech Coalition, 535 U.S. 234 (2002).

Although CIPA does not permit any experimentation, the District Court expressly found that a variety of alternatives less restrictive are available at the local level:

"[L]ess restrictive alternatives exist that further the government's legitimate interest in preventing the dissemination of obscenity, child pornography, and material harmful to minors, and in preventing patrons from being unwillingly exposed to patently offensive, sexu-ally explicit content. To prevent patrons from accessing visual depic-tions that are obscene and child pornography, public libraries may enforce Internet use policies that make clear to patrons that the library's Internet terminals may not be used to access illegal speech. Libraries may then impose penalties on patrons who violate these poli-cies, ranging from a warning to notification of law enforcement, in the appropriate case. Less restrictive alternatives to filtering that fur-ther libraries' interest in preventing minors from exposure to visual depictions that are harmful to minors include requiring parental con-sent to or presence during unfiltered access, or restricting minors' unfil-tered access to terminals within view of library staff. Finally, optional filtering, privacy screens, recessed monitors, and placement of unfil-tered Internet terminals outside of sight-lines provide less restrictive alternatives for libraries to prevent patrons from being unwillingly exposed to sexually explicit content on the Internet." 201 F. Supp. 2d, at 410.

Those findings are consistent with scholarly comment on the issue arguing that local decisions tailored to local circumstances are more appropriate than a mandate from Congress. The plurality does not reject any of those findings. Instead, assuming that such erroneous blocking presents constitutional difficulties, it relies on the Solicitor

General's assurance that the statute permits individual librarians to disable filtering mechanisms whenever a patron so requests. In my judgment, that assurance does not cure the constitutional infirmity in the statute.

Until a blocked site or group of sites is unblocked, a patron is unlikely to know what is being hidden and therefore whether there is any point in asking for the filter to be removed. It is as though the statute required a significant part of every library's reading materials to be kept in unmarked, locked rooms or cabinets, which could be opened only in response to specific requests. Some curious readers would in time obtain access to the hidden materials, but many would not. Inevitably, the interest of the authors of those works in reaching the widest possible audience would be abridged. Moreover, because the procedures that different libraries are likely to adopt to respond to unblocking requests will no doubt vary, it is impossible to measure the aggregate effect of the statute on patrons' access to blocked sites. Unless we assume that the statute is a mere symbolic gesture, we must conclude that it will create a significant prior restraint on adult access to protected speech. A law that prohibits reading without official consent, like a law that prohibits speaking without consent, "constitutes a dramatic departure from our national heritage and constitutional tradition." Watchtower Bible & Tract Soc. of N. Y., Inc. v. Village of Stratton, <u>536 U.S. 150</u>, 166 (2002).

II

The plurality incorrectly argues that the statute does not impose "an unconstitutional condition on public libraries." On the contrary, it impermissibly conditions the receipt of Government funding on the restriction of significant First Amendment rights.

The plurality explains the "worthy missions" of the public library in facilitating "learning and cultural enrichment." It then asserts that in order to fulfill these missions, "libraries must have broad discretion to decide what material to provide to their patrons." Thus the selection decision is the province of the librarians, a province into which we have hesitated to enter:

"A library's need to exercise judgment in making collection decisions depends on its traditional role in identifying suitable and worthwhile material; it is no less entitled to play that role when it collects material from the Internet than when it collects material from any other source. Most libraries already exclude pornography from their print collections because they deem it inappropriate for inclusion. We do not subject these decisions to heightened scrutiny; it would make little sense to treat libraries' judgments to block online pornography any differently, when these judgments are made for just the same reason." (Rehnquist Opinion—see above).

As the plurality recognizes, we have always assumed that libraries have discretion when making decisions regarding what to include in, and exclude from, their collections. That discretion is comparable to the "business of a university ... to determine for itself on academic grounds who may teach, what may be taught, how it shall be taught, and who may be admitted to study." Sweezy v. New Hampshire, 354 U.S. 234 (1957). As the District Court found, one of the central purposes of a library is to provide information for educational purposes: "Books and other library resources should be provided for the interest, information, and enlightenment of all people of the community the library serves." 201 F. Supp. 2d, at 420 (quoting the American Library Association's Library Bill of Rights). Given our Nation's deep commitment "to safeguarding academic freedom" and to the "robust exchange of ideas," Keyishian v. Board of Regents of Univ. of State of N.Y., 385 U.S. 589, 603 (1967), a library's exercise of judgment with respect to its collection is entitled to First Amendment protection.

A federal statute penalizing a library for failing to install filtering software on every one of its Internet-accessible computers would unquestionably violate that Amendment. Cf. Reno v. American Civil Liberties Union, 521 U.S. 844 (1997). I think it equally clear that the First Amendment protects libraries from being denied funds for refusing to comply with an identical rule. An abridgment of speech by means of a threatened denial of benefits can be just as pernicious as an abridgment by means of a threatened penalty.

The issue in this case . . .involves the use of its treasury to impose controls on an important medium of expression. In an analogous situation, we specifically held that when "the Government seeks to use an existing medium of expression and to control it, in a class of cases, in ways which distort its usual functioning," the distorting restriction must be struck down under the First Amendment. Legal Services Corporation v. Velazquez, 531 U.S. 533, 543 (2001). The question, then, is whether requiring the filtering software on all Internet-accessible computers distorts that medium. As I have discussed above, the over- and underblocking of the software does just that.

The plurality argues that the controversial decision in Rust v. Sullivan, 500 U.S. 173 (1991), requires rejection of appellees' unconstitutional conditions claim. But, as subsequent cases have explained, Rust only involved and only applies to instances of governmental speech–that is, situations in which the government seeks to communicate a specific message. The discounts under the E-rate program and funding under the Library Services and Technology Act (LSTA) program involved in this case do not subsidize any message favored by the Government. As Congress made clear, these programs were designed "[t]o help public libraries provide their patrons with Internet access," which in turn "provide[s] patrons with a vast amount of valuable information." These programs thus are designed to provide access, particularly for individuals in low-income communities, see 47 U.S.C. § 254, to a vast amount and wide variety of private speech. They are not designed to foster or transmit any particular governmental message.

Even if we were to construe the passage of CIPA as modifying the E-rate and LSTA programs such that they now convey a governmental message that no "'visual depictions' that are 'obscene,' 'child pornography,' or in the case of minors, 'harmful to minors,'" 201 F. Supp. 2d, at 407, should be expressed or viewed, the use of filtering software does not promote that message. As described above, all filtering software erroneously blocks access to a substantial number of Web sites that contain constitutionally protected speech on a wide variety of topics (describing erroneous blocking of speech on churches and religious groups, on politics and government, on health issues, on education and careers, on sports, and on travel). Moreover, there are "frequent instances of underblocking," id., at 448, that is, instances in which filtering software did not prevent access to Web sites with depictions that fall within what CIPA seeks to block access to. In short, the message conveyed by the use of filtering software is not that all speech except that which is prohibited by CIPA is supported by the Government, but rather that all speech that gets through the software is supported by the Government. And the items that get through the software include some visual depictions that are obscene, some that are child pornography, and some that are harmful to minors, while at the same time the software blocks an enormous amount of speech that is not sexually explicit and certainly does not meet CIPA's definitions of prohibited content. As such, since the message conveyed is far from the message the Government purports to promote–indeed, the material permitted past the filtering software does not seem to have any coherent message–Rust is inapposite.

The plurality's reliance on National Endowment for Arts v. Finley, <u>524 U.S. 569</u> (1998), is also misplaced. That case involved a challenge to a statute setting forth the criteria used by a federal panel of experts administering a federal grant program. Unlike this case, the Federal Government was not seeking to impose restrictions on the administration of a nonfederal program. As explained above, Rust would appear to permit restrictions on a federal program such as the NEA arts grant program at issue in Finley.

Further, like a library, the NEA experts in Finley had a great deal of discretion to make judgments as to what projects to fund. But unlike this case, Finley did not involve a challenge by the NEA to a governmental restriction on its ability to award grants. Instead, the respondents were performance artists who had applied for NEA grants but were denied funding. See 524 U.S., at 577. If this were a case in which library patrons had challenged a library's decision to install and use filtering software, it would be in the same posture as Finley. Because it is not, Finley does not control this case.

Also unlike Finley, the Government does not merely seek to control a library's discretion with respect to computers purchased with Government funds or those computers with Government-discounted Internet access. CIPA requires libraries to install filtering software on every computer with Internet access if the library receives any discount from the E-rate program or any funds from the LSTA program. If a library has 10 computers paid for by nonfederal funds and has Internet service for those computers also paid for by nonfederal funds, the library may choose not to put filtering software on any of those 10 computers. Or a library may decide to put filtering software on the 5 computers in its children's section. Or a library in an elementary school might choose to put filters on every single one of its 10 computers. But under this statute, if a library attempts to provide Internet service for even one computer through an E-rate discount, that library must put filtering software on all of its computers with Internet access, not just the one computer with E-rate discount.

This Court should not permit federal funds to be used to enforce this kind of broad restriction of First Amendment rights, particularly when such a restriction is unnecessary to accomplish Congress' stated goal. The abridgment of speech is equally obnoxious whether a rule like this one is enforced by a threat of penalties or by a threat to withhold a benefit.

I would affirm the judgment of the District Court.

References

Greenhouse, L. (2003), "Court Upholds Law to Make Libraries Use Internet Filters," *The New York Times,* June 24, p. A22.

Multnomah Public Library et al. v. *U.S* (2002) 201 F. Supp. 2d 401 (ED Pa).

Censorship, the Internet, and the Child Pornography Law of 1996: A Critique[1]

Jacques N. Catudal

When the law speaks universally, then, and a case arises on it which is not covered by the universal statement, then it is right, where the legislator fails us and has erred by over-simplicity, to correct the omission—to say what the legislator himself would have said had he been present, and would have put into his law if he had known.

Aristotle, N. Eth. V, 10, 1137b19-24.

Introduction

Agreement over the proposition that children have protection against those who would exploit them by producing child pornographic materials, especially now that such materials are quickly and widely distributed over the Internet, is not sufficient to secure agreement over the means by which to provide protections: the Child Pornography Prevention Act (CPPA) of 1996. After describing the CPPA, I shall argue that it is much more harmful than beneficial and, accordingly, that it ought to be significantly *amended*. However, some may regard as sacrilegious, or treasonous, or perhaps, as just plain wicked the mere idea of attacking any measure that really (or even putatively) protects children. So I begin by stating unequivocally that it is not my intention to offend the religious, political, or moral sensibilities of any person. In the end, I am as committed to the protection of children as any person

This essay originally appeared in *Ethics and Information Technology*, 1: 105–116, 1999. Copyright © 1999 by Kluwer Academic Publishers. Reprinted with permission.

[1] This paper was presented at the Eighth Annual Meeting of the Association for Practical and Professional Ethics, Washington National Airport Hilton Hotel, Washington, D.C. (25–27 February 1999). An earlier version was presented at a conference titled The Tangled Web: Ethical Dilemmas of the Internet, Dartmouth College, Hanover, NH (8 August 1998).

is, but with the qualification that, if possible, such protection not be accorded at the expense of forfeiting the Constitutional rights of adults.

Three main objections are presented against CPPA. First, CPPA is so broad in its proscriptions as to violate the First Amendment rights of adults; the same protections made available to children by CPPA can be provided by an amended version of the law that does not violate the First Amendment rights of adults. Second, CPPA altogether fails to provide minors and their legal guardians with the privacy rights needed to combat the harms associated with certain classes of prurient material on the Internet. So, it isn't just that CPPA provides protections to children at the expense of violating the rights of adults, it's also that the protections it provides are inadequate. Third, technological advances in home computing,[2] and Congress' failure to appreciate how prurient material may be accessed over the Internet combine with CPPA to wrongfully expose an increasing number of individuals to possible prosecution and personal ruin.

Several other objections will be registered along the way, including one aimed at the draconian punishments the law metes out to violators. But ultimately, my objective is to offer the outlines of an amended version of the law that promises not to violate the rights of adults, that affords children and adults equal and effective protection against the very harmful practices the current law cannot eradicate, and that prescribes punishments that are consistent with the tolerance necessary to support a more democratic and humane vision of the Internet.

Definitions and Scope

In conducting what might otherwise be an abstract, esoteric, and unwieldy discussion of censorship on the Internet, it will be useful to introduce and define a number of key terms and distinctions, not only for achieving greater clarity and control over the discussion, but for setting the moral and political backdrop against which it takes place. Accordingly, I begin by distinguishing between "censorship by suppression" and "censorship by deterrence." Both forms of censorship presuppose that some authorized person or group of persons (1) has judged some text (or type of text)[3] to be objectionable on moral, political, or other grounds and, (2) banned that text (or type of text), i.e., prohibited by law or decree any access to the text. The difference in the forms of censorship bears on effecting the prohibition. *Censorship by suppression* effects the prohibition by preventing the objectionable material itself from being revealed, published, or circulated; it may do this by *blocking* the material (e.g., by impeding the sending or receiving of the material), by *removing* the material to inaccessible archives, or by *destroying* the material. *Censorship by deterrence* does not prevent material from being published; indeed, material may

---

[2] The main advances I have in mind since CPPA was enacted are significantly faster processor speeds, significantly larger RAM and ROM sizes and data access times, and much faster rates of data transmission over the Internet.

[3] The word 'text' is used broadly to include print and electronic modes of expression.

be quite available to all. The prohibition is rather effected by threats of arrest, prosecution, conviction, and punishment, usually severe punishment, against those who would make objectionable material available and against those who would acquire it. Heavy fines and long imprisonment terms are typical of the prescribed legal punishments. Additionally, deterrence may be provided by threats of various forms of social disenfranchisement and personal disgrace (e.g., excommunication, professional and/or public censure, loss of reputation, loss of social standing, public humiliation, etc). In fact, violations of the censorship decree may or may not *actually* lead to arrest, prosecution, sentencing, or any degree of personal ruin; what is key is that the *threat* of these actions be taken so seriously as to wholly deter the acquisition of the objectionable material. Governments may accomplish this through "high profile" convictions,[4] or by leaking information or misinformation to the press. For example, the mere rumor that the Justice Department is reviewing thousands of America On Line (AOL) member accounts for possible violation of child pornography laws and has so far prepared more than 400 arrest warrants to be executed in the next few weeks would be quite sufficient to deter many individuals from accessing the banned materials. Censorship by suppression and censorship by deterrence are both exercised in cyberspace, though it is with the second that I shall be particularly concerned in this discussion.

The topic of Internet censorship, or more specifically, of prohibitions against acquiring or using certain words or pictures, or against expressing certain ideas deemed morally, politically, or otherwise objectionable, in email, websites, ftp sites, Usenet groups, chat rooms, and so on, presents us with a morass of unruly and distinct issues. Internet censorship can be directed by governments, through acts, statutes, and decrees that outlaw the posting of certain kinds of material, such as obscene or child pornographic materials; or it can be instituted by the private sector, say, by Internet service providers (ISPs) who refuse or suspend services to users engaged in activities that violate their terms of use.[5] Corporations, profit and non-profit, also practice censorship, as when private colleges and universities prohibit faculty, students, and staff from using certain words in their email communications—among others, those inadvertently made famous in the annals of American law by the comedian George Carlin.[6] Being so multifarious, instances of censorship on the Internet are best evaluated on a case by case basis. The focus in this essay is on recent federal legislation aimed at prurient material available on the Internet.

---

[4] See the discussion of the separate legal cases of Paul Fraser and David Hilton, pp. 109–110.

[5] A case in point is the ISP Mindspring that shut down the 'Nuremberg Files' website in February 1999. You may recall that on February 2nd, a Portland federal court awarded Planned Parenthood $107 million in damages resulting from the activities of the anti-abortionist website 'Nuremberg Files.' What is interesting is that the federal court refused Planned Parenthood's request to shut down the website; that action was taken independently by Mindspring, for activities it considered threatening and harassing, i.e., activities that violated its policies.

[6] My reference is to a comedic monologue by George Carlin titled "The Seven Dirty Words You Can't Say On Television." The daylight radio broadcast of the Carlin monologue was the subject of a Supreme Court case known as *FCC v. Pacifica Foundation* (1978). In that case, the Court ruled that the FCC did have the authority to regulate content over the airwaves and, specifically, to sanction radio stations that broadcast "indecent" material.

I use the expression "prurient material" to refer to material that is "sexually arous-ing" or that "appeals to an inordinate interest in sex." My usage covers pornographic, child pornographic, and obscene material or, in other words, all sexually arousing mate-rial whether such material currently finds protection in American law or not.[7]

Second, references to prurient material available in cyberspace are to visual mate-rial. Thus, there is no discussion of prurient sound files (e.g., WAV files). Again, of the visual material, I'm only concerned with still images, not with moving images (e.g., not with AVI or MPG files), and only with those still images that are found in Usenet. Usenet is one of several data communication services that constitute the Internet; oth-ers include the World Wide Web, email, and file transfer.[8] Usenet is a collection of more than 35,000 topically named discussion groups or "newsgroups." It has been estimat-ed that it is accessed by more than 15 million people a day in more than 100 countries.[9]

So, at bottom, I shall be exclusively concerned with recent federal legislation aimed at a very particular kind of file found in some newsgroups, viz., the binary file. The binary file is a file containing instructions in a computer-readable format, capable of conversion into a graphical (and, therefore, viewable) format such as JPEG or GIF; my focus is on such binary files as one may find in the "alt" hierarchy of newsgroups that partially constitute Usenet. The "alt" designation, which consti-tutes one of several top-level Usenet classes, is short for "alternative," suggesting that the newsgroups it includes exist outside of the standard newsgroup cate-gories such as <comp>, <rec>, <soc>, and so on. Any of the newsgroups listed in Figure 1 may contain the binary files that are the subject of this essay.[10] So my dis-cussion addresses a federal law aimed at prohibiting access to "alt" binary files of just the sort that, when they are converted to graphical format, constitute a par-ticular kind of prurient image. Likewise, I am concerned here with only some laws.

A reasonably complete examination of recent American (federal) law aimed at regulating access to prurient material in cyberspace would yield three acts. Even though I shall be focusing on "The Child Pornography Prevention Act (CPPA) of 1996," no account would be complete without at least passing reference to "The Communications Decency Act (CDA) of 1996" and "The Child On-line Protection Act

---

[7] Specifically, my use does not preserve the legal distinction between obscene and non-obscene sexually explicit material as set forth in *Miller v. California* (1973), nor the distinction set forth in *United States v. X-citement Video, Inc.* (1994) between protected non-obscene "pornography" and prohibited "child pornography." Constitutionally protected pornographic images, that is, porno-graphic images that pass the three-prong Miller test, loose all protection whenever minors are depicted as engaging in sexually explicit acts, precisely to prevent the sexual exploitation of minors.

[8] My focus on Usenet avoids, among other complications, those introduced by commercial pornographic ventures on the World Wide Web.

[9] Throughout this discussion, I rely on *Webster's New World Dictionary of Computer Terms* (6th edition), edited by Bryan Pfaffenberger (New York: Simon & Schuster, 1997) for the definition of technical terms.

[10] Your Internet service provider (ISP) isn't obligated to carry any of the "alt" Usenet groups; for better or for worse, depending on your point of view, your access to what is available on the Internet may already be limited. (I suggest you ask your ISP whether the service engages in censorship.) Further, not all "alt" newsgroups contain prurient material, for example, (alt.binaries.pictures.aviation); indeed, there are many "alt" newsgroups without a prurient orientation at all. On the other hand, it is also true both that Figure 1 does not contain anything like an exhaustive list of the "'alt" groups devoted to prurient material (some of the more offending or disturbing group names are not included), and that many Usenet groups devoted to the exchange of prurient material do not belong to the "alt" class of newsgroups.

alt.binaries.erotica	alt.binaries.nospam.sappho	alt.binaries.pictures.erotica.lolita
alt.binaries. erotica. blondes	alt.binaries.nospam.teenfem	alt.binaries.pictures.erofica.supermodels
alt.binaries.erotica.bondage	alt.binaries.pictures.brunette	alt.binaries.pictures.erotica.tasteless
alt.binaries.erofica.cartoons	alt.binaries.pictures.celebrities	alt.binaries.pictures.erotica.teen.female
alt.binaries.erotica.male	alt. binaries .pictures . erotica. amateur	alt.binaries.pictures.erotica.voyerism
alt.binaries. erotica. female	alt. binaries. pictures. erotica.exhibitioni sm.	alt.binaries.pictures.erotica.young

Figure 1 Selected "alt" newsgroups.

(COPA) of 1998." As is well known, CDA was found to be unconstitutional by the Supreme Court of the United States in June of 1997. COPA is intended to be its constitutionally more robust successor, though on 1 February 1999, U. S. District Judge Lowell A. Reed, Jr. blocked COPA; the Justice Department had until the end of March to appeal Judge Lowell's decision. This appeal will constitute a final determination on just how robust COPA really is.

In addition to the laws already mentioned, it's important to note two recent bills, one introduced in the House by Rep. Frank (R., New Jersey), H. R. 368, the "Safe Schools Internet Act," its counterpart in the Senate introduced by John McCaine (R., Arizona), S. 97, the "Children Internet Protection Act." Both bills, if passed into law, would require public elementary and secondary schools to install blocking software on computers connected to the Internet. Frank's bill would also force public libraries to install blocking software on computers with Internet access.

The Child Pornography Prevention Act of 1996

The Supreme Court's June 1997 decision striking down CDA as unconstitutional, and the more recent District Court decision blocking COPA, may have given many netizens a false sense of victory, since CPPA remains in effect. Indeed, CPPA passed constitutional muster in Federal District Court (Northern California) in August 1997[11] and, on 27 January 1999, was upheld by the 1st Circuit Court of Appeals in Boston, overturning another District Court ruling made last year.[12] CPPA aims at regulating the use of computers in the production and dissemination of child pornography and is, upon close inspection, remarkably restrictive.[13] The Act makes it a crime to knowingly send, receive, distribute, reproduce, sell, or possess with intent to sell, by any means, including computer, any child pornography, and makes it a crime to possess more than three child pornographic images. Significantly, the Act greatly broadens the definition of "child pornography" to include entire cate-

---

[11] An appeal, filed by the Free Speech Coalition, is pending before the 9th Circuit Court of Appeals.

[12] On 30 March 1998, Judge Gene Carter of the Federal District Court in Portland, Maine, issued an opinion stating that key portions of the Child Pornography Prevention Act were unconstitutional.

[13] The Child Pornography Prevention Act was introduced in the Senate by Orin Hatch (R., Utah) as S. 1237 during the first session of the 104th Congress, specifically on 13 September 1995, and in the House of Representatives a year later, on 30 September 1996, by Joseph Kennedy (D., Massachusetts). The bill amends several sections of title 18, United States Code, dealing with child pornography.

gories of images that many would judge *not* to be *child* pornographic, and that some would judge *not* to be *pornographic* at all. So, many who now believe themselves engaged in a legal activity, following the demise of CDA and the recent blocking of COPA, may in fact be breaking the law. For the moment, CPPA is the most robust and stringent federal law we have regulating prurient material on the Internet.

One of CPPA's more controversial features is that it extends the definition of child pornography to include visual depictions of sexually explicit conduct that do not involve minors. Its definition of "child pornography" is as follows:

> *"child pornography" means any visual depiction, including any photograph, film, video, picture, or computer or computer-generated image or picture, whether made or produced by electronic, mechanical, or other means, of sexually explicit conduct, where—*
>
> (A) *the production of such visual depiction involves the use of a minor engaging in sexually explicit conduct;*
>
> (B) *such visual depiction is, or appears to be, of a minor engaging in sexually explicit conduct; or*
>
> (C) *such visual depiction has been created, adapted, or modified to appear that an identifiable minor is engaging in sexually explicit conduct; or*
>
> (D) *such visual depiction is advertised, promoted, presented, described, or distributed in such a manner that conveys the impression that the material is or contains a visual depiction of a minor engaging in sexually explicit conduct;*

Paragraph (A) re-asserts the prohibition against the object traditionally regarded as constituting child pornography. What has always been (and continues to be) outlawed are images of *actual* children posing in lewd or lascivious ways[14] or, images of *actual* children engaged in sexual conduct.[15] I call these "Category A" images; they occur in many newsgroups—and possessing more than three of them is illegal. However, to appreciate what is controversial in CPPA, consider the following description of what I shall dub a "Category B" image.

The photograph is of a very young looking 19-year-old woman in pigtails, wearing only white knee socks and red "Mary Janes," seated on the floor of what appears

---

[14] Hence, the uproar on 17 February 1999, led by the Conservative watchdog group, Morality in Media, concerning a billboard advertisement featuring children's underwear by Calvin Klein. The issue turns on whether the photograph (depicting two very young children wearing only Klein's brand of underwear) is *plausibly interpreted* to be sexually suggestive or lewd. Note that the firm withdrew its advertisement the next day. Another series of Calvin Klein billboards was the subject of a similar protest two years ago; in that case, the depictions involved pubescent kids "posing suggestively" in Calvin Klein jeans.

[15] Though "sexual conduct" is not defined in CPPA, the terms "sexual act" and "sexual contact" are defined in section 2246 of title 18, United States Code.

to be her bedroom, surrounded by teddy bears, dolls, and other toys. She is wide-eyed and smiling; her pigtails are held together by large red ribbons.

Instances of this "Little Girl" genre of pornography can be found in the newsgroups. The "Little Girl" type does not, by definition, involve little girls or minors of any age; the type is characterized by young looking adults or by computer-generated simulations of children. What is significant about Category B images of the "Little Girl" type, and often overlooked by critics of the law, is that CPPA outlaws them *only in that case where they are "pandered" as child pornography*; in other words, CPPA provides a defendant with an affirmative defense if he or she can show that the offending material was not distributed "in such a manner as to convey the impression that it is or contains a visual depiction of a minor engaging in sexually explicit conduct." In this regard, then, CPPA is consistent with the Supreme Court's decision in *New York v. Ferber* (1982) that "...valid alternatives to banned child pornography include pictures of adults who look younger than they are, or simulations" (*Ferber*, 458 U. S. at 763). This is not what many critics of the law would have you believe, including the American Civil Liberties Union.[16] As we shall see, CPPA's provision of this affirmative defense not only deflects a potentially devastating criticism but, more importantly, helps us better understand the issues that subtend it and that may have moved its authors.

In any case, we are left with the "Little Girl" genre of pornography, which only becomes child pornography when pandered as such.[17] Now, while such a genre might strike some as perverse or deranged, or as just plain silly, one putative reason for allowing its existence is to *protect* children from sexual exploitation (and worse harms).[18] For it may be assumed, plausibly, that among some segment of humanity there will always be an interest in, or desire for, depictions of naked minors, or of minors engaged in sexual activity. Assume further that such an interest or desire will almost always be regarded as problematic; the question then is how best to deal with the problem.

One way, consistent with the Supreme Court's statement in Ferber concerning young-looking adults and "simulations," would be to make more severe the penalties for use of Category A images, while permitting Category B images. The prediction is that children would be better protected because, from the pornographer's point of view, it would make little sense to risk long incarceration and heavy fines for producing Category A images, given the legality of Category B images; but there are difficulties with this approach.

First, to be effective—by which I mean to really protect children—the particular Category B image would have to be convincing or, more exactly, arousing, as an instance of simulated *child* pornography. It will not do to use 28-year-old models who look like 28-year-old models, no matter what the setting or what the props.

---

[16] American Civil Liberties Union, "Free Speech Advocates Appeal Decision Upholding So-Called 'Porn Prevention Law'," 3 October 1997 (http://www.aclu.org/news/n100397b.htm).

[17] There are other such genres that make use of the "young looking adult," among them the "school girl," "the cheerleader," and "the doll." See also, n. 26.

[18] I am not attributing this rationale to the Supreme Court; the Court, no doubt, was more concerned about the First Amendment issue.

Young looking 18 year olds might be very much in demand by pornographers. Yet, even they might not look young enough if the purpose were to depict very young children. As Dr. Victor Cline stated before the Senate Committee on 4 June 1996, "most pedophiles and child molesters have special preferences with respect to child pornography, in terms of age, physical appearance, and sexual acts or poses of depicted minors."[19] Indeed, prepubescent youth would be left wholly unprotected by this approach.

Another way of putting the point is to say that Category A and Category B images represent two different kinds of prurient image, where the difference consists of the type of audience whose sexual feelings are being aroused. Thus, audiences aroused by a Category A image (say, an actual naked 7-year-old boy) may not be aroused by a Category B image (say, of the "Little Girl" sort earlier described), and vice versa. And so, I believe, the strategy could leave the very young unprotected.

Second, it could be argued that permitting Category B images will sanction or condone an attitude toward "simulated children" as objects of sexual gratification that will be transferable to actual children; for this reason alone, some might conclude that we ought not permit Category B images. While I am not prepared to support such an argument, the empirical question(s) it suggests really ought to be studied. However, such study is made impossible by CPPA itself, to the extent that it would require the use of illegal images.

For example, on 29 January 1999, Paul V. Fraser, a psychotherapist from Rome, New York, was convicted of possessing a large, computer-based collection of child pornographic images. Fraser's defense was that "the materials were for his work with a volunteer county committee called the Pornography Interdiction Work Group *and* that the district attorney's office knew what he was doing."[20] The point to note, assuming Fraser's defense to be truthful, is that such a defense is legally irrelevant. As the prosecutor in the case has stated, "Fraser was never authorized to collect such materials."[21] There are many other cases like Fraser's, including that of a reporter who collected child pornographic materials for a story he was writing and, most significantly, a computer repairman, David Hilton, from Norway, Maine, who initiated a collaboration with law enforcement by repeatedly turning over child pornographic materials he had obtained on the Internet, and by advising authorities on the location of child pornographic sites. The law prohibits all persons from possessing three or more child pornographic files, with the exception of persons officially authorized to enforce the law. In any case, Fraser is probably correct in maintaining that his conviction "will have a chilling effect, if not completely halt any legitimate research in the area of child pornography on the Internet."[22]

---

[19] "Child Pornography Threatens the Physical and Mental Health and the Well-being of Children," *Child Pornography Prevention Act of 1995*, http://thomas.loc.gov/cgi-bin/ cpquery/l?cpIO4:./temp/, 5 August 1998, p. 4. Its important to note that Dr. Cline's work in "the treatment of sexual addictions" is featured by the Conservative group Morality in Media. See, for example, <http://www.mim.org>.

[20] Associated Press, "Therapist Convicted of Child Porn", <http://wire.ap.org>, 10 February 1999, 23:05 EST.

[21] *Ibid.*

[22] *Ibid.*

While I shall later argue that legalizing Category B images would not preclude providing as much protection to minors as CPPA currently provides, given certain modifications in the law, it is with the prohibition against "Category C" images that serious difficulties with the law begin to emerge. Category C images are those that appear to depict an identifiable minor engaging in sexually explicit conduct. They include the innocent picture of an identifiable child altered to create the impression or appearance that the child is engaging in sexual conduct; and the flawlessness of the alteration is not to be minimized, given currently available software. The legal case of the moment is precisely the case just mentioned, that of David Hilton. Hilton was arrested in the Fall of 1997 and "charged with possessing 63 illegal pictures downloaded from the Internet." At least one of those pictures was a Category C image, "a 'morphed' photo featuring the head and upper body of a nude young girl, affixed to the body of an adult who was engaged in sexual intercourse."[23]

On 30 March 1998, Judge Gene Carter of the Federal District Court in Portland, Maine issued an 11-page opinion in the context of *United States v. Hilton*, stating that key portions of the Child Pornography Prevention Act were unconstitutional. "Carter found that the key term, 'appears to be' a minor, is impermissibly vague because an ordinary viewer's determination of the age of a person depicted in the image would be highly subjective."[24] He stated that "the law's definition of pornography 'creates substantial uncertainty' for viewers presented with sexual materials depicting adults." Perhaps most significantly, the court found that the definition of child pornography "would improperly 'sweep within its provisions' much material that is constitutionally protected," i.e., nonobscene pornography.[25]

Carter's decision was appealed to the U.S. Court of Appeals for the First Circuit in Boston; on 30 January 1999, the Court of Appeals upheld CPPA. "The Appeals Court stated that CPPA is not so vague that a consumer could not understand what type of pornography is illegal."[26] However, note that Judge Carter's objections had not been directed at the vagueness of CPPA itself, i.e., at the words used to articulate the law, nor were they directed at vagueness concerning the "type" of pornography that is made illegal. The issue of vagueness arises in the context of a viewer's ability to determine whether a particular photograph is or is not of the type that CPPA makes illegal. It is that issue that is central to Carter's objections and that the Court of Appeals has simply chosen to circumvent.

The main difficulty with this part of the law is discussed in Argument 2. It has mainly to do with my analysis of the harms created by the production and distribution of prurient images of the Category C type. The view I later develop is that the best way to protect against these harms is to provide stronger privacy protections for children and adults. For the moment, it may be sufficient to reflect on the

---

[23] Carl S. Kaplan, "Differing Rulings on Child Porn Law Set Up Potential Supreme Court Case," *Cyber Law Journal of The New York Times*, http://www.nytimes.com/ (10 April 1998), p. 2.

[24] Carl S. Kaplan, *ibid*.

[25] Carl S. Kaplan, *ibid*.

[26] David Sharp, "Court Upholds Child Porn Law," Associated Press, <http://wire.ap.org>, 30 January 1999, 03:36 EST.

fact that any picture of any child or adult found on the Internet can be altered to produce a prurient image.[27] It's something to think about before putting your kid's picture on your website.

Section D of CPPA is mainly addressed to providers (not necessarily producers) of pornography. In the context of the Internet, it may be interpreted to suggest a distinct type of image; I call it the Category "D" image. The typical Category D image is that of a fully clothed minor not engaged in sexually explicit behavior, nor posing in a lewd or sexually offensive manner. The most striking feature of the Category D image (as such) is that it unambiguously depicts a minor; and the significance of this feature is perhaps best appreciated by comparison to the function served by website "teasers." The latter are images that one first encounters on the homepage (or "initial point of entry") of pornographic websites. The homepage is designed to entice or excite the viewer into clicking on to the next page, which may contain photographs of the same, or of a more explicit nature. Typically, at some point in the "tease," the viewer is asked to provide a credit card number as a condition of going any further.

As I noted, I am not concerned in this essay with issues pertaining to the World Wide Web, or with commercial distribution of prurient materials, though the issue of the prurient homepage is a very serious one. The child who mistakenly types in the wrong top-level generic domain, say, ".com," rather than ".gov," in trying to get to the White House website is not well served. However, this issue would be more fittingly handled in a discussion of COPA.

Nonetheless, Category D images may also be found in newsgroups, when, for example, photographs are scanned from a magazine or book, and posted to a newsgroup in such a way as to preserve the temporal order or sequence of the action depicted in the photographs, or when the individual frames of a video are posted as separate "snapshots" in a way that preserves the temporal sequence of the action. Often, the first few images in such a series may contain fully clothed adolescents who are not posing in a lewd manner, nor engaged in sexual conduct of any sort; for example, two fully clothed 14-year-old kids may just be sitting on a couch, talking. These are followed by increasingly revealing photographs such that, at some point, there is no question as to the child pornographic nature of the pictures. The question is whether the initial photographs, those perfectly decent and innocent images, are child pornographic? Couldn't the argument be made that, insofar as they are found in a newsgroup devoted to the exchange of prurient images, such images are child pornographic?

I believe that the sponsors of the Child Pornography Prevention Act don't think the questions fundamentally important or relevant. Their contention is that the most effective way to protect children against the harms created by child pornography is to ban any material whose effect would be "to whet the appetites" of child sexual abusers. With this contention, we begin to understand the motivation for banning images depicting not only minors, but "apparent" minors, simulations, morphed images, and "innocent" images of the sort just described.

---

[27] This includes those faculty photographs that some administrators insist on posting to the faculty pages of university websites, with or without a faculty member's knowledge and, therefore, consent.

Argument 1: CPPA Violates the First Amendment

Obviously, the perspective here shifts from banning child pornography so that children do not become the victimized subjects of such images, to protecting children from those whose appetites are sustained by child pornography. In the former case, the objective is to censor child pornographic images (photographs or drawings of actual minors), on the assumption that the depicted minor is harmed by their production. In the most horrific of instances, such as the child pornography ring that terrorized Belgium a few years ago, the harm to the victims included physical pain and death. But psychological harm to those whose victimization was neither physically brutal nor violent, victims, that is, tricked into revealing their bodies, need be no less horrific, for even then victims may later report having felt tremendous fear, even terror; and, in the long-term, there may be damage to the victim's self-esteem, as well as severe lasting mental distress. The harm may also assume a social dimension where the victim's reputation is affected.

Now, in citing these physiological, psychological, and social harms to children depicted in child pornographic images, I say that it "may" happen, not that it always does or must. While I don't wish to discuss here the admittedly controversial thesis that there can be child erotic images whose production does not harm the children depicted in them, images that are visually (aesthetically) remarkable, I do wish to raise the question of what harm minors are caused by images in which they are not *actually* depicted in sexually explicit conduct (Category B images), or if actually depicted, so depicted in the absence of lewdness, lasciviousness, or sexual conduct of any sort (Category D images).

Of course, the sponsors of the Child Pornography Prevention Act have an answer. Their objective is to censor child pornography (in their broad definition of the term) not only because the depicted minor is harmed *by their production*, but because their availability leads to still further harms to minors *by whetting the appetites of child sexual abusers*. Thus, CPPA's ultimate objective is eradicating "the secondary effects" of child pornography, specifically, child sexual abuse. Of course, this is not to assert that the sponsors of the law believe that child pornography is the sole cause of child sexual abuse, but that it is *a* cause.

In upholding the Child Pornography Prevention Act in August 1997, U. S. District Judge Samuel Conti wrote the following:

> The court finds that the CPPA is designed to counteract the effect that such material has on its viewers, on children, and to society as a whole, and is not intended to regulate or outlaw the ideas themselves. If child pornography is targeted by the regulation, it is due to the effect of the pornography on innocent children, not to the nature of the materials themselves, especially if that pornography contains computer generated images of children.[28]

---

28 American Civil Liberties Union, *ibid.*

But surely Judge Conti cannot believe that an image that is otherwise constitutionally protected (that is, that passes the three-pronged Miller test) looses protection when its effect is to cause children to be sexually abused. For it may very well be, however disturbing, that an 11-year-old boy's school photograph would whet the appetites of a pedophile; yet, surely we don't want to ban such photographs.[29] It should not be a crime for a parent to post this photograph to a website, though I do believe it is not advisable. But let's be charitable to the proponents of the law: they would not ban *any* image that might cause a pedophile to sexually abuse children, but only those that are *child pornographic*; but what are these? They cannot be defined as those that would cause a pedophile to sexually abuse children, on pain of vicious circularity.

Further, the difficulty in accepting Judge Conti's argument is that it begs a fundamental question, namely, whether there is any plausible evidence to establish a causal link between the consumption of child pornography by an individual and subsequent predatory sexual behavior aimed at children?[30] Even in the strongest case, where we assume the individual in question is a pedophile, and where we grant that the pedophile's appetites are "whetted" or "inflamed" by child pornographic images, what evidence have we for claiming that such an appetite will be sated at the horrifying expense of actual children?

Note that one might even concede Dr. Shirley O'Brien's point, cited in the Senate's report on child pornography, that "a direct relationship exists between pornographic literature and the sexual molestation of young children. Law-enforcement officers say they routinely find pornographic materials when they investigate sex crimes against children."[31] Indeed, it is O'Brien who must be credited with advancing the idea of the "cycle" of child pornography. The idea is that children's defenses may be lowered by sharing with them pictures of other children engaged in sexual

---

[29] There exists what may be termed a "school girl" genre of child pornography that may be either of the Category "A" (i.e., actual child) or "B" (young-looking adult) type. Many of these photographs are of fully clothed girls (that is, of girls in school uniforms) who are neither engaged in sexual activity or lewdly posing. Indeed, they may simply be walking on their way to school, or playing in the school yard. It is not the photographs that are disturbing here.

[30] In "Healing Sexual and Pornography Addictions," one of the Government's expert witnesses at hearings looking into child pornography, Victor B. Cline (a licensed clinical psychologist from Salt Lake City, Utah) testified that "Some of the 'experts' who publicly suggest that pornography has no effects are just unaware of the research and studies suggesting harm. Others really do not believe what they are asserting. Still others will only reluctantly admit to the possibility of harm from 'violent pornography'." First, I think that Cline's remark may have the effect of "poisoning the well." Second, some researchers (not surprisingly, the wave of researchers that responded critically to the report issued by the 1986 Attorney General's Commission on Pornography) suggest that pornography (even child pornography) may have socially beneficial effects; other researchers suggest harmful effects. I find no consensus with regard to the more specific question of whether the use of child pornography by an individual can cause that individual to sexually abuse a child. At this time, it is simply misleading to suggest that there is a consensus one way or the other. By the way, there's a difficulty here for Conservatives—for the more they press a causal connection, the less they can argue for the moral agency of the pedophile; and the latter is as important to them as preserving the moral agency of homosexuals by maintaining that they choose their sexual orientation. Conservatives cannot have it both ways.

[31] "Child Pornography Threatens the Physical and Mental Health . . ." *ibid.*, p. 2. The question remains, what is the nature of this "direct relationship"?

activity; in turn when the former children eventually engage in sexual activity, pictures may be made of the event, pictures that may later be used to weaken the defenses of other children, and so on.

What all of this suggests, however, is not that child pornography causes pedophiles to sexually abuse children, but that pedophiles may *use* child pornography to sexually abuse children. Yet, instead of simply criminalizing the *production* of Category A images, and criminalizing the use of all categories of images defined in the CPPA to sexually abuse children, Congress chose instead to prohibit the production of all categories of images. So, *my claim is that prohibiting the production of Categories B and D images doesn't protect children anymore than does prohibiting the use of these same images to sexually abuse children. However, prohibiting the production of these categories of images does violate the First Amendment rights of adults, whereas prohibiting their use to sexually abuse children does not.* There is a compromise that allows us to protect children and that simultaneously allows us to protect the First Amendment rights of adults; but this is not what Congress chose to do.

In fact, there is a reason why it was important for some in Congress to prohibit the production of Categories B and D images, and it has little to do with protecting children. What it does have to do with is more a matter of how rapid advances in computer hardware and software have made it exceptionally difficult to win convictions in cases of child pornography. In *United States v. Kimbrough* (1995), "the first ever federal trial involving charges of importation of child pornography by computer," the Justice Department was confronted with a new defense strategy; it argued that "the Government had the burden of proving that each item of alleged child pornography did, in fact, depict an actual minor rather than an adult made to look like one," and further, "that the defendant should be acquitted if the government did not meet that burden."[32] While the government was able "to meet that burden" in *United States v. Kimbrough*, Deputy Assistant Attorney General Kevin Di Gregory testified before the Senate Committee, "If the government must continue to prove beyond a reasonable doubt that mailed photos, smuggled magazines or videos, traded pictures, and computer images being transmitted over the Internet, are indeed actual depictions of an actual minor engaging in the sex portrayed, then there could be a built-in reasonable doubt argument in every child exploitation/ pornography prosecution." And that is what best explains the motivation behind the construction and passage of CPPA.

Argument 2: CPPA's Protections Are Inadequate

Of course, we do need to protect children from the sort of exploitation presented by child pornography, but greater familiarity with prurient material on the Internet argues against construing minors as a special class of individuals needing protec-

---

[32] "B. Computer-Generated Child Pornography Poses the Same Threat to the Well-Being of Children as Photographic Child Pornography," *Child Pornography Prevention Act of 1995*, http://thomas.loc.gov/cgi-bin/cpquery/1?cp104:/temp/cp104o4dl:e43450: (5 August 1998), p. 4.

tion. Indeed, there are thousands of adults who, unknowingly, have had revealing pictures of themselves taken and posted to the Internet for the whole world to see. The technologies of concealment and magnification (I mean here, for example, miniature still and motion cameras, high-power telephoto lenses, night-vision lenses, and other high-tech monitoring devices) have come a very long way, not merely in their technical aspects but, as significantly, in their affordability for an increasing number of consumers.[33] And so images taken of unsuspecting persons who are showering or bathing, changing clothes at home or trying on clothes at a department store, tanning on the beach in New Jersey or on Crete, driving in an automobile or walking at the mall—all of these types, and many more, are now found in the Usenet groups.

On the other hand, intimate photographs taken by a former boyfriend or ex-husband, whether yesterday or 20 years ago, did not require the camera to be concealed; they perhaps only required an implicit trust, all too easily rendered moot with the passage of time and/or circumstances. Prurient images of sleeping subjects, or of subjects passed out from too much alcohol, don't require concealed cameras either. The point is that adults have a right to as much protection from embarrassing and damaging violations of personal privacy as do minors.

Further, adults can be baited or tricked just as easily as children into revealing their bodies, i.e., without fully understanding the import of their actions. Flattery, affection, curiosity, sexual excitement, alcohol, and the dangerous pleasure that comes from doing something new, risqué, or forbidden—one or more of these may lead one to lower one's guard, so to speak. The passing pleasure can quickly become a long-lasting horror.

Nor do you have to be a celebrity, such as Alyssa Milano, Brad Pitt, or Hilary Clinton, to need protection from exceptionally lewd and disturbing forms of morphing. Indeed, celebrities have Cyber-Trackers, an organization recently formed, amid great publicity, to hunt down websites that carry celebrity fakes;[34] and in some states celebrities may benefit from new protections especially tailored to fit the privacy needs of public figures. But consider that just about any photograph of any identifiable person can be convincingly manipulated in such a way as to portray the pictured person in a sexually compromising position. So the problem addressed

---

[33] The advance of these technologies of concealment and magnification also increasingly undermines any recourse one might have to "the reasonable expectation of privacy" as traditionally construed. How reasonable is the expectation of privacy in a world around which revolve government and commercial satellites equipped with high-resolution cameras? For example, it is public knowledge that Canada's RADARSTAT-2 has "the ability to zero in on objects as small as three meters," and that U. S. military and intelligence satellites can do considerably better than that ("Canada, U. S. in Standoff Over Too-Smart Satellite," *San Jose Mercury News* (18 February 1999, 4:00 p.m. PST) <http://www.mercurycenter.com/breaking/docs/074537.htm>).

[34] Lynn Milano, Alyssa's mother, says she recently founded Cyber-Trackers upon being told by Alyssa's 12-year-old brother that prurient fake photographs of his sister were on the Internet and being emailed to him. Cyber-Trackers has combated the sale of prurient fakes by threatening legal action against ISPs that carry them. Mitchel Karmarck, Alyssa Milano's attorney, states, "If you're profiting off of someone else's name or image, you're gonna be found and you're gonna be prosecuted, unless you cease doing so" (WTXF, FOX Philadelphia Evening News, 21 February 1999,10:00 p.m.). Note that Karmack here seeks to protect his client's *proprietary interest* in her name and likeness; the issue for many celebrities is money. The private citizen will probably appeal to a right of privacy to protect other interests, such as peace of mind and reputation, though it's conceivable that a proprietary interest may also be involved.

by the prohibition of Category C images in CPPA isn't just a problem for children. We all need protection, children and adults, for the power that resides in the Internet-savvy user is simply awesome. What is needed, in this context, is a law that prohibits what is harmful to all human beings, irrespective of age, of gender, of race, and not just what is "harmful to minors."

Congress' appeal to what is "harmful to minors" is too obscure and, in any case, too narrow. It is also much too transparent, particularly at a time in our history when increasing numbers of politicians are demanding that minors be tried as adults for capital offenses. What we need, and what is bound to present us with a truly difficult challenge, is a comprehensive law that can better balance, on the one hand, the privacy rights of individuals, and on the other, the free speech rights of individuals. That is the challenge.

Still, it might be argued that this plea for greater privacy protections, while perhaps having some merit, misses the point of providing greater protections against the harms caused by child pornography and, in particular, by Category C images. The greatest of these harms are those associated with child sexual abuse, and greater privacy protections are simply irrelevant to combating this offense.

I must disagree. First, in so far as child pornography is thought to contribute to child sexual abuse, minors can be provided with full legal protection by making illegal the use of any prurient material for the purpose of seduction. Second, part of the harm that is done to a minor depicted in a Category C image stems from the fact that his or her privacy may have been violated. This recognition is important because a privacy violation of this sort may constitute a logically or conceptually prior harm to the sexual abuse that results from the use of the image, in the sense that the image contributes to the possibility of the abuse. In other words, the seduction of children involving the use of Category C images, as suggested by O'Brien's "cycle of child pornography," is deterred if the production and distribution of such images is made illegal; I am suggesting that such production and distribution should be made illegal, whether or not such images may be used to seduce children, on the grounds that they violate the privacy of the identifiable minors depicted in them. So, by addressing the issue of privacy violations, we also address the issue of sexual abuse; but the privacy issue as it arises in the context of Category C images is most effectively addressed by applying the protections to all persons, and not just children. In that way, we avoid the difficulties noted in Judge Carter's legitimate objections to CPPA, most notably, the viewer's ability to determine whether the image is of an adult or a minor. With comprehensive privacy protections, such difficulties would not arise.

Argument 3: CPPA Can Harm Our Children

There is another profoundly serious, if somewhat ironic, side to the law we have been discussing. The very people who might be harmed by this law are the very people it was meant to protect, and/or their parents. This is so partly because the people who made the law (1) have lost touch with the reality of the pubescent child growing up in this America and (2) show little understanding of how the Internet works.

Typical middle-class, computer-literate, pubescent children are not only inundated with sexual imagery—on TV, in the movies, on bus stop billboards, and on the Internet—but also interpret their world in sexual terms. The typical 12-year-old does have a sexual appetite; but the collision of that appetite with the Internet is something to be concerned about, especially when it's understood just how easy Congress has made it for that child to become a felon.

Remember that among its provisions, which are particularly aimed at regulating the use of computers for the exchange of prurient material, CPPA makes it illegal to possess more than 3 child pornographic images. There are two points we need to consider in connection with this provision: First, to a 12-year-old boy, for example, the image of a 16-year-old girl is the image of a significantly older woman and, indeed, an image that may be "preferable" to that of an "aged" 18 or 21 year old. So, it shouldn't be surprising to find computer-literate pubescent minors cruising binary newsgroups for what the government defines as child pornography. Second, it is exceptionally easy for the computer-literate pubescent child to download 3 such files. Indeed, such a child could download 30, or 300, or even 3,000 files, in no time at all—and each might be convertible to a full color, high quality, image. Indeed, to anyone with a computer that isn't more than a year old connected to the Internet via a home cable modem (as an increasing number of families have), downloading 3,000 binary files in less than an hour is easily accomplished, and that will include the time it takes to convert the file from binary to viewable JPEG or GIF.[35]

Of course, it's going to take our 12 year old considerably more time to view the files than it did to download them. Prior to this viewing, our 12 year old doesn't know what's been downloaded; the names of the newsgroups serve only as rough indications of their content. Even if the newsgroups more likely to contain child pornographic files were avoided, it's just about guaranteed, given Congress' definition, and the fact that all kinds of people from all over the world post all kinds of prurient files to (and across) the newsgroups, that among the 3,000 downloaded pictures, 3 or more are going to be child pornographic. And recall that it is a violation of the law to possess 3 or more child pornographic files—it doesn't matter whether you've viewed them or not. (The crime is not in the viewing, but in the possession, transmission, etc.). So, it's likely that our 12 year old has violated the law without knowing it; or rather that you, the parent and rightful owner of the computer, have violated the law, and we know that ignorance of the law is no excuse.

What we are talking about here is not the commission of a misdemeanor; it is a grave crime, a felony punishable by 10 years in prison. The parent will, of course, proclaim his innocence, through lawyers who may or may not understand how the Internet works, and/or who may or may not have a knowledge of applicable law. In any case, it won't matter because the parent will be guilty; there are no extenuating circumstances that can be appealed to.

---

[35] Maximum data transmission speed on the @Home cable network, for example, is 10 megabits per second. Actual data transmission speed depends on such factors as processor speed, amount of Random-Access Memory, amount of available storage space, and time of day or night.

The local (and perhaps even the national) media will no doubt report, truly, that you had thousands of pornographic pictures in your computer; few people would understand the relative meaninglessness of this fact. The media will know about your case because arrests are a matter of public record and/or because the District Attorney needs to let people know that she's doing her job. In any case, when word gets around, you will surely seem to be the scum of the earth to your neighbors and to some of your friends, particularly if you try to blame your own kid for the situation. Some might even call you a pedophile or a child molester; many will think it. Some might say that a person like you doesn't deserve children—shouldn't be trusted with children—and some might try to do something about it on grounds that you are unfit to be a parent.

Congress could not have considered how quickly computer technology develops; nor could Congress have considered the children and younger people who use this technology daily. This law is devastating the lives of very good people; and such a law, no matter how effective it may be in preventing harm from coming to children (and that is questionable) is, on moral and prudential grounds alone, unacceptable.

Conclusion

An amended law would prohibit the production of Category A photographs, and forbid the use of all categories of child pornography for the purpose of encouraging any minor to engage in sexual conduct. Additionally, an amended law would provide privacy protections to all identifiable individuals, adults and minors, by requiring the consent of depicted individuals before any image involving nudity could be posted to any newsgroup. The judgment as to whether an image depicting an identifiable individual is or is not of a prurient nature would ultimately reside with the depicted person. Again, where more than one identifiable individual is depicted, the judgment by any one individual that the image is prurient would be sufficient to prohibit publication of the image. Here it may be argued that there would be no issue of requiring the consent of minors, or more appropriately, of their legal guardians, since prurient images of them remain illegal; however, since not all photographs of minors involving nudity are prurient, the provision requiring consent would guard against violations of privacy of a sort closely related to that involved in the non-consensual publication of prurient images.

These features of an amended law represent only a few of the elements of a more comprehensive and more just approach to dealing with the problems presented by child pornography and, more generally, by the prurient. Naturally, the features are not without problems, and a great deal of work remains to be done. It should be clear, however, that in the age of the Internet, the problem of child pornography, like so many others arising in a visual medium, must be construed to involve violations of privacy; indeed, such violations should be counted among the most basic of the harms we should seek to prevent. It is therefore surprising that in the zealous rush to stamp out prurience (by appeal to the notion of material "harmful to minors"), privacy violations have not been given any consideration.

References

American Civil Liberties Union. Free Speech Advocates Appeal Decision Upholding So-Called "Porn Prevention Law." <http://www.aclu.org/news/nlO039b.htm>, 3 October 1997.

Associated Press. Therapist Convicted of Child Porn. <http:// wire.ap.org>, 10 February 1999.

V. Cline. Child Pornography Threatens the Physical and Mental Health and the Well-Being of Children. *Child Pornography Prevention Act of 1995*. <http://thomas.loc.gov/cgibin/cpquery/l?cplO4:./temp/>, 5 August 1998.

C.S. Kaplan. Differing Rulings on Child Porn Law Set Up Potential Supreme Court Case. *Cyber Law Journal of The New York Times*, <http://www.nytimes.com/>, 10 April 1998.

B. Pfaffenberger, editor. *Webster's New World Dictionary of Computer Terms*, 6th edition. New York, Simon & Schuster, 1997.

San Jose Mercury News. Canada, U.S. in Standoff Over Too-Smart Satellite. <http://www.mercurycenter.com/breaking/ docs/074537.htm>, 18 February 1999.

D. Sharp. Court Upholds Child Porn Law. *Associated Press*, <http://wire.ap.org>, 30 January 1999.

United States Code. Title 18, Section 2246, <http:Mcweb2. loc.gov/law/GLINvl/GLIN.html>.

B. Computer-Generated Child Pornography Poses the Same Threat to the Well-Being of Children as Photographic Child Pornography. *Child Pornography Prevention Act of 1995*, <http://thomas.loc.gov/cgi-bin/cpquery/1?cpl 04:./tamp/-cp104o4dl:e43450:>, 5 August 1998.

WTXF, FOX Philadelphia Evening News, 21 February 1999, 10:00 p.m.

Agents of Harm or Agents of Grace: The Legal and Ethical Aspects of Identifying Harm and Assigning Responsibility in a Networked World[1]

Tomas A. Lipinski, Elizabeth A. Buchanan, and Johannes J. Britz

Introduction and Background

In general, an action for defamation requires a showing that the plaintiff has been exposed to contempt or public ridicule, thus injuring professional standing in the community.[2] The four elements of a claim for defamation are: (1) a false and defamatory statement, (2) that is published to one or more third parties without privilege, (3) by a publisher who is at least negligent in communicating the information, and (4) that results in presumed or actual damage.[3] In traditional analog environments, information intermediaries, such as a library or bookstore, are not responsible for the defamatory statements contained within material located on its shelves for loan or *purchase*. This is because U.S. law draws a distinction between a true *publisher* of a defamatory statement and a mere *distributor* of a defamatory statement. Examples of such distributors include libraries, bookstores, and news vendors.[4] In virtual space, one would like to apply distributor status to web site or bulletin board operators and extend such protections as a result of such status. However, in cyberspace, parties traditionally secure from such actions may be exposed to liability given the unsettled nature of the Internet legal environment; furthermore this is compounded by technological advances that often blur the legal distinction between the actual information creator (author or publisher) and a mere conduit (distributor) of that information; electronic publishing is a good case in point.[5] A library, web site, news vendor, or bulletin board moderator, all arguably traditional distributors, might in the former instance cut, paste, graft, or otherwise edit content onto an in-house publication distributed to library patrons or to web site visitors, or in the latter instance monitor board postings according to standards of relevance or etiquette. By these actions the intermediary has moved beyond the function of a mere conduit or distributor and now acts more like a publisher or editor of a book or newspaper. So too, the web site operator or bulletin board moderator that cuts, pastes, or edits content might be held to the same level of legal responsibility in online settings.

This is not to say that a distributor (intermediary) shares no liability whatsoever for the defamatory content it distributes, but rather the intermediary becomes liable only when it knows or should have known the defamatory content of the material.[6] "The words 'reason to know' are used throughout the Restatement of this Subject [Restatement (second) of Torts] to denote the fact that the actor has information from which a person of reasonable intelligence or of the superior intelligence of the actor would infer that the fact in question exists, or that such person would govern his conduct upon the assumption that such fact exists."[7] It does not require that one is under a duty to use reasonable diligence to ascertain the existence or non-existence of the fact in question, this would be a higher, "should know" standard.[8]

Thus, when a distributor is made aware of the defamatory content of material under its control or receives material from a publisher or other source of dubious quality or reputation, e.g., it has frequently published defamatory material in the past, the "reason to know" standard is met. If the material is distributed nonetheless, the distributor takes the risk of becoming liable to those subsequently defamed by the material.[9] There have been no recent cases against traditional distributors such as libraries, but two very old cases do exist from the turn of the century; in these cases, libraries that failed to take action after receiving a removal request notice from the publisher were found liable,[10] public policy concerns notwithstanding. As a practical matter, given the short duration of the statute of limitations for action arising in tort, traditional distributors such as libraries or bookstores are seldom targets of litigation.

Typically, those who act as a publisher or republisher[11] of defamatory material are also liable with the speaker or writer of the defamation. The law imposes this burden on the intermediary-as-publisher for several reasons. First, the publisher may benefit economically from the publication and so should share in its social cost. Second, the publisher may have resources or be in the most efficient position to intercede in preventing the harm, i.e., it can halt or cease publication of the harmful material. Finally, it serves as a form of risk allocation. If authors would bear the sole burden of harm, future speakers might be less willing to speak and future speech might be chilled. To what extent can a failure to act constitute a publication, transforming as it were, the acts or omissions of an intermediary into a publisher for purposes of liability? Under the existing law a person who fails to remove a defamatory matter posted on land or chattels, can become liable for its continued publication. However, steps to remove the defamatory material need not be "unreasonable if the burden of the measures outweighs the harm to the plaintiff. However, when removal is not unduly difficult or onerous, he may easily remove the defamation, he may be found liable if he intentionally fails to remove it."[12]

Finally, those who merely supply the equipment or facilities that one may use for facilitating the communication process are not responsible for the defamatory messages that one may send. However, unlike a telephone or telegraph entity, a person who uses the World Wide Web to convey a defamatory message does more than simply use the technology as a delivery vehicle. The sender of a defamatory message in the online environment could be said to use it as a publishing vehicle or, at least given the circumstances, such can be assumed when one posts messages to a discussion board or website. The posting of a website can constitute a "publication" of that website for purposes of the copyright law.[13] Of course, one can use the web only to send and receive defamatory messages and, in those cases when the online intermediary acts as only a common carrier, there is no liability. However, as discussed above, the failure to intentionally remove a defamatory matter may give rise to liability for its continued posting or publication. How soon after notice must action be taken before a failure to remove the material or message is viewed as a "publication?" A recent Australian case involved a message left on several public bus shelters for thirty days.[14] Earlier cases involved time periods as short as several days (lampoon of plaintiff posted on the wall of a private club[15]) to several hours (derogatory comment regarding chastity of plaintiff's spouse written on a bathroom tavern wall[16]).

Moreover, it could still be argued that using the web as a communication delivery system, such as chat rooms, discussion boards, etc., places the web operator beyond the common carrier analogy such as a telephone carrier, since the telephone carrier seldom if ever records the content of the calls it passes, let alone allows others to hear a replay of the defamatory statement, i.e., the capacity in web settings that allows users to review chat logs, discussion board transcripts, etc. In any event, most of the material posted or sent in online environments does not fit the one to-one-common carrier model of immunity that developed under past law. Rather than one-to-one, the form of communication is one-to-many. In addition, the message is "published" in the sense that what is sent or posted resides on the system for some amount of time, often for many others to see, or at least publication occurs when the message remains available after notice of objection is made. Such messages are more like traditional publications, and when such events occur, the owner who fails to remove defamatory matter posted on property under his or her control is subject to liability, or at least the potential for liability for its continued publication. Under prior analysis, a defamatory leaflet posted on another's property can subject the owner to liability for its continued posting[17] and likewise, might also impose liability on online property owners as well, including website or board operators, for example, for similar liability.

Applying Defamation in the Online Environment

Courts have not shied away from applying these concepts in online settings. An early case in the United States applied the distributor and publisher distinction and concluded that an online service provider *could not be responsible* for defamatory messages posted on discussion boards operated by third parties, even though the messages and discussion board resided on its system. The court observed: "CompuServe has no more editorial control over such a publication than does a public library, bookstore, or newsstand, and it would be no more feasible for CompuServe to examine every publication it carries for potentially defamatory statements than it would be for any other distributor to do so."[18]

There has been much written about the *Cubby* case, and it is often mischaracterized. *Cubby* never stood for the proposition that an online service provider or a bulletin board operator could never be held liable as a distributor, nor that an online service provider or a bulletin board operator might act in the capacity of publisher or re-publisher in its own right. Any reading into the *Cubby* case of such a message is illusory at best, plain erroneous at worst. A bulletin board operator or website owner could be liable for defamation that it re-posts (re-publishes); it might even create the material itself. Furthermore, if someone else posted the material, if the operator or owner who allowed it to be posted failed to remove it when the owner knows or should have known of the defamatory character of the message, the operator may then face liability as a distributor.

Another possible way for an online service provider to be liable for the acts of a bulletin board operator is based on a theory of *vicarious liability*. If the online service provider has the ability to control the acts of the bulletin board operator, then the bulletin board operator is deemed the agent of the online service provider and the online service provider shares in the legal responsibility for the acts of the bulletin board operator. In *Cubby,* the board operators were found to be independent contractors and, while there might be some financial obligation by the board operator to the online service provider (rental revenue that the service provider receives based on number of visits or postings, for example), independent contractors are thought to act beyond the control of those who commission them.

In online settings these distinctions become blurred. For example, it is unclear whether a link to another site that contains defamatory material makes the linking site also liable to the defamed party. If a link is analogous to speech, then is a link equivalent to repeating what is at the site, or at least the equivalent of calling attention to it, so that others are encouraged to read it? At least one case has arisen concerning this issue, *Curzon-Brown v. San Francisco Community College District et al.,*[19] but has not resulted in any decided opinion. Could a traditional distributor like a board operator or website designer linking to a site of defamatory material be cast in the role of a re-publisher, as one who republishes a defamatory statement is also liable? A mere link would appear unlikely to be a republication[20] but a link provided in the context of a website containing other recommended links for patrons, students or site visitors to consult places the information intermediary into the role of editor, or at least "promoter," or arguably an "endorser" function that may serve as to trigger publisher/re-publisher liability.

The developing law is often inconsistent, with one infamous decision holding that an online service provider was liable for the defamatory postings of a third party on its system.[21] Looking to traditional media (print, radio, etc.) for guidance one finds a conflict of opinion. One case held that a radio broadcast that called attention to a defamatory magazine was not liable for "republication or publication."[22] Yet the Restatement of Torts includes an example that suggests that a person who gives a copy of his or her newspaper to another, calling attention to the defamatory article is liable as is the publisher of it.[23]

To some extent, *Stratton Oakmont, Inc.,* is consistent with developing case law, as intermediaries such as a library, or bulletin board operator or online service provider can be liable for defamation when it either acts as a publisher or re-publisher, or when, having knowledge or reason to know of such content, nevertheless distributes the defamatory content, for example, by posting it on a website. The *Stratton Oakmont, Inc.* court concluded that the online service provider acted more like a publisher than a mere distributor. This is so for several reasons. First,

Prodigy claimed to edit content in its advertising literature with a promise to be a family-oriented network. Second, Prodigy had promulgated content guidelines. Third, Prodigy used a software-screening program to control offensive content. Finally, and unlike CompuServ in the *Cubby* case, Prodigy exercised control over its board leaders in enforcing its content guidelines. While there is some disagreement over whether the court adopted a set of facts that was less than accurate, the courts' application of the law to the facts it did observe is consistent with the law of defamation: Those who edit content, like a newspaper publisher, are responsible for the defamatory comments contained in the resulting material when it is published. The controversy raised by *Stratton Oakmont, Inc.* is whether the board operator's actions were truly representative of an editor merely because the Stratton Oakmont tried to restore some sense of propriety to online board discussion.

The Underlying Rationale of Section 230

The specific facts of *Stratton Oakmont, Inc.* must be recalled in order to understand fully the context of the legislation that the U.S. Congress enacted, in addition to viewing the new statute as a response to the developing judicial confusion. While it is true that when Congress added Section 47 U.S.C. § 230(c) to the federal communication law, Congress made it clear that one purpose of the new law was to overrule the decision in *Stratton Oakmont*.[24] The overall context of new Section 230, enacted as part of the Communications Decency Act, was to make sure that information intermediaries, like board operators or online service providers are immune from any liability as a publisher when the intermediary undertakes actions to limit the content of information made available on its system, that this action is not viewed by courts as willingness to be treated as an editor. Under Section 230, the intermediary is immune from publisher liability when it makes available content-controlling technologies like filtering or screening software on its systems, either for use by customers (Section 230(c)(2)(B)) or when it employs that technology itself to limit content (Section 230(c)(2)(A)).

However, such an intermediary could still be liable as a distributor under the plain language of the statute. The point is that Congress did not want online intermediaries to be punished for good faith attempts to limit content themselves or when the intermediary provided the tools for others (such as parents who desire to limit their children's access to controversial material online) to control content, especially when that control, due to the limitations of existing technology, is less than successful. It was thought in Congress' mind that such content-controlling technologies could help make the Internet a kinder, gentler place.

While it could, in theory, be argued that an online service provider could still be treated as a publisher when it acts in an editorial capacity other than by the use of filtering or screening technologies (Section 230(c)(2)), Congress did not make this distinction. In fact, it specifically states in Section 230(c)(1) that "[n]o provider or user of an interactive computer service shall be treated as the publisher or speaker *of any information* provided by another information content provider." Regardless of whether such technology is used, if the content is derived from some other source, even if the board or website operator incorporated (edited) the material into its own work, it could not be treated as the editor-publisher of that material. That is the broad scope of the "immunity" granted by Section 230(c)(1).

However, the plain language of the statute does not preclude that the board operator or online service provider could itself be liable as a publisher for material that does not emanate from another content provider but that it created itself, as speaker. Nor does it preclude liability for third party sources of information emanating from sources other than from another "information content provider," the Section 230(c)(1) proviso. In other words, while "[n]o provider or user of an interactive computer service shall be treated as the publisher or speaker of any information provided by another information content provider," some information might come from sources other than said "information content provider." However, this might depend on how one interprets the definition of information content provider in Section 230(f)(3): "any person or entity that is responsible, in whole or in part, for the creation or development of information provided though the Internet or any other "interactive computer service."[25] In other words, an online intermediary who took content from an analog source, scanned it, and posted it would not be protected under 230 since the information would not have been provided by another information content provider as the print sourced published was *not* "provided through the Internet or any other 'interactive computer service.'" It differs from the definition of interactive computer service in Section 230(f)(2). If the information content provider includes anyone who posts information, then indeed the third party source proviso of Section 230(c)(1) is broad, as it would include online carriers, publishers and mere speakers. However, it would seem more consistent with the purpose of Section 230(c) that the definition is meant to included only publishers ("any person responsible, in whole or in part, for the creation or development of information provided though the Internet") and carriers or those providing access to carriers ("or any other interactive computer service"), but not these speakers. (Under Section 230(f)(2), an interactive computer service means "any information service, system, or access software provider that provides or enables computer access by multiple users to a computer service, including specifically a service or system that provides access to the Internet and such systems operated or services offered by libraries or educational institutions").[26]

At least one court has limited the broad sweeping content provided to online, Internet, or any other interactive computer service, and excluded print source publishers and speakers. While it may appear that section 230 immunity for material created by another is limitless, the Court of Appeals for the Ninth Circuit concluded that the operative section 230(c)(1) language "provided by another information content provider" when considered in conjunction with the statutory definition of "information content provider" requires that the third party content be "provided through the Internet or any other interactive computer services."[27] This prevents someone who sends a "private" message that the provider posts from claiming immunity or from taking a defamatory or otherwise harmful message first released in print form and re-publishing it online. In the first instance, the email message was not *provided through the Internet or any other interactive computer service* and in the second instance, though provided for mass distribution by the newspaper or book publisher, it was not done so *"through the Internet or any other interactive com-*

puter service." Under the facts of the case, the service provider, Cremer, received a private email from Smith hypothesizing that Batzel possessed various art work misappropriated by the Nazis during WWII from persons of Jewish heritage and that Batzel was a descendent of a leading figure of the Nazi party. Cremer posted the message "on an open website." In the court's view of the issue, the message, while received via email, might not have met the statutory requirement of being "provided" for that purpose, i.e., posting. The court thus remanded the case for further proceedings and established the following rule: "We therefore hold that a service provider or user is immune from liability under § 230(c)(1) when a third person or entity that created or developed the information in question furnished it to the provider or user under circumstances in which a reasonable person in the position of the service provider or user would conclude that the information was provided for publication on the Internet or other 'interactive computer service.'"[28]

According to Street, those information or service providers that "claim to exercise editorial control or do in fact exercise editorial control... are likely to be treated as publishers and held liable for defamation in the materials they publish."[29] However, this is not the interpretation the courts have given this simple language and its straightforward legislative purpose. Finally, an interactive service provider could be liable as a distributor if it met the conditions of distributor liability as discussed earlier.

Section 230 and the Developing Law

In passing the new immunity law, Congress commented that "[t]hese protections apply to all interactive computer services, as defined in new subsection 230(f)(2), including non-subscriber systems such as those operated by many businesses for employee use."[30] While Section 230(f)(2) defines an interactive computer service as "any information service, system, or access software provider that provides or enables computer access by multiple users to a computer server, including specifically a service or system that provides access to the Internet and such systems operated or services offered by libraries or educational institutions,"[31] subsequent case law interpreted Section 230 as offering complete immunity for all harms associated with third party content creation on the Internet from any source, not just from another information content provider.[32] This is true even if the content derived from a third party and was reposted by the board operator. Only the original information content provider can be liable, never a re-poster of a message. A case such as *Barret v. Clark*[33] "represents exceptionally broad interpretation of Section 230. The decision provides "reposters" of information with complete immunity, even if it is alleged that the reposter knew the information was false or acted in 'reckless disregard of the truth.'"[34] Section 230 provides immunity for online content "provided by" a third party.

Although these developments have been criticized,[35] expansion of Section 230 immunity continues, even to intermediaries such as public libraries and in contexts other than defamation. In *Kathleen R. v. City of Livermore*,[36] the court granted the defendant's motion for summary judgment when a library patron (the plaintiff) claimed that a lack of filtering software on Internet access terminals caused her child to be exposed to harmful materials. The court relied in part on Section

230 in providing tort (nuisance theory) immunity from harmful material that the library, as a conduit, made accessible through its connection to the Internet, i.e., the library did not create the content nor provide a link, nor was the mere provision of Internet access deemed a publication. In fact, any tort liability (including invasion of privacy, fraud, and negligence for example) resulting from the content of a third party that might be available through the library website would not be imputed to the library in the *Kathleen R. v. City of Livermore* example, and the same argument could be made to insulate any other online service provider performing a similar access function.[37] Section 230 would provide a complete bar.

Arguably the law immunizes the interactive computer service provider when it acts as a traditional publisher or re-publisher when dealing with content from others, but do circumstances exist where the service provider acts as an editor to such an extent as to be considered an author in its own right or as a distributor? "The issue is in what circumstances will courts rule that a defamatory statement, authored by a third party, was effectively adopted by the service provider as its own and thus was 'provided by' the service provider, rather than by 'another information content provider,' for purposes of Section 230(c)(1)?"[38]

The possibility of this occurrence was recognized, as one way that the immunity provided by Section 230 would become inapplicable by the district court in *Zeran*.[39] However, in another district, the court of *Does v. Franco Productions*,[40] relying on language in *Blumenthal v. Drudge*,[41] which interpreted Section 230 immunity to apply even in those circumstances where the "interactive service provider has an active, even aggressive role in making available content prepared by others," made it clear that the Section 230 immunity applies to any content created by a third party regardless of the subsequent treatment of that defamatory content by the online service provider on its website. The *Does v. Franco Productions* court observed: "As such, Plaintiffs' new characterization of GTE and PSINet as web hosts neither prevents these defendants from being deemed service providers protected by immunity under the CDA [Communications Decency Act] nor makes them content providers unprotected by the CDA's immunity."[42] It would appear based on developing precedent that even when the intermediary such as a bulletin board operator or online service provider made some affirmative statement of incorporation or endorsement of the defamatory statement, there is little likelihood of tort liability for defamation or other harms, and even if it would make such endorsement, the no liability for third party content rule the courts appear to be developing would bar liability in any event.

In fact, based upon the developing case law, such an online intermediary is never liable for third party content, as publisher or as distributor. However, this is not to say that the courts would not eventually carve out or identify circumstances consistent with Section 230 and the existing case law under which an intermediary such as a board operator or service provider would be responsible for the content derived from third party sources it places on its site or links from its site. This might occur if the intermediary incorporates content, for instance, in a travel site rating certain destinations. The Carib Inn, a resort in the Caribbean, sued America Online for alleged defamatory remarks made by an AOL subscriber who reported that her diving instructor was "stoned" during her dive at the resort.[43] What if the board operator mined the Internet for various ratings and made some of its own as a part of its new mega travel site? It still might depend on how broadly the courts continue to construe Section 230 immunity; in other words, a broad view of Section 230 immunity would suggest that, no matter how it is presented, any online material that originated with a third party would not support a claim of liability against the board or site operator or intermediary.

It would appear that the only time a service provider could be held responsible is if one of its own employees made the defamatory statement itself, i.e., in the Carib case, if one of the board operators defamed the resort, perhaps based upon their own experience. But again, if the definition of information content provider under Section 230(f)(3) would include information made by an employee of an interactive computer service, statements coming from employees could be deemed to have come from another information content provider, i.e., the employee, and the service provider, would be immune. It can only be assumed that the reach of Section 230 immunity must end somewhere, however, courts have yet to define its limits. In such a case, it could only be hoped that the service provider would be considered as the speaker of its own content and, specifically, of that of its employee, or if it incorporated a comment posted by another speaker not considered to be a separate information content provider, a scenario not exempted by the explicit language of the statute.

Courts are continuing to immunize intermediaries such as the providers of interactive computer services under Section 230. In *Patentwizard, Inc. v. Kinkos, Inc.,*[44] the district court concluded that Kinkos was an "internet service provider" under the statute and that the alleged poster of a defaming message in a chat room by a Kinkos customer who was known as "Jimmy" was an "information content provider." Even though Kinkos was a brick and mortar entity, that is, Kinkos was a provider of facilities where Internet service was provided, Section 230 protected it from so-called virtual "premise liability," that is, Jimmy physically sat in a Kinkos store and typed his message, but the message was posted in cyberspace. As a result, Section 230 insulated Kinkos from liability for its conduct in disseminating Jimmy's statements, nor could primary liability be asserted against Kinkos for the alleged defamatory matter that was published by Jimmy.[45]

Moreover, courts have made clear that the immunity provided to providers of interactive computer services includes entities beyond the community of Internet Service Providers: "[a]s such, internet service providers (ISPs) are only a subclass of the broader definition of interactive service providers."[46] In a claim for invasion of privacy, right of publicity, defamation, and negligence by Christine Carafano (aka Chase Masterson) who portrays the character Leeta on Star Trek Deep Space Nine, against Matchmaker system, a service accessed from the World Wide Web that permits members to search a database containing profiles of posted other members, the district court concluded that Matchmaker fell within the definition of interactive computer service even though it did not provide nor enable computer access to the Internet but was a website operator. The litigation resulted from a series of obscene communications received by Carafano, *aka* Masterson, after her home address and phone were posted on the Matchmaker system. The district court also concluded that Matchmaker was an information content provider as well, as unlike a bulletin board operator it "takes an active role in developing the information that gets posted" by for example creating a template of 72 questions that Matchmaker members use to create their profile.[47] The issue in this case is whether the immunity provided by Section 230 applies in situations where the interactive "computer service provider" is also an "information content provider." While the mere right to edit is not the same as the ability to create, it is significant to observe that the *Carafano* court, after recalling the service provider versus content provider distinction discussed in *Blumenthal* v. *Drudge,* concluded that when Matchmaker acts as an information content provider, the immunity of Section 230 does not apply.[48] However the court subsequently granted the defendant's motion for summary judgment on the privacy, defamation (while Section 230 did not shield the defendants, the plaintiff failed to show the defamatory publication was made with actual malice), right of publicity, and negligence claims.

Section 230 immunity extends to those cases where a service provider fails to remove defamatory statements from property under its control. This was made clear in *Smith* v. *Intercosmos Media Group, Inc.*[49] The result was the proper one because under principles of the evolving law of online defamation, an intermediary would normally be treated as the publisher of the defamatory content created and posted (i.e., published initially) by another if that intermediary failed to end its display on property under its control. Allowing liability to attach to its conduct would be to allow the precise result Section 230 was designed to avoid, that is, treating an interactive service provider, such as Intercosmos, as a publisher. Thus Section 230 also immunizes after-the-fact reticence to act.[50]

In a similar after-the-fact, fail-to-act case, reflective perhaps of the content of discourse on the Internet in a post 9-11 world, Section 230 again protected a service provider defendant for its failure to prevent messages from being removed or posted in the first instances.[51] The two AOL chat rooms in question were the "Beliefs Islam" and the "Koran." According to the plaintiff, AOL was required to take steps against the posting of harassing messages as it was required to do so by its Terms of Service, which includes a Member Agreement and Community Guidelines. True, while the member documentation prohibited the sending of harassing messages, hate speech, disruptive (to the flow of chat) language, the same agreement stated that AOL had the sole discretion of whether or not to enforce the standards. Moreover, the Member Agreement states in specific that such language is "not intended to confer, and do[es] not confer, any rights or remedies upon any person."[52] The plaintiff sued AOL claiming that its refusal to enforce these standards constituted a breech of contract (though at the time of the litigation, plaintiff was no longer a subscriber) and a violation of the public accommodation provisions of the Civil Rights Act of 1964, known commonly as Title II.

For both claims the court concluded that the complaint should be dismissed. Unfortunately, "[i]n light of this plain contractual language, plaintiff cannot claim that AOL breached a duty to protect him from the harassing speech of others; the Member Agreement expressly disclaims any such duty."[53] Again Section 230 was found to bar further proceedings as that section immunizes service providers from liability as a publisher, i.e., for engaging in publisher-like conduct such as deciding whether to publish, withdraw, postpone, or alter content.[54] "In sum, § 230 bars plaintiff's claim under Title II because it seeks to treat AOL as the publisher of the allegedly harassing statements of other AOL members.... Accordingly, under § 230, plaintiff may not seek recourse against AOL as publisher of the offending statements; instead, plaintiff must pursue his rights, if any, against the offending AOL members themselves."[55] Moreover, even if Section 230 did not bar such a claim, the court concluded that a chat room does not constitute a "place of public accommodation," a Title II prerequisite, because the Title II precedent requires that a place of accommodation be a physical locale and does not apply to a virtual room.[56]

Legal Implications

Who then remains liable for defamatory information posted in Internet environments and what are the results of these suggested misapplications of Section 230? Online intermediaries such as Internet service providers or bulletin board operators, whether acting as publishers (including re-publishers) or distributors, are immune from any legal responsibility for defamatory content deriving from others on their boards or sites, save possibly for material that it creates. There are several problems with this.

First, it results in a disparity in treatment between the levels of responsibility imposed upon online intermediaries versus their traditional analog counterparts. Traditional intermediaries are held to a higher standard, while online intermediaries are immunized from liability.

Second, in most online settings (unless the board operator is not also treated as a service provider), the only party from which to seek remedy by an aggrieved plaintiff is the actual speaker of the defamatory content. The intermediary is now immune, whether it is a distributor or publisher. In the online setting, this has grave implications for the future freedom of Internet speech. Consider Internet communication, especially that which might be considered questionable as to its defamatory nature, that appears from anonymous posters. The fact that plaintiffs in defamation suits will need to pursue remedy against the actual speaker when that speaker has spoken (posted) anonymously, means that one's right to speak from a veil of anonymity is jeopardized and must be balanced against the plaintiff's right to seek redress. Would it not have been a simpler Internet if, similar to the immunity/liability pattern established under 17 U.S.C. § 512 for secondary liability under the copyright law, intermediaries were responsible for the defamatory messages contained on their boards or sites when they fail to remove such messages after proper notice? However, there is no legal incentive for intermediaries to do this now under Section 230. Whether there is a moral incentive will be discussed momentarily.

Finally, the difference between commonwealth legal standards, which are historically pro-plaintiff and the U.S. legal standard, which at least in online settings might be described as a speaker-only liability standard, underscores the need for a uniform standard on the Internet that transcends the geographic boundaries of traditional defamation law.

Approaches in other Countries

In defamation matters, England is known as a plaintiff's jurisdiction.[57] This might be true for several reasons. First, the publication rule states that each time a defamatory item is made available and received by an individual there is a separate publication of it. In *Godfrey v. Demon Internet Ltd.*, the court stated: "In my judgment the defendant, whenever it transmits and whenever there is transmitted from the storage of its news server a defamatory posting, publish that posting to any subscriber to its ISP who accesses the newsgroup containing that posting. Thus, every time one of the defendant's customers accesses "soc.culture.thai" and sees that posting defamatory of the plaintiff there is a publication to that customer."[58] This can be compared to the recent application of the "publication" rule in Internet settings in the United States. In contrast, the United States rule is more accurately described as a "single publication" rule. In *Firth v. State of New York*,[59] the plaintiff claimed that the continued availability of the article on the Internet constituted a republication that would trigger the statute of limitations anew each day. The court disagreed and observed that while its availability on the Internet was indeed a publication, without some alteration or modification, its continued posting would not be a new publication for purposes of the statute of limitations.

Second, in many commonwealth jurisdictions there is no distinction between distributor and publisher. Liability for defamation is based on the concept of strict liability.[60] As a result, English law assumes the statement is false, and the defendant must prove the truthfulness or assert some other form of defense.[61] One example of an affirmative defense was enacted by England in 1996 as part of the Defamation Act of 1996. The language appears to parallel the concept of distributor in the United States: "In defamation proceedings a person has a defence [sic] if he shows that (a) he was not the author, editor, or publisher of the statement complained of, (b) he took reasonable care in relation to its publication, and (c) he did not know, and had no reason to believe, that what he did cause or contribute to the publication of a defamatory statement." A defendant must prove all three elements to avail him or her self of the codification of what was essentially the defense of "innocent distributor."[62] The definition of publisher is further explained to exclude those who are only involved in the "printing, producing, distributing, or selling printed material containing the statement." However, the reasonable care (second element) is defined as a somewhat higher or at least more complex standard than the "know or reason to know" distributor standard in the United States: "In determining for the purposes of this section whether a person took reasonable care, or had reason to believe that what he did caused or contributed to the publication of a defamatory statement, regard shall be had to (a) the extent of his responsibility for the content of the statement or the decision to publish it, (b) the nature or circumstances of the publication, and (c) the previous conduct or character of the author, editor, or publisher."[63]

The problem for the defendants in the leading English case is that, once the defendants received notice of a defamatory posting and chose not to remove it from their Usenet news servers, any defense available to them under the Defamation Act became in the court's words "hopeless." Obtaining guidance from the Consultation Document the *Godfrey v. Demon Internet Ltd.* court quoted: "The defence [sic] of innocent dissemination has never provided an absolute immunity for distributors, however mechanical their contribution. It does not protect those who knew that the material they were handling was defamatory, or who *ought* to have known of its nature. Those safeguards are preserved, so that the defence [sic] is not available to a defendant who knew that his act involved or contributed to publication defamatory of the plaintiff. It is available only if, having taken all reasonable care, the defendant had no reason to suspect that his act had that effect."[64] As a result the court concluded that the defendants could not be considered as innocent distributors. As observed earlier, the Restatement (Second) of Torts, contains almost identical language protecting innocent distributors such as news vendors and libraries. Moreover, most of the cases cited in support of the U.S. Restatement position are English cases that were, incidentally, also cited by the *Godfrey* v. *Demon Internet Ltd. Court*.[65]

Several Australian cases resulted in either success at trial or were settled.[66] An earlier Australian case concluded that liability was appropriate where the defendant failed to remove a defamatory publication and could be applicable to Internet settings.[67] A recent case, *Gutnick* v. *Dow Jones & Co.*,[68] raises an issue of increasing importance in cross-border international disputes. It relies on an English precedent from the 1840s to the effect that defamation arises where the item is first obtained. In Internet settings, this would mean the location (country) from which a reader accesses the posting. The court concluded that this was not New Jersey where Dow Jones is located, but Australia where it was read.[69] The court was unmoved by the defendant's objection of setting a precedent that defendants must rise and litigate across the globe: This "must be balanced against the world-wide inconvenience caused to litigants, from Outer Mongolia to the Outer Barcoo, frequently not of notable means, who would at enormous expense and inconvenience have to embark upon the formidable task of suing in the USA . . . where the libel laws are, in many respects, tilted in favour [sic] of defendants, or, if you will, in favour [sic] of the constitutional free speech concepts and rights developed in the USA which originated in the liberal construction by the courts of the First Amendment."[70]

The High Court of Australia, the equivalent of the United States Supreme Court, recently upheld the lower court decision denying Dow Jones' request to stay the proceedings on the grounds of *forum non conveniens*,[71] with the result that the case may now proceed to trial.[72] The case represents the first high appellate court decision from any country regarding the trans-national problems associated with civil liability of Internet content providers. The concern among international media content providers and distributors is that all publishers worldwide are now subject to the law of the most restrictive country, not only in defamation law, but also in other speech related harms, as a result of the ability, according to the Australian High Court, of plaintiffs to exert jurisdiction over remote defendants. The court misses the point when it comments: "the spectre [sic] which Dow Jones sought to conjure up in the present appeal, of a publisher forced to consider every article it publishes on the World Wide Web against the defamation laws of every other country from Afghanistan to Zimbabwe is seen to be unreal when it is recalled that in all except the most unusual of cases, identifying the person about whom material is to be published will readily identify the defamation law to which that person may resort."[73] First, defamation law's singular plaintiff is not the only legal remedy generated from speech-related harms. Second, this would still require a publisher to undertake a tremendous amount of pre-publication inquiry, as a plaintiff in defamation may have a reputation in more than a single jurisdiction, and so may be harmed beyond a single jurisdiction. The content presented by a publisher about a particular individual, the future plaintiff, will now depend on the strictness of the subject's (the named person, or in other speech-related harms, the listener) national law of defamation, hate speech, etc., and not the principles of free speech with which the speaker-author has become culturally conditioned to conform vis-à-vis his or her own legal system, but that of an unfamiliar environment. The rule will force each speaker to consider the impact of his or her speech in the context not of the pulpit or podium from which he or she speaks, but from the perspective of the potential listener. This results in the establishment of an international "heckler's veto."[74]

Moreover, other speech-related harms such as a civil remedy against hate speech, for example, do not require a specific person as a target of the alleged harm. As the High Court here suggests, it would in practice still open a publisher to liability in multiple jurisdictions as a person, especially in today's connected world, might be known in more than one country and so might have a "reputation" to defend in many places. How a publisher is to know where a publication's subject might have an interest and thus might suffer harm is not explained by the High Court. "This does not only open the door to forum shopping, it also exposes the publisher/content provider to widely differing legal regimes."[75] All a plaintiff needs do is travel to the next jurisdiction where his or her reputation is established, demonstrate that others have read the article (according to the Australian court, publication occurs where the article is perceived, that is the loci of the arm), and file suit. Though as van Hoek points out the common law doctrine of *estoppel* should be used to quell dangers of multiple litigation: "This latter problem is countered in the judgment by a substantive law remedy, rather than by a means of private international law: any justification of the conduct of Dow Jones under US law would not automatically absolve Dow Jones of liability but should be entered as a defense under Australian law. It remains to be seen whether this actually provides an adequate solution."[76] Moreover, by the High Court's own discussion, it is impossible for a publisher to guarantee that its publication might not reach some readers in a more "strict" or limiting defamation jurisdiction than his or her own.[77]

The High Court appeared to suggest that because of realities of media penetration in the 21st century, publishers should expect the potential for such litigation and characterized the Internet as little different from other sorts of communication: "It must be recognized, however, that satellite broadcasting now permits very wide dissemination of radio and television and it may, therefore, be doubted that it is right to say that the World Wide Web has a uniquely broad reach. It is no more or less ubiquitous than some television services."[78] The court analogy of media fails. The difference between the web and worldwide television for example, even satellite TV is two fold, first the broadcast is not normally perpetually available as is a posting on a website. Second, there is some intermediate act on the part of the disseminator, i.e., the broadcast or transmission of the program. With the web publication, once posted it remains only for the reader to access it. Of course, scenarios of exception could be constructed for this counter analogy as well, but just as with the analogy forwarded by the court, less than perfect analogies are not a sound basis for legal or policy decision-making. The reality is that a person today, because of the power of dissemination of the Internet as well as other mass media, can literally achieve celebrity status overnight, the likelihood of his or her having a reputation in multiple jurisdictions with multiple standards of harm is indeed possible. In such a case, potential liability in defamation for the publication of material relating to such a person on the Internet may indeed have a chilling effect on free speech merely because one jurisdiction has more restrictive defamation or other speech laws than others.[79] Similarly, there may be more restrictive jurisdictions facing Australian publishers as well.[80] The High Court then appears to throw up its proverbial legal hands and observes that such "problems are the result of the absence of uniformity in defamation laws, combined with an ability to access and broadcast material across national boundaries [which is not limited to the Internet] and the absence of international treaties or reciprocal laws to govern those issues."[81] A telling comment for sure, as trans-border information flows resulting from new communication technologies have been around for most of the last quarter to half century for sure, yet there is no common ground for resolution of these issues. And the *Dow Jones & Company, Inc.* v. *Gutnick*, court offers little guidance on solving those problems other than to apply the law of its jurisdiction in a rather singular way, i.e., without much consideration internationally to its repercussions, which as a sovereign state deciding an issue within its own borders is its right of course. Unfortunately, its response, like the content posted by Dow Jones and other web publishers, belongs to the vast community of World Wide Web users who transcend any border.

The court posed what is perhaps at the heart of the harm versus speech controversy: "defamation seeks to strike a balance between … society's interest in freedom of expression and the free exchange of information and ideas … [and] an individual's interest in maintaining his or her reputation in society free from unwarranted slur or damage."[82] Where one chooses to strike this balance might depend on how high one places a value on the right to speak versus the weight of verbal (written or spoken) or visual (depictions such as cartoons, paintings, motion pictures) or other communicative harms—a classic example of cultures in conflict. In the context of the World Wide Web publishing, should the readership by citizens of one country, in the present case a few hundred subscribers in Australia, in essence dictate what the rest of subscribers worldwide may read? What is the greater harm, that a community of readers in Australia be prevented from thinking less of Joseph Gutnick or that subscribers worldwide be able to read about it? One can easily see the legal and ethical difficulties in answering these sorts of questions. Yet, echoing the High Court's call, perhaps what is needed is an international standard.[83]

However, this does not get the argument very far, as each participant in the debate would wonder what countries' laws and norms/values would dominate the discussion and subsequent policies. How would a civil discourse around these issues proceed? Would the extensive free speech perspectives of the U.S. once again be accused of trumping other perspectives in deference to its own cultural agenda? How would private commercial interests be represented? Would it make sense to have the law of the jurisdiction where publication is created at least have some sway in the debate? (The High Court offers the following observation: "Because the vastly disproportionate location of webservers in the United States when compared to virtually all other countries (including Australia) this would necessarily have the result, in many cases, of extending the application of a law of the United States (and possibly the jurisdiction and forum of its courts) to defamation proceedings brought by Australian and other foreign citizens in respect of local damage to their reputations by publication on the Internet."[84]

Of course the Gutnick litigation is not the first time the Internet facilitated a clash of attitudes and clash of respective culture's legal constructions, in particular, the United States and France. The case arose out of the ability of French citizens to access from the Yahoo! Website (or via link through Yahoo.fr) approximately 1,000 "messages, images, and text relating to Nazi objects, relics, insignia, emblems, and flags, or which evoke Nazism;" also available on the site were excerpts from Adolf Hitler's *Mein Kampf* and an infamous anti-Semitic report produced by the Czarist secret police in the early 1900s, *The Protocol of the Elders of Zion,* as well as material or links to material expounding theories of Holocaust denial.[85] The French court found Yahoo! in violation of the French Criminal Code, section R645-1, which prohibits exhibition of Nazi propaganda and artifacts for sale.

Which right is more important? The right to speak or the right not to hear or to be protected from hearing, viewing, reading, etc. offensive material, assuming an alignment of what is offensive cross-culturally can be achieved? Of course one might not characterize the entire Yahoo! website as "speech," i.e., the sale of Nazi paraphernalia. Yet that also may be part of the difference in cultural-legal attitudes.[86] In response Yahoo! commenced litigation in the United States claiming that because it could not fulfill the terms of the French Court order, i.e., to block French citizen's access to the material "without banning Nazi related material from Yahoo.com altogether. Yahoo! contend[ed] that such a ban would infringe impermissibly upon its rights under the First Amendment to the United States Constitution."[87] The French court considered the technical difficulties of fulfilling its order but did not view the difficulties as insurmountable. Its dismissal of these concerns defies logic when considered in spite of the fact that the court's own expert panel pointed out the problems of compliance with such demands. One solution was to require that all who desire to access the prohibited material make a declaration that he or she is not French.[88] The enforcement problems associated with this solution might be characterized as threefold: technical (false or disguised IP address, software exists to mask locations on the Internet), practical (a person could simply make an untruthful declaration, and would not a person in France, seeking Nazi memorabilia, also be likely to lie in order to obtain it?), and policy (privacy issues, for example, of requiring a person to reveal identity information before being able to access certain material).

Yahoo! sought declaratory judgment from a U.S. court that the French Court's order is "neither cognizable nor enforceable under the laws of the United States." A federal district court granted Yahoo!'s request,[89] though the case is now pending appeal before the Ninth Circuit.[90] The U.S. district court wrestled with similar demons of conflicting cultural and jurisprudential attitudes as did the Australian High Court. "What is at issue here is whether it is consistent with the Constitution and laws of the United States for another nation to regulate speech by United States residents within the United States on the basis that such speech can be accessed by Internet users in that nation."[91] What the U.S. district court foresaw but the Australian High Court spent little time discussing, was the implications of its decision: "There is little doubt that Internet users in the United States routinely engage in speech that violates, for example, China's laws against religious expression, the laws of various nations against advocacy of genre equality or homosexuality, or even the United Kingdom's restriction on freedom of the press."[92] The impact of decision reaches far beyond the narrow confines if its specific legal issue.[93] If local law determines the standard by which the content and character of all Internet expression is based, then any organized church with a website should expect to be hauled into court in China, or a porn site operator drawn into the court system of a Muslim country.

Of course "[a] basic function of a sovereign state is to determine by law what forms of speech and conduct are acceptable within its border."[94] China has chosen this route and attempts enforcement not by litigation but by regulation of all landline access to its country,[95] but with Internet connectivity now using satellite technology, this will undoubtedly become more difficult. This approach, while solving the international cultural-legal clash, may limit considerably the amount of information available to a country's citizenry and may again pit a choice of whose paternalism should prevail: a country's own values as reflected by its laws limiting the information content available to its citizens (government knows best for its citizens) vs. a broad international opinion of free information allowing each individual as a citizen of the world to decide for him or herself the merits of particular speech (information wants to be free approach). The U.S. court observed that "[w]hat makes this case uniquely challenging is that the Internet in effect allows one to speak in more than one place at the same time."[96] Of course it can be argued that a national government speaks the will of its people, and so its place on the cultural-legal continuum of protected vs. banned expression should be respected. However, this appears suspect in countries where media is often restricted, such as China and some Muslim states. However unacceptable this might be from an ethical perspective, considering the issue of true representation of and by some governments, from a legal perspective, this is acceptable, as a sovereign state has the right to control conduct within its borders, as U.S. citizens would be bound by Australian or French law, while acting within the borders of those countries. The problem in the Gutnick and Yahoo! litigations is the specter of courts in one nation binding the conduct of citizens of another: "However, an entirely different case would be presented if the French court ordered the party not to engage in the same expression in the United States on the basis that French citizens (along with anyone else in the world with the means to do so) later could read, hear, or see it. While the advent of the Internet effectively has removed the physical and temporal elements of this hypothetical, the legal analysis remains."[97] Another unacceptable response would be to allow prospective defendants in one country to pre-empt such litigation as it arises in a foreign jurisdiction for fear that it may later be used to mandate remedy by foreign plaintiffs in the defendant's own country.[98]

The U.S. District Court, like the Australian High Court observed the problem caused by the lack of an international protocol: "Absent a body of law that establishes international standards with respect to speech on the Internet and on appropriate treaty or legislation addressing enforcement of such standards to speech originating within the United States, the principle of comity is outweighed by the Courts' obligation to uphold the First Amendment."[99] Of course, it might also be wise to point out that there exists at present international protocols that guarantee the right of all world citizens to express as well as to receive information on all viewpoints and perspectives, protocols to which both Australia and France are parties.[100]

Anonymous and Defamatory Speech on the Internet

If a link is not speech for purposes of speaking or republishing a defamatory comment, then the only party left to hold responsible and thus, sue, is the speaker. And what of cases whether the speaker chooses to speak anonymously; under what conditions should the identity of the anonymous speaker be revealed? A handful of cases involving anonymous speakers on the Internet have arisen.[101]

The following factors have been developed by the courts and are used to determine whether a subpoena ordering the release of an anonymous user's identity should be enforced or quashed: jurisdiction, good faith both as to party (internal) and as to claim (external), and necessity (basic and in some cases absolute).[102] In other words, the plaintiff seeking the identity of an anonymous poster must first demonstrate the legal merits of the action. "Legal merit" is established by showing that the court has jurisdiction over the defendant and that the claim would survive a motion for summary judgment (external good faith). The defendant must act in good faith as a party to the action (internal good faith). Courts would reject the subpoena requested as an exploratory device to identify unrelated anonymous persons, as this would be an abuse of the subpoena power. Internal good faith can also be demonstrated by showing that the plaintiff made fair attempts to determine the identity of the anonymous speaker without recourse to the subpoena. There must also be some sense of urgency or necessity in that the information (the identity of the anonymous poster) is needed in order to proceed with the litigation (basic necessity) or absolute necessity, i.e., that there is no other source of the information.

Absolute necessity is often required in cases where the anonymous person is not a party to the action, that is, he/she is not the poster of a defamatory statement. This would arise in a case where a party to a lawsuit, based upon the postings of an anonymous speaker, believes that the anonymous speaker has information that might exonerate or promote their case. That party needs to know who the anonymous poster is in order submit them to discovery proceedings, further subpoena, material witness order, etc., even though the plaintiff is not suing the anonymous speaker.

The theory behind the subpoena-anonymous speaker cases is that an aggrieved person should have a right to seek redress in a court by proper means. However, this right according to the case law should be balanced against a person's right to speak freely and anonymously if one so chooses—in any setting, including the Internet. The right to speak anonymously and the right to speak anonymously on the Internet is recognized by the developing U.S. precedent, where the right of free speech is strong, but the right of anonymous speech might be less protected in those countries where speaker rights are also less developed, especially in cases involving race, hate, or other similar speech harms.[103]

In *In re Verizon Internet Services, Inc.,*[104] the motion of Verizon to quash a subpoena served on it by the RIAA (Recording Industry Association of America) seeking "the identity of an anonymous user of the conduit functions of Verizon's Internet service who is alleged to have infringed copyrights by offering hundreds of songs for downloading over the Internet" was denied.[105] This case, in a predictable result continues the trend of individuals seeking remedy in the aftermath of Congress' insulation of online intermediaries, that is, to seek redress directly from the individual perpetrator of the harm. This case also demonstrates Congressional (vis-à-vis federal statute) attitudes toward protecting online intermediaries not only from the tort-based harms of Section 230 cases to copyright infringement. Intellectual property rights are one of the rights specifically *not* covered by Section 230. However, as part of the Digital Millennium Copyright Act (DMCA), the US Congress enacted Section 512 that similar to Section 230 provides some legal protection to online intermediaries. Section 512 does not provide complete immunity but limits the remedy to injunctive relief only, also excluding award of attorney's fees.

The case also demonstrates that anonymity is not a shield for tortfeasors. These cases are monitored by free speech advocates for the potential negative impact on the rights of individuals to engage in anonymous speech. However, the court in *In re Verizon Internet Services, Inc.,* concluded that the Section 512(h) subpoena provision did not "offend the First Amendment."[106] While the court acknowledged that the First Amendment protects anonymous expression on the Internet it does not shield those who engage in copyright infringement as "the degree of protection is minimal where the alleged copyright infringement is the expression at issue."[107] "Verizon's customers should have little expectation of privacy (or anonymity) in infringing copyrights."[108] The court believed that the procedural safeguards built into Section 512(h), such as the requirement that a person making a subpoena request "in effect, plead a prima facie case of copyright infringement," sufficient to protect those limited speech rights.[109]

In fact, the court concluded that provisions of Section 512 "are precisely the type of procedural requirements other courts have imposed—in non-copyright cases—to compel a service provider to reveal the identity of anonymous Internet users."[110] The court observed that in the five years since the Section 512 was enacted there has been little abuse or misuse of its subpoena power and in a somewhat utilitarian statement concluded that: "Judged in relation to the statute's plainly legitimate sweep, and in light of the extent of copyright piracy over the Internet, any impact on expressive and associational rights on the Internet is negligible."[111]

While the law has established guidelines for determining the liability of intermediaries in traditional analog environments, in the online settings this traditional approach has broken down, with the only party bearing responsibility being the actual speaker. As a result, there is increased pressure to locate and hold accountable those speakers, including anonymous speakers. Can an ethical discussion shed light on the questions of responsibility for the genus of harmful speech in online settings and can it redirect where legislative reform should perhaps be directed?

Morality Versus Legality?

It is evident from the aforementioned legal discussion that we are dealing with a rather complex and multifaceted legal, and by implication, moral dilemma. It can be anticipated that an ethical reflection might not provide clear-cut answers to the legal issues that were raised, precisely because of the diversity of ethical approaches and decision-making processes involved in moral reflection. However, it is important to suggest a moral framework that can be used to guide legal discourse. This is based on the assumption that the law is founded on a minimum moral consensus in any society.

This moral argument is structured in the following way: First, it is illustrated, by means of appropriate examples, that the current legal discourse is unsatisfactory from a moral perspective. It is furthermore argued that a moral reflection presupposes a proper understanding of the different roles and functions of ISPs. This forms the second part of the argument, where the notion of responsibility is elaborated. Three responsibility levels are distinguished and applied to ISPs.

On which moral norms should the responsibility of ISPs then be founded? Based on the views of Kant (1956), Habermas (1993), Rawls (1973) and Singer (1979),[112] it is argued that there can indeed be a shared foundation for moral discourse and decision making. We therefore reject moral relativism and argue in favor of human rights (specifically the right to freedom of expression and privacy) as a universal moral framework to regulate the Internet and by implication ISPs. From this the question, we assert how these human rights can be applied to the responsibilities of ISPs. Two main approaches in the Western philosophical tradition are used to build this argument. These approaches are the communitarian (collectivists) view, which is based on the ideas of Hegel, and the liberalists (individualist) approach, which is more in the Lockian tradition. It is argued that both of these approaches (in their extreme versions) are unsatisfactory and a balanced approach is proposed. The preference is however toward the individual and his/her rights to freedom of expression and privacy.

Due to the fact that the development and application of modern technology (which includes the Internet) puts into question the classical model of negative retrospective responsibility, it is therefore necessary to supplement this notion of retrospective responsibility by a notion of positive prospective responsibility. Indeed, Jonas has asserted "Modern technology has introduced actions of such novel scale, objects and consequences that the framework of former ethics can no longer contain them...."[113] It is illustrated that both models of moral reasoning can be applied to ISPs depending on their specific function and role. This retrospective/prospective argument is based on the views of Jonas (1984), Bayertz (1995), and Mitcham (1987).[114]

Unsatisfactory Legal Discourse

From a moral perspective, it can be argued that the current international legal situation regarding defamation and an ISP's responsibility is very deficient. The ultimate question with which we are dealing is who must bear legal responsibility and what are the grounds thereof? From a moral perspective, it seems that the drawing of accountability lines regarding cyber-defamation is very difficult; while the law seeks to minimize ambiguities and gray areas, a moral reflection exposes such areas for philosophical debate, including multiple ways of defining and understanding "responsibility" and "accountability" as concepts themselves. Moreover, rather than thinking of the liability-responsibility only in dyadic or dichotomous terms as the current legal perspectives enables us to, a moral reflection allows us to consider a continuum of liability and responsibility.

This deficient legal position is primarily due to the fact that the law portrays ISPs as publishers, distributors, *or* common carriers which reflects a traditional paradigm of legal thinking reflecting a rather narrow and limited understanding of the nature and functions of an ISP as well as speech issues. This explains the rather extreme and undesirable positions in the current legal discourse on cyber defamation and the allocation of legal accountability toward ISPs: That is, the legal positions must assert *either* strict responsibility or non-responsibility, as in the cases discussed above. A shared responsibility between, for instance, an ISP and the speaker himself/herself has not been explored. Perhaps it is easier to assume a shared responsibility on moral terms over legal terms.

This legal position on ISPs and their responsibility regarding defamation is as noted unsatisfactory from a moral perspective for a number of reasons, including the fact that a strict legal mandate of ISP liability will not only certainly have a worldwide effect on free speech and freedom of expression on the Internet but could also, in certain contexts, imply unfair treatment of ISPs and their members. Conversely, and of great import from a moral viewpoint, the failure to require ISPs to be legally accountable for defamation could lead to a situation where the common good or "civil discourse"[115] will not be served or honored, and where individuals, who are affected by defamation and hate speech, will have no form of moral or legal protection in cyberspace. We indicated above that the current legal remedies leave only the speaker or agent of speech as the one to sue and this seems quite undesirable, for obvious reasons.

Notably, ISPs are *not* value-free or value-neutral forums operating on morally-neutral grounds, and thus, to absolve them from any liability based on existing and emerging legal precedent gives us cause for concern. An ISP is *not* simply an inanimate object, but it is a living, dynamic entity that can assume responsibility for its acts. The emerging U.S. case law seems to deny this, perhaps in line with a growing American sensibility to protect industry and private interests over individual rights. Yet, as Internet communications continue to become more and more prevalent and readily available across the world, we must acknowledge the power they indeed have over societies and how they are shaped in technological *and* philosophical terms. Just as television has been critiqued and yes, blamed, for its influence over society, the Internet too faces such critiques. While different cultures embrace the Internet on their own terms, the issues under consideration throughout this paper will also continue to be examined and critiqued on a cultural basis. Whether the law or moral discourse, or , hopefully, a combination of the two, will drive decisions surrounding defamation, liability, and ultimate responsibility is yet to be seen.

Nature, Functions, and Accountability of ISPs

The inherent nature of the Internet is debatable. Where does it lay in the communications media schema? O'Neill has provided a brief yet informative discussion of this issue.[116] For a proper understanding of the moral accountability surrounding an ISP, it is important to first ask the question: How must an ISP be categorized? When one looks at the definitions and functions of publishers (editors), distributors (e.g., bookstores) and common carriers (telephone lines), it is clear that an ISP, in terms of its functions, does not fit specifically into one of these categories. It can *either, and sometimes simultaneously,* act as a common carrier, distributor, or publisher —depending on its role in a specific context. Moral consideration of this context is critical in assessing responsibility. Blanket immunity, stemming from Section 230, then fails to contextualize appropriately.

It is also important to understand how defamation can occur via an ISP. Four ways can be distinguished: via e-mail sent to single users, and this same message can be forwarded to others, contributing to defamation on the part of the one who forwarded the message; secondly, via comments posted on listservs; thirdly, via comments posted on Usenet boards; and lastly, by means of defamatory comments on websites.[117] This leads to the following questions: When can ISPs be held liable for defamation and to what extent? The answer to these questions are not *a priori,* as the law may have it, and depends on variables such as the level of knowledge that the ISP has about the content of the message as well as what role (carrier, publisher, distributor) it assumed and to what extent it assumed this role.

A Moral Perspective on Responsibility

To begin answering these questions from a moral perspective, it is important to clarify what is meant by responsibility. Responsibility, which originates from the Latin word *respondeo,* relates to accountability, blame, and punishment. It is a state of being accountable or answerable, to a relationship or obligation. It implies a relationship of trust between at least two people, entities, or things, or, in other words, it is a second-level normative concept, by which we mean is it always linked to a set of values/norms (cultural or social, temporal, universal, etc) on which responsibility is based and judged—one must be responsible *for something.* While this fundamental understanding of responsibility can cross borders, the attribution of responsibility can become more complex and confusing when there is a clash of norms. For example, a potential clash exists between freedom of speech and defamation, while another potential clash exists between one's right to expression and one's right to privacy. We saw these clashes in action in our earlier discussion of France and its prohibition of Nazi memorabilia online.

Three different levels of responsibility that can be assigned to ISPs can be distinguished. The first is a *functional* responsibility. It relates to the ability to communicate information in an effective and reliable manner. Functional responsibility does not exclude moral responsibility, but these responsibilities are however limited to their *functional role* as common carriers of information. In other words, their only moral obligation is to see that information is communicated in an effective and reliable process. Information that is not communicated effectively can cause, for example, damages, as in lost revenue or work stoppage. Most ISPs favor this functional role responsibility and thereby limit their moral responsibility. This functional responsibility role applies, however, when ISPs are only considered common carriers, which, we've argued, is not the case.

The second level of responsibility is *legal responsibility* and is primarily based on the minimum moral consensus within a society (cultural differences notwithstanding), as natural law theory would assert. Clarity and consensus on the moral responsibilities of ISPs are therefore important to determine the legal responsibilities of ISPs. Responsibilities of ISPs do not start with a law ascribing and assigning these responsibilities—moral consensus must exist first and inform the law. Legal systems are more restricted in the sense that they operate to protect the interest of society and maintain stability within the society at large. There is typically a limited number of cases regarding ISPs where serious harm is done to people, though these cases are growing, as our legal discussion above illustrated. Although legal responsibility is mostly based on a moral foundation, it can differ from moral responsibility. For example, one has no choice but to obey the law; thus, one can be held legally responsible even in cases where one is acting morally responsible. We are seeing this dilemma playing out in the legal discourse in the United States.

Thirdly, *moral responsibility* protects a broader realm of human interest and is based on a set of shared core values to which society or a group of people adheres. Moor, for instance, names life and happiness, ability, freedom, knowledge, resources, and security.[118] His goal is to find core values that apply internationally and imply mutual acceptance. As Moor identified, a significant problem surrounds the identification and acceptance of this set of core values/norms that can be used to regulate the Internet. Moreover, Habermas[119] correctly states that a norm is only justified if it is equally good for each person or group concerned. To this end, he proposes an ethical approach grounded in dialogue and based on a communicative, intersubjective approach to identify this common norm/s to enable global moral reasoning. Based on this approach, we suggest that *human rights* provide the best universal moral framework to regulate the Internet. Human rights provide a cross-cultural validity; for example, the universal acceptance of a need for security and acknowledgement of human autonomy. These core values can be articulated through the right to privacy and the right to freedom of expression. These core values—security and human autonomy—will be used as the measure against which we evaluate moral responsibility and the ISP.

A Balanced Approach Between the Communitarian and Libertarian Approaches

Based on these core values, we support the application of this third level of responsibility, moral responsibility, when considering ISPs and defamatory speech. There are different approaches to reasoning for moral responsibility. The first is the *communitarian approach,* which emphasizes the collective responsibility to one's society as a whole—sometimes at the expense of the freedom and rights of individuals.[120] This communitarian approach has the undesirable effect of limiting individual freedom of speech on the Internet. The recent United States Supreme Court decision[121] (July 2003) to uphold the Children's Internet Protection Act (CIPA), which requires filtering of children's access to the Internet, is a prime example of this form of reasoning to protect society as a whole. This was not the reasoning, however, in the dismissal of *Kathleen v. City of Livermore.*

The second approach, a *libertarian approach,* emphasizes the right of the individual and regards these rights to be of more importance than the interests of the community. According to this approach, which is supported by liberalists (or egoists), the right of the individual must be respected as opposed to the interests of the community. This approach can lead to an absolutism of privacy and freedom of expression, and this would imply that ISPs have absolutely no responsibility regarding defamation or defamatory speech. In the case of the person being defamed, his or her rights are therefore neglected and disregarded in favor of another's absolute rights. Moreover, extreme individual freedom (of expression, for instance) can create serious social harm and even social chaos.[122]

In the most extreme forms, both aforementioned approaches fail to provide a solution to the dilemma surrounding freedom of expression versus the interest of the community. The solution must rather be sought in a balance between the communitarian and liberalist approaches, between individual autonomy and collective interests. To achieve this balance, the default condition must support the individual's right to freedom of expression, until that freedom harms society. Harm is derived from the fact that all humans are of equal value and have certain rights that must be protected and respected. Harm is done where there are intentional actions (for example, speech) which has the effect of injuring/harming this "human beingness" of a person.

One's right to privacy must be acknowledged, protected, and accepted as a primary principle; therefore, freedom of expression and privacy can be seen as manifestations of the core values of human autonomy and security in any society and must be regarded as a cornerstone in moral reasoning regarding anonymous speech on the Internet.

The Different Roles of ISPs and the Assigning of Retrospective and Prospective Responsibilities

The Internet is a complex entity, with many stakeholders and role players; the ISP itself is indeed complex, as it too holds many roles and responsibilities. In the assigning of moral responsibility to an ISP, this complexity must be considered. Firstly, the moral responsibility is not restricted to functional responsibility. To lessen the responsibility to the functional level is to compare the ISP to a common carrier and thus, neglect their role as distributor or even creator of information. Within the functional role, the ISP must only provide the means of transmission and assure that communications take place effectively. What transpires between individuals is not a moral concern. The main moral concern within the functional model is the protection of privacy. We can see the clash between the moral and the legal in the aforementioned Verizon case, where Verizon abided by the law over the privacy interests of the individual.

Secondly, apart from the common carrier model, ISPs can also be considered distributors, such as bookstores and libraries, and thus assume the same level of moral responsibility. This distribution is expressed through web pages, chat rooms, and bulletin boards. Recall that the default condition upholds the individual's right to expression and to privacy, but when harm is done through a web page, chat room, or bulletin board, moral responsibility toward society applies.

In assigning this moral responsibility to the ISP, the following must be considered: The level and type of harm; legal assertions; and the core values. It is furthermore argued that we use retrospective reasoning[123] in the assignment of responsibility. This entails that an ISP must act when notified, not before. In contrast, prospective reasoning questions the default condition by violating the right to expression and to privacy, as it requires individuals and institutions to look forward to prevent harm from happening; in the realm of the Internet, this is done through the use of filters, for example. Prospective reasoning is furthermore hampered by practical considerations, such as management, unreliable software, time, and financial constraints. Prospective reasoning also fails, as it actually can inhibit moral responsibility, due to the fact that once you accept this responsibility, the law can more easily hold you retrospectively responsible.

Thirdly, an ISP can also act as an editor, creator, and publisher of information. In these roles, the ISP assumes a greater level of moral responsibility to individuals *and* to society. Both retrospective and prospective reasoning are favored here. For example, if an ISP is a creator of harmful information, such as a threat or a defamatory remark, it must look forward in order to prevent potential harm, as well as act retrospectively, and remove the harmful material.

Thus, it can be argued that moral responsibility differs from functional and legal responsibility. Yet, it is significant that moral responsibility plays a role in both other types of responsibility. Moreover, moral responsibility is a second level normative concept, and is complex. When applied to an ISP, it becomes even more complex due to the clash between individual rights and societal interests, as well as the different functional roles the ISP can hold. It is argued that individual rights are the default condition, until societal harm is done. Preference is furthermore given to retrospective reasoning, except when an ISP holds the role of creator or publisher.

Moral Framework for the Legal Discourse

Based on the aforementioned moral approach it is proposed that any legal discourse on the topic of the responsibility of ISPs regarding freedom of expression and defamation must first take the following into consideration:

- The recognition of the autonomy and freedom of the individual. Individuals have certain rights, above and beyond the commercial or private interests of the ISP or other entity, which must form the default in legal reasoning

- Human rights imply also a responsibility and duty toward society. One must participate in and contribute to the society responsibly and fairly to maintain a balance of rights. Rights are therefore prima facie and can be overruled in cases where harm is done to other individuals or society

- In assigning responsibility to ISPs, the different roles and functions of ISPs must be kept in mind. These roles and functions should determine the assigning of retrospective or prospective responsibility.

Conclusion

In conclusion, the above moral considerations lead us to suggest that the current legal paradigm is remiss in its approach to the role of the ISP. An emergent definition of the ISP and its role is necessary from the moral perspective in order to protect all of the stakeholders in their various positions in this new arena of communication.

Two potential proposals can be envisioned: Restore the distributor liability as it was before case law began interpreting Section 230 as a complete immunity provision. This would be a "know or reason to know" standard and makes intermediaries responsible in limited circumstances. Second, consider imposing a "should know standard." This would impose some duty to investigate. However, it is a standard that is not imposed on print publishers, yet it might be justified in the Internet context as the natural content control features of traditional publishing are not widespread on the Internet, thus a higher level of vigilance may be needed.

Further discussion will certainly continue around these issues, as legal and moral precedent and consideration expands. Our goal throughout this paper was to provide a solid foundation from which to deliberate on defamation, responsibility, and the major stakeholders and related issues involved in these complex relationships.

Notes

1. An earlier version of this paper appeared as "Sticks and Stones and Words That Harm: Liability vs. Responsibility, Section 230 and Defamatory Speech in Cyberspace," *Ethics and Information Technology* 4 (2), 143–158 (2002).

2. 1 W. Page Keeton et al., *Prosser and Keeton on the Law of Torts* 117 (5th Ed. 1984).

3. F. Lawrence Street, *Law of the Internet* § 6-2(b), at 625 (2000)

4. James M. Talbot, *New Media: Intellectual Property, Entertainment and Technology Law* § 10.4, at 10-4 (1999); Kent D. Stuckey, *Internet and Online Law*, § 2.03[3], at 2–33, (2000).

5. Cynthia L. Counts and C. Amanda Martin, Libel in Cyberspace: A Framework for Addressing Liability and Jurisdictional Issues in This New Frontier, 59 *Albany Law Review* 1083 (1996); James M. Talbot, *New Media: Intellectual Property, Entertainment and Technology Law* § 10.15 (1999).

6. Restatement (Second) of Torts 2d § 581.

7. Restatement (Second) of Torts 2d § 12.

8. Restatement (Second) of Torts 2d § 12, comment a.

9. Restatement (Second) of torts 2d § 581, comment e.

10. *Martin* v. *Trustees of the British Museum*, 10 T.L.R. 338 (1894); *Vizzetelly* v. *Mudie's Select Library, Ltd.*, [1900] 2 Q.B. 170.

11. Restatement (Second) of Torts § 578.

12. Restatement (Second) of Torts 2d § 577, comment p.

13. *Getaped.com* v. *Canqemi,* 2002 WL 338110 (S.D.N.Y. 2002).

14. *Urbanchich* v. *Drummoyne Municipal Council*, 1988 N. S. W. LEXIS 8802 (1988).

15. *Byrne* v. *Dean,* [1937] 1 KB 818.

16. *Heller* v. *Bianco,* 244 P.2d 757 (Calif. 1953).

17. Restatement of Torts § 577: "((1) Publication of defamatory matter is its communication inten-tionally or by a negligent act to one other than the person defamed. (2) One who intentionally and unreasonably fails to remove defamatory matter that he knows to be exhibited on land or chattels in his possession or under his control is subject to liability for its continued publication").

18. *Cubby* v. *CompuServ,* 776 F. Supp. 135, 140 (S.D.N.Y.1991).

19. *Curzon-Brown* v. *San Francisco Community College District et al.*, No. 307335, demurer filed (Cal. Super. Ct.,) San Francisco County, January 21, 2000); Student Group Seeks Dismissal of "Libel-by-Linking" Lawsuit, Computer & Online Industry Litigation Reporter, May 16, 2000, at 10.

20. Brenda Sandburg, Hyperlink Blast Sparks a Libel Suit, *The National Law Journal*, February 21, 2000, at A4.

21. *Stratton Oakmont, Inc.* v. *Prodigy Services Co.,* 1995 NY Misc. LEXIS 229, 23 Media L. Reporter (BNA) (N.Y. Sup. Ct. May 24, 1995).

22. *MacFadden* v. *Anthony,* 117 N.Y.S.2d 520 (Sup. 1952).

23. Restatement (Second) of Torts, § 581, comment c, illustration 3 (1977).

24. Conference Report, House Report 104–458, 104th Congress, 2nd Session 194 (1996) (Conference Report on the Telecommunications Act of 1996).

25. 47 U.S.C. § 230(f)(1) (2000).

26. 47 US.C. § 230(f)(2) (2000).

27. *Batzel* v. *Smith,* 2003 U.S. App. LEXIS 12736 (9th Cir. 2003).

28. *Batzel* v. *Smith,* 2003 U.S. App. LEXIS 12736, *44-*45 (9th Cir. 2003).

29. F. Lawrence Street, *Law of the Internet* § 6-2(A), at 625(2000); Harvey L. Zuckman et al., *Modem Communications Law*, § 5.10, at 612 (1999).

30. Conference Report, House Report 104–458, 104th Congress, 2nd Session, 194 (1996) (Conference Report on the Telecommunications Act of 1996).

31. 47 U.S.C. § 230(f)(2) (2000).

32. *Zeran* v. *America Online, Inc.,* 129 F.3d 327 (4th Cir.1997), cert. denied, 524 U.S. 937 (1998) (defamation); *Blumenthal* v. *Drudge,* 992 F. Supp 2d 44 (D.D.C. 1998) (defamation); *Lunney* v. *Prodigy Services Co.,* 94 N.Y. 2d 242, 723 N.E. 2d 539, 701 N.Y.S. 2d 684 (1999); cert. denied 120 S. Ct. 1832 (1999); *Blumenthal* v. *Drudge,* 992 F. Supp 2d 44 (D.D.C. 1998) (defamation); *Ben Ezra, Einstein & Co.* v. *American Online, Inc.,* 206 F. 3d 980 (10th Cir. 2000) (defamation and negligence); *Stoner* v. *eBay. Inc.,* No. 305666 (Cal. Super. Ct., San Francisco County, Nov. 7, 2000) (business law); *Doe* v. *American Online, Inc.,* 783 So. 2d 1010 (Florida 2001) (negligence).

33. *Barret* v. *Clark,* 2001 WL 881259, *9 (Cal. Super. Ct 2001)(unpublished).

34. 31 Laurin H. Milles and Leslie Paul Machado, ISP Immunity Provisions Broadly Interpreted. *The National Law Journal*, C19, C20, April 15, 2002.

35. Ian C. Ballon, Defamation and Preemption under the Telecommunications Act of 1996: Why the Rule in *Zeran* v. *America Online is Wrong,* 2 *Cyberspace Lawyer* 6 (July/August, 1997); David Wiener, Negligent Publication of Statements Posted on Electronic Bulletin Boards: Is There Any Liability Left After Zeran?, 39 *Santa Clara Law Review* 905 (1999), Michelle J. Kane, Business Law: 1. Electronic Commerce: b) Internet Service Provider Liability: *Blumenthal* v. *Drudge,* 14 *Berkeley Tech. LJ.* 483 (1999), Michael H. Spencer, Defamatory E-Mail and Employer Liability: Why Razing *Zeran* v. *America Online* Is a Good Thing, 6 *Richmond Journal of Law and Technology* 25 (2000).

36. *Kathleen R.* v. *City of Livermore,* V-015266-4 (Calif. Sup. Ct. October 21, 1998); see also, Brief of Amici Curiae American Civil Liberties Union, *Kathleen R.* v. *City of Livermore,* V-015266-4 (available at www.aclu.org/court/ kathleenrvslivermore.html).

37. *Ben Ezra, Weinstein & Co.* v. *American Online, Inc.,* No. Civ 97-485 Lh/Lfg (D.N.N. 1999) (4 Electronic Commerce & Law Reporter (BNA), March 17, 1999; *Doe* v. *America Online,* 718 So.2d 385 (Fla. App. 1998).

38. Kent D. Stuckey, Internet And Online Law, § 2.03[3], at 2-74 (2000).

39. *Zeran* v. *America Online, Inc.,* 958 F. Supp. 1124, 1133, 1134, at n. 20 (E.D. Va. 1997), aff'd 129 F.3d 327 (4th Cir. 1997).

40. *Does* v. *Franco Productions,* 2000 U.S. Dist. LEXIS 8645 (N.D. Ill. 2000).

41. *Blumenthal* v. *Drudge,* 992 F. Supp. 44, 52 (D.D.C 1998).

42. *Does* v. *Franco* Productions, 2000 U.S. Dist. LEXIS 8645,at *16-*17 (N.D. Ill. 2000).

43. *Bowker* v. *America Online, Inc.,* No. 95L 013509, Verified Petition for Discovery (Cir. Ct. Cook Cty. Ill., filed Sept. 12, 1995), available at www.courttv.comllibrary/cyberlaw/ aoldefamatioll.html

44. 163 F. Supp. 2d 1069 (S.D. 2001).

45. 163 F. Supp. 2d at 1071.

46. *Carafano* v. *Metrosplash.com.Inc.,* 207 F.Supp. 2d 1055, 1065-1066 (C.D. Cal. 2002).

47. 207 F.Supp. 2d at 1067.

48. 207 F.Supp. 2d at 1068.

49. 2002 U.S. Dist. LEXIS 24251 (E.D. La. 2002).

50. 2002 U.S. Dist. LEXIS 24251, at *10-*12.

51. *Noah* v. *AOL Time Warner, Inc.,* 2003 U.S. Dist. LEXIS 8242 (E.D. Va. 2003) ("claim[ ] that the ISP wrongfully refused to prevent participants in an online chat room from posting or submitting harassing comments that blasphemed and defamed plaintiff's Islamic religion and his co-religionists").

52. As quoted at 2003 U.S. Dist. LEXIS 8242, at *6-*7.

53. 2003 U.S. Dist. LEXIS 8242, at *37-*38.

54. 2003 U.S. Dist. LEXIS 8242, at * 12, quoting *Zeran* v. *AOL.*

55. 2003 U.S. Dist. LEXIS 8242, at * 21.

56. 2003 U.S. Dist. LEXIS 8242, at * 24.

57. Scott Sterling, International Law of Mystery: Holding Internet Service Providers Liable for Defamation and the Need for a Comprehensive International Solution, 21 *Loyola Los Angeles Entertainment Law Review* 327, 337 (2001).

58. *Godfrey* v. *Demon Internet Ltd.,* [1999] 4 All E.R. 342, [2000] 3 WLR. 1020.

59. *Firth* v. *State of New York,* 84 Misc.2d 105 (N.Y. Ct. Cl. 2000). See also *Van Buskirk* v. *The New York Times Co.,* 2000 WL 1206732 (S.D.N.Y. Aug. 24, 2000) (holding "single publication rule" applies to Internet publications).

60. F. Lawrence Street and Mark P. Grant, *Law of the Internet,* § 6.10, at 6-17 (2001).

61. Scott Sterling, International Law of Mystery: Holding Internet Service Providers Liable for Defamation and the Need for a Comprehensive International Solution, 21 *Loyola Los Angeles Entertainment Law Review* 327, 338 (2001).

62. Defamation Act, 1996, ch. 31, section 1(1).

63. Defamation Act, 1996, ch. 31, section 1(3).

64. *Godfrey* v. *Demon Internet Ltd.,* [1999] 4 All E.R. 342, [2000] 3 WL.R. 1020.

65. The Restatement of Torts, 2d § 581, Reporter's Notes to Comment c lists: "This is supported, as to news vendors, by *Cardozo* v. *True,* 342 So.2d 633 (Fla. App. 1977); *Balabanoff* v. *Fossani,* 192 Misc. 615, 81 N.Y.S.2d 732 (1948); *Emmens* v. *Pottle,* 16 Q.B.D. 354 (1885); *Weldon* v *"The Times" Book Co.,* 28 TLR. 143 (1911). See, also: Libraries: *Martin* v. *Trustees of the British Museum,* 10 T.L.R. 338 (1894); *Vzzetelly* v. *Mudie's Select Library, Ltd.,* [1900] 2 Q.B. 170. The *Godfrey* v. *Demon Internet Ltd.* court comments and cites: "The situation is analogous to that of the bookseller who sells a book defamatory of the plaintiff (see *Weldon* v. *Times Book Co Ltd* (1911) 28 TLR 143, the case about the books on Gounod), to that of the circulating library who provided books to subscribers (see *Vzzetelly* v. *Mudie's Select Library Ltd* [1900] 2 QB 170 esp at 178–181 per Romer L J, the case about the book on Stanley's search for Emir Pasha in Africa) and to that of distributors (see *Bottomley* v. *F W Woolworth & Co Ltd* (1932) 48 TLR 521, the case about the detective story magazine containing the article Swindlers and Scoundrels. *Horatio Bottomley, Editor and Embezzler* and *Sun Life Assurance Co* of *Canada* v *W H Smith & Son Ltd* (1933) 150 LT 211, [1933] All ER Rep 432, the case about newspaper posters announcing More Grave Sun Life of Canada Disclosures).

66. *Rinas* v. *Hardwick,* 1 Media L. Rep. 67 (S.C. of Western Australia, 1994); Malcolm McDonald, Internet Libel Case Settled Out of Court, NZ *Infotech Weekly* (Wellington), March 23, 1998, at p. 2.

67. *Urbanchich* v. *Drummoyne Municipal Council,* 1988 N. S. W LEXIS 8802 (1988).

68. Jurisdiction for Defamation: Place of Publication or Place of Review, Cyberspace Lawyer, June 2001, atp. 18.

69. *Gutnick* v. *Dow Jones & Company,* [2001] VSC 305 (available at www.austlii.edu.au/au/cases/vicNSC/2001l305.rtf).

70. *Gutnick* v. *Dow Jones & Company,* [2001] VSC 305 (available at www.austlii.edu.au/au/cases/vicNSC/2001l305.rtf).

71. The doctrine or principle that where, in a broad sense, the ends of justice strongly indicate that the controversy may be more suitably tried elsewhere, jurisdiction should be declined and the parties relegated to relief to be sought in another forum. *Universal Adjustment Corp.* v *Midland Bank,* 281 Mass 303, 184 NE 152, 87 ALR 1407. The doctrine that an American court has power to decline to assume jurisdiction where the litigation is between aliens or nonresidents, or can more appropriately be conducted in a foreign tribunal. *Ballentine's Law Dictionary* (1969) (no pagination in LEXIS*NEXIS version).

72. *Dow Jones & Company, Inc. v. Gutnick,* [2002] HCA 56, 10 December, 2002, M3/2002, available at http://austlii.edu/au/au/cases/cth/high_ct/2002/56.rtf.

73. *Dow Jones & Company, Inc. v. Gutnick,* at p. 19, ¶ 54.

74. "This argument ignores the fact that most Internet fora—including chat rooms, newsgroups, mail exploders, and the Web—are open to all comers. The Government's assertion that the knowledge requirement somehow protects the communications of adults is therefore untenable. Even the strongest reading of the 'specific person' requirement of 223(d) cannot save the statute. It would confer broad powers of censorship, in the form of a *heckler's veto,* upon any opponent of indecent speech who might simply log on and inform the would-be discoursers that his 17-year-old child—a 'specific person . . . under 18 years of age" 47 U.S.C. A. § 223(d)(1)(A) (Supp. 1997)—would be present." *ACLU* v. *Reno,* 521 U.S. 844, 880 (1997).

75. Aukje A.H. van Hoek, Australia's High Court Upholds Local (Private Law) Jurisdiction in Case of Defamation over the Internet, *International Enforcement Law Reporter*, May, 2003 (no pagination in LEXIS document).

76. Aukje A.H. van Hoek, Australia's High Court Upholds Local (Private Law) Jurisdiction in Case of Defamation over the Internet, *International Enforcement Law Reporter*, May, 2003 (no pagination in LEXIS document) (emphasis added).

77. *Dow Jones & Company, Inc. v. Gutnick,* at p. 29–30, ¶¶ 84-87 ("The nature of Web makes it virtually impossible to ensure with complete effectiveness the isolation of any geographic area on the Earth's surface from access to a particular website. Id., at p. 29, ¶ 84.).

78. *Dow Jones & Company, Inc. v. Gutnick,* at p. 39, ¶ 14.

79. *Dow Jones & Company, Inc. v. Gutnick,* at p. 54, ¶ 152.

80. *Dow Jones & Company, Inc. v. Gutnick,* at p. 54, ¶ 152 ("This approach could subject Australian defendants to the more restrictive defamation laws of foreign jurisdictions." Footnote omitted.).

81. *Dow Jones & Company, Inc. v. Gutnick,* at p. 54, ¶ 152.

82. *Dow Jones & Company, Inc. v. Gutnick,* at p. 6, ¶ 23.

83. *Dow Jones & Company, Inc. v. Gutnick,* at p. 41, ¶ 119–87 ("It may do this especially if that judgment was secured by the application of laws, the enforcement of which would be regarded as unconstitutional or otherwise offensive to a different legal culture. However, such results are still less than wholly satisfactory. They appear to warrant national legislative attention and to require international discussion in a forum as global as the Internet itself." *Dow Jones & Company, Inc. v. Gutnick,* at p. 58, ¶¶ 165–166).

84. *Dow Jones & Company, Inc. v. Gutnick,* at p. 47, ¶¶ 133.

85. (See, High Court of Paris, May 22, 2000, Interim Court Order No. 00/05308, 00/05309 (translation attested accurate by Isabell Camus, February 16, 2001, as observed in *Yahoo! Inc.* v. *La Liguecontre le Racisme et L'Antisitisme,* 169 F. supp. 2d 1181 (N.D. Cal. 2001) and Interim Court Order, 22 May, 2000, provided by Center for Democracy and Technology, available at http://www.cdt.org (English translation of order issued by County Court of Paris, France (translator unknown).

86. Sakur Mizuno, When Free Speech and the Internet Collide: Yahoo!-Nazi-Paraphernalia Case, *International Trade Law Journal* 56 (2001) (no pagination in LEXIS) ("What this case boils down to is the fundamental differences between the French and the American jurisprudence, and what is, and is not acceptable activity in the context of the Internet"). See also Id., compar-

ing the Free Speech clause of the U.S. Constitution and the French Declaration of the Rights of Man and of the Citizen, that is incorporated into the French Constitution and that provides for a limited right of speech, i.e., a speaker is "responsible for such abuses of this freedom."

87. 169 F. Supp. 2d at 1186.

88. See discussion of the case in, Sakur Mizuno, When Free Speech and the Internet Collide: Yahoo!-Nazi-Paraphernalia Case, *International Trade Law Journal* 56 (2001) (no pagination in LEXIS).

89. 169 F. Supp. 2d at 1186 and 1194.

90. See, In the News: French Court Acquits Yahoo! of Criminal Charges Stemming from Sale of Nazi memorabilia by Yahoo!-hosted websites in U.S., Entertainment Law Reporter, March 2003. As the headline announces, a French court acquitted Yahoo! of criminal liability early in 2003.

91. 169 F. Supp. 2d at 1186.

92. 169 F. Supp. 2d at 1186–1187. See also, *Yahoo! Inc. v. La Liguecontre le Racisme et L'Antisitisme,* 145 F. Supp. 2d 1168, 1179, at n. 7 (N.D. Cal. 2001) ("As Yahoo! and others have pointed out, a content restriction imposed upon an Internet service provider by a foreign court just as easily could prohibit promotion of democracy, gender equality, a particular religion or other viewpoints which have strong support in the United States but are viewed as offensive or inappropriate elsewhere").

93. James M. Hirschhorn, Fortress America on the Internet, *New Jersey Law Journal*, January 13, 2003 ("Its reasoning subjects American web sites to the libel laws of Singapore, the anti-racism laws of France or the sedition laws of China. This poses an obvious danger that American publishers will be deterred from posting material that violates foreign law, with the result that the American audience will be limited to reading what is deemed acceptable for foreigners who do not enjoy American freedom of expression.")

94. 169 F. Supp. 2d at 1186.

95. See, Editorial, *New Jersey Law Journal*, January 6, 2003.

96. 169 F. Supp. 2d at 1192.

97. 169 F. Supp. 2d at 1194.

98. This was rejected by a federal district in a dispute between Dow Jones and Harrods Department Store. See, *Dow Jones & Company, Inc. v. Harrods, Ltd.,* 237 F. Supp. 2d 394 (S.D.N.Y. 2002) ("Validating this proposition would make it appropriate and commonplace for litigants to resort to federal courts under the DJA [the federal Declaratory Judgment Act] to obtain declaration of non-liability and injunctive relief whenever a party alleges that it faces even a mere prospect of a lawsuit or contingent liability in a foreign jurisdiction whose laws or procedures may conflict in some with fundamental rights enjoyed under United States law. Thus, under Dow Jones' hypothesis, the DJA would confer upon an American court a preemptive style of global jurisdiction branching worldwide and able to strike down offending litigation anywhere on Earth… The Court finds nothing in the United States Constitution, nor in the DJA or in customary practice of international law, that comports with such a robust, Olympian perspective of federal judicial power." Id., at 411.)

99. 169 F. Supp. 2d at 1193 (also observing a footnote that no opinion is made as to whether such treaty or legislation would be constitutional, footnote n. 12).

100. See, e.g., International Covenant on Civil and Political Rights, art. 19(2), December 16, 1966, 993 U.N.T.S. 171; European Convention for the Protection of Human Rights and Fundamental Freedoms, at 10(1), November 4, 1950, 213 U.N.T.S. 221; Universal Declaration of Human Rights, art 19, December 10, 1948, U.N. GAOR, 3rd Sess., Pt. 1, Resolutions, at 71 U.N. Doc. A/810 (1948) ("Everyone has the right to freedom of opinion and expression, this right includes freedom to hold opinions without interference and to seek, receive and impart information and ideas through any media and regardless of frontiers.")

101. *Columbia Insurance Co.* v. *See scandy.com,* 185 ER.D. 573 (N.D. Cal. 1999); *In re Subpoena Duces Tecum to America Online, Inc.,* 52 Va. Cir. 26 (2000); *Doe* v. *2TheMart.com, Inc.,* 140 E Supp. 2d 1088 (WD. Wash. 2001); *Dendrite International, Inc.* v. *John Doe No.3,* 775 A.2d 756 (N.J. Super. Ct. 2001); *Doe* v. *2TheMart.com, Inc.,* 140 E Supp. 2d 1088 (WD. Wash. 2001).

102. Tomas A. Lipinski, To Speak or Not to Speak: Developing Legal Standard for Anonymous Speech on the Internet, 5 *Informing Science* 95 (2001).

103. R. Buys (ed.) (2000) *Cyberlaw: The Law of the Internet in South Africa.* Van Shaick: Pretoria, 357–362.

104. 2003 U.S. Dist LEXIS 6778 (D.C. D.C. 2003).

105. *In re Verizon Internet Services, Inc.,* at *1.

106. *In re Verizon Internet Services, Inc.,* at *34.

107. *In re Verizon Internet Services, Inc.,* at *44.

108. *In re Verizon Internet Services, Inc.,* at *65.

109. *In re Verizon Internet Services, Inc.,* at *52.

110. *In re Verizon Internet Services, Inc.,* n. 22, at *54.

111. *In re Verizon Internet Services, Inc.,* at *61-*62.

112. J. Rawls (1973). *A Theory of Justice.* Oxford: Oxford University Press ; J. Habermas, (1993) *Moral Consciousness and Communication Action.* Cambridge, MA: MIT Press, 1993; P. Singer (1979). Practical Ethics. Cambridge: Cambridge University Press; I. Kant (1956) *Critique of Practical Reason.* Translated by L.W. Beck. New York: Bobbs-Merrill

113. H. Jonas (1984) *The Imperative of Responsibility.* Chicago: University of Chicago Press; C. Mitcham (1987) Responsibility and Technology. The Expanding Relationship In P T Durbin (ed), *Technology and Responibility.* Dordrecht: D Reidel Publishing Company: 3–39.

114. K. Bayertz (1995) Herkunft der Verantwortung In Idem *Verantwortug: Prinzip oder Problem?* Darmstadt: Wissenshaftliche Buchgesellschaft: 3–71; H.Jonas (1984) The Imperative of Responsibility. Chicago: University of Chicago Press; C. Mitcham (1987) Responsibility and Technology. The Expanding Relationship In P. T. Durbin (ed), Technology and Responsibility. Dordrecht: D. Reidel Publishing Company: 3–39.

115. R. Spinello, "Internet Service Providers and Defamation: New Standards of Liability," in *Readings in CyberEthics* (Eds. R. Spinello and H. Tavani), Sudbury, MA: Jones and Bartlett, 2001.

116. R. O'Neill, "Free Speech in Cyberspace," *Journal of Information Ethics,* 7(1), 15–23.

117. R. Spinello, "Internet Service Providers and Defamation: New Standards for Liability," in *Readings in Cyberethics* (Eds. R. Spinello and H. Tavani), Sudbury, MA: Jones and Bartlett, 2001.

118. J. Moor, "Reason, Relativity, and Responsibility in Computer Ethics," in *Readings in Cyberethics* (Eds. R. Spinello and H. Tavani), Sudbury, MA, Jones and Bartlett, 2001.

119. Habermas, J. (1993). *Moral Consciousness and Communication Action.* Cambridge, MA: MIT Press, 1993.

120. Van den Hoven, M.J., Towards a theory of privacy in the information age, *Computers & Society,* 27(3):33–37 (1997). Communitarianism as a movement is popularized by Robert Bellah in his book *Habits of the Heart* (1996) and Amitai Etzioni (1994) in *The Spirit of Community.*

121. *United States* v. *American Library Association*, 2003 U.S. Lexis 4799.

122. An example of this comes from South Africa; two university students sent an email after the 9/11 terrorist attacks suggesting that South Africa was indirectly involved in the attacks. Upon dissemination of this email, South Africa's stock market responded very negatively and the currency dropped in value dramatically. *Beeld Morning Newspaper,* September 25, 2001.

123. Bayertz, K. (1995). *Verantwortung: Prinzip oder Problem?* Darmstadt: Wissenschaftliche Buchgesellschaft.

Introduction to Chapter 3:
Intellectual Property in Cyberspace

In the information age there may be no more contentious issue than the scope of ownership rights to intellectual property. This type of property consists of "intellectual objects," such as original musical compositions, poems, novels, inventions, product formulas, and so forth. Unlike physical objects, intellectual ones are nonexclusive and "non-rivalrous," since they can be used by many people simultaneously and their use by some does not preclude their use by others. Furthermore, although the development and creation of intellectual property objects may be time-consuming and costly, the marginal cost of reproducing intellectual products is usually quite low. Intellectual property is protected by a regime of sophisticated laws such as patent, copyright, and trademark statutes, spurring innovation by giving the authors or inventors a limited monopoly for their creations.

The primary axis of discussion in this chapter is copyright law, which exists to protect creative or literary works such as novels, music, and even software programs. These laws now give individual authors ownership to their work for the lifetime of the author plus 70 years before falling into the public domain. Copyright laws have traditionally made provisions for "first sale" and "fair use" in order to balance the public interest with the enclosure of intellectual property. For example, the author's rights to the fruit of his/her creation are balanced with a fair use provision that allows small segments of copyrighted works to be quoted for research purposes, for critical reviews, and for educational purposes without getting the author's permission. Copyright laws are also predicated on an important distinction between ideas, which cannot be "owned" by anyone, and the expression of those ideas. Only what is "fixed in a tangible medium of expression" is protected by copyright law.

The Internet is obviously changing views on intellectual property and the future of copyright protection. John Perry Barlow (1994) has been predicting that the Net and digital technology will mean free information and the end of copyright law as we know it. According to Barlow, only myopic individuals, living in a world of "glassy-eyed denial," are blind to the new realities and possibilities of digital data and network technology.

Barlow's prediction may one day come to pass, but for the time being intellectual property issues of varying complexity still dominate the headlines about cyberspace. Content providers and software developers insist on safeguarding "their property" and engage in sometimes in futile struggles against piracy and against free riders who frequent the Web.

Paul Goldstein (1994) has conjured the metaphor of a "celestial jukebox" to envision the Web of the not-too-distant future, where individuals will have easy access to a plethora of free or nominally priced digital products such as CDs, books, journals, television shows, and many other forms of information and entertainment. Many hurdles must be overcome such as copyright disputes, trademark claims, restrictions on hyperlinking, and so forth before this utopian vision can be realized. Movie and recording studios, for example, see the awesome advantages of distributing their content online but worry that encryption and other sophisticated technologies cannot adequately protect the information.

Encryption is certainly part of the solution but it is by no means foolproof. Its limitations were recently made manifest in the now infamous DeCSS case. DVD movie files are encrypted with a format known as CSS (Content Scrambling System). A young teenager in Norway (with the help of some friends he met on the Internet) developed a program known as DeCSS to decrypt CSS. These young "hackers" claimed that they did not intend to pirate movies but to play DVD movies on Linux systems, which, unlike Mac and Windows Operating systems, do not come equipped with CSS capability. The movie studios joined together in a major lawsuit against the purveyors of DeCSS code.

This seminal lawsuit, *Universal City Studios* v. *Remeirdes* (2000), triggered some difficult questions, which are presented in "A Note on the DeCSS Case." Excerpts from the Digital Millennium Copyright Act (DMCA), which was enacted by the U.S. Congress in September 1998, precede this case study. A controversial section of that law, the anti-circumvention provisions, are challenged in the DeCSS case on constitutional grounds. These provisions criminalize the use of technologies that circumvent technical protection or encryption systems along with "trafficking" in such technologies.

The DeCSS case should be read in conjunction with the relevant sections of the DMCA. It is a primary test case for considering the scope and constitutionality of the DMCA's anti-circumvention provisions. Does this legislation give copyright holders too much discretionary power to block or interfere with the fair use of their work by consumers? And does it interfere with the free speech rights of those who create or disseminate code such as DeCSS?

Another issue addressed in the DMCA legislation is intermediary liability, that is, the liability of third parties for the copyright infringements of others. Some adjustments have been made in the law of contributory infringement for Online Service Providers (OSPs) (see section 512). According to Samuelson (1999), under this law OSPs "can qualify for one of a number of exemptions from liability ('safe harbors') if they are willing to terminate service to repeat infringers, to accommodate standard technological measures adopted by copyright industries to protect works, and to abide by certain other conditions." OSPs must also remove material from their sites once they are notified that the material infringes copyright.

In addition to digital movies, MP3 music files are also vulnerable to piracy. To explore this problem, this chapter includes another short case study called "Digital Music and Peer-to-Peer File Sharing." It reviews the functionality of peer-to-peer technologies such as KaZaA, and highlights the ethical problems faced by those who share music files. This case also describes the music industry's anti-piracy campaign, which resulted in a flood of lawsuits against people accused of illicitly distributing music over peer-to-peer networks on the Internet.

With the next reading, "A Politics of Intellectual Property: Environmentalism for the Net?," we turn from the intricacies of copyright law to some philosophical reflections about the politics of intellectual property. James Boyle, author of *Shamans, Software, and Spleens*, argues that we need a "political economy" of intellectual property. A main theme of his book is that society's justification for strong intellectual property protection is rooted in our romanticized notion of "authorship." Society sees the author as an original creator, crafting something new. By granting this new work protection, we can justly reward its author and set that work apart from the public domain. According to Boyle (1996), "it is the *originality* of the author, the novelty which he or she adds to the raw materials provided by culture and the common pool which 'justifies' the property right. . . ."

In "Politics of Intellectual Property," Boyle expresses his concern that a romanticized "original author" model is inducing us to overprotect intellectual property. As a result, the public domain is disappearing, "first in concept and then, increasingly, as a reality." We need, therefore, a political movement that will save this shrinking public domain just as the American environmental movement in the 1960s and 1970s saved the physical environment from further degradation.

The next two readings continue to question the appropriate level of protection and philosophical underpinnings of intellectual property rights. Like Boyle, Michael McFarland has concerns about preserving our intellectual commons. In "Intellectual Property, Information, and the Common Good," he maintains that we must not focus too narrowly on individual property rights lest we lose sight of the common good. Relying on Aristorelian and natural law ethics, he argues that the purpose of information must be taken into account when we construct policies and laws governing its distribution. According to McFarland, "information is about communication; it is meant to be shared." A recognition of the social nature of information will lead to more balanced legislation that will protect the rights of individuals without neglecting the common good.

Shelly Warwick asks about the ethical suitability of copyright law in her essay "Is Copyright Ethical." This essay examines the relationship between intellectual property rights and ethics; it probes a seldom-asked question: is the concept of private ownership of intellectual property inherently ethical? Echoing Boyle and McFarland, she expresses concern that the interests of individual creators are protected, and suggests that an economic rather than an ethical rationale drives this extension of rights.

John Snapper also questions the importance of copyright policy on the Web and contends that plagiarism is a more critical problem than copyright piracy. He concludes that "weakened copyright protections can still provide an adequate economic incentive for the publication industry." This does not imply that copyrights and patents have no place on the Web—the trick is to find the right level of protection against free riders while preserving incentives for web-based publishers.

Implicit in the next reading, "An Ethical Evaluation of Web Site Linking," is a more traditional approach to property issues. This article explores the issue of "deep linking," which raises a number of complex intellectual property issues. The most critical question concerns the appropriate scope of property rights for a web site and how to properly balance those rights against the common good of free and open communication on the Web. The author contends that there is no presumptive claim to the liberty of deep linking, since deep linking may be disrespectful of property rights in certain situations. Drawing support from the major theories that justify property ownership, the case is put forth that a web site must be considered as a form of intellectual property. The essay then probes the specific rights implied by this form of ownership along with the implications for activities such as hyperlinking.

Finally, it must be recognized that the impetus for intellectual property protection also comes from the software industry. This industry has carefully guarded its "crown jewels," that is, its precious source code.[1] Software licenses preclude illicit copying, fixing flaws, or even engaging in reverse-engineering. But the advent of open source code has begun to

---

[1] Software is written in high-level languages such as Java, C++, or BASIC. This source code is compiled or translated into machine readable object code or binary code (1s and 0s) that can only be understood by a computer.

change all this. According to Moody (2001), "the open source movement poses a challenge not just to Microsoft but to the entire software industry." Open source software developers not only distribute the software free of charge, but also share their source code, hoping that others will modify the code, fix flaws, or even make major enhancements. No one considered open source code too seriously until the appearance of Linux, an open source code operating system that is rapidly gaining in popularity and beginning to pose some threat to the dominance of Windows.

In the first of two key articles on this important development, "Ethical Issues in Open Source Software," Grodzinsky, Miller, and Wolf argue that the current social and ethical structure in the Open Source Software (OSS) Community stems from its roots in academia. The individual developers experience a level of autonomy similar to that of a faculty member in a university environment. The authors also underscore the difficulty of disguising low quality open source software as high quality software, because the open source model offers strong accountability. This article provides valuable background on licensing options available for open source software developers, and it explicitly considers the ethical dimensions of the open source movement.

Finally, Eric Raymond's influential essay "The Cathedral and the Bazaar" contrasts traditional development methods (the "cathedral") with the principles of more open and free development (the "bazaar"). While this essay may not end the debate, it clearly summarizes the many advantages of the open source code revolution. This alternative avenue for software development may have significant social implications since open code, easily customized by users, does not lend itself to the same level of regulatory control as traditional source code.

Discussion Questions

1. What is the DMCA and exactly what does it prohibit? Explain the "anti-circumvention" provisions of the DMCA in § 1201 (a). What is your assessment of these provisions? Does the DMCA violate the First Amendment to the Constitution?

2. How do you assess the implicit claim made by the defendants in the DeCSS trial that there is an unrestricted right to link to other web sites, even sites with unlawful material? [See also "An Ethical Evaluation of Web Site Linking."]

3. Assess the conclusions in Boyle's essay regarding the disappearance of the public domain. Cite evidence that this conclusion is true (or false). In your view, are we falling into the trap of overprotecting intellectual property as Boyle suggests?

4. Do you agree with Snapper's argument that plagiarism may be more important than copyright on the Web?

5. Will P2P systems like KaZaA ultimately suffer the same fate as Napster? Should they?

6. Write a critical review of Raymond's essay on open source code. What are the advantages and disadvantages of open code? [See also "Ethical Issues in Open Source Software"].

7. Do you agree with Samuel Johnson's comment regarding an open source software developer's willingness to work without compensation? "No one but a blockhead ever wrote, except for money."

References

Barlow, John. "The Economy of Ideas: A Framework for Rethinking Copyrights and Patents," *Wired,* March, 1994, pp. 47–50.

Boyle, James. *Shamans, Software and Spleens.* Cambridge: Harvard University Press, 1996

Goldstein, Paul. *Copyright's Highway.* New York: Hill and Wang, 1994.

Moody, Glyn. *Rebel Code.* Perseus Publishing, Cambridge, 2001.

Samuelson, Pamela. "Good News and Bad News on the Intellectual Property Front," *Communications of the ACM,* March, 1999, pp. 19–24.

Suggestions for Further Reading

Alderman, John. (2001). *Sonic Boom: Napster, MP3 and the New Pioneers of Music.* Cambridge, MA: Perseus Books.

Baase, Sara (2003). "Protecting Software and other Intellectual Property." Chapter 5 in *A Gift of Fire: Social, Legal, and Ethical Issues in Computing.* 2nd ed. Upper Saddle River, NJ: Prentice Hall.

Barlow, John. (1994). "The Economy of Ideas: A Framework for Rethinking Copyrights and Patents, *Wired,* (March), pp. 47–50.

Boyle, James. (1996). *Shamans, Software and Spleens.* Cambridge: Harvard University Press.

Johnson, Deborah. (2001). "Property Rights in Computer Software." Chapter 6 in *Computer Ethics,* 3rd ed. Upper Saddle River, NJ: Prentice Hall.

Lessig, Larry. (2001). *The Future of Ideas.* New York: Random House.

Littman, Jessica. (2001). *Digital Copyright.* New York: Prometheus Books.

Moore, Adam (ed.). (1997). *Intellectual Property: Moral, Legal and Intellectual Dilemmas.* Lanham, Md.: Rowman & Littlefield.

Samuelson, Pamela. (1999). "Intellectual Property and the Digital Economy: Why the Anti-circumvention Regulations Need to be Revised," 14 *Berkeley Tech. Law Journal* 519.

Spinello, Richard. (2003). "The Future of Intellectual Property." *Ethics and Information Technology,* Vol. 5: 1–16.

Spinello, Richard. (2003). "Intellectual Property in Cyberspace." Chapter 4 in *CyberEthics: Morality and Law in Cyberspace.* 2nd ed. Sudbury, MA: Jones and Bartlett.

Tavani, Herman. (2004). "Intellectual Property Disputes in Cyberspace." Chapter 8 in *Ethics & Technology: Ethical Issues in an Age of Information and Communication Technology.* Hoboken, NJ: John Wiley and Sons.

Digital Millennium Copyright Act[1]

Public Law 105-304
105th Congress
SEC. 103. Copyright Protection Systems and Copyright Management
(a) In General.–Title 17, United States Code, is amended by adding at the end the following new chapter:
CHAPTER 12–COPYRIGHT PROTECTION AND MANAGEMENT SYSTEMS
Sec. 1201. Circumvention of copyright protection systems
(a) Violations Regarding Circumvention of Technological Measures.
(1)   (A) No person shall circumvent a technological measure that effectively controls access to a work protected under this title. The prohibition contained in the preceding sentence shall take effect at the end of the 2-year period beginning on the date of the enactment of this chapter.

(B) The prohibition contained in subparagraph (A) shall not apply to persons who are users of a copyrighted work which is in a particular class of works, if such persons are, or are likely to be in the succeeding 3-year period, adversely affected by virtue of such prohibition in their ability to make noninfringing uses of that particular class of works under this title, as determined under subparagraph (C).

(C) During the 2-year period described in subparagraph (A), and during each succeeding 3-year period,the Librarian of Congress, upon the recommendation of the Register of Copyrights, who shall consult with the Assistant Secretary for Communications and Information of the Department of Commerce and report and comment on his or her views in making such recommendation, shall make the determination in a rulemaking proceeding on the record for purposes of subparagraph (B) of whether persons who are users of a copyrighted work are, or are likely to be in the succeeding 3-year period, adversely affected by the prohibition under subparagraph (A) in their ability to make noninfringing uses under this title

---

This Act is Public Law 105-304 passed by the 105th Congress and signed into law on October 28, 1998.

[1] These excerpts from the DMCA have been prepared by the editors.

of a particular class of copyrighted works. In conducting such rulemaking, the Librarian shall examine—

(i) the availability for use of copyrighted works;

(ii) the availability for use of works for nonprofit archival, preservation, and educational purposes;

(iii) the impact that the prohibition on the circumvention of technological measures applied to copyrighted works has on criticism, comment, news reporting, teaching, scholarship, or research;

(iv) the effect of circumvention of technological measures on the market for or value of copyrighted works; and

(v) such other factors as the Librarian considers appropriate.

(D) The Librarian shall publish any class of copyrighted works for which the Librarian has determined, pursuant to the rulemaking conducted under subparagraph (C), that non-infringing uses by persons who are users of a copyrighted work are, or are likely to be, adversely affected, and the prohibition contained in subparagraph (A) shall not apply to such users with respect to such class of works for the ensuing 3-year period.

(2) No person shall manufacture, import, offer to the public, provide, or otherwise traffic in any technology, product, service, device, component, or part thereof, that—

(A) is primarily designed or produced for the purpose of circumventing a technological measure that effectively controls access to a work protected under this title;

(B) has only limited commercially significant purpose or use other than to circumvent a technological measure that effectively controls access to a work protected under this title; or

(C) is marketed by that person or another acting in concert with that person with that person's knowledge for use in circumventing a technological measure that effectively controls access to a work protected under this title.

(3) As used in this subsection—

(A) to 'circumvent a technological measure' means to descramble a scrambled work, to decrypt an encrypted work, or otherwise to avoid, bypass, remove, deactivate, or impair a technological measure, without the authority of the copyright owner; and

(B) a technological measure 'effectively controls access to a work' if the measure, in the ordinary course of its operation, requires the application of information, or a process or a treatment, with the authority of the copyright owner, to gain access to the work.

....

(e) Law Enforcement, Intelligence, and Other Government Activities.—

This section does not prohibit any lawfully authorized investigative, protective, information security, or intelligence activity of an officer, agent, or employee of the United States, a State, or a political subdivision of a State, or a person acting pursuant to a contract with the United States, a State, or a political subdivision of a State. For purposes of this subsection, the term 'information security' means activities carried out in order to identify and address the vulnerabilities of a government computer, computer system, or computer network.

(f) Reverse Engineering.—

(1) Notwithstanding the provisions of subsection (a)(1)(A), a person who has lawfully obtained the right to use a copy of a computer program may circumvent a technological measure that effectively controls access to a particular portion of that program for the sole purpose of identifying and analyzing those elements of the program that are necessary to achieve interoperability of an independently created computer program with other programs, and that have not previously been readily available to the person engaging in the circumvention, to the extent any such acts of identification and analysis do not constitute infringement under this title.

....

Sec. 1202. Integrity of Copyright Management Information

(a) False Copyright Management Information.—No person shall knowingly and with the intent to induce, enable, facilitate, or conceal infringement—

(1) provide copyright management information that is false, or

(2) distribute or import for distribution copyright management information that is false.

(b) Removal or Alteration of Copyright Management Information.—No person shall, without the authority of the copyright owner or the law—

(1) intentionally remove or alter any copyright management information,

(2) distribute or import for distribution copyright management information knowing that the copyright management information has been removed or altered without authority of the copyright owner or the law, or

(3) distribute, import for distribution, or publicly perform works, copies of works, or phonorecords, knowing that copyright management information has been removed or altered without authority of the copyright owner or the law, knowing, or, with respect to civil remedies under section 1203, having reasonable grounds to know, that it will induce, enable, facilitate, or conceal an infringement of any right under this title.

(c) Definition.—As used in this section, the term 'copyright management information' means any of the following information conveyed in connection with copies or phonorecords of a work or performances or displays of a work, including in digital form, except that such term does not include any personally identifying information about a user of a work or of a copy, phonorecord, performance, or display of a work:

(1) The title and other information identifying the work, including the information set forth on a notice of copyright.

(2) The name of, and other identifying information about, the author of a work.

(3) The name of, and other identifying information about, the copyright owner of the work, including the information set forth in a notice of copyright.

(4) With the exception of public performances of works by radio and television broadcast stations, the name of, and other identifying information about, a performer whose performance is fixed in a work other than an audiovisual work.

(5) With the exception of public performances of works by radio and television broadcast stations, in the case of an audiovisual work, the name of, and other identifying information about, a writer, performer, or director who is credited in the audiovisual work.

(6) Terms and conditions for use of the work.

(7) Identifying numbers or symbols referring to such information or links to such information.

(8) Such other information as the Register of Copyrights may prescribe by regulation, except that the Register of Copyrights may not require the provision of any information concerning the user of a copyrighted work.

....

TITLE II—ONLINE COPYRIGHT INFRINGEMENT LIABILITY LIMITATION

Sec. 202. Limitations on liability for Copyright Infringement
(a) In General.—Chapter 5 of title 17, United States Code, is amended by adding after section 511 the following new section:

Sec. 512. Limitations on liability relating to material online
(a) Transitory Digital Network Communications.—A service provider shall not be liable for monetary relief, or, except as provided in subsection (j), for injunctive or other equitable relief, for infringement of copyright by reason of the provider's transmitting, routing, or providing connections for, material through a system or network controlled or operated by or for the service provider, or by reason of the intermediate and transient storage of that material in the course of such transmitting, routing, or providing connections, if—

(1) the transmission of the material was initiated by or at the direction of a person other than the service provider;

(2) the transmission, routing, provision of connections, or storage is carried out through an automatic technical process without selection of the material by the service provider;

(3) the service provider does not select the recipients of the material except as an automatic response to the request of another person;

(4) no copy of the material made by the service provider in the course of such intermediate or transient storage is maintained on the system or network in a manner ordinarily accessible to anyone other than anticipated recipients, and no such copy is maintained on the system or network in a manner ordinarily accessible to such anticipated recipients for a longer period than is reasonably necessary for the transmission, routing, or provision of connections; and

(5) the material is transmitted through the system or network without modification of its content.

(b) System Caching.—

(1) Limitation on liability.—A service provider shall not be liable for monetary relief, or, except as provided in subsection (j), for injunctive or other equitable relief, for infringement of copyright by reason of the intermediate and temporary storage of material on a system or network controlled or operated by or for the service provider in a case in which—

(A) the material is made available online by a person other than the service provider;

(B) the material is transmitted from the person described in subparagraph (A) through the system or network to a person other than the person described in subparagraph (A) at the direction of that other person; and

(C) the storage is carried out through an automatic technical process for the purpose of making the material available to users of the system or network who, after the material is transmitted as described in subparagraph (B), request access to the material from the person described in subparagraph (A), if the conditions set forth in paragraph (2) are met.

(2) Conditions.—The conditions referred to in paragraph (1) are that—

(A) the material described in paragraph (1) is transmitted to the subsequent users described in paragraph (1)(C) without modification to its content from the manner in which the material was transmitted from the person described in paragraph (1)(A);

(B) the service provider described in paragraph (1) complies with rules concerning the refreshing, reloading, or other updating of the material when specified by the person making the material available online in accordance with a generally accepted industry standard data communications protocol for the system or network through which that person makes the material available, except that this subparagraph applies only if those rules are not used by the person described in paragraph (1)(A) to prevent or unreasonably impair the intermediate storage to which this subsection applies;

(C) the service provider does not interfere with the ability of technology associated with the material to return to the person described in paragraph (1)(A) the information that would have been available to that person if the material had been obtained by the subsequent users described in paragraph (1)(C) directly from that person, except that this subparagraph applies only if that technology—

(i) does not significantly interfere with the performance of the provider's system or network or with the intermediate storage of the material;

(ii) is consistent with generally accepted industry standard communications protocols; and

(iii) does not extract information from the provider's system or network other than the information that would have been available to the person described in paragraph (1)(A) if the subsequent users had gained access to the material directly from that person;

(D) if the person described in paragraph (1)(A) has in effect a condition that a person must meet prior to having access to the material, such as a condition based on payment of a fee or provision of a password or other information, the service provider permits access to the stored material in significant part only to users of its system or network that have met those conditions and only in accordance with those conditions; and

(E) if the person described in paragraph (1)(A) makes that material available online without the authorization of the copyright owner of the material, the service provider responds expeditiously to remove, or disable access to, the material that is claimed to be infringing upon notification of claimed infringement as described in subsection (C)(3), except that this subparagraph applies only if—

(i) the material has previously been removed from the originating site or access to it has been disabled, or a court has ordered that the material be removed from the originating site or that access to the material on the originating site be disabled; and

(ii) the party giving the notification includes in the notification a statement confirming that the material has been removed from the originating site or access to it has been disabled or that a court has ordered that the material be removed from the originating site or that access to the material on the originating site be disabled.

(c) Information Residing on Systems or Networks At Direction of Users—

(1) In general.—A service provider shall not be liable for monetary relief, or, except as provided in subsection (j), for injunctive or other equitable relief, for infringement of copyright by reason of the storage at the direction of a user of material that resides on a system or network controlled or operated by or for the service provider, if the service provider—

(A) (i) does not have actual knowledge that the material or an activity using the material on the system or network is infringing;

(ii) in the absence of such actual knowledge, is not aware of facts or circumstances from which infringing activity is apparent; or

(iii) upon obtaining such knowledge or awareness, acts expeditiously to remove, or disable access to, the material;

(B) does not receive a financial benefit directly attributable to the infringing activity, in a case in which the service provider has the right and ability to control such activity; and

(C) upon notification of claimed infringement as described in paragraph (3), responds expeditiously to remove, or disable access to, the material that is claimed to be infringing or to be the subject of infringing activity.

....

(3) Elements of notification.—

(A) To be effective under this subsection, a notification of claimed infringement must be a written communication provided to the designated agent of a service provider that includes substantially the following:

(i) A physical or electronic signature of a person authorized to act on behalf of the owner of an exclusive right that is allegedly infringed.

(ii) Identification of the copyrighted work claimed to have been infringed, or, if multiple copyrighted works at a single online site are covered by a single notification, a representative list of such works at that site.

(iii) Identification of the material that is claimed to be infringing or to be the subject of infringing activity and that is to be removed or access to which is to be disabled, and information reasonably sufficient to permit the service provider to locate the material.

(iv) Information reasonably sufficient to permit the service provider to contact the complaining party, such as an address, telephone number, and, if available, an electronic mail address at which the complaining party may be contacted.

(v) A statement that the complaining party has a good faith belief that use of the material in the manner complained of is not authorized by the copyright owner, its agent, or the law.

(vi) A statement that the information in the notification is accurate, and under penalty of perjury, that the complaining party is authorized to act on behalf of the owner of an exclusive right that is allegedly infringed.

(B) (i) Subject to clause (ii), a notification from a copyright owner or from a person authorized to act on behalf of the copyright owner that fails to comply substantially with the provisions of subparagraph (A) shall not be considered under paragraph (1)(A) in determining whether a service provider has actual knowledge or is aware of facts or circumstances from which infringing activity is apparent.

(ii) In a case in which the notification that is provided to the service provider's designated agent fails to comply substantially with all the provisions of subparagraph (A) but substantially complies with clauses (ii), (iii), and (iv) of subparagraph (A), clause (i) of this subparagraph applies only if the service provider promptly attempts to contact the person making the notification or takes other reasonable steps to assist in the receipt of notification that substantially complies with all the provisions of subparagraph (A).

(d) Information Location Tools.—

A service provider shall not be liable for monetary relief, or, except as provided in subsection (j),for injunctive or other equitable relief, for infringement of copyright by reason of the provider referring or linking users to an online location containing infringing material or infringing activity, by using information location tools, including a directory, index, reference, pointer, or hypertext link, if the service provider—

(1)   (A) does not have actual knowledge that the material or activity is infringing;

(B) in the absence of such actual knowledge, is not aware of facts or circumstances from which infringing activity is apparent; or

(C) upon obtaining such knowledge or awareness, acts expeditiously to remove, or disable access to, the material;

(2)   does not receive a financial benefit directly attributable to the infringing activity, in a case in which the service provider has the right and ability to control such activity; and

(3)   upon notification of claimed infringement as described in subsection (c)(3), responds expeditiously to remove, or disable access to, the material that is claimed to be infringing or to be the subject of infringing activity, except that, for purposes of this paragraph, the information described in subsection (c)(3)(A)(iii) shall be identification of the reference or link, to material or activity claimed to be infringing, that is to be removed or access to which is to be disabled, and information reasonably sufficient to permit the service provider to locate that reference or link.

(e) Limitation on liability of nonprofit educational institutions.—

(1) When a public or other nonprofit institution of higher education is a service provider, and when a faculty member or graduate student who is an employee of such institution is performing a teaching or research function, for the purposes of subsections (a) and (b) such faculty member or graduate student shall be considered to be a person other than the institution, and for the purposes of subsections (c) and (d) such faculty member's or graduate student's knowledge or awareness of his or her infringing activities shall not be attributed to the institution, if—

(A) such faculty member's or graduate student's infringing activities do not involve the provision of online access to instructional materials that are or were required or recommended, within the preceding 3-year period, for a course taught at the institution by such faculty member or graduate student;

(B) the institution has not, within the preceding 3-year period, received more than two notifications described in subsection (c)(3) of claimed infringement by such faculty member or graduate student, and such notifications of claimed infringement were not actionable under subsection (f); and

(C) the institution provides to all users of its system or network informational materials that accurately describe, and promote compliance with, the laws of the United States relating to copyright.

....

(g) Replacement of Removed or Disabled Material and Limitation on Other Liability.—

(1) No liability for taking down generally.—Subject to paragraph (2), a service provider shall not be liable to any person for any claim based on the service provider's good faith disabling of access to, or removal of, material or activity claimed to be infringing or based on facts or circumstances from which infringing activity is apparent, regardless of whether the material or activity is ultimately determined to be infringing.

(2) Exception.—Paragraph (1) shall not apply with respect to material residing at the direction of a subscriber of the service provider on a system or network controlled or operated by or for the service provider that is removed, or to which access is disabled by the service provider, pursuant to a notice provided under subsection (c)(1)(C), unless the service provider—

(A) takes reasonable steps promptly to notify the subscriber that it has removed or disabled access to the material;

(B) upon receipt of a counter notification described in paragraph (3), promptly provides the person who provided the notification under subsection (c)(1)(C) with a copy of the counter notification, and informs that person that it will replace the removed material or cease disabling access to it in 10 business days; and

(C) replaces the removed material and ceases disabling access to it not less than 10, nor more than 14, business days following receipt of the counter notice, unless its designated agent first receives notice from the person who submitted the notification under subsection (c)(1)(C) that such person has filed an action seeking a court order to restrain the subscriber from engaging in infringing activity relating to the material on the service provider's system or network.

(3) Contents of counter notification.—To be effective under this subsection, a counter notification must be a written communication provided to the service provider's designated agent that includes substantially the following:

(A) A physical or electronic signature of the subscriber.

(B) Identification of the material that has been removed or to which access has been disabled and the location at which the material appeared before it was removed or access to it was disabled.

(C) A statement under penalty of perjury that the subscriber has a good faith belief that the material was removed or disabled as a result of mistake or misidentification of the material to be removed or disabled.

(D) The subscriber's name, address, and telephone number, and a statement that the subscriber consents to the jurisdiction of Federal District Court for the judicial district in which the address is located, or if the subscriber's address is outside of the United States, for any judicial district in which the service provider may be found, and that the subscriber will accept service of process from the person who provided notification under subsection (c)(1)(C) or an agent of such person.

....

(i) Conditions for Eligibility.—

(1) Accommodation of technology.—The limitations on liability established by this section shall apply to a service provider only if the service provider—

(A) has adopted and reasonably implemented, and informs subscribers and account holders of the service provider's system or network of, a policy that provides for the termination in appropriate circumstances of subscribers and account holders of the service provider's system or network who are repeat infringers; and

(B) accommodates and does not interfere with standard technical measures.

(2) Definition.—As used in this subsection, the term 'standard technical measures' means technical measures that are used by copyright owners to identify or protect copyrighted works and—

(A) have been developed pursuant to a broad consensus of copyright owners and service providers in an open, fair, voluntary, multi-industry standards process;

(B) are available to any person on reasonable and nondiscriminatory terms; and

(C) do not impose substantial costs on service providers or substantial burdens on their systems or networks.

....

(k) Definitions.—

(1) Service provider.—(A) As used in subsection (a), the term 'service provider' means an entity offering the transmission, routing, or providing of connections for digital online communications, between or among points specified by a user, of material of the user's choosing, without modification to the content of the material as sent or received.

(B) As used in this section, other than subsection (a), the term 'service provider' means a provider of online services or network access, or the operator of facilities therefor, and includes an entity described in subparagraph (A).

(2) Monetary relief.—As used in this section, the term 'monetary relief' means damages, costs, attorneys' fees, and any other form of monetary payment.

Note on the DeCSS Case

In the fast-paced world of cyberlaw the first summer of the new millennium will be remembered for two controversial cases. The first was the well-publicized dispute over Napster, a company that facilitated the sharing of MP3 music files on a massive scale. The music industry sought an injunction to prevent Napster users from sharing these copyrighted music files. Napster fared poorly in its confrontation with the legal system and was eventually driven into bankruptcy.

The second case involved a decryption program known as DeCSS. It received much less attention than the Napster trial, since the subject matter probably seemed more arcane to the general public. Both cases, however, are closely related and have the potential to shape the precarious landscape of intellectual property law in cyberspace. In the DeCSS case the concern was not the copying of music files but the piracy or illegal downloads of digital movies.

The initial phase of the DeCSS trial concluded in mid-August, 2000, and it tested the scope and constitutionality of the anti-circumvention provisions included in section 1201 of the Digital Millennium Copyright Act (DMCA). The questions triggered by that case go to the heart of the intellectual property rights debate. Is DeCSS no more than a piracy tool that enables widespread copying of DVD files? Or does it merely enable "fair use" of DVD media by allowing DVD formatted movies to be played on computers with unsupported operating systems such as Linux?

Technical Background

DVDs (or Digital Versatile Discs) are 5-inch discs that hold a full-length motion picture. They provide higher clarity and quality than the video cassettes that are played on VCRs. All DVDs contain digital information, and this allows copies of a motion picture contained on a DVD to be stored on a hard disk drive in the computer system's memory or to be transmitted over the Internet. Moreover, there is no degradation of quality and clarity when such digital copies are produced.

Since DVDs are so vulnerable to illicit copying they have been protected with an access control system that encrypts the contents. This system, known as the Content Scramble System or CSS, was developed by Matshusita Electric Industrial

This article was prepared by the editors and appeared for the first time in the first edition of *Readings in CyberEthics*. It has been revised for this new edition.

Co. and Toshiba Corporation. The DVD industry, including manufacturers of DVD players, and content providers (i.e., the movie studios) have jointly adopted this standard. All movies in this digital format are distributed on DVDs protected with CSS.

These movies can only be viewed on a DVD player or specially configured PC that has a licensed copy of CSS that contains the keys for decryption. This is a complex system that requires a series of keys that operate in a hierarchical pattern. The first is the master key that is unique to each DVD manufacturer. This key reads and decodes the main disk key on the DVD disk. Once this has been decoded, the disk key is used to read the title keys corresponding to the portions of the video that is about to be played. This title key is then used to unscramble the actual content.

If computer users want to watch DVD movies on their personal computers instead of a dedicated DVD player, those computers must be using a Mac or Windows operating system. CSS does not support any other operating system at the present time.

In the fall of 1999 Jan Johansen of Larvik, Norway decided that he wanted to watch DVD movies on a computer that ran the Linux operating system. With the help of two friends he met on the Internet, Johansen set out to create a software program that would play DVDs on a Linux system. This meant, of course, that it would be necessary to crack the CSS encryption code.

Cracking this code was not a major hurdle for Johansen and his friends, and within a short time a decryption program called DeCSS (or Decode CSS) was born. This program allows a user to decode a DVD disk. Once the DVD file is decoded, it can be downloaded with the help of a compression program called DivX, which can compress huge DVDs into manageable files that can be stored on a computer's hard drive and disseminated on the Internet like any other digital file. According to Hartigan (2000), "With a high speed connection, it is possible to download a full-length movie in one or two hours, a process that would have taken days without DivX, and the quality is near picture-perfect."

Johansen posted the executable object code of DeCSS on the Web in order to ensure its widespread distribution. Soon web sites began posting both the DeCSS source code and object code while many other sites provided links to this program. As DeCSS proliferated through cyberspace, the movie industry, fearful that its movies would be transmitted in cyberspace in a Napster-like fashion, concluded that it needed to take legal action.

The Lawsuit

In November, 1999 Eric Corley wrote an article about DeCSS for a web site known as 2600.com. This is a well known "hacker" web site associated with the print magazine, *2600: The Hacker Quarterly*. This magazine has published articles detailing security flaws or giving instructions on how to penetrate the security of certain commercial systems. Corley's story about the saga of DeCSS and the opposition of the movie industry included copies of both the source code and object code of DeCSS along with links to other web sites with DeCSS. According to Corley, he included the code and the links because "in a journalistic world, . . . you have to show your evidence, . . . and particularly in the magazine that I work for, people want to see specifically what it is that we are referring to" (Trial Transcript, 2000). On the 2600 web site, however, DeCSS was described as "a free DVD decoder" that enables "people to copy DVDs" (*Universal City Studios* v. *Corley*, 2001).

The movie industry demanded the removal of the DeCSS code and sought an injunction against Corley (along with two other defendants, Remeirdes and Kazan). In a statement supporting this lawsuit Jack Valenti, president of the Motion Picture Association, said "This is a case of theft. . .the posting of the de-encryption formula is no different from making and then distributing unauthorized keys to a department store" (Dow Jones, 2000). In January 2000 a federal district court issued a preliminary injunction preventing the 2600 web site from posting the DeCSS code. The defendants complied but they continued to post links to other web sites where the DeCSS code could be found. At the plaintiff's request the scope of the preliminary injunction was broadened to include those hyperlinks, which were then removed from the 2600.com web site by the defendants.

At trial, the plaintiffs portrayed DeCSS as little more than a "piracy tool," and a supportive government brief called it a "digital crowbar" that could be used to decrypt movies in DVD format for distribution over the Internet. The movie industry's lawyers argued that DeCSS violated the anti-trafficking provision of the DMCA. The court also heard the defendant's arguments that DeCSS simply preserves "fair use" in digital media by allowing DVDs to work on computer systems that are not running Mac or Windows operating systems. The defendants' lawyers claimed that consumers should have the right to use these disks on a Linux system, and this required the development of a program like DeCSS. Their contention was that DeCSS existed to facilitate a reverse-engineering process that would allow the playing of movies on these unsupported systems. According to the defendants, this code had not been written to facilitate copying or the transmission of DVD files throughout cyberspace.

The Defendants also claimed that the DMCA was unconstitutional, reasoning that although DeCSS is computer code, it is still protected free expression. But the DMCA discriminates against DeCSS on the basis of its content. The defense team argued that computer programs, including object or source code, represent a form of expressive free speech that deserves full First Amendment protection. A computer scientist appearing as an expert witness proclaimed that an injunction against the use of code would adversely affect his ability to express himself. The implication was that Congress could not legally restrict the ability to transmit this code (through laws like the DMCA) lest they violate the First Amendment.

Finally, the defense argued that the ban on linking was also tantamount to suppressing another important form of First Amendment expression. Hyperlinks, despite their functionality, are a vital part of the expressiveness of a web page and therefore their curtailment clearly violates the First Amendment. In a supportive brief for the defense, the Openlaw Participants (2000) wrote that "Plaintiffs' attempts to bar 2600 from linking to outside sites would bar speech precisely for the message the links convey."

But in the end the district court accepted the plaintiff's claim that posting of DeCSS violated the DMCA's anti-trafficking provision, 1201 (a) (2). The court concluded that DeCSS "was created solely for the purpose of decrypting CSS" and that its distribution was tantamount to "publishing a bank vault combination in a national newspaper" (*Universal City Studios* v. *Remeirdes*, 2000). It dismissed the defendants' claims that the distribution of DeCSS fell under the reverse engineering exception or that the conduct of the defendants should be protected under the fair use doctrine.

The court also asserted that by linking to sites with DeCSS code the defendants were "trafficking" in DeCSS, so that the defendants were also liable for these linking activities. The Court reasoned that links to DeCSS were "the functional equivalent of transferring the DeCSS code to the users themselves" (*Universal City Studios v. Remeirdes,* 2000). As a consequence, the court issued a permanent injunction prohibiting the defendants from posting DeCSS or linking to web sites containing DeCSS code.

The Appeal

The case was promptly appealed by Corley and 2600 Enterprises (the other defendants dropped out). Legal scholars, worried about the implications of this case for free speech rights in cyberspace, came to the defense of Corley by writing Amici Curiae briefs. But all of this was to no avail. In November 2001, the U.S. Court of Appeals for the Second Circuit affirmed the judgment of the District Court. The appeals court agreed that posting DeCSS or hyperlinking to sites with DeCSS violated the DMCA. As a consequence it left the permanent injunction in place.

The Second Circuit agreed with Judge Kaplan of the district court that computer code is a form of speech and hence merits First Amendment protection. The Second Circuit further noted that code such as DeCSS has both speech and functional components. The DMCA, however, seeks only to regulate the latter element. Any restriction on the dissemination of DeCSS is content-neutral because the intent is not to suppress the content of the expression but to advance a particular government interest, that is, the protection of copyrighted material. According to the appeals court,

> As a communication, the DeCSS code has a claim to being "speech" and as "speech," it has a claim to being protected by the First Amendment. But just as the realities of what any computer code can accomplish must inform the scope of its constitutional protection, so the capacity of a decryption program like DeCSS to accomplish unauthorized—indeed, unlawful—access to materials in which the Plaintiffs have intellectual property rights must inform and limit the scope of its First Amendment protection (Universal City Studios v. Corley, 2001).

Judge Kaplan had further argued that the application of the DMCA to hyperlinks to web sites containing the DeCSS code did not violate the First Amendment rights of the defendants. He reasoned that this restriction was content-neutral, that is, it was justified because of the hyperlink's functionality and without regard for the "speech component" of the link. The appeals court concurred: "The linking prohibition is justified solely by the functional capability of the hyperlink" (*Universal City Studios v. Corley,* 2001). The appeals court also addressed the concern that strict liability for linking might unduly impair free expression. It applauded Judge Kaplan's standard of limited liability. According to that standard, those liable or responsible for linking to unlawful material must: (a) know at the relevant time that the offending material is on the linked-to site; (b) know that it is circumvention technology that may not lawfully be offered; (c) create or maintain the link for the purpose of disseminating the technology (*Universal City Studios* v. *Remeirdes, 2000*). The defendants had claimed that the test should include an "intent to cause, or aid, or abet, harm" requirement (*Universal City Studios* v. *Corley, 2001*), but the Second Circuit concluded that this requirement went too far. In their viewpoint Judge Kaplan's standard was acceptable.

Finally, the Second Circuit registered some concern about the impact of these rulings on free speech rights. But in its view the court was compelled to tolerate "some impairment of communication in order to permit Congress to prohibit decryption that may lawfully be prevented. . . ." (*Universal City Studios* v. *Corley, 2001*).

Questions

Beyond the narrow legal questions addressed in this case there are obviously much larger issues pertaining to the First Amendment and its apparent conflict with property rights. To what extent should the First Amendment protect computer code, which is considered a form of speech? Is an injunction against DeCSS tantamount to prior restraint of a public discussion about the functionality of the CSS program? Does the First Amendment also support a basic "freedom-to-link," an unrestricted right to link to other web sites? And is that right unfairly truncated by the DMCA?

This case also raises other questions about the application of the DMCA. How can "fair use" be preserved if copyrighted material is in encrypted form and programs like DeCSS are outlawed? According to Harmon (2000), critics of the anti-circumvention provision "worry that it goes far beyond the specific copyright challenges of the digital age to give copyright holders broad new powers over how the public uses their material." Is there a better way to balance the rights of copyright holders who rely on protective devices with free speech rights and the fair use concept? Or is the DMCA necessary to protect fragile digital content such as movies or music?

References

Dow Jones News Service, (2000) "Hollywood Studios Join Legal Battle to Stop DVD Copying," January 15.

Harmon, A. (2000) "Free Speech Rights for Computer Code," *The New York Times,* July 31, 2000, p. C1.

Hartigan, P. (2000) "Download War: The Sequel," *The Boston Globe,* August 19.

Openlaw Participants (2000) Amicus Curiae Brief, *Universal City Studios* v. *Remeirdes* (2000) 111 F. Supp. 294 [S.D.N.Y.].

Trial Transcript (2000) *Universal City Studios* v. *Remeirdes* 111 F. Supp. 294 [S.D.N.Y.].

Universal City Studios v. *Remeirdes* (2000) 111 F. Supp. 294 [S.D.N.Y.].

Universal City Studios v. *Corley* (2001) 273 F. 3d 429 [2d Cir.]

Digital Music and Peer-to-Peer File Sharing

Richard A. Spinello

The Peer-to-Peer Architecture

Internet content such as books, movies, music, documents, or even web pages are typically disseminated by means of the client server model. For example, in this model a movie or music file is "served" from a central system based on a request from a user's client system, usually a personal computer. As the Internet has expanded, the burden on servers has increased considerably.

However, an alternative architecture that has greatly facilitated music distribution is peer-to-peer (P2P) computing. Unlike the server-based technology, with peer-to-peer any computer in the network can function as the distribution point. In this way one central server is not inundated with requests from multiple clients. P2P systems, therefore, enable communications among individual personal computers relying on the Internet infrastructure. For example, a user can prompt his or her personal computer to ask other PCs in a peer-to-peer network if they have a certain digital file. That request is passed along from computer to computer within the network until the file is located and a copy is sent along to the requester's system.

There is nothing inherently wrong with P2P technology, but if the file being shared has a copyright, the transmission from one PC to the other may not be legal. Copyright law does not allow the reproduction of copyrighted material without the copyright holder's protection. Unlike server-based technology, however, it is much more difficult to enforce copyright laws with a P2P system, since it is difficult to trace the movements of files in this network and there is no central server to shut down.

Music is a prime candidate for this type of file sharing thanks to an Internet protocol know as MP3. Music has always been stored on physical media such as an album or a CD, but digitization and the MP3 format permit the proliferation of "containerless" music. MP3 is an audio compression file format, so when users refer to "MP3s" they mean compressed digital music files. The compression allows for near-CD-quality files that are as much as 20 times smaller than standard music

This essay appears for the first time in *Readings in CyberEthics* (2nd ed.). Copyright © (2003) by Richard A. Spinello.

CD files. MP3 files are often created through a technique known as "ripping" whereby a standard music CD is inserted into the computer, and, with the help of an MP3 encoding program, the CD's contents are compressed and copied to the computer's hard drive. Users can listen to this music on portable MP3 players or on their hard drives with media player software produced by companies such as RealNetworks. Thanks to the MP3 architecture, users can easily download, store, and share music more efficiently than ever before.

The most famous program for music sharing was Napster, but Napster was not a true P2P application since it relied on a central server for support. That server stored Napster's centralized directory of music files. The music files themselves were stored on the computer systems of Napster's users, but Napster relied on a central index located on a server to match user search requests and the location of music files across the Napster network. Once that server is disabled the whole network is effectively shut down. But unlike a server-oriented technology, P2P treats all nodes in the network as equals and disabling one node will have minimal impact on the network.

For the music industry this lethal combination of easily reproducible digital music files, the MP3 format enabling storage, and the P2P architecture making illicit distribution difficult to detect, is a recipe for disaster. Now that Napster has been neutralized, the industry is most concerned about true P2P sites such as Morpheus, Grokster, and KaZaA.

These systems work as follows: let us assume that user A installs software such as KaZaA, which enables that individual to search the systems of other KaZaA clients for a particular music file. Once the music file is located the user can access that file and download a copy. In exchange for this privilege, user A usually creates a folder of MP3 files for sharing with other KaZaA users. In order to accelerate the peer-to-peer exchange of information certain peers are temporarily elevated to supernode status depending upon their bandwidth. These supernodes mediate in searches for files so that they can be found more quickly. The KaZaA program might call on the web server for an "auto update" (the software checks to see if a more recent version is available) or a starting list of supernodes (when KaZaA is initiated, the client retrieves a list of these supernodes.) Finally, unlike Napster, P2P systems allow for the exchange of other material besides MP3 files, including digital movies or electronic books and documents.

KaZaA is the most popular music sharing software with 275 million users (as of September, 2003) and about 3 million new users added each week (Delaney, 2003). The software was created under the leadership of Niklas Zennstrom who co-founded a Dutch company called KaZaA, BV in order to distribute the KaZaA software. Zennstrom sold the software to Sharman Networks (located on a South Pacific island called Vanuatu) in early 2002, partly out of concern over impending lawsuits. Sharman's servers are in Denmark and its employees are contracted through an Australian company called LEF. Around the same time, control of the software code was transferred to Blastoise, a company with operations on an island off the coast of Britain known for its status as a tax haven.

Despite this extraordinary subterfuge, Zennstrom believed that since KaZaA did not require his company to host a central directory, it would be "tougher to blame him for illegal swapping by others" (Delaney, 2003). Unlike Napster, companies that distribute P2P software can claim immunity from liability when their users share copyrighted files because the system is decentralized and it is impossible for those companies to know what these software users are doing.

KaZaA, BV was sued in a Netherlands court for contributory copyright infringement. In the U.S., liability for contributory infringement can be imposed on anyone who "with knowledge of the infringing activity, induces, causes, or materially contributes to the infringing conduct" of the guilty party (*Gershwin Publishing* v. *Columbia Artists Mgmt*, 1971). KaZaA, BV lost the first round of the case, but in March 2002, a Netherlands court of appeals overturned the lower court ruling and held that KaZaA should not be held liable for the unlawful acts of those who use its software. According to the appeals court,

> *The KaZaA application does not depend on any intervention by KaZaA, BV. The program is expanded and functions even better by means of the services provided by KaZaA plus it can be better controlled that way. These services, however, are not necessary for the locating and exchanging of files. . . .With the present state of standardization, it is not possible to technically detect which files are copyrighted and which are not. Thus, it is not possible for KaZaA (or any other software) to incorporate a blockage against the unlawful exchange of files (Amsterdam Appellate Court, 2002).*

The Music Industry Fights Back

In the fall of 2003, the RIAA (Recording Industry Association of America) filed lawsuits against 261 individuals accused of illegally distributing music over the Internet. This anti-piracy campaign represented the music industry's attempt to fight back against rampant file sharing on the web by shifting the focus away from P2P companies to users of file-sharing programs. The industry had always been reluctant to sue its own customers, but music industry executives felt they had no choice as more and more users downloaded KaZaA or other P2P software. The decision to sue came in the wake of a decision by a federal judge in California in April, 2003, which declined to shut down two peer-to-peer systems, Grokster and Morpheus. According to France (2003), "The devastating ruling meant that it would be impossible to kill music web sites in court, leaving the industry with only one legal option: suing consumers."

The initial lawsuits have targeted only the heaviest users of file-sharing programs. For example, of the dozen lawsuits filed in San Francisco one named a young man who shared more than 1,700 music files, including songs by Tori Amos, Bob Marley, and Red Hot Chili Peppers (Wingfield, 2003). Industry representatives hope that these lawsuits will have a pedagogical effect as users come to realize that what they are doing is illegal.

The music industry's campaign, however, was met with widespread criticism and skepticism. In part, the reason for this is that the vast majority of Internet users see no problem with the actions of music file-sharers. A New York Times/CBS News poll revealed that only 36% of the US population believe that file sharing is a form of stealing (Harmon and Schwartz, 2003). As a result, the file sharing trend among all demographic segments of the population shows no signs of abating. Also, according to Harmon and Schwartz (2003), "experts argue that legal prohibition alone is rarely effective in getting people to behave differently if it runs counter to strong societal beliefs." Many users refuse to be intimidated and have continued file sharing, while software developers are accelerating their efforts to develop new systems that will allow users to share their music files more covertly. Nonetheless, the music industry seems committed to undermining P2P networks by resorting to whatever legal methods are at their disposal.

References

Amsterdam Appellate Court (2002), BUMA & STEMRA v. KaZaA, March 28.

Delaney, K. (2003). "KaZaA Founder Peddles Software to Speed File Sharing," *The Wall Street Journal,* September 8, p. B1.

France, M. (2003). "Striking Back: How the Music Industry Charted its Crusade against Web Pirates," *Business Week,* September 29, pp. 94–96.

Gershwin Publishing v. *Columbia Artists Mgmt* (1971), 443 F 2d 1159, [2nd Cir].

Harmon, A. and J. Schwartz (2003). "Despite Suits, Music File-Sharers Shrug Off Guilt and Keep Sharing," *The New York Times,* September 19, pp. A1, C2.

Wingfield, N. (2003). "The High Cost of Sharing," *The Wall Street Journal,* September 9, p. B1.

A Politics of Intellectual Property: Environmentalism for the Net?

James Boyle[1]

This article argues that we need a politics, or perhaps a political economy, of intellectual property. Using the controversy over copyright on the Net as a case-study and the history of the environmental movement as a comparison, it offers a couple of modest proposals about what such a politics might look like—what theoretical ideas it might draw upon and what constituencies it might unite.

I   "Code is Code"—The Logic of the Information Relation

Everyone says that we are moving to an information age. Everyone says that the ownership and control of information is one of the most important forms of power in contemporary society. These ideas are so well-accepted, such clichés, that I can get away with saying them in a *law review article* without footnote support. (For those blessedly unfamiliar with law reviews, this is a status given to only the most staggeringly obvious claims; the theory of evolution,[2] and the orbit of the earth around the sun,[3] probably would not qualify.)

Beyond the claim that the information society exists, however, there is surprisingly little theoretical work. Sadly for academics, the best social theorists of the information age are still science fiction writers and, in particular, cyberpunks—the originators of the phrase "cyberspace" and the premier fantasists of the Net. If one wants to understand the information age, this is a good place to start.

Cyberpunk science fiction succeeded as a genre largely because it combined a particular plot aesthetic with a particular conceptual insight. The plot aesthetic was simple; the bad boy/film noir world of the romantic lowlife. When juxtaposed to the 2-dimensional priggishness of the normal science fiction hero, the cigarette smoking, drugged-out petty outlaws and mirror-shaded ninja-chicks of cyberpunk seemed rebellious, cynical and just, well, *cool*. The character-type is a familiar one;

James Dean could easily have played the hero of *Neuromancer*.[4] The conceptual insight is not so familiar. Cyberpunk is built on the extrapolation of two principal technologies, computers and the Web on the one hand, and genetic engineering on the other. The theme of cyberpunk is that the information age means the homologisation of all forms of information—whether genetic, electronic, or demographic. I grew up believing that genes had to do with biology, petri dishes, and cells and that computers had to do with punch cards and magnetic disks. It would be hard to imagine two more disparate fields. In contrast, cyberpunk sees only one issue—code—expressed in binary digits or the Cs, Gs, As, and Ts on a gene map.

II   Intellectual Property is the Legal Form of the Information Age

The cyberpunk writers also offer us a legal insight. The more one moves to a world in which the message, rather than the medium, is the focus of conceptual and economic interest, the more central does intellectual property become. Intellectual property is the legal form of the information age. Like most property regimes, our intellectual property regime will be contentious in distributional, ideological, and efficiency terms. It will have effects on market power, economic concentration, and social structure. Yet, right now, we have no politics of intellectual property in the way that we have a politics of the environment or of tax reform. We lack a conceptual map of issues, a rough working model of costs and benefits, and a functioning coalition—politics of groups unified by common interest perceived in apparently diverse situations.

Why don't we have such a politics? One reason is that with a few exceptions, the mass media coverage of the information age has been focused firmly on "cyberporn" and its potential censorship. This is rather like thinking that the most important feature of the industrial revolution was that it allowed the mass-production—and then the regulation—of pornographic magazines. Given the magnitude of the changes occurring, and the relatively small differences between pornography on-line and pornography anywhere else, a more trivial emblematic concern would have been hard to find. It is intellectual property, not the regulation of cyber-smut, that provides the key to the distribution of wealth, power, and access in the information society. The intellectual property regime could make—or break—the educational, political, scientific, and cultural promise of the Net. Indeed, even if our *only* concern were censorship, it would be perverse to concentrate exclusively on the direct criminalization of content by governments. The digital world gives new salience to private censorship—the control by intellectual property holders of distribution of and access to information. The recent Scientology cases are only the most obvious manifestation of this tendency.[5]

The media were not the only ones to miss the boat. Lawyers and legal academics largely followed suit. With a few exceptions, lawyers have assumed that intellectual property was an esoteric and arcane field, something that was only interesting (and comprehensible) to practitioners in the field.[6] There is some question whether this attitude was ever defensible; it certainly is not now. In terms of ideology and rhetorical structure, no less than practical economic effect, intellectual property is the legal form of the information age. It is the *locus* of the most important decisions in information policy. It profoundly affects the distribution of political and economic power in the digital environment. It has impacts on issues ranging from education to free speech. The "value" protected[7] by intellectual property in the world economy is in the hundreds of billions of dollars and growing all the time.

There are structural reasons why these tendencies will continue. The first crucial aspect of the current information economy is the increasing homologization of *forms* of information. Think of the many ways in which it now does not make sense to distinguish between electronic and genetic information—any more than between red books or green books. Precisely because we conceive of them as (and have the capability to treat them as) information, both present the same issues of regulation—privacy, access, public goods problems, and so on. As a result, they have literally begun to overlap—think of the storing (and then the sale?) of the human genome on computer disk, or of the private gene databases that add value to information developed through publicly funded research and then demand patent options as the prerequisite for access by outsiders.[8] Read about the mathematical-biological/computer-science discipline of bio-informatics, a discipline that is premised on the belief that information is information, whether the medium is a double helix or an optical disk.[9]

We are now used to the idea that Microsoft retains rights over the lines of code sitting on computer hard drives around the world. We can even produce a utilitarian justification to explain why. It is a lot stranger to think that women all over the country may carry in their bodies a string of genetic information—brca1, the so-called breast cancer gene—that has been patented by Myriad Genetics or that the Commerce Department tried to patent the genes of a Guyami Indian woman who possessed an abnormal resistance to leukemia.[10] From the point of view of the information economy, though, the two cases are very similar; in each case, strings of code are subject to intellectual property rights granted in the belief that they will inspire further innovation and discovery. The fact that this can be done in the face of the profound shock most people feel at the ownership of human genes is a testament to the universalizing logic of the information relation. (Whether it is also a good thing is a different question.)

The process is not simply a legal one and the overlaps go in both directions. Scan the science pages and see articles about the possibility of using DNA sequences as incredibly powerful parallel processing "computers."[11] Think of the software designers who create electronic ecologies and then use those strings of computer code that have proved themselves as survivors—harnessing a form of "natural" selection that Darwin would have recognized but could never have imagined.[12] Put it all together and then compare this "reality" to the way that we thought about computers on the one hand and biology on the other, just twenty years ago. In the international information economy, the medium is not the message. The medium is *irrelevant*.

The second crucial aspect of the information economy is a corollary of the homologization of forms of information: the decreasing proportion of product cost and intellectual attention devoted to medium (diskettes, cell-lines) rather than message (software, decoded DNA sequences). A moment's thought will show that *both* of these aspects will give increased importance to intellectual property. Reconceiving new areas of science, commerce, and research as "information issues" simply gives us more fields in which it is likely we will spy the public goods problems that intellectual property is supposed to solve. And the diminishing portion of product cost devoted to medium rather than message means that, within any given area, the public goods problems grow all the more salient. (The price of the program rises, at least relative to the falling price of the diskette onto which it can be copied.)

When I say that we lack a politics of intellectual property, I don't mean to imply that this is the only type of "information politics"—more like the most neglected. Look at the recent past. From the net roots campaign against the Communications Decency Act to the titanic industry lobbying over the Telecommunication Bill in which the CDA was embedded, there have been many moments of political struggle and agitation over digital commerce and communications regulation.[13] There have been conferences, both Polyannish and despairing, over the use of the Net by nonprofit groups, and thoughtful warnings of the dangers posed by disparate access to information technologies. These are serious points; the issue of access in particular. But in most cases, they are isolated applications to a new technology of a familiar political worldview or calculation of self-interest. Libertarians don't want newspapers censored; their attitude to the Net is the same (though the interactive quality of the technology, and the proprietary feeling that novelty gives first adopters have certainly given more people a stake in the protection of the system). Non-profit groups have to adjust to changes in communications technology, just like changes in tax law, or the regulation of lobbying. Communications conglomerates have an attitude toward bandwidth that seems indistinguishable from most commercial entities' attitude toward publicly held real estate; rationally enough, they want more, they want it free (ideally, they want it subsidized), and they want to be able to exploit it without strings. The left sees a resource with new importance—access to information technology—and makes about it the points that it makes about access to health care or education.[14] I don't mean to minimize these concerns, and certainly don't want to make the claim that they are somehow less fundamental than the ones I describe here. But I do think that, precisely because of their comfortable familiarity, they miss some of the *differences* in the politics of the information age, the ideas we have not thought about so often or so well.

III   The Conceptual Structure of an Intellectual Land-Grab

Elsewhere, I have argued at unseemly length that there are structural tendencies in our patterns of thinking and discourse about intellectual property that lead us generally to "over" rather than "under-protect."[15] I will summarize, rather than attempt to justify those claims here. (A chart that might be helpful is provided in Table 3.1.)

One of the roots of the problem is a conceptual one. The economic analysis of information is beset by internal contradiction and uncertainty; information is both a component of the perfect market and a good that must be produced within that market. Under the former characterization, information is supposed to move

Table 3.1   Tensions in an Intellectual Property System

Subject Matter	Information	Innovation
Economic Perspective	Efficiency	Incentives
Paradigmatic Conception of Problems	Transaction Cost Problems. Barriers to the free flow of information lead to the inhibition of innovation/inadequate circulation of information	Public Goods Problems. Inadequate incentives for future production leads to the inhibition/inadequate circulation of information
Reward (if any) for...	Effort/Investment/Risk	Originality/Transformation
View of the Public Domain	Finite Resources for future creators	Infinite Resources for future creators
Vision of the Productive Process	Development based on existing material. "Poetry can only be made out of other poems; novels out of other novels. All of this was much clearer before the assimilation of literature to private enterprise."[23]	Creation *ex nihilo* "Copyright is about sustaining the conditions of creativity that enable an individual to craft *out of thin air* an *Appalachian Spring*, a *Sun Also Rises*, a *Citizen Kane*."[24]
Normative Starting Point	Free speech/Free circulation of ideas and information.	Property rights—the creator's "natural" right, the reward for past creation, the incentive to produce again.

toward perfection—a state in which it is costless, instantly available, and so on. Under the latter characterization, information must be commodified so as to give its producers an incentive to produce. But each property right handed out to ensure the production of information is a transaction cost when seen from the perspective of market efficiency.[16]

The most succinct encapsulation of the problem comes from an article co-written by the current head of the President's Council of Economic Advisors, who in a former life was one of the most distinguished scholars of information economics. "There is a fundamental conflict between the efficiency with which markets spread information and the incentives to acquire information."[17] This problem is often, though not always, "solved" by ignoring it. A pre-theoretical classification is made, conventionally ascribing a certain problem to one or other realm and the discussion then continues on that basis. Thus for example, we tend to look at the field of intellectual property with a finely honed sensitivity to "public goods" problems that might lead to underproduction, while underestimating or failing to mention the efficiency costs and other losses generated by the very rights we are granting. Some conventional ascriptions visibly switch over time. The contemporary proponents of legalizing insider trading use the idea of the efficient capital market to minimize or defend the practice. The first generation of analyses saw the insider trade as the entrepreneur's incentive and reward for Faustian recombinations of the factors of production. An alternative method for smoothing over the tensions in the policy analysis is for the analyst to acknowledge the tension between efficiency and incentives, point out that there are some limitations imposed on intellectual property rights, to conclude that there are both efficiency-promoting and incentive-promoting aspects to intellectual property law, and then to imply that an optimal balance has been struck.[18] (This is rather like saying that because fishermen throw some fish back, we can assume over-fishing is not occurring.)

In general, then, I would claim there is a tendency to think that intellectual property is a place to apply our "public goods/incentives theory" rather than our "anti-monopoly/free-flow of information" theory.[19] All by itself, this might push rhetoric and analysis toward more expansive property rights. The tendency is compounded, however, by two others.

First, courts are traditionally much less sensitive to First Amendment, free speech, and other "free flow of information arguments" when the context is seen as private rather than public, property rather than censorship. Thus, for example, the Supreme Court will refuse to allow the state to ban flag burning, but is quite happy to create a property right in a general word such as "Olympic," convey it to a private party, and then allow the private party selectively to refuse public usage of the word. Backed by this state-sponsored "homestead law for the language,"[20] the US Olympic Committee has decreed that the handicapped may have their "Special Olympics," but that gay activists may not hold a "Gay Olympics."[21] This, it seems, is not state censorship but private property. (Emboldened, Justice Rehnquist advocated privatizing the flag.)[22]

Second, intellectual property rights are given only for "original" creation. But the idea of the original author or inventor implicitly devalues the importance of the raw materials with which any creator works—the rhetorical focus on originality leads to a tendency to undervalue the public domain. After all, the novelist who, as Paul Goldstein puts it, "craft[s] out of thin air" does not need a rich and fertile public domain on which to draw. The ironic result is that a regime that lauds and proposes to encourage the great creator may in that process actually function to take away the raw materials that future creators need to produce their little piece of innovation. One interesting thought experiment is to wonder whether Bill Gates could have developed the highly derivative program of MS-DOS if, at the time that he developed it, the current set of expansive copyright and patent protections for software had been in place. My book provides a lengthy discussion of this tendency so I will not dwell on it here.

Tensions In an Intellectual Property System

I have arranged these tensions in two vertical sets. Each set is not a list of corollaries, indeed they are sometimes internally contradictory. Thinking of the subject of intellectual property as "information" rather than "invention" does not commit oneself to Northrop Frye's views about the nature of artistic creation. It certainly does not entail the idea that intellectual property should protect investment and labor—in fact, the "efficiency" perspective tends to eschew intellectual property rights altogether. Let me also acknowledge that any particular portion of information regime is likely to mix and match the columns, like a restaurant patron picking four from column B and one from column A. *Nevertheless,* the members of each column are most likely to be found in popular and scholarly discourse when linked to their vertical neighbors. **Under the guise of resolving these problems, the effect of the author's vision is to make the items in the middle column either disappear or recede in importance.**

So much for the background—now a brief case study. The difficulty is not in finding an example of intellectual property expansion, but in knowing which one to pick. The last few years have seen the expansion of first copyright and then patent to cover software, the patenting of life-forms and human genes, the extension of copyright term limits. Speaking not to the level of protection, but to the current conception of intellectual property law, it is interesting to note that current legislation proposes that the Copyright Office and the Patent Office should cease to be part of the government, being converted instead to government corporations or "performance-based organizations" that would thus be forced to pay greater attention to their "users" and might even be funded through user fees.[25] The idea that the rights-holders are the true "users" or "clients" of the office is a striking one. On the international level we have seen the use of the GATT to turn intellectual property violations into trade violations, thus codifying a particular vision of intellectual property and sanctifying it with the label of "The Market."[26] The example I will pick, however, is the Clinton Administration's proposal for copyright on the Net, which is now hanging somewhere in legislative limbo.

IV   A Brief Case Study: Copyright on the Net

If the information society has an iconic form (one could hardly say an embodiment), it is the Internet. The Net is the anarchic, decentralized network of computers that provides the main locus of digital interchange. While Vice-President Gore, the Commerce Department, and the National Telecommunications and Information Administration were *planning* the "information superhighway," the Net was *becoming* it.

Accordingly, if the government produced a proposal that laid down the ground rules for the information economy that profoundly altered the distribution of property rights over this extremely important resource and that threatened to "lock in" the power of current market leaders, one would expect a great deal of attention to be paid by lawyers, scholars, and the media. Nothing could be further from the truth. The appearance of the Clinton Administration "White Paper"[27] on intellectual property on the National Information Infrastructure produced almost no press reaction. The same was true of the introduction and eventual stalling of the White Paper's legislative proposals in both the House and the Senate.[28] Given the potential ramifications of the legislation, this alone, it seems to me, would be strong evidence for the proposition that greater scrutiny of our intellectual policy making is needed. But the problem lies deeper.

Elsewhere I, and many others, have written about the problems with the White Paper's account of current law, its distressing tendency to misstate, minimize, or simply ignore contrary cases, policy, and legislative history, and its habit of presenting as settled, that which is in fact a matter of profound dispute.[29] There have also been thoughtful analyses of some of the potential negative *effects* of the White Paper and its implementing legislation, particularly focusing on the consequences for libraries, for software innovation, and for privacy.[30] Defenders of the White Paper have argued that its proposals are necessary to protect content on, and encourage fuller use and faster growth of, the Net.[31]

From my point of view, however, the really depressing thing about the report is that it fails to accomplish its stated goal—to examine what level of intellectual property rights would be necessary in cyberspace. It fails in a way that is both revealing and disturbing. The problem isn't simply the tendency to give a pro-author account of the existing law. Even if the White Paper's summary of intellectual property law were accurate, there might well be reasons why a different level of protection might be appropriate in the digital environment. For example, the global reach and ease of access that the Net offers clearly facilitate illegitimate copying. But they also cut down enormously on advertising and on the costs of distribution, potentially yielding a higher percentage return for a lower level of investment. Thus, with some products, more intellectual property protection might be required while with others a lower level of protection would still produce an adequate return to encourage future production.

Some "digital products" require enormous investments of time and energy, are of lasting value, require no "tied" subsidiary services to make them work, and can be copied for pennies. Others require little investment precisely because of their digital nature, do not require extensive research and development, or can be protected by denial of access (databases and search engines) by preemptive release of "demo" or partially disabled shareware versions (DOOM) by being first to market, by "tying arrangements" such as help lines, technical assistance or paid advertising (Netscape), and so on. The point is that the digital environment is complicated; the same technical factors that make copying easier also yield other ways for producers to recover their investments or to encourage further innovation. Rather than take these complexities seriously, the White Paper simply assumes that, on the Net, a right-holder needs all the rights available outside the Net, plus some new ones as well. To the point that there are multiple ways for producers to secure an adequate return on their investment of time and ingenuity, the White Paper opines weakly that not everyone will choose to enforce to the full the rights the report proposes to give them. This is rather like responding to the argument that a capital gains tax cut is not necessary to stimulate investment, with the rejoinder that some investors may decide to give the extra money to charity. Yes, it may happen, but that doesn't go to the question of whether the change was necessary in the first place.

More important than the individual positions taken, however, are the logical fallacies and baseline errors with which the White Paper is loaded. Intellectual property rights are limited monopolies conferred in order to produce present and future public benefit—for the purposes of achieving those goals, the "limitations" on the right are just as important as the grant of the right itself. To put it more accurately, since there is no "natural" absolute intellectual property right, the doctrines that favor consumers and other users, such as fair use, are just as much a part of the basic right as the entitlement of the author to prevent certain kinds of copying. Even the source of the Congress's authority in intellectual property matters—Article 1, Section 8, Clause 8 of the Constitution—mentions two limitations on intellectual property rights; one is functional, "To promote the Progress of Science and useful Arts," and the other is temporal, "by securing for limited times to authors and inventors." Thus, intellectual property is a particularly inappropriate area to talk about property rights as if they were both natural and absolute. Yet this the White Paper does with a dogged consistency and an unlikely passion. Observe in the following quotation how the White Paper first sets up its own inflated idea of intellectual property as the baseline, then implies that right-holders actually have an absolute property right in the continuation of that level of protection. Amazingly, the "limitations" that define intellectual property rights instead become a "tax" on right-holders:

"Some participants have suggested that the United States is being divided into a nation of information "haves" and "have nots" and that this could be ameliorated by ensuring that the fair use defense is broadly generous [sic] in the NII context. The Working Group rejects the notion that copyright owners should be taxed—apart from all others—to facilitate the legitimate goal of universal access."[32]

Of course, given the goals of copyright law, it would have made just as much sense if the argument had been reversed, taking the fair use rights of users and consumers as the baseline. The White Paper wants to give expansive intellectual property rights because it believes, wrongly in my view, that this is the best way to encourage private companies to fund the construction of the information superhighway. In response, a more skeptical Working Group might have said:

"Some reports have suggested that the difficulties of encouraging companies to develop the National Information Infrastructure could be ameliorated by ensuring that intellectual property rights are broadly generous and fair use rights curtailed in the NII context. The Working Group rejects the notion that consumers, future creators and other holders of fair use rights should be taxed—apart from all others—to facilitate the legitimate goal of encouraging investment in the information superhighway."

But the White Paper not only illustrates the pervasive power of baseline fallacies in information economics, it also shows how the "original author" vision downplays the importance of fair use and thus encourages an absolutist rather than a functional idea of intellectual property. In a footnote to the passage quoted above, the Working Group explains further. "The laws of economics and physics protect producers of equipment and tangible supplies to a greater extent than copyright owners." A university, for example, has little choice but to pay to acquire photocopy equipment, computer paper, and diskettes . . . It may, however, seek subsidization from copyright owners by arguing that its copying and distribution of their works should, as a fair use, not be compensated."[33]

This completes the picture given above. Fair use rights are a "subsidy" sought by universities. But wait a minute. Even if the only goal of intellectual property law were to encourage future innovation and information production, this argument would be fallacious. Future creators need some raw material to work with, after all. Fair use is one important method of providing that raw material. It can also be seen as part of the implicit quid pro quo of intellectual property; we will give you this extremely valuable legal monopoly, backed with state power and enforced through the courts (and by the FBI). In return, we will design the contours of your right so as to encourage a variety of socially valuable uses. The White Paper wants to give copyright holders the "quid" while claiming that the "quo" is a tax, or a forced subsidy.

Only the unfamiliarity of intellectual property conceals the ludicrousness of the argument. It's as if a developer had negotiated a fat package of cash grants and tax breaks as the price of building a new stadium in Washington D.C., but then wanted to claim the benefits of the deal while insisting that to make him fulfill his side of the bargain would be to confer a "subsidy" on the city.[34]

The press reaction to the White Paper was respectful (and a little foggy around the edges). Obviously at a loss to know whom to contact, the reporters got reactions from the Business Software Alliance, the recording industry, and the publishers' lobbyists. Surprisingly enough, all these groups felt this was a fine document, the result of meticulous analysis and a good basis for the future. Only later did the press begin to contact those who would be negatively affected by the proposed changes: libraries, on-line service providers, teachers, and so on. The coverage in the media demonstrated two vital things about the future of intellectual property.

First, it is still possible to get away with arguments that if made about any other area of regulation would arouse howls of derision—or at least well-informed skepticism. Compare press reactions to proposals for a flat-tax or arguments that property owners should be compensated for the costs of complying with environmental regulation. Second, the press and the public simply have no idea of the likely "sides" or "interests" involved in such a decision. If a labor law is passed, the *Washington Post* doesn't only call the Chamber of Commerce, on environmental issues they don't only call the Sierra Club. Yet on intellectual property issues, they call only the largest property holders. The idea that startup software developers, academics, librarians, civil libertarians, and so on might have a distinct perspective on these issues simply hasn't emerged into popular consciousness.

V   The Analogy to Environmentalism

Assume for a moment the need for a politics of intellectual property. Go further for a moment, and accept the idea that there might be a special need for a politics to protect the public domain. What might such a politics look like? Right now, it seems to me that, in a number of respects, we are at the stage that the American environmental movement was at in the 1950s. There are people who care about issues we would now identify as "environmental"—supporters of the park system, hunters, birdwatchers, and so on. (In the world of intellectual property we have startup software engineers, libraries, appropriationist artists, parodists, biographers, biotech researchers, etc.) There are flurries of outrage over particular crises—burning rivers, oil spills. (In the world of intellectual property, we have disconnected stories about Microsoft's allegedly anti-competitive practices, the problematic morals of patenting human genes, the propriety of using copyright to shut down certain critics of the Church of Scientology.) Lacking, however, is a general framework, a set of analytical tools with which issues should—as a first cut—be analyzed, and as a result, a perception of common interest in apparently disparate situations—cutting across traditional oppositions. (Hunter vs. Birdwatcher, for example.)[35] What kinds of tools are we talking about?

Crudely speaking, the environmental movement was deeply influenced by two basic analytical frameworks. The first was the idea of ecology; the fragile, complex, and unpredictable interconnections between living systems. The second was the idea of welfare economics—the ways in which markets can fail to make activities internalize their full costs. The combination of the two ideas yielded a powerful and disturbing conclusion. Markets would *routinely* fail to make activities internalize their own costs, particularly their own environmental costs. This failure would, *routinely*, disrupt or destroy fragile ecological systems, with unpredictable, ugly, dangerous and possible irreparable consequences. These two types of analysis pointed to a *general* interest in environmental protection and thus helped to build a large constituency that supported governmental efforts to that end. The duck-hunter's preservation of wetlands as a species habitat turns out to have wider functions in the prevention of erosion and the maintenance of water quality. The decision to burn coal rather than gas for power generation may have impacts on everything from forests to fisheries.

Of course, it would be silly to think that environmental policy was fuelled only by ideas rather than by more immediate desires. As William Ruckelshaus put it, "With air pollution there was, for example, a desire of the people living in Denver to see the mountains again. Similarly, the people living in Los Angeles had a desire to see one another."[36] (Funnily enough, as with intellectual property, changes in communications technology also played a role. "In our living rooms in the middle sixties, black and white television went out and color television came in. We have only begun to understand some of the impacts of television on our lives, but certainly for the environmental movement it was a bonanza. A yellow outfall flowing into a blue river does not have anywhere near the impact on black and white television that it has on color television; neither does brown smog against a blue sky."[37])

Nevertheless, the ideas I mentioned, ecology and welfare economics, were extremely important for the environmental movement. They helped to provide its agenda, its rhetoric and the perception of common interest underneath its coalition politics. Even more interestingly, for my purposes, those ideas—which began as inaccessible, scientific, or economic concepts, far from popular discourse—were brought into the mainstream of American politics. This did not happen easily or automatically. Popularizing complicated ideas is hard work. There were brilliant books like *Silent Spring* and *A Sand County Almanac,* television discussions, documentaries on Love Canal or the California kelp beds, op-ed pieces in newspapers and pontificating experts on TV. Environmental groups both shocking and staid played their part, through the dramatic theatre of a Greenpeace protest, or the tweedy respectability of the Audubon society. Where once the idea of "The Environment" (as opposed to 'my lake', say) was seen as a mere abstraction, something that couldn't stand against the concrete benefits brought by a particular piece of development, it came to be an abstraction with both the force of law and of popular interest behind it.

To me, this suggests a strategy for the future of the politics of intellectual property. In both areas, we seem to have the same recipe for failure in the structure of the decision-making process. Decisions in a democracy are made badly when they are primarily made by and for the benefit of a few stake-holders (land-owners or content providers). It is a matter of rudimentary political science analysis or public choice theory to say that democracy works badly when the gains of a particular action can be captured by a relatively small and well-identified group while the losses—even if larger in aggregate—are low-level effects spread over a larger, more inchoate group.[38] (This effect is only intensified when the transaction costs of identifying and resisting the change are high.) Think of the costs and benefits of acid rain producing power-generation or, less serious, but surely similar in form, the costs and benefits of retrospectively increasing copyright term limits on works for which the copyright had already expired pulling them back out of the public domain. There are obvious benefits to the heirs and assigns of authors whose copyright has expired, in having the Congress put the fence back up around this portion of the intellectual commons.[39] There are obviously *some* costs—for example, to education and public debate—in not having multiple, competing, low cost editions of these works. But these costs are individually small and have few obvious stake-holders to represent them.

Beyond the failures in the decision-making process lie failures in the way that we think about the issues. The environmental movement gained much of its persuasive power by pointing out that there were structural reasons that we were likely to make bad environmental decisions; a legal system based on a particular notion of what "private property" entailed, and an engineering or scientific system that treated the world as a simple, linearly related set of causes and effects. In both of these conceptual systems, the environment actually *disappeared*; there was no place for it in the analysis. Small surprise then that we did not preserve it very well. I have argued that the same is true about the public domain. The fundamental aporia in economic analysis of information issues, the source-blindness of an "original author"-centered model or property rights, and the political blindness to the importance of the public domain as a whole (not "my lake," but "The Environment") all come together to make the public domain disappear, first in concept and then, increasingly, as a reality.

I have said all of this in an attempt to show that there is something larger going on under the *realpolitik* of land grabs by Disney and campaign contributions by the Recording Industry of America. But it would be an equal and opposite mistake to think that this is just about a dysfunctional discourse of intellectual property. In this part of the analysis, too, the environmental movement offers some useful practical reminders. The ideas of ecology and environmental welfare economics were important, but one cannot merely write a *Silent Spring* or *A Sand County Almanac* and hope that the world will change. Environmentalists piggy-backed on existing sources of conservationist sentiment—love of nature, the national parks movement, hikers, campers, birdwatchers. They built coalitions between those who might be affected by environmental changes. They even discovered, though very slowly, the reality of environmental racism.

Some of these aspects, at least, could be replicated in the politics of intellectual property. The coalitions developed to combat the White Paper and its implementing legislation offer some nice examples of the possibilities and pitfalls. Other strategies also come to mind. For environmental problems, some of the transaction costs of investigation and political action are overcome through expert agents, both public and private. I pay my taxes to support the EPA or my charity dollars to Greenpeace, and hope they do a good job of tracking environmental problems. (In the latter case, I know at least that the makers of Zodiac rubber boats will be given a boost.) Right now there is not a single public or private organization whose main task is to protect and preserve the public domain. This should change.

Conclusion

I have argued that the idea of an information age is indeed a useful and productive concept, that there is a homologizing tendency for all "information issues" to collapse into each other as information technology and the idea of "information" to move forward in reciprocal relationship. The range of information issues expands and the value of the "message" increases, at least in comparison to the diminishing marginal cost of the medium. This, in turn, gives greater and greater importance to intellectual property. Yet despite its astounding economic importance and its impact on everything from public education to the ownership of one's own genetic information, intellectual property has no corresponding place in popular debate or political understanding. The belief seems to be that information-age politics means fighting censorship on the Web too.

Apart from the normal presumption in favor of informed democratic participation in the formation of entire property regimes, I argued that there are particular reasons why this comparative political vacuum is particularly unfortunate. Drawing on some prior work, I claimed that our intellectual property discourse has structural tendencies toward over-protection, rather than under-protection. To combat that tendency, as well as to prevent the formation and rigidification of a set of rules crafted by and for the largest stakeholders, I argued that we need a politics of intellectual property. Using the environmental movement as an analogy, I pointed out that a successful political movement needed both a set of (popularizable) analytical tools and coalition built around the more general interests those tools revealed. Welfare economics and the idea of ecology showed that "the environment" literally disappeared as a concept in the analytical structure of private property claims, simplistic "cause and effect" science, and markets that do not force the internalization of negative externalities. Similarly, I claimed the "public domain" is disappearing, both conceptually and literally, in an IP system built around the interests of the current stakeholders, and the notion of the original author, around an over-deterministic practice of economic analysis and around a "free speech" community that is under-sensitized to the dangers of private censorship. In one very real sense, the environmental movement invented the environment so that farmers, consumers, hunters, and birdwatchers could all discover themselves as environmentalists. Perhaps we need to invent the public domain in order to call into being the coalition that might protect it.[40]

Is the environmental analogy of only rhetorical or strategic value, then? For my part, though I would be happy to acknowledge its imperfections, I would say that it also shows us some of the dangers inherent in the kind of strategies I have described. Right now, even under a purely instrumental economic analysis, it is hard to argue that intellectual property is set at the appropriate level. Just as the idea of "activities internalizing their full costs" galvanized and then began to dominate environmental discourse, the economic inadequacy of current intellectual property discourse has been emphasized by skeptics.[41] But the attraction of the economic analysis conceals a danger. The problems of efficiency, of market oligopoly, and of future innovation are certainly important ones, but they are not the only problems we face. Aldo Leopold expressed the point powerfully and presciently nearly fifty years ago in a passage entitled "Substitutes for a Land Ethic."

> "One basic weakness in a conservation system based wholly on economic motives is that most members of the land community have no economic value... When one of these non-economic categories is threatened, and if we happen to love it, we invent subterfuges to give it economic importance... It is painful to read those circumlocutions today."[42]

I believe that there are powerful arguments why a Pay-as-you-read architecture on the Net would be economically inefficient even with minimal transaction costs. I can make arguments that point out the economic problems with our current treatments of "sources" of genetic information, or what have you. I can even say with complete truthfulness that I believe my arguments to be better than those on the "other side." But under Leopold's gentle chiding I am reminded of the dangers of embracing too closely a language that can express only some of the things that you care about.

Let me conclude by dealing with two particular objections to my thesis here. First, that my whole premise is simply wrong; intellectual property is not out of balance, the public domain is not systematically threatened, economic analysis is both determinate and clear in supporting the current regime, the general tendency both internationally and domestically has not been toward the kind of intellectual land-grab I describe, or—if it has—the tendency exists for some very good reasons. Elsewhere I have tried to refute those claims but to some extent the point is moot. Even if I was wrong, the basic idea of democratic accountability over public disposal of *extremely* valuable rights would seem to demand a vastly more informed politics of intellectual property in the information age. If such accountability is to exist, the public domain should be more systematically discussed and defended than has heretofore been the case.

The second objection is more fundamental. How can I compare the politics of intellectual property to the politics of the environment? For some, the difference in seriousness of the two problems robs the analogy of its force. After all, environmental problems could actually destroy the biosphere and this is just, well, intellectual property. My response to this is partly that this is *an analogy.* I am comparing the form of the problems rather than their seriousness. Still, I have to say I believe that part of this reaction has to do with a failure to adjust to the importance that intellectual property has and is going to have in an information society. Again and again, one meets a belief that this is a technical issue with no serious human, political, or distributional consequences. Yet a "bad" intellectual property regime of the kind that I am talking about could:

- Lead to extraordinary monopoly and concentration in the software industry, as copyright and patent trump antitrust policy. Right now the effects are mainly those that would concern the actual drafters of the antitrust laws, who worried about the effects that concentration of wealth and economic power had on the republic, rather than their more modern "consumer-welfare" oriented exegetes. There is some reason, however, to believe that there could be costs even a Chicago-school antitrust analysis would find distasteful.
- Extend intellectual property rights even further over living organisms, including the human genome, transgenic species, and the like. This clearly has some ethical, medical, and religious ramifications, while the spectre of a first world-dominated land grab over the human genome would surely be enough to shock those who believed that the deep sea bed was the common heritage of mankind.
- "Privatise" words, or aspects of images or texts that are currently in the public domain, to the detriment of public debate, education, equal access to information, and the like.
- Impose a pay-as-you-read architecture on the Net without considering some of the costs resulting from that decision.

And so on, and so on. The list could be extended. Some of these things have not yet come to pass, and not all of them will. There are court and regulatory decisions that cut against the protectionist tendency I have described. Recent organizing efforts around the Net, cultural property, pharmaceutical, and fair use issues have improved the discourse markedly. Nevertheless, I think that the current situation is enough to warrant what one might call precautionary alarmism. It would be a shame for the fundamental property regime of the information economy to be constructed behind our backs. We need a politics—a political economy—of intellectual property and we need it now.

Endnotes

1. © James Boyle 1997. This article draws on ideas first developed in my book, *Shamans, Software and Spleens: Law and The Construction of the Information Society* (1996). Those who study intellectual property will realize how extensive a debt this article owes to David Lange's classic piece "Recognizing the Public Domain," 44 *Law and Contemporary Problems* 147 (1981). Thanks are also due to Keith Aoki, John Perry Barlow, Robert Gordon, Jessica Litman, Peter Jaszi, Bruce Sterling, and to the Yale and Columbia Legal Theory Workshop Series. Please don't quote or cite 'til I get the bugs out.

2. See Charles Darwin, *On the Origin of Species by Means of Natural Selection* (1859) but see *Genesis* 1:1–29 contra.

3. See Nicolaus Copernicus, *Concerning the Revolutions of the Celestial Spheres* (1543) but see Claudius Ptolemaeus, *Almagest* (c. 170 A.D.) *contra*.

4. *See generally* William Gibson, *Neuromancer* (1984).

5. *Church of Scientology Int'l* v. *Fishman*, 35 F.3d 570 (9th Cir. 1994); *Religious Technology Center* v. *Netcom On-Line Communications Servs.*, 907 F. Supp. 1361, 1377–1378 (D. Cal. 1995). *Religious Technology Center* v. *Arnaldo Pagliarina Lerma*, 908 F. Supp. 1362, 1368 (E.D. Va. 1995). ("Although the RTC brought the complaint under traditional secular concepts of copy-right and trade secret law, it has become clear that a much broader motivation prevailed—the stifling of criticism and dissent of the religious practices of Scientology and the destruction of its opponents.") The documents filed in the case have excited considerable comment on the Web. (Declan McCullagh, Scientology, critics collide in Internet copyright case FOCUS, vol. 25, no. 1, October 1995, page 4.)

6. This attitude is in marked contrast to lawyers' assumptions about, say, the jurisprudence of the First Amendment, or the Education Department's rulings on race-conscious scholarships. Though these are also complicated areas of law or regulation, many lawyers and laypeople feel that a basic under-standing of them is a sine qua non of political consciousness. In many cases, in fact, the language of liberal legalism defines the central issues of public debate—a fact that presents its own problems.

7. And, in an important sense, created.

8. See, e.g., Karen Riley, *"Rockville Biotech Firm Takes Next Step in Genetics Journey,"* Wash. Times., June 9, 1995, at B7.

9. For an introduction to the biological applications of information theory, see *Biological Information Theory and Chowder Society FAQ*, and the archives of the Usenet newsgroup *bionet.info-theory*.

10. "In the forests of Panama lives a Guyami Indian woman who is unusually resistant to a virus that causes leukemia. She was discovered by scientific 'gene hunters,' engaged in seeking out native peoples whose lives and cultures are threatened with extinction. Though they provided basic medical care, the hunters did not set out to preserve the people, only their genes—which can be kept in cultures of 'immortalized' cells grown in the laboratory. In 1993, the US Department of Commerce tried to patent the Guyami woman's genes—and only abandoned the attempt in the face of furious protest from representatives of indigenous peoples." Tom Wilkie, *"Whose gene is it anyway?",* Indep., Nov. 19, 1995, at 75.

11. See, e.g., Frank Guarnieri et al., *"Making DNA Add,"* Science, July 12, 1996, at 220.

12. See, e.g., Julian Dibbell, *"The Race to Build Intelligent Machines,"* Time, Mar. 25, 1996, at 56.

13. See Communications Decency Act of 1996, Pub. L. No. 104-104, 110 Stat. 133 (codified at vari-ous sections of 47 U.S.C. and 18 U.S.C.); *see also generally ALA-led Coalition Challenges CDA*, Am. Libr., Apr. 1996, at 13.

14. Given the fate of these arguments in the contemporary political arena, maybe I should reiterate them: Distribution of this good (education, health care, wired-ness) through a market system is going to have a lot of serious negative effects on those who cannot pay, effects that will track and actually intensify existing inequalities of class, race, and gender. Given the importance of the resource in question, its relevance to the citizens' status *qua* citizen, and the corrosive effects of such inequalities on the well-being of the polity, something should be done to mitigate or

eliminate the problem of access. All of this seems profoundly true, but it is hardly a new argument. In fact, subject matter aside, it would have been completely familiar to the authors of the Federalist Papers.

15. For the arguments behind this claim, see James Boyle, *Shamans, Software and Spleens: Law and the Construction of the Information Society* (1996). There are specific areas in which the situation might be reversed, such as "unoriginal" databases. These, however, are the exception rather than the rule.

16. In the book, I explore the reasons that this problem is not "solved" when one moves to the reality of imperfect markets. The abstract idea of "trade-offs" also proves insufficient to generate the determinacy of result which most analysts claim for their work.

17. Sanford J. Grossman & Joseph E. Stiglitz, *"On the Impossibility of Informationally Efficient Markets,"* 70 Am. Econ. Rev. 393, 405 (1980). I cannot here go into the full joys of this debate, but those who talk confidently about the economic efficiency of the fine details of intellectual property doctrine would do well to look at the absolutely basic disputes between information economists. For example, Kenneth Arrow argues that, without intellectual property rights, too little information will be produced because producers of information will not be able to capture its true value. (Even with intellectual property rights he believes that certain kinds of information generation may need direct government subsidy on a 'cost-plus' basis.) Kenneth Arrow, *"Economic Welfare and the Allocation of Resources for Invention,* in Rate and Direction of Inventive Activity: Economic and Social Factors," 609, 617 (National Bureau of Economic Research ed., 1962). Fama and Laffer, on the other hand, argue that, without intellectual property rights, too much information will be generated, because some information will be produced only in order to gain some temporary advantage in trading, thus redistributing wealth but not achieving greater allocative efficiency. Eugene F. Fama & Arthur B. Laffer, *"Information and Capital Markets,"* 44 J. Bus. 289 (1971). In other words, in the absence of information property rights, there may be an inefficiently *high* investment of social resources in information-gathering activities, activities that merely slice the pie up differently, rather than making it bigger. Hirshleifer gives a similar analysis of patent law, ending up with the conclusion that patent law may be *either* a necessary incentive for the production of inventions or an unnecessary legal monopoly in information that overcompensates an inventor who has already had the opportunity to trade on the information implied by his or her discovery. Jack Hirshleifer, *"The Private and Social Value of Information and the Reward to Inventive Activity,"* 61 Am. Econ. Rev. 561 (1971). The difficulty of yielding definite results is compounded by the fact that some professional economists seem to have a naive, pre-realist understanding of law. They often talk as though there was a natural suite of property rights that automatically accompanied a free market. They make strong and unexplained assumptions that certain types of activities (for example, trading on a superior information position) would "naturally" be allowed and involve no "harm" to others, but that certain others (for example, trading on coercion through superior physical strength) will not be. There is a fascinating study to be done on these remnants of classical economics still present in a supposedly neo-classical analysis. The same kind of error also creeps into the work of some lawyer-economists. See, e.g., Saul Levmore, *"Securities and Secrets: Insider Trading and the Law of Contracts,"* 68 Va. L. Rev. 117 (1982).

18. Some are more sophisticated. "In principle, there is a level of copyright protection that balances these two competing interests optimally...We shall see...that various doctrines of copyright law, such as the distinction between idea and expression and the fair use doctrine, can be understood as *attempts* to promote economic efficiency..." William M. Landes & Richard A. Posner, *"An Economic Analysis of Copyright Law,"* 18 J. Legal Stud. 325, 333 (1989) (emphasis added). Despite the qualifying phrases, one leaves the article with the sense that the copyright law has hit the appropriate balance between efficiency and incentives. This level of comfort with the current regime is to be compared with the open skepticism displayed by an economist such as Hirshleifer. See Jack Hirshleifer, *"The Private and Social Value of Information and the Reward to Inventive Activity,"* 61 Am. Econ. Rev. 561, 572 (1971). (Because of the possibility of speculation on prior knowledge of invention and the uncertainties of "irrelevant" risks, patent protection may or may not be necessary in order to produce an appropriate incentive to invention.) It will be interesting to watch the Supreme Court's attitude toward these issues over the next few years, given the identity of one of the original skeptics. See Stephen Breyer, *"The Uneasy Case for Copyright: A Study of Copyright in Books, Photocopies, and Computer Programs,"* 84 Harv. Law Rev. 281 (1970).

19. In one sense, the current configuration of Federal bureaucracies mirrors the tensions I have been describing in this article; the FTC and the Justice Department tend to view information issues from within an efficiency perspective, accepting the need for economic incentives but more skeptical of the monopoly effects of extensive intellectual property rights. The Commerce Department—and the administration, on the other hand—take a strong incentive-focused approach to most issues. As a result, the battle to regulate the information economy is a fascinating fusion of organizational *persona,* economic theory, and political turf war. See, e.g., Federal Trade Commissioner Christine A. Varney, Antitrust in the Information Age, Remarks before the Charles River Associates Conference on Economics, in Legal & Reg. Proc., May 4, 1995.

20. Felix Cohen's phrase. *"Transcendental Nonsense and the Functional Approach,"* 25 Colum. L. Rev. 809 (1935), *reprinted* in *The Legal Conscience: Selected Papers of Felix S. Cohen* (Lucy K. Cohen ed., 1970), at 33, 42.

21. *San Francisco Arts and Athletics Inc., et al.* v. *United States Olympic Committee,* 483 U.S. 522.

22. "Only two terms ago in *San Francisco Arts and Athletics, Inc. v. United States Olympic Committee,* the Court held that Congress could grant exclusive use of the word "Olympic" to the United States Olympic Committee... As the Court stated 'when a word [or symbol] acquires 'value as the result of organization and the expenditure of labor, skill and money' by an entity, that entity constitutionally may obtain a limited property right in the word [or symbol].' Surely Congress or the States may recognize a similar interest in the flag." *Texas* v. *Johnson,* 491 U.S. 397, 429–30 (1989).

23. Northrop Frye, *Anatomy Of Criticism: Four Essays,* 96–97 (1957).

24. Paul Goldstein, *Copyright,* 38 J. Copyright Soc'y of the U.S.A. 109, 110 (1991) (emphasis added.)

25. Omnibus Patent Act of 1996, S. 1961, 104th Cong.; Morehead-Schroeder Patent Reform Act, H.R. 3460, 104th Cong. (1996).

26. Employing child labor or violating environmental regulations will give a nation's industry what might seem to be an unfair competitive advantage, but will not trigger trade sanctions. See, e.g.,

Robert Howse and Michael J. Trebilcock, "The Fair Trade-Free Trade Debate: Trade, Labor, and the Environment," 16 Int'l Rev. L. & Econ. 61 (discussing the absence from the GATT/World Trade Organization framework of provisions for sanctions in response to other nations' environmental and labor practices); *but see* North American Agreement on Labor Cooperation, Sept. 13, 1993, Can.-Mex.-U.S., ann. 1, 32 I.L.M. 1499 (1993). Refusing to accept and enforce our vision of intellectual property law, however, is cause for international action. See generally J. H. Reichman, *"Compliance with the TRIPS Agreement: Introduction to a Scholarly Debate,"* 29 Vand. J. Transnat'l L. 363 (1996).

27. *Information Infrastructure Task Force, Intellectual Property and the National Information Infrastructure: The Report of the Working Group on Intellectual Property Rights* (1995) [hereinafter White Paper]. See also James Boyle, *"Sold Out,"* N.Y. Times, Mar. 31, 1996; *"Is Congress Turning the Internet into an Information Toll Road?,"* Insight, Jan. 15, 1996, at 24. This section of the article is a revised version of the analysis provided in *Shamans* and in those articles.

28. The relevant Bills are HR 2441 and S. 1284.

29. This tendency is to be contrasted unfavorably with the most thoughtful defense of the White Paper—which argued that its protections would be necessary to put "cars on the Information superhighway" but was careful to acknowledge that some of the White Paper's legal theories were controversial, and then to defend them on their own terms rather than to offer them as propositions so obvious they needed no defense. Jane C. Ginsburg, "Putting Cars on the 'Information Superhighway': Authors, Exploiters and Copyright in Cyberspace," 95 Colum. L. Rev. 1466, 1476 (1995) [e.g., defending White Paper's embrace of the RAM copy theory but pointing that this approach has been "questioned or even strongly criticized"]; See also Jessica Litman, "The Exclusive Right to Read," 13 Cardozo Arts & Ent. L. J. 29 (1994).

30. See David Post, *"New Wine, Old Bottles: The Case of the Evanescent Copy,"* Am. Lawyer, May 1995; Niva Elkin-Koren, *"Copyright Law and Social Dialogue on the Information Superhighway":* Pamela Samuelson, *"Legally Speaking: The NII Intellectual Property Report,"* Communications of the ACM, December 1994, at 21. *"The Case Against Copyright Liability of Bulletin Board Operators,"* 13 Cardozo Arts & Ent. L.J. 345 (1995). Evan St. Lifer and Michael Rogers, *"NII White Paper Has Librarians Concerned About Copyright,"* Library Journal News, Oct. 1, 1995. Vic Sussman, *"Copyright Wrong,"* U.S. News & World Report, Sept. 18, 1995; Andrea Lunsford & Susan West Schantz, *"Who Should Own Cyberspace,"* Columbus Dispatch, Mar. 26, 1996; Many of these points were also made in testimony. *Intellectual Property and the National Information Infrastructure: Public Hearing Before the White House Information Infrastructure Task Force,* Sept. 22, 1994 (testimony of Jessica Litman, Professor of Law, Wayne State Univ.). *Comments of Professor Mary Brandt Jensen, August 26th 1994. Comments of Professor Neil Netanel and Professor Mark Lemley, University of Texas School of Law, September 2, 1994.*

31. Jane C. Ginsburg, *"Putting Cars on the 'Information Superhighway': Authors, Exploiters and Copyright in Cyberspace,"* 95 Colum. L. Rev. 1466 (1995).

32. White Paper at 84.

33. Id at n. 266.

34. Generally such arguments turn on disagreements over the current law baseline from which "subsidies" or "taxes" are calculated. The remarkable thing about occasional passages such as this in the

White Paper is that they suggest that any fair use rights would be a subsidy to users. Not all of the White Paper's discussion is this extreme, however. Some of the debate still turns on differences of opinion about the meaning of fair use jurisprudence. Elsewhere I have given my account of the deficiencies in the White Paper's account of current law. See *The Debate on the White Paper.*

35. Although this may be an oversimplification, it does not seem to be a *controversial* oversimplification. "First, the basic analytical approach and policy values underlying environmental law came from a fundamental paradigm shift born of Rachel Carson in 1961, perhaps assisted unwittingly by Ronald Coase, redefining the scope of how societal governance decisions should be made. What we might call the Rachel Carson Paradigm declared that, although humans naturally try to maximize their own accumulation of benefits and ignore negative effects of their actions, a society that wishes to survive and prosper must identify and take comprehensive account of the real interacting consequences of individual decisions, negative as well as positive, whether the marketplace accounts for them or not. Attempts to achieve such expanded accountings, as much as anything, have been the common thread linking the remarkable range of issues that we call environmental law." Zygmunt J.B. Plater, *"From the Beginning, a Fundamental Shift of Paradigms: A Theory and Short History of Environmental Law,"* 27 Loy. L.A. L. Rev. 981-2 (1994). See also Rachel Carson, *Silent Spring* (1961). I would replace Coase by Pigou, and mention Leopold as well as Carson, but otherwise agree. Focusing on Leopold also has another beneficial effect. It emphasizes the extent to which environmentalism was driven in addition by a belief that the economic valuation, and "commodification," of environmental resources was not only incomplete but actually wrong. See A. Leopold, *A Sand County Almanac* (1949).

36. William D. Ruckelshaus, *"Environmental Protection: A Brief History of the Environmental Movement in America and the Implications Abroad,"* 15 Envtl. L. J. 455, 456 (1985).

37. Id.

38. There are other, more context-specific, problems. Both environmental disputes and intellectual property issues are seen as "technical," which tends to inhibit popular participation. In both areas, opposition to expansionist versions of stake-holders' rights can be off-puttingly portrayed as a stand "against private property." This is a frequent claim in intellectual property disputes, where defenders of the public domain are portrayed as "info-commies" or enemies of "the free market." (The latter is a nicely ironic argument to make in favor of a state licensed monopoly.) Indeed, the resurgence of a non-positivist, property owners takings jurisprudence in the Supreme Court seems to indicate that this idea still has great force even in the environmental area.

39. Although it is beyond me how retrospective, and even post-mortem, copyright term extension is to be squared with the idea that intellectual property rights should be given only when they will stimulate the production of new work; barring the idea of sooth-saying or other worldly communication, the incentive effects would seem to be small.

40. For a path-breaking formulation see David Lange, *"Recognizing the Public Domain,"* 44 Law and Contemp. Probs. 147 (1981). I have also been influenced by Jessica Litman's work on the subject.

41. This economic skepticism links works otherwise very different in tone. Compare Stephen Breyer, *"The Uneasy Case for Copyright: A Study of Copyright in Books, Photocopies, and Computer Programs,"* 84 Harv. L. Rev. 281 (1970); Pamela Samuelson, *"The Copyright Grab,"* WIRED 4.01 (1996); Boyle, *Shamans* supra.

42. Aldo Leopold, *A Sand County Almanac* 210-211 (1949).

Intellectual Property, Information, and the Common Good

Michael C. McFarland, SJ

1. Introduction

Intellectual property is an odd notion, almost an oxymoron. Property usually refers to tangible assets over which someone has or claims control. Originally it meant land. Now it could also refer to a car, a milling machine, a jacket, or a toothbrush. In all these cases the property claim is of control of the physical entity. If I claim a plot of land as my property, I am saying I can control who has access to that land and what they do there. I can build a fence around it, rent it out, or drill for oil on it. If a car is my property, I get the keys to it. I can exclude others from using it and use it myself for whatever I want, as long as I do not threaten the lives or property of others. Intellectual property is different because its object is something intangible, although it usually has tangible expression. The intellectual property in a book is not the physical paper and ink, but the arrangement of words that the ink marks on the paper represent. The ink marks can be translated into regions of magnetic polarization on a computer disk, and the intellectual property, and whatever claims there are to that property, will be the same. The owner of a song claims control, not of the CD on which the song is recorded, but of the song itself, of where, when, and how it can be performed and recorded. But how can you build a fence around a song? What does it mean to "own" an idea? Where are the locks that keep other people from "driving" it?

Intellectual property has always been closely tied to technology. Technology arises from intellectual property in the form of new inventions. But technology also supports intellectual property by providing new, more powerful and more efficient ways of creating and disseminating writing, musical composition, visual art, and so on. In fact it was the technology of the printing press that originally gave rise to intellectual property as a legal and moral issue. Before, when it took almost as

This essay originally appeared in the *Proceedings of the Fourth Annual Ethics and Technology Conference*, Boston College, Chestnut Hill, MA, 1999, pp. 88–95. Copyright © 1999 by Michael McFarland, S.J. Reprinted with permission.

much of an effort to reproduce a document as it took to create it, there was little need to impose limits on copying. It was only when inexpensive reproductions became feasible that it was seen as necessary to give authors more control over how their works were used by creating copyrights (Samuelson, 1991).

Computer technology has created a new revolution in how intellectual property is created, stored, reproduced, and disseminated; with that revolution has come new challenges to our understanding of intellectual property and how to protect it. Of course computers have given rise to a whole new category of intellectual property, namely computer software. A major commercial program can take a team of one hundred or more highly skilled and highly paid programmers years to create and can sell for hundreds, or even hundreds of thousands, of dollars per copy. Yet someone with access to such a program can make a copy in moments at practically no cost. There is clearly great incentive for the user to make copies without paying for them, while the creator in many cases insists on being paid for each copy in order to recoup the investment in creating the product, plus a reasonable (or unreasonable) profit. In addition, as more and more traditional forms of intellectual property, such as writing, music and other sound, movies and videos, photographs, and so on, are being made publicly available on computer networks, they can be copied, manipulated, reworked, excerpted, recombined, and distributed much more easily than before. Without some form of legal and moral protection, the creator or "owner" of such creative products has much less control over how they are used and by whom, and less opportunity to benefit from them. The question is, how much protection is required, and when and to what extent should it apply? (Samuelson, 1991)

This paper addresses that question. First it presents some cases that illustrate the range of possible intellectual property rights. Next it examines the traditional justifications for such rights. It then critiques those justifications, not to refute them, but to show their limits. Finally it proposes a different way of looking at the problem, using traditional natural law ethics. This gives a more complete and balanced way of analyzing these cases.

2. Conflicts over Intellectual Property: Five Cases

The types of claims asserted over intellectual property have been many and diverse, some eminently reasonable, others seemingly quite extreme. The following cases give some idea of the diversity of such claims.

Case 1:   Plagiarism. Educators, especially those in higher education, are seeing an increasing number of cases of plagiarism from the Internet and other electronic sources. Students will often take all or part of an article or essay that they have located online and hand it in as their own work, with or without additions or modifications of their own.

Plagiarism, of course, has been a problem for a long time, but the easy access to vast amounts of electronic information dramatically increases the possibilities, and the temptations. Not only is there more material available, but it is much easier to find and access. Furthermore it can be downloaded and included in a document with a few brief commands. It is not even necessary to retype it.

This violates the traditional canons of academic honesty. Students are assigned essays to sharpen their research and writing skills, and so that they will develop and express their own understanding and synthesis of the material. Copying someone else's essay does none of this. Furthermore it is almost universally accepted that when one incorporates another's work into one's own, one must clearly identify it as copied and give credit to the original author.

Case 2: Software Piracy. In April, 1994, an MIT student, David LaMacchia, was indicted for allegedly setting up and running a computer bulletin board that allowed people on the Internet to exchange copies of commercial software. The system was set up so that anyone on the Internet could post a copy of a program, which was then available for downloading for free by anyone who chose to do so. The site had become quite popular. Investigators claimed that they found software worth millions of dollars on the system. LaMacchia was accused of wire fraud and the interstate transportation of stolen property. If convicted he could have been sent to prison and assessed fines of up to $250,000. At the time this was billed as "the largest case of computer piracy in the country" (Rakowsky, 1994).

Ultimately the case was thrown out on a technicality. LaMacchia did not benefit monetarily from the arrangement and did not download any of the software himself. Therefore his offense did not come under existing law. However, the judge commented that "if the indictment is to be believed, one might at best describe his actions as heedlessly irresponsible, and at worst as nihilistic, self-indulgent, and lacking in any fundamental sense of values" (Zuckoff, 1994). He suggested that the law needed to be rewritten to cover cases like this.

This is just one instance of the widespread practice of making and using copies of commercial software, such as operating systems, word processors and other office productivity tools, games, and so on, without giving any compensation to those who created, published, distributed, and sold it. Software publishers estimate that more than half of all copies of their products in use in the United States are unauthorized. It can be as high as ninety percent in some foreign countries.

In the United States and most other countries, the producers of software can copyright it, meaning that they can control its distribution and use. It is illegal to make and use copies without authorization, and software publishers have won some substantial judgments against offenders, particularly large corporations. For the most part, however, they have not gone after individual users because the potential return is so small in relation to the cost.

Case 3: Repackaging Data and Databases. A company named ProCD published a CD-ROM containing a large compilation of telephone listings. A University of Wisconsin graduate student put all the data on the CD-ROM onto his Web site and charged users to access it. The company sued, claiming it had invested $10 million in collecting the data, putting it into an easily accessible form, packaging and marketing it, while the student was cutting into their sales and making profits himself with almost no effort (Samuelson, 1996b). ProCD won, but only on the narrow grounds that the student had violated the shrink-wrap license agreement that came with the CD-ROM.

If the student had obtained the information through a network or a third party, presumably he would not have been held liable. Traditionally databases have not been covered by copyright unless they involved some creativity in the way the data was selected or put together. This was established in Feist Publications, Inc. v. Rural Telephone Service Co., where the plaintiff Feist took without permission directory listings published by Rural Telephone and included them in its own directory. The court found that no matter how much effort the telephone company had put into compiling the listings, it was not original and therefore not protected (Hayden, 1991).

There has been much debate recently about whether databases and the data in them should receive more protection than currently afforded by copyright law. The European Union, for example, issued a directive requiring that its member states pass laws giving database developers control over how their databases and data are used. The United States has proposed legislation with similar intent, both internally and for adoption by the World Intellectual Property Organization (WIPO) (Samuelson, 1996b). Individual concerns have also been asserting stronger claims to ownership of data. For example the National Basketball Association (NBA) has sued STATS, Inc. to prevent the latter from publishing minute-by-minute scores of NBA games while they are in progress, claiming that the scores and other statistics are the NBA's property. The NBA won at the trial court level, but the case is being appealed. If the NBA's claims are upheld, either in court or by legislation, it will have a tremendous impact on the public availability of not just sports scores and statistics, but also stock prices, weather data, travel schedules, and so on.

Case 4: Reverse Engineering. Computer software never runs in isolation. It has to interact with hardware, with operating systems, and often with other applications. In order for it to work correctly, the developers must know in great detail how the other pieces of the system operate, and especially how they are designed to interface. Makers of hardware, operating systems, and other software generally publish specifications about how they are supposed to work and how to interface with them, but these are frequently incomplete, obscure, and inaccurate. Developers often find they must study the actual code or hardware design of the system their product must work with in order to get the interface right. Since the original code or design, as written by the designers, is usually jealously guarded, developers who need to learn about the system must take object code, the cryptic code that actually executes on the computer, or the actual chips in the case of hardware, and translate them back into human-readable form to divine how they really work. This is known as reverse engineering.

Reverse engineering is often a necessity for reliable software design. Reputable companies are very careful to extract only the specifications necessary for a correct interface and not to copy any of the original code itself. However, the practice has been challenged in a number of lawsuits, on the grounds that the company doing the reverse engineering could use the insight gained to produce a competing program without doing the expensive design work required in the original. To date courts have allowed reverse engineering, as long as certain reasonable restrictions are observed (Behrens, 1998).

Case 5:   Copying in Transmission. The Internet, like most large computer networks today, uses a so-called "store and forward" architecture. Unlike a classical analog phone system, where there is a direct connection from the sender all the way through to the receiver, a message in a store and forward system is sent from computer to computer until it finally reaches its destination. No computer in the chain has complete knowledge of or control over the route the message will follow. It knows enough to select the next computer to send it to. For the sake of reliability, each computer keeps a copy of the message after sending it and holds the copy until it has received verification that the message has reached its destination. That way it can resend it if the earlier attempt failed. This procedure is used for all kinds of network transactions, including email, file transfers, and Web pages.

Generally the copying of messages in transit is automatic and transparent. The copy is made by the software as a routine part of the transmission procedure and deleted when the transaction is complete. However, it is certainly possible to keep the copy, and sometimes that is done for diagnostic purposes, as part of a system backup, or to monitor the volume, nature, or content of network traffic. For example, it is routine for some companies to save copies of all emails that pass through their computers.

Store and forward transmission is a well-established and universally accepted technology. However, with the growing concern over the protection of electronic intellectual property, it has begun to be questioned. For example, the online version of *The Wall Street Journal* is meant to be available only to those who have paid for a subscription to it. Suppose a reader with a paid subscription is reading that day's Journal over the Web, the normal means of access. In addition to the copy on the reader's computer, there have been several other copies made on other computers to facilitate transmission. Ordinarily these will come and go without the notice of anyone, although it would certainly be possible to grab them and store them for use on the intermediate computers. Are the intermediate copies in violation of the copyright? As another example, suppose an employee of a large company emails a photo from Playboy to a co-worker without obtaining permission from the magazine, which is known to guard its assets jealously. The company's server archives all email, so not only does the recipient have an unauthorized copy of the photo, but so does the corporation. Does that put the company at the mercy of Playboy's lawyers?

These cases represent a range of possibilities that test the limits of intellectual property rights for electronic data. The first two seem fairly straightforward. Few would argue that taking someone else's work and passing it off as one's own without proper attribution is justifiable. In the second case too, it seems unfair to take and use software that has cost millions of dollars to develop and is sold for hundreds of dollars per copy, without giving some reasonable compensation to the developer. There are some who argue that all software should be free. But even among them, the most responsible voices, at least, do not advocate the Robin Hood approach of taking and redistributing commercial software, but rather work to create viable alternatives in the public domain (Mann, 1999).

The other three are more problematic. Am I violating someone's intellectual property if I call a friend before the game is over to tell him I just saw Mark McGwire hit his seventieth home run, or if I look up the email addresses of several friends online, put them in my own database and send it to another friend? The practice of reverse engineering and the copying involved in store and forward technology both seem justified, indeed necessary, in some circumstances.

It was surprising, therefore, and to many disturbing, that the Clinton administration proposed in 1996 to extend intellectual property rights over electronically stored information far beyond current copyright law. Had the proposal been enacted, it would have made all instances of copying in our five cases illegal if done without authorization (Samuelson, 1996a). Fortunately many of the most worrisome aspects of the proposal were not accepted, either in the WIPO treaty of December, 1996 or in the new U.S. copyright law passed last year. However, there are powerful interests behind the push to extend intellectual property rights, particularly in the entertainment and software industries, so the pressure will no doubt continue (Samuelson, 1999). It is important, therefore, to try to understand the ethical basis for intellectual property rights in order to make sound judgments about their legitimacy and proper extent.

3. Philosophical Justification for Intellectual Property

Justin Hughes, in his masterful article, "The Philosophy of Intellectual Property" (Hughes, 1988), gives two basic justifications for intellectual property rights. The first, which he calls the Lockean justification, is often called the labor theory of property. According to Locke, a person acquires property rights to something by investing labor in it. For example if someone goes out into the forest, cuts down a tree and saws it into firewood, that wood becomes his property. Even though he did not own the tree or the land it was on and did nothing to plant the tree or make it grow, by putting the work into turning the tree into something useful, the product becomes his. He can use it as he wants, whether to sell or to heat his house, and, more importantly, he can exclude others from its use. This theory works well in a commercial environment. Not only does it offer a credible justification for private property, but it also provides incentives for people to work hard and therefore create wealth.

It is interesting that Locke never applied this line of reasoning to intellectual property, but the extension is obvious. It takes much thought, time, and effort to create a book, a musical composition, or a computer program. Those who worked to create it have the strongest claim to the benefits of its use, over anyone else who contributed nothing to the project.

The labor theory is often used today, implicitly at least, to justify claims to intellectual property rights. For example, software developers who want to discredit "pirates" who use their products without paying cite the enormous time and effort that goes into developing a piece of commercial software and the unfairness of others benefiting from it without compensating the developer.

The other justification Hughes discusses is what he calls the Hegelian, or personality, theory of intellectual property. In this view an essay, book, musical piece, or other creative work is an act of self-expression or self-realization, and thus is an extension of the creator's person. As such it belongs to the creator, not just as an object of possession, but as a part of the self. Thus basic human freedom demands that creators be able to control what is done with their creations, just as they should be able to determine other aspects of their personal lives. If someone writes a very personal poem for a special friend, for example, it should not be published or, worse yet, sold without the author's consent. That would seem like a violation of the author's person, rather than just an unfair business deal.

The personality theory does figure in some current claims to intellectual property. For example, Richard Stallman, hacker supreme and passionate advocate of free software, has copyrighted his Emacs text editor and other parts of the GNU software project. The purpose of the copyright (or copyleft, as he likes to call it) is not so that he can sell it and be compensated for his labor, since he does not believe software should be sold, but to prevent others from selling it. He claims control over the conditions of use and distribution of his code to guarantee that a company does not incorporate it into a product that they then sell for profit. That would be taking Stallman's creative work and using it in a way that subverts his own values, which he sees, quite rightly, as a violation of his person. As another example, a songwriter who is an ardent environmentalist, might object strenuously to one of her songs being used in a commercial for, say, a logging company, even though the company was willing to pay royalties, because she did not want to be personally identified with the company's abuse of the environment.

The labor theory and the personality theory give a credible justification for at least some claims to intellectual property rights. In the Case 1 example, plagiarism is wrong under both theories. Under the labor theory, the student is claiming credit for work someone else did. The analysis under the personality theory is even more important. The student was asked to produce an essay that is a personal synthesis and analysis of the subject, not just to produce for the teacher the best possible essay, where the essay is regarded as a product whose origin is of no consequence. For the student to present someone else's work as his own is to misrepresent himself, to violate the integrity of his person. In the second case, as noted earlier, the tremendous investment of labor and capital (another form of labor) put into the development of commercial software gives the developers some right to control how it is used, including the right to charge for its use if they so choose.

The real question is how far those rights extend. If one invests a certain amount of labor in gathering a collection of addresses or statistics, does one therefore gain exclusive rights to that data, so that no one else can use them without permission? Does the "owner" of a creative product have absolute control of that product, even so far as to exclude beneficial or incidental uses that do not conflict directly with the owner's interests? On a basic common sense level, we would say no. People other than the owners have an interest in intellectual property. For example facts that are commonly accessible cannot be owned by a few individuals just because they record them in a database. As another example, the sharing of design ideas and knowledge can increase efficiency in the integration and interoperation of different products, promote healthy competition, and lead to new ideas and greater creativity. In general, the more widely and efficiently intellectual products are disseminated, the more people benefit from them. It seems that there must be a balance between the legitimate claims of the developers of intellectual products and the public's interest in their widest possible availability (Samuelson, 1997). Without that balance, there is a danger of absolutizing the claims to ownership and control to the detriment of other interested parties, something we have noted in recent legislative proposals.

4. A More Balanced View

The fundamental problem with intellectual property as an ethical category is that it is purely individualistic. It focuses on the creator/developer of the intellectual work and what he or she is entitled to. There is truth in this, but not the whole truth. It ignores the social role of the creator and of the work itself, thus overlooking their ethically significant relationships with the rest of society. The balance is lost.

If we start with the idea of property, then the issue naturally becomes ownership and control, because that is what property is about. It is necessary to step outside that framework to get a more complete view of the issues. The way I propose to do that is to use the traditional, but now much neglected, theory of natural law.

Natural law, which goes back at least as far as Aristotle's *Nicomachean Ethics,* begins by asking what is the good. For Aristotle the good of something was inherent in its nature; it was the fulfillment of its purpose. Thus an acorn exists to become a tree. That is its purpose. It finds its fulfillment, its virtue, in growing into that tree. Human beings are by nature rational and social beings. Their fulfillment, then, and their happiness come from living rationally in society. Aristotle identifies a number of particular virtues that support this, the most important of which are friendship and love.

We might ask, then, what is the nature of all those creative products we call intellectual property, especially the ones that can be stored and transmitted electronically? What do a mystery novel, an autobiography, a demographic study, a table of stock prices, a photo, a painting, a piece of music, the design of an automobile, and a web browser all have in common? All are information in some sense. Anything that can be stored on a computer is information, including the computer programs that process that information. Software can be examined, manipulated, and modified like any other information.

What is the purpose of information? It certainly can be self-expression, such as a personal reflection, a painting, or a song. It can also be a product meant to perform some useful function, such as a machine design or a computer program. However, at an even more fundamental level, information is about communication. That is its purpose. *The Oxford English Dictionary* (Short Version), for example, defines information as "Communication of the knowledge of some fact or occurrence" and "knowledge or facts communicated about a particular subject, event, etc." If information is not the communication itself, it is something meant to be communicated. A story or essay is written to be read, even if only by the author. A song is meant to be heard. A program is meant to be run, which means it must convey some instructions to a computer and produce some discernible effect. In athletics they keep score because players and fans care who wins, and they keep statistics because they want to measure individual achievements. These are worthless unless they are communicated. The nature and purpose of information is communication. That is also therefore its good, its virtue. Any adequate ethics of information must take that into account.

Another essential characteristic of information is that it is dynamic and cumulative. Because it is the product of human thought and not itself corporeal, information is constantly changing, growing, combining, and creating offshoots. An intellectual work never springs pure and original from a single human mind. There are always influences. The language, the characters, the themes, and the structure of a novel all have their predecessors. Programmers always learn from other programmers, as anyone who has followed their intense conversations can appreciate. One of the strongest arguments for "free software" is not just that people do not have to pay for it, but that other programmers can examine it and learn from it. Software is not really free, according to free software advocates, unless its human-readable source code is available for distribution (Mann, 1999).

The purpose, or the good, of these intellectual works is to be communicated and shared. Of course ethics is about people, not databases or automobile designs. But knowing the purpose of information tells us something very important about the purpose, or the virtue, of information producers. It is not just production that matters, but communication as well. They are not fulfilling their purpose, that is, they are not virtuous, unless their work is shared in an appropriate way; the more effective the sharing, the more virtuous they are.

I emphasize that the sharing must be done "in an appropriate way" because on a more specific level, different intellectual works have different purposes. It is not usually the purpose of a diary to be published as widely as possible. That in fact would be a perversion of its purpose in most instances. The purpose of a diary is to give an honest, intimate account of the life of the writer. Intimacy requires privacy, which means the writer needs tight control over who sees the diary. It would certainly be wrong for a friend who has been entrusted with it to publish it without the writer's permission. On the other hand, the main purpose of a scientific study is to increase the common store of knowledge. Even if there is a secondary purpose of recovering some of the costs of producing and publishing the study, the virtuous publisher will strive to make the study as available as possible to anyone who would benefit from it.

This approach allows us to make sound, balanced judgments about cases such as those at the beginning of this paper, because it allows us to consider each in light of both general principles and the particular characteristics of the case. In the first case, as we said earlier, the purpose of the paper is for the student to achieve a personal understanding and synthesis of the subject under consideration and to communicate that effectively to the teacher. Simply finding and submitting someone else's work subverts that purpose. It is a failure.

Commercial software of the type considered in Case 2 is more complex ethically because it has multiple purposes. It is meant to perform useful functions for its users. Without that it is worthless. But it also represents a large capital investment and tens or even hundreds of person-years of labor on the part of its developers. The most just, and therefore the most virtuous, distribution scheme would be the one that would provide maximum value to the user community while giving the developers enough compensation to make their labor and investment worthwhile. We still have not found the ideal solution, but we can be sure it is not for a few people to buy the program and make it available to hundreds of thousands of others who contribute nothing, nor is it for the developers to charge outrageous prices because they happen to have a monopoly.

In Case 3 the street addresses are by their nature public. They exist to help people locate homes and businesses. If they are not public they cannot fulfill their purpose. If someone invests a great deal of labor and creativity to make the data available in a particularly useful and attractive way, they might be able to sell that particular arrangement of the data. But they should not be able to prevent someone from sharing the data itself. Batting averages have that same public character; the same analysis applies.

As we said earlier with regard to Case 4, software cannot run in isolation; and software cannot be developed in isolation. It requires extensive information sharing for proper interfacing. Furthermore, like any design process, software development flourishes where there is a free sharing of ideas and experience. That is why patent holders are required to disclose fully their design in exchange for exclusive use of it over a limited period. Of course commercial software development is also competitive, and it would be wrong for a company to copy another company's program and sell it for less. But beyond that there should be as free an exchange of information and ideas as possible.

Finally, information services like the one described in Case 5 exist to communicate information. Those that rely on networks to do their business also rely on the network technology. If the technology requires making and storing copies of the information, that is quite justifiable. It is the nature of the communication. Of course the purpose of those copies is to facilitate communications. Any other use might well be challenged.

5. Conclusion

Producers of information who want to maximize their control over its use, and therefore their ability to profit from it, find intellectual property a very attractive concept because it focuses primarily on the producers and their claims of ownership. These claims are not invalid. As we saw there are some convincing justifications for them. But they are incomplete.

To get a more adequate perspective, we need to step back and ask about the significance and purpose of this information. When we do this, we gain a very important insight that tends to be lost when we only think in terms of rights and property. That is that information is about communication; it is meant to be shared. Ethical policies for the use and distribution of information must take into account the social nature of information, even as they recognize the legitimate claims of the producers. It is in this balance, Aristotle's median, that virtue is found.

This approach has two advantages. First, it gives a theoretical basis for considering the interests of the rest of society, in addition to those of the developers. That is harder to do when we just talk about property, because those who are not producers have no claim to property if they have not somehow invested in it. Yet as we have seen there are some types of information that ought to be freely available, so non-owners do have a claim on it. Of course a utilitarian system would also take into account the overall good of society. But utilitarianism does not recognize individual rights, and individual rights are important. For example a utilitarian analysis might find that it is good to publish a private diary because many people would enjoy it, outweighing any embarrassment to the writer. But that does not seem right, because it violates basic values of human respect.

The other advantage is that this natural law approach allows a nuanced analysis of individual cases, while still being guided by general principles. We can differentiate between a personal diary and a stock market report, between an original program that needs to work in the same environment as a competitor and a clone. We can make useful judgments in real cases.

Admittedly this approach does not lead to any startlingly new conclusions. In a sense it just tells us what we already know. That is, intellectual property claims can only go so far. They must be balanced against the common good. Moreover there are different types of intellectual property and they must be treated differently. But the theory's consistency with sound common sense is its virtue. The ultimate standard for ethics is the collective moral wisdom of the community. If a system gives us the same conclusions as the best minds in our society, it is probably a pretty good system. That is, more can be said for some of the more extreme proposals that have been advanced in the name of intellectual property.

References

Behrens, B. and R. Levary: 1998, "Practical Legal Aspects of Software Reverse Engineering," *Communications of the ACM*, Vol. 41, 2, 27–29.

Hayden, J.: 1991, "Copyright Protection of Computer Databases after Feist," *Harvard Journal of Law & Technology*, Vol. 5, 215–243.

Hughes, J.: 1988, "The Philosophy of Intellectual Property," *The Georgetown Law Review*, Vol. 77, 287–366.

Mann, C.: 1999, "Programs to the People," *Technology Review*, Vol. 102, 1, 36–42.

Rakowsky, J.: 1994, "MIT Student Is Called Software Piracy Plotter," *The Boston Globe*, April 8, 1.

Samuelson, P.: 1991, "Digital Media and the Law," *Communications of the ACM*, Vol. 34, 10, 23–28.

Samuelson, P.: 1996a, "The Copyright Grab," *Wired*, Vol. 4, 1, 134. Also available on the Web at http://www.wired.com/wired/archive/4.01/whitepaper.html

Samuelson, P.: 1996b, "Legal Protection for Database Contents," *Communications of the ACM*, Vol. 39, 12, 17–23.

Samuelson, P.: 1997, "The Never Ending Struggle for Balance," *Communications of the ACM*, Vol. 40, 5, 17–21.

Samuelson, P.: 1999, "Good News and Bad News on the Intellectual Property Front," *Communications of the ACM*, Vol. 42, 3, 19–24.

Zuckoff, M.: 1994, "Software Piracy Charges Dismissed against Student," *The Boston Globe*, December 30, 1.

Is Copyright Ethical? An Examination of the Theories, Laws, and Practices Regarding the Private Ownership of Intellectual Work in the United States

Shelly Warwick

I. Introduction

The Constitution of the United States empowers Congress to secure for authors and inventors the exclusive rights to their writings and discoveries for a limited time in order to promote the progress of science and the useful arts (Article 1, §8). In revising the Copyright Act in 1909, Congress stated that the rights of copyright holders were solely created by government grant and had no other basis (H.R. REP. No. 2222). It would seem then that copyright law was created by the government as an instrument of policy. Policy usually is based on a choice of preferred outcomes, and that choice may be based on considerations other than the moral or the ethical. Given then that copyright law expresses policy, why does the software industry decry the lack of ethics of individuals and nations who pirate computer programs, and why do database producers cry unfair when the public domain material in their databases is copied by others?

This paper examines the relationship between intellectual property rights and ethics, focusing for the most part on copyright. The focus is on two key questions: 1) What is the relationship between ethics and copyright law and practice in the United States, and 2) is the concept of private ownership of intellectual property inherently ethical? These questions are important because access to an overwhelming number of the elements of daily life is now controlled by intellectual property law. Is non-conformance with these laws a calculated risk against being

This essay originally appeared in the *Proceedings of the Fourth Annual Ethics and Technology Conference*, Boston College, Chestnut Hill, MA, 1999, pp. 135–146. Copyright © 1999 by Shelly Warwick. Reprinted with permission.

caught—equivalent to parking at a meter beyond the specified time period—or is it a matter of ethics?

To provide a basis for this examination, some varying constructions of rights, property, and intellectual property will be presented along with a brief history of copyright in the United States. The copyright legislation passed by the 105th Congress will be discussed as well as some current international aspects of intellectual property. Then, with both theory and practice at hand, we will proceed to the ethical examination. Sadly we will be unable to reach a conclusion on whether all aspects of intellectual property are a matter of ethics, but will have found that copyright in the United States is an economic regime that pays homage to ethics only when it wishes to invoke a higher ground than economic damages for reasons to obey copyright law.

II. What Are Rights and How Do They Arise?

An excellent summary of various approaches to rights is provided by Waldron (Waldron, 1984) who elaborates rights theories as being of two kinds, those based on some perceived intrinsic quality (natural rights theories) or on some value that a society wishes to achieve (utilitarian theories). He argues that rights cannot be discussed without considering the topic of political morality, which may be based on rights, duty, or goals. While Waldron thinks that rights can exist outside of positive law, he acknowledges that much of the debate on the basis of rights has incurred within that framework. He points to Bentham as the key liberal theorist of natural rights, who derived all rights from the right of subsistence and viewed rights as the child of law through the marketplace. Most modern jurists recognize that the legal system includes rules that allow individuals to harm others without redress, and therefore reject the meta-theory of liberalism, accepting that ". . . to the extent others have legal liberties, one has no security" (Singer, 1969, p. 985).

Dworkin (1984) views rights as trumps ". . . over some background justification for political decisions that states a goal for the community as a whole." He goes on to state that the concept of rights is needed in a political theory only when some decision that injures some people finds *prima-facie* support in the claim that it will make the community as a whole better off. Dworkin views rights as the legal means for achieving the values of a society.

Perhaps one of the most influential refutations of liberalism and clear discussion of rights has been provided by Wesley Hohfeld (1923), who explored the basic contractions within legal and political theory and caused jurists to realize that all legal decisions were not based on an inherent logic of rights, but on politics, morality, and the competing goals of liberty and security. In short the modern view of rights is that they are created by law and stem from no "natural" source. Rawls' (1972) theory of justice as fairness is in accord with this thinking, but adds the concept of fairness and the priority of liberty to the fashioning of positive law. While many modern thinkers have rejected the assertion of liberal theorists and of Locke, Locke's position that certain rights are natural (exist prior to the state and whether or not the state recognizes them) still has a profound resonance in most discussions of rights, and had a major influence on the founding of the United

States. The Declaration of Independence is a clear statement of the liberal philosophy, asserting that rights stem not from a sovereign or state, but from a creator (which would make them natural and moral), and that they are inalienable (unable to be given away or transferred), which means that the state can not subsume these rights.

III. Property Rights

The traditional legal basis for property is well defined and discussed by Cohen (1935) who defines property rights as the relationship between individuals in reference to things. He asserts that the owners of all revenue producing property are granted the power to tax the future of social product. This power, along with the power to command the service of a large number of individuals who are not economically independent, is viewed as the basis for political sovereignty. Four approaches to the development of private property are presented: 1) Occupation, where rights develop based on discovery or tenancy; 2) Labor, where rights accrue through use or work; 3) Personality, or the need for a sphere for an individual to exercise their right to act as a free personality; and 4) Economic, which views private property as the means to maximize productivity. However, Cohen point out that private ownership often encourages the sacrifice of long-term social interests for immediate individual profit.

In discussing occupancy, Cohen observes that no matter how property was obtained, the longer one holds it, the stronger the expectation to continue to do so, and that the law finds value in protecting legitimate expectations. In terms of the self-evident nature of property through labor, Cohen comments that economic goods are never the result of one person's work and that consideration must be given even to those that "guarded the peace while work was being done." Cohen gives little value to those who derive the right of property from the right of an individual to act as a free personality and not depend on others for their material goods. Cohen characterizes the economic basis of private property as a means to maximize productivity, but comments that this often results in an emphasis on short-term gains and a sacrifice of social interests to profits, and perhaps less productivity in the long-term. In short, there appears to be a common sense basis for all approaches to property, and at the same time a common sense limitation. He concludes, "The issue before thoughtful people is therefore not the maintenance or abolition of private property, but the determination of the precise lines along which private enterprise must be given free scope and where it must be restricted in the interests of the common good" (Cohen, 1985, p. 304).

Another detailed discussion of property and rights is presented by Waldron (1988) who poses two questions: 1) What individual interests are served by the existence of private property, and 2) are any of these interests so important from a moral point of view that they justify a government duty to protect them? Waldron examines utilitarian arguments for private property, which are based on the concept that society will benefit more if material resources are controlled by individuals than if they were controlled by the state or the community as a whole. He points out two defects in this approach: It treats all human desires and interests as equal, even if they cause pain and suffering to others, and that they care little about how the sum of happiness is achieved, and have no concern with justice or equality. "The owner of a resource is simply the individual whose determination as to the use of the resource is taken as final in a system of this kind" (Waldron, 1988, p. 35).

A major proponent of the utilitarian nature of property rights is Demsetz (1967), who defines a property owner as one who "... possesses the consent of fellowmen to allow him to act in particular ways." Property rights are defined as rights that specify how persons may be benefited and harmed, and who must pay to modify the actions taken by various persons and are put forth as a means of achieving a greater internalization of externalities or a means of bringing new factors into the equation and as they arise along with the emergence of new benefits or harmful effects. Coase, whose thinking is at the core of much of Demsezt's theories, views rights as a factor of production, the cost of which must be factored into any costing processes and states that it is desirable that "the only actions performed were those in which what was gained was worth more than what was lost" and that the choice of social arrangement and individual decisions may lead to changes that improve some decisions but worsen others (Coase, 1960).

From these various points of view on the origin and purpose of private property and the control of scarce resources, it can be seen that the state has the role of adopting an approach for rulemaking that can be to: 1) support the expectations of those who have property; 2) follow an over-riding principle; or 3) strive to achieve a desired end (policy). While it would be convenient if each state followed a single course, we'll find as we examine the history of copyright in the United States that the government tends to utilize all three approaches when making rules, including those concerning intellectual property and copyright.

IV. Theories of Intellectual Property and Copyright

Intellectual property is a term that has recently come into extensive use and is often used without definition (Brown et al., 1990; Miller, 1979), or defined as that which is covered by patent, copyright, or trademarks (Rozek, 1990). Abbott (1990, p. 312) states that intellectual property rights are "... the legally protected property interests individuals possess in the fruits of their intellectual endeavors" while Sherwood (Sherwood, 1990) views intellectual property as a compound of the results of private activity (ideas, inventions, and creative expression) and the public willingness to bestow the status of property on these results.

Most scholars accept that copyright is a bundle of property rights that produce/protect a limited monopoly (Ringer et al., 1965). The basis for these rights, however, is hotly debated, as is the purpose of the rights and what protection should (or should not) be provided intellectual property in the future. Two views dominate copyright theory. The first approach views copyright as a "natural" right either based on labor, echoing Locke, or personality, echoing Hegel. The second approach treats copyright as a state policy to achieve set goals (such as an increased creativity, progress in the useful arts, an orderly market for products of mind, a means for expanding foreign trade, or the like). The first approach, the natural right of an author to the fruits of his or her labor, has been asserted since the dawn of copyright in England (Birrell, 1899; Lowndes, 1840; Warburton, 1974) and is still asserted by those who feel labor should be a key element in determining the control of works (Hicks, 1987; Ginsburg, 1990; Goldstein, 1992). Equally voracious are those who feel copyright should promote the useful arts or public access to information (Litman, 1992, Patterson et al., 1991; Samuelson, 1997) and those who see it as a means to insure an orderly market for works of the mind (Demsetz, 1967, Gordon, 1990; Landes et al., 1989). It might be noted here that almost no one feels that copyright, as currently formulated in the United States, is adequate to whatever role they assign it. From those who proclaim that information wants to be free and that copyright will die a natural death due to electronic communication (Schlachter, 1996) to strong protectionists (Ginsburg, 1990; Goldstein, 1992), copyright law is contradictory and needs focus.

Branscomb (1984) identifies a basic conflict in U.S. copyright law in that it addresses the ideal of shared resources while practicing the principles of management of scarcity through the choices of the marketplace, while Patterson (1984) castigates it for lack of a fundamental principle. Though some theorists like Gordon (1989) believe copyright is consistent with other laws of property in its provision and protection of rights, others like Hettinger (1993) question every assumption about copyright, citing a reward for labor as a choice of social policy. Hettinger refers to copyrights, patents, and trade secrets as intellectual objects and points to the key difference between intellectual objects and real objects, which is that intellectual objects do not dissipate with use and can be used by more than one person at the same time. Hettinger also sees a contradiction in a political system that places value on freedom of expression and then has intellectual property laws that make ideas and expression private. While he acknowledges that the concept that a person is entitled to the fruit of her labor is a most powerful idea, he states that most intellectual labor is built on the labor of others, which would make it difficult to assign rights to a specific individual. In recapping Locke's theory of ownership, which is based upon an individual's ownership of his or her own body and the resultant ownership of what the body makes, Hettinger points to the need to distinguish between what is attributable to the object and to the body. Intellectual products, states Hettinger, are fundamentally social products and there is no reason for the last contributor to get all the rewards. Hettinger puts forth the concept that an individual is *entitled* to rewards for labor is a myth, and that rewarding labor may be a social policy, but is not a moral right. Hettinger also states that there is a gap between saying that one has the right to use the fruits of his or her labor and the claim that one should receive whatever the market will bear. He argues that if property rights in the thing created were always the reward for labor, parents would deserve property rights in their children even when the children achieve adulthood. Hettinger also refutes the utilitarian argument that intellectual property laws are necessary for competition, and claims that it slows down the diffusion of ideas in the name of promoting diffusion. He further questions whether the current intellectual property laws have actually increased either the amount of intellectual property available or its use. Hettinger (p. 35) raises the central ethical question as to "why one person should have the exclusive right to possess and use something which all people could possess and use concurrently?"

Chief among those arguing the economic basis of copyright are Landes and Posner (1989) who view copyright law as a means of promoting efficient allocation of resources and see "striking the correct balance between access and incentives as the central problem of copyright law."They believe too much protection will raise the cost of creation, while too little will provide little incentive. They state that the "optional amount of copyright protection is greater for classes of work that are more valuable socially." A refutation of Landes and Posner is offered by Palmer (1990) who bases much of his arguments on the economic theories of Coase and Demsetz and states, in short, that the marketplace and individual arrangements, such as licenses and trade agreements, would allow authors to profit from their intellectual property without the need for copyright. Palmer (1990, p. 279) takes the position often adopted by advocates of expanded fair use that "the central element in the spontaneous emergence of property rights is scarcity . . . but that copyright depends not on scarcity but on law."

Another approach to copyright has been to protect an author's moral rights, or rights of paternity or attribution (the rights of the author to be identified as the creator of the work) and rights of integrity (which prevent a work from being altered without the author's permission) (Jacobs, 1993; Nimmer, 1995). The crucial difference in these approaches is that property or economic rights can be sold or assigned while moral rights remain with the author even if the economic rights are conveyed to others. The United States and England have long been associated with economic rights while France and the Scandinavian countries are associated with moral rights. Once it is understood that copyright in the United States pertains only to economic rights, its nature as a utilitarian policy and not an ethical construct becomes clear.

V. History of Copyright in the United States

The legal basis for copyright in the United States is Article 1, Section 8 of the Constitution, which empowers Congress "to promote the progress of science and the useful arts, by securing for limited times to authors and inventors the exclusive right to their respective writings and discoveries." The model for the first Copyright Act, that of 1790, was the English Statue of Anne, which is generally recognized as intending to regulate trade rather than recognize author's rights or promote learning (Patterson, 1968; Rose, 1993). Copyright in England and the rest of Europe was essentially based on the assertion that the sovereign had the rights to all things within his domain and the rights of others were solely based on the pleasure of the crown (Rose, 1993). The Constitution, by reserving for citizens all rights not explicitly granted to Congress or the states, raised the people to the role of sovereign. The limited nature of the rights conferred by the 1790 act, which granted to authors the rights to print, reprint, publish, and vend their writings for 14 years, makes more sense when it is understood that the rights not granted to authors are reserved to the people as sovereign. Transformative or productive uses of the protected works, such as translations, abridgements, and derivations, were not prohibited as these were not considered copies, but uses of the work (Patterson, 1968). Copyright protection was only granted to citizens of the United States.

United States copyright law has been consistently revised to embrace new media and to provide a wider range of rights to copyright holders, usually in reaction to copying not prohibited by the current law but deemed unjust or unethical by the Courts or Congress. For example, the right to create derivative works, including translations, was not granted to authors until after Harriet Beecher Stowe had failed in an action against a German translator of *Uncle Tom's Cabin* (*Stowe v. Thomas*). Protection to works created by citizens of nations was granted in 1891, and then with the provision that the work be printed in the United States. The United States recognized, if a bit late, the need for reciprocal international copyright and became a founding member of the Universal Copyright Convention (UCC) in 1951, and later a signatory to the Berne Convention in 1989. The growing importance of copyright within international trade and the tendency to try to force intellectual products into a framework constructed for consumable goods is exhibited by the Trade Related Aspects of Intellectual Property (TRIPs) agreement of the General Agreement of Tariffs and Trade, which the United States adopted in 1994.

The last major revision of copyright law took place in 1976 after over 20 years of studies and debate (Henry, 1976). The intent of Congress was to create a law so inclusive that as new media arose, the works created in them would automatically be eligible for copyright protection without the necessity of revising copyright law. At the time this law was crafted, the photocopier was the major new technology and computers were things that took up huge spaces and were only owned by large organizations.

Current copyright law, as per the Copyright Act of 1976 as amended, protects all "original works of authorship fixed in a tangible medium of expression." Copyright holders have the exclusive right to reproduce, distribute, sell or lease works, and to prepare derivative works, and to publicly perform literary, musical, dramatic and choreographic works, pantomimes, motion pictures and other audio visual works, as well as to display these and pictorial, graphic, or sculptural works, including individual images of a motion picture or other audiovisual work (U.S.C. 17 §106). In 1980 software was deemed a type of copyrightable work, and in 1984 the designs for semiconductors (computer chips) were given *sui generis* protection.

In 1997 and 1998 the 105th Congress passed three major copyright laws, the No Electronic Theft (NET) Act, the Sonny Bono Term Extension Act (SBCTEA) and the Digital Millennium Copyright Act (DMCA). The NET Act extended the concept of financial gain to receipt of anything of value and made willful infringement of works having a total value of more than $1,000 a criminal offense, even if the infringer did not profit. Prior to this act, copyright infringement was a civil matter. The Sonny Bono Term Extension Act extended the term of copyright to match that of the European Union, extending the term of copyright by 20 years, so that the basic term of copyright is now the life of the author plus 70 years. This act was retroactive, extending the term of works already created. Both the NET and SBCTEA clearly indicate that copyright in the United States is becoming more a tool for securing property interests than a mode of encouraging new works, especially since the latter provides an additional term of protection for works already created. The DMCA was passed to implement the 1996 Word Intellectual Property treaties, making it a crime to circumvent technological protections put in place by the copyright owner. This provision takes effect two years after the enactment of the DMCA, during which period the Librarian of Congress is to conduct a rule-making proceeding to determine appropriate exceptions to the prohibition (17 U.S.C. §1201). There is no explicit exemption for fair use, and, therefore someone who disabled protection to access the information would be committing a criminal act even if the use of the information would be fair. The impact of this provision can best be appreciated if one remembers that until the No Electronic Theft Act of 1997, infringement of copyright was a civil not a criminal matter. The worst penalty an infringer could expect would be to be told to stop making copies and to pay a fine. Under the new law, a person who evades a technological protection could go to jail. This law was very strongly backed by content providers, including print publishers. In a similar vein, this law makes it a criminal act to manufacture or import any device that has as its main purpose the circumvention of technological protection. The DMCA also provides penalties for changing or deleting Copyright Management Information (CMI) when providing a copy of a work, provides some protection to internet service providers against copyright liability, makes some technical corrections to copyright law, and mandates the Librarian of Congress to begin a rule-making process for the use of copyright protected works in distance learning environments.

These most recent copyright laws can perhaps best be understood in an international framework. The European Union, which includes Britain, recently adopted an Intellectual Property Directive that established the life of the author plus 70 years as the basic period of protection, and in December of 1996, two World Intellectual Property Organization (WIPO) treaties were adopted in Geneva that called for, among other things, the protection of technological safeguards used by copyright holders (WIPO, 1996). The push for this, and even more stringent measures, was spearheaded by the United States (Samuelson, 1997).

What Copyright Doesn't Cover

Copyright protection is not provided to ideas, procedures, processes, systems, methods of operation, concepts, principles, discoveries, short phrases, facts, or works created by the United States government. There are a number of exceptions to the rights of copyright holders, most of which are applicable to a limited class of actors, such as libraries, educational institutions, cable television systems, and radio stations. Two exemptions are available to the general public, the right of first sale and fair use. The right of first sale allows a person who has purchased a copy of a work protected by copyright to lend, sell, or otherwise transfer that copy of the work to someone else. The fair use exemption is more complex in that it allows copying for purposes such as criticism, comment, news reporting, teaching, scholarship, or research, with whether the use is fair to be determined based on: (1) The purpose and character of the use, including whether such use is of a commercial nature or is for nonprofit educational purposes; (2) the nature of the copyrighted work; (3) the amount and substantiality of the portion used in relation to the copyrighted work as a whole; and (4) the effect of the use upon the potential market for or value of the copyrighted work (U.S.C. 17 §107). While fair use is generally perceived as establishing rights of use, or as a limitation on the rights of a copyright holder, Patterson (1992) contends that it has actually broadened the rights of the copyright holder and that prior to the 1909 Act, fair use did not apply to consumers because fair use was a defense for infringement that only applied to those who made commercial use of the work, not individual use.

VI. Is Copyright Ethical?

The ethics of copyright can be approached in two ways: (1) If, as Hettinger suggests, every creator stands on the shoulders of giants, what is the essential morality in allowing the last contributor to reap the full reward or to have the right to prevent others from building on her contribution; and (2) If, as postulated by Locke, an individual is entitled to what he or she creates, what are the ethics of limiting a creator's rights in regard to his or her creation? Theoretically copyright law in the United States takes the first view, stating that authors have no natural right in their creation but only the rights that the state has conferred by reason of policy to encourage the creation of new works (H.R. REP. No. 2222). This approach assumes that the content of products of mind (not the objects in which they are embedded) belong to society as a whole, but that society would benefit more if more such products were available, and that in order to encourage production, the creator of such products should be given rights that will allow him or her to reap some economic benefits from the creation. As Branscomb (1984) observed, this is encouraging access by legislating scarcity.

Earlier United States copyright law was better aligned with the encouragement theory and the ethical position that creative works belonged to society as a whole. Only the exact copying of a work was prohibited, not new works based on a previous work. Subsequent authors were free to adapt novels to the stage, abridge scholarly works for the masses, and translate works into other languages without paying a license fee to the creator or to whomever the creator had transferred his or her copyright. However as copyright law has expanded to grant creators more rights, the law has all but abandoned the concept of allowing, let alone encouraging, transformative or productive use. Copyright no longer has a consistent theory, let alone an ethical position. It has become what is often called an equitable rule of reason, which attempts to balance the rights of authors with the rights of users. It is often not clear whether this balance is to be obtained by granting rights via law or by recognizing the intrinsic rights of each. However, if copyright is indeed only a matter of law, there should be no rights other than those granted by the law. What both creators and users then have are expectations, but, as Cohen (1985) observed, the law finds value in protecting legitimate expectations.

But whose expectations are legitimate? The creator who envisions riches for building a better mouse-trap or the users who expect to be able to use the designs of that mouse trap to build an even better one or learn about how mice can be trapped? If both expectations are legitimate, we have a dilemma, but is it an ethical dilemma or a policy dilemma? Copyright law avoids taking an ethical position or even deciding which group holds the highest trump, but endeavors to effect a compromise between the expectations of creators and users by creating a period where the expectations of the creators are recognized by law (the period of copyright protection) followed by a period where the expectations of users are recognized (when a work enters the public domain.). This perhaps was an equitable rule of reason when the term of copyright was 14 years with a possible renewal of another 14 years (as provided in the Copyright Act of 1790) but is it as equitable now that copyright exists for the life of the author plus 70 years? Is it even consistent with encouragement theory to extend the term of protection for works already created?

One could argue that the continual extension of the term of copyright protection and the expansion of authors' rights indicates a shift of ethical perceptions in the United States and that the "right" of creators to benefit from their work is now perceived as more legitimate. Or one could argue that copyright has lost whatever mooring it once had to either ethics or theory and is a law unduly influenced by those who would benefit most from stronger protection. For example, many of those who argued for an expanded term of copyright often spoke of literary work as an author's legacy to their family (echoing the arguments of the Stationer's Company who pointed to the widows and orphans of authors as they lobbied for perpetual copyright) (Rose, 1993). What drove term expansion, however, were the interests of corporate copyright holders such as Walt Disney who feared the entry of Mickey Mouse into the public domain (Litman, 1994).

Given the strong connection between a creator and her work (especially in the literary genre), it is difficult to assert that granting no rights to the creator is ethical. Likewise given the fact that almost all works, including those that are literary, owe a debt to the sum of works that have gone before, it is difficult to assert that granting exclusive perpetual rights in a work to a creator is ethical. However, the arguments for personal ownership and control of intellectual works are appealing, since they are in accord with the concept of ownership as awarded to physical works, since original works can satisfy all four approaches to private property: occupancy, labor, personality, and a means to an economic end. However intellectual works are different from physical objects. One of the problems of the current copyright system is that it was created at a time when intellectual property was easily fixed in real objects, so it was not necessary to confront the difference between the container and the content. This is no longer the case with the advent of technologies that allow intellectual works to be easily copied and shifted from media to media. Not only can the enforcement of copyright become more difficult, but the non-consumable and non-exclusive nature of intellectual property becomes evident, along with its low marginal cost of reproduction (Hettinger, 1993). Intellectual property laws tend to stuff creative works back into containers, creating an artificial scarcity (Branscomb, 1984).

Copyright, in as much as it attempts to balance the interests of creators and society, could be considered based on ethics. However, while such ethical considerations might have been present in the minds of those who crafted copyright law, they were never stated either in the Constitution or in the law. This discussion becomes more complex when applied to factual works. Copyright has never protected facts or ideas. It only protects expression. Therefore a scholar who has labored for years to research a subject such as Lincoln's death may find his work utilized without credit and have no recourse under law (*Eisenschiml v. Fawcett Pub*). As the judge observed, "Whatever we may think of the ethics of Millard [the second author] in utilizing various portions of plaintiff's [first author] works with only a scant credit reference, or the ethics of the defendant [the publisher] in publishing the article after first eliminating the credit reference, we conclude, in view of the findings we must hold there was not a sufficient copying to amount to an infringement." In short, plagiarism may be unethical but it is not illegal if it can be justified by fair use, which does not specify that the source of work used must be cited.

If copyright does not protect facts, it also does not protect labor. While many circuit courts incorrectly interpreted the 1909 Copyright Act as protecting compilations of information based on labor, this was clearly found unconstitutional by the Supreme Court in *Feist v. Rural Telephone*, which ruled that unoriginal arrangements of facts had no more protection than a single fact. In light of this decision, there has been a major effort by information compilers and database developers to have a law passed in the United States that would protect compilations of facts based on labor and investment. The current proposal (H.R. 354, The Collections of Information Privacy Act) would prohibit even legitimate purchasers and subscribers of compilations from using substantial amounts of data in the resource. It would also allow renewal of the protection as long as the compilation received new inputs of either labor or investment. This protection mimics protection already granted in the European Union by the EU Database Directive (European Parliament, 1996). This new legislation would **not** protect the labor of original researchers who discover and interpret facts, since works like articles and monographs would still be protected by copyright as it is now constituted. What would be protected is the labor and investment of those who compiled facts, often from the articles of original research. While it is tempting to discuss at length the effect such legislation would have on scholarly research and the cost of education, we will merely state that we've done this elsewhere (Warwick 1998) and focus here on the ethical question. Where is the ethics of stating that intellectual creations are the sum of the labor of many and belongs to society, then having a policy of encouraging creativity by offering creators of original work protection only for their expression, while providing additional protections to those who produce unoriginal works clearly based on the work of others? If more socially valuable works should be given more protection (Landes and Posner, 1989), then why should a creator of a phone directory receive more protection than the creator of a prize-winning science article? How is social value being measured? While some may argue that database protection is lesser protection than copyright protection, there is nothing in the proposed United States legislation or the EU Directive that prohibits works from being protected under both regimes, in fact this is anticipated.

As stated before, the United States has traditionally protected the economic rights of creators, not their moral rights. However in 1990, authors of visual works were granted the rights of attribution and integrity. These rights were designated as being separate from copyright and for a term that expired with the death of the creator. However, unlike moral rights in France, they can be waived. It is difficult from an ethical viewpoint to understand how visual artists have moral rights and not creators in other media, such as text or music. Is it perhaps the fact that an original painting or sculpture are usually unique, one-of-a-kind items that lose value (artist and financial) in reproduction so that the original needs to be preserved as created? If so, then an underlying value of copyright law would be that works that retain value through reproduction should receive less protection. In that case factual works should receive the least amount of protection.

Once moral rights are recognized as distinct from economic rights, a possible way out of the copyright maze presents itself. One could declare that society owns the economic rights of creative works while the author retains the moral rights. Then society, in the form of the United States government, would be taking a consistent ethical position even if it chose to craft a policy of providing an inducement to create more works by providing economic incentives in the form of economic copyright protection. Though if one was going to analyze copyright as an inducement to create more works, it would be sensible to find out how many more works, if any, were created only because a longer period of copyright protection was available. Surely there are other, and perhaps more effective, means to induce the protection of creative works. However there is a constitutional problem. While Congress is empowered to "promote the progress of science and the useful arts," this empowerment requires doing so by "securing for limited times to authors and inventors the exclusive right to their respective writings and discoveries." Many claim this limits the ability of Congress to provide other means of encouragement. However, the Constitution does not state whether the exclusive rights are moral or economic. Nor does it distinguish between the economic rights of the creators and of those to whom the rights have been transferred.

Copyright clearly illustrates Waldron's (1988) contention that the utilitarian arguments for private property are defective in that they treat all interests as equal, even if pain and suffering is caused to others. The interests of the very few members of society who are authors and publishers are weighed evenly with the interests of the vast body of citizens who are not creators. The interests of a few publishers who would not make an additional 5% profit unless additional protections are provided is often weighted equally with those of thousands of students who will not do as well as their classmates because they would not be able to afford access to information if additional protection raised the cost of research. The issue of group rights to intellectual property has also been raised in regard to the cultural symbols and folklore of Native Americans and indigenous peoples (Dougherty, 1998; Farley, 1997) and in biological patents (Shiva, 1993, 1990; Ritchie, Dawkins and Vallianatos, 1996).

The ethics of copyright have also been raised when the rights granted by copyright have come into conflict with those of freedom of speech, freedom of the press and privacy. For example Martin Luther King Jr.'s "I Have A Dream" speech was ruled to be in the public domain (*Estate Of Martin Luther King, Jr., Inc., v. CBS, Inc.*) and the unlicensed use of Zapruder's copyright video of President John F. Kennedy's assassination permitted based on the public interest in the topic (*Time Inc. v.. Bernard Geis Assoc. Inc*). Conversely J.D. Salinger was found to have the right to limit the use of his unpublished letters, and their use in a scholarly biography was found not to be fair, though Salinger had donated those letters to a library for study (*Salinger v. Random*

House, Inc.). This prompted an amendment to the Copyright Act that expressly extended fair use to unpublished works. Are these contortions and amendments of copyright law an attempt to fine tune public policy or to create an ethical law? Probably some of both.

Another area where the rights granted by United States copyright law are raised to the area of ethics rather than policy are in the international arena. The copying of intellectual property in countries that have not declared this illegal has been branded "piracy" and a great effort has been made to export United States copyright law to the People's Republic of China, Taiwan, and Latin America (Beam 1995; Lara, 1998; Slotkin, 1996; Yeh, 1996), even where the tradition of copying is part of recognizing established values (Alford, 1995). While it is undoubtedly true that producers and distributors of intellectual property who are citizens of the United States suffer economic harm through loss of sales in those countries that do not stringently protect or enforce intellectual property rights, one wonders how that which is stated as a policy choice in the United States can be raised to a level of ethics when applied to the action of citizens of other countries. The moral and ethical pose often adopted by the United States in the international copyright arena is perhaps ironic, considering that for almost half its existence the United States was a major intellectual property pirate, printing literary and scholarly works with little or no compensation to their British creators. Indeed in the 1800s, protecting the copyright of non-United States nationals was viewed by the average citizen as an undesirable policy and one that would drive up the price of books (Putnam 1891a, 1891b; 1891c).

Ethics are often raised as well in regard to copying software. The Software Publisher's Association (SPA), which merged with the Information Industry Association (IIA) in January of 1999 to form the Software & Information Industry Association (SIIA), offers a guide on Software Use and the Law (SPA 1997) that states it is intended to provide "a basic understanding of the issues involved in ethical software use." The same document declares that it is "wrong" for a school to duplicate software. While copying software, except for backup or archival purposes, is clearly illegal, does this automatically make such actions unethical? Unless one considers all laws ethical, and that breaking any law to be unethical, illegality and unethicality can not be automatically equated. One also might question whether the efforts by the SIIA and its predecessor organizations to have Congress enact legislation that provides greater rights to creators (and their assigns) than to users were prompted by an ethical position or by a desire for greater profits.

VII. Summary

United States copyright law is theoretically based on policy created within a framework that valued the interests of the people as a whole over the interests of individual creators. The original framework is being slowly dismantled to give more weight to the interests of individual creators. This shift in policy is often defended based on the ethics of allowing a creator control over her work. However, this ethical position does not generally extend to moral rights. Moral rights, of course, only benefit creators, not publishers or distributors. This calls into question whether the extension of rights is based on an ethical position or in reaction to pressures exerted by those whose profits depend on the protections granted by copyright. Copyright was created as a policy, not an ethical construct, but many treat the law as if it is, or should be, such a construct. Copyright law as currently constituted does not appear to have a consistent ethical basis nor to provide a consistent policy to promote learning and the useful arts.

References

Abbott, A.F.: 1990, "Developing A Framework For Intellectual Property To Advance Innovation," In R. W. Rushing & C. G. Brown (Eds.), *Intellectual Property Rights In Science, Technology, and Economic Performance: International Comparisons,* 32–46, (Westview Press, Boulder Co.).

Alford, W.: 1995. *To Steal a Book is an Elegant Offense: Intellectual Property Law in Chinese Civilization* (Stanford University, Stanford).

Barlow, J.P.: 1994, "The Economy Of Ideas: A Framework For Rethinking Patents And Copyrights In The Digital Age (Everything You Know About Intellectual Property Is Wrong)," *Wired,* March, 85–129.

Beam, A.: 1995, "Piracy of American Intellectual Property in China," *Detroit College of Law Journal of International Law and Practice,* vol. 4, 335–365.

Birrell, A.: 1899, *Seven Lectures On The Law And History Of Copyright In Books* (Putnam., New York).

Branscomb, A.W.: 1984, *The Accommodation Of Intellectual Property Law To The Introduction Of New Technologies.* (433–9810.0 ed.). (Office of Technology Assessment of the U.S. Congress, Washington, D.C.)

Brown, C.G., & Rushing, F.W.: 1990, "Intellectual property rights in the 1990s: Problems and solutions," In F. W. Rushing & C. G. Brown (Eds.), *Intellectual Property Rights In Science, Technology, and Economic Performance: International Comparisons,* pp. 32–46. (Westview, Boulder, Co.).

Coase, R.H.: 1960, "The Problem of Social Cost," *The Journal of Law & Economics,* 3, 1–44.

Cohen, F.: 1935, "Transcendental Nonsense and the Functional Approach," *Columbia Law Review,* 35(6), 809–849.

Copyright Act of 1790.

Copyright Act of 1909.

Copyright Act of 1976.

Demsetz, H.: 1967, "Toward A Theory Of Property Rights," *The American Economic Review, 57* (2), 347–359.

Digital Millennium Copyright Act. (1998). P.L. 105-304.

Dougherty, T.: 1998, "Group Rights to Cultural Survival: Intellectual Property in Native American Cultural Symbols," *Columbia Human Rights Law Review,* vol. 29, 355.

Dworkin, R.: 1984, "Rights as Trumps," In J. Waldron (Ed.), *Theories of Rights,* 153–167 (Oxford University Press, London).

Eisenschiml v. Fawcett Pub. (7th Cir.) 246 F.2d 598; 1957 U.S. App. LEXIS 5399.

Estate Of Martin Luther King, Jr., Inc., v. CBS, Inc, (N.D. GA, Atlanta Div., 1998), 13 F. Supp. 2d 1347; 1998 U.S. Dist. LEXIS 11287; 47 U.S.P.Q.2D (BNA) 1611.

European Parliament and Council of the European Union: 1996. *EU Databases Directive.*

Farley, C.: 1997, "Protecting Folklore of Indigenous Peoples: Is Intellectual Property the Answer?" *Connecticut Law Review* vol. 30, 1–25.

Feist v. Rural Telephone Co. (111 S. Ct. 1282; 1991 U.S. LEXIS 1856).

Ginsburg, J.C.: 1990, "Creation and Commercial Value: Copyright Protection of Works of Information," *Columbia Law Review,* 90(7), 1865–1938.

Goldstein, P.: 1992, "Copyright," *Law and Contemporary Problems,* 55(2), 79–91.

Gordon, W.: 1990, "Toward a Jurisprudence of Benefits: The Norms of Copyright and the Problem of Private Censorship," *The University of Chicago Law Review,* 57, 1009–1049.

Gordon, W.J.: 1989, "An Inquiry into the Merits of Copyright: The Challenges of Consistency, Consent, and Encouragement Theory," *Stanford Law Review,* vol. 41 (July), 1343–1469.

H.R. 354. Collections of Information Antipiracy Act. 106th Cong. Lst Sess. (1999).

H.R. REP. No. 2222, 60th Cong., 2d. Sess. 7. (1909) *(Report accompanying the Copyright Act of 1909).*

Hettinger, E.C.: 1993, "Justifying Intellectual Property Rights," *Philosophy and Public Affairs,* vol. 18, pp. 31–52.

Hicks, J.B.: 1987, "Copyright and Computer Databases: Is Traditional Compilation Law Adequate? *Texas Law Review,* vol. 65, 5, 993–1028.

Hohfeld, W.N.: 1923, *Fundamental Legal Conceptions As Applied In Judicial Reasoning And Other Legal Essays By Wesley Newcomb Hohfeld.* (Yale University Press, New Haven).

Kost, R.J.: 1987, "The End of Copyright," In Network Advisory Committee (Ed.), *Intellectual Property Rights in an Electronic Age: Network Planning Paper No. 16,* Proceedings of the Library of Congress Network Advisory Committee Meeting, April 22-24, 1987, 19–25 (Network Development and MARC Standards Office Library of Congress, Washington, D.C.).

Landes, W.M., and Posner, R.A.: 1989, "An Economic Analysis of Copyright Law," *Journal of Legal Studies,* vol. 28, 325–363.

Lara, G: 1998, "The Privacy of American Films in China: Why the U.S. Art Form is Not Protected by Copyright Laws in the People's Republic of China," *UCLA Journal of International Law and Foreign Affairs.*

Litman, J.: 1992, "Copyright and Information Policy," *Law and Contemporary Problems,* vol. 55(2), 185–209.

Litman, J.: 1994, "Mickey Mouse Emeritus: Character Protection and the Public Domain," *University of Miami Entertainment & Sports Law Review,* vol. 11, 429–435.

Lowndes, J.L.: 1840, *An Historical Sketch of the Law of Copyright; with Remarks on Sergeant Talfourd's Bill: And an Appendix Of The Copyright Laws Of Foreign Countries.* (Saunders and Benning, London).

Miller, J.K.: 1979, *Applying The New Copyright Law: A Guide For Educators And Librarians.* (American Library Association, Chicago, IL).

No Electronic Theft (NET) Act (1997). PL 105–147.

Palmer, T.G.: 1990, "Intellectual Property: A Non-Posnerian Law and Economics Approach," *Hamline Law Review,* vol. 12, 261–304.

Patterson, L.R., and Lindberg, S.W.: 1991, *The Nature of Copyright: A Law of Users' Rights.* (University of Georgia Press, Athens, GA).

Patterson, L.R.: 1968, *Copyright In Historical Perspective* (Vanderbilt University Press, Nashville, TN).

Patterson, L.R.: 1984, *Copyright and New Technology: The Impact On The Law Of Privacy Antitrust And Free Speech.* (Office of Technology Assessment, United States Congress, Washington, D.C.).

Public Law No. 103-465 (1994). The Trade-Related Aspects of Intellectual Property (TRIPs) of the General Agreement on Tariffs and Trade (GATT).

Putnam, G. H.: 1891a, "Literary Property, An Historical Sketch." In G. H. Putnam (Ed.), *The Question of Copyright,* 36–95 (G.P. Putnam's Sons, New York).

Putnam, G. H.: 1891b, "International Copyright Will Not Increase The Prices Of Books." In G.H. Putnam (Ed.), *The Question of Copyright,* 356–375 (G.P. Putnam's Sons, New York).

Putnam, G. H.: 1891c, "The Contest For International Copyright." In G.H. Putnam (Ed.), *The Question of Copyright,* 376–398 (G.P. Putnam's Sons, New York).

Rawls, J.: 1972, *A Theory of Justice.* (Oxford University Press, New York).

Ringer, B.A., and Gitlin, P.: 1965, *Copyrights.* (Rev. Ed. ed.). (Practicing Law Institute, New York.)

Ritchies, M., K. Dawkins and M. Vallianatos: 1996, "Intellectual Property Rights and Biodiversity: The Industrialization of Natural Resources and Traditional Knowledge," *St. John's Journal of Legal Commentary,* vol. 11, 431–452.

Rose, M.: 1993, *Authors and Owners: The Invention Of Copyright.* (Harvard University Press, Cambridge, MA).

Rozek, R.P.: 1990, "Protection Of Intellectual Property Rights: Research And Development Decisions And Economic Growth," In F. W. Rushing and C. G. Brown (Eds.), *Intellectual Property Rights In Science, Technology, And Economic Performance: International Comparisons,* 32–46 (Westview, Boulder, Co).

Salinger v. Random House, Inc (2nd Cir. 1987), 818 F.2d 252; 1987 U.S. App. LEXIS 7173; 2 U.S.P.Q.2D (BNA) 1727.

Samuelson, P.: 1997, "The U.S. Digital Agenda at WIPO," *Virginia Journal of International Law Association,* vol. 37, 369–439.

Schlachter, E. *The Intellectual Property Renaissance in Cyberspace: Why Copyright Law Could Be Unimportant on the Internet.* (un pub)

Sherwood, R.M.: 1990, *Intellectual Property And Economic Development.* (Westview Press, San Francisco).

Shiva, V.: 1993, "Intellectual Piracy and the Neem Tree," *The Ecologist,* vol. 23, 223–227.

Shiva, V.: 1990, "Biodiversitry, Biotechnology, and Profit: The Need for a Peoples' Plan to Protect Biological Diversity," *The Ecologist,* vol. 20, 44–47.

Singer, J.W.: 1982, "The Legal Rights Debate in Analytical Jurisprudence from Bentham to Hohfeld," *Wisconsin Law Review,* vol. 975–1059.

Slotkin, S.: 1996, "Trademark Piracy in Latin America: A Case Study on Reebok International Ltd.," *Loyola of Los Angeles International & Comparative Law Journal,* vol. 18, 671–682.

The Sonny Bono Copyright Extension Act of 1998. PL 105-298.

Sony Corporation of America v. Universal City Studios, Inc., 464 U.S. 417; 104 S. Ct. 774; 1984 U.S. LEXIS 19.

SPA: 1997: *www.spa.org/piracy/sftuse.htm*

Time Inc. v. Bernard Geis Assoc. Inc. (S.D.N.Y. 1968) 293 F. Supp. 130; 1968 U.S. Dist. LEXIS 12385; 159 U.S.P.Q. (BNA) 663.

Trade Related Aspects of Intellectual Property (TRIPs) Agreement of the General Agreement of Tariffs and Trade: 1994.

Waldron, J.: 1984, "Introduction," In J. Waldron (Ed.), *Theories of Rights,* 1–20. (Oxford University Press, London).

Waldron, J.: 1988, *The Right To Private Property.* (Clarendon Press, Oxford).

Warburton, W.: 1747, "A Letter from an Author to a Member of Parliament Concerning Literary Property. London, 1747." Reprinted 1974 in *Horace Walpole's Political Tracts, 1747–1748 with Two by William Warburton.* (Garland Publishing., New York).

Warwick, S.: 1998, "Beyond Copyright: Database Protection And The Web." In Williams, Martha, (Ed.) *Proceedings of the Nineteenth National Online Meeting New York Hilton May 12–14, 1998,* 455–463, (Information Today, New York).

WIPO: 1996, WIPO Copyright Treaty. World Intellectual Property Organization, CRNR'DC/94. *http://www.wipo.org/eng/diplconf/distrib/94dc.htm*

Yeh, M.: 1996, "Up Against a Great Wall: The First Struggle Against Intellectual Property Piracy in China," *Minnesota Journal of Global Trade* vol. 5, 503–530.

On the Web, Plagiarism Matters More than Copyright Piracy

John W. Snapper

Plagiarism and Piracy

Although commonly confused, the values inherent in copyright policy are different from those inherent in scholarly standards for the proper accreditation of
ideas. Piracy is the infringement of a copyright, and plagiarism is the failure to give
credit.[1] They are confused because the most common examples of these wrongs
involve both sorts of wrongs. But it is not hard to give examples that separate
them. It would be *plagiarism but not piracy* for me to take the works of an obscure
19th century poet and try to pass them off as my own. Since the copyright will have
expired on such works, this is not piracy. But it remains plagiarism of the sort that
could be grounds for dismissal from a journalism post. It would be *piracy but not
plagiarism* if I were to edit a volume of modern poetry and forget to get copyright
permission for one item in the volume. Assuming that the credits were properly
given to the author and source publication, this is not plagiarism. All the same, it
would certainly be grounds for action under copyright law. We may base a more
sophisticated distinction between plagiarism and piracy on the commonplace
notion that copyrights grant control over the means of expression, but never grants

This essay originally appeared in *Ethics and Information Technology,* 1: 127–136, 1999. Copyright © 1999 by Kluwer Academic
Publishers. Reprinted with permission.

[1] These contrasting definitions of plagiarism and piracy are consistent with most legal language, although there are some legal
discussions where the notions are confused or the words are defined differently. See K.R. St. Onge, *The Melancholy Anatomy of
Plagiarism,* University Press, 1988, for a survey of various definitions.

control over information or ideas.[2] It may be plagiarism to take information without giving credit, even if there is no piracy of a form of expression.[3]

The increasing use of Web-based electronic publication has created new contexts for both piracy and plagiarism. Situations emerge daily for which we have no clear standard either for copyright or for scholarly accreditation. Consider for instance, the common practice of downloading html tags that define the layout of a Web page. I see a page layout with moving figures that I like. I download that page and use it as a template for my personal publication. I do not include any words, pictures, or information from the original site, only the html tags and java script that give the site its special look. Is this action a copyright infringement? As a scholar, am I obligated to give credit to the source of the layout code? The situation is not at all clear. And we should not expect that the establishment of a copyright standard will settle the issue for scholarly accreditation, since these are separate sorts of wrongs. An analysis of this sort of example requires that we identify the values inherent in the condemnations of piracy and plagiarism, and then see if those values suggest a way to deal with the new situations.

Our investigation into values is much easier for the copyright issues than for accreditation issues. Copyright is now defined in statutory law. The US statutes have an explicit basis in the US Constitution.[4] International copyright law has an explicit basis in international agreements.[5] If we dislike some feature of the law or believe that the law has failed to promote the traditional copyright values, then we know how to go about revising the law. The investigation into plagiarism is, however, much more difficult. We are faced with a mishmash of differing academic statements of principles, an ill-defined tradition in the writing community, and an inconsistent history of recognition in common law.[6] Although in many cases, we "know it when

---

[2] "In no case does copyright protection for an original work of authorship extend to any idea ..." 1976, Copyright Act of 1976 #102b. The "idea/expression dichotomy" is central to all discussion of copyright law, but almost all commentators begin their discussion by noting that the dichotomy is at best fuzzy, and at worst simply confused. A US Supreme Court application of this dichotomy to a denial of protection for the content of an electronically published database (in *Feist Publications, Inc.* v *Rural Telephone Service Co.,* 499 U.S. 340 (1991)) has led to considerable discussion and some legislative attempts (e.g., HR 2652, introduced 1997) to provide protection for databases. This is presently a very "hot topic" in intellectual property law.

[3] *Narell* v. *Freeman* 872 F.2nd 907, nicely illustrates the point. Freeman wrote a book that freely borrowed from a prior study by Narell. This is a clear example of plagiarism. Since there was only minor direct quotation, however, the copyright claim was dismissed. Laurie Sterns calls this a "paradigm" of the distinction between plagiarism and copyright infringement, "Copy Wrong: Plagiarism, Process, Property, and the Law," *California Law Review 80,* 1992, p. 542.

[4] *US. Constitution,* Article I.8

[5] The Universal Copyright Convention of 1974, The Berne Convention of 1986, and the Copyright Law of 1976 amended by the Berne Convention Implementation Act of 1988, are all conveniently collected in *Selected Statutes and International Agreements on Unfair Competition, Trademark, Copyright and Patent,* ed P. Goldstein et al., Foundation Press, 1995.

[6] For an overview with many legal citations, see Laurie Sterns supra. This is an excellent article that should be studied with care by any reader interested in the issues raised in the present paper. Ms. Sterns provides an insightful critique of the plagiarism/piracy dichotomy that differs from the approach of the present article in several interesting ways.

we see it,"[7] plagiarism remains a notion with no generally recognized body of classical examples. And if we believe that we have discovered a need for revision of its standards, then we have nothing better to do than to put forth our ideas in articles such as this. Perhaps due to the difficulty with investigating plagiarism, there is very little literature on the subject, especially in contrast to the huge literature on copyrights. The issue of copyright on the Web has received considerable attention and plagiarism per se is largely ignored. For these reasons, the present paper concentrates on a study of the values inherent in the condemnation of plagiarism, rather than the presently heated debate over piracy on the Web.

What's the Harm in Plagiarism?

We may assess a standard through an appreciation of the harm done by an infringement of the standard. It would seem (at first glance, anyway) that a copyright infringement harms the copyright owner. The copyright owner suffers from loss of the revenue that is customarily paid for permission to copy. In contrast, it is not clear at first glance that anyone is harmed by plagiarism.

The obvious candidate for a plagiarism harm is the author who receives no credit. But it is hard to see what harm that author may have suffered. Unless there is also copyright infringement, an author has few legal grounds for claiming economic loss for a plagiarized use of his work. There is no direct financial harm. And, given the strong tradition of refusing to grant property protection over ideas and information (as opposed to copyright protection over the means of expression), it is unlikely that we would want to grant an author any financial interest in the uncopyrighted content of a paper.[8] Perhaps there is an indirect financial harm to the author who fails to gain a reputation as ideas are taken without giving "due credit." But this harm is notoriously hard to assess.[9] Undoubtably, those scholars who provide citation counts as evidence of their scholarly reputations are "wronged" when their work is uncited. But this purported wrong certainly does not rise even near to the level of harm that demands legal protections through the criminalization of plagiarism. A possible loss of potential reputation is hardly sufficient grounds for the ethical indignation that academics express over incidents of plagiarism. And in the case of plagiarism from, for instance, the work of a defunct 19th century cor-

---

[7] The most famous use of this criterion is Judge Stewart's claim that he knew pornography when he saw it, in *Jacobelis* v. *Ohio*, 378 US 197 (1964). That fact that it is extremely doubtful that Judge Stewart did indeed know pornography when he saw it should throw doubt on the criterion.

[8] This is a slight exaggeration, ignoring such areas of intellectual property as trade secret protection. In particular, consider the case of *International News Service* v *Associated Press*, 39 SC 38, in which a news service was forbidden to base its publication upon the reports of a rival news service, even though there was no copying of the form of expression and hence no copying. This is an example of what is commonly called "pseudo-property," based on common law and outside the limits of copyright protection. It would take us too far afield to consider these alternatives in this paper. For an introductory discussion, see Charles McManis, *Unfair Trade Practices 3rd Ed.*, West Publishing, 1992, Ch. 6. Note that the *INS* case is not strictly a plagiarism case as defined in this paper, since proper citation would in no way diminish the pseudo-property claim of the prior news service.

[9] See Arthur Austin "The Reliability of Citation Counts in Judgments on Promotion, Tenure, and Status," *Arizona Law Review*, 35, 1993, for an interesting discussion of how academics establish their reputation through a count of the number of times they are cited.

poration, there seems to be no grounds whatsoever for worry about loss of potential reputation. We may also consider cases of "self-plagiarism" in which an author uses material that he or she has previously published in another source. Although such action may be "justified" by an author's sense of modesty, it does create a break in the citation trail. It is plagiarism in the sense of the present paper.

I suggest that the actual harm done by plagiarism is not harm to the author so much as harm to the reading public. When citations are left out of documents, the reader is deprived of one of the most fruitful ways of seeking additional resources related to the paper topic. It is also often of great importance for scholarship that sources can be traced backwards and verified. Consider, for instance, the study of the Bermuda Triangle[10] that traces the stories back to their unreliable sources. This trace is important for the assessment of the Triangle. Consider the importance of identifying the source of "Protocols of the Elders of Zion," and continuing to trace stories back to this source when certain views appear in modern works. Plagiarism destroys the scholarly trails and causes significant harm to the scholarly effort itself. Like the creation of false data and false histories, plagiarism cheats the public by presenting claims with a misleading or hidden provenance. Whereas piracy is a property violation, plagiarism is akin to "fraud"[11] carried out against the reader.[12] Whereas a victim of piracy has the legal standing to institute a case of copyright infringement, it is the academic and journalistic communities themselves that protest plagiarism even in the absence of a "victimized author."

If this analysis of the harm of plagiarism is correct, then it would appear that the Web heightens the need for protections against plagiarism. The underlying problem is that the Web makes provenance difficult to establish, and consequently makes it more important that we work harder to preserve provenance. One of the problems is "invisible revisability."[13] To take a personal example, a biographer seeking information on the author of the present paper might have discovered that I received a PhD in 1967, according to the vita linked to my Web home page. That date was a typographic error that I have now corrected. The problem is not that some false information was published. False information is as common in the hardcopy print media as it is in the electronic media. The problem is that I corrected the date and left no trace of the correction. In contrast, a print correction

---

[10] Larry Kusche's study is a fine example of good search for sources that have gotten out of hand: *The Bermuda Triangle Mystery Solved*, Prometheus Books, 1995.

[11] The term "fraud" seems particularly apt, since like the term "plagiarism" it is only vaguely defined in the legal tradition. Broadly speaking, it is an intentional, material misrepresentation that actually misleads and causes damages, see Prosser *On Torts*. It would, indeed, be hard to treat plagiarism as fraud, since it would be hard to assess damages. On a related topic, see Stern, supra at note 49, on the relation between plagiarism and commercial "palming off."

[12] Peter Shaw, "Plagiarism," *American Scholar* 51, 1982, gives an example of a scientist who received a slap on the wrist for plagiarism, and then was fired when it was discovered that he had also faked data. It is clear which form of fraud is taken more seriously in science.

[13] The term is, so far as I can trace it, introduced by Andrew Harnack and Gene Kleppinger in "Beyond the MLA Handbook: Documenting Electronic Sources on the Internet," presented at the 23rd Conference, Kentucky Philological Association, March 1996, and posted at <falcon.eku.edu/honors/beyondmla>. Revised November 1996, accessed July 1998. This is an important source document for readers interested in citation standards.

would be visible by a comparison of earlier and later editions of the source. A biographer who used the false date taken from the Web might be accused of bad scholarship, as the Web source was invisibly altered. And a later scholar, tracing back the information might be puzzled about an odd discrepancy over dates with no apparent source.

There has been considerable effort in recent years by a number of organizations to address the problem of invisible revisability by the establishment of standards for scholarly references. For instance, the Modern Language Association,[14] the American Psychological Association,[15] and the International Standardization Organization[16] are all involved in the creation of standards for Web citations, including guards against invisible revisability.[17] Most of these guards are intuitive. In citing a Web publication, you should, for instance, refer to both the URL of the site where you found the publication and also to a location where the publication is archived. This works, of course, if the archiving is secure, as it would be for a major newspaper published in both electronic and hard-copy versions. In response to the perceived need to archive, we now see the creation of a new industry that provides archiving services to Web users.[18] Some academic organizations strengthen the call for archived sources by refusing to accept citations to Web sources that are not securely archived. This is a fine standard, but a standard that may seem overly restrictive to someone seeking information that is most easily obtained through a search of my Web-based vita.

It is obvious that these standards for citation are definitionally tied to the notion of plagiarism: On one level, plagiarism is failure to follow the standards for citation. As we establish the standards for citation, we alter the notion of plagiarism. In order to guard against invisible revisability, the Web seems to require more stringent standards for citations. It would seem that more stringent standards create a higher scholarly obligation. And that higher obligation may entail a more serious sense of plagiarism with a heightened sense of the seriousness of the offense. This is a realistic scenario, which may in fact be played out as the Web, which is well recognized as a dangerous source for information, becomes a more important source of information. We shall see.

---

[14] See Harnack and Kleppinger, *ibid.*

[15] See Mary Elleng Guffey, "APA Style Electronic Formats," Business Communication Quarterly March 1997, revised and posted at <www.westwords.com/guffey/apa_z.html>, accessed July 1998. See Xia Li and Nancy Crane, *Electronic Style: A guide to Citing Electronic Information* (1993). Also see note #1 in Harnack and Kleppinger, supra, bemoaning the lack of discussion in the Publication Manual of the American Psychological Association.

[16] See "Excerpts from ISO Standard 690-2 (1997) posted at <www.nlc-bnc.ca/iso/tc46sc9/standard/696-2c.html>, accessed July 1998.

[17] The "Electronic References and Scholarly Citations of Internet Sources" Web site at <www.gu.edu.au/gint.WWWVL/OnlineRefs.html> is an invaluable source for research into changing standards for Web citations.

[18] For a lengthy discussion of the needs and problems in archiving and of the industry response, see Cross Industry Working Team white paper (May 1997) on "Managing Access to Digital Information: An Approach Based on Digital Objects and Stated Operations," posted at <www.xiwt.org/documents/MagagAccess/ManagAcess.html>, accessed July 1998. This white paper draws attention to a wide range of interesting intellectual property issues for Web publications.

I would like to expand the discussion of invisible revisability to a more general concern for electronic provenance. Invisible revisability is only one example of the volatile nature of electronic information. Consider, as a further problem, the new practice of publishing encrypted documents with a key made available to subscribers. If a publisher permits a "cryptolope" document to "go out of print" without ever publishing an unencrypted form of the document, there is a real possibility that the document will have disappeared as completely as the ancient Greek books lost at the destruction of the library at Alexandria. Electronic publications can be even more ephemeral than hard-copy publications.[19] And as a final concern, let us note that an author can easily alter archived primary sources. For instance, consider a claim based on an email correspondence. (This is an area of concern addressed by all the organizations that are presently looking into citations for Web-based sources of information.) The fraudulent author can alter the archived version email message that stands as evidence for a claim. This fraud is simply the electronic version of the use of forged documentary evidence in traditional print media, except that the electronic version is much more difficult to expose. As the problems of electronic provenance make fraud easier and more dangerous to scholarship, it would seem reasonable for the scholarly community to heighten its sensitivity to plagiarism. This may take many forms, including a higher standard for citation against which to assess plagiarism, or a heightened reaction among academics to incidents of plagiarism.[20]

What's the Use of Copyright?

A focus on the rights of the producer rather than the expectations of the reader is what distinguishes piracy from plagiarism in the sense of the present paper. As noted above, copyright piracy harms the copyright owner. The harm is almost always viewed as a crime against property. The most common harm is the victim's loss of revenue from unauthorized copying, which is commonly called "theft." We may also consider unauthorized alteration of a copyrighted text. Although this is also a crime against property, it more closely resembles vandalism than theft. But in any event, it is clear that the copyright owner is the victim in these property crimes and torts.

The observation that copyright shows concern for the owner rather than the user, however, is only a starting point for a study of the issues regarding copyrights in Web publication. Our copyright policies are legal conventions that establish the relevant notion of property. The real issue for copyright is the social utility of these

---

[19] It is a mark of the ephemeral nature of Web information that I have not been able to access a primary reference on cryptolopes: the IBM InfoMarket 1995 site at (www.infomarket.ibm.com). To all appearances, the site has been eliminated, without links to a new site. The problem of cryptolopes is also discussed in the XIWT white paper, supra.

[20] Academic responses to scholarly improprieties are notoriously mild. Although universities tend to scold errant professors and sweep wrongs under the carpet, newspapers and magazines take plagiarism and piracy much more seriously. For an interesting discussion of academic practices, see Marilyn V. Yarbrough "Do As I Say, Not As I Do: Mixed Messages for Law Students," *Dickenson Law Review* 100.3 (1996).

conventions.[21] In particular, the problem before us is whether those conventions are as useful in the context of electronic Web publication as in the context of hard-copy publication. It is simply impossible in a short paper to do justice to the huge volume of recent studies of this copyright issue. The study of copyrights on the Web is almost an industry, with a steady stream of excellent law review articles, books, organization white papers, and suggestive legal decisions. I will make no attempt here to address even a reasonable portion of the range of complex copyright issues raised by the Web publication. Rather, I will draw attention to one particular aspect of electronic publication that, I believe, suggests that Web publication can remain a viable industry with fewer copyright protections. The argument is that a shift from hard-copy publication to Web-based publication creates a new economic environment in which slightly weakened copyright protections can still provide an adequate economic incentive for the publication industry. At the start, however, let me note three important qualifications to this argument.

First, it is my personal (unscientific) impression that the majority of legal scholars propose strengthened, rather than weakened, intellectual property protections for electronic publication. All reasonable commentators recognize that copyright policy must find a balance between (a) overly stringent protections that interfere with an author's right to base new studies on previously copyrighted works and (b) overly weak protections that fail to provide economic encouragement for the creation of new copyrightable works. My review of the literature leads me to the impression that the mood among most (but not all) legal scholars is that the Web creates an environment in which we need a new balance with additional protections against the ease with which works are electronically copied and distributed. We may take the attitude of the Working Group on Intellectual Property Rights as typical in this regard. Responding to a number of arguments (although not the argument of this paper), the WGIPR concludes that "weakening copyright owners's rights in the NII [national information infrastructure] is not in the public interest; nor would a dramatic increase in their rights be justified."[22] In contrast to the WGIPR call for an undramatic increase in rights, the present paper goes against the majority view by suggesting an undramatic reduction in rights.

Secondly, the present paper seems to echo a generally unconvincing argument presented by S. Breyer in 1970.[23] Breyer argued that changes in technology lowered

---

[21] This remark assumes a utilitarian assessment of copyright policy, and ignores any suggestion that an author might have a natural right to the fruit of his or her labor. This paper is no place to argue this fundamental issue, and we simply adopt the standard utilitarian approach without argument. A natural rights attitude may be common among novelists and journalists who take pride in their work, but the mainstream of legal and philosophical literature is united in agreeing with Thomas Jefferson's observation (in the context of a patent dispute) that intellectual property is "given not of natural right, but for the benefit of society," in the "Letter to Isaac M'Pherson, Aug 13, 1813," *The Writings of Thomas Jefferson,* Taylor & Maury, 1854, vol. 6, p. 181. As an incidental matter, it reinforces the argument of this paper to note that I first took this passage from a secondary source that misquoted Jefferson. I have corrected the quotation.

[22] From the last page of the Introduction to The Report. The Report was prepared by the Working Group on Intellectual Property Rights (chaired by Assistant Secretary of Commerce, Bruce Lehman) for the White House National Information Infrastructure Task Force (chaired by Secretary of Commerce, Ronald Brown), and submitted to Congress in 1995. It is available at <www.uspto.gov/web/offices/com/doc/ipnii>, accessed Aug 1998.

[23] S. Breyer, "The Uneasy Case for Copyright," *Harvard Law Review* 84, 1970.

the cost of publication to the point that most copyright protections were no longer needed to encourage publication. Although the argument received some attention, it is generally believed that Breyer failed to appreciate the economics of the publication industry. The present argument differs from Breyer's argument in several ways. Obviously Web publication is a far cry from the emerging technology contemplated by Breyer in 1970. But more to the point, whereas Breyer advocated a broad overhaul of the copyright system, the present argument only advocates some slight weakening of copyright protection in some contexts.

Thirdly, as with most complex policies, copyright policy has a myriad of social utilities. Its intended utility, as stated in the US Constitution for US copyright policy, is that copyright policy is "to promote the progress of science and the useful arts," which suggests that copyright policy is to be judged on whether that policy is an incentive to the publication of new scientific and technical work. Although we may count the increased publication of scientific information among the social utilities of a successful copyright policy, this is obviously not the sole utility of copyright policy in today's world. Among the other utilities, for instance, are the encouragement of work in the fine arts and (in the software industry) the encouragement of the development of industrial processes. Without in the least bit suggesting that this is the only social utility to copyright policy, however, I focus here on how copyright policies provide financial incentives for the publication of original documents. This supposed utility is indeed the first social utility of copyright that is considered by most commentators. In particular, I ask what level of protection against "free riders" is needed to provide publishers an incentive to publish new documents in the Web environment.

A focus on publishers may seem odd to some creative writers. These writers are more interested in providing incentives to authors to write than in providing incentives to publishers to publish. From that writer's perspective, it has been argued that the Web opportunity for more self-publication by writers on their works shifts copyright concern away from protections for publishers to the need to protect writers.[24] In contrast, the following analysis shows little concern for authors who post their own works on their own Web sites. (I must admit a certain lack of sympathy for authors who loudly demand economic rights to works self-published on the Web. This sort of activity hardly seems to require the economic incentives of copyright protection.[25]) My emphasis on economic protections for the publication industry may betray my academic background. Whereas the writers of cookbooks and mystery novels are in the business for the collection of royalties on their works,

---

[24] Joan Latchaw and Jeffrey Galin argue in "Shifting Boundaries of Intellectual Property: Authors and Publishers Negotiating the WWW," *Computers and Composition,* 15.12, 1998 that the Web creates a context in which the "power" of authors and publishers is shifting to give greater emphasis to the concerns of authors.

[25] Given that damages for copyright infringement are based on a calculation of lost income or potential income, it is doubtful that there would be a significant reward for a copyright infringement for non-commercial Web publication of a self-published free-access manuscript. It would be another matter, of course, if there was some potential commercial value to the original site. See note 32 following on the need to recognize lost commercial value when the original site is usually accessed by way of a link from a site that includes commercial advertisements.

academics in fields such as my own rarely write in the expectation of direct profit from their efforts. With some outstanding exceptions, the fact is that successful
academic writers rarely depend on royalties to do much more than finance a nice
summer vacation or a new car now and then. Although academics write a great
deal and profit from their writings with academic recognition, they rarely expect
to make much money from copyright licenses. What I need, as an academic, is a
healthy academic publishing industry that wants to publish my writings. So the
question raised by Web technology is what sort of copyright policy is needed to
encourage electronic publishers?[26] Are these the same copyright policies as are needed to encourage hard-copy publishers?

Once the issue is presented in terms of the economic incentives for the publication industry, we see an immediate difference between the needs of the industry in the hard-copy and electronic realms. Electronic publication lowers both the
cost and the financial risk of publication, and therefore suggests that the electronic
publication industry needs fewer copyright protections than the hard-copy publication industry. In preparing this paper, I spoke to several publishers who have moved
or are moving into electronic publication. A typical story concerns the publication
of a small journal in Chicago that focuses on African-American fine arts. The publisher informs me that the annual budget in 1997 for the publication of his journal
in hard-copy was about $300k, of which about half goes to support the editorial staff,
marketing, solicitation of articles, etc. The other half goes to the production of the
journal, including typesetting, purchase of paper, printing, etc. This latter cost is
reduced from $150k to $10k by the shift to electronic publication. Basically, his costs
are cut in half by the shift to electronic publication. This, however, is only one part
of the saving. In addition, the publication risks are immensely reduced. In hard-copy
publication, the editor must estimate the size of a printing run. If he overesti-
mates, he suffers a considerable financial loss as the edition sits unsold in the warehouse. If he underestimates, he suffers the financial loss of lost opportunity,
including the opportunity to raise his advertising rates for a more widely distributed
journal. Run-size is not at issue for electronic publication. Whether he distributes
his product over the Web or through the sale of CDROMs, the publisher needs only
a small inventory and can produce the product quickly to meet demand. And finally,
the publisher sees a new form of profit opportunity through on-line sale of subsidiary products. The publisher sees the possibility of both direct marketing from
the journal site and of some form of compensation from advertisers who sell items
over the Web to customers who link from the journal site. For the publisher of a
small art journal, electronic publication provides new economic opportunities at
considerably lower economic risk.

If we view the copyright as providing such protections against piracy as are needed to ensure a profit for the publication of documents, then the above example seems
to suggest that we can lower the level of copyright protection. The example does

---

[26] "The motive force behind legal protection for published works did not emanate from authors, scholars, and scientists; it came
from booksellers, printers, and publishers." Stern, supra at 535.

not, however, suggest elimination of copyright protection. Even if publishing costs are cut by something over half, they do not go away. The small journal publisher still needs some protections against piracy. We cannot use this example to suggest the elimination of copyright protection. What the example might suggest, however, is a lower level of protection. In particular, I suggest that we might expand the notion of "fair use" to permit more unauthorized electronic copying of articles, for instance for distribution as an electronic text to students in a university class. We might also loosen the standards for "similarity" so as to permit unauthorized publication of an article that is substantially similar, although not identical, to a copyrighted electronic manuscript. We might generally recognize that an author and publisher both independently have copyright authority to authorize republication, and no longer recognize the sale by an author of full copyright authority. In any event, the example suggests that piracy is less important in the context of Web publication than it is in the context of hard-copy publication.[27] And this contrasts directly with the conclusions drawn above on the importance of plagiarism in the Web environment.

The example is suggestive, but by itself, it hardly provides a conclusive argument. From my personal discussions with a number of publishers, I think the example is fairly typical for journals shifting from hard-copy to Web publication. The situation radically changes if we consider, for instance, the somewhat futuristic possibility of distributing movies over the Web. The major cost to the film studios are costs of making the master copy. Although the Web opens up the possibility that studios may do their own distribution over the Web (which would be a significant change from the present financial structure of the industry), we could not make the same claims as we did for the journal that costs are cut by over half. The Web-based distribution of computer games,[28] the Web-based distribution of computer software, the Web-based distribution of music, and the Web-based presentation of college classes[29] each have special needs that distinguish them from the electronic journal industry, and we must be careful not to overgeneralize from the experience of electronic journals. The computer pornography industry is an interesting case in point for our study: It functions

---

[27] Fred Cate et al. in "Copyright Issues in Colleges and Universities" argue the opposite point: ". . . copying a page from an article or a frame from a motion picture might previously have been thought fair because it involved copying only a small portion of a larger work where no market existed for that portion alone. Today however a use might be found.... As computers create markets for smaller and smaller fragments of works, uses that were fair in print may cease to be so in the context of digital information." *Academe,* May/June 1998, p. 44.

[28] The protection needs of each industry in this list is discussed in the report of the Working Group on Intellectual Property Rights. The Report is rapidly acquiring the status of a benchmark for discussions of the varying needs for copyright protection.

[29] There has been considerable theoretical discussion and some legislative action addressing the need to accommodate electronic classrooms through redefinition of fair use. Ellen Schrecker in her editorial introduction to the "Technology and Intellectual Property" issue of *Academe,* May/June 1998, argues that Web-based courses and "distance learning" in general are quite expensive, largely due to equipment costs. She rejects the commonplace claim that distance learning is a cheap alternative to traditional education. Henrietta Shirk and Howard Smith provide a nice overview of changing standards for fair use in electronic classes in "Emerging Fair Use Guidelines for Multimedia: Implications for the Writing Classroom," in *Computers and Composition* 15.2 1998.

well and earns a profit for its publishers, even though the industry makes few attempts to claim copyrights on its Web sites. Projections on the emerging industry of electronic book publication also provide evidence that Web-based publication does not need the same level of copyright protections against piracy as does hard-copy publication.[30]

The analysis above treats piracy is a form of "free-riding" in which the pirate takes advantage of the efforts of the original author without having the investment of resources by the original author. Although this is the most common focus of discussion of copyright issues, we must recognize that there are certainly other ways to analyze the harm of piracy. In particular, we should take note of the popular use of copyright to protect against unauthorized alteration of a manuscript. The most recent revisions of the copyright law add recognition of this "moral right" of the author to the traditional economic rights of the copyright holder. Exercising this right, one of the Web-based papers that I read in preparation for this paper included the notice that the author held the copyright, but would permit replication on condition that "the paper is copied fully, without alteration." Given the usual academic standard for "fair use" quotation of passages from published papers, it is unclear what sort of copying this author intended to preclude. All the same, this sort of concern is clearly in the mind of many authors,[31] and it is not primarily a financial concern. In fact, this is a concern that views piracy as something very close to plagiarism, except that it views alteration of a text as a harm against the author rather than against the reader. In both cases, the issue is the purity of the textual information source.

Bringing It All Together

The above observations provide evidence for a claim that the Web creates an environment that heightens the dangers of plagiarism and lessens the dangers of piracy. Let us not overstate the situation. The evidence is suggestive, but does not justify a radical revision of our present system. Indeed, at some level our observations justify a continuation of the present legal system that formally recognizes the crime of piracy while largely ignoring plagiarism. It is much easier to quantify and calculate the harm caused by piracy than by plagiarism, as these wrongs are defined above. In calculating damages for piracy, the courts calculate the loss in value to the original work, as well as the unfair profit made by the free-riding pirate. It is not clear how we would calculate the harm caused by plagiarism. The

---

[30] *The Wall Street Journal* tells us that a publisher of electronic books predicts that electronic distribution will permit him to cut the retail price by 30% and still double profits. This is entirely in keeping with the projections for the shift to electronic journal publishing that are reported above.

Joshua Kwan, "Nascent Electronic Book Field Already Seems Crowded," *Wall Street Journal,* July 30, 1998.

[31] The US Copyright Act of 1976, as originally enacted, shows little concern for an author's "moral right" (in contrast to "economic rights") to prevent alterations to a work. This concern, however, received considerable attention in other countries. The Berne Convention Article 6b is a very powerful statement of moral rights: "Independent of the author's economic rights, and even after the transfer of said rights, the author shall have the right to claim authorship of the work and to object to any distortion, mutilation, or other modification of, or other derogatory action in relation to, the said work, which would be prejudicial to his honor or reputation." When the US Copyright Act was amended to bring it into agreement with the Berne Convention, a strong statement of moral rights was added as section 106A.

courts certainly do not want to enter into sterile arguments over who gets credited for what. And therefore, we should expect that the law should deal with the former more aggressively than the latter. In contrast, we should not be surprised by the fact that academics seem willing to infringe copyrights as an everyday matter at their photocopy machines, while those same academics complain loudly when they see signs of plagiarized data in academic papers. Although plagiarism is aggravated and piracy is lessened by the use of electronic publication, it does not follow that our present legal and ethical responses to these wrongs need an immediate overhaul. It is more likely that, as the Web becomes a more and more important tool for research and distribution of information, we will see a slight shift in the importance that is attached to piracy and plagiarism. To return, for instance, to the question of citation counts, we can take note of the fact that electronic databases are making it easier to establish citation counts. Whereas it used to be the case that only the legal profession had the sort of reference records that made citations easy to establish, it is now the case that electronic databases are making citation counts possible in fields such as theoretical physics. Although it remains the case that this concern for a loss of potential reputation cannot justify the seriousness with which academics treat plagiarism, we must note how Web-based databases are changing the game to heighten concern for the reference trail. And we may need to respond to the change with new standards.

The point is nicely illustrated by a look at the practice of digital archiving of files taken from the Web. One obvious guard against the volatility of electronic provenance is the archiving of Web-based information. If it is plagiarism to present information without citing the source, then scholars should be able to keep a copy of the source as a guard against its disappearance in change on the volatile Web. But it may be piracy to make the copy needed to avoid the charge of plagiarism, particularly if we make a complete copy of a lengthy document. It would seem reasonable, therefore, that copying for the sake of archiving electronic information be seen as "fair use." Indeed this is very close to the definition of fair use as traditionally defined in Sections 106 and 107 of the Copyright Act, which permits a copy for preservation that does not diminish "the potential market for or value of the copyrighted work." The doctrine concerning fair use archiving was not originally designed to meet the present problem, but rather recognized the practice by "libraries and archives" (as opposed to individuals) that make (photographic, but not electronic) copies for "the purposes of preservation and security." It would appear that the need to strengthen guidelines for Web-based citations in the Web environment entails a broader recognition in copyright policy for electronic archival copying of files in personal archives that are not, strictly speaking, libraries. Indeed the present trend in copyright law is to recognize more fair use copying for archival purposes.[32] In order to protect the scholarly community against plagiarism in cyberspace, we may need to lessen the property protections of the copyright owner in cyberspace.

---

[32] S 1146 introduced in the Senate in 1997 amends the fair use section of the copyright law to explicitly recognize digital archiving.

I suggest that a heightened concern for Web plagiarism combined with a lessened need for economic protection of Web publishers might entail a number of Web-based extensions of the fair use policy. For example, we might consider the apparent volatility of a Web site as relevant to whether it is fair use to digitally download a file from that site. On this grounds, it is fair use to download a Web home-page that is not obviously archived in any manner. In contrast, books published by MIT press are not frequently available both on-line and in bookstores. The existence of the hard-copy version would speak against the fair use right to digitally copy the book. That a work is firmly archived (on standards that are yet to be defined) becomes part of the copyright owner's expectation for economic protection. This is, of course, only one example of the way in which the Web environment may lead to a broadened notion of free use and of weakened copyright protection. These sorts of examples suggest that as a general matter, many of the new issues for cyberspace's use of files should be decided in favor of broader rather than more restricted fair use policy.[33]

We must be very leery of any extension of the present argument that would lead to copyright policies that seriously harm the economic incentive for commercial Web publication. I do not suggest a policy under which a scholar who cited a Web source could make a downloaded version of the source available as an attachment to a scholarly study.[34] This is explicitly not fair use as presently defined. It would practically eliminate all copyright protections, greatly diminishing the revenue opportunity of a pay-to-access Web site that holds a copyrighted source file. (We can imagine a system where secondary users could distribute original sources under a system of mandatory licensing of copyrighted electronic documents, with automatic distribution of royalties such as are presently used by the music industry. That we can imagine these new systems of protections for Web sites, of course, does not mean that we should implement them. For now, it is enough to take note of them.) The present paper suggests the we can loosen the notion of fair use for some cases of digital copying, not that we embark on a rampant elimination of copyright protections.

Let us now return to the issue raised in the first section of this paper: Let us consider the uncited and unauthorized copying of the layout code that establishes the look of a Web site, without the copying of the words or pictures that appear on the site. I suggest that this should not be seen as a serious incident of plagiarism. The

---

[33] A broad range of relevant issues are discussed in the Interim Report of the Conference on Fair Use (1996/97) available at <www.usptol.gov/web/offices/dcom/olia/confu>, accessed August 1998. CONFU does note the scholarly need for archives. It goes much further to consider issues for the definition of fair use on the Web that go beyond the scope of the present paper, including quite specific proposals for fair use guidelines. It suggests, for instance, a 1000 word limit on passages copied from lengthy documents.

[34] The issue here is files that are downloaded and attached to a published document. A closely related issue is the practice of linking a reference to the site that is the original source of the reference. On this matter, see Walter A. Effross, "Withdrawal of the Reference: Rights, Rules, and Remedies for Unwelcome Web-Linking," *South Carolina Law Review* 49, Summer 1998. This volume is available over the Web on a link from <www.law.sc.edu/sclr/vol49_4.htm>. It is noteworthy that I was made aware of this article through a reference that went directly to the location of the html version of the paper, rather than to the above site of the *South Carolina Law Review*. The article discusses the journal's remedies for loss of commercial value in such direct linkages, which ignore the mother journal.

point is that, for most purposes, there is little or no scholarly value in knowing the original source of the html tags. We may be able to construct examples where a historian of the fine arts has an interest in the creator of the code, but these examples are a bit recherché. On the whole, this sort of copying seems unimportant on the values inherent in guards against plagiarism. In contrast, however, we might very well see this as piracy. On the theory that a copyright protects the programmer's opportunity to make a profit from the labor that goes into the writing of a manuscript, we may recognize that the code to define a graphics template is, under certain circumstances, "copyrightable subject matter." Our discussion, however, suggests that as the Web makes the distribution of documents easier and cheaper, then, we can afford to set fairly high criteria for a text as copyrightable subject matter. On a "sweat-of-the-brow" test for copyright claim on layout code,[35] we should only extend copyright protection to layout code if the code is of considerable length and represents considerable development cost.

References

Austin, Arthur. The Reliability of Citation Counts in Judgments on Promotion, Tenure, and Status. *Arizona Law Review* 35, 1993.

Breyer, S. The Uneasy Case for Copyright. *Harvard Law Review* 84, 1970.

Cate, Fred. et al. Copyright Issues in Colleges and Universities. *Academe,* May/June 1998.

Cross Industry Working Team. Managing Access to Digital Information: An Approach Based on Digital Objects and Stated Operations. <www.xiwt.org/documents/MagagAccess/ManagAcess.html>, May 1997, accessed July 1998.

Electronic References and Scholarly Citations of Internet Sources. <www.gu.edu.au/gint.WWWVL/OnlineRefs.html>.

Guffey, Mary Ellen. APA style Electronic Formats. *Business Communication Quarterly,* <www.west-words.com/guffey/apa_z.html>, March 1997, accessed July 1998.

Harnack, Andrew and Kleppinger, Gene. Beyond the MLA Handbook: Documenting Electronic Sources on the Internet. 23rd Conference, Kentucky Philological Association, <falcon.eku.edu/honors/beyond-mla>, November 1996, accessed July 1998.

International Standardization Organization. Excerpts from ISO Standard 690-2, <www.nlc-bnc.ca/iso/tc46sc9/standard/6962c.html>, 1997, accessed July 1998.

Jefferson, Thomas. Letter to Isaac M'Pherson, Aug 13, 1813. *The Writings of Thomas Jefferson.* Taylor & Maury, vol. 6. 1854.

Kusche, Larr. *The Bermuda Triangle Mystery Solved.* Prometheus Books, 1995.

Kwan, Joshua. Nascent Electronic Book Field Already Seems Crowded. *Wall Street Journal,* July 30, 1998.

Latchaw, Joan and Galin, Jeffrey. Shifting Boundaries of Intellectual Property: Authors and Publishers Negotiating the WWW. *Computers and Composition* 15(12), 1998.

Li, Lia and Crane, Nancy. *Electronic Style: A Guide to Citing Electronic Information,* 1993.

---

[35] A sweat-of-brow test has a long and controversial history in copyright law. Generally the test has not stood up well in recent decisions, see Feist supra. The present suggestion is quite radical in this respect.

McManis, Charles. *Unfair Trade Practices, 3rd Ed.* West Publishing, 1992.

Prosser, I.R. et al. *Casebook on Torts.* Foundation Press, 1982.

Schrecker, Ellen. Technology and Intellectual Property. *Academe,* May/June 1998.

Shawl, Peter. Plagiarism. *American Scholar* 51, 1982.

Shirk, Henrietta. and Smith, Howard. Emerging Fair Use Guidelines for Multimedia: Implications for the Writing Classroom. *Computers and Composition* 15(2), 1998.

St. Onge, K.R. *The Melancholy Anatomy of Plagiarism.* University Press, 1988.

Sterns, Laurie. Copy Wrong: Plagiarism, Process, Property, and the Law. *California Law Review* 80, 1992.

Working Group on Intellectual Property Rights for the White House National Information Infrastructure Task Force. <www.uspto.gov/web/offices/com/doc/ipnii>, 1995, accessed Aug. 1998.

Yarbrough, Marilyn V. Do As I Say, Not As I Do: Mixed Messages for Law Students. *Dickenson Law Review* 100(3), 1996.

Law Cases

Feist Publications, Inc. v Rural Telephone Service Co., 499 U.S. 340, 1991.

International News Service v Associated Press, 39 SC 38, 1918.

Jacobelis v. Ohio, 378 US 197, 1964.

Narell v. Freeman 872 F.2nd 907.

An Ethical Evaluation of Web Site Linking

Richard A. Spinello

As the World Wide Web has grown in popularity, the propriety of linking to other web sites has achieved some prominence as an important moral and legal issue. Hyperlinks represent the essence of Web-based activity, since they facilitate navigation in a unique and efficient fashion. But the pervasive activity of linking has generated notable controversies. While most sites welcome and support incoming links, others block them or seek to license them in some way. Particularly problematic are so-called "deep links," which bypass the home page along with the extensive advertising and promotional material that is usually found there. While some contend that a site's mere presence on the web is implicit permission for virtually any form of linking, others argue that at least in some circumstances deep linking is unfair and constitutes misappropriation of intellectual property.

In this paper we will explore the issue of *deep linking* from a distinctly moral vantage point. While legal scholars have vigorously debated this issue, it has received little attention from moralists. But deep linking raises a plethora of complex property issues with subtle moral implications, and hence it deserves our careful scrutiny. The most fundamental question concerns the appropriate scope of property rights for a web site and how those rights can be properly balanced against the common good of free and open communications on the Web. It is our contention that there is no presumptive claim to the liberty of deep linking at will, since it may be disrespectful of property rights in certain situations. In order to defend this position we first make the case that a web site is a form of intellectual property, drawing support from the major theories that justify property ownership. Once we have established that a web site is really property, we consider the specific rights implied by such ownership. We conclude that on the basis of those rights, a prima facie case can be made that because of the potential for negative effects, users should not presume that deep linking is acceptable unless they first seek out the permission of the target web site.

This essay originally appeared in *Computers and Society,* Vol. 30, No. 4 (December) 2000: 25–32. Copyright © 2000 by Richard A. Spinello. Reprinted with Permission.

We also fully appreciate the dangers inherent in propertizing the web and the need to encourage the most flexible forms of linking. Therefore, we argue that any arbitrary or unnecessary restrictions against deep linking should be eschewed for the sake of the common good of open communications, flexibility, and maximum porosity in the Internet environment. While web site authors may indeed have a property right in their creative work, they have a correlative obligation to promote the sharing and free flow of information when their specific ownership rights are not put in jeopardy by deep linking.

The Technical Aspects of Web Site Linking

A web site refers to a combination of text, graphics, or media content that has been put into an area of the Internet known as the World Wide Web. Each web site has a unique address or URL (Universal Resource Locator) such as www.bc.edu. A web site typically consists of multiple pages that are organized and controlled from a beginning or home page. It is important to note, however, that a web site is more than these logical protocols. It has a physical dimension as well, since a web site is located on a machine running server software, which is connected to other systems over a network. A logical web site is stored on such a physical server that may be owned and controlled by someone else, such as an Internet Service Provider. In some cases, of course, the creator of the logical web site also owns the physical server. While this distinction may complicate matters to some extent, in our treatment of property rights we are referring to the logical web site and its content, and assuming that if the creator of that site does not own the server on which it is located, he or she has the authority to use that server for the purpose of building and operating a web site.

Quite simply, a link is a connection within the same web site or between two different web sites. For example, a hyperlink within a web page may contain the URL for another web site, which is activated with the click of the mouse. While most links take the user to the other web site's home page, it is possible to bring the user to subordinate pages within that web site. This practice has become known as "deep linking." The hyperlink text itself can appear in many forms. It can be the name of the linked to web site or a description of what is to be found at that web site (usually the name or description appears in highlighted text). It can even take the form of a revealing graphic or image such as a company logo. There are two types of links: an HREF link that instructs the browser to locate another web site and provide its contents for the user, and an IMG or image link. An IMG link instructs a browser to enhance the text on the user's Web page with an image contained in a separate file usually located at a completely different web site. For instance, if one is writing a narrative on Monet, the French Impressionist painter, one can include an image of a Monet painting from the Boston Museum of Fine Art's on-line image file to provide an illustration that will accompany that narrative.

The mechanics of the more common HREF linking are simple enough. A link is merely a short line of HTML code such as the following:

```
<A HREF="http://www.bc.edu">Boston College<A>.
```

The "<A HREF" piece of code tells the browser that this is a link to another Web page to which the user should be taken. The address or URL of that web page (http://www.bc.edu) follows. And the words "Boston College" represent the text that appears on the screen—this is the only thing that the user actually sees. When the browser encounters this line of code, it is thereby instructed to locate the Boston College web page. It then sends a copy of the web page to the user's browser. For the sake of clarity in this discussion we will refer to the site that is being linked to as the "target" web site. The site containing the hypertext link will be called the "source site."

The value and social benefits of linking are manifold and beyond dispute. Most web pages have multiple links to other web pages and they are also the target of many other links. Links from one web site to another permit instantaneous access to multiple sources of information. They are an indispensable tool for search engines that allow users to search for products across a variety of web site databases. Linking also allows users to easily follow a complex and intricate trail of research, and each user can determine how extensively or deeply to follow that trail. Linking is the essence of the World Wide Web, and there is little doubt that legal or technological constraints on linking would have substantial negative ramifications for the web. Although most users concede that there is nothing wrong with linking even without getting the target site's permission, there are problems with the way in which some source sites do their linking. Some of the more serious and common problems are highlighted in the following two case studies.

Two Case Studies

The Ticketmaster v. Microsoft Case

In 1997 Ticketmaster Group Inc. filed suit against Microsoft for federal trademark infringement and unfair competition. Microsoft operates a web site called Seattle Sidewalk, which functions as a guide to recreational and cultural activities in the Seattle metropolitan area. Seattle Sidewalk provided abundant links to related web sites including a link to Ticketmaster, which operates a popular ticket selling web site. That link, however, bypassed the Ticketmaster home page and went directly to the respective pages for purchases to events listed in the Seattle Sidewalk page. For instance, a listing on the Seattle Sidewalk page for the Seattle Symphony would include a direct link to a Ticketmaster sub-page that would allow users to purchase their symphony tickets.

This is a prime example of deep linking, and Ticketmaster raised a number of objections to this practice. According to Ticketmaster, by bypassing its home page, Seattle Sidewalk users were not being exposed to the extensive advertising and promotional announcements that were posted there. This diminished the value of that advertising and ultimately the rates that could be charged to future advertisers. A second problem with this mode of linking concerned Ticketmaster's relationship with MasterCard, which was promised to receive greater prominence than other payment methods. But unless Ticketmaster could control how users navigated this site, it could not keep its commitment to MasterCard. Ticketmaster also complained that Microsoft was able to generate advertising revenues on the basis of this link because Microsoft posted a banner advertisement on the same page on which it displayed the Ticketmaster name and link. And, according to Wagner (1997), Ticketmaster alleged that the links were done in such a way that they "presented information incorrectly and out of context."

This case certainly raised the fundamental problem with deep linking that circumvents advertising and other identifying or promotional features on the home page. Deep linking not only reduces the value of the target site's advertising, but deprives that web site of its proper exposure and recognition. On the other hand, it could be argued that Ticketmaster had no real quarrel here. Its web site information is at least quasi-public. Ticketmaster therefore should not interfere with the web's free flow of information. In its legal defense, Microsoft argued "that Ticketmaster breached an unwritten Internet code in which any web site operator has the right to link to anyone else's site" (Tedeschi, 1999). Microsoft also argued that it had a First Amendment right to publish this public information.

There was an out-of-court settlement to this lawsuit in February 1999. Although the terms of that settlement were not disclosed, Microsoft did agree to link to Ticketmaster's home page instead of to its sub-pages. The settlement was actually a disappointment for those searching for a firm legal precedent about controversial linking activities. As a result, at least in the United States, there are currently no unambiguous legal guidelines on the practice of deep linking.

Since the Ticketmaster case there have been several other contentious disputes that have reinforced the problem of deep linking for commercial web sites. For instance, Universal Studios insisted that a web site called Movie-List remove direct links to movie previews on the Universal site. Universal had no problem with linking to its overall package of information about a film, but not directly to a trailer. According to a Universal spokesperson, it was important to pursue this matter as a means of "protecting our property in all media" (Kaplan, 1999). And eBay has recently taken a strong stand against auction search engines such as AuctionWatch. These sites collect data about products for sale on eBay and other auction sites and then include links to those items. But eBay is pursuing legal action to block these search engines from gaining direct access to items within its auction database. It claims that AuctionWatch unfairly profits from its investment and devalues the eBay brand, since buyers are not exposed to its upper level pages.

Maria's On-Line Art Gallery

This case is purely hypothetical but does represent a realistic example of the problems that non-commercial web sites can experience with deep linking. Maria is a young up-and-coming artist who decides to set up a web site to display scanned images of her most recent art works. On the home page she explains the rationale behind this exhibit and describes how these works, which center on three basic themes, must be examined sequentially for the proper effect. She is willing to allow links to her site but wants those links to be to the home page so that viewers and art critics will have an opportunity to read her explanation of the exhibit and to look at the works in their proper context and sequence. Nevertheless, deep linking to this site is rampant, especially to one work that seems provocative and somewhat sensational when considered in isolation, but has a much different meaning when viewed in its proper context. Several art critics who have seen only this work, thanks to a few maverick source sites that include it in their on-line collections, criticize Maria's exhibit on the basis of this one painting, and her reputation suffers.

To be sure, deep linking may be the source of other difficulties that are not illustrated by these cases. Nonetheless, the problems that emerge in the Ticketmaster case and the hypothetical case of Maria's art gallery are representative of the moral (and legal) issues triggered by deep linking.

Web Sites as Intellectual Property

Given the potential for harm cited in these cases, what should be done about deep linking? To some extent, the resolution of this normative question depends upon whether or not a web site can be classified as private property and, if so, what specific rights should belong to the property owner. When authors create web sites and put them on the World Wide Web, do those sites in effect become part of the Internet commons and does this give others an implied license to link to those sites in any way they choose? Or are they still the intellectual property of their owners despite their quasi-public and social nature? Before we explicitly consider this question, it is instructive to review the prominent theories of intellectual property that have been invoked to justify property rights. These theories can help us to address the issue of whether or not there is a justification for classifying a web site as private intellectual property. Moreover they can assist us in determining what set of specific rights or privileges are implied by such a classification.

There are three theories that one encounters in the traditional literature about intellectual property, and each of them has a convenient label:

1. Utilitarianism
2. The Lockean or labor-desert theory
3. The personality theory

We cannot concern ourselves here with the viability of these theories, though we acknowledge that each has certain deficiencies. As Fisher (1998) has observed, none of these theories can provide a determinate means for resolving questions of legal entitlements or complicated ownership issues—"rather, each is best understood and employed as a language, a paradigm helpful in identifying considerations that ought to be taken into account when determining who should own what." They are, therefore, simply fruitful avenues of reflection for helping us think critically about intellectual property and ownership questions. Despite their ultimate indeterminacy, they do enable us to make more nuanced and reasoned judgments about intellectual property issues.

The utilitarian approach assumes that the utility principle, sometimes expressed as "the greatest good of the greatest number" should be the basis for determining property entitlements. It has several variations but the main argument is based on the premise that people need to acquire, possess, and use things in order to achieve some degree of happiness and fulfillment. Since insecurity in one's possessions does not provide such happiness, security in possession, use, and control of things is necessary. Furthermore, security of possession can only be accomplished by a system of property rights. Also, utilitarian philosophers such as Bentham justified the institution of private property by the related argument that knowledge of future ownership is an incentive that encourages people to behave in certain ways that will increase socially valuable goods. It would certainly appear that the basic utilitarian argument can be easily extended to intellectual property. According to the Landes/Posner model, since intellectual products can often be easily replicated due to low "costs of production," there is a danger that creators will not be able to cover their "costs of expression" (e.g., the time and effort involved in writing a novel or producing a music album). Creators cognizant of this danger are reluctant to produce socially valuable works unless they have ownership or the exclusive prerogative to make copies of their productions. Thus, intellectual property rights induce creators to develop works they would not otherwise produce without this protection, and this contributes to the general good of society (Fisher, 1998).

The second approach, sometimes referred to as the labor-desert theory, is based on the premise that the person who works upon common or unowned resources has a right to the fruits of his or her labor. John Locke stated this simple thesis in the Fifth Chapter of his *Second Treatise on Government* where he brings property to the center of political philosophy. According to Locke, people have a natural right or entitlement to the fruits of their labor. Thus, if someone takes common, unusable land and through the sweat of the brow transforms it into valuable farm land, that person deserves to own this land. Locke's basic argument is that labor is an unpleasant and onerous activity and hence people do it only to reap its benefits; as a result, it would be unjust not to let people have these benefits they take such pains to procure. In short, property rights are required as a return and suitable reward for the laborers' painful and strenuous work. Locke, however, stipulates a proviso that one can acquire such a property right only as long as one leaves "enough and good enough" left for others.

Although Locke had in mind physical property such as land, it would seem that this theory is naturally applicable to intellectual property as well. In this case the relevant resource is common knowledge (i.e., unowned facts, ideas, algorithms, etc.), and one's intellectual labor that contributes value to this common pool of knowledge should entitle one to have a natural property right in the finished product such as a novel, a computer program, or a musical composition. Even if this sort of labor is not so unpleasant and difficult, Hughes (1997) argues that a property right is still deserved since that labor creates something of social value. Further, the granting of most intellectual property rights will satisfy the Lockean sufficiency proviso. Nozick (1974) contends that the proper interpretation of this proviso is that ownership of property through labor is acceptable if others do not suffer any net harm. He argues that patents, for example, satisfy this proviso since without this incentive, that is, without the prospect of a long, heavily protected monopoly around one's invention, there would probably be no invention and everyone would be worse off.

The basis of the third and final approach is that property rights are essential for proper personal expression. This theory has its roots in Hegel's philosophy. Hegel argued that property was necessary for the realization of freedom, as individuals put their personality into the world by producing things and engaging in craftsmanship. According to Reeve (1986), "Property enables an individual to put his will into a thing." Property then is an expression of personality, a mechanism for self-actualization. This theory seems particularly apt for intellectual property. As human beings freely externalize their will in various things such as novels, works of art, or poetry, they create property to which they are entitled because those intellectual products are a manifestation of their personality or selfhood. It is an extension of their being and as such belongs to them. While not all types of intellectual property entail a great deal of personality, the more creative and individualistic one's intellectual works are, the greater one's "personality stake" in that particular object and the more important the need for some type of ownership rights (Hughes, 1997).

It seems plausible that by relying on these general "avenues" of theoretical reflection, a convincing case can be put forward that a web site should be considered as the proprietary and private property of its creator(s). From a Lockean perspective, there ought to be property rights in web sites because their value is based predominantly on the labor and energy involved in constructing and setting up the site. The production of a web site is most often a labor-intensive activity and this effort should confer a property right for those who have made the substantial investment of time and effort to build that site. In addition, if we follow the value-added logic that is hinted at in Locke, the production of a web site from common intellectual resources clearly creates social value and therefore deserves a fitting reward.

Further, a property right in a web site would appear to be consistent with Locke's sufficiency proviso, though this certainly depends on how society chooses to interpret and implement that property right. It also depends on what we mean by the intellectual resources, which belong to the commons. If we follow Hughes' interpretation (which is slightly different from Nozick), it refers to the set of all "reachable" ideas, that is, ideas that are available to us or within our grasp. According to Hughes (1997), the development and expression of most ideas inspires people to reach new ones and thus expands the commons rather than depletes it. Following this interpretation, propertizing a web site should not worsen the lot of others since the idea(s) that it embodies may stimulate new ideas for other potential web site developers. For instance, by granting eBay a property right in its web site, we do nothing that will impede others from developing their own novel ideas (based perhaps on what they see at the eBay site) that will in turn result in new and unique web sites providing similar services. Also, the raw materials (such as graphics, text, standard musical harmonies, algorithms, etc.) that are woven together into a multi-media web site remain (or should remain) part of the commons and available for other web site creators. As a consequence, as long as the property right is properly implemented, it should not yield any net harm to persons since the resources available for their use will not be constricted in any meaningful way when that property right is bestowed. Indeed, the U.S. legal system does appear to recognize some type of property right in a web site, and yet this has done nothing to interfere with the extraordinary pace of new web site development.

Likewise, the utilitarian argument that ownership rights are justified because they maximize social utility and provide an incentive to build future web sites is also apposite. It surely seems reasonable to conclude that the prospect of future ownership and all that it entails is an incentive for the creation and embellishment of web sites, many of which require a high cost of expression. While it may be too much to say that no web site would ever be created without the prospect of ownership, it seems obvious that without such an incentive, the rate of creation would be reduced, especially for commercial web sites where there is an expectation of ownership and control in order to generate the revenues that will pay for this investment. Also, the quality of web sites would be diminished since there is generally a strong correlation between quality and a high cost of expression, and the higher the cost, the more web authors look to ownership rights to help ensure a return on their investment. Without the protection of ownership, there would likely be a preponderance of "cheap" web sites, that is, sites of lower quality with a reduced cost of expression. To some extent, then, a recognition of private property rights in a web site does provide an incentive to develop new, high quality sites, since developers will be motivated by the realization that they will retain firm control over the accessibility to these sites and reap the tangible and intangible rewards of ownership.

And finally, to varying degrees, a web site is often a creative expression or manifestation of one's personality and for this reason too should be considered as a form of property. Many web pages, particularly those created by individuals, clearly reflect the personality of their creators. According to Radin's (1982) theory, one could argue that web pages like other intellectual products "are closely bound up with personhood because they are part of the way we constitute ourselves as continuing personal entities in the world." It is true that not every web page will have the same level of self-expression. Hardy (1996) notes that corporate web pages will have fewer "personal attributes," but even here a "corporate personality" is often expressed by a web page. Hence given that both individuals and corporations do have some "personality stake" in a web page, its creators deserve a property interest in such pages to safeguard that stake (Hughes, 1997).

Thus, all three theories seem to converge and support the notion that a web site is a form of intellectual property. According to our analysis, a property right is warranted as an incentive for future creation, a reward for one's labor and the social value created by that labor, and as a means of protecting whatever personality stake is included in this intellectual product. This result is also consistent with our common moral sense. We realize that as the virtual world begins to displace the physical one, a web site is an important information asset that will become a principal wellspring of wealth and advantage for both corporations and individuals.

Deep Linking Revisited

Even if a web site is a form of private intellectual property, what does it mean to say that one "owns" this property? What is included in the bundle of rights that belong to a web site author? We cannot assume that just because someone has a property claim on a web site that any deep linking activities involving that site are moral-ly forbidden. What are the specific intellectual property rights implied by one's "own-ership" of a particular web site? For example, it seems intuitively evident that a property right would include the right to prevent blatant copying or the prepara-tion of derivative works. Therefore an on-line bookseller cannot simply copy the content of amazon.com's web pages, but must create its own original web page that performs the same function of selling books. But what else is included in this prop-erty right? Is there any basis for the claim that there is also a right to determine how others link to a web site?

In order to answer this question we must consider what is implied by the "own-ership" of property. According to Honore (1961), ownership is defined as "the great-est possible interest in a thing which a mature system of law recognizes." This definition acknowledges that property ownership is not absolute, but it also suggests that there is a set of powers, rights, and privileges that constitute ownership. Along these lines, Honore (1961) argues that the liberal notion of ownership (as opposed to absolute ownership) includes the following elements: the right to possess; the right to use; the right to manage; the right to income; the right to capital; the right to secu-rity; the right of transmissibility; the absence of term; the prohibition of harmful use; liability to execution; and residuary character. A full treatment of each of these ele-ments is well beyond the scope of this paper, but two elements seem especially per-tinent for our analysis, especially in light of the case studies discussed above: *the right to manage* and *the right to income*. The right to manage is the right to decide how and by whom a thing shall be used, while the right to income means the right to appropriate the value generated by allowing others to use one's property.

There are many varieties of ownership based on the various subsets of these elements, but according to Becker (1977), the rights to security in possession, secu-rity in use, security in income, and security in management are among the most fundamental of these elements. They are at the core of what we commonly mean by ownership of physical or intellectual property. It seems reasonable to assume that a web site author should possess this full subset of rights, but we will con-centrate on the right to earn income and the right to manage. To exclude these rights from ownership would suggest a diluted version of ownership that seems difficult to justify. More importantly, it would be inconsistent with the theoretical ration-ale that we have used to justify that ownership.

Let us first consider the right to earn income, which is clearly at stake in many deep linking disputes. In Hohfeldian terms, this is in part a power right, which rep-resents "the existence of a state of affairs such that one person (the right holder) may morally (or legally) alter at will some of the rights, duties, liberties, power or immunities of another person (the liability bearer)" (Becker, 1977). In this case it would mean that the web site owner has the power to curtail the rights and liber-ties of other stakeholders with respect to that web site and to set the conditions for activities such as linking when the revenue-generating potential of that site is at stake.

If labor has engendered a property right in a web site, it follows that one should have one of the most basic rights of ownership, that is, the right to derive income from that site, especially since that income is the primary reward for that labor and an incentive for future creations. By making the investment of labor, energy, and capital, the owner is surely entitled to maximize the return on that investment, which is realized by the right to earn income by allowing others to use that site. Any restrictions on that particular right would be tantamount to a disincentive for investing heavily in the socially valuable activity of new web site creation. It seems evident then that a property right based on the labor-desert rationale would surely be hollow unless the property owner can get a return on his or her investment as enabled by the right or "power" to earn income.

If this is so, what does it imply about the activity of deep linking? The Ticketmaster case presented the general problem. Web site X derives revenues from advertisements, which appear primarily on its home page, but web site Y links to a subordinate page and completely bypasses those ads. Consequently, many users who visit site X do not see these ads. This has the effect of reducing the eyeball contact with the advertising and this will negatively effect the rates that can be charged to advertisers. Therefore deep linking to site X undercuts its revenues and thereby interferes with its right to earn income from that site. In summary, Y's activities or liberties with respect to site X impede X's efforts to derive a material benefit from allowing others to use its property, and this is inconsistent with its right to earn income.

The hypothetical case of Maria's on-line gallery is different since there are no advertising revenues at stake. What is at stake is Maria's prerogative to control her web site. In Honore's terms, the basic property right at stake in this case is the right to manage, to determine how people use her web site for the purpose of preserving her creative integrity. This too is in part a power right that allows Maria to alter the liberties of others with respect to her site. In this situation her ability to control how her material is presented to viewers is compromised by source sites that engage in deep linking without permission. If we justify property rights through the personality theory, which has a special relevance in Maria's case, it follows that the need for web artists and authors to maintain some control over their personal expression is of paramount importance. Maria's strong personal and emotional attachment to her virtual gallery demands that she have a property interest in her work and that interest must take the form of *managing* how her art will be viewed by others. The essence of the personality theory is the right to control the public disclosure of one's works since they embody one's personality. This can only be effectively realized by the *right to manage,* i.e., to determine how and in what manner they will be accessed by others. Through that right to manage Maria will be able to better protect her expressive integrity.

Moreover, this issue is connected to Maria's First Amendment right to free expression. As Hughes (1997) has noted, "freedom of expression is meaningless without assurances that the expression will remain unadulterated." Deep linking can sometimes be used as a tool for editing the target site's works, and this can create the perverse effect of undermining the integrity of the creator's work. Authors like our fictional Maria should have the right to use this medium of expression as effectively as possible and this means the moral prerogative to demand that others refrain from deep linking when it caricatures or distorts their creative efforts and expression.

In summary, then, if ownership is to have any real meaning for the web site author, it must include these basic elements cited by Honore, including the right to manage and to derive income. The bottom line is that if a web site is to be regarded as property with a legitimate owner, that owner has the right to control his or her intellectual product, that is, to set the rules and conditions for how that web site will be accessed and used by others.

Of course one can make a counterargument here that these particular rights of control, specifically, the right to income and the right to manage, should be restricted in some way because of serious disutilities or negative externalities for other Internet stakeholders. A claim may be presented that the scope of these property rights should be limited for the sake of curbing those externalities. But are there significant disutilities that would warrant the abridgement of these particular rights?

Although certain disutilities can be identified when we take away an unrestricted liberty to deep link, none are grave enough to justify the limitation of these basic ownership rights to manage and derive income from one's possessions. Granted, users are sometimes inconvenienced by the need to enter a site through the home page and work their way down to their desired location. Deep linking does make it considerably easier for users to access material and information, and it does take better advantage of the Internet's extraordinary flexibility. More significantly, perhaps, a case can be made that the functionality of deep linking is quite significant for Internet users since the construction of those links is itself an act of creative self-expression in which certain users unlock the value and meaning of the Internet. As we have already demonstrated, producing a web site is an important creative activity that is enhanced by the use of techniques such as deep linking.

While we recognize the functionality and value of deep linking along with the inconvenience of putting any limitations on this activity, we must consider two key points. First, we are certainly not arguing that deep linking should not be allowed to the vast majority of web sites, only that one should not presume a right to link in this way without permission. If the target site is reasonable and there is little or no harm involved, deep links will most likely be permitted. Also, despite the role that deep linking can play in the expressive activity of web site production, the target site's ownership rights should still take precedence. There is little justification for circumscribing a legitimate property right in order to facilitate someone else's self-expression. We can find many analogies in the non-virtual world that would support this view. For instance, putting together an anthology of 20th century poetry is also a creative activity, but that does not mean that the compiler of the anthology should not be required to seek permission of the poets or copyright holders just because to do so would be an inconvenience and would interfere with his or her creative activity.

Furthermore, according to Becker (1977), the disutilities that might provoke us to limit property rights should be on a much grander scale than the ones we have cited. They should usually involve complete inaccessibility to or monopolization of some scare resource. Becker argues that the labor argument "produces a presumption in favor of allowing people to acquire full ownership, . . .

[and] once the disutilities of exhaustibility, accumulation, and harmful use are take care of, other disutilities serious enough to outweigh the labor and liberty arguments are likely to be rare." Nothing of the sort is going on when we require that users seek out permission before deep linking. There are no substantial disutilities that would warrant limiting one's ownership based on hard work. Hence the property right in one's web site should trump the interests of other Internet stakeholders when deep linking to that site is damaging in some objectively meaningful way such as the loss of revenue or the impairment of creative integrity.

Respecting the Common Good

Although we have argued with some insistence on behalf of a web site author's property rights, there is another side to the equation when intellectual property issues are considered from a moral perspective. The web site author as property owner should not completely neglect or ignore the interests of other stakeholders. There is always a danger that when one focuses exclusively on his or her individual property rights, the needs and interests of those other parties will be shortchanged. This is incompatible with the moral point of view, which requires respect for the perspective and projects of others. Further, too narrow a focus on the individual's rights ignores the social role of creative activity. There is a need, therefore, to balance these web site property rights that we have identified with proper respect for the common good of the web. Without this kind of balance, there is a tendency to absolutize ownership claims to the detriment of the larger purpose served by the Internet and the connectivity that it provides for its users. As McFarland (1999) maintains, "Ethical policies for the use and distribution of information must take into account the social nature of information, even as they recognize the legitimate claims of the producers. It is in this balance . . . that virtue is found."

But what is the common good in this case and how can it best be articulated? It is probably made manifest by examining the ultimate purpose of the World Wide Web: the sharing and dissemination of information. For this purpose to be fully realized, web sites and the information that they contain should be made as widely available as possible in the most efficient manner.

What implications does all of this have for these routine activities such as linking? As we have already intimated, there must be some recognition that linking is a vital activity for the web, which furthers the goal of open communication, that is, the free exchange and free flow of ideas and information. Given a moral obligation to respect the common good and the social nature of information, some reasonable limits should be imposed on the property right enjoyed by web site authors. One way of achieving this balance is to assume that there is an implied license to link to any target site's home page, since this sort of linking has not been the source of so much contention. The target site should prevent such links or demand permission only under unusual circumstances. In our estimation, it would be too burdensome and counterproductive to insist upon such explicit permission for every HREF link. The necessity of seeking such permission could dramatically curtail the linking that occurs on the web and thereby impair the common good of the free flow of information. Even deep linking should be permitted and facilitated in cases where there is no harm that accrues to the target web site, such as a loss of revenues or a threat to the site's integrity. Web sites that suffer no such appreciable harm should allow deep linking out of regard for the free flow of information. As a result, deep linking should not be blocked for arbitrary or trivial reasons since it does have unusual functionality and serves as a valuable means to the ends of openness and information sharing.

If web site authors block or demand permission for deep links only for legitimate reasons such as the ones cited here, they will be acting prudently, respectful of the moral imperative to balance their own important property rights with the interests of others and the web's ultimate purpose. In our estimation, these prima facie rules represent a reasonable way of harmonizing one's legitimate property rights in a web site with respect for the Internet's common good.

Conclusion

Although deep linking may appear on the surface to be a benign activity that captures and fulfills the meaning of the Web, it has become fraught with controversy for the reasons enumerated in this paper. This issue is complex and even has a certain symbolic import since the creation of web sites through deep links and other techniques seems to obscure our traditional notion of authorship, which assumes an irreducible point of reference. Nonetheless we argue here against any presumptive claim on behalf of source sites that boast a right to deep link to other sites at will, and we defend this position with the following argument:

1. Deep linking can be harmful for target web sites in some circumstances. For example, it can lead to lost advertising revenues or damage to one's creative integrity.
2. Because of this potential harm, a presumptive claim to the liberty of deep linking without permission is unjustified. This is based on the assumption that a web site is private intellectual property and not common property and that, as a result, liberties with respect to web site access are constricted.
3. The notion that a logical web site is a form of intellectual property can be defended by invoking traditional justifications for property rights: utilitarianism, labor-desert, and personality-based theories. All three theories offer firm support for the conception of a web site as private intellectual property. A property right is warranted as an incentive for future creation (utilitarianism), a reward for labor and the social value created by that labor, and as a means of protecting whatever personality stake is included in an intellectual product.
4. If a web site is property, according to the liberal theory of ownership, ownership rights should include (among others) the right to earn income and the right to manage. Ownership that did not include these basic rights would be empty, especially given the theoretical rationale used to justify that ownership in the first place. These two rights endow property owners with the power to set conditions for how their sites will be accessed and utilized. This would appear to preclude potentially disruptive activities such as deep linking unless the source site obtains permission of the owner.

5. However, the moral point of view has an other-directed component and requires that intellectual property owners also consider the common good. The good or ultimate end of the Web is the sharing of information. Hence web site property owners should not block deep links for arbitrary or insignificant reasons but only when material or meaningful harm can be demonstrated. In this way property rights in a web site will be properly harmonized with the common good.

6. In conclusion, we argue here for a limited and balanced property right in a web site that does impose a moral duty on other web sites to engage in deep linking activities with care, to consider the possible harm that those activities can bring about, and to seek permission for deep linking unless it is abundantly clear that deep links cause no damage and are welcome by the target site.

References

Becker, L. (1977) *Property rights: philosophic foundations.* Routledge & Kegan Paul, London.

Fisher, W. (1998) Property and contract on the internet. http://cyber.law.harvard.edu/ipcoop/98fish.html

Hardy, T. (1996) The ancient doctrine of trespass to web sites. *Journal of Online Law,* art. 7.

Honore, A.M. (1961) Ownership, in *Oxford essays in jurisprudence,* (ed. A.G. Guest), 107–147, Oxford University Press, New York.

Hughes, J. (1997) The philosophy of intellectual property, in *Intellectual Property,* (ed. A. Moore), 107–177, Rowman & Littlefield, Lanham, MD.

Jakab, P. (1997) Facts and law of web linking. Twelfth Annual Computer Law Institute, State Bar of Georgia.

Kaplan, C. (1997) Editors feud over whether linking is stealing. *CyberLaw Journal,* November 27.

Kaplan, C. (1999) Is linking always legal? The experts aren't sure. *CyberLaw Journal,* August 6.

McFarland, M. (1999) Intellectual property, information, and the common good. Proceedings, Fourth Annual Ethics and Technology Conference, Boston College, 88–95.

Nozick, R. (1974) *Anarchy, state and utopia.* Basic Books, New York.

Radin, J. (1982) Property and personhood. *Stanford Law Review,* 34, 957.

Reeve, A. (1986) *Property.* Humanities Press, Atlantic Heights, NJ.

Tedeschi, B. (1999) Ticketmaster and Microsoft settle suit on internet linking. *The New York Times,* February 15.

Wagner, M. (1997) Suits attack web fundamentals. *Computerworld,* May 5, 125.

Ethical Issues in Open Source Software

Frances S. Grodzinsky, Keith Miller, and Marty Wolf

Introduction

Open Source Software (OSS) and the emergence of an entire Open Source Movement have practical, political, economic and ethical ramifications for software development and software use. In this article we examine ethical issues that have been raised by open source software and its challenge to commercial software models. First we will trace the history and impetus of the open source movement, examining its fore-runners, including UNIX, Stallman's Free Software Foundation, and Linux. Next we will define Open Source and examine its development model. Lastly, we present the ethical issues raised by OSS and attempt to demonstrate how human values are interwoven with the economic and technical choices that OSS affords.

A Brief History of Software Development

The field of software development, like many technological fields, has its roots inter-twined with academia. Academia has a long-standing tradition of sharing ideas and results, as long as appropriate credit is given to the originators. This tradition is most easily observed in the rich collection of scholarly journals used by the research community. These journals provide a forum for the dissemination of ideas and results. In addition, they provide a vehicle for researchers to advance new ideas and enhance the quality of existing theories. These traditions are deeply engrained in the Computer Science and Software Engineering academic communities.

The field of software development also shares a close connection with industry. The first ties occurred with hardware developers. IBM, for example, in conjunction

This essay originally appeared in the *Journal of Information, Communication and Ethics in Society*, Vol. 1, No. 4 (October) 2003: 193–205. Copyright © 2003 Troubador Publishing Ltd. Reprinted with permission.

with researchers at Harvard University, built its first computer in 1944. Over the next 15 years, IBM would bundle hardware, software, and services in a single package, rarely distinguishing among the various components. Then in 1969 IBM adopted a new marketing policy in which software and services were marketed separately from hardware. Therefore, in order to have any opportunity for profitability for the programming division, the source code would need to be kept confidential. This separation became complete in 1981 when IBM partnered with Intel and Microsoft to develop the personal computer (The History of IBM). Hewlett Packard (HP) was another company that first marketed hardware and then later software. In 1966, HP's first computer was developed to control a variety of laboratory instruments. In 1969, HP marketed its first time-sharing operating system (About HP, 2003).

Perhaps the most interesting connection between software development, industry, and academia surrounds the history of Unix. Unix was first developed in the early 1970s at AT&T Bell Labs in New Jersey, USA, largely due to the efforts of K. Thompson, D. Ritchie, M. D. McIlroy, J. F.Ossanna (Ritchie, 1996). One of their design goals was to develop a portable operating system. Thompson demonstrated the portability of Unix by mailing magnetic tapes containing Unix source code and utilities to friends (Moffitt, 2002). At the same time, AT&T gave away source code and licenses to universities for Unix Level 6. AT&T even published two books that contained the source code along with commentary.

The Computer Science Department at the University of California, Berkeley, was one such licensee that used the source code extensively for research projects. Eventually, they enhanced the Unix source code to include many new features and were freely distributing their enhanced versions. People throughout the world added many additional features, some of which are used to run the Internet today. Throughout the 1980s there was confusion as to just what "Unix" meant. There were lawsuits and counter lawsuits over which parts of Unix software source code could be freely given away and which parts required a royalty even to use in binary form. As we will see later, these issues largely went away in the early 1990s when Linus Torvalds introduced Linux.

While these developments were taking place in industry, the hacker culture was developing at many of the major research laboratories across the United States. The hacker culture involved people who loved to program and enjoyed being clever about it. By the early 1970s this culture was engrained at the Massachusetts Institute of Technology and had a significant impact on Richard Stallman's attitudes about software development. He says, "Whenever people from another university or a company wanted to port and use a program, we gladly let them. If you saw someone using an unfamiliar and interesting program, you could always ask to see the source code, so that you could read it, change it, or cannibalize parts of it to make a new program" (Stallman, 1999). The idea that source code could be freely exchanged, changed and used appealed to him as an efficacious software development technique. However, that system of development began to break down in the late 1970s and early 1980s as the changes noted above were taking place in industry. A further impact was the fact that industry was hiring many of the best software developers and programmers from the computing labs, and those indi-

viduals were taking the software they developed with them. To Stallman, suc-
cumbing to this industrial model of software development was tantamount "to making the world a worse place" (Stallman, 1999). In response to commercialization
within the software development industry, Stallman began the GNU project in
1984 with a goal of "creating a new software sharing community" (Stallman, 1999).
The GNU project goal was to develop an entire Unix-like operating system, complete with all the utilities in order to build a community of developers dedicated
to writing free software. All of the source code would be freely available for modification and use by anyone who was willing to make further changes.

The Free Software Foundation (FSF) was started in 1985 largely to support this
objective (The GNU Project, 2002). By the early 1990s, the GNU project had succeeded
in many ways. Useful software development and environment tools, plus the General
Public License (GPL), had been developed under the auspices of the Free Software
Foundation. However, GNU still lacked the core of an operating system—the kernel.
However, when Linus Torvalds developed and released the Linux kernel under the
GNU GPL the picture was completed. With the Linux kernel and the tools developed
by GNU, the world now had a complete, functional operating system with all of the
source code freely available for inspection, modification, and improvement.

As the Linux kernel developed and matured, people began to take note of the
software development methodology used to create it. In 1998, those who advocated
the software development process that is afforded by shared source code started
a movement called the Open Source Initiative (OSI). The Open Source Initiative
shares many of the same goals as the Free Software Foundation (Open source initiative, 2002). However its focus is grounded in the development methodology that
arises when source code is open and free to all who want it. On the other hand,
the FSF is a proponent of a philosophy that puts the notion of free software first.
According to the FSF there are four freedoms that are essential for free software:

1. Freedom to run the program, for any purpose.
2. Freedom to study how the program works, and adapt it to your needs.
3. Freedom to redistribute copies so you can help your neighbor.
4. Freedom to improve the program, and release your improvements to the public, so that the
   whole community benefits.

Requiring that all derivative works of GPL software also be licensed under the
GPL, if and when they become published, propagates these freedoms. This protection is known as copy left and prevents source code from being swallowed up
in a commercial venture (See Appendix B).

The OSI is less focused on philosophical tenets emphasized by Stallman and more
focused on promoting open source as a development methodology. This promotion
is evident in the emergence of other important software cultures including the Perl
culture under Larry Wall, John Osterhout's Tcl and Guido van Rossum's Python languages. "All three of these communities expressed their ideological independence
by devising their own, non-GPL licensing schemes" (Raymond, 2000).

Ethical Issues in OSS

What motivates a developer to write OSS? In the previous section we have alluded to the philosophy of Richard Stallman and members of the Open Source Initiative. Linus Torvalds believes that good software development starts by the scratching of a personal itch: the curiosity and desire to see if something can be done. In *The Cathedral and the Bazaar,* Eric Raymond depicts the OSS developer as one who has found the golden mean between underutilization and over-utilization caused by ill-formulated project goals. Raymond's "happy programmer," conforms to the Aristotelian model of one, who while enjoying the freedom to experiment and excel, brings forth imaginative and creative software (Raymond, 2001). Which, if any of these depictions still holds true? We will begin by examining the Open Source Software Development Community including the Open Source Definition as a social contract. Then we will explore some of the ethical issues that might explain the motivations of the OSS movement: autonomy, quality, and accountability. Finally we will close this section with analysis of whether Open Source can be considered a public good.

The Open Source Software Development Community

The Open Source Software development community emerged out of a parting of the ways with Richard Stallman and the Free Software Foundation. While the details of the contentious debate are beyond the scope of this paper, we will try to articulate some of the major points. Stallman's vision was one of a community of programmers who were doing something for the good of humankind. Although he acknowledges that open source and free software belong to the same category of software, Stallman maintains that there was an ideological shift within those advocating for open source. Stallman asserts that while the GNU Project holds onto the concept of freedom, the OSS community tries to appeal to businesses. Because business values profit above all, he argues that values of community and freedom are lost in the OSS development model. Citing examples of proprietary software that work with Linux, Stallman wonders if OSS developers will shun or support them (Stallman, 1999).

Open Source advocates argue that OSS is primarily a development methodology grounded in the philosophy of making source code open and free to all who want it. Developers self-select according to their interest in a project. Users and developers co-exist in a community where software grows and expands based on personal needs. These enhancements make the project more globally desirable as it fits more and more requirements. Linus Torvalds, the epitome of the open source developer says

- Release early and often
- Delegate everything you can
- Be open (Raymond, 2001, p.309)

It usually takes one interested developer to write a piece of core code to get a project going. Torvalds believes that it is the responsibility of the originator of the project to listen to the users who will find the bugs and those who will fix them.

In this type of scenario, "users are rewarded by the daily improvement in the work" (Raymond, 2001, p. 315).

Creators of OSS typically use the software themselves as it is being developed; therefore, the users are involved in the software development from the beginning. When software is created solely for commercial gain, there is always a danger that the customer is treated merely as a means to a financial end: financial enrichment of the software developer. Open source software removes that temptation.

Empirical evidence suggests that developers are less concerned with the ideological split between the FSF and the OSS, than with the idea of making free software available to all. Eric Raymond explains, "A side effect of the rapid growth of Linux was the induction of a large number of new hackers for which Linux was their primary loyalty and the FSF's agenda primarily of historical interest" (Raymond, 2000). He maintains that it was the Netscape announcement in February 1998 that it would distribute Navigator 5.0's source code that changed the environment dramatically. The idea that "free software" could be exploited within the commercial community excited the hacker culture and caused the parting of the ways between free software and open source advocates.

As with all software, quality is a major issue when evaluating Open Source Software. It has been argued that with open source software "you get what you pay for." If a developer is not paid for creating and maintaining a piece of software, then he/she may not feel the same obligation to do a quality job. Linus Torvalds argues that programmers tend to find projects that interest them, and if the programmer loses interest in a piece of code, there is usually a co-developer out there willing and able to continue on the project. The reason that Linux is so successful is that it interests people to develop a complete, open operating system. While it is true that there might be less success in developing a less glamorous project, developers would usually not undertake it, rather than do a shoddy job. Their reputations among their peers are at stake. In the hacker community, "one's work is one's statement...and there's a strong ethos that quality should (indeed must) be left to speak for itself...Boasting or self-importance is suppressed because it behaves like noise tending to corrupt the vital signals from experiments in creative and cooperative behavior" (Raymond, 2000).

Thus within the community of those working on the project, individual interest and work contribute to a larger goal: a working project for all. In addition, because it is open source, others may take advantage of the software once it is available on line. Floridi and Saunders in their paper entitled "Internet Ethics: the Constructionist Values of Homo Poieticus" maintain that a collaborative project relies on an "unsuspected but evident interest, shared by a growing community" and the coordination of efforts to produce a global product based on "local specific components." They name this phenomenon "distributed constructionism." They maintain that the Internet facilitates communication amongst users irrespective of distance and creates an environment that encourages and facilitates production of OSS like Linux (Floridi et al., 2003).

The Open Source Definition: A Social Contract
The formalization of the OSS community came about with the development of the Open Source Definition and the OSI. In 1997, Bruce Perens published a set of guide-

lines to articulate the developers' commitment to open source software and its users (Perens, 2002). The Debian Free Software Guidelines were incorporated into and became the basis of the Open Source Definition (See Appendix A). The OSI published licenses that met the Open Source Definition and declared that software distributed under any of these licenses would be "OSI Certified." The OSI offers copies of these licenses for anyone to use and modify for their own business model. The Mozilla Public License has been the one most often used since 1998. Most of these licenses give permission for the software to be used. Some ask that a copyright and year be included when redistributing the software. Most of them present the software "as is" and indemnify themselves against liability.

The social contract articulated in the guidelines is fairly clear about what the OSS is offering to others. But what do OSS developers expect in return? What motivates developers to contribute to an open source project? Is it altruism, i.e., do they consider it a "pro bono" project that contributes to the public good? Is it a reaction against corporate greed? Does it make them feel part of a select community with special talents? Clearly all of these play a part in OSS developer motivation to abide by this contract. Beyond that, however, there is also a sense that developers see their involvement as "enlightened self interest" (Kollock, 1999). Their contributions lead to software that they want and often need. OSS is an alternative for users; developers are themselves users of computing, almost always heavy users. Developers and users participate voluntarily in a development environment that emphasizes cooperation and mutual support under the OSI guidelines. They have found the environment satisfying enough to make OSS a major challenger to commercial software.

Autonomy

One perceived attraction for OSS developers is the autonomy of the developer. While developers who embrace OSS do gain a measure of autonomy not available to developers working on commercial software, the claim for complete autonomy doesn't appear to be valid. OSS developers work as volunteers, and can join or quit an effort strictly on their own initiative. These volunteers are not coerced into participation, and willingly contribute. Therefore, one might assume that the OSS developer can be depicted as a libertarian ideal, unshackled by corporate controls. However, there are several types of control in OSS, even though no single developer is in charge of an OSS project. As an OSS developer, the developer cannot be sure that his/her contribution will be accepted into the canonical version that is continuously evolving. This contribution may be embraced or rejected in the short term, and if accepted may be changed or replaced later. The developer is free to contribute or not, but any single developer cannot claim ultimate control over the use of his/her contribution. In *Homesteading the Noosphere,* Eric Raymond states, "the open-source culture has an elaborate but largely unadmitted set of ownership customs. These customs regulate who can modify software, the circumstances under which it can be modified, and (especially) who has the right to redistribute modified versions back to the community" (Raymond, 2000).

Open source software has the seemingly useful feature that at any point, any one with appropriate technical skills can modify the code and take the project in a direction that diverges from the direction others are taking it (called "code forking"). Thus, one of the perceived benefits of a piece of open source software is that it has the opportunity to evolve rapidly into competing programs where, presumably, Darwin's theories of evolution can take over: the best piece of software for the current environment will survive. If code forking is prevalent, we might expect to see many innovations occur in open source software development. However, Raymond gives two very pragmatic reasons for the low incidence of code forking in many successful OSS projects. The first major reason for projects to persist is a fear of diluting the developer community for the project—both child projects have fewer developers, thus weakening the entire project, especially relative to the parent project. Secondly, shortly after a code fork the child projects cannot exchange code. In addition, Raymond adds that "there is strong social pressure against forking projects" in the open source community. According to Raymond the open source community is best viewed as a gift culture where one's social status is determined by what one gives away. In addition to the practical concerns, forking a project cuts right to the core of the culture—it damages someone's reputation.

Thus, given both the pragmatic and cultural pressure to avoid code forking, the developers of an open source project must take special care to avoid the symptoms of groupthink. A newcomer to open source development has very little in terms of reputation to bring to the table when he/she proposes a new piece of code or a new tack on development for a project. Project leaders, who are less open to new ideas and ways of doing things, may miss the innovation of the newcomer's idea. Not only will the project lose the good idea, but it also faces the potential of losing a good developer. Thus, open source project leaders and developers must show a great willingness to take in new ideas, evaluate them thoughtfully, and respond constructively in order to nurture both the idea and the developer of the idea.

Project leaders must exercise similar abilities when a subgroup comes with an idea that is controversial. Care must be taken that the larger group does not ride roughshod over the smaller group's idea. Again, in addition to losing out on a good idea and potentially driving people away from the project, doing so will discourage future innovators from taking their ideas forward. Note that the proprietary software development model is not subject to this argument. The innovative developer who meets resistant project leaders or management is typically free to leave the organization, and he/she regularly does. In fact there are social norms that actually encourage this type of behavior; we call these people entrepreneurs.

So it appears that the autonomy experienced by an open source developer is much like the autonomy experienced by a university faculty member: freedom to choose which projects to work on. Thus, an open source developer has increased autonomy when compared to a corporate developer. Whereas, the corporate developer might find a supportive social structure to take a project in a new direction, the social structure in the Open Source community often works to suppress this type of entrepreneurial endeavor.

Software Quality

Quality software, in the traditional sense, is software that meets requirement specifications, is well tested, well documented, and maintainable (Schach, 2002). Advocates of OSS claim that its developers/users are motivated to do quality work because not only are they developing software for their own use, but their reputations among their peers also are at stake. Critics of OSS claim that volunteers will not do professional quality work if there is no monetary compensation. They also claim that documentation and maintenance are non-existent. While it is true that documentation and maintenance are concerns, OSS advocates assert that OSS meets users' requirements, is tested by its developers and is constantly being upgraded. Documentation evolves as more and more users become interested in the software and use it. For example, books on Linux can be found everywhere.

The question of whether OSS is of higher or lower quality than comparable commercial software is essentially an empirical rather than a philosophical question. The answer to this question is not readily available, but we can cite some preliminary anecdotal evidence on this issue. The Apache web server is OSS that competes with commercial web servers. The web server market is a potentially lucrative one, and we expect commercial software developers to compete for that market with high quality software. Yet despite commercial alternatives, according to third party observers (Netcraft, 2002) the OSS Apache server is by far the most used web server. According to an August, 2002 survey, 63% of web servers on the Internet are Apache. At least in this market segment, it appears that OSS is sufficiently high quality for most users. Of course, Apache is free and other servers aren't; the cost motivation might explain some of Apache's popularity. But if the Apache server were of significantly lower quality than commercial alternatives, then it would be surprising to see its widespread use. This raises the question of whether market-dominance and popularity should be a benchmark for software quality. Does the fact that Microsoft Windows runs on some 90% of home computers assure us of its quality? We would argue that popularity and quality might be linked if it can be shown that there is a level of expertise about software quality in the people making the choices. System administrators have more expertise than an average user of a home computer system. Therefore, when a majority of these professionals choose an OSS alternative, it deserves notice.

The Apache example illustrates an important distinction among OSS users. Initially, first adopters of OSS are its developers and as the code becomes more known, OSS gains users who were not involved in the development. These users adopt the OSS for many reasons, but some of these new users (particularly non-programmers), appreciate the product, though they may not understand or care about the process that developed it. All users of OSS gain if the software delivers needed functionality.

If an OSS project pleases its developers, but does not gather a following outside the developing community, that may be fine with the developers; if a commercial project only pleases its developers, it is a financial failure. The OSS model has different kinds of successes, and fewer outright failures. The rewards for developers in an OSS project are likely to be less tangible than rewards for a successful commercial product, but that does not make the rewards less real. The public has potential gains in the OSS movement that do not require large investments by the public.

Another distinction between OSS projects and commercial projects is the lack of a release date. While open source developers anticipate frequent releases, there are no release deadlines. The announcements of a release date by a commercial vendor impose pressure on developers to cut corners, thus increasing the possibility of errors in the software. Furthermore, such a deadline has a tendency to impose on the autonomy of the developer.

Finally, we note that both open source and proprietary developers share the same professional ethical responsibility to develop solid, well-tested code. The social pressure in the open source community to avoid code forking provides incentives for project leaders to ensure that the code is the best it can be. On the other hand, when an open source developer believes there is too much risk associated with a particular piece of code, he/she can rewrite it and release it. While there is a reputation risk in doing so, there is the opportunity to publicly demonstrate that the forked product is superior. In a proprietary model, however, a developer's main avenue of recourse is to "blow the whistle" on his/her manager or employer. To do so entails grave personal risk to one's livelihood, professional standing, lifestyle, and family. Worse yet, the developer will likely not have the opportunity to demonstrate the wisdom of his/her ways.

Open Source and Accountability

In her article entitled *Computing and Accountability*, Helen Nissenbaum cites four barriers to accountability: 1) the problem of many hands, 2) bugs, 3) computer as scapegoat, and 4) ownership without liability. She asserts that these barriers can lead to "harm and risks for which no one is answerable and about which nothing is done" (Nissenbaum, 1994). We will examine how OSS may have addressed barriers 1 and 2. Number 3 is a general issue and number 4 does not apply because there is no software ownership per se in open source. The Open Source Definition #1 addresses her fourth point (See Appendix A).

"Where a mishap is the work of 'many hands,' it can be difficult to identify who is accountable because the locus of decision making is frequently different from the mishap's most direct causal antecedent; that is, cause and intent do not converge" (Johnson and Nissenbaum, 1995). In open source, however, if a developer were to write irresponsible code, others contributing to the open source software would be unlikely to accept it. So, in this case, there is built-in individual accountability. If a developer were part of a large company, where all programming parts contribute to a large commercial venture, it then would fall on both the company and the individual to accept responsibility for the problematic software product. Often this is not done. So the many hands problem referred to by Nissenbaum in "Computing and Accountability" can be reduced in OSS because parts of code can be ascribed to various developers, and their peers hold them accountable for their contributions.

Nissenbaum argues that accepting bugs as a software fact of life has issues regarding accountability (Nissenbaum, 1994). The open source approach to software development treats the bug problem with a group effort to detect and fix problems. Torvalds states, "given enough eyeballs, all bugs are shallow" (Raymond, 2001, p. 315). The person that finds a bug in OSS may not be the person to fix it. Since many adept developers examine OSS code, bugs are found and corrected more quickly than in a development effort where only a few developers see the code. In this group effort, accountability is not lost in the group, but is instead taken up by the entire group. The question of whether or not this group accountability is as effective as individual responsibility is, again, empirical. The examples of Apache and Linux (Webcab Solutions, 2003) offer at least anecdotal evidence that some OSS demonstrates high reliability.

Don Gotterbarn is also concerned about issues of professional accountability in OSS (Wolf et al, 2002). In addition to worries about sufficient care in programming and maintaining OSS, Gotterbarn points out that an OSS licensing agreement forces the authors of the software to relinquish control of the software. If someone puts OSS to a morally objectionable use, then the developers have no right to withdraw the software from that use.

Gotterbarn's objection has some theoretical interest, for the OSS licensing agreements clearly state that no one who follows the OSS rules can be blocked from using the software. But if we accept the idea that software developers have a moral duty to police the use of the software they distribute, especially when the software is utility software, we fall into a practical and theoretical thicket. How is a vendor to know the eventual use of software, especially when the software is utility software (such as an operating system or a graphics package)? Are software developers empowered to judge the ethics of each customer or perspective customer? These responsibilities are overreaching ethically, and far too ambitious in a practical sense.

Furthermore, the relinquishment of control argument has practical significance only if existing competing software models include effective control over the use of software. (That is, should OSS be held to a higher standard than commercial software in relation to ethical responsibility for downstream use?) We are unaware of any action by existing commercial software vendors to police the uses to which their software is put. Commercial software vendors are certainly concerned that people who use their software have paid for it. Once paid for, vendors concerned about ethical use do not police commercial software.

Is Open Source a Public Good?

The claim that OSS is a revolutionary idea, a departure from previous models of intellectual property, is worth examining. Although clearly distinct from a commercial model of software development, OSS can be seen as a continuation of previously accepted traditions in academics in general, and in mathematics in particular.

Academia has long had the tradition of sharing ideas without direct payments. Scholarly journals do not pay authors (and in fact may charge them for pages printed). Law has not protected mathematical formulae and formal descriptions of natural laws. Copyright covers the expression of ideas, but not the ideas themselves; patent has (at least traditionally) protected the practical application of ideas, but not the physical laws underlying the ideas. So, if software is viewed as an extended mathematical object, akin to a theorem, then OSS could be a natural extension of the long tradition of free ideas in mathematics. Does that make it a public good?

Peter Kollack, a sociologist at the University of California at Los Angeles, examines the idea of public goods on line in his paper entitled *The Economies of Online*

Cooperation: Gifts and Public Goods in Cyberspace. He defines public goods as those things that are non-excludable and indivisible. Because the Open Source Definition prohibits discrimination against persons or groups or against fields of endeavor (See Appendix A), it supports the definition of a public good being non-excludable. Public goods in cyberspace can benefit the users of cyberspace irrespective of whether they have contributed to these goods or whether these goods have come from groups or individuals. The fact that one person using OSS does not affect its availability to the whole supports Kollack's idea of indivisibility. He maintains that "[a]ny piece of information posted to an online community becomes a public good because the network makes it available to the group as a whole and because one person's 'consumption' of the information does not diminish another person's use of it" (Kollock,1999). If a user downloads a copy of Linux, for example, it does not diminish its availability for other users. So by this definition, we concur that OSS is a public good.

However, is there an active interest among developers to create a public good? Are OSS developers actually motivated to do good by contributing software to the public, and by maintaining it in a group effort? Some developers argue that they can customize OSS, and if others find the customizations useful, then they have provided a public good. However, there could be another possible motivation for OSS. It might be a philosophical or instinctive animus toward existing commercial software developers. Bertrand Meyer recites with dismay the many negative statements by OSS advocates about commercial software development and developers (Meyer, 2000). Some see "Microsoft bashing" as a central theme of the OSS movement. Since most OSS competes directly with Microsoft products, some friction between OSS advocates and the largest commercial software corporation seems inevitable. But if OSS development is motivated primarily by its opposition to commercial software producers, then its ethical underpinnings are less benign than if OSS is motivated primarily by an altruistic desire to help computer users. Since the OSS movement is, by design, decentralized and evolving, it seems impossible to gauge with any precision the motivations of all its members. But the often-repeated disdain for commercial business practices seems more in tune with the hacker culture than with a culture of altruism. So, we would argue that for the most part, the altruism involved in the creation of a public good in the case of OSS is more of a by-product of developers who are interested in creating tools that are of use for themselves. Customization and expansion of Linux, for example, came from developers who wanted applications for their own use and then shared their code.

Nowhere can OSS be considered more of a public good than in the academic community. Computer Science departments are expected to be on the cutting edge of technology in their curricular offerings. The price of commercial software, even with educational discounts, often straps a department's budget. Academic institutions have strong financial motivations to adopt open source software. GNU compilers, for example, have largely replaced proprietary versions that cost the university software fees as well as licensing fees. Linux is appearing as the operating system of choice often replacing Solaris. As more and more applications run on Linux, universities will have less incentive to buy from vendors who offer a UNIX platform.

They will buy cheaper hardware and run Linux. One caveat to this scenario is the availability of staff that can support the Linux platform and the availability of documentation for OSS.

Using OSS at a university raises interesting ethical questions. One could argue that a university should expose its students to multiple perspectives so students develop skills to make judgments about the world around them. A university that exposes its students to a single point of view fails to help a student develop these skills. Thus, a university should provide a learning environment where future computer science professionals are exposed to both proprietary and open source software, and be given experiences to develop software evaluative skills. Part of this evaluation would come from using the software and evaluating the effectiveness from a user's perspective. However, an important part of the evaluative process, at least for computer science students, involves accessing the source code. Open source software makes looking at the source code easy. While it is true that some proprietary software vendors are willing to share their source code with universities for educational purposes, others are not. It is precisely when the software vendor is unwilling to share source code with university faculty, or makes it onerous on the university, that the university is faced with an ethical dilemma: How does it respond to proprietary software vendors that interfere with its duty to educate its students? OSS provides a partial solution to that problem. These questions are further complicated by the relationship that software companies often share with many universities. It is not uncommon for a software company to make generous contributions to a computer science department for access to the department's graduates, or to sponsor a faculty member's research. Faculty at these institutions must take care not to let the largess interfere with their ethical responsibilities to their students.

If a university is part of the open source community, we might expect them to be a contributor as well as a user of OSS. For many places of higher education, especially research institutions, this is not an issue as university faculty and students develop much open source software. But those institutions, whose faculty and students are not making such contributions, are faced with making the choice of contributing in some other way.

One approach might be a cash donation to an appropriate foundation that supports open source development for the value the software brings to the educational environment. This is not always easy to do. Anecdotally, a federal employee who wanted to do this reported two problems: 1) Accountants in her agency balked at making a contribution; they thought it might be illegal, and 2) She tried but could not get additional clarifying information from the OSS foundation. Contact people listed at the foundation did not return her emails and phone calls. She ended up not making a donation and feeling bad about it. It may be argued that merely exposing students to open source software may fulfill the university's ethical obligation to support OSS since doing so meets the OSS community's goal of building the OSS user community.

Finally, we explore an issue that is becoming part of the mission of many institutions of higher education: service learning. The choice between open source software and proprietary software plays into service learning as well. Consider a scenario where a software engineering class is to produce a piece of software for a local charity. The choice between open source alternatives and proprietary alternatives is not to be taken lightly. Seemingly, open source software makes good sense for both the students and the charitable organization. The cost is low and, presumably, the quality is sufficient. Yet there are long-term costs that are faced by the charity (as well as any business making such a choice). How expensive will it be to maintain the software? Is there enough open source expertise available to maintain it? And, finally, what documentation and user training can be expected if OSS is the software of choice. An extension of the service model might offer some on-going support to these charities.

Conclusion

OSS is no longer an academic curiosity. We have demonstrated that certain OSS products are making a significant niche for themselves in computing environments. Both Apache and Linux are increasing in popularity. The OSS model is distinct from commercial software development from several viewpoints: as a software engineering process, as an economic plan, and as a marketing strategy. In both models, however, developers have certain obligations and responsibilities to their users. In our analysis we have argued that open source software's successes may be due in part to the sheer number of people who get involved, and to the users who are engaged from the start of development.

We have found that the authors of OSS have complex motivations, some laudatory, and others less so. OSS has produced some successes, and the public has benefited from these. There are questions about reliability and professionalism, but evidence against the quality of OSS is not, as yet, convincing to us. It does not appear likely that OSS will displace commercial software in the foreseeable future, and we have not uncovered any ethical imperative that it should. Yet, OSS has distinct economic advantages for many especially in the academic arena. It can help bridge the digital divide and can involve growing numbers of people in computing, both as developers and users. Developers of OSS strive to be the best they can to contribute to the sustainable whole and thus secure their reputation ethically among their peers.

OSS and commercial software can coexist, each giving the public the goods it desires. Both advocates and critics of OSS have an ethical obligation to respect each other and to avoid inaccurate and mean-spirited accusations. All software developers have ethical obligations for quality and openness (Software Engineering Code of Ethics, 1999). OSS is a novel development of traditional ideas of sharing academic intellectual property, but OSS exists in a world dominated by commercial enterprise. As such, OSS challenges the status quo in a way that can be a constructive check on excesses of traditional free enterprise systems. In a time when many for-profit corporations have disappointed the public with their lack of ethical behavior, OSS has the potential to be a positive ethical force in the world of computing. Hackers who get involved in OSS development can contribute to the sustainable whole and, thus ethically secure their reputation among their peers. This is a way to publicly excel at hacking without illegal and unethical harm to others.

References

About HP: History and Facts. www.hp.com/hpinfo/abouthp/histnfacts/. Accessed 2003.

Barr, J. Live and let license: A primer on software licensing in the Open Source context www.itworld.com/AppDev/350/LWD010523vcontrol4, May 23, 2001.

Floridi, L. and Sanders, J. W., Internet Ethics: the Constructionist Values of Homo Poieticus. In *The Impact of the Internet on Our Moral Lives,* Cavalier, R., ed. New York: SUNY, 2003.

Johnson, D.J. and Nissenbaum H., eds., *Computers, Ethics and Social Values.* New Jersey: Prentice Hall, 1995.

Kollock, P. The Economies of Online Cooperation: Gifts and Public Goods in Cyberspace. In *Communities in Cyberspace,* Smith, M. and Kollock, P., eds. London: Routledge, 1999.

Meyer, B. The Ethics of Free Software. *Software Developers Online.* www.sdmagazine.com/documents/s=746/sdm0003d/0003d.htm, login required, March 2000.

Miller, R. 90% Windows, 5% Mac, 5% Linux? Not true! *The Register.* www.theregister.co.uk/content/4/19661.html, June 13, 2001.

Moffitt, N. Nick Moffitt's $7 History of Unix. www.crackmonkey.org/unix.html. Accessed 2002.

Netcraft Web Server Survey. www.netcraft.com/survey, 2002.

Nissenbaum, H. Computing and Accountability. *Communications of the ACM,* 37, 1, January 1994.

Open Source Initiative (OSI). www.opensource.org, 2002.

Perens, B. Debian Social Contract. www.debian.org/social_contract.html, 2002.

Raymond, E. S. Homesteading the Noosphere. tuxedo.org/~esr/writings/cathedral-bazaar, 2000.

Raymond, E. S. "The Cathedral and the Bazaar," in *Readings in Cyberethics,* eds. Spinello and Tavani, Sudbury, MA: Jones and Bartlett, 2001.

Ritchie, D. M. The Evolution of the Unix Time-sharing System. cm.bell-labs.com/cm/cs/who/dmr/hist.html, 1996.

Schach, Stephen, *Object Oriented and Classical Software Engineering* (fifth ed). New York: McGraw Hill, 2002. p. 137.

Software Engineering Code of Ethics and Professional Practice(5.2). seeri.etsu.edu/TheSECode.htm, 1999.

Stallman, R. M. The GNU Operating System and the Free Software Movement. In Open Sources: Voices from the Open Source Revolution, Stone, M., Ockman, and DiBona, C., eds. www.oreilly.com/catalog/opensources/book/stallman.html, 1999.

The GNU Project and the Free Software Foundation (FSF). www.gnu.org and www.fsf.org, 2002.

The History of IBM. www-1.ibm.com/ibm/history/index.html Accessed Spring 2003.

WebCab Solutions - Linux Reliability. www.webcab.co.uk/solutions/linux/reliability.html. Accessed 2003.

Wolf, M. J., K. Bowyer, D. Gotterbarn, and K. Miller. Open Source Software: Intellectual Challenges to the Status Quo, panel presentation at 2002 SIGCSE Technical Symposium, *SIGCSE Bulletin,* 34(1), March 2002, pp. 317–318 and www.cstc.org/data/resources/254/wholething.pdf.

Appendix A

Open Source Definition

Open source doesn't just mean access to the source code. The distribution terms of open-source software must comply with the following criteria:

1. **Free Redistribution**

   The license shall not restrict any party from selling or giving away the software as a component of an aggregate software distribution containing programs from several different sources. The license shall not require a royalty or other fee for such sale.

2. **Source Code**

   The program must include source code, and must allow distribution in source code as well as compiled form. Where some form of a product is not distributed with source code, there must be a well-publicized means of obtaining the source code for no more than a reasonable reproduction cost—preferably, downloading via the Internet without charge. The source code must be the preferred form in which a developer would modify the program. Deliberately obfuscated source code is not allowed. Intermediate forms such as the output of a preprocessor or translator are not allowed.

3. **Derived Works**

   The license must allow modifications and derived works, and must allow them to be distributed under the same terms as the license of the original software.

4. **Integrity of the Author's Source Code**

   The license may restrict source-code from being distributed in modified form only if the license allows the distribution of "patch files" with the source code for the purpose of modifying the program at build time. The license must explicitly permit distribution of software built from modified source code. The license may require derived works to carry a different name or version number from the original software.

5. **No Discrimination Against Persons or Groups**

   The license must not discriminate against any person or group of persons.

6. **No Discrimination Against Fields of Endeavor**

   The license must not restrict anyone from making use of the program in a specific field of endeavor. For example, it may not restrict the program from being used in a business, or from being used for genetic research.

7. **Distribution of License**

   The rights attached to the program must apply to all to whom the program is redistributed without the need for execution of an additional license by those parties.

8. **License Must Not Be Specific to a Product**

   The rights attached to the program must not depend on the program's being part of a particular software distribution. If the program is extracted from that distribution and used or distributed within the terms of the program's license, all parties to whom the program is redistributed should have the same rights as those that are granted in conjunction with the original software distribution.

9. The License Must Not Restrict Other Software

The license must not place restrictions on other software that is distributed along with the licensed software. For example, the license must not insist that all other programs distributed on the same medium must be open-source software.

http://www.opensource.org/docs/definition_plain.html

Appendix B

"To copyleft a program, we first state that it is copyrighted; then we add distribution terms, which are a legal instrument that gives everyone the rights to use, modify, and redistribute the program's code or any program derived from it but only if the distribution terms are unchanged. Thus, the code and the freedoms become legally inseparable." (www.FSF.org)

The Cathedral and the Bazaar

Eric Raymond

The Cathedral and the Bazaar

Linux is subversive. Who would have thought even five years ago (1991) that a world-class operating system could coalesce as if by magic out of part-time hacking by several thousand developers scattered all over the planet, connected only by the tenuous strands of the Internet?

Certainly not I. By the time Linux swam onto my radar screen in early 1993, I had already been involved in Unix and open-source development for ten years. I was one of the first GNU contributors in the mid-1980s. I had released a good deal of open-source software onto the net, developing or co-developing several programs (nethack, Emacs's VC and GUD modes, xlife, and others) that are still in wide use today. I thought I knew how it was done.

Linux overturned much of what I thought I knew. I had been preaching the Unix gospel of small tools, rapid prototyping, and evolutionary programming for years. But I also believed there was a certain critical complexity above which a more centralized, a priori approach was required. I believed that the most important software (operating systems and really large tools like the Emacs programming editor) needed to be built like cathedrals, carefully crafted by individual wizards or small bands of mages working in splendid isolation, with no beta to be released before its time.

Linus Torvalds's style of development—release early and often, delegate everything you can, be open to the point of promiscuity—came as a surprise. No quiet, reverent cathedral-building here—rather, the Linux community seemed to resemble a great babbling bazaar of differing agendas and approaches (aptly symbolized by the Linux archive sites, who'd take submissions from anyone) out of which a coherent and stable system could seemingly emerge only by a succession of miracles.

The fact that this bazaar style seemed to work, and work well, came as a distinct shock. As I learned my way around, I worked hard not just at individual projects, but also at trying to understand why the Linux world not only didn't fly apart in confusion but seemed to go from strength to strength at a speed barely imaginable to cathedral-builders.

By mid-1996 I thought I was beginning to understand. Chance handed me a perfect way to test my theory, in the form of an open-source project that I could consciously try to run in the bazaar style. So I did—and it was a significant success.

This is the story of that project. I'll use it to propose some aphorisms about effective open-source development. Not all of these are things I first learned in the Linux world, but we'll see how the Linux world gives them particular point. If I'm correct, they'll help you understand exactly what it is that makes the Linux community such a fountain of good software—and, perhaps, they will help you become more productive yourself.

The Mail Must Get Through

Since 1993 I'd been running the technical side of a small free-access Internet service provider called Chester County InterLink (CCIL) in West Chester, Pennsylvania. I co-founded CCIL and wrote our unique multiuser bulletin-board software—you can check it out by telnetting to locke.ccil.org. Today it supports almost three thousand users on thirty lines. The job allowed me 24-hour-a-day access to the net through CCIL's 56K line—in fact, the job practically demanded it!

I had gotten quite used to instant Internet email. I found having to periodically telnet over to locke to check my mail annoying. What I wanted was for my mail to be delivered on snark (my home system) so that I would be notified when it arrived and could handle it using all my local tools.

The Internet's native mail forwarding protocol, SMTP (Simple Mail Transfer Protocol), wouldn't suit, because it works best when machines are connected full-time, while my personal machine isn't always on the net, and doesn't have a static IP address. What I needed was a program that would reach out over my intermittent dialup connection and pull across my mail to be delivered locally. I knew such things existed, and that most of them used a simple application protocol called POP (Post Office Protocol). POP is now widely supported by most common mail clients, but at the time, it wasn't built-in to the mail reader I was using.

I needed a POP3 client. So I went out on the net and found one. Actually, I found three or four. I used one of them for a while, but it was missing what seemed an obvious feature, the ability to hack the addresses on fetched mail so replies would work properly.

The problem was this: Suppose someone named 'joe' on locke sent me mail. If I fetched the mail to snark and then tried to reply to it, my mailer would cheerfully try to ship it to a nonexistent 'joe' on snark. Hand-editing reply addresses to tack on '@ccil.org' quickly got to be a serious pain.

This was clearly something the computer ought to be doing for me. But none of the existing POP clients knew how! And this brings us to the first lesson:

1. *Every good work of software starts by scratching a developer's personal itch.*

Perhaps this should have been obvious (it's long been proverbial that "necessity is the mother of invention") but too often software developers spend their days grinding away for pay at programs they neither need nor love. But not in the Linux world—which may explain why the average quality of software originated in the Linux community is so high.

So, did I immediately launch into a furious whirl of coding up a brand-new POP3 client to compete with the existing ones? Not on your life! I looked carefully at the POP utilities I had in hand, asking myself, "Which one is closest to what I want?" Because

2. *Good programmers know what to write. Great ones know what to rewrite (and reuse).*

While I don't claim to be a great programmer, I try to imitate one. An important trait of the great ones is constructive laziness. They know that you get an A not for effort but for results, and that it's almost always easier to start from a good partial solution than from nothing at all.

Linus Torvalds, for example, didn't actually try to write Linux from scratch. Instead, he started by reusing code and ideas from Minix, a tiny Unix-like operating system for PC clones. Eventually all the Minix code went away or was completely rewritten—but while it was there, it provided scaffolding for the infant that would eventually become Linux.

In the same spirit, I went looking for an existing POP utility that was reasonably well coded to use as a development base.

The source-sharing tradition of the Unix world has always been friendly to code reuse (this is why the GNU project chose Unix as a base OS, in spite of serious reservations about the OS itself). The Linux world has taken this tradition nearly to its technological limit; it has terabytes of open sources generally available. So spending time looking for some else's almost-good-enough is more likely to give you good results in the Linux world than anywhere else.

And it did for me. With those I'd found earlier, my second search made up a total of nine candidates—fetchpop, PopTart, get-mail, gwpop, pimp, pop-perl, popc, pop-mail, and upop. The one I first settled on was 'fetchpop' by Seung-Hong Oh. I put my header-rewrite feature in it, and made various other improvements, which the author accepted into his 1.9 release.

A few weeks later, though, I stumbled across the code for 'popclient' by Carl Harris, and found I had a problem. Though fetchpop had some good original ideas in it (such as its background-daemon mode), it could only handle POP3 and was rather amateurishly coded (Seung-Hong was at that time a bright but inexperienced programmer, and both traits showed). Carl's code was better, quite professional and solid, but his program lacked several important and rather tricky-to-implement fetchpop features (including those I'd coded myself).

Stay or switch? If I switched, I'd be throwing away the coding I'd already done in exchange for a better development base. A practical motive to switch was the presence of multiple-protocol support. POP3 is the most commonly used of the post-office server protocols, but not the only one. Fetchpop and the other competition didn't do POP2, RPOP, or APOP, and I was already having vague thoughts of perhaps adding IMAP (Internet Message Access Protocol, the most recently designed and most powerful post-office protocol) just for fun.

But I had a more theoretical reason to think switching might be as good an idea as well, something I learned long before Linux.

3. *"Plan to throw one away; you will, anyhow."* (Fred Brooks, "The Mythical Man-Month," Chapter 11)

Or, to put it another way, you often don't really understand the problem until after the first time you implement a solution. The second time, maybe you know enough to do it right. So if you want to get it right, be ready to start over at least once [JB].

Well (I told myself) the changes to fetchpop had been my first try. So I switched.

After I sent my first set of popclient patches to Carl Harris on 25 June 1996, I found out that he had basically lost interest in popclient some time before. The code was a bit dusty, with minor bugs hanging out. I had many changes to make, and we quickly agreed that the logical thing for me to do was take over the program.

Without my actually noticing, the project had escalated. No longer was I just contemplating minor patches to an existing POP client. I took on maintaining an entire one, and there were ideas bubbling in my head that I knew would probably lead to major changes.

In a software culture that encourages code-sharing, this is a natural way for a project to evolve. I was acting out this principle:

4. *If you have the right attitude, interesting problems will find you.*

But Carl Harris's attitude was even more important. He understood that

5. *When you lose interest in a program, your last duty to it is to hand it off to a competent successor.*

Without ever having to discuss it, Carl and I knew we had a common goal of having the best solution out there. The only question for either of us was whether I could establish that I was a safe pair of hands. Once I did that, he acted with grace and dispatch. I hope I will do as well when it comes my turn.

The Importance of Having Users

And so I inherited popclient. Just as importantly, I inherited popclient's user base. Users are wonderful things to have, and not just because they demonstrate that you're serving a need, that you've done something right. Properly cultivated, they can become co-developers.

Another strength of the Unix tradition, one that Linux pushes to a happy extreme, is that a lot of users are hackers too. Because source code is available, they can be effective hackers. This can be tremendously useful for shortening debugging time. Given a bit of encouragement, your users will diagnose problems, suggest fixes, and help improve the code far more quickly than you could unaided.

6. *Treating your users as co-developers is your least-hassle route to rapid code improvement and effective debugging.*

The power of this effect is easy to underestimate. In fact, pretty well all of us in the open-source world drastically underestimated how well it would scale up with number of users and against system complexity, until Linus Torvalds showed us differently.

In fact, I think Linus's cleverest and most consequential hack was not the construction of the Linux kernel itself, but rather his invention of the Linux development model. When I expressed this opinion in his presence once, he smiled and quietly repeated something he has often said: "I'm basically a very lazy person who likes to get credit for things other people actually do." Lazy like a fox. Or, as Robert Heinlein famously wrote of one of his characters, too lazy to fail.

In retrospect, one precedent for the methods and success of Linux can be seen in the development of the GNU Emacs Lisp library and Lisp code archives. In contrast to the cathedral-building style of the Emacs C core and most other GNU tools, the evolution of the Lisp code pool was fluid and very user-driven. Ideas and prototype modes were often rewritten three or four times before reaching a stable final form. And loosely-coupled collaborations enabled by the Internet, a la Linux, were frequent.

Indeed, my own most successful single hack previous to fetchmail was probably Emacs VC (version control) mode, a Linux-like collaboration by email with three other people, only one of whom (Richard Stallman, the author of Emacs and founder of the Free Software Foundation) I have met to this day. It was a front-end for SCCS, RCS, and later CVS from within Emacs that offered "one-touch" version control operations. It evolved from a tiny, crude sccs.el mode somebody else had written. And the development of VC succeeded because, unlike Emacs itself, Emacs Lisp code could go through release/test/improve generations very quickly.

Release Early, Release Often

Early and frequent releases are a critical part of the Linux development model. Most developers (including me) used to believe this was bad policy for larger than trivial projects, because early versions are almost by definition buggy versions and you don't want to wear out the patience of your users.

This belief reinforced the general commitment to a cathedral-building style of development. If the overriding objective was for users to see as few bugs as possible, why then you'd only release a version every six months (or less often), and work like a dog on debugging between releases. The Emacs C core was developed this way. The Lisp library, in effect, was not, because there were active Lisp archives outside the FSF's control where you could go to find new and development code versions independently of Emacs's release cycle [QR].

The most important of these, the Ohio State elisp archive, anticipated the spirit and many of the features of today's big Linux archives. But few of us really thought very hard about what we were doing, or about what the very existence of that archive suggested about problems in the FSF's cathedral-building development model. I made one serious attempt around 1992 to get a lot of the Ohio code formally merged into the official Emacs Lisp library. I ran into political trouble and was largely unsuccessful.

But by a year later, as Linux became widely visible, it was clear that something different and much healthier was going on there. Linus's open development policy was the very opposite of cathedral-building. Linux's Internet archives were burgeoning, multiple distributions were being floated. And all of this was driven by an unheard-of frequency of core system releases. Linus was treating his users as co-developers in the most effective possible way:

7. *Release early. Release often. And listen to your customers.*

Linus's innovation wasn't so much in doing quick-turnaround releases incorporating lots of user feedback (something like this had been Unix-world tradition for a long time), but in scaling it up to a level of intensity that matched the complexity of what he was developing. In those early times (around 1991), it wasn't unknown for him to release a new kernel more than once a day! Because he cultivated his base of co-developers and leveraged the Internet for collaboration harder than anyone else, this worked.

But how did it work? And was it something I could duplicate, or did it rely on some unique genius of Linus Torvalds? I didn't think so. Granted, Linus is a damn fine hacker. How many of us could engineer an entire production-quality operating system kernel from scratch? But Linux didn't represent any awesome conceptual leap forward. Linus is not (or at least, not yet) an innovative genius of design in the way that, say, Richard Stallman or James Gosling (of NeWS and Java) are. Rather, Linus seems to me to be a genius of engineering and implementation, with a sixth sense for avoiding bugs and development dead-ends and a true knack for finding the minimum-effort path from point A to point B. Indeed, the whole design of Linux breathes this quality and mirrors Linus's essentially conservative and simplifying design approach.

So, if rapid releases and leveraging the Internet medium to the hilt were not accidents but integral parts of Linus's engineering-genius insight into the minimum-effort path, what was he maximizing? What was he cranking out of the machinery?

Put that way, the question answers itself. Linus was keeping his hacker/users constantly stimulated and rewarded—stimulated by the prospect of having an ego-satisfying piece of the action, rewarded by the sight of constant (even daily) improvement in their work.

Linus was directly aiming to maximize the number of person-hours thrown at debugging and development, even at the possible cost of instability in the code and user-base burnout if any serious bug proved intractable. Linus was behaving as though he believed something like this:

8. *Given a large enough beta-tester and co-developer base, almost every problem will be characterized quickly and the fix obvious to someone.*

Or, less formally, "Given enough eyeballs, all bugs are shallow." I dub this: "Linus's Law."

My original formulation was that every problem "will be transparent to somebody." Linus demurred that the person who understands and fixes the problem is not necessarily or even usually the person who first characterizes it. "Somebody finds the problem," he says, "and somebody else understands it. And I'll go on record as saying that finding it is the bigger challenge." But the point is that both things tend to happen rapidly.

Here, I think, is the core difference underlying the cathedral-builder and bazaar styles. In the cathedral-builder view of programming, bugs and development problems are tricky, insidious, deep phenomena. It takes months of scrutiny by a dedicated few to develop confidence that you've winkled them all out. Thus the long release intervals, and the inevitable disappointment when long-awaited releases are not perfect.

In the bazaar view, on the other hand, you assume that bugs are generally shallow phenomena—or, at least, that they turn shallow pretty quickly when exposed to a thousand eager co-developers pounding on every single new release. Accordingly you release often in order to get more corrections, and as a beneficial side effect you have less to lose if an occasional botch gets out the door.

And that's it. That's enough. If "Linus's Law" is false, then any system as complex as the Linux kernel, being hacked over by as many hands as the Linux kernel, should at some point have collapsed under the weight of unforeseen bad interactions and undiscovered "deep" bugs. If it's true, on the other hand, it is sufficient to explain Linux's relative lack of bugginess and its continuous uptimes spanning months or even years.

Maybe it shouldn't have been such a surprise, at that. Sociologists years ago discovered that the averaged opinion of a mass of equally expert (or equally ignorant) observers is quite a bit more reliable a predictor than that of a single randomly-chosen one of the observers. They called this the "Delphi effect." It appears that what Linus has shown is that this applies even to debugging an operating system—that the Delphi effect can tame development complexity even at the complexity level of an OS kernel.

One special feature of the Linux situation that clearly helps along the Delphi effect is the fact that the contributors for any given project are self-selected. An early respondent pointed out that contributions are received not from a random sample, but from people who are interested enough to use the software, learn about how it works, attempt to find solutions to problems they encounter, and actually produce an apparently reasonable fix. Anyone who passes all these filters is highly likely to have something useful to contribute.

I am indebted to my friend Jeff Dutky for pointing out that Linus's Law can be rephrased as "Debugging is parallelizable." Jeff observes that although debugging requires debuggers to communicate with some coordinating developer, it doesn't require significant coordination between debuggers. Thus it doesn't fall prey to the same quadratic complexity and management costs that make adding developers problematic.

In practice, the theoretical loss of efficiency due to duplication of work by debuggers almost never seems to be an issue in the Linux world. One effect of a "release early and often policy" is to minimize such duplication by propagating fed-back fixes quickly [JH].

Brooks (the author of "The Mythical Man-Month") even made an off-hand observation related to Jeff's: "The total cost of maintaining a widely used program is typically 40 percent or more of the cost of developing it. Surprisingly this cost is strongly affected by the number of users. More users find more bugs."

More users find more bugs because adding more users adds more different ways of stressing the program. This effect is amplified when the users are co-developers. Each one approaches the task of bug characterization with a slightly different perceptual set and analytical toolkit, a different angle on the problem. The "Delphi effect" seems to work precisely because of this variation. In the specific context of debugging, the variation also tends to reduce duplication of effort.

So adding more beta-testers may not reduce the complexity of the current "deepest" bug from the developer's point of view, but it increases the probability that someone's toolkit will be matched to the problem in such a way that the bug is shallow to that person.

Linus coppers his bets, too. In case there are serious bugs, Linux kernel versions are numbered in such a way that potential users can make a choice either to run the last version designated "stable" or to ride the cutting edge and risk bugs in order to get new features. This tactic is not yet formally imitated by most Linux hackers, but perhaps it should be; the fact that either choice is available makes both more attractive. [HBS]

When Is a Rose Not a Rose?

Having studied Linus's behavior and formed a theory about why it was successful, I made a conscious decision to test this theory on my new (admittedly much less complex and ambitious) project.

But the first thing I did was reorganize and simplify popclient a lot. Carl Harris's implementation was very sound, but exhibited a kind of unnecessary complexity common to many C programmers. He treated the code as central and the data structures as support for the code. As a result, the code was beautiful but the data structure design ad-hoc and rather ugly (at least by the high standards of this old LISP hacker).

I had another purpose for rewriting besides improving the code and the data structure design, however. That was to evolve it into something I understood completely. It's no fun to be responsible for fixing bugs in a program you don't understand.

For the first month or so, then, I was simply following out the implications of Carl's basic design. The first serious change I made was to add IMAP support. I did this by reorganizing the protocol machines into a generic driver and three method tables (for POP2, POP3, and IMAP). This and the previous changes illustrate a general principle that's good for programmers to keep in mind, especially in languages like C that don't naturally do dynamic typing:

9. *Smart data structures and dumb code work a lot better than the other way around.*

Brooks, Chapter 9: "Show me your [code] and conceal your [data structures], and I shall continue to be mystified. Show me your [data structures], and I won't usually need your [code]; it'll be obvious." Actually, he said "flowcharts" and "tables." But allowing for thirty years of terminological/cultural shift, it's almost the same point.

At this point (early September 1996, about six weeks from zero) I started thinking that a name change might be in order—after all, it wasn't just a POP client any more. But I hesitated, because there was as yet nothing genuinely new in the design. My version of popclient had yet to develop an identity of its own.

That changed, radically, when fetchmail learned how to forward fetched mail to the SMTP port. I'll get to that in a moment. But first: I said above that I'd decided to use this project to test my theory about what Linus Torvalds had done right. How (you may well ask) did I do that? In these ways:

- I released early and often (almost never less often than every ten days; during periods of intense development, once a day).
- I grew my beta list by adding to it everyone who contacted me about fetchmail.
- I sent chatty announcements to the beta list whenever I released, encouraging people to participate.
- And I listened to my beta testers, polling them about design decisions and stroking them whenever they sent in patches and feedback.

The payoff from these simple measures was immediate. From the beginning of the project, I got bug reports of a quality most developers would kill for, often with good fixes attached. I got thoughtful criticism, I got fan mail, I got intelligent feature suggestions. Which leads to:

10. *If you treat your beta-testers as if they're your most valuable resource, they will respond by becoming your most valuable resource.*

One interesting measure of fetchmail's success is the sheer size of the project beta list, fetchmail-friends. At the time of last revision (August 2000) it has 249 members and is adding two or three a week.

Actually, as I revise in late May 1997, the list is beginning to lose members from its high of close to 300 for an interesting reason. Several people have asked me to unsubscribe them because fetchmail is working so well for them that they no longer need to see the list traffic! Perhaps this is part of the normal life-cycle of a mature bazaar-style project.

Popclient becomes Fetchmail

The real turning point in the project was when Harry Hochheiser sent me his scratch code for forwarding mail to the client machine's SMTP port. I realized almost immediately that a reliable implementation of this feature would make all the other mail delivery modes next to obsolete.

For many weeks I had been tweaking fetchmail rather incrementally while feeling like the interface design was serviceable but grubby—inelegant and with too many exiguous options hanging out all over. The options to dump fetched mail to a mailbox file or standard output particularly bothered me, but I couldn't figure out why. (If you don't care about the technicalia of Internet mail, the next two paragraphs can be safely skipped.)

What I saw when I thought about SMTP forwarding was that popclient had been trying to do too many things. It had been designed to be both a mail transport agent (MTA) and a local delivery agent (MDA). With SMTP forwarding, it could get out of the MDA business and be a pure MTA, handing off mail to other programs for local delivery just as sendmail does.

Why mess with all the complexity of configuring a mail delivery agent or setting up lock-and-append on a mailbox when port 25 is almost guaranteed to be there on any platform with TCP/IP support in the first place? Especially when this means retrieved mail is guaranteed to look like normal sender-initiated SMTP mail, which is really what we want anyway.

(Back to a higher level...)

Even if you didn't follow the preceding technical jargon, there are several important lessons here. First, this SMTP-forwarding concept was the biggest single payoff I got from consciously trying to emulate Linus's methods. A user gave me this terrific idea—all I had to do was understand the implications.

> **11.** *The next best thing to having good ideas is recognizing good ideas from your users. Sometimes the latter is better.*

Interestingly enough, you will quickly find that if you are completely and self-deprecatingly truthful about how much you owe other people, the world at large will treat you like you did every bit of the invention yourself and are just being becomingly modest about your innate genius. We can all see how well this worked for Linus!

(When I gave my talk at the Perl conference in August 1997, hacker extraordinaire Larry Wall was in the front row. As I got to the last line above he called out, religious-revival style, "Tell it, tell it, brother!" The whole audience laughed, because they knew this had worked for the inventor of Perl, too.)

After a very few weeks of running the project in the same spirit, I began to get similar praise not just from my users but from other people to whom the word leaked out. I stashed away some of that email; I'll look at it again sometime if I ever start wondering whether my life has been worthwhile.

But there are two more fundamental, non-political lessons here that are general to all kinds of design.

12. *Often, the most striking and innovative solutions come from realizing that your concept of the problem was wrong.*

I had been trying to solve the wrong problem by continuing to develop popclient as a combined MTA/MDA with all kinds of funky local delivery modes. Fetchmail's design needed to be rethought from the ground up as a pure MTA, a part of the normal SMTP-speaking Internet mail path.

When you hit a wall in development—when you find yourself hard put to think past the next patch—it's often time to ask not whether you've got the right answer, but whether you're asking the right question. Perhaps the problem needs to be reframed.

Well, I had reframed my problem. Clearly, the right thing to do was (1) hack SMTP forwarding support into the generic driver, (2) make it the default mode, and (3) eventually throw out all the other delivery modes, especially the deliver-to-file and deliver-to-standard-output options.

I hesitated over Step 3 for some time, fearing to upset long-time popclient users dependent on the alternate delivery mechanisms. In theory, they could immediately switch to .forward files or their non-sendmail equivalents to get the same effects. In practice the transition might have been messy.

But when I did it, the benefits proved huge. The cruftiest parts of the driver code vanished. Configuration got radically simpler—no more groveling around for the system MDA and user's mailbox, no more worries about whether the underlying OS supports file locking.

Also, the only way to lose mail vanished. If you specified delivery to a file and the disk got full, your mail got lost. This can't happen with SMTP forwarding because your SMTP listener won't return OK unless the message can be delivered or at least spooled for later delivery.

Also, performance improved (though not so you'd notice it in a single run). Another not insignificant benefit of this change was that the manual page got a lot simpler.

Later, I had to bring delivery via a user-specified local MDA back in order to allow handling of some obscure situations involving dynamic SLIP. But I found a much simpler way to do it.

The moral? Don't hesitate to throw away superannuated features when you can do it without loss of effectiveness. Antoine de Saint-Exupéry (who was an aviator and aircraft designer when he wasn't being the author of classic children's books) said:

13. *"Perfection (in design) is achieved not when there is nothing more to add, but rather when there is nothing more to take away."*

When your code is getting both better and simpler, that is when you know it's right. And in the process, the fetchmail design acquired an identity of its own, different from the ancestral popclient.

It was time for the name change. The new design looked much more like a dual of sendmail than the old popclient had; both are MTAs, but where sendmail pushes then delivers, the new popclient pulls then delivers. So, two months off the blocks, I renamed it fetchmail.

There is a more general lesson in this story about how SMTP delivery came to fetchmail. It is not only debugging that is parallelizable; development and (to a perhaps surprising extent) exploration of design space is, too. When your development mode is rapidly iterative, development and enhancement may become special cases of debugging—fixing "bugs of omission" in the original capabilities or concept of the software.

Even at a higher level of design, it can be very valuable to have the thinking of lots of co-developers random-walking through the design space near your product. Consider the way a puddle of water finds a drain, or better yet how ants find food: exploration essentially by diffusion, followed by exploitation mediated by a scalable communication mechanism. This works very well; as with Harry Hochheiser and me, one of your outriders may well find a huge win nearby that you were just a little too close-focused to see.

Fetchmail Grows Up

There I was with a neat and innovative design, code that I knew worked well because I used it every day, and a burgeoning beta list. It gradually dawned on me that I was no longer engaged in a trivial personal hack that might happen to be useful to few other people. I had my hands on a program every hacker with a Unix box and a SLIP/PPP mail connection really needs.

With the SMTP forwarding feature, it pulled far enough in front of the competition to potentially become a "category killer," one of those classic programs that fills its niche so competently that the alternatives are not just discarded but almost forgotten.

I think you can't really aim or plan for a result like this. You have to get pulled into it by design ideas so powerful that afterward the results just seem inevitable, natural, even foreordained. The only way to try for ideas like that is by having lots of ideas—or by having the engineering judgment to take other peoples' good ideas beyond where the originators thought they could go.

Andy Tanenbaum had the original idea to build a simple native Unix for IBM PCs, for use as a teaching tool (he called it Minix). Linus Torvalds pushed the Minix concept further than Andrew probably thought it could go—and it grew into something wonderful. In the same way (though on a smaller scale), I took some ideas by Carl Harris and Harry Hochheiser and pushed them hard. Neither of us was "original" in the romantic way people think is genius. But then, most science and engineering and software development isn't done by original genius, hacker mythology to the contrary.

The results were pretty heady stuff all the same—in fact, just the kind of success every hacker lives for! And they meant I would have to set my standards even higher. To make fetchmail as good as I now saw it could be, I'd have to write not just for my own needs, but also include and support features necessary to others outside my orbit. And do that while keeping the program simple and robust.

The first and overwhelmingly most important feature I wrote after realizing this was multidrop support—the ability to fetch mail from mailboxes that had accumulated all mail for a group of users, and then route each piece of mail to its individual recipients.

I decided to add the multidrop support partly because some users were clamoring for it, but mostly because I thought it would shake bugs out of the single-drop code by forcing me to deal with addressing in full generality. And so it proved. Getting RFC 82sed dress parsing right took me a remarkably long time, not because any individual piece of it is hard but because it involved a pile of interdependent and fussy details.

But multidrop addressing turned out to be an excellent design decision as well. Here's how I knew:

14. *Any tool should be useful in the expected way, but a truly great tool lends itself to uses you never expected.*

The unexpected use for multi-drop fetchmail is to run mailing lists with the list kept, and alias expansion done, on the client side of the Internet connection. This means someone running a personal machine through an ISP account can manage a mailing list without continuing access to the ISP's alias files.

Another important change demanded by my beta testers was support for 8-bit MIME (Multipurpose Internet Mail Extensions) operation. This was pretty easy to do, because I had been careful to keep the code 8-bit clean. Not because I anticipated the demand for this feature, but rather in obedience to another rule:

15. *When writing gateway software of any kind, take pains to disturb the data stream as little as possible—and *never* throw away information unless the recipient forces you to!*

Had I not obeyed this rule, 8-bit MIME support would have been difficult and buggy. As it was, all I had to do was read the MIME standard (RFC 1652) and add a trivial bit of header-generation logic.

Some European users bugged me into adding an option to limit the number of messages retrieved per session (so they can control costs from their expensive phone networks). I resisted this for a long time, and I'm still not entirely happy about it. But if you're writing for the world, you have to listen to your customers—this doesn't change just because they're not paying you in money.

A Few More Lessons from Fetchmail

Before we go back to general software-engineering issues, there are a couple more specific lessons from the fetchmail experience to ponder. Nontechnical readers can safely skip this section.

The rc (control) file syntax includes optional "noise" keywords that are entirely ignored by the parser. The English-like syntax they allow is considerably more readable than the traditional terse keyword-value pairs you get when you strip them all out.

These started out as a late-night experiment when I noticed how much the rc file declarations were beginning to resemble an imperative minilanguage. (This is also why I changed the original popclient "server" keyword to "poll").

It seemed to me that trying to make that imperative minilanguage more like English might make it easier to use. Now, although I'm a convinced partisan of the "make it a language" school of design as exemplified by Emacs and HTML and many database engines, I am not normally a big fan of "English-like" syntaxes.

Traditionally programmers have tended to favor control syntaxes that are very precise and compact and have no redundancy at all. This is a cultural legacy from when computing resources were expensive, so parsing stages had to be as cheap and simple as possible. English, with about 50% redundancy, looked like a very inappropriate model then.

This is not my reason for normally avoiding English-like syntaxes; I mention it here only to demolish it. With cheap cycles and core, terseness should not be an end in itself. Nowadays it's more important for a language to be convenient for humans than to be cheap for the computer.

There remain, however, good reasons to be wary. One is the complexity cost of the parsing stage—you don't want to raise that to the point where it's a significant source of bugs and user confusion in itself. Another is that trying to make a language syntax English-like often demands that the "English" it speaks be bent seriously out of shape, so much so that the superficial resemblance to natural language is as confusing as a traditional syntax would have been. (You see this bad effect in a lot of so-called "fourth generation" and commercial database-query languages.)

The fetchmail control syntax seems to avoid these problems because the language domain is extremely restricted. It's nowhere near a general-purpose language; the things it says simply are not very complicated, so there's little potential for confusion in moving mentally between a tiny subset of English and the actual control language. I think there may be a wider lesson here:

16. *When your language is nowhere near Turing-complete, syntactic sugar can be your friend.*

Another lesson is about security by obscurity. Some fetchmail users asked me to change the software to store passwords encrypted in the rc file, so snoopers wouldn't be able to casually see them.

I didn't do it, because this doesn't actually add protection. Anyone who's acquired permissions to read your rc file will be able to run fetchmail as you anyway—and if it's your password they're after, they'd be able to rip the necessary decoder out of the fetchmail code itself to get it.

All that fetchmailrc password encryption would have done is give a false sense of security to people who don't think very hard. The general rule here is:

17. *A security system is only as secure as its secret. Beware of pseudo-secrets.*

Necessary Preconditions for the Bazaar Style

Early reviewers and test audiences for this paper consistently raised questions about the preconditions for successful bazaar-style development, including both the qualifications of the project leader and the state of code at the time one goes public and starts to try to build a co-developer community.

It's fairly clear that one cannot code from the ground up in bazaar style [IN]. One can test, debug and improve in bazaar style, but it would be very hard to originate a project in bazaar mode. Linus didn't try it. I didn't either. Your nascent developer community needs to have something runnable and testable to play with.

When you start community-building, what you need to be able to present is a plausible promise. Your program doesn't have to work particularly well. It can be crude, buggy, incomplete, and poorly documented. What it must not fail to do is (a) run, and (b) convince potential co-developers that it can be evolved into something really neat in the foreseeable future.

Linux and fetchmail both went public with strong, attractive basic designs. Many people thinking about the bazaar model as I have presented it have correctly considered this critical, then jumped from it to the conclusion that a high degree of design intuition and cleverness in the project leader is indispensable.

But Linus got his design from Unix. I got mine initially from the ancestral popclient (though it would later change a great deal, much more proportionately speaking than has Linux). So does the leader/coordinator for a bazaar-style effort really have to have exceptional design talent, or can he get by on leveraging the design talent of others?

I think it is not critical that the coordinator be able to originate designs of exceptional brilliance, but it is absolutely critical that the coordinator be able to recognize good design ideas from others.

Both the Linux and fetchmail projects show evidence of this. Linus, while not (as previously discussed) a spectacularly original designer, has displayed a powerful knack for recognizing good design and integrating it into the Linux kernel. And I have already described how the single most powerful design idea in fetchmail (SMTP forwarding) came from somebody else.

Early audiences of this paper complimented me by suggesting that I am prone to undervalue design originality in bazaar projects because I have a lot of it myself, and therefore take it for granted. There may be some truth to this; design (as opposed to coding or debugging) is certainly my strongest skill.

But the problem with being clever and original in software design is that it gets to be a habit—you start reflexively making things cute and complicated when you should be keeping them robust and simple. I have had projects crash on me because I made this mistake, but I managed not to with fetchmail.

So I believe the fetchmail project succeeded partly because I restrained my tendency to be clever; this argues (at least) against design originality being essential for successful bazaar projects. And consider Linux. Suppose Linus Torvalds had been trying to pull off fundamental innovations in operating system design during the development; does it seem at all likely that the resulting kernel would be as stable and successful as what we have?

A certain base level of design and coding skill is required, of course, but I expect almost anybody seriously thinking of launching a bazaar effort will already be above that minimum. The open-source community's internal market in reputation exerts subtle pressure on people not to launch development efforts they're not competent to follow through on. So far this seems to have worked pretty well.

There is another kind of skill not normally associated with software development that I think is as important as design cleverness to bazaar projects—and it may be more important. A bazaar project coordinator or leader must have good people and communication skills.

This should be obvious. In order to build a development community, you need to attract people, interest them in what you're doing, and keep them happy about the amount of work they're doing. Technical sizzle will go a long way toward accomplishing this, but it's far from the whole story. The personality you project matters, too.

It is not a coincidence that Linus is a nice guy who makes people like him and want to help him. It's not a coincidence that I'm an energetic extrovert who enjoys working a crowd and has some of the delivery and instincts of a stand-up comic. To make the bazaar model work, it helps enormously if you have at least a little skill at charming people.

The Social Context of Open-Source Software

It is truly written: The best hacks start out as personal solutions to the author's everyday problems, and spread because the problem turns out to be typical for a large class of users. This takes us back to the matter of Rule 1, restated in a perhaps more useful way:

18. *To solve an interesting problem, start by finding a problem that is interesting to you.*

So it was with Carl Harris and the ancestral popclient, and so with me and fetchmail. But this has been understood for a long time. The interesting point, the point that the histories of Linux and fetchmail seem to demand we focus on, is the next stage—the evolution of software in the presence of a large and active community of users and co-developers.

In "The Mythical Man-Month," Fred Brooks observed that programmer time is not fungible; adding developers to a late software project makes it later. He argued that the complexity and communication costs of a project rise with the square of the number of developers, while work done only rises linearly. This claim has since become known as "Brooks's Law" and is widely regarded as a truism. But if Brooks's Law were the whole picture, Linux would be impossible.

Gerald Weinberg's classic "The Psychology Of Computer Programming" supplied what, in hindsight, we can see as a vital correction to Brooks. In his discussion of "egoless programming," Weinberg observed that in shops where developers are not territorial about their code, and encourage other people to look for bugs and potential improvements in it, improvement happens dramatically faster than elsewhere.

Weinberg's choice of terminology has perhaps prevented his analysis from gaining the acceptance it deserved—one has to smile at the thought of describing Internet hackers as "egoless." But I think his argument looks more compelling today than ever.

The history of Unix should have prepared us for what we're learning from Linux (and what I've verified experimentally on a smaller scale by deliberately copying Linus's methods [EGCS]). That is, that while coding remains an essentially solitary activity, the really great hacks come from harnessing the attention and brainpower of entire communities. The developer who uses only his or her own brain in a closed project is going to fall behind the developer who knows how to create an open, evolutionary context in which feedback exploring the design space, code contributions, bug-spotting, and other improvements come back from hundreds (perhaps thousands) of people.

But the traditional Unix world was prevented from pushing this approach to the ultimate by several factors. One was the legal constraints of various licenses, trade secrets, and commercial interests. Another (in hindsight) was that the Internet wasn't yet good enough.

Before cheap Internet, there were some geographically compact communities where the culture encouraged Weinberg's "egoless" programming, and a developer could easily attract a lot of skilled kibitzers and co-developers. Bell Labs, the MIT AI Lab, UC Berkeley—these became the home of innovations that are legendary and still potent.

Linux was the first project to make a conscious and successful effort to use the entire world as its talent pool. I don't think it's a coincidence that the gestation period of Linux coincided with the birth of the World Wide Web, and that Linux left its infancy during the same period in 1993–1994 that saw the takeoff of the ISP industry and the explosion of mainstream interest in the Internet. Linus was the first person who learned how to play by the new rules that pervasive Internet access made possible.

While cheap Internet was a necessary condition for the Linux model to evolve, I think it was not by itself a sufficient condition. Another vital factor was the development of a leadership style and set of cooperative customs that could allow developers to attract co-developers and get maximum leverage out of the medium.

But what is this leadership style and what are these customs? They cannot be based on power relationships, and even if they could be, leadership by coercion would not produce the results we see. Weinberg quotes the autobiography of the 19th-century Russian anarchist Pyotr Alexeyvich Kropotkin's *Memoirs of a Revolutionist* to good effect on this subject:

Having been brought up in a serf-owner's family, I entered active life, like all young men of my time, with a great deal of confidence in the necessity of commanding, ordering, scolding, punishing and the like. But when, at an early stage, I had to manage serious enterprises and to deal with [free] men, and when each mistake would lead at once to heavy consequences, I began to appreciate the difference between acting on the principle of command and discipline and acting on the principle of common understanding. The former works admirably in a military parade, but it is worth nothing where real life is concerned, and the aim can be achieved only through the severe effort of many converging wills.

The "severe effort of many converging wills" is precisely what a project like Linux requires—and the "principle of command" is effectively impossible to apply among volunteers in the anarchist's paradise we call the Internet. To operate and compete effectively, hackers who want to lead collaborative projects have to learn how to recruit and energize effective communities of interest in the mode vaguely suggested by Kropotkin's "principle of understanding." They must learn to use Linus's Law. [SP]

Earlier I referred to the "Delphi effect" as a possible explanation for Linus's Law. But more powerful analogies to adaptive systems in biology and economics also irresistibly suggest themselves. The Linux world behaves in many respects like a free market or an ecology, a collection of selfish agents attempting to maximize utility, which in the process produces a self-correcting spontaneous order more elaborate and efficient than any amount of central planning could have achieved. Here, then, is the place to seek the "principle of understanding."

The "utility function" Linux hackers are maximizing is not classically economic, but is the intangible of their own ego satisfaction and reputation among other hackers. (One may call their motivation "altruistic," but this ignores the fact that altruism is itself a form of ego satisfaction for the altruist.) Voluntary cultures that work this way are not actually uncommon; one other in which I have long participated is science fiction fandom, which unlike hackerdom has long explicitly recognized "egoboo" (ego-boosting, or the enhancement of one's reputation among other fans) as the basic drive behind volunteer activity.

Linus, by successfully positioning himself as the gatekeeper of a project in which the development is mostly done by others, and nurturing interest in the project until it became self-sustaining, has shown an acute grasp of Kropotkin's "principle of shared understanding." This quasi-economic view of the Linux world enables us to see how that understanding is applied.

We may view Linus's method as a way to create an efficient market in "egoboo"—to connect the selfishness of individual hackers as firmly as possible to difficult ends that can only be achieved by sustained cooperation. With the fetchmail project I have shown (albeit on a smaller scale) that his methods can be duplicated with good results. Perhaps I have even done it a bit more consciously and systematically than he.

Many people (especially those who politically distrust free markets) would expect a culture of self-directed egoists to be fragmented, territorial, wasteful, secretive, and hostile. But this expectation is clearly falsified by (to give just one example) the stunning variety, quality, and depth of Linux documentation. It is a hallowed given that programmers hate documenting; how is it, then, that Linux hackers generate so much of it? Evidently Linux's free market in egoboo works better to produce virtuous, other-directed behavior than the massively-funded documentation shops of commercial software producers.

Both the fetchmail and Linux kernel projects show that by properly rewarding the egos of many other hackers, a strong developer/coordinator can use the Internet to capture the benefits of having lots of co-developers without having a project collapse into a chaotic mess. So to Brooks's Law, I counter-propose the following:

19. *Provided the development coordinator has a medium at least as good as the Internet, and knows how to lead without coercion, many heads are inevitably better than one.*

I think the future of open-source software will increasingly belong to people who know how to play Linus's game, people who leave behind the cathedral and embrace the bazaar. This is not to say that individual vision and brilliance will no longer matter; rather, I think that the cutting edge of open-source software will belong to people who start from individual vision and brilliance, then amplify it through the effective construction of voluntary communities of interest.

Perhaps this is not only the future of open-source software. No closed-source developer can match the pool of talent the Linux community can bring to bear on a problem. Very few could afford even to hire the more than two hundred (1999: six hundred, 2000: eight hundred) people who have contributed to fetchmail!

Perhaps in the end the open-source culture will triumph not because cooperation is morally right or software "hoarding" is morally wrong (assuming you believe the latter, which neither Linus nor I do), but simply because the closed-source world cannot win an evolutionary arms race with open-source communities that can put orders of magnitude more skilled time into a problem.

On Management and the Maginot Line

The original "Cathedral and Bazaar" paper of 1997 ended with the vision above—that of happy networked hordes of programmer/anarchists outcompeting and overwhelming the hierarchical world of conventional closed software.

A good many skeptics weren't convinced, however, and the questions they raise deserve a fair engagement. Most of the objections to the bazaar argument come down to the claim that its proponents have underestimated the productivity-multiplying effect of conventional management.

Traditionally-minded software-development managers often object that the casualness with which project groups form and change and dissolve in the open-source world negates a significant part of the apparent advantage of numbers that the open-source community has over any single closed-source developer. They would observe that in software development, it is really sustained effort over time and the degree to which customers can expect continuing investment in the product that matters, not just how many people have thrown a bone in the pot and left it to simmer.

There is something to this argument, to be sure; in fact, I have developed the idea that expected future service value is the key to the economics of software production in *The Magic Cauldron*.

But this argument also has a major hidden problem; its implicit assumption that open-source development cannot deliver such sustained effort. In fact, there have been open-source projects that maintained a coherent direction and an effective maintainer community over quite long periods of time without the kinds of incentive structures or institutional controls that conventional management finds essential. The development of the GNU Emacs editor is an extreme and instructive example; it has absorbed the efforts of hundreds of contributors over fifteen years into a unified architectural vision, despite high turnover and the fact that only one person (its author) has been continuously active during all that time. No closed-source editor has ever matched this longevity record.

This suggests a reason for questioning the advantages of conventionally-managed software development that is independent of the rest of the arguments over cathedral vs. bazaar mode. If it's possible for GNU Emacs to express a consistent architectural vision over fifteen years, or for an operating system like Linux to do the same over eight years of rapidly changing hardware and platform technology;

and if (as is indeed the case) there have been many well-architected open-source projects of more than five years duration—then we are entitled to wonder what, if anything, the tremendous overhead of conventionally-managed development is actually buying us.

Whatever it is certainly doesn't include reliable execution by deadline, or on budget, or to all features of the specification; it's a rare "managed" project that meets even one of these goals, let alone all three. It also does not appear to be ability to adapt to changes in technology and economic context during the project lifetime, either; the open-source community has proven far more effective on that score (as one can readily verify, for example, by comparing the thirty-year history of the Internet with the short half-lives of proprietary networking technologies, or the cost of the 16-bit to 32-bit transition in Microsoft Windows with the nearly effortless up-migration of Linux during the same period, not only along the Intel line of development but to more than a dozen other hardware platforms including the 64-bit Alpha as well).

One thing many people think the traditional mode buys you is somebody to hold legally liable and potentially recover compensation from if the project goes wrong. But this is an illusion; most software licenses are written to disclaim even warranty of merchantability, let alone performance—and cases of successful recovery for software nonperformance are vanishingly rare. Even if they were common, feeling comforted by having somebody to sue would be missing the point. You didn't want to be in a lawsuit; you wanted working software.

So what is all that management overhead buying?

In order to understand that, we need to understand what software development managers believe they do. A woman I know who seems to be very good at this job says software project management has five functions:

- To define goals and keep everybody pointed in the same direction.
- To monitor and make sure crucial details don't get skipped.
- To motivate people to do boring but necessary drudgework.
- To organize the deployment of people for best productivity.
- To marshal resources needed to sustain the project.

Apparently worthy goals, all of these; but under the open-source model, and in its surrounding social context, they can begin to seem strangely irrelevant. We'll take them in reverse order.

My friend reports that a lot of resource marshalling is basically defensive; once you have your people and machines and office space, you have to defend them from peer managers competing for the same resources, and higher-ups trying to allocate the most efficient use of a limited pool.

But open-source developers are volunteers, self-selected for both interest and ability to contribute to the projects they work on (and this remains generally true even when they are being paid a salary to hack open source). The volunteer ethos tends to take care of the "attack" side of resource-marshalling automatically; people bring their own resources to the table. And there is little or no need for a manager to "play defense" in the conventional sense.

Anyway, in a world of cheap PCs and fast Internet links, we find pretty consistently that the only really limiting resource is skilled attention. Open-source projects, when they founder, essentially never do so for want of machines or links or office space; they die only when the developers themselves lose interest.

That being the case, it's doubly important that open-source hackers organize themselves for maximum productivity by self-selection—and the social milieu selects ruthlessly for competence. My friend, familiar with both the open-source world and large closed projects, believes that open source has been successful partly because its culture only accepts the most talented 5% or so of the programming population. She spends most of her time organizing the deployment of the other 95%, and has thus observed first-hand the well-known variance of a factor of one hundred in productivity between the most able programmers and the merely competent.

The size of that variance has always raised an awkward question: Would individual projects, and the field as a whole, be better off without more than 50% of the least able in it? Thoughtful managers have understood for a long time that if conventional software management's only function were to convert the least able from a net loss to a marginal win, the game might not be worth the candle.

The success of the open-source community sharpens this question considerably by providing hard evidence that it is often cheaper and more effective to recruit self-selected volunteers from the Internet than it is to manage buildings full of people who would rather be doing something else.

Which brings us neatly to the question of motivation. An equivalent and often-heard way to state my friend's point is that traditional development management is a necessary compensation for poorly motivated programmers who would not otherwise turn out good work.

This answer usually travels with a claim that the open-source community can only be relied on to do work that is "sexy" or technically sweet; anything else will be left undone (or done only poorly) unless it's churned out by money-motivated cubicle peons with managers cracking whips over them. I address the psychological and social reasons for being skeptical of this claim in "Homesteading the Noosphere." For present purposes, however, I think it's more interesting to point out the implications of accepting it as true.

If the conventional, closed-source, heavily-managed style of software development is really defended only by a sort of Maginot line of problems conducive to boredom, then it's going to remain viable in each individual application area for only so long as nobody finds those problems really interesting and nobody else finds any way to route around them. Because the moment there is open-source competition for a "boring" piece of software, customers are going to know that it was finally tackled by someone who chose that problem to solve because of a fascination with the problem itself—which, in software as in other kinds of creative work, is a far more effective motivator than money alone.

Having a conventional management structure solely in order to motivate, then, is probably good tactics but bad strategy; a short-term win, but in the longer term, a surer loss. So far, conventional development management looks like a bad bet now against open source on two points (resource marshalling, organization), and like it's living on borrowed time with respect to a third (motivation). And the poor beleaguered conventional manager is not going to get any succour from the monitoring issue; the strongest argument the open-source community has is that decentralized peer review trumps all the conventional methods for trying to ensure that details don't get slipped.

Can we save defining goals as a justification for the overhead of conventional software project management? Perhaps; but to do so, we'll need good reason to believe that management committees and corporate roadmaps are more successful at defining worthy and widely-shared goals than the project leaders and tribal elders who fill the analogous role in the open-source world.

That is, on the face of it, a pretty hard case to make. And it's not so much the open-source side of the balance (the longevity of Emacs, or Linus Torvalds's ability to mobilize hordes of developers with talk of "world domination") that makes it tough. Rather, it's the demonstrated awfulness of conventional mechanisms for defining the goals of software projects.

One of the best-known folk theorems of software engineering is that 60% to 75% of conventional software projects either are never completed or are rejected by their intended users. If that range is anywhere near true (and I've never met a manager of any experience who disputes it), then more projects than not are being aimed at goals that are either (a) not realistically attainable, or (b) just plain wrong.

This, more than any other problem, is the reason that in today's software engineering world the very phrase "management committee" is likely to send chills down the hearer's spine—even (or perhaps especially) if the hearer is a manager. The days when only programmers griped about this pattern are long past; "Dilbert" cartoons hang over executives' desks now.

Our reply, then, to the traditional software development manager, is simple— if the open-source community has really underestimated the value of conventional management, why do so many of you display contempt for your own process?

Once again the existence of the open-source community sharpens this question considerably—because we have fun doing what we do. Our creative play has been racking up technical, market-share, and mind-share successes at an astounding rate. We're proving not only that we can do better software, but that joy is an asset.

Two and a half years after the first version of this essay, the most radical thought I can offer to close with is no longer a vision of an open-source-dominated software world; that, after all, looks plausible to a lot of sober people in suits these days.

Rather, I want to suggest what may be a wider lesson about software (and probably about every kind of creative or professional work). Human beings generally take pleasure in a task when it falls in a sort of optimal-challenge zone; not so easy as to be boring, not too hard to achieve. A happy programmer is one who is neither underutilized nor weighed down with ill-formulated goals and stressful process friction. *Enjoyment predicts efficiency.*

Relating to your own work process with fear and loathing (even in the displaced, ironic way suggested by hanging up Dilbert cartoons) should therefore be regarded in itself as a sign that the process has failed. Joy, humor, and playfulness are indeed assets; it was not mainly for the alliteration that I wrote of "happy hordes" above, and it is no mere joke that the Linux mascot is a cuddly, neotenous penguin.

It may well turn out that one of the most important effects of open source's success will be to teach us that play is the most economically efficient mode of creative work.

Acknowledgments

This paper was improved by conversations with a large number of people who helped debug it. Particular thanks to Jeff Dutky, who suggested the "debugging is parallelizable" formulation, and helped develop the analysis that proceeds from it. Also to Nancy Lebovitz for her suggestion that I emulate Weinberg by quoting Kropotkin. Perceptive criticisms also came from Joan Eslinger and Marty Franz of the General Technics list. Glen Vandenburg pointed out the importance of self-selection in contributor populations and suggested the fruitful idea that much development rectifies "bugs of omission;" Daniel Upper suggested the natural analogies for this. I'm grateful to the members of PLUG, the Philadelphia Linux User's group, for providing the first test audience for the first public version of this paper. Paula Matuszek enlightened me about the practice of software management. Phil Hudson reminded me that the social organization of the hacker culture mirrors the organization of its software, and vice-versa. Finally, Linus Torvalds's comments were helpful and his early endorsement very encouraging.

For Further Reading

I quoted several bits from Frederick P. Brooks's classic *The Mythical Man-Month* because, in many respects, his insights have yet to be improved upon. I heartily recommend the 25th Anniversary edition from Addison-Wesley, which adds his 1986 "No Silver Bullet" paper. The new edition is wrapped up by an invaluable 20-years-later retrospective in which Brooks forthrightly admits to the few judgments in the original text that have not stood the test of time. I first read the retrospective after the first public version of this paper was substantially complete, and was surprised to discover that Brooks attributes bazaar-like practices to Microsoft! (In fact, however, this attribution turned out to be mistaken. In 1998 we learned from the Halloween Documents that Microsoft's internal developer community is heavily balkanized, with the kind of general source access needed to support a bazaar not even truly possible.)

Gerald M. Weinberg's *The Psychology Of Computer Programming* (New York, Van Nostrand Reinhold 1971) introduced the rather unfortunately-labeled concept of "egoless programming." While he was nowhere near the first person to realize the futility of the "principle of command," he was probably the first to recognize and argue the point in particular connection with software development.

Richard P. Gabriel, contemplating the Unix culture of the pre-Linux era, reluctantly argued for the superiority of a primitive bazaar-like model in his 1989 paper "Lisp: Good News, Bad News, and How To Win Big." Though dated in some respects, this essay is still rightly celebrated among Lisp fans (including me). A correspondent reminded me that the section titled "Worse Is Better" reads almost as an anticipation of Linux. The paper is accessible on the World Wide Web at http://www.naggum.no/worse-is-better.html.

De Marco and Lister's *Peopleware: Productive Projects and Teams* (New York; Dorset House, 1987) is an under-appreciated gem that I was delighted to see Fred Brooks cite in his retrospective. While little of what the authors have to say is directly applicable to the Linux or open-source communities, the authors' insight into the conditions necessary for creative work is acute and worthwhile for anyone attempting to import some of the bazaar model's virtues into a commercial context.

Finally, I must admit that I very nearly called this paper "The Cathedral and the Agora," the latter term being the Greek for an open market or public meeting place. The seminal "agoric systems" papers by Mark Miller and Eric Drexler, by describing the emergent properties of market-like computational ecologies, helped prepare me to think clearly about analogous phenomena in the open-source culture when Linux rubbed my nose in them five years later. These papers are available on the Web at http://www.agorics.com/agorpapers.html.

Epilog: Netscape Embraces the Bazaar

It's a strange feeling to realize you're helping make history....

On January 22, 1998, approximately seven months after I first published "The Cathedral and the Bazaar," Netscape Communications, Inc. announced plans to give away the source for Netscape Communicator. I had had no clue this was going to happen before the day of the announcement.

Eric Hahn, Executive Vice President and Chief Technology Officer at Netscape, emailed me shortly afterwards as follows: "On behalf of everyone at Netscape, I want to thank you for helping us get to this point in the first place. Your thinking and writings were fundamental inspirations to our decision."

The following week I flew out to Silicon Valley at Netscape's invitation for a day-long strategy conference (on Feb 4, 1998) with some of their top executives and technical people. We designed Netscape's source-release strategy and license together.

A few days later I wrote the following:

> Netscape is about to provide us with a large-scale, real-world test of the bazaar
> model in the commercial world. The open-source culture now faces a dan-
> ger; if Netscape's execution doesn't work, the open-source concept may be
> so discredited that the commercial world won't touch it again for another
> decade.

On the other hand, this is also a spectacular opportunity. Initial reaction to the move on Wall Street and elsewhere has been cautiously positive. We're being giv-en a chance to prove ourselves, too. If Netscape regains substantial market share through this move, it just may set off a long-overdue revolution in the software industry.

The next year should be a very instructive and interesting time.

And indeed it was. As I write in mid-1999, the development of what was later named "Mozilla" has been only a qualified success. It achieved Netscape's original goal, which was to deny Microsoft a monopoly lock on the browser market. It has also achieved some dramatic successes (notably the release of the next-generation Gecko rendering engine).

However, it has not yet garnered the massive development effort from outside Netscape that the Mozilla founders had originally hoped for. The problem here seems to be that for a long time the Mozilla distribution actually broke one of the basic rules of the bazaar model; they didn't ship something potential contribu-tors could easily run and see working. (Until more than a year after release, build-ing Mozilla from source required a license for the proprietary Motif library.)

Most negatively (from the point of view of the outside world) the Mozilla group has yet to ship a production-quality browser—and one of the project's principals caused a bit of a sensation by resigning, complaining of poor management and missed opportunities. "Open source," he correctly observed, "is not magic pixie dust."

And indeed it is not. The long-term prognosis for Mozilla looks dramatically better now (in August 2000) than it did at the time of Jamie Zawinski's resignation letter—but he was right to point out that going open will not necessarily save an existing project that suffers from ill-defined goals or spaghetti code or any of the software engineering's other chronic ills. Mozilla has managed to provide an example simultaneously of how open source can succeed and how it could fail.

In the mean time, however, the open-source idea has scored successes and found backers elsewhere. 1998 and late 1999 saw a tremendous explosion of interest in the open-source development model, a trend both driven by and driving the con-tinuing success of the Linux operating system. The trend Mozilla touched off is continuing at an accelerating rate.

Endnotes

[JB]   In Programming Pearls, the noted computer-science aphorist Jon Bentley comments on Brooks's observation with, "If you plan to throw one away, you will throw away two." He is almost certainly right. The point of Brooks's observation, and Bentley's, isn't merely that you should expect your first attempt to be wrong, it's that starting over with the right idea is usually more effective than trying to salvage a mess.

[QR]   Examples of successful open-source, bazaar development predating the Internet explosion and unrelated to the Unix and Internet traditions have existed. The development of the info-Zip compression utility during 1990–1992, primarily for DOS machines, was one such. Another was the RBBS bulletin board system (again for DOS), which began in 1983 and developed a sufficiently strong community that there have been fairly regular releases up to the present (mid-1999) despite the huge technical advantages of Internet mail and file-sharing over local BBSs. While the info-Zip community relied to some extent on Internet mail, the RBBS developer culture was actually able to base a substantial on-line community on RBBS that was completely independent of the TCP/IP infrastructure. John Hasler has suggested an interesting explanation for the fact that duplication of effort doesn't seem to be a net drag on open-source development. He proposes what I'll dub "Hasler's Law": The costs of duplicated work tend to scale sub-quadratically with team size—that is, more slowly than the planning and management overhead that would be needed to eliminate them.

This claim actually does not contradict Brooks's Law. It may be the case that total complexity overhead and vulnerability to bugs scales with the square of team size, but that the costs from duplicated work are nevertheless a special case that scales more slowly. It's not hard to develop plausible reasons for this, starting with the undoubted fact that it is much easier to agree on functional boundaries between different developers' code that will prevent duplication of effort than it is to prevent the kinds of unplanned bad interactions across the whole system that underlie most bugs.

The combination of Linus's Law and Hasler's Law suggests that there are actually three critical size regimes in software projects. On small projects (I would say one to at most three developers) no management structure more elaborate than picking a lead programmer is needed. And there is some intermediate range above that in which the cost of traditional management is relatively low, so its benefits from avoiding duplication of effort, bug-tracking, and pushing to see that details are not overlooked actually net out positive.

Above that, however, the combination of Linus's Law and Hasler's Law suggests there is a large-project range in which the costs and problems of traditional management rise much faster than the expected cost from duplication of effort. Not the least of these costs is a structural inability to harness the many-eyeballs effect, which (as we've seen) seems to do a much better job than traditional management at making sure bugs and details are not overlooked. Thus, in the large-project case, the combination of these laws effectively drives the net payoff of traditional management to zero.

[HBS]   The split between Linux's experimental and stable versions has another function related to, but distinct from, hedging risk. The split attacks another problem: the deadliness of deadlines. When programmers are held both to an immutable feature list and a fixed drop-dead date, quality goes out the window and there is likely a colossal mess in the making. I am indebted to Marco Iansiti and Alan MacCormack of the Harvard Business School for pointing me at evidence that relaxing either one of these constraints can make scheduling workable.

One way to do this is to fix the deadline but leave the feature list flexible, allowing features to drop off if not completed by deadline. This is essentially the strategy of the "stable" kernel branch; Alan Cox (the stable-kernel maintainer) puts out releases at fairly regular intervals, but makes no guarantees about when particular bugs will be fixed or features back-ported from the experimental branch.

The other way to do this is to set a desired feature list and deliver only when it is done. This is essentially the strategy of the "experimental" kernel branch. De Marco and Lister cited research showing that this scheduling policy ("wake me up when it's done") produces not only the highest quality but, on average, shorter delivery times than either "realistic" or "aggressive" scheduling.

I have come to suspect (as of early 2000) that in earlier versions of this paper I severely underestimated the importance of the "wake me up when it's done" anti-deadline policy to the open-source community's productivity and quality. General experience with the rushed GNOME 1.0 in 1999 suggests that pressure for a premature release can neutralize many of the quality benefits open source normally confers.

It may well turn out to be that the process transparency of open source is one of three coequal drivers of its quality, along with "wake me up when it's done" scheduling and developer self-selection.

[IN] An issue related to whether one can start projects from zero in the bazaar style is whether the bazaar style is capable of supporting truly innovative work. Some claim that, lacking strong leadership, the bazaar can only handle the cloning and improvement of ideas already present at the engineering state of the art, but is unable to push the state of the art. This argument was perhaps most infamously made by the Halloween Documents, two embarrassing internal Microsoft memoranda written about the open-source phenomenon. The authors compared Linux's development of a Unix-like operating system to "chasing taillights," and opined "(once a project has achieved "parity" with the state-of-the-art), the level of management necessary to push towards new frontiers becomes massive."

There are serious errors of fact implied in this argument. One is exposed when the Halloween authors themselves later observe that "often [...] new research ideas are first implemented and available on Linux before they are available/incorporated into other platforms."

If we read "open source" for "Linux," we see that this is far from a new phenomenon. Historically, the open-source community did not invent Emacs or the World Wide Web or the Internet itself by chasing taillights or being massively managed—and in the present, there is so much innovative work going on in open source that one is spoiled for choice. The GNOME project (to pick one of many) is pushing the state of the art in GUIs and object technology hard enough to have attracted considerable notice in the computer trade press well outside the Linux community. Other examples are legion, as a visit to Freshmeat on any given day will quickly prove.

But there is a more fundamental error in the implicit assumption that the cathedral model (or the bazaar model, or any other kind of management structure) can somehow make innovation happen reliably. This is nonsense. Gangs don't have breakthrough insights—even volunteer groups of bazaar anarchists are usually incapable of genuine originality, let alone corporate committees of people with a survival stake in some status quo ante. Insight comes from individuals. The most their surrounding social machinery can ever hope to do is to be responsive to breakthrough insights—to nourish and reward and rigorously test them instead of squashing them.

Some will characterize this as a romantic view, a reversion to outmoded lone-inventor stereotypes. Not so; I am not asserting that groups are incapable of developing break-through insights once they have been hatched; indeed, we learn from the peer-review process that such development groups are essential to producing a high-quality result. Rather I am pointing out that every such group development starts from—is necessarily sparked by—one good idea in one person's head. Cathedrals and bazaars and other social structures can catch that lightning and refine it, but they cannot make it on demand.

Therefore the root problem of innovation (in software, or anywhere else) is indeed how not to squash it—but, even more fundamentally, it is how to grow lots of people who can have insights in the first place.

To suppose that cathedral-style development could manage this trick but the low entry barriers and process fluidity of the bazaar cannot would be absurd. If what it takes is one person with one good idea, then a social milieu in which one person can rapidly attract the cooperation of hundreds or thousands of others with that good idea is going to inevitably out-innovate any in which the person has to do a political sales job to a hierar-chy before he can work on his idea without risk of getting fired.

And, indeed, if we look at the history of software innovation by organizations using the cathedral model, we quickly find it is rather rare. Large corporations rely on university research for new ideas (thus the Halloween Documents authors' unease about Linux's facility at coopting that research more rapidly). Or they buy out small companies built around some innovator's brain. In neither case is the innovation native to the cathedral culture; indeed, many innovations so imported end up being quietly suffocated under the "massive level of management" the Halloween Documents authors so extol.

That, however, is a negative point. The reader would be better served by a positive one. I suggest, as an experiment, the following;

- Pick a criterion for originality that you believe you can apply consistently. If your definition is "I know it when see it," that's not a problem for purposes of this test.
- Pick any closed-source operating system competing with Linux, and a best source for accounts of current development work on it.
- Watch that source and Freshmeat for one month. Every day, count the number of release announcements on Freshmeat that you consider "original" work. Apply the same definition of "original" to announcements for that other OS and count them.
- Thirty days later, total up both figures.

The day I wrote this, Freshmeat carried twenty-two release announcements, of which three appear they might push state of the art in some respect. This was a slow day for Freshmeat, but I will be astonished if any reader reports as many as three likely innovations a month in any closed-source channel.

[EGCS]   We now have history on a project that, in several ways, may provide a more indicative test of the bazaar premise than fetchmail; EGCS, the Experimental GNU Compiler System.

This project was announced in mid-August of 1997 as a conscious attempt to apply the ideas in the early public versions of "The Cathedral and the Bazaar." The project founders felt that the development of GCC, the Gnu C Compiler, had been stagnating. For about twenty months afterwards, GCC and EGCS continued as parallel products—both drawing from the same Internet developer population, both starting from the same GCC source base, both using pretty much the same Unix toolsets and development environment. The projects differed only in that EGCS consciously tried to apply the bazaar tactics I have previously described, while GCC retained a more cathedral-like organization with a closed developer group and infrequent releases.

This was about as close to a controlled experiment as one could ask for, and the results were dramatic. Within months, the EGCS versions had pulled substantially ahead in features; better optimization, better support for FORTRAN and C++. Many people found the EGCS development snapshots to be more reliable than the most recent stable version of GCC, and major Linux distributions began to switch to EGCS.

In April of 1999, the Free Software Foundation (the official sponsors of GCC) dissolved the original GCC development group and officially handed control of the project to the EGCS steering team.

[SP]   Of course, Kropotkin's critique and Linus's Law raise some wider issues about the cybernetics of social organizations. Another folk theorem of software engineering suggests one of them; Conway's Law—commonly stated as "If you have four groups working on a compiler, you'll get a 4-pass compiler." The original statement was more general: "Organizations which design systems are constrained to produce designs which are copies of the communication structures of these organizations." We might put it more succinctly as "The means determine the ends," or even "Process becomes product."

It is accordingly worth noting that in the open-source community, organizational form and function match on many levels. The network is everything and everywhere: Not just the Internet, but the people doing the work form a distributed, loosely coupled, peer-to-peer network that provides multiple redundancy and degrades very gracefully. In both networks, each node is important only to the extent that other nodes want to cooperate with it.

The peer-to-peer part is essential to the community's astonishing productivity. The point Kropotkin was trying to make about power relationships is developed further by the "SNAFU Principle": "True communication is possible only between equals, because inferiors are more consistently rewarded for telling their superiors pleasant lies than for telling the truth." Creative teamwork utterly depends on true communication and is thus very seriously hindered by the presence of power relationships. The open-source community, effectively free of such power relationships, is teaching us by contrast how dreadfully much they cost in bugs, in lowered productivity, and in lost opportunities.

Further, the SNAFU principle predicts in authoritarian organizations a progressive disconnect between decision-makers and reality, as more and more of the input to those who decide tends to become pleasant lies. The way this plays out in conventional software development is easy to see; there are strong incentives for the inferiors to hide, ignore, and minimize problems. When this process becomes product, software is a disaster.

Introduction to Chapter 4: Privacy in Cyberspace

Perhaps no ethical issue involving computers and cybertechnology has received more attention in the news media and popular press than concerns about the loss of privacy. Surveys conducted by *Business Week*, Harris Associates, Equifax, and others suggest that most Americans either are "concerned" or "very concerned" about their privacy. Other surveys and studies suggest that individuals worry about having to give up pieces of their privacy in order to use the Internet. What is personal privacy, and why is it important? How exactly does cybertechnology threaten privacy? What is data mining, and what kinds of threats does it pose to personal privacy? Is a new theory of privacy needed for the cyber era? These and related questions are considered in the readings in Chapter 4.

What is Personal Privacy?

Privacy is a concept that is neither clearly understood nor easily defined. We often hear remarks that one's privacy has been "lost," "diminished," "intruded upon," "invaded," "violated," "breached," and so forth. Each of these descriptions, in turn, reflects the insights and biases of one or more models or theories of privacy. For example, some theories see privacy as an "all-or-nothing" concept—i.e., privacy is something that one either has (totally) or does not have; others view privacy as a repository of information possessed by an individual, which can be eroded gradually. Still others see privacy in terms of a spatial metaphor, such as a zone, that can be intruded upon or invaded by individuals and organizations. And other theories view privacy in terms of confidentiality that can be violated, or trust that can be breached. Several interesting models of privacy either directly correspond to, or approximately fit, one or more of the metaphors just described. Some of those theories are considered in the readings included in this chapter.

Certain privacy analysts have suggested that privacy be viewed as an individual's presumed or stipulated *interest* in protecting personal information, personal property, or personal space rather than as a moral or legal right. Others have suggested that personal privacy be viewed in terms of an economic interest, and that information about individuals be thought of as personal property that can be bought and sold in the commercial sphere. Many Western European nations have preferred to approach questions involving individual privacy as issues of *data protection* —i.e., as an interest in protecting personal information—rather than in terms of a normative concept that needs philosophical analysis (see the reading by Dag Elgesem included in this chapter). In the United States, on the other hand, extensive legal and philosophical arguments drive discussions involving the concept of privacy as a legal right.[1]

The Theory of Privacy

In the first reading of this chapter, James Moor points out that in the United States, the concept of privacy has evolved from earlier concerns involving intrusion into one's personal space and interference with an individual's personal affairs to current concerns that center on control over and access to personal information. The conception of privacy in terms of intrusion is rooted in a very influential article by Warren and Brandeis (1890), which argued that privacy consists in "being let alone." In the 1960s the concept of privacy became more closely aligned with concerns stemming from interference in personal affairs. This view of privacy is articulated in two U.S. Supreme Court cases—one involving reproductive rights and contraception (*Griswold* v. *Connecticut*, 1965), and the other involving abortion (*Roe* v. *Wade*, 1973). Since in the 1970s, much of the focus on privacy issues has been directed at concerns about the kind of personal *information* that is gathered via computerized techniques and then exchanged between and mined from computer databases. Privacy analysts distinguish the issues of "informational privacy" from privacy concerns related both to intrusion and interference, which are sometimes described as "psychological privacy" (Regan, 1995) or "associative privacy" (DeCew, 1997). In this chapter, we focus on informational privacy.

Two theories of informational privacy have received considerable attention in recent years—the *control theory* and the *restricted access theory*. According to the control theory, one has privacy if and only if one has control over information about oneself (see, for example, Fried, 1984; and Rachels, 1995). And according to the restricted access theory, one has privacy if access to information about oneself is limited or restricted in certain contexts (see, for example, Allen, 1988; and Gavison, 1984).

One strength of the the control theory is that it recognizes that an individual with privacy can grant, as well as deny, others access to his/her

---

[1] To appreciate more fully the differences between these two distinct approaches to understanding the concept of privacy, compare relevant portions of the reading by Dag Elgesem, in Chapter 4, to the relevant section of Jean Camp's article "Web Security and Privacy: An American Perspective," included in Chapter 5.

information. And one strength of the restricted access theory is that it recognizes the importance of contexts or "zones" for protecting privacy. However, critics have pointed out certain weaknesses in each theory. The control theory has at least two major flaws—On a practical level, one is never able to have complete control over every piece of information about oneself. And a theoretical or conceptual difficulty arises for control theorists who suggest that one could conceivably reveal every bit of personal information about oneself while retaining personal privacy. Complete disclosure of personal information while maintaining privacy certainly counters a traditional view of privacy. One problem with the restricted access theory, on the other hand, is that it tends to underestimate the role of control required in one's having privacy. So it would seem that neither of these two theories is fully adequate. However, each theory offers an insight into what is essential for individuals to have privacy. Can aspects of these two different accounts of privacy somehow be successfully incorporated into one coherent theory?

In the first reading in Chapter 4, "Towards a Theory of Privacy for the Information Age," James Moor sets out to integrate essential elements of both the control and restricted access theories; he appropriately calls this comprehensive theory the *control/restricted access theory*. Building on his earlier work on privacy (see, for example, Moor, 1990), he shows why it is important both to restrict access (i.e., set up "zones" of protection) and to grant limited controls to individuals. Moor then illustrates how his theory can be implemented into a privacy policy via a set of principles, which includes the "Publicity Principle."

The second reading, by Dag Elgesem, describes the structure of rights in the European Union (EU) 1995 Directive on the protection of individuals with regard to the processing of personal data. It also critically analyzes some philosophical theories of privacy. Elgesem argues that the restricted access theory of privacy, a variation of which he attributes to Moor, is too narrow to be an adequate conception of privacy. He then proposes a theory of privacy and data protection in which he introduces the notion of "channels" or "social arenas" for the flow of personal information. Elgesem believes that his theory of privacy is better suited for characterizing the central issues raised in the EU Directive than alternative privacy theories.

In the chapter's third reading, "Privacy Protection, Control of Information, and Privacy-Enhancing Technologies," Herman Tavani and James Moor respond to Elgesem by arguing that confusion regarding privacy occurs whenever we fail to distinguish between the *concept* of privacy and the *management* and *justification* of privacy. Tavani and Moor also argue that whereas the concept of privacy is best understood in terms of restricted access to information, the management of and justification for privacy require individual controls. Individual control mechanisms must allow for *choice*, *consent*, and *correction*. To illustrate these distinctions, the authors include some examples of Privacy-Enhancing Technologies (or PETS). These examples show how an individual can both (a) exercise control over one's personal information but not have privacy, and (b) have privacy without having total control over one's personal information. Tavani and Moor conclude that, in addition to individual controls such as those provided by PETs, stronger privacy policies that both establish and enforce zones of privacy are needed to guarantee privacy protection for individuals.

The fourth reading, by Helen Nissenbaum, explores some of the difficulties of protecting personal privacy in public contexts. She states this problem "falls outside the scope of dominant theoretical approaches" to privacy. Traditional privacy theories, Nissenbaum points out, emphasize the connection between privacy and the protection of information in the personal or "intimate" sphere. She notes that cybertechnology generates a kind of personal information that is not currently protected by privacy norms because it is considered to be in "a sphere other than intimate." Nissenbaum exposes two assumptions underlying this problem, both of which she believes are misleading: (1) There is a realm of public information about persons to which no privacy norms apply, and (2) An aggregate of information does not violate privacy if its parts, taken individually, do not. To avoid the conceptual traps that result from these two misleading assumptions, Nissenbaum argues for a conception of privacy that would "extend consideration to all information," including information gathered in the public sphere.

Data Mining and the Knowledge Discovery Process

The first four readings in this chapter are primarily concerned with conceptual and theoretical aspects of privacy; the fifth and sixth readings examine a specific technology that has raised concerns for personal privacy in both on- and off-line contexts. This relatively new technique of information gathering is called "Knowledge Discovery in Databases" (KDD), but is referred to more commonly as *data mining*. What exactly is this data-gathering technique, and how is it different from other data-collecting schemes?

Because personal data has been gathered and manipulated long before the advent of computers and the Internet, one may ask why the use of computerized techniques make a significant difference. First, consider the amount of data that now can be collected because of computers and cybertechnology. Also consider the speed at which that data can be transferred, as well as the indefinite duration of time the data can be stored. As a result of these and other factors, personal privacy is threatened in ways that it was not in the pre-computer era. We should also note that electronic records in one database can easily be merged with or matched against records in another database. Because of concerns related to the easy flow of personal information between and across computer databases, laws such as the Privacy Act of 1974 in the United States and the 1995 Directive in Europe (see the reading by Elgesem in this chapter) have been enacted to set limits on the ways in which electronic records containing personal information can be transferred and exchanged. However, these laws apply only to the exchange of a specific kind of information in electronic records—the kind of personal information that is deemed to be confidential (e.g., electronic records that contain information about one's financial affairs, health status, etc.). As Helen Nissenbaum points out in the fourth reading in this chapter, we now have good reasons to worry about how some information that has generally been categorized as *public* in character, and thus assumed not to be in need of normative or legal protection, is so easily gathered.

Although intimate or confidential information is protected by existing privacy laws and policies, much of the personal information that can now be gathered online does not enjoy legal or normative protection. Legally protected personal information in computer databases typically exists in the form of explicit electronic records. However, data-mining techniques are now used to search for and "mine" personal information in patterns that are merely implicit in data. In many cases, the newly discovered data-mined patterns pertaining to individuals are "non-obvious" to those individuals ultimately affected. As a result, decisions about individuals can be made based on certain patterns that identify these individuals with a certain group—and possibly a "non-obvious group" that many of the identified individuals had no idea even existed. These seemingly innocuous pieces of data, which are exempt from legal or normative protection, can sometimes generate non-obvious groups of people. For example, an individual with impeccable credit might be denied an automobile loan based solely on his or her identification with a "risky" consumer group because of certain behavioral patterns revealed in one or more data-mining applications. Recall Nissenbaum's concern with the misleading assumption: *An aggregate of information does not violate privacy if its parts, taken individually, do not.* This assumption can be found in the rationale underlying many who engage in data-mining activities. And when combined with the other assumption that Nissenbaum finds misleading—*There is a realm of public information about persons to which no privacy norms apply*—we see how the central problems associated with data mining arise.

In this chapter we include two readings on privacy concerns involving data mining, one by Anton Vedder and one by Joseph Fulda. Although neither reading examines data mining issues that are particular to the Internet per se, each proposes a solution to the problem of data mining in general.[2] In the fifth reading, "KDD, Privacy, Individuality, and Fairness," Vedder points out that the KDD process can produce group profiles that confront us with morally problematic situations. He also shows why current privacy laws and theories are inadequate to address these difficulties, because they approach the issue with what Vedder describes as far too narrow a conception of "personal data." As a proposed resolution, the author introduces the notion of "categorial privacy."

Fulda offers a different kind of solution to data-mining privacy problems in the chapter's sixth reading. In a paper entitled "Data Mining and Privacy," Fulda invites us to consider two distinct, but related, questions: (1) "Is it possible for data that do not in themselves deserve legal protection to contain implicit knowledge that does deserve legal protection?" and (2) "[I]f so, what balance must be struck between the freedom to use whatever knowledge one has at one's disposal to further one's own ends and...the freedom not to have one's personal data mined into knowledge that will be used as a means to someone else's ends?" Fulda suggests that answers to these questions are crucial in providing an adequate solution to privacy problems involving data mining. Essentially, Fulda believes that a solution to the problem exists in developing a theory of privacy rights that is (a) based generally on tort law (in the United States), and (b) updated for the information age.[3]

Workplace Privacy, Surveillance, and Autonomy

The last two readings in Chapter 4 examine privacy concerns related to surveillance, employee monitoring, and autonomy. These privacy issues involve concerns about the use of computing devices to engage in surveillance activities such as the tracking of individuals' online behavior (e.g., through "cookies" technology) and employee monitoring in the workplace. The idea of supervisors monitoring their subordinates' workloads and workplace productivity is hardly new. But computer technology has made possible a kind of "invisible supervisor" who can track certain kinds of employee tasks and functions in a way that could not have been measured so precisely in the pre-computer era. So-called "informational workers" have perhaps been the most vulnerable group to this relatively new form of workplace surveillance. Because the very tools that information workers use to carry out their workplace assignments—i.e., computing and electronic devices used to book airline flights, take incoming phone requests

---

[2] These two readings were selected because of the interesting "solutions" they offer to the problem. For more information about data-mining activities that are specific to the Internet, such as issues involving the use of meta-search engines, "softbots," and electronic agents to harvest information from the Web, see Fulda (1998) and Tavani (1999).

[3] The interested reader can further compare the American perspective on privacy (Fulda) to the European view (Vedder) in terms of the solution that each offers to privacy issues involving data mining by consulting the readings by Elgesem, in Chapter 4, and Camp, in Chapter 5, to shed some additional light on these two very different perspectives on privacy.

for merchandise, etc.—these employees are subject to computerized monitoring in ways that employees in other professions and trades are not.

Certain businesses argue that computerized employee monitoring increases workplace productivity, keeps the business competitive, and helps prevent employee fraud, abuse, and theft. Opponents of monitoring counter that computerized monitoring violates employee autonomy and privacy and eliminates the possibility of trust on the part of employees. However, they propose that if the monitoring occurs, it should at least conform to a "code of ethics" (see, for example, Marx and Sherizen, 1986) in which clear and explicit guidelines are followed. First, employees must be told that their activities are being monitored. Workers would also be permitted to verify the accuracy of any information gathered about them by computers. An adequate code for monitoring, according to Marx and Sherizen, would also require that a statute of limitations be set for how long the information about an employee can be kept on file.

In the sixth reading, Lucas Introna considers issues of privacy, autonomy, and fairness related to workplace surveillance. Introna asks whether employees can legitimately resist increasing scrutiny now that modern technologies provide unprecedented opportunities for surveillance. He points out that while surveillance technologies have become less expensive, they also have become more overt and more diffused. In fact, Introna notes that surveillance is being "built into" technology itself and into the very fabric of many of our organizational processes. He argues that the distribution of privacy rights and transparency rights (in defense of surveillance) is a matter of "distributive justice." Introna then suggests that we can use the Rawlsian notion of "the veil of ignorance," introduced in John Rawls' classic work *A Theory of Justice*, to develop a framework of distributive justice that would fairly distribute transparency and privacy between the collective (i.e., the interests of the corporation or organization) and the individual (viz., the worker), respectively.

Although Introna's essay focuses on issues involving workplace surveillance, it also raises the broader concern of certain tensions that exist between the *collective* and the *individual*. In the final reading of Chapter 4, "Privacy and the Varieties of Informational Wrongdoing," Jeroen van den Hoven considers the privacy debate from the vantage point of collectivists (Communitarians) and individualists (Liberalists). He raises the question of how competing claims for personal freedom and autonomy and the needs for the community must be balanced. The problem arises, van den Hoven points out, because of a tension between those who strive to protect an individual's personal information and those who want to make information more readily available in order to benefit the community. Although many arguments have been advanced in defense of privacy rights for individuals, some authors (see, for example, Etzioni, 1999) have also recently expressed the need to be concerned with privacy policies as they affect the interests of the greater community.

Among the privacy issues not directly considered in Chapter 4 are those involving email privacy. For example, should employers be able to monitor and read an employee's email messages? What can an employee reasonably expect for privacy in his or her email? What kinds of privacy protections can ordinary users expect in email communications? Although privacy issues involving email per se are not examined in this chapter, the reading by Jean Camp in Chapter 5 discusses certain privacy and security issues that affect email communications. Interested readers may elect to read that article in conjunction with one or more readings in Chapter 4.

Privacy issues related to the use of biometric technologies in public places are examined in readings included in Chapter 5. These readings, by Irma van der Ploeg and Philip Brey, discuss privacy as well as security issues of biometrics

Discussion Questions

1. What is personal privacy, and why is privacy such a difficult concept to define? Describe the key aspects of James Moor's "restricted access/limited control theory" of privacy. In what ways can this theory be viewed as an improvement over earlier privacy theories?

2. How does the theory of privacy advanced by Dag Elgesem, which represents the European Union (EU) perspective, differ from Moor's theory? What are some of the key differences between the notion of "data protection," as practiced by the EU countries, and the concept of individual privacy as understood in the United States?

3. Describe the strategy that Moor and Tavani use to respond to Elgesem's critique of the restricted access/limited control theory of privacy. In particular, what roles do they believe the notions of *choice, consent,* and *correction* play in the "management of privacy"? What are Privacy Enhancing Technologies or PETs? Do PETs provide Internet users with adequate privacy protection?

4. What does Helen Nissenbaum mean by the "Problem of Protecting Privacy in Public"? How is this problem exacerbated by current uses of cybertechnology? Do you agree with Nissenbaum's assessment of the problem?

5. What is Knowledge Discovery in Databases (KDD), and why does Anton Vedder believe that this technology raises problems for individual privacy and fairness? Why does Vedder also believe that a new scheme of privacy protection, called *categorical privacy,* is needed to respond to problems introduced by the use of KDD?

6. What exactly is *data mining,* and why has it been considered by many privacy advocates to be an especially serious threat to individual privacy? How, according to Joseph Fulda, can at least some privacy problems associated with data-mining practices in the United States be resolved through a theory of privacy rights based on tort law?

7. Summarize the arguments that Lucas Introna presents for and against the use of computer technology to monitor employees? How does Introna appeal to John Rawls' notion of a "veil of ignorance" to make the case against a presumption in favor of employee monitoring? What does Introna mean by an "asymmetry of power" on the part of employees in the debate over computerized monitoring in the workplace? Do you agree with Introna's position on this issue?

8. Why does Jeroen van den Hoven believe that the privacy debate in Western democracies can be analyzed in terms of the dispute between communitarianism and classical liberalism? Have individual privacy rights gone too far, as some communitarian critics suggest? Do claims involving individual privacy rights and expectations now threaten the "collective good"? How does van den Hoven respond to the communitarian position? Does an individual's right to privacy change in the post-September 11 World?

References

Allen, Anita (1988). *Uneasy Access: Privacy for Women in a Free Society.* Totowa, NJ: Rowman and Littlefield.

DeCew, Judith W. (1997). *In Pursuit of Privacy: Law, Ethics, and the Rise of Technology.* Ithaca, New York: Cornell University Press.

Etzioni, Amatai (1999). *The Limits of Privacy.* Basic Books, New York.

Fried, Charles (1984). "Privacy." F. D. Schoeman, ed. *Philosophical Dimensions of Privacy.* New York: Cambridge University Press.

Fulda, Joseph S. (1998). "Data Mining and the Web," *Computers and Society,* Vol. 28, No. 1, March pp. 42–43.

Gavison, Ruth (1980). "Privacy and the Limits of the Law," *Yale Law Journal,* Vol. 89, 1980.

Moor, James H. (1990). "Ethics of Privacy Protection." *Library Trends,* Vol. 39, Nos. 1 & 2, pp. 69–82.

Rachels, James (1995). "Why Privacy Is Important." D.G. Johnson and H. Nissenbaum, eds. *Computing, Ethics and Social Values.* Upper Saddle River, NJ: Prentice Hall, pp. 351–357.

Regan, Prescilla M. (1995). *Legislating Privacy: Technology, Social Values, and Public Policy.* The University of North Carolina Press, Chapel Hill, North Carolina.

Tavani, Herman T. (1999). "Informational Privacy, Data Mining, and the Internet." *Ethics and Information Technology,* Vol. 1, No. 2, pp. 137–145.

Warren, Sammuel and Louis Brandeis (1890). "The Right to Privacy," *Harvard Law Review,* Vol. 14, No. 5.

Suggestions for Further Readings

Agre, Philip and Marc Rotenberg, eds. (1997). *Technology and Privacy: The New Landscape.* Cambridge, MA: MIT Press.

Bennett, Colin J. (2001). "Cookies, Web Bugs, Webcams, and CUE Cats: Patterns of Surveillance on the World Wide Web," *Ethics and Information Technology,* Vol. 3, No. 3, pp. 197–210.

Bennett, Colin J., and Rebecca Grant, eds. (1999). *Visions of Privacy:* Policy Choices for the Digital Age. Toronto: University of Toronto Press Incorporated.

Chaum, David (1991). "Achieving Electronic Privacy," *Scientific American,* August, pp. 96–101.

Clarke, Roger. (1999). "Internet Privacy Concerns Confirm the Case for Intervention," Communications of the ACM, Vol. 42, No. 2, pp. 60–67.

Cranor, Lorrie F. (1999). "Internet Privacy," *Communications of the ACM,* Vol. 42, No. 2, pp. 28–31.

DeCew, Judith W. (1999). "Alternatives for Protecting Privacy While Respecting Patient Care and Public Health Needs," *Ethics and Information Technology,* Vol. 1, No. 4, pp. 249–255.

Diffie, Whitield and Susan Landau (1998). *Privacy on the Line. The Politics of Wiretapping and Encryption.* Cambridge, MA: MIT Press.

Edgar, Stacey L. (2003). "Privacy." Chapter 7 in *Morality and Machines: Perspectives on Computer Ethics.* 2nd ed. Sudbury, MA: Jones and Bartlett.

Elgesem, Dag (1996). "Privacy, Respect for Persons, and Risk." C. Ess, ed. *Philosophical Perspectives on Computer-Mediated Communication.* New York: State University of New York Press.

Fulda, Joseph S. (1999). "A New Standard for Appropriation, with Some Remarks on Aggregration," *University of New Brunswick Law Journal,* Vol. 48, pp. 313–323.

Gandy, Oscar H. (1993). *The Panoptic Sort: A Political Economy of Personal Information.* Boulder, CO: Westview Press.

Garfinkel, Simson (1999). *Database Nation. The Death of Privacy in the 21st Century.* Cambridge, MA: O'Reilly and Associates, Inc.

Gotterbarn, Don (1999). "Privacy Lost: The Net, Autonomous Agents, and 'Virtual Information,'" *Ethics and Information Technology,* Vol. 1, No. 2, pp. 147–154.

Introna, Lucas D. (1997). "Privacy and the Computer: Why We Need Privacy in the Information Society," *Metaphilosophy,* Vol.28, No. 3, July, pp. 259–275.

Loudon, Kenneth C. (1986). *Dossier Society: Value Choices in the Design of a National Information System.* New York: Columbia University Press.

Marx, Gary (2001). "Murky Conceptual Waters: The Public and the Private," *Ethics and Information Technology,* Vol. 3, No. 3, pp. 157–169.

Marx, Gary and Sanford Sherizen (1986). "Monitoring on the Job," *Technology Review,* November/December.

Moor, James H. (1999). "Using Genetic Information While Protecting the Privacy of the Soul," *Ethics and Information Technology,* Vol. 1, No. 4, pp. 257–263.

Nissenbaum, Helen (1998). "Protecting Privacy in an Information Age," *Law and Philosophy,* Vol. 17, pp. 559–596.

O'Connell, Brian M. (1999). "Employment Privacy: Where Utopia Meets Reality," *Australian Journal of Professional and Applied Ethics,* Vol. 1, No. 1, pp. 96–102.

Parent, W. (1983). "Privacy, Morality, and the Law," *Philosophy and Public Affairs,* Vol. 12, No. 5, pp. 269–288.

Reiman, Jeffrey (1984). "Privacy, Intimacy, and Personhood." F. D. Schoeman, ed. *Philosophical Dimensions of Privacy.* New York: Cambridge University Press.

Sipior, Janice C. and Burke T. Ward (1995). "The Ethical and Legal Quandaries of Email Privacy," *Communications of the ACM,* Vol. 38, No. 12, December, pp. 28–31, pp. 33–39.

Spinello, Richard A. (1997). "The End of Privacy." R. E. Long, ed. Rights to Privacy. New York: H. W. Wilson, Co.

Spinello, Richard A. (2003). "Regulating Internet Privacy." Chapter 5 in *CyberEthics: Morality and Law in Cyberspace.* 2nd ed. Sudbury, MA: Jones and Bartlett.

Tavani, Herman T. (2000). "Privacy-Enhancing Technologies as a Panacea for Online Privacy Concerns: Some Ethical Considerations," *Journal of Information Ethics,* Vol. 9, No. 2, pp. 26–36.

Tavani, Herman T. (2004). "Privacy and Cyberspace." Chapter 5 in Ethics and Technology: *Ethical Issues in an Age of Information and Communication Technology.* Hoboken, NJ: John Wiley and Sons.

Vedder, Anton H. (1999). "KDD: The Challenge to Individualism," *Ethics and Information Technology, Vol. 1, No. 4, pp. 275–281.*

Westin, Anthony F. (1967). *Privacy and Freedom.* New York: Atheneum Press.

Toward a Theory of Privacy for the Information Age

James H. Moor

Greased Data

When we think of ethical problems involving computing, probably none is more paradigmatic than the issue of privacy. Given the ability of computers to manipulate information—to store endlessly, to sort efficiently, and to locate effortlessly—we are justifiably concerned that in a computerized society our privacy may be invaded and that information harmful to us will be revealed. Of course, we are reluctant to give up the advantages of speedy and convenient computerized information. We appreciate the easy access to computerized data when making reservations, using automatic teller machines, buying new products on the web, or investigating topics in computer databases. Our challenge is to take advantage of computing without allowing computing to take advantage of us. When information is computerized, it is *greased* to slide easily and quickly to many ports of call. This makes information retrieval quick and convenient. But legitimate concerns about privacy arise when this speed and convenience lead to the improper exposure of information. Greased information is information that moves like lightning and is hard to hold onto.

Consider, for example, listed telephone numbers that have been routinely available through a telephone operator and a telephone book but that now are available along with address information in giant electronic phone books on the internet. The Hanover, New Hampshire telephone book (the telephone book for where I live) is rather hard to locate in most places in the world, but now anyone in the world with access to the internet can easily find out my phone number, who my wife is, and where I live. One can even retrieve a map of my residential area. I don't consider this to be a breach of privacy, but I use it to point out how the same information, which has technically been public for a long time, can dramatically change levels of accessibility practically speaking when put into electronic form on computer networks. It is ironic that my name may be hard to find in the internet phone book in that it is listed there anachronistically in an abbreviated form. "James" is

This essay originally appeared in *Computers and Society,* Vol. 27, No. 3 (September) 1997: 27–32. Copyright © 1997 by James H. Moor. Reprinted by permission.

abbreviated as "Jas," an abbreviation I never use and have seen only in old print phone books, presumably introduced to save print space but mindlessly copied when put on the internet. Don't tell anyone.

The greasing of information makes information so easy to access that it can be used again and again. Computers have elephant memories—big, accurate, and long term. The ability of computers to remember so well for so long undercuts a human frailty that assists privacy. We, humans, forget most things. Most short term memories don't even make it to long term memory. Every time I go to a busy supermarket I am a new customer. Who can remember what I bought the last time I was there? Actually, a computer does. Most of the time I shop at a cooperative food store that gives a rebate at the end of the year. When I buy food, I give the checkout person my account number (I can remember at least that most days). The checkout person scans my purchases, which appear on a screen by the name of the item and its price. This information is definitely greased. It appears as quickly as the checker can move the items across the barcode reader. Then my total is displayed and the information is added to my grand total of purchases of which I get a certain percentage back each year. Notice that in addition to the total of my purchases, the market also has information about what I have purchased. It helps the market keep track of its inventory. But, it also means that the store has a profile on my buying habits. They know how much wine I purchase, my fondness for Raisin Bran cereal, and the kind of vegetables I prefer. In principle, such evidence could be subpoenaed if my eating habits were relevant to a court case. Does this accumulation of information violate my privacy? I suppose not, but it is greased so that it moves easily and is more accessible over a longer period of time than ever before. Practically speaking, the information is never forgotten. A documented history of purchases generates the possibility for an invasion of privacy that does not exist without it.

In the case of my food shopping, the collection of information is obvious to me. I can see my eating habits and my limited willpower flash on the display screen as the calories tumble by on the conveyor. But information about us can be collected subtly when we don't realize it. The greasing of information allows other computers to capture and manipulate information in ways we do not expect. Consider a final personal example to illustrate this. Not long ago I lived for a few months in Edinburgh. On days I didn't feel like cooking, I would sometimes order pizza. The pizza was delivered to my apartment and hence was a convenient way to get a quick meal. However, I was somewhat taken aback the second time I phoned the pizza establishment. Without my placing an order the pizzamakers already seemed to know my address and my favorite pizza. Did I want to have another medium pepperoni and mushroom delivered? I hadn't been in Edinburgh very long. How could they possibly know my taste (or lack of taste) so quickly? The answer, of course, was their use of caller ID. No mystery here. I had called before and given information about my pizza preference and my delivery address, and they had linked it with my phone number. When I called the second time, my phone number was captured electronically by the pizza parlor and used to select the other information from my first call. Had my privacy been invaded? Probably not, but I confess that I initially felt some mild indignation that my pizza profile had been stored away without my knowing it. If I were a frequent customer in a fine restaurant and the waiter had memorized my tastes, I would feel complimented that he remembered me. But, as efficient as the caller ID/computer system was, I found no gain in self worth by having a pizza parlor computer recall my intake of pepperoni and mushroom pizza.

I mention these three examples, the internet phone book, the supermarket refund policy based on bar code data, and the pizza parlor caller ID, not because they represent some deep treachery but because they are perfectly ordinary activities and illustrate how effortlessly information is collected and transmitted without any of us giving it a second thought. Once information is captured electronically for whatever purpose, it is greased and ready to go for *any* purpose. In a computerized world we leave electronic footprints everywhere, and data collected for one purpose can be resurrected and used elsewhere. The problem of computer privacy is to keep proper vigilance on where such information can and should go.

For the most part the need for privacy is like good art, you know it when you see it. But sometimes our intuitions can be misleading and it is important to become as clear as possible what privacy is, how it is justified, and how it is applied in ethical situations. In this paper I will assemble pieces of an overall theory of privacy and try to defend it. In the computer age during a period when information technology is growing rapidly and its consequences are difficult to predict more than a few days in advance, if at all, it is more important than ever to determine how privacy should be understood and guarded.

Grounding Privacy

From the point of view of ethical theory, privacy is a curious value. On the one hand, it seems to be something of very great importance and something vital to defend, and, on the other hand, privacy seems to be a matter of individual preference, culturally relative, and difficult to justify in general. Is privacy a primary value? How can we justify or ground the importance of privacy?

I will discuss two standard ways of justifying privacy, both of which I have used before, and describe the limitations of these two approaches. Then I will present a third way to justify the importance of privacy that I now find more defensible. Philosophers frequently distinguish between instrumental values and intrinsic values. Instrumental values are those values that are good because they lead to something else that is good. Intrinsic values are values that are good in themselves. Instrumental values are good as means; intrinsic values are good as ends. My computer is good as a means to help me write papers, send e-mail, and calculate my taxes. My computer has instrumental value. However, the joy I gain from using my computer is good in itself. Joy doesn't have to lead to anything to have value. Joy has intrinsic value. And, as philosophers since Aristotle have pointed out, some things, such as health, have both instrumental and intrinsic value. This familiar philosophical distinction between instrumental and intrinsic values suggests two common ways to attempt to justify privacy.

Almost everyone would agree that privacy has instrumental value. This is its most common justification. Privacy offers us protection against harm. For example, in some cases if a person's medical condition were publicly known, then that person would risk discrimination. If the person tests HIV+, an employer might be reluctant to hire him and an insurance company might be reluctant to insure him.

Examples of this nature are well known and we need not amass examples further to make a convincing case that privacy has instrumental value. But, so do tooth-picks. To justify the high instrumental value of privacy we need to show that not only does privacy have instrumental value but that it leads to something very, very important. One of the best known attempts to do this has been given by James Rachaels. Rachaels suggests that privacy is valuable because it enables us to form varied relationships with other people [Rachels, 1975, p. 323]. Privacy does enable us to form intimate bonds with other people that might be difficult to form and maintain in public. But the need to relate to others differently may not ground pri-vacy securely because not everyone may want to form varied relationships and those who do may not need privacy to do it. Some people simply do not care how they are perceived by others.

The justification of privacy would be more secure if we could show that it has intrinsic value. Deborah Johnson has suggested a clever way of doing this. Johnson proposes that we regard "privacy as an essential aspect of autonomy" [Johnson, 1994, p. 89]. So, assuming that autonomy is intrinsically valuable and privacy is a nec-essary condition for autonomy, we have the strong and attractive claim that pri-vacy is a necessary condition for an intrinsic good. If privacy is not an intrinsic good itself, it is the next best thing. But, is it true that "autonomy is inconceivable with-out privacy"? [Johnson, 1994, p. 89]

I have proposed a thought experiment about Tom, an electronic eavesdropper, which, I believe, shows Johnson's claim to be incorrect [Moor, 1989, pp. 61–62]. In this thought experiment, Tom is very good with computers and electronics and has a real fondness for knowing about you—all about you. Tom uses computers secret-ly to search your financial records, your medical records, and your criminal records. He knows about your late mortgage payments, your persistent hemorrhoids, and that driving while intoxicated charge that you thought was long forgotten. Tom is so fascinated with your life that he has clandestine cameras installed that record your every movement. You know nothing about any of this, but Tom really enjoys watching you, especially those instant replays. "For Tom, watching your life is like following a soap opera—The Days of Your Life" [Moor, 1989, p. 62]. I think most of us will agree that there is something repugnant about Tom's peeping. But what is it? It is not that he is directly harming you. He doesn't use any of this information to hurt you. He doesn't share the information with anyone else or take advantage of you in any way whatsoever. Moreover, you have complete autonomy, just no pri-vacy. Thus, it follows that privacy is not an essential condition for autonomy. It is conceivable to have autonomy without privacy. Nevertheless, I would agree that some people, including myself, regard privacy as intrinsically valuable, not mere-ly instrumentally valuable.

Now let me consider a third approach to justifying the importance of privacy. I wish to maintain that there is a set of values, which I call the "core values," which are shared and fundamental to human evaluation. The test for a core value is that it is a value that is found in all human cultures. Here is the list of some of the val-ues that I believe are at the core: *life, happiness, freedom, knowledge, ability, resources,* and *security.* My claim is an empirical one. I am claiming that all sustainable human cultures will exhibit these values. I am not suggesting for a moment that all cultures are moral or that these goods are fairly distributed in every culture. Regrettably, they almost never are. (An ethical theory requires an account of fairness as well as an account of the core values.) What I am claiming is that every viable culture will exhibit a preference for these values. Consider the most primitive, immoral culture you can imagine. As barbaric and repulsive as it is, its members must find nourishment and raise their young if the culture is to survive. These activities require at least implicit acknowledgment of the core values. To abandon the core values completely is to abandon existence.

Is privacy a core value? I wish it were. It would make the justification of privacy so much easier. But, upon reflection it is clear that it is not in the core. One can easily imagine sustainable and flourishing human cultures that place no value on privacy. Consider a man and a woman who live together but give each other no privacy and who could care less about privacy. Presumably, many couples live this way and have no trouble existing. Now imagine a family or a small tribe with equal disinterest in privacy. Everybody in the group can know as much as they want about everybody else. They might believe that their society functions better without secrets. An anti-Rachaelsean in the society might maintain that they have better and more varied human relationships just because they can know everything about everybody! The concept of privacy has a distinctly cultural aspect that goes beyond the core values. Some cultures may value privacy and some may not.

How then should we justify privacy? How is it grounded? Let me propose a justification of privacy by using the core values. The core values are the values that all normal humans and cultures need for survival. Knowledge, for example, is crucial for the ongoing survival of individuals and cultures. The transmission of culture from one generation to the next by definition involves the transmission of knowledge. I emphasize the core values because they provide a common value framework, a set of standards by which we can assess the activities of different people and different cultures [Moor, 1998]. The core values allow us to make transcultural judgments. The core values are the values we have in common as human beings. To focus on the core is to focus on similarities. But now let's focus on the differences. Individuals and cultures articulate the core values differently depending on environment and circumstances. The transmission of knowledge is essential for the survival of every culture, but it is not the same knowledge that must be transmitted. Resources such as food are essential for everyone, but not everyone must prefer the same kind of food. So, though there is a common framework of values, there is also room for much individual and cultural variation within the framework. Let's call the articulation of a core value for an individual or a culture the "expression of a core value."

Although privacy is not a core value per se, it is the expression of a core value, viz., the value of security. Without protection, species and cultures don't survive and flourish. All cultures need security of some kind, but not all need privacy. As societies become larger and highly interactive, but less intimate, privacy becomes a natural expression of the need for security. We seek protection from strangers who may have goals antithetical to our own. In particular, in a large, highly computerized culture in which lots of personal information is greased, it is almost inevitable that privacy will emerge as an expression of the core value, security.

Consider once again the dichotomy between instrumental and intrinsic values. Because privacy is instrumental in supporting all of the core values, it is instrumental for important matters; and because privacy is a necessary means of support in a highly computerized culture, privacy is instrumentally well grounded for our society. Moreover, because privacy is an expression of the core value of security, it is a plausible candidate for an intrinsic good in the context of a highly populated, computerized society. Tom, the electronic eavesdropper who doesn't harm his subject when he spies, nevertheless seems to be doing something wrong intrinsically. The subject's security is being violated by Tom even if no other harm befalls the person. People have a basic right to be protected, which from the point of view of our computerized culture, includes privacy protection.

I have argued that using the core value framework, privacy can be grounded both instrumentally and intrinsically—instrumentally, as a support of all the core values, and intrinsically, as an expression of security. I am, however, concerned that the traditional instrumental/intrinsic understanding may be misleading. Traditionally, instrumental/intrinsic analyses push us in the direction of a search for a summum bonum, a greatest good. We try to find the one thing to which all other things lead. In the core value approach that I am advocating, some values may be more important than others, but there is not a summum bonum. Rather the model is one of an intersupporting framework. The core values, as the beams of a truss, are in support of each other. Asking whether a core value or the expression of a core value is instrumental or intrinsic is like asking whether a beam of a truss is supporting or supported. It is essentially both. The core values for all of us are mutually supporting. Some people will emphasize some values more than others. An athlete will emphasize ability, a businessperson will emphasize resources, a soldier will emphasize security, a scholar will emphasize knowledge, and so forth. However, everyone and every culture needs all of the core values to exist and flourish. Privacy, as an expression of security, is a critical, interlocking member in our systems of values in our increasingly computerized culture.

The Nature of Privacy

Understanding privacy as the expression of the core value of security has the advantage of explaining the changing conception of privacy over time. Privacy is not mentioned explicitly either in the United States Declaration of Independence or in its Constitution [Moor, 1990]. It is strange that a value that seems so important to us now was not even mentioned by the revolutionary leaders and statesmen who were so impressed with the ideals of individual freedoms. The concept of privacy has been evolving in the U.S. from a concept of non-intrusion (e.g., the Fourth Amendment to the U.S. Constitution offering protection against unreasonable governmental searches and seizures), to a concept of non-interference (e.g., the Roe v. Wade decision giving a woman the right to choose to have an abortion), to limited information access (e.g., Privacy Act of 1974 restricting the collection, use, and distribution of information by Federal Agencies). Privacy is a concept that has been dramatically stretched over time. In our computer age, the notion of privacy has become stretched even further. Now the concept of privacy has become so informationally enriched [Moor, 1998] that "privacy" in contemporary use typically refers to informational privacy, though, of course, other aspects of the concept remain important.

Consider a useful distinction that helps to avoid some misunderstandings about the nature of privacy. The term "privacy" is sometimes used to designate a situation in which people are protected from intrusion or observation by natural or physical circumstances. Someone spelunking by herself would be in a naturally private (and probably dangerous) situation. Nobody can see her in the cave she is exploring. In addition to natural privacy there is normative privacy. A normatively private situation is a situation protected by ethical, legal, or conventional norms. Consultations with a lawyer or doctor would be normatively private situations. Obviously, many normatively private situations are naturally private as well. We send mail in sealed envelopes. When an unauthorized entry is made into a normatively private situation, privacy has not only been lost, it has been breached or invaded.

Now if we put the evolving conceptions of privacy together with distinction between normative and natural privacy, we get a useful account of the nature of privacy.

> An individual or group has normative privacy in a situation with regard to others if and only if in that situation the individual or group is normatively protected from intrusion, interference, and information access by others. [Culver, Moor, et al., 1994, p. 6]

I use the general term "situation" deliberately because it is broad enough to cover many kinds of privacy: private *locations* such as one's diary in a computer file, private *relationships* such as e-mail to one's pharmacy, and private *activities* such as the utilization of computerized credit histories.

The situations that are normatively private can vary significantly from culture to culture, place to place, and time to time. This doesn't show that the privacy standards are arbitrary or unjustified, they are just different. For example, at a private college, faculty salaries are kept confidential, but at some state colleges faculty salaries, at least salaries above a certain level, are published. Presumably, the private colleges believe that protecting salary information will reduce squabbling and embarrassment, whereas state colleges (or the state legislatures) believe that the taxpayers who support the institution have the right to know how much faculty members are being paid. These are different but defensible policies for protecting and releasing information.

Clearly some personal information is very sensitive and should be protected. We need to create zones of privacy, a variety of private situations, so that people can ensure that information about themselves that might be damaging if generally released will be protected. With different zones of privacy, one can decide how much personal information to keep private and how much to make public. Notice that on my account the notion of privacy really attaches to a situation or zone and not to the information itself. For instance, if an Internal Revenue Service employee uses a computer to call up and process a movie star's income tax return, then the employee is not invading the star's privacy. He is allowed in this situation to investigate the star's tax return. However, if that same employee were to call up that same star's tax return on his computer after hours just to browse around, then the employee would be violating the star's privacy although the employee may gain no new information! The employee has legitimate access in the first situation but not the second.

The theory I am proposing is a version of the restricted access view of privacy [Moor, 1990, pp. 76–80]. The major opposing view is the control theory of privacy. One proponent of this view, Charles Fried, writes, "Privacy is not simply an absence of information about us in the minds of others, rather it is the *control* we have over information about ourselves" [Fried, 1984, p. 209]. I agree that it is highly desirable that we control information about ourselves. However, in a highly computerized culture this is simply impossible. We don't control vast amounts of information about ourselves. Personal information about us is well greased and slides rapidly through computer systems around the world, around the clock. Therefore, to protect ourselves we need to make sure the right people and only the right people have *access* to relevant information at the right time. Hence, the restricted access view puts the focus on what we should be considering when developing policies for protecting privacy. However, the restricted access account, at least in the form I am proposing it, has all of the advantages of the control theory for one of the goals in setting policies to give individuals as much control (informed consent) over personal data as realistically possible. For this reason I will label my account as a "control/restricted access" theory of privacy.

The control/restricted access conception of privacy has the advantage that polices for privacy can be fine tuned. Different people may be given different levels of access for different kinds of information at different times. A good example occurs in a modern, computerized hospital. Physicians are allowed access to on-line medical information while secretaries are not. However, physicians are generally not allowed to see all the information about a patient that a hospital possesses. For example, they don't have access to most billing records. In some hospitals some medical information such as psychiatric interviews may be accessible to some physicians and not others. Rather than regarding privacy as an all or nothing proposition—either only I know or everybody knows—it is better to regard it as a complex of situations in which information is authorized to flow to some people some of the time. Ideally, those who need to know do, those who don't don't.

The control/restricted access also explains some anomalies about private situations. Usually, when we consider privacy, we are thinking about situations in which individuals possess possibly damaging personal information they want to keep others from knowing. But situations can be private in other circumstances. Imagine a situation in a restaurant with scores of people dining. A couple begins to argue loudly and eventually each shouts to the other about a marital problem they are having. They go into excruciating detail about various kinds of sexual dysfunction and bodily needs. Everyone can hear them and many patrons of the restaurant feel uncomfortable as they proceed with their meal. Finally, the waiter, who thinks he can help, cannot stand it anymore. He walks over to the couple and asks whether they would like his advice. The couple in unison tell him, "No, it's a private matter."

As ironic as their comment may be, it does make sense on several levels. In private situations, the access to information can be blocked in both directions. This couple did not want to allow information from the waiter although they themselves had been indiscreet in revealing details to the entire population of the restaurant. Moreover, in our culture some activities are required to be done in private. Discussions of one's intimate marital problems may be one of them. Privacy is a form of protection and it can protect the general population as well as individuals.

Setting and Adjusting Policies for Private Situations

So far I have commented on the greasing effect computerization has on information and the potential problems for privacy computerization poses. I have proposed a justification for privacy as an expression of one of the core values and as an essential member of the central framework of values for a computerized society. I have characterized the nature of privacy as an evolving concept that has become informationally enriched with the development of computing. And I have argued that privacy is best understood in terms of a control/restricted access account. Now it is time to focus on practical policies for the protection of privacy. As an example, I will use information gathered from genetic testing. This is an interesting case because, practically speaking, genetic testing would not be possible without information technology, and with information technology, genetic testing is one of the greatest potential threats to our individual privacy. Improper disclosure of our genetic information may be the ultimate violation of our privacy.

Suppose a patient decides to have herself tested for a breast cancer gene. She does not have breast cancer, but breast cancer runs in her family and she wants to know whether she is genetically disposed to have breast cancer. She goes to the hospital for tests for the gene and the results are positive. The results are put in her medical record so that the information is available to physicians to encourage aggressive testing for the disease in the future. The information will be computerized, which means that many heath care providers throughout the state may have access to the information. The patient's health insurance company will also have access to it. Information of this kind could be detrimental to the patient when obtaining life insurance or future health insurance, and eventually, if the information slides through enough computer networks, it could be detrimental to the patient's children when obtaining insurance and applying for employment though they have shown no signs of the disease and have never been tested.

In formulating policies, we should try to minimize excess harm and risk. In cases like this, it may be hard to do. Clearly, the medical records should be treated confidentially but that may not be enough to protect the patient. Because the records are computerized, and hence well-greased, information will be sent rapidly along networks and gathered by third parties who may find their own self-interested uses for it. New legal policies might be helpful here, including the passage of statutes protecting patients from discrimination on the basis of genetic testing. Also, the hospital might consider setting up a zone of privacy for patients who want only predictive testing done. There is a difference between predictive genetic testing in which the patient is tested for genetic information that may be indicative of future disease and diagnostic testing in which the patient is tested for genetic information that may confirm a diagnosis of an existing disease. The hospital could establish a private situation for predictive testing so that the patient's records were not incorporated into the regular medical file. These records would be computerized but not accessible to all of those who have access to the general medical record. This is a way of adjusting the access conditions to increase the level of privacy for the patient. Of course, the patient should be told what will happen to the test information. The patient might prefer to have the information included in her medical record.

One of the principles that should guide the establishment of policies for privacy is the Publicity Principle.

> The Publicity Principle: Rules and conditions governing private situations should be clear and known to the persons affected by them.

In effect, we can plan to protect our privacy better if we know where the zones of privacy are and under what conditions and to whom information will be given. If an employer can read one's e-mail, then applying for a new job is done more discreetly by not using e-mail. The publicity principle encourages informed consent and rational decision making.

Once policies are established, known circumstances sometimes arise that invite us to breach the policy. Obviously, policy breaches should be avoided as much as possible as they undermine confidence in the policy. However, sometimes truly exceptional circumstances occur. Suppose that after some predictive genetic tests are run, new information about the consequences of the test results are uncovered. New scientific evidence in combination with the test results show that the patient surely must have transmitted a devastating disease to her offspring but that the disease can be treated effectively if caught in time. In such circumstances it would seem that the hospital should notify not only the patient but also her adult offspring even though that was not part of the original agreement. The harm caused by the disclosure will be so much less than the harm prevented that the breach is justified.

> The Justification of Exceptions Principle: A breach of a private situation is justified if and only if there is a great likelihood that the harm caused by the disclosure will be so much less than the harm prevented that an impartial person would permit breach in this and in morally similar situations.

These exceptional circumstances should not be kept secret from future users of the policy. Hence, we need a principle for disclosure and adjustment in the policy statement itself.

> *The Adjustment Principle: If special circumstances justify a change in the parameters of a private situation, then the alteration should become an explicit and public part of the rules and conditions governing the private situation.*

In this example, those who continued to have predictive genetic testing would know what information would be released in the stated exceptional circumstances. They would know the possible consequences of their decision to have predictive genetic testing and could plan accordingly. The control/restricted access theory can give individuals as much personal choice as possible while still being concerned about information flow beyond individual control.

Conclusion

In a computerized society, information is greased. It moves like lightning and will have applications and reapplications that are impossible to imagine when initially entered into a computer. In a computerized society the concern for privacy is legitimate and well grounded. Privacy is one of our expressions of the core value of security. Individuals and societies that are not secure do not flourish and do not exist for long. It is, therefore, imperative that we create zones of privacy that allow citizens to rationally plan their lives without fear. The zones of privacy will contain private situations with different kinds and levels of access for different individuals. It is important to think of privacy in terms of a control/restricted access account, because this conception encourages informed consent as much as possible and fosters the development of practical, fine grained, and sensitive policies for protecting privacy when it is not.

References

Culver, Charles, James Moor, William Duerfeldt, Marshall Kapp, and Mark Sullivan. "Privacy." *Professional Ethics 3.* Nos. 3 & 4 (1994): 3–25.

Fried, Charles. "Privacy." *Philosophical Dimensions of Privacy.* Ed. F. D. Schoeman. New York: Cambridge University Press, 1984. 203–222.

Johnson, Deborah G. *Computer Ethics.* 2nd ed. Englewood Cliffs, New Jersey: Prentice Hall, 1994.

Moor, James. "Ethics of Privacy Protection." *Library Trends* 39.1 & 2 (1990): 69–82.

Moor, James. "How to Invade and Protect Privacy with Computers." *The Information Web.* Ed. Carol C. Gould. Boulder: Westview Press, 1989. 57–70.

Moor, James. "Reason, Relativity, and Responsibility in Computer Ethics." Reader in *Global Information Ethics.* Ed. Terrell Ward Bynum and Simon Rogerson. Oxford: Basil Blackwell, 1998.

Moor, James. "What is Computer Ethics?" *Metaphilosophy* 16.4 (1985): 266–275.

Rachels, James. "Why is Privacy Important?" *Philosophy and Public Affairs 4.* Summer (1975): 323–333.

The Structure of Rights in Directive 95/46/EC on the Protection of Individuals with Regard to the Processing of Personal Data and the Free Movement of Such Data

Dag Elgesem

Introduction

The Directive 95/46/EC of the European Parliament and of the Council of 24 October 1995 on the protection of individuals with regard to the processing of personal data and the free movement of such data is about to be implemented in the form of national legislation all over Europe. This Directive will be instrumental in shaping the European standard concerning privacy rights. In order to understand and to assess the situation for individual rights with regard to the processing of personal data in Europe, an analysis of this Directive is indispensable. The first aim of the present paper is to contribute to the interpretation of the Directive. Secondly, the paper is a contribution to the philosophical theory of privacy. Modern data protection legislation, of which the Directive is a central example, raises a whole set of conceptual and ethical issues. Unfortunately, much of the philosophical discourse on privacy has taken only a superficial interest in these problems.[1]

The paper has three parts. In the first part the structure of rights in the Directive is described. I start by way of a discussion of the question of how the Directive handles the problem of further processing of personal data collected for a different purpose. It turns out that an important part of the Directive's structure of individual rights has to be brought to bear in order to answer this question. Special attention is given to the principle that personal data shall not be further processed in ways that are incompatible with the purpose for which they were originally processed. This principle plays an important role in the Directive. I argue that the point of the

---

This essay originally appeared in *Ethics and Information Technology*, 1: 283–293, 1999. Copyright © 2000 by Kluwer Academic Publishers. Reprinted by permission.

[1] There are of course exceptions, e.g., DeCew (1997). DeCew's account is discussed in a later section.

principle is that data shall not be processed in ways that the data subject could reasonably expect. It is not possible to give, I suggest, an interpretation of the principle that does not refer to the data subject's perception of the situation.

In the second part I discuss some of the most widely discussed philosophical accounts of privacy. According to one theory, privacy should be identified with the individual's control concerning the flow of personal information. According to another theory, we have privacy to the extent that other people's access to us is restricted. Such philosophical accounts of privacy usually try to say *what* privacy is, i.e., what the state is that is protected by pieces of privacy legislation. By confronting these philosophical characterisations of privacy with the issues raised by the Directive, it becomes clear, I think, that they need to be supplemented in various ways. They simply do not have much light to shed on many of the important privacy issues with which the Directive is concerned.

In the third part of the paper I present some of my own ideas for a philosophical theory of individual rights in connection with the processing of personal data. It is argued, first, that a general notion of channels for the flow of personal information should be an element in such a theory. Secondly I argue that data protection can be seen as a special form of restrictions on the flow of personal information in one type of such channels. Third, I argue that this rudimentary theory of privacy is able to shed light on the similarities as well as the differences between privacy protection in private arenas and data protection in the sense of the Directive. Fourth, it is argued that the question about the data subject's reasonable expectation concerning the processing of information about himself is a fundamental one in the theory of privacy.

The Directive on the Question of Further Processing of Personal Data

Under what conditions is it legitimate to process personal data that are collected for a different purpose? This is a central question in the modern discussion of data protection. After all, the bulk of processing of personal data uses information that is already available as the result of other information processes. Hence, the questions about what constitutes a different purpose and what the conditions are on which further processing for a different purpose is legitimate, are crucial. The Directive addresses this question explicitly in Article 6, where it is stressed that all personal data "must be collected for specified, explicit and legitimate purposes and not further processed in a way that is incompatible with those purposes." This principle needs interpretation. It is not at all clear what processing in "a way that is incompatible with those purposes" means. I will return to a discussion of the relevant notion of 'incompatibility' later. First, however, it is necessary to have a look at some of the other provisions of the Directive that pertain to individual rights. These principles also contribute to the regulation of the further processing of personal information.

Let me start the discussion by way of some general remarks on the structure of the Directive. In the first article, the two objectives of the Directive are stated. First, its aim is to "protect the fundamental rights and freedom of natural persons, and in particular the right to privacy with respect to the processing of personal data" (Article 1). Secondly, this protection is meant make the flow of personal information within the European Community easier. The perspective of the Directive is that a uniform level of protection of individual rights will promote the flow of personal information within the Community.

The central concept in the directive is that of 'processing of personal data.' While earlier pieces of legislation focused on the recording of data, this directive is organised around the much broader notion of the *processing* of personal data. The recording of information is here only a special kind of processing of personal data. 'Processing personal data' is defined as "any operation or set of operations which is performed upon personal data, whether or not by automatic means, such as collection, recording, organisation, storage, adaptation or alteration, retrieval, consultation, use, disclosure by transmission, dissemination or otherwise making available, alignment or combination, blocking, erasure or destruction" (Article 2). The focus in the Directive is thus on the flow of *information*, rather than on the storage of information.

Data Quality

The Directive has several layers of provisions. The first layer is a set of principles pertaining to data quality. The notion of the *purpose* for which the data are processed is of central importance here. Article 6 begins with the principle mentioned already, that information shall be processed fairly and lawfully, for a specific purpose, and not further processed in a way incompatible with those purposes. In addition to this, there are standard principles pertaining to the quality of the data themselves, i.e., that data shall be adequate, relevant, and not excessive in relation to the purposes for which they are collected and further processed. Furthermore, data must be accurate and kept up to date, and they must not be kept longer than necessary for the purpose for which they were collected. Importantly, it is stated that it is the responsibility of the controller[2] of the processing to see to it that these requirements are met.

One important function of such requirements of data quality is the protection of the data subject's reasonable expectations concerning the processing of data about himself. Personal data are often used as the basis for making decisions concerning the individual. If the data are incorrect, outdated or not relevant, the decision can turn out to be incorrect. But these provisions are also motivated by considerations related to the fairness of the processing. It would certainly be very unreasonable if the data subject himself had been given the responsibility of controlling the quality of the data.

Legitimate Purposes

Next, the Directive lists the purposes for which the processing of personal data are considered to be legitimate. This is the case if either "(a) the data subject has unam-

---

[2] 'Controller' shall mean the natural or legal person, public authority, agency, or any other body that alone or jointly with others determines the purposes and means of the processing of personal data (Article 2).

biguously given his consent; or (b) processing is necessary for the performance of a contract to which the data subject is party; or (c) processing is necessary for compliance with a legal obligation to which the controller is subject; or (d) processing is necessary in order to protect the vital interests of the data subject; or (e) processing is necessary for the performance of a task carried out in the public interest or in the exercise of official authority vested in the controller or in a third party to whom the data are disclosed; or (f) processing is necessary for the purposes of the legitimate interests pursued by the controller or by the third party or parties to whom the data are disclosed," unless the processing violates the data subject's right to privacy (Article 7).

The requirements listed above do not put very clear limits to the processing of personal data, however. But the last two clauses are worth noting, because later, in Article 14, the data subject is given the right to *object* to processing of personal data under conditions (e) and (f). The processing of personal data for commercial purposes is a central example of group (f). I will return to the right to object later.

Sensitive Data

But even if a processing is legitimate, it is not necessarily permitted if the data is of a sensitive nature. Personal data "revealing racial or ethnic origin, political opinions, religious beliefs, trade-union membership, and the processing of data concerning health or sex life" are singled out as particularly sensitive. These "special categories of data" are sensitive in the sense that the dissemination of such data can be particularly harmful to the data subject's interests. The processing of these special types of data shall be *prohibited*, according to the Directive, unless certain conditions are met. In the normal case, the processing of such data is permitted only if the data subject has given his 'explicit consent.' But the Directive accepts in addition a number of other reasons for processing sensitive data. In particular, the processing of such data is permitted if the processing "is necessary in order to protect the vital interests of the data subject or another person where the data subject is physically or legally incapable of giving his consent." Also, the processing of personal data is permitted if it is carried out in the course of the "legitimate activities with appropriate safeguards by a foundation, association, or any other non-profit-seeking body with a political, philosophical, religious or trade-union aim." In addition, the processing of medical data within the health system for purposes of treatment etc. is not prohibited (Article 8). There are also other purposes for which the processing of sensitive data is permitted, but it is not possible to go into all the details here.

The Right to Be Informed

The data subject is, in the Directive, given the right to be informed about the processing of personal data concerning himself. He is entitled to information about the identity of the controller, the purpose of the processing, and the recipients of the data. Furthermore, he shall be informed about his right to access and to rectify data concerning himself. In this connection, the Directive distinguishes between the situation where the data are obtained from the data subject directly, and the situation where the data are obtained from other sources. The latter category includes also the further processing of data that were originally collected from the data subject. In cases of processing based on information from other sources than the data subject, the subjects concerned shall also be informed about the categories of information that are processed.

The Data Subject's Right to Access and to Object

The Directive gives the individual a general right to access and to correct information about himself. Furthermore, data subjects are given the right to object to the processing of data for certain purposes, as mentioned above. In addition to this, the data subject has the right to object to the processing of personal data relating to him, "which the controller anticipates being processed for purposes of direct marketing." Furthermore, data subjects have the right to refuse to be "subject to a decision which produces legal effects concerning him or significantly affects him and which is based solely on automated processing of data intended to evaluate certain personal aspects relating to him, such as his performance at work, creditworthiness, reliability, conduct, etc."

The structure of the right to object should be noted. The processing of personal data for the purpose of direct marketing, for example, is permitted provided that the data subject does not object. Hence, this introduces a form of passive consent. I return to this and other forms of individual control in the discussion below.

The Reprocessing of Personal Data

Let us consider how these principles apply to the problem of the further processing of data for a different purpose. As mentioned several times already, according to Article 6, in the section on principles relating to data quality, it is stressed that all personal data "must be collected for specified, explicit and legitimate purposes and not further processed in a way that is incompatible with those purposes." It is added that the "[f]urther processing of data for historical, statistical or scientific purposes shall not be considered as incompatible provided that Member States provide appropriate safeguards." Note, first, that in general the further processing of information for a different purpose will always also be a case of processing of information that is not collected from the data subject. This is important, because in accordance with Article 11, it is not always necessary to inform the data subject in such cases, i.e. if the data are further processed for the purposes of research. I will return to this later.

Let us consider different types of cases where data are further processed for new purposes. Let us assume, furthermore, that the new processing is consistent with the purpose for which the data were collected. There are then three cases to consider. First, suppose that the data are *not* sensitive in the sense defined by Article 8, i.e., it is not personal data 'revealing racial or ethnic origin, political opinions, religious beliefs, trade-union membership, and the processing of data concerning health or sex life.' New processing of such data is legitimate, according to the Directive, on the conditions that the general requirements on data quality and the legitimacy of processing are all met, and, in addition, that the data subject is given information about the identity of the controller, etc. Furthermore, if the data are processed in the public or commercial interest or for the purpose of direct marketing, the data subject will normally have the right to object to the further processing.

But suppose, instead, that the data *are* sensitive. Suppose the initial processing was permitted because the data subject had consented to it. If, now, the further processing was consistent with the purpose for which it was originally processed, the further processing can take place. Since this is a case of processing of data that have not been obtained from the data subject, the controller in accordance with Article 11 has a duty to inform the data subject about the further processing. Furthermore, the data subject has the right to access and correct the information, and to object to the processing on the conditions in Article 14.

According to Article 8, any processing of sensitive data is forbidden unless the data subject has consented or the processing is justified for other reasons. However, it is unclear whether it is necessary in this case for the controller to obtain the data subject's consent to the further processing. The reason why this is unclear is the following. By supposition, the data subject has consented to the initial processing and the further processing is not inconsistent with the purpose of this initial processing. If, now, the further processing really is consistent with the initial purpose, it could be argued that he had already consented to the further processing in virtue of his consent to the initial processing. On the other hand, if he has not consented to the further processing in virtue of consenting to the initial processing, could the purposes then really be consistent in the first place? The answer to these questions depends, obviously, on interpretation of the notion of incompatibility. I will return to this question later. It is clear, however, that an acceptable interpretation will have show how it is possible for a processing to be compatible with the original purpose even though the data subject has not consented to the further processing.

Before I go on to discuss the interpretation, let me also mention the processing of personal data for the purposes of research. Interestingly, the processing for purposes of research is said not to be incompatible with the purpose for which it was collected. "Further processing of data for historical, statistical or scientific purposes shall not be considered incompatible [with the purpose for which they were processed initially, DE] provided that Member States provide appropriate safeguards" (Article 6). Furthermore, if the data is not collected from the data subject, the duty to inform does not apply in the case of new processing of personal information for purposes of research. Article 11 states that the general duty to inform "shall not apply where, in particular for processing for statistical purposes or for the purposes of historical or scientific research, the provision of such information proves impossible or would involve a disproportionate effort or if recording or disclosure is expressively laid down by law." I will return to both of these points in the following discussion.

Suppose the information is not sensitive and that it is very difficult to inform the data subject. Since processing for purposes of research is not inconsistent with the purpose for which it was processed initially, it is not necessary to inform the data subjects. Neither is it necessary to obtain the data subject's consent to the processing. The data subject does in this case have the right to access the data, but he does not have the right to object to the processing. Assume, instead, that the data that are used in the research process are sensitive and that the initial processing was justified because the data subjects had consented to this processing. This further processing of data for research purposes is a case of processing of information that are not collected from the data subject. If, now, it is difficult to inform the data subjects, according to Article 11 the research can then be undertaken without informing the data subjects. But Article 8, on the other hand, requires that every processing of sensitive data be made legitimate in virtue of the data subject's consent, or by one of the other conditions. Note that research is not among the conditions that can justify processing of sensitive data. The problem, now, is that consent of course requires information. I can see two possible solutions. Perhaps Article 8 will override the exemption from the duty to inform in Article 11. In this case the answer is that the controller has to obtain data subject's consent. But perhaps, because the new processing is not incompatible with the initial processing, the data subject is considered to have consented to the further processing in virtue of his consent to the initial processing. Again, the interpretation of the principle that the further processing shall not be inconsistent with purpose for which the data were processed initially turns out to be of central importance.

I will now turn to a discussion of the interpretation of this principle. It should be clear from the discussion above that this is not a purely academic issue. As we have seen, the interpretation of the conditions for the further processing of data collected for other purposes depends on the interpretation of this principle.

Using Personal Data for a Different Purpose

The notion of further processing of data in a way that is not incompatible with the purpose for which it was collected is a difficult one to interpret. I have indicated some of the problems above. Another difficulty is this: It is hard to believe that the double negation in the formulation of the principle is accidental. Hence, the locution 'not inconsistent with' is probably not meant to be read as equivalent in meaning to 'consistent with.' The explication should be able to make sense of this distinction.

How should we, then, interpret the principle that further processing of personal data shall not be incompatible with the purpose for it was originally processed? Note first the purpose in question, i.e., the purpose for which the information was initially processed, cannot be the subjective purpose of the data subject. The purpose with which the data subject gave up information about himself could be different from the purpose for which the data was collected. First, data sometimes can be legitimately collected without active participation of the data subject. Hence, in such cases there would be no purpose for which the data was processed. Furthermore, in the cases where the data subject is the source of information, the data subject can give up information with all kinds of deceptive purposes. Suppose, for example, that the data subject gives false information to a public agency in order to obtain a social benefit. If, now, the agency used the personal data to check the accuracy of the information that the data subject had given, that would certainly not be compatible with the purpose of the data subject. However, this use of the information would be compatible with the purpose of the agency and with the purpose for which the data were originally processed. The purpose in question is, of course, the purpose of the processing. I will argue below, however, that a plausible explication of the relevant notion of incompatibility cannot be given that does not make reference to the data subject's reasonable expectations concerning how information about himself will be processed.

Let us have a look at some plausible candidates for an explication of the notion of incompatibility. Firstly, 'incompatibility' cannot mean *logical* consistency. To say that process P1 is inconsistent with purpose P2 is only to say that both cannot both be true in the same world, i.e. that P1 does logically imply the negation of P2. Under this interpretation, the claim would be that data should not be used in ways that are inconsistent with the purpose for which they were collected. But this would be an almost empty claim. It would only rule out combinations of purposes that are impossible for logical reasons.

Secondly, 'incompatible' cannot mean that the purposes are practically inconsistent. Under this interpretation, the claim would be that data should not be used for purposes that are impossible to achieve simultaneously. Again this would be an incredibly weak rule without any bite whatsoever. In fact, anything that is practically possible would go through. Of course, the Directive intends something of a more substantial nature.

Thirdly, 'incompatible' cannot mean simply that the two purposes are different. Such an interpretation would also have unacceptable consequences. Under this interpretation, the rule would be that data should not be used for purposes that are different from the purpose for which it was collected. But the Directive itself mentions a counterexample, namely that of research. Under this interpretation the rule would therefore be unreasonably strict.

The problem with the explications considered so far is that they are not bringing in the perspective of the data subject. I argued previously that the purpose mentioned in the principle is not the subjective purpose with which the data subject gives up information about himself. This point does not stand in the way however, of making reference to the expectations the data subject reasonably ought to have concerning the processing. My suggestion for an interpretation of the principle is the following: Let us say that process P2 is *compatible* with purpose P1, if the data subject could, on the basis of his knowledge of P1, reasonably expect P2. If we accept this, we would say that P2 is *incompatible* with P1 if the data subject could, on the basis of P1, reasonably expect process P2 would not be undertaken. What the principle says, I suggest, is that personal data shall not be processed in a way that the data subject, on the basis of his knowledge of the purpose for which the data were originally collected, could reasonably expect not to take place.

Let us apply this suggestion to the problem discussed previously. The problem arises in those situations where the data subject has consented to the initial processing of sensitive data. What kinds of processing are ruled out by the principle in such situations? Does the Directive require, for example, that the data subject's consent has to be obtained anew when data are to be further processed for a new purpose? On the interpretation suggested previously, the answer is that it will depend on whether or not the data subject could reasonably expect that the data would be further processed *without his consent*. The processing would be impermissible, according to the principle, if the data subject could reasonably expect that the processing would not take place. Under the suggested interpretation, the principle thus gives a fairly clear answer in the problematic cases described above. I count this as a point in the favour of the interpretation.

Furthermore, on this interpretation, 'compatible with' is to be distinguished from 'not incompatible with,' because 'expectation' is an intentional notion. It is certainly possible for a person not to expect a processing not to happen without expecting it to happen. The Directive itself mentions that further processing of personal data for research purposes shall not be considered inconsistent with the purpose for which the data were processed initially. The point is, I suggest, to say that the data subject cannot reasonably expect that personal data will not be the subject of research. The point is not, I think, to say that the data subject always should expect personal data to be subject to research. That seems like an unreasonably strong principle. There are thus important differences between 'not incompatible with' and 'compatible with.'

If the suggested interpretation is correct, this has consequences both for the interpretation of the Directive and for the philosophy of privacy. It is important to the interpretation of the Directive because it shows that at the heart of its structure lies a complex, intentional notion pertaining to the reasonable expectations of the data subject. Second, the interpretation suggests that the notion of the individual's reasonable expectations deserve attention within the philosophy of privacy. I will return to this in the section below. In the following section I will turn to a discussion of the problems of data protection in the light of various philosophical accounts of privacy.

Data Protection and the Philosophy of Privacy

In this section I will try to relate important positions in the philosophical literature on privacy to the problems that the Directive tries to tackle. I will not try to show that these accounts are wrong. However, I will argue that these theories are not able to shed much light on the privacy issues raised by the Directive. First I will discuss the so-called restricted access account of privacy. Then I will critically consider the idea that privacy is a form of control.

Privacy as Restricted Access

The basic idea of the restricted access account is that, "in its most suggestive sense, privacy is a limitation of other's access to the individual." [3] Furthermore, the account is guided by an interest in giving a *neutral* definition that does not pre-empt any important questions concerning the value of privacy. Gavison distinguishes three forms of restricted access: informational access, attention paid to an individual, and physical access. Allen, another proponent of this line of approach, defines privacy as "a degree of inaccessibility of persons, of their mental states, and of information about them to the senses and surveillance of others." [4] She then goes on to

---

[3] R. Gavison. "Privacy and the Limits of Law." In *F.D. Schoeman, editor,* Philosophical Dimensions of Privacy. Cambridge University Press, Cambridge, p. 350, 1980.

[4] A.L. Allen. Uneasy Access. *Privacy for Women in a Free Society.* Rowman and Littlefield, Totowa, NJ, 1988.

say that "privacy a descriptive, neutral concept, denoting conditions that are neither always desirable and praiseworthy, nor always undesirable and unpraisewor-
thy."[5] I do agree that restricted access is an aspect of privacy. However, the account
is in my view not sufficiently rich as a theory of what privacy is.

Consider, first, the following objection. Suppose a person is locked up in a cell
where he is constantly watched by a group of guards, but that the guards do not
allow anybody else to see the person. In this case, there is restricted access to the
person in both an informational and a physical sense. Since we here have restricted access but not privacy, the objection goes, inaccessibility is not sufficient for
privacy. In response to this, Allen says: "But to take the prison example as a proof
that inaccessibility is not a sufficient condition is to fall prey to the fallacy of equiv-
ocation. Such examples show only what no one doubts: inaccessibility in one
respect does not always entail privacy in other respects." [6] Allen maintains, therefore, that it is accurate to say that the prisoner has privacy with respect to those
whose access is restricted, but not with respect to the guards. In this way privacy
is made a relational concept. It only makes sense to speak of a person's privacy
relative to other persons, Allen seems to suggest. Gavison also views privacy as a
relational concept when she describes privacy "as a situation of an individual vis-
à-vis others."[7]

In James Moor's sophisticated version of the restricted access view of privacy,
the central notion is that of a *private situation*. On this account, a situation can be
either physically or normatively private. In the case of a normatively private situation, 'the individual or group is normatively protected from intrusion, interference
and information access by others.'[8]

A general problem with the restricted access view is that it is difficult to see how
it draws the distinction between private and public situations. This account rests
on the premise that it is possible to make a clear distinction between private and
public situations. But it seems that, on this view, we have to admit that we always
have some degree of privacy, since there will always be billions of people who have
physically restricted access to us. But precisely because all situations are private
to some degree, it is difficult to see exactly how the private situations are distinguished from the public ones on this theory. The problem is that we need more than
the notion of restricted access to characterise the class of private situations. Hence,
the restricted access view is not a complete account of privacy.

A second limitation of the restricted access view is that every case of dissemination of information about oneself must be counted as a loss of privacy, since one
makes oneself more accessible to others. There is, intuitively, a big difference
between the situation where your privacy is violated, say your phone is tapped, and
the situation where you tell your friend an intimate secret. In order to account for

---

[5] *Ibid.:* 3.

[6] *Ibid.:* 15.

[7] *Ibid.:* 349.

[8] Moor 1998: 45. Other aspects of the restricted access account are discussed in Moor 1989 and Moor 1990. I have offered some critical remarks in Elgesem 1996.

the differences between these situations, we have to bring in the notion of consent to the transfer of personal information, i.e. a notion of control. But the restricted access account explicitly rejects the use of notions pertaining to control in the characterisation of privacy.[9] It is difficult, therefore, to see how it will account for this aspect of privacy.

As mentioned above, I do not consider these objections to be refutations of the restricted access account. Perhaps it can be developed into a more sophisticated theory. What the objections tend to show, however, is that a more resourceful theoretical framework should be developed. But let us turn, now, to the question of whether this account has anything interesting to say about the protection of the "right to privacy with respect to the processing of personal data", i.e., the problems of the Directive.

The restricted access view is clearly relevant, because the questions of restricted *informational* access are quite central in the Directive. In particular, the restrictions on the processing of sensitive data are concerned with restricting access to the individual. There are, however, many norms in the Directive pertaining to data protection that are not adequately described as restricting access to individuals. The functions of the norms of data quality, for example, or the individual rights of information and access, are not at all concerned with the restriction of access to the data subject. The function of such norms is primarily to make it possible for the data subject to form reasonable expectations about how information about himself is processed.

We should conclude, I think, that the restricted access account is not necessarily wrong, but that it is too narrow. At least it seems clear that it does not capture important functions of norms pertaining to data protection.

Privacy as Control

The basic idea of the control account is just as simple as that of the restricted accesses account. The classical definition is due to Westin, who says: "Privacy is not simply an absence of information about us in the minds of others, rather it is the control we have over information about ourselves."[10] One attractive feature of this account is the way it distinguishes between situations where a person's privacy is *violated* and situations where the person *reveals* personal information about himself. The difference is, on the control account, that there is a loss of control in the first case while in the second case the person exercises his control.

This is a plausible explanation, but it has also been the subject of criticism. It would seem, for example, that a person who confesses intimate details about his life to a priest, say, thereby loses privacy, since he no longer has any control over the further dissemination of information. The control account would have to say, the objection continues, that there was no loss of privacy involved in this case. There was, on the contrary, an exercise of control. But this objection fails, I think. The con-

---

[9] Note that Moor 1998 argues that his version of the restricted access theory is compatible with the view that privacy gives the individual control.

[10] *A. Westin. Privacy and Freedom.* Athenum, New York, p. 208, 1967.

trol theorist can reply that there was an exercise of control that resulted in a loss of control in later situations. The loss might not have been severe, however. The priest is, after all, bound by norms of confidentiality, etc. Hence, it seems true to say that the man still had quite a lot of control after the confession. But, of course, control comes in degrees and it seems clear that the man by confessing has given up some control. But this is something that I think the control theorist can admit.

There is a further question here that is worth considering. The problem is that it is difficult to see how this approach has the resources to distinguish between actual and potential violations of privacy. By defining privacy as control over personal information, threats of privacy violations also seem to be counted as actual violations of privacy. Suppose, for example, that person A has visual access to B's bedroom if he uses a pair of binoculars, but that A never exploits this opportunity. In some sense B has lost control over the dissemination of information about himself, since it now is up to A to decide whether information about B is disseminated. On the control account, it seems that we have to say that B's privacy is already violated. But this must be wrong. What the control theorist could say in reply to this, I think, is that a loss of privacy has not occurred until A actually interferes with B's control.

I think the notion of control is a central one in the theory of privacy. But even if we qualify the crude statement of the theory in the two directions suggested above, it is still far from rich enough to account for all of the dimensions of control that arise in the Directive. There are at least five levels of individual control that have to be distinguished in the Directive. First, there are the norms of data quality in Article 6, i.e., that data must be collected for a specific purpose, that they must be adequate, relevant and not excessive in relation to the purpose, accurate, and up to date. These norms—when implemented—confer a certain degree of control on the data subject in virtue of protecting the integrity of the processing. Their function is to make sure that the data subject is not treated unfairly just because of the processing of data. It is also a prerequisite for being able to form stable expectations about how information about himself will be processed. Secondly, the directive gives the data subject the right to access and to correct information about himself. This confers more control on the data subject than do the norms at the first level. These rights on the part of the data subject make it possible for him to control information about himself more actively. Third, still more control is given to the data subject when he is actively informed about the processing of information about himself. Article 10 in the Directive requires that the data subject shall be informed about the identity of the controller, the purposes of the processing, and the types of information that is processed. To be fully informed about this is an important prerequisite both for being able to take part in the control of the flow of personal data, and to know for what purposes information about himself will be processed. Fourth, the Directive also in some cases uses *passive* consent. In Article 14, the data subject is given the right to object to processing for certain purposes. This is the case, for example, with processing for the purpose of direct marketing. The processing of personal data for such purposes is considered legitimate, hence permitted *unless* the data subject objects to the processing. Fifth, informed consent plays an important role in the Directive. It uses a rather strong form of consent. 'The data subject's consent' means "any freely given specific and informed indication of his wishes by which the data subject signifies his agreement to personal data relating to him being processed." Most important, the data subject's consent is considered by the Directive to be the normal way to make the processing of sensitive data legitimate.

Again, the point is that these are forms of control that a theory of privacy in this area has to take into consideration. But there is an additional dimension of control in the Directive. Consider again Article 6 on data quality. It is explicitly stated that it is the responsibility of the controller to see to it that these requirements are met, i.e., to see to it that personal data are accurate, relevant, etc. The controller has to control the quality of the data. In contrast, in the cases of the rights to consent to the processing, to access and correct information, and to object to the processing, the data subject is himself controlling the quality and flow of information. There is an important distributive issue here concerning the burden of control. Is it fair, for example, that the data subject himself has to object to processing for purposes of direct marketing? I will not go into this question here. Again, the point is to indicate that the questions relating to control in this area are too complex to be adequately handled by the simple theory that privacy is informational control.

I will however end this section by way of some remarks on the interesting recent contribution to the discussion, due to DeCew. Her suggestion is that we can characterise privacy in terms of "types of information and activity in which individuals might reasonably expect others not to interfere."[11] According to her broad conception, privacy has three aspects. The first aspect is informational privacy, i.e., the protection of personal communications. The second aspect is called accessibility privacy, and covers restrictions on physical as well as informational access to individuals. Inspired by Ferdinand Shoeman, DeCew argues that privacy also has a third and often overlooked aspect that she calls *expressive privacy*. "Here privacy protects a realm for expressing one's self-identity or personhood through speech or activity. It protects the ability to decide to continue or to modify one's behavior when the activity in question helps define oneself as a person, shielded from interference, pressure, and coercion from government or from other individuals."[12]

This characterisation of privacy in terms of the three aspects is helpful. Consider informational privacy, which is the kind of privacy protected by the Directive. The function of this kind of privacy, according to DeCew, is to protect the individual against the use of personal information to 'pressure or embarrass one, to damage one's credibility or economic status, and so on. Informational privacy thus shields individuals from intrusions as well as fear of threats of intrusions, and it also affords individuals control in deciding who has access to the information and for what purposes."[13] As DeCew points out, information privacy and accessibility privacy overlaps, because information privacy obviously restricts access to the indi-

---

[11] J. DeCew. In Pursuit of Privacy. Cornell University Press, Ithaca, p. 75, 1997.

[12] *Ibid.*: 77.

[13] *Ibid.*: 75

vidual and is therefore also a kind of accessibility privacy.[14] Hence, DeCew provides reasons for rejecting the cleavage between theories that defines privacy as control and those that identify it with restricted control.

DeCew is right, I think, that privacy is a broad and multifaceted cluster concept. In the final section of the paper I will however suggest a somewhat different kind of characterisation of privacy. DeCew's account characterises privacy in terms of the function of various pieces of legislation pertaining to the protection of privacy, i.e., *what* it is that is protected by the various pieces of legislation and why it is so protected. In the next section I will suggest that it is also fruitful to investigate the different aspects of privacy in terms of *how* it is protected in different arenas. A central question will concern the relationship between data protection and the protection of privacy in private domains. I will start, therefore, by considering how the Directive conceives of this relationship.

Channels for the Flow of Personal Information

The Relationship between Privacy and Data Protection in the Directive

As mentioned above, the Directive has a certain view on the relationship between its own norms pertaining to data protection and the right to privacy. In Article 1 it is said, "In accordance with this Directive, Member States shall protect the fundamental rights and freedoms of natural persons, and in particular the right to privacy with respect to the processing of personal data." Hence, the right to privacy is seen as the underlying value that the Directive is designed to protect. Nowhere does the Directive try to define privacy, however, and, furthermore, the right to privacy is not *identified* with the norms in the Directive. Indeed, at several places the Directive mentions that it might be necessary to supplement or derogate from its provisions in order to reconcile the right to privacy with other interests. It is said, for example, that exemptions and derogation from the Directive are acceptable for "the processing of personal data carried out solely for journalistic purposes or the purpose of artistic or literary expression only if they are necessary to reconcile the right to privacy with the rules governing freedom of expression." And in Article 7 it is stated that personal data may be processed for purposes of various legitimate interests "except where such interests are overridden by the interests or fundamental rights and freedoms of data subject which require protection under Article 1." The fundamental rights in question include the right to privacy. The Directive recognises in this way that it might turn out that additional provisions have to be formulated in order to provide a more adequate protection of the right to privacy.

The idea, then, is that there is an underlying right to privacy, which is protected by the norms of the Directive, but that these norms in themselves do not define the right to privacy. In different areas, or at different stages of the technological

---

[14] *Ibid.*: 76.

development, different norms are presumably required in order to protect the same right to privacy. This distinction is a sound one, I think, and for the purposes of the Directive, this picture is adequate and helpful. From a more theoretically ambitious perspective, however, this is not sufficient.

Channels for the Flow of Personal Information

There are different social arenas or 'channels,' as I prefer to call them, for the flow of personal information. Examples are private homes, public streets, or registers with medical records in a hospital. Different channels are characterised by different sets of *restrictions* on the flow of such information. There can be restrictions on the *audience* that has access to the channel, and restrictions on the *type of information* that is allowed to flow in the channel. The private sphere is protected by restrictions on the audience that have access to it, through legal and social norms pertaining to the protection of privacy. However, there are no similar public norms that restrict the type of information that flows in this private channel. On a public street, in contrast, there are no restrictions on the audience that has access to the channel, while there *are* restrictions on the type of information that is allowed to be generated. Compare this to a medical register, my third example of a channel for the flow of personal information, which is subject to restrictions both on the audience and on the type of information that is allowed to flow in the channel.

I said above that the information that is allowed to flow in a private home is not subject to restrictions by *public* norms. I emphasise 'public,' because there are of course restrictions on the flow of information also in our private homes. I do not read my wife's letters, for example. There is, however, a fundamental difference between restrictions that obtain in virtue of public norms, and those that are subject to negotiation and agreement among those involved in the channel. In private channels, for example in a private home, it is up to those who live there to determine who shall have access and what kind of information that shall be generated there. In the case of a register in a hospital, on the other hand, both who shall have access and what kind of information is allowed to flow there is determined by *public* norms.

To sum up, my suggestion is that it is important to distinguish three types of channels. First, there are private channels, like private homes, characterised by restrictions on the audience that have access to the channel but without restrictions on the type of information that flows in it. Secondly, there are public channels, like a public street, that have restrictions on the type of information that flows in the channel but without restrictions on the audience. Third, there are channels for the processing of information for a specific purpose. The Directive is of course concerned with the protection of individual integrity in channels of the third kind.

Data Protection and the Protection of Privacy

The philosophical discussion on privacy has primarily been concerned with the protection of private channels. The relationship to problems of privacy, as they arise in channels established for the purposes of specific activities, is often assumed to of the same kind. But it is important, I think, to see that there are important differences between the protection of privacy in the two areas. First, a private channel is not set up for a particular purpose. Of course, purposeful information processing takes place in such channels, but there is no overall purpose for which information is processed.

Second, in a private channel the identity of those who get access to the information is crucial. Information is disseminated as a part of the development of personal relationships. With the processing of personal data in channels established for a purpose, in contrast, the identity of those who get access to the information does not matter. Suppose I give up personal information at the hospital in the form of a blood sample. It does not matter to me exactly who analyses the sample and writes it down in my file. What matters is that there are general rules of confidentiality that are respected by all those who work in the hospital. Again, in a private channel the dissemination of intimate information to another person will often play a role in the development of a personal relationship. In a channel for the processing of data for a specific purpose, however, the dissemination of intimate information does not have such functions. Or, to use DeCew's notion of expressive privacy, a private channel is, but a purpose-specific channel is usually not "a realm for expressing one's self-identity or personhood."[15]

Third, in a channel where data is processed for a specific purpose, the data subject forms expectations about how the data will be used on the basis of his knowledge of that purpose. An important function of the protection of privacy in such channels is to secure that these reasonable expectations are not frustrated. When a patient gives up information in a hospital, for example, he can reasonably expect that the information is used for purposes related to his treatment, there is restricted access to the information, and that the information is not used for other than medical purposes. The patient does not have detailed knowledge of or control over how the information is processed. Rather, he has to accept a package of procedures for the processing of personal information. In a private channel, in contrast, there is no overall purpose on which to form expectations. Instead, the terms of communication are the subject of agreement between those interacting in the channel.

The Directive and the Protection of Channels

This last point brings us back to the Directive and the problem of the further processing of data. An important function of the protection of privacy in channels with a purpose is, I have suggested, to enable the data subject to form stable expectations concerning the future use of information about himself. And, in the first section it was argued that the notion of the data subject's reasonable expectations concerning the further processing of data was essential to the interpretation of the Directive's use of the notion of 'incompatibility.' Indeed, I do believe that the question of what it is to be able to form reasonable expectations concerning the further processing of data should be a central one in the theory of privacy.

I do believe, however, that the protection of individuals in this area also has another dimension. In the discussion above, I argued that there are different levels of

---

[15] *Ibid.*: 77.

individual control corresponding to different instruments for the protection of individuals in the Directive. The role of some of these forms of protection and control is to protect and support the data subject's reasonable expectations about how data about him will be processed. The requirements of information quality and security, the right to access and correction, and the duty to inform the data subject about the processing of data all have this function. These are requirements that apply to all channels no matter what their purposes are.

But in a large group of cases, in addition, the data subject's active or passive consent is required. In particular, for the processing of sensitive information, the consent of the data subject is required. For example, consent is a sufficient condition for making processing legitimate, and also for making processing of sensitive information permitted. But there are also other conditions that can justify the processing of personal data. The Directive mentions at least 5 conditions that can justify the processing of sensitive data. The processing of such data is permitted if, for example, the processing is necessary to protect vital interests of the data subject and he is incapable of giving his consent. Or, to mention another example, "the processing is required for the purpose of preventive medicine, medical diagnosis, the provision of care or treatment or the management of health care services, and where those data are processed by health care professionals subject under national law" (Article 8).

There are thus two very different ideals in the Directive pertaining to the protection of individual rights in the processing of personal data. First, there is the ideal that the data subject shall be able to form reasonable expectations concerning how personal data will be processed. This is secured by provisions in the Directive pertaining to data quality and to security. Call this the ideal of *predictability*. Second, there are the questions concerning the *justification* of the different kinds of processing. Call this the ideal of justifiability. It is important here to distinguish the idea that a certain processing is a justifiable social activity, from the idea that the processing is justified to the data subjects concerned. According to the Directive, processing of personal data shall always be justifiable in the first sense, i.e., as a legitimate social activity. But, as mentioned, the processing does not always have to be *justified* to the data subject, i.e., the processing can be legitimate and permissible also without the consent of the data subject. Hence, even though the ideal of predictability and the ideal of justifiability overlap to some extent, they do not overlap completely.

To sum up, three different questions have to be distinguished: 1) Is the processing predictable, 2) Does the processing constitute a socially justifiable activity, and (3) Is the processing justified to the data subject, i.e., has he actively or passively consented? The Directive demands affirmative answers to questions 1 and 2 in order for a processing to be legitimate. In addition, it is a sufficient condition for the processing of sensitive information to be permissible that the processing is justified to the data subject, i.e., an affirmative answer to question 3 can be given. In general, an affirmative answer to question 3 implies an affirmative answer also to questions 1 and 2. Conversely, a negative answer to question 1 implies a negative answer also to questions 2 and 3. On the basis of this, the important *ethical* questions will be in which cases a consent from the data subject is required in order for the processing to be morally justifiable, and when processing is justifiable in the absence of such a justification to the data subject. This question cannot be answered at a general level, I think. Each case has to be considered separately.

References

Allen, Anita L. *Uneasy Access. Privacy for Women in a Free Society.* Rowman and Littlefield, Totowa, NJ, 1988.

DeCew, Judith. *In Pursuit of Privacy.* Cornell University Press, Ithaca, 1997.

Elgesem, Dag. "Privacy, Respect for Persons, and Risk." In Charles Ess, editor, *Philosophical Perspectives on Computer-Mediated Communication*, pp. 45–66. State University of New York Press, Albany, NY, 1996.

Gavison, Ruth. "Privacy and the Limits of Law." In F. D. Schoeman, editor, *Philosophical Dimensions of Privacy*, pp. 346–402. Cambridge University Press, Cambridge, 1984.

Moor, James. "How to Invade and Protect Privacy with Computers." In Carol Gould, editor, *The Information Web: Ethical and Social Implications of Computer Networking*, pp. 57–70. Westview, Boulder, CO, 1989.

Moor, James. "The Ethics of Privacy Protection." *Library Trends*, 39(1/2: Summer/Fall): 69–82, 1990.

Moor, James. "Towards a Theory of Privacy in the Information Age." In M. J. van den Hoven, editor, *Proceedings of CEPE97.* Rotterdam, 1998.

Westin, Alan. *Privacy and Freedom.* Atheneum, New York, 1967.

Privacy Protection, Control of Information, and Privacy-Enhancing Technologies

Herman T. Tavani and James H. Moor

The present study is organized into two main parts. In Part I, we respond to a recent criticism that the restricted access theory of privacy does not adequately explain the role that control of personal information plays in protecting one's privacy. In defending a version of the restricted access theory, we put forth a tripartite model that differentiates the *concept* of privacy from both the *justification* and the *management* of privacy. This distinction is important, we argue, because it enables us to avoid conflating the concept of privacy, which we define in terms of protection from intrusion and information gathering [Moor 1990; 1997] from the concept of control, which (a) is used to justify the framing of policies that provide privacy protection and (b) is essential to the management of privacy. Separating privacy from control is necessary, we further argue, to preserve the identity of both notions. After showing why the notion of individual control, as expressed in three different ways—*choice*, *consent*, and *correction*—plays an important role in the management of privacy, we conclude Part I with an account of why individual controls alone are not sufficient to guarantee the protection of personal privacy and why certain external controls, such as those provided by privacy policies, are also needed.

To illustrate some of the key points made in the first part of this essay, we consider examples of privacy-enhancing technologies (or PETs) in Part II. We argue that even if PETs provide individuals with a means of controlling their personal information, these tools do not necessarily ensure privacy protection. Because PETs do not provide online users with a zone of privacy protection that incorporates external controls, i.e., controls beyond those at the individual level, we conclude that the use of PETs can actually blur the need for privacy protection, rather than provide it.

Part I: The Theory of Privacy

In this section, we defend a version of the restricted access theory of privacy [Moor, 1990; 1997] against recent attacks that such a theory does not explain the important role that one's ability to control personal information plays in protecting per-

This essay originally appeared in the *Proceedings of the Third Conference on Computer Ethics–Philosophical Enquiry* (CEPE 2000), Dartmouth College, Hanover, NH, pp. 293–304. Copyright © 2000 by Herman T. Tavani and James H. Moor. Reprinted by permission.

sonal privacy [Elgesem, 1996; 1999]. We begin with a critique of privacy as understood mainly in terms of control over personal information.

The Role of Control in the Theory of Privacy

In our private lives we wish to control information about ourselves. We wish to control information that might be embarrassing or harm us. And, we wish to control information that might increase our opportunities and allow us to advance our projects. The notion of privacy and the notion of control fit together. But how do they fit together? There is a tradition, especially with regard to the privacy of information, to define privacy in terms of control. Alan Westin maintains, "Privacy is the claim of individuals, groups, or institutions to determine for themselves when, how, and to what extent information about them is communicated to others" [Westin, 1967 p. 7]. Arthur Miller says, "... the basic attribute of an effective right of privacy is the individual's ability to control the circulation of information relating to him..." [Miller, 1971 p. 25]. Charles Fried states, "Privacy is not simply an absence of information about us in the minds of others, rather it is the *control* we have over information about ourselves" [Fried, 1984 p. 209]. More recently, Dag Elgesem suggests, "In my view, to have personal privacy is to have the ability to *consent* to the dissemination of personal information" [Elgesem, 1996 p. 51].

We believe this tradition of identifying the concept of privacy with control is misleading. Control of personal information is extremely important as, of course, is privacy. But, these concepts are more useful when treated as separable, mutually supporting concepts than as one. A good theory of privacy has at least three components: an account of the concept of privacy, an account of the justification for privacy, and an account of the management of privacy. This tripartite structure of the theory of privacy is important to keep in mind because each part of the theory performs a different function. To give an account of one of the parts is not to give an account of the others. The concept of privacy itself is best defined in terms of restricted access, not control [Moor, 1990; Moor, 1997]. Privacy is fundamentally about protection from intrusion and information gathering by others. Individual control of personal information, on the other hand, is part of the justification of privacy and plays a role in the management of privacy. Privacy and control do fit together naturally, just not in the way people often state.

These philosophical distinctions have practical import. We can have control but no privacy, and privacy but no control. We should aim to have both control and privacy. When we blur the distinctions, we are vulnerable to losing one of them. For example, as we shall argue later, providing privacy-enhancing technologies (PETs) that seem to promote individual control may actually blur the need for stronger privacy protection, not provide it.

A fundamental problem about defining the concept of privacy in terms of individual control of information is that it greatly reduces what can be private. We control so little. As a practical matter we cannot possibly control vast amounts of information about us that circulates through myriads of computer networks and databases. The current globalization of these information processes exacerbates the problem. If privacy depends, by definition, on our individual control, we simply don't have significant privacy and never will in a computerized world.

On the contrary, it seems more reasonable to maintain that sensitive personal information ought to be private even if its owner is not in a position to control it. A patient should not lose her right to have her medical records protected when she is under anesthesia. A resident of the U.S. who is required to give personal information to the Census Bureau should not thereby lose his right to privacy of the personal information he has surrendered. In general, loss of control should not entail the loss of the right to privacy, which it would if individual control really were a necessary condition for the right to privacy.

Virtually all societies establish normatively private situations, zones of privacy, which limit access to people or aspects about them under certain conditions [Moore, 1984]. The details of these normatively private situations vary somewhat from culture to culture, but they are intended to protect individuals and foster social relationships whether the individuals have control in the situations or not.

We often think of normatively private situations in terms of physical locations. A house is a normatively private situation. Outsiders are expected to knock and get permission to enter. But situations other than locations, situations that involve relationships, activities, and information, can be normatively private as well. Religious confessions are typically private wherever they are given. Voting is often a private activity whether it is by paper ballot or voting machine or Internet. Medical records and information are private. All of these examples are private situations—zones in which protection of privacy is reasonably expected and normatively protected. The normative aspect of these private situations restricts access by individuals, groups, or governments. This restricted access expresses a right of protection. It prohibits intrusion and information processing by someone or something. Of course, it is prudent to supplement normative protection with security measures. Doors have locks and databases have passwords. But, if the locks and passwords are circumvented, the right to privacy is not diminished even if the contents are disclosed.

Normative Privacy and the Restricted Access Theory

Normative privacy (the right to privacy) needs to be distinguished from natural or descriptive privacy (privacy that exists as a matter of fact). Simply being alone doesn't provide a sufficient claim to the right to privacy any more than having a right to privacy can guarantee privacy as a matter of fact. In this essay we are primarily concerned with privacy as a normative concept. It is easy to confuse the two. A critic of the restricted access theory objects, "But it seems that, on this view, we have to admit that we always have some degree of privacy, since there will always be billions of people who have physically restricted access to us. But precisely because all situations are private to some degree, it is difficult to see exactly how the private situations are distinguished from the public ones on this theory" [Elgesem, 1999 p. 289]. The reply to this objection is that the relevant public/private distinction is drawn normatively, not descriptively. Public streets are unrestricted normatively to virtually everyone, whereas a house is restricted normatively to everyone except its residents. The fact that a public street is empty at night does not make it less (normatively) public any more than the fact that a large family lives in a house in a densely populated area makes the house less (normatively) private *vis-à-vis* outsiders.

The restricted access model provides a framework for discussing privacy on the Internet in a way in which a control theory of privacy does not. Individuals cannot control the packet switching of their personal information or what happens to it once it arrives at a remote destination. Individual control of the flow of information is out of the question; individual protection is not. We can determine what information sent over the Internet requires protection. That is, the restricted access model does not force us to make an all or none choice such that the Internet must be either completely public or completely private [see, for example, Tavani, 2000b]. In general, diverse private and public situations can be imbedded in and overlap each other in complex ways. Consider a simple example in the real world. A woman in a public building may be having a private phone conversation while being publicly viewed holding a purse whose contents are private. We have no trouble making such public/private distinctions in ordinary life and we can designate private situations involving information on the Internet in similar ways. Information on the Web is generally public. Web sites are typically designed to solicit public attention. Nevertheless, we can be selective within this public framework. For example, we can insist that consumer and medical transactions be protected as private while allowing other Internet information to remain public. Although there is some conventionality in how we carve up zones of privacy in social situations, including Internet use, overall the carving should produce a set of zones that offer sufficient protection of personal information. We need to think carefully, not so much in terms of what information we can individually control, though that is important, but about what information and activities need to be protected on the Internet.

In defining a private situation it is necessary to define who has access to what under which circumstances. The privacy of medical information in a modern hospital represents a good example of the complexity of the restrictions that must be placed on a privacy situation. Physicians are allowed to see most if not all the medical records of only a select number of patients. HMOs may see only part of the medical records of more patients. Financial officers can see the financial records for the medical services. These restrictions bar most people from gaining access, and possibly nobody can see all of the records. These restrictions in access also often forbid revelation of private matters to others by those who do have access. A physician who has access to medical records is still bound by confidentiality and cannot freely reveal the contents of those records. The restricted access analysis of privacy permits a fine-grained analysis of privacy among various individuals in a situation including possible demands of confidentiality on those who do have access.

In a similar manner, sensitive transactions on the Internet must be identified and protected. Different parties may have different levels of access and confidentiality restrictions. E-commerce, to pick an obvious example, should be designated as a zone of privacy. Merchants should be required to treat consumer information confidentially. Legal and social sanctions should be established for those who do not comply. In effect, this is what the European Union Directive on Privacy is aimed at—the creation of zones of privacy with sanctions to protect personal information.

Pressuring commercial partners, such as the United States, to share this perspective is an attempt to extend a secure zone of privacy. Recently, there are encouraging signs, such as announcements from the Federal Trade Commission and the Safe Harbor Agreement, that the U.S. is moving closer to treating more situations on the Internet as normatively private.

With the constant evolution of information technology, new zones of privacy continually need to be created and access relationships defined to maintain high levels of protection. In a time in which e-commerce is expanding exponentially, data mining is routine, surveillance from space at one meter resolution is commercially available, biometric identification is poised to become commonplace, and the human genome is about to be mapped and sequenced, it is imperative to rethink and revise what the zones of privacy should be [Moor, 1999b; Tavani, 1999b, 1999c]. Moreover, these new zones of privacy need to be created to protect individuals especially when individuals lack control of personal information and cannot protect themselves.

Thus far, we have argued that the right to privacy cannot be adequately conceptualized in terms of the control of information but rather is better understood in terms of a theory of restricted access. Citizens may not control whether they provide income tax information, but the information they are forced to furnish should be accessible only to tax authorities bound by confidentiality. And, we have argued that new zones of privacy with protections need to be established as technology develops because individual control by itself is not likely to be sufficient for adequate protection. Filing income tax information electronically should be normatively protected because the filer cannot control the flow of such personal information over the Internet.

The Use of Control in the Justification and Management of Privacy

We have gone to some length to separate the notion of individual control from the basic concept of privacy in order to preserve the identity of both, but now we wish to emphasize the importance of control in the other areas of the tripartite theory of privacy. Individual control plays a central role in the justification and in the management of privacy. Thus, in the overall theory of privacy, control and privacy are complementary notions that reinforce each other.

A straightforward *justification* for having privacy is the protection it affords us to plan our lives, to decide what benefits we wish to seek, and what harms we wish to avoid. It allows us to decide what projects we will undertake and what risks we will assume. Privacy allows us to seek medical care we might not otherwise seek and to buy products without advertising our buying habits. Private situations permit intimacy and the development of close personal relationships. In short, privacy offers us control over our lives. Privacy is not an unqualified good, as people can also use zones of privacy to commit robberies and beat their spouses. But all things considered, privacy, perhaps privacy subject to carefully monitored court ordered intervention, provides protection that most of us would impartially support. This individual control generated from policies of privacy leads to greatly increased human happiness and autonomy [Moor, 1999a].

Individual control in turn helps us to manage our own privacy. Individual control for the *management* of privacy typically expresses itself in one of three ways: *choice*, *consent*, and *correction*. We control privacy in part by choosing situations that offer the desired level of access ranging from total privacy to unabashed publicity. And in seeking a level of privacy we may not only choose the level of access but choose the level of risk as well. Two situations can have the same actual level of privacy but one may be more *secure*, i.e., offer less risk of access.

The management of privacy through choice need not involve normatively private situations but just prudent choosing, so that the flow of information is controlled and prevents access. If people don't want others to see them jog, they should choose to jog when others are not around. No right of privacy is at stake here, but privacy can be chosen. However, the existence of normative situations, zones of privacy, can affect what choices one has in seeking privacy. Zones of privacy offer more possibilities for protection, assuming the privacy rights are honored and enforced, i.e., they are reasonable and secure. Therefore in creating zones of privacy, it is important to inform people under what conditions they operate and with what level of security so that people may take advantage of them as they wish. To this end, we advocate the *Publicity Principle* that states that the rules and conditions governing private situations can be clear and known to the persons affected by them [Culver et al., 1994]. If office e-mail is not a normatively private situation, as it is not in the U.S., then employees need to know that employers have the right to examine it. People so informed and seeking privacy in e-mail can choose an e-mail system with a zone of privacy.

Another way privacy is managed by control is through consent. In many normatively private situations, individuals have the right to waive their right to privacy and allow access by others. This is sometimes thought to be incompatible with the restricted access view. Dag Elgesem explains, "There is, intuitively, a big difference between the situation where your privacy is violated, say your phone is tapped, and the situation where you tell your friend an intimate secret." To account for the difference, he says, we have to bring in "the notion of consent to the transfer of personal information, i.e., a notion of control. But the restricted access account explicitly rejects the use of notions pertaining to control in the characterisation of privacy" [Elgesem, 1999 p. 289]. However, this line of criticism dissipates once we distinguish the concept of privacy, defined by restricted access, from the management of privacy. The presence or absence of consent makes a crucial difference between a proper action and a violation of a right. Giving consent is a familiar way of granting access to an otherwise restricted situation. We can invite a stranger into our private house. No incompatibility exists between the restricted access definition of privacy and the notion of consent to suspend restrictions in access. Consent is a means of control that manages privacy and justifies what without it would be an invasion of privacy.

Control also plays a role in another area in the management of privacy: the correction of personal information. A general principle that characterizes fair information practices is that data subjects should be able to access their personal information with an ability to amend if necessary [Bennett, 1992 pp. 101–111, Bennett and Grant,

1999 p. 6]. This principle is clearly a way for an individual to control personal information and suggests a safeguard against maintaining harmful erroneous information that has been collected within a zone of privacy. Such individual control of personal information resulting in the correction of data is consistent with a restricted access account of the concept of privacy and needs to be part of good privacy management practice.

All of the aspects of individual control—choice, consent, and correction—are important ingredients in the management of privacy. They are important in fair information practices that characterize various national and international privacy regulations. But all have their limits. There is only so much individual choosing, consenting, and correcting that one can do. The management of privacy requires controls beyond individual control that will ensure restrictions in access and the purposes for which the normatively private situations are created. Additional controls, such as good national and international privacy policies and laws with enforcement, are necessary in order to fully protect privacy. As an example, we consider privacy-enhancing technologies (PETs) and their limitations in Part II of this essay.

Part II: Privacy-Enhancing Technologies

We next consider the role of *privacy-enhancing technologies* or PETs in the protection of personal privacy. Following a brief discussion of what PETs are and why they are viewed by some as a means for resolving online privacy concerns, we examine some of the ways in which PETs enable individuals to manage personal privacy—*viz.*, through individual control mechanisms such as choice and consent. We then consider whether PETs, even if they provide users with a certain level of control over their personal information, actually ensure users that their privacy will be protected.

What Exactly Are PETs and Why Are They Appealing?

According to Burkert [1997 p. 125], PETs can be understood as "technical and organizational concepts that aim at protecting personal identity." As organizational concepts, PETs can perhaps be thought of in terms of industry-standard guidelines for privacy protection, such as those adopted by the Platform for Privacy Protection (P3P). For example, *online privacy seal programs*, such as TRUSTe, can inform users of an online vendor's privacy policies and assure those users that a vendor's stated policies are backed and enforced by reputable third-parties. In their technical sense, on the other hand, PETs can be viewed as specific *online tools* used by individuals to control the amount of personal information they disclose in online activities. Although Burkert's definition correctly distinguishes between the technical and organizational functions that PETs perform, his definition would also seem to imply that all PETs are aimed at protecting the *identity* of persons. Clearly, a primary function of certain kinds of PETs is to protect personal identity. However, one of the oldest, most effective PETs, encryption, can be used simply to protect the informational content of messages, not the identity of persons. Unfortunately, Burkert's definition, despite the fact that it draws a very important distinction for helping us to divide PETs into two useful categories, does not seem to take into account that PETs perform tasks other than simply protecting one's identity.

Because PETs have come to be understood and debated primarily in their technical sense, i.e., as tools that can assist users either in concealing their identity while online or in securing the content of information they communicate electronically, we will focus our discussion mainly on the sense of PETs as privacy-enhancing tools. As tools, PETs perform a host of functions. For example, Cranor [1999 p. 30] notes that some PETs can function as "anonymizing agents" and "pseudonym agents." Whereas certain PETs, such as anonymizing tools (e.g., the *Anonymizer*) and pseudonym agents (e.g., *Lucent Personalized Web Assistant*) have been designed with the goal of enabling users to navigate the Internet either anonymously or pseudonymously, other PETS have been developed to allow users to communicate online via correspondences that are encrypted with either digital-signature or blind-signature technologies. Much has been written about the technical details and nuances of various PETs, so there is no need to repeat that discussion here. Our primary concern in this essay is in determining whether PETs provide online users with adequate privacy protection.

The appeal of using PETs is obvious. PETs provide users with control over their own information. PETs offer users choices about what information they wish to release. Users may consent or not to the acquisition of personal information. The fundamental PET, encryption, offers users privacy with increased security. What could be better in the management of privacy? On the one hand, certain privacy advocates and consumer groups have argued that stronger privacy legislation is needed to protect the interests and rights of online users. On the other hand, groups representing the e-commerce sector have lobbied for voluntary controls and industry self-regulation as an alternative to new privacy legislation. Generally, the respective solutions proposed by one camp have been unacceptable to the other. Now, some members of each camp appear ready to embrace PETs as a compromise resolution. PETs are clearly advantageous for managing personal privacy. Nobody denies that. But we wish to argue that PETs are not formidable guard dogs of privacy but tools with serious limitations.

The adequacy of PETs can be challenged in terms of their technological effectiveness or on the basis of their security and public-policy implications [Tavani, 2000a]. With respect to issues of technical adequacy, some have noted that "anonymizing tools" do not always ensure that users will have total anonymity while they interact with the Web, whereas others have questioned the effectiveness of PETs as reliable encryption technologies. And with respect to public policy and security, some government officials and law-enforcement agents have argued that anonymity tools are potentially dangerous for national security because (a) they allow terrorists to carry out certain criminal activities online that would be extremely difficult to trace back to the party or parties responsible for those activities and (b) they allow criminals and terrorists to communicate via encrypted messages that possibly cannot be decoded by appropriate law enforcement agencies. However, we will not pursue the lines of argumentation based on either technical or security-related inadequacies involving PETs. Rather, our interest in this essay is in whether PETs can enable individuals to protect their privacy while they are engaged in online activities. We begin by looking at PETs as tools for controlling personal information with respect to individual choice.

PETs and the Role of Individual Choice in Controlling Personal Information

Burkert [1997 p. 125] notes that, among other things, PETs "give direct control over revelation of personal information to the person concerned." Because PETs offer users a certain degree of choice with respect to disclosing personal information in online transactions, which otherwise those users might not have, it would seem that the PETs provide users with much more privacy protection than was afforded them in the earlier systems of voluntary controls and industry self-regulation. But even if PETs provide users with a means of controlling information about themselves, do these tools provide users with adequate privacy protection? How, for example, are users supposed to learn about the existence of PETs in the first place. At present, responsibility for learning about the existence of these tools would clearly seem to be incumbent upon online users themselves, since there is no requirement for online entrepreneurs either to inform users of the existence of PETs or to make such tools available to users. In this sense, then, PETs would fail to satisfy the Publicity Principle, which requires that the rules and conditions governing a scheme for protecting privacy must be open and public. Because the Publicity Principle is a crucial aspect of any normative policy designed to protect personal privacy, PETs would have to meet the conditions of such a principle if they are to be considered an adequate form of privacy protection.

And, who is responsible for distributing PETs, if they are not automatically bundled with either operating-system or application software or if they are not provided as part of the Web interfaces of online vendors? Should online entrepreneurs be responsible for providing them, or should consumers be required to locate PETs and then be further responsible for installing them on their systems? Is it reasonable to expect online users to be responsible for these tasks?

Consider the case of one of the earlier and more popularly known privacy-enhancing tools, PGP (Pretty Good Privacy). PGP enabled ordinary users to send encrypted e-mail messages, and the PGP tool cookie.cutter enabled users to avoid having "cookie" files sent to their computers. Although PGP was available free of charge, the onus was on users, first to discover that PGP applications existed and then to track down the location of those tools and download them on to their computers. Currently, the latest versions of most Web browsers allow users to reject cookies without having to install separate privacy-enhancing software to do so. Of course, if the default setting on Web browsers and the default policies on Web sites were such that no information about users could be collected unless those users explicitly consented, we could ask whether tools such as PETs would even be needed.

Independent of questions about how users are supposed to find out about the existence of PETs and about how those tools should be made available to users, other problems regarding the aspect of choice need to be addressed and resolved if PETs are to ensure adequate privacy protection for users. For although PETs may allow users a certain measure of control over their personal information in an initial online transaction, they do not necessarily ensure that users will have any say (control) about how information about them is subsequently used once that information has been disclosed to an online vendor.

Consider, for example, a recent case involving the e-commerce Web site *Toysmart.com*. Online consumers who engaged in transactions with Toysmart were assured, via an online *trust seal*—i.e., a type of PET that would seem to fall under Burkert's category of PETs as organizational concepts—that their personal data would be protected. This vendor's policy stated that personal information disclosed to Toysmart would be used internally, but would not be sold to or exchanged with external vendors. However, in the spring of 2000, Toysmart was forced to file for bankruptcy. Ceasing operations in May 2000, Toysmart decided to solicit bids for its assets, which included the names of customers in its databases. Parties interested in purchasing that information believed that they were under no obligation to adhere to the privacy policy that Toysmart had established with its clients. So the party or parties who took over Toysmart, or who purchased Toysmart's databases, would, in principle, be free to do whatever they wished with the personal information in that vendor's databases. Thus personal information about Toysmart's clients might no longer be protected, despite the fact that such information was given to that online vendor by clients who were operating under the belief that information about them would be protected indefinitely. And these clients would seem to have been justified in holding such a belief because of specific agreements they made with Toysmart under the provisions of a privacy policy involving a type of PET in the form of a trust seal.

The Toysmart incident illustrates a case in which individuals exercised control over their personal information in one context—i.e., in controlling whether they would elect to disclose information about themselves to Toysmart in online transactions—based on specific conditions stated in Toysmart's privacy policy. However, it also turned out that these individuals were not able to be guaranteed that the personal information they disclosed to Toysmart would be protected in the future. Thus it would seem that, beyond the limited control of personal information provided by PETs and by the specific privacy policies of certain online vendors, additional controls in the form of policies and laws are needed in order to ensure that a zone of privacy is established and enforced to protect individuals in subsequent uses of the personal information they disclose in one or more online activities.

PETs and the Principle of Informed Consent

Another important question involving PETs, which is also related to the control of personal information, has to do with whether individuals can make *informed* decisions about the disclosure of their personal data in online transactions. Traditionally, the principle of informed consent has been the model or standard for disclosure involving personal data. But in certain online commercial activities, including those involving the use of PETs, it would seem that the informed consent principle might not be adhered to as strictly as one might assume. For instance, users who willingly consent to provide information about themselves for use in one context often have no idea as to how that information might be used subsequently. That is, they do not always realize that the information they disclose for one purpose, or in one online transaction, might also have secondary uses. Although this particular problem is not unique to PETs, or for that matter to online activities, concerns about the secondary use of a consumer's personal data are nonetheless exacerbated by certain online activities, including e-commerce transactions. So it would seem that regardless of whether users consent to the initial collection of their personal information, they must also be given an explicit choice of whether or not to consent to the future use of that information in secondary applications. Unfortunately, not all PETs provide users with this explicit option.

One argument that has been advanced by some online entrepreneurs is that no one is forcing users to reveal personal data and that the disclosure of such data is done on a completely voluntary basis. However, even if it is granted that a user has willingly consented to disclose personal data to an e-commerce vendor for use in a specific business transaction, i.e., in some specific context, does it follow that the user has *ipso facto* granted permission to use that information for additional purposes (i.e., secondary uses)? Does the online vendor now "own" that information, and is the vendor now free to do with that information whatever he or she chooses? Consider the case of various data-mining activities in the commercial sector. Specific information given by a consumer for use in one context, say in an application for an automobile loan, is collected and stored in a data warehouse, and then the data is subsequently "mined" for implicit consumer patterns. As a result of data-mining activities, an individual could eventually be "discovered" to be a member of a newly created category or group—conceivably one that the user has no idea even exists. And based solely on his or her identification in such a newly discovered category or group, that individual might be denied a consumer loan, despite the fact that this particular individual's credit history is impeccable [Tavani 1999a].

Another argument that might be advanced by online entrepreneurs, especially in defense of the secondary use of personal information as in the case of data-mining practices, is: If the user has put information about him or herself into the public domain of the Internet, i.e., disclosed the data as part of an online questionnaire for a transaction, then that information is no longer private. Of course, one response to this line of reasoning could be to question whether users, who in the process of consenting to disclose personal data in response to queries in online business transactions, understood clearly all of the conditions in which the data they had consented to reveal could be used, including certain future uses to which that data might also be put. For example, if users are queried as to whether they are willing to have their personal data "mined," many would likely be perplexed by this question since they might never have heard of the practice of data mining. Also we can certainly ask whether the businesses that collect personal data could possibly know in advance exactly how that data will be used—viz., to which uses that data would be put in secondary and future applications. This being the case, it would seem that online businesses *could not* adequately inform users about exactly how their personal data will be used. What kind of *informed* choice, then, could these users make in such a case? Can we—indeed should we—assume that most consumers understand the intricacies of a technique such as data mining?

Some online entrepreneurs have responded to charges involving privacy violations by pointing out that in most cases users are now provided with the means either to "opt-in" or "opt-out" of having their personal data collected, as well as having that data made available for secondary use. Currently, however, the default seems to be such that if no option is specified by the user when that individual discloses personal data for use in one context, that disclosed personal data would also be available for secondary use. We can certainly ask whether that presumption is a reasonable one. We can also ask whether having the ability simply to opt-in or opt-out of disclosing personal information is itself sufficient to protect personal privacy.

Because users can *choose* whether to grant or withhold information about themselves in online transactions—i.e., either opt-in or opt-out—it would certainly seem that users have at least some means of controlling their personal information, at least initially. And in some cases, users might also retain some say about how their information is used subsequently since they can elect to "sell" their personal information in return for certain financial incentives (in the form of discounts and rebates) currently offered by some e-commerce sites. Unfortunately, less affluent persons might be more inclined than would their wealthier counterparts to sell their personal data. This factor would seem to suggest that those users who are members of lower socioeconomic groups will, by virtue of their economic status, have less choice in (i.e., less control over) whether to sell their personal data. Informed consent should be free, not coerced. So the use of PETs would also seem to raise issues of social equity [Tavani, 2000c] as well as concerns involving the protection of personal information. Of course, our main concern in this section of the present essay has been with whether PETs necessarily provide adequate privacy protection for online users. We conclude that they do not.

PET Owners Beware

We have distinguished the concept of privacy from the notion of control. The concept of privacy is defined in terms of restricted access, whereas control has a central role in the justification and management of privacy. One practical payoff in making this distinction is that one can resist the temptation to think that because one has increased control, one has increased privacy. The conclusion is not a conceptual truth as it would be on the control theory of privacy. PETs give us increased control but it remains an open question whether privacy is increased.

Moreover, although PETs give us more control through choice and consent, there are good reasons to be skeptical about how easy and effective PETs are to use. For example, the controls for cookies are more hidden than ever in the most recent versions of Web browsers. The average user may not know what choices are available or how to get into a position to make them. A user may be coerced into giving consent to accept cookies because not doing so would make his browsing activities possibly sluggish.

PETs, though important tools, are not adequate to fully protect personal privacy. National and international policies and laws are also needed to set up zones of privacy to ensure that personal information continues to be protected once it has been given in one or more online transactions. The restricted access theory of privacy, defended in this essay, describes the kinds of rules and principles—e.g., as stated in the Publicity Principle—of protection that need to be established.

References

Bennett, C. J. [1992] *Regulating Privacy*. Ithaca, NY: Cornell University Press.

Bennett, C. J., and R. Grant, eds. [1999] *Visions of Privacy: Policy Choices for the Digital Age*. Toronto: University of Toronto Press Incorporated.

Burkert, H. [1997] "Privacy-Enhancing Technologies: Typology, Critique, Vision." In *Technology and Privacy: The New Landscape*, edited by P. E. Agre and M. Rotenberg. Cambridge, MA: MIT Press.

Cranor, L. F. [1999] "Internet Privacy." *Communications of the ACM*, **42** (2): 29–31.

Culver, C., J. Moor, W. Duerfeldt, M. Kapp, and M. Sullivan. [1994] "Privacy." *Professional Ethics*, **3** (3 & 4): 3–25.

Elgesem, D. [1996] "Privacy, Respect for Persons, and Risk." In *Philosophical Perspectives on Computer-Mediated Communication*, edited by C. Ess. New York: State University of New York Press.

Elgesem, D. [1999] "The Structure of Rights in Directive 95/46/EC on the Protection of Individuals with Regard to the Processing of Personal Data and the Free Movement of Such Data." *Ethics and Information Technology*, **1** (4): 283–293.

Fried, C. [1984] "Privacy." In *Philosophical Dimensions of Privacy*, edited by F. D. Schoeman. New York: Cambridge University Press.

Miller, A. R. [1971] *The Assault on Privacy: Computers, Data Banks, and Dossiers*. Ann Arbor: University of Michigan Press.

Moor, J. H. [1989] "How to Invade and Protect Privacy with Computers." In *The Information Web*, edited by C. C. Gould. Boulder: Westview Press.

Moor, J. H. [1990] "Ethics of Privacy Protection." *Library Trends*, **39** (1 & 2): 69–82.

Moor, J. H. [1997] "Towards a Theory of Privacy in the Information Age." *Computers and Society*, **27** (3): 27–32.

Moor, J. H. [1999a] "Just Consequentialism and Computing." *Ethics and Information Technology*, **1** (1): 65–69.

Moor, J. H. [1999b] "Using Genetic Information While Protecting the Privacy of the Soul." *Ethics and Information Technology*, **1** (4): 257–263.

Moore, B. [1984] *Privacy: Studies in Social and Cultural History*. Armonk, New York: M. E. Sharpe, Inc.

Tavani, H. T. [1999a] "Informational Privacy, Data Mining and the Internet." *Ethics and Information Technology*, **1** (2): 137–145.

Tavani, H. T. [1999b] "KDD, Data Mining, and the Challenge for Normative Privacy." *Ethics and Information Technology*, **1** (4): 265–273.

Tavani, H. T. [1999c] "Privacy Online." *Computers and Society*, **29** (4): 11–19.

Tavani, H. T. [2000a] "Privacy and Security." Chap. 4 in *Internet Ethics*, edited by D. Langford. New York: St. Martin's Press.

Tavani, H. T. [2000b] "Privacy and the Internet." In *Privacy and the Constitution*, edited by M. Placencia. Hamden, CT: Garland Publishing, Inc.

Tavani, H. T. [2000c] "Privacy-Enhancing Technologies as a Panacea for Online Privacy Concerns: Some Ethical Considerations," *Journal of Information Ethics*, **9** (2): 26–36.

Westin, A. R. [1967] *Privacy and Freedom*. New York: Atheneum.

Acknowledgments

We would like to express our thanks to Dag Elgesem whose careful critiques of the restricted access account have led us to a more clearly developed theory of privacy. We are also grateful to Michael Scanlan for some helpful comments on a version of this essay presented at the Conference on Computer Ethics–Philosophical Enquiry (CEPE 2000), Dartmouth College, July 14–16, 2000.

Toward an Approach to Privacy in Public: Challenges of Information Technology

Helen Nissenbaum

This article highlights a contemporary privacy problem that falls outside the scope of dominant theoretical approaches. Although these approaches emphasize the connection between privacy and a protected personal (or intimate) sphere, many individuals perceive a threat to privacy in the widespread collection of information even in realms normally considered "public." In identifying and describing the problem of privacy in public, this article is preliminary work in a larger effort to map out future theoretical directions.

Many influential approaches to privacy emphasize the role of privacy in safeguarding a personal or intimate realm where people may escape the prying and interference of others. This *private realm*, which is contrasted with a *public realm*, is defined in various ways. It is delimited by physical boundaries, such as the home; by personal relationships, such as family, friends, and intimates; and by selected fields of information, such as personal, sensitive, or embarrassing information. Privacy is worthy of safeguarding, these approaches argue, because intimacy is important; privacy is worth protecting because we value the sanctity of a personal realm.

This article does not dispute the importance of securing intimate and personal realms. Nor does it challenge the compelling connection between privacy norms and the ability to protect these realms against unwarranted intrusion. It argues, however, that an account of privacy is not complete that stops with the intimate and personal realms. The widespread use of information technology, such as in personal profiling, to assemble and transmit vast stores of information—even so-called "public" information—has shown that an adequate account of privacy should neither neglect the nonintimate realm nor explicitly exclude it from consideration. Loud calls of public protest in response to information harvesting strongly indicate that

This essay originally appeared in *Ethics & Behavior,* 7(3), 1997, 207–219. Copyright © 1997, Lawrence Erlbaum Associates, Inc. Reprinted by permission.

implicit norms of privacy are not restricted to personal zones. I henceforth call this challenge to existing theoretical frameworks the problem of protecting "privacy in public."

Privacy and the Personal Realm—Background

The idea that privacy functions to protect the integrity of a private or intimate realm spans scholarly work in many disciplines, including legal, political, and philosophical discussions of privacy. James Fitzjames Stephen (1873), a 19th century British legal theorist, wrote in his treatise on law, "there is a sphere, nonetheless real because it is impossible to define its limits, within which the law and public opinion are intruders likely to do more harm than good" (p. 160). The political scientist Carl Friedrichs (1971) remarked that the goal of legal protections is "primarily that of protecting the private sphere against intruders, whether government or not" (p. 105). Law in many countries recognizes realms that are basically off-limits. In the United States, for example, constitutional prohibitions on unreasonable searches and seizure, protection against self-incrimination, and guarantees of freedom of conscience delineate for each citizen a personal zone that is free from the prying and interference of government. This zone covers the home and personal effects as well as certain areas of his life such as family, "conscience," sexual and marital relations, and reproduction.[1] Tort Law has also helped insulate this personal zone against intrusion by nongovernmental agents.

Prominent among contemporary philosophical works on privacy is Charles Fried's. Fried (1984) argued that privacy is important because it renders possible important human relationships. Privacy provides "the necessary context for relationships which we would hardly be human if we had to do without—the relationships of love, friendship and trust" (p. 211). Although Fried conceived of privacy as control over all information about oneself, he defended a moral and legal right to privacy that extends only over the far more limited domain of intimate, or personal, information. He accepted this narrowing of scope because even a limited domain of intimate or personal information provides sufficient "currency" for people to differentiate relationships of varying degrees of intimacy. The danger of extending control over too broad a spectrum of information is that privacy may then interfere with other social and legal values. Fried wrote, "The important thing is that there be some information which is protected" (p. 214), namely, information about the personal and intimate aspects of life. According to Fried, the precise content of the class of protected information will be determined largely by social and cultural convention. Prevailing social order "designates certain areas, intrinsically no more private than other areas, as symbolic of the whole institution of privacy, and thus deserving of protection beyond their particular importance" (p. 214).

Other philosophers also have focused on the interdependence between privacy and a personal or intimate realm. Robert Gerstein (1984), for example, contended

---

[1] For an excellent discussion, see DeCew (1986).

that "intimacy simply could not exist unless people had the opportunity for privacy. Excluding outsiders and resenting their uninvited intrusions are essential parts of having an intimate relationship" (p. 217). Ferdinand Schoeman (1984) noted that "one's private sphere in some sense can be equated with those areas of a person's life which are considered intimate or innermost" (p. 412). Privacy's purpose, he wrote, is to insulate "individual objectives from social scrutiny. Social scrutiny can generally be expected to move individuals in the direction of the socially useful. Privacy insulates people from this kind of accountability and thereby protects the real of the personal" (p. 415). Schoeman, unlike Fried (1984) however, holds that there are domains of life that are essentially private and not merely determined to be so by social convention.

The views of Schoeman, Fried, and Gerstein, though differing in detail, rest on a common core. Each held that properly functioning, psychically healthy individuals need privacy. Privacy assures these people a space in which they are free of public scrutiny, judgment, and accountability, and in which they may unselfconsciously develop intimate relationships with others.

Other philosophical discussions are less motivated by this underlying conception of human need and more by a perceived need to sharpen the concept and definition of privacy. William Parent (1983), for example, rejected the many over-broad definitions and offered in their place a definition of privacy as "the condition of not having undocumented personal knowledge about one possessed by others" (p. 269). By personal facts Parent means "facts which most persons in a given society choose not to reveal about themselves (except to close friends, family, . . .) or facts about which a particular individual is acutely sensitive" (p. 270). By "undocumented" Parent means information that has not appeared in a "newspaper, court proceedings, and other official documents open to public inspection" (p. 270). A person's right to privacy restricts access by others to this sphere of personal, undocumented information unless, in any given case, there are other moral rights that clearly outweigh privacy. Although many other writers who have highlighted the connection between privacy and the personal realm have not attended merely to the status of the "non-personal" realm, Parent is explicit in excluding it. If information is not personal information or if it is documented, then action taken with respect to it simply does not bear on privacy.

Raymond Waks (1989), who is also motivated by the need for a more precise definition with clear boundaries, laid down this foundation:

> At the heart of the concern to protect "privacy" lies a conception of the individual and his or her relationship with society. The idea of private and public spheres or activity assumes a community in which not only does such a division make sense, but the institutional and structural arrangements that facilitate an organic representation of this kind are present. (p. 7)

The work of a theory of privacy is to define legitimate boundaries between these spheres. Like Parent (1983), Waks (1989) did not extend the conception of privacy to freedom of action (such as the right to abortion) but placed at the core of his definition of the right to privacy its "protection against the misuse of personal sensitive information" (p. 10).

Tom Gerety (1977), too, sought more rigor in his proposed definition of privacy. According to Gerety, the problem of privacy as a legal and moral concept

> comes not from the concept's meagerness but from its amplitude, for it has a protean capacity to be all things to all lawyers. . . . A legal concept will do us little good if it expands like a gas to fill up the available space. (p. 234)

Gerety characterized privacy as a "legal island of personal autonomy in the midst of a sea of public regulation and interaction" (p. 271). The scope of this autonomy is limited to the "intimacies of personal identity" (p. 281). This, and only this, is the domain of privacy.

Violating Privacy in Public—The Case of Lotus Marketplace: Households

The approaches described earlier are problematic not because they develop normative accounts of privacy that protect the personal and intimate realms from interference, but because they neglect the relevance to privacy of realms other than the intimate and sensitive. Some, like Parent's and Gerety's, go even further to explicitly deny it. In excluding all but the personal and intimate, they effectively disarm their normative accounts of privacy against one of the most vexing challenges that information technology currently poses. Almost 12 years ago, Hunter (1985) predicted, "Our revolution will not be in gathering data—don't look for TV cameras in your bedroom—but in analyzing the information that is already willingly shared" (p. 32). Hunter's comment makes an almost paradoxical point: We are complicit in an invasion of our own privacy that ultimately we find objectionable. The invasion is not from the realm of the intimate but from the realm that is generally not given serious consideration by many noted theorists of privacy.[2]

Lotus Marketplace: Households,[3] a case that has attracted a great deal of attention among privacy policy advocates, illustrates the distance between public perception of what counts as an unwarranted invasion of privacy and what may be inferred from some of the theoretical positions outlined earlier. In April 1990, Lotus Development Corporation, a developer and marketer of popular software, and Equifax Inc., a company that collects and sells information about consumer financial transactions, announced their intention to produce a comprehensive database called "Lotus Marketplace: Households" that would contain actual and inferred information about approximately 120 million individuals in the United States. It

---

[2] There are exceptions. Schoeman may be the clearest case. In contemporary work on policy issues, privacy advocates and policy analysts such as Regan, Rotenberg, and Goldman have been very vocal in these issues.

[3] For a fuller description of the case see Culnan and Smith (1995).

would include name, address, type of dwelling, marital status, gender, age, household income, lifestyle, and purchasing propensity. The two companies expected that the database, which was to have been recorded and sold in the format of a CD-ROM, would be widely adopted by marketers and mailing companies.[4]

They did not, however, anticipate the vigorous public outcry against Lotus Marketplace: Households. An estimated 30,000 letters of protest expressed its displeasure. Defenders were astonished. How was it possible to construe Lotus Marketplace as an invasion of privacy when the information it contained was taken from public sources only and not by violating any sensitive or personal realms? It was to be compiled from information already "out there" and would use no intrusive means to gain information of a personal or intimate nature—no hidden cameras in bedrooms. Information was to be harvested from public records and from records of transactions that individuals carried out in the public arena and made no efforts to hide. No private zones would be breached, the integrity of home and family would be respected, embarrassing personal facts would not be revealed. Defenders argued, furthermore, that opposition to Lotus Marketplace violated the right of its creators to pursue profitable enterprise.

Nevertheless, in January 1991, executives of Lotus Development Corporation and Equifax Inc. announced that they were canceling Lotus Marketplace, insisting that their decision was prompted by negative public reaction and misunderstanding and not because of any real threat to privacy. Normative theories of privacy like the ones advanced by Parent, Gerety, and Waks were compatible with the views expressed by the executives. Gerety (1977), for example, in commenting on compilations of nonintimate data wrote, "In these matters privacy affords us a convenient rhetoric of advocacy and legitimacy. Nonetheless, it is not the issue at bottom" (p. 291). And Parent (1983) wrote that as long as the information is neither personal, nor undocumented, it "cannot without glaring paradox be called private" (p. 271).

Although privacy advocates and activists may regard the outcome of Lotus Marketplace: Households a victory for privacy, in hindsight the victory appears thin. The loud and determined public outcry carried the day. But if the course of electronic profiling was stalled, it was stalled only temporarily. Personal data services satisfying virtually any conceivable need proliferate at a furious pace. Since Lotus Marketplace, no single case has served as an equivalent lightening rod for public action. Despite the absence of dramatic reaction, however, measures of public opinion continue to show the persistent sense that databases of so-called "public" information do violate privacy. For example, in June 1994, when ABC's *Nightline* anchor Ted Koppel conducted a poll, 73% of respondents said they viewed the sale of records to mail-order companies to be an invasion of privacy. Following Parent, Gerety, and Waks, one may attribute this public reaction to fuzzy thinking. A better alternative, if we are to develop a more meaningful concept of privacy, is to give serious consideration to the concerns expressed in public reactions to Lotus Marketplace and to the opinions from the *Nightline* polls (and others). Precision may be a worthy goal of scholarship, but not at the cost of missing a significant and persistent worry.

---

[4] Other industry analysts were also very encouraging. An interesting example is Esther Dyson, now head of the Electronic Frontier Foundation, in a *Forbes* magazine column (Dyson 1990).

There is a reason, I think, in this divergence of theoretical implications and observed public opinion. Here is where information technology enters the picture. Whereas prior to the proliferation of databases of so-called "public" information normative theories that focused on protecting a personal realm offered a good approximation to the actual threats to privacy (namely, government intruding into personal lives), it now no longer covers the full sense of what is valuable about privacy, and fails to capture aspects of privacy that we care about. Where previously, physical barriers and inconvenience might have discouraged all but the most tenacious from ferreting out information, technology makes this available at the click of a button or for a few dollars. This has dramatically expanded the scope of what is possible with even public information. As a result, dominant legal and philosophical theory, which has been serviceable until now, is no longer in step with moral norms. Theory tells us Lotus Marketplace is permissible; our norms tell us "no."

Two Misleading Assumptions

I argued earlier that if a theory of privacy is not able to give an account of personal information in the so-called "public realm," then it is unable to meet one of the central challenges of information technology. Although ultimately our aim should be to generate an alternative theoretical framework, or an extension of existing theory, which would meet these new challenges, the following discussion attempts only to clear a way toward this more ambitious goal. It directs attention to two commonly held, but misleading assumptions about the nonintimate realm and its relation to privacy. These assumptions, cast by supporters as truisms, stand in the way of an adequate conception of privacy.

Erroneous Assumption 1: There is a realm of public information about persons to which no privacy norms apply.

This assumption holds that there is a category of information about persons that is perfectly public (public in a normative sense), which is "up for grabs" for anyone with an interest in and use for it, for which "anything goes." This category, generated by default, consists of information accepted by broad consensus in a given society not belonging to the personal, sensitive, or intimate zone, and not acquired by eavesdropping, spying, or other means generally considered intrusive. Widespread use and abuse of information about persons rests on this assumption.

I argue later that even if, on the one hand, there is broad consensus on what information may be classified personal and intimate, there is, on the other hand, little, if anything, that people universally would admit into a completely public realm if by that we mean that it is governed by no norms of privacy whatever.[5]

---

[5] Reiman (1984) wrote,

> Privacy is a social practice. It involves a complex of behaviors that stretches from refraining from asking questions about what is none of one's business to refraining from looking into open windows one passes on the street, from refraining from entering a closed door without knocking, to refraining from knocking down a locked door without a warrant. (p. 310)

For another account of privacy norms, see Schoeman (1994).

Let us consider what might be meant by a category of information for which "anything goes." What might this category include? How might we define it? One possibility is to define the category of public information in terms of a category we understand more directly; namely, that of a public place. Accordingly, public information would include any information observed and recorded in a public place, in keeping with Reiman's (1984) suggestion that the social practice of privacy "does not assert a right never to be seen even on a crowded street" (p. 319). It would be reasonable to conclude, therefore, that information harvested in a public place is "up for grabs" and not covered by norms of privacy.

This proposal would only work if at least two things hold: one, that judgment confirms the inference from public space to public (in this strong sense) information, and two, judgments about information are indeed derivable from judgments about the nature of the place. It is not clear, however, that either of these hold. In the first place, the idea that we judge information to be public merely because it is acquired in a public arena is readily challenged. Consider Schoeman's (1994) remarks,

> Just because something happens in public does not mean it becomes a public fact: the Central Park rape occurred in public as did the trial of the accused, but the victim maintains a measure of privacy as to her identity. In less dramatic cases, the notion of civil inattention directs us to the same realization. (p. 81)

In general, even if we agree that a number of familiar places are not part of the "intimate" and private realms, we would not therefore agree that any information harvested from them is completely public. This would mean that facts gleaned from arenas such as public schools, supermarkets, parks, and libraries belong in a category of public information in the strongest sense. By contrast, even quintessential public places—a public square or sidewalk—are governed by some norms of privacy. It would be within one's rights to reply "none of your business" to a stranger who asks your name.

In the second place, at times our public sentiments suggest that the idea of private information may not be derivable from ideas of public space. This is demonstrated in cases where a change of determination occurs as a result of a traumatic incident or public discussion. In 1988, for example, after a newspaper published videotape rental records of then-nominee to the Supreme Court, Robert Bork, the U.S. Congress passed the Video Privacy Protection Act of 1988, which reversed the status of video rental records from public to private (see Regan, 1995). Even though the setting did not change—transactions still occurred in the video rental store—a societal judgment shifted video rentals records from public to private. In other words, privacy norms are not necessarily derivable from setting but can come prior.

Another contender for a category of information that is "up for grabs" is information found in public records such as birth and death records, real estate records, and court records. Here too, however, people are beginning to question the inference that if information is in a public record then it is perfectly public. These doubts have been expressed not only by members of the public but by public officials. In two recent court cases in New Jersey, the New Jersey Supreme Court explicitly asserted that we may not conclude, just because information exists in a public record, that the information is not subject to restrictions in distribution and use.

In *Higg-A-Rella Inc. v. County of Essex*, the Court recognized that the form of public records—computerized versus paper—can affect de facto privacy protection. Even though it ruled in favor of Higg-A-Rella in its bid to gain access to computerized records of municipal tax-assessment data, it stated that

> *Release of information on computer tape in many instances is far more reveal-ing than release of hard copies, and offer the potential for far more intrusive inspections. Unlike paper records, computerized records can be easily retrieved, researched, and reassembled in novel and unique ways, not previously imag-ined.* (Higg-A-Rella, Inc. v. County of Essex, 1995, p. 52)

In another ruling, *Doe v. Poritz*, the New Jersey Supreme Court noted that "an indi-vidual's right in controlling the dissemination of information regarding personal matters does not dissolve simply because that information may be available to the public in some form" (*Doe v. Poritz*, 1995, p. 83). The court thereby does not allow us to infer from the presence of information in a public record that it is entirely "up for grabs." By the same token, in states where the names of rape victims are part of the public records, there is support for the idea that victims of rape, or for that matter, victims and families of victims of other crime, retain some measure of con-trol over the information about them. Just because people are able to learn these facts by referring to public records does not imply a right to distribute and use the information in any way they choose.

The free dissemination of drivers' records information has also come under public scrutiny and opposition. The murder of actress Rebecca Schaeffer and, as a result, better public understanding of the status of drivers' records, led to a revi-sion in the law. Previously, state departments of motor vehicles treated drivers' records as public records—no-holds barred. The Driver's Privacy Protection Act of 1993, which was incorporated into the Violent Crime Control and Law Enforcement Act of 1994, changed this by limiting access to these records. It allows drivers to opt out of lists that previously were freely disseminated by departments of motor vehi-cles. Here, too, is an example of the way concern over privacy has led to a reevalu-ation of the norms associated with "public records."[6]

What I have tried to show is that even for two of the most plausible contenders for the category of personal information "up for grabs," there are significant prob-lems. At root, I believe, is a mismatch between intuitively held privacy norms as applied to information and the much touted private–public dichotomy. A promis-ing alternative rejects the relevance of the dichotomy to information about persons in favor of the idea of a multiplicity of contexts. Information learned in one con-text belongs in that context and is public vis à vis that context. We do not have a dichotomy of two realms but a panoply of realms; something considered public in relation to one realm may be private in relation to another, "disclosure of information

---

[6] For a more complete discussion, see Regan (1995, p. 103).

to groups, even potentially large groups, might still be considered private provided still larger groups were excluded" (Schoeman, 1984). People count on this contextual integrity as an effective protection of privacy. Nightclub patrons may not mind being seen by other patrons but may reasonably object to having their actions reported outside of that context. Shoppers may not object to using open shopping carts but may sense violation if inquisitive neighbors noted and reported elsewhere on their purchases. Similarly, information such as the number and identities of a person's children, the gender and identity of one's live-in partner, and so forth, are facts freely available in some contexts (that is, are "public" in some realms) but considered private in others.[7]

Two philosophers, Schoeman and Rachels, offer additional reasons for protecting contextual integrity. Whereas Fried argued for a single dimension stretching from intimate, on the one end, to public, on the other, Schoeman and Rachels suggested a multiplicity. Privacy, in enabling individuals to maintain contextual integrity, enables them to develop a variety of distinct relationships. Schoeman (1984) wrote, "People have, and it is important that they maintain, different relationships with different people. Information appropriate in the context of one relationship may not be appropriate in another" (p. 408). Rachels (1984) argued that

> "the value of privacy [is] based on the idea that there is a close connection between our ability to control who has access to us and to information about us, and our ability to create and maintain different sorts of social relationships with different people." (p. 292)

Erroneous Assumption 2: An aggregation of information does not violate privacy if its parts, taken individually, do not.

At first hearing, the logic behind the assumption may seem unassailable. Consider the rhetoric: Assemble innocuous bits of information and you will have an innocuous assemblage of information, a "benign composite of humdrum data." The assumption plays an important role in defending a position that databases of nonsensitive information are nonsensitive. On closer scrutiny, however, the assumption, and along with it the many activities it supports, are questionable. When bits of information are aggregated, compiled, and assembled, they can be invasive of privacy even if when taken individually they are not. (The remarks that follow are merely suggestive. A fuller discussion, which develops when and why aggregations may violate privacy, is beyond the scope of what I am able to cover in this article.)

Experience with databases of personal information has left no doubt that the value of information can be seriously affected by combining and compiling it with other information. Metaphorically speaking, with information one *can* sew a silk purse out of a sow's ear. Ware (1991) noted, "A whole industry thrives on assem-

---

[7] Some may argue that if information is in public, then it is obviously up for grabs. This conclusion is far from compelling. As we see in the case of intellectual property, an intellectual work can be viewed (sung, displayed) in public but still be controlled in important ways by its author or owner. In a similar way, despite public display or availability, subjects may continue to maintain control. I do not mean by this that privacy rights are a form of intellectual property rights but that they share this feature.

bling and selling data;" countless businesses profit from hawking assemblages and compilations of otherwise worthless bits of personal information. A single fact about someone takes on a new dimension when it is combined with other facts about the individual, or when it is compared with similar facts about other individuals. Applying ingenuity to one-dimensional bits of information can transform mere "noise" and statistical data into rich portraits of people. Through the powers of information technology we acquire the capability not only to collect and store vast amounts of information, but to bring order to it, to manipulate it, and to draw meaningful inferences from it. By these actions we are able to inject shape and also value into a riot of formless data.

At the same time, the capacity to manipulate information in these ways may have significant bearing on the humans who are its subjects. First, the act of compiling almost always involves shifting information from one context to another; it involves using information in a manner not explicitly announced when the information was initially collected. This means that unless the subjects of the information have explicitly granted permission to move it around, they have effectively lost control over it. Moreover, as suggested earlier, although the broadcast of information in one context is perfectly apt, it may be highly inappropriate, demeaning, or awkward when broadcast in another.

The act of compiling information may also transform harmless bits into a picture that can embarrass and hurt. Even when there is no call for this degree of accountability, even when discrete bits of information are all that are needed to carry out efficient transactions with a given agency or business, these bits may be conjoined with other bits to form rich portraits capable of revealing character, identity, personality, and lifestyle. "In the information age, our public acts disclose our private dispositions, even more than a camera in the bedroom would," writes Larry Hunter (1985). The subjects of these portraits, or profiles, may well ask what right those who compile the information have to the insights and access to their lives and personalities that these portraits provide. Moreover, portraits are developed not for the purpose of developing friendship or intimate association, but to manipulate, motivate, and judge; to make decisions that will affect the lives of their subjects in important ways.

To sense the nature of this affront, imagine oneself the subject of general but constant surveillance. Although assurances that it covers only nonintimate realms may provide some consolation, the omnipresent record-taking opens one to unbearable exposure.

Conclusion: Implications for a Theory of Privacy

This article urges a conception of privacy that would extend consideration to all information, including information gathered in so-called public realms. If successful, it would also block two misleading assumptions that both implicitly and explicitly have been invoked by those who would justify compilation of complex databases of nonintimate information. Existing theories that limit the scope of privacy to a personal zone or to intimate and sensitive information fail to capture elements of common real-world judgments. Public reaction to Lotus Marketplace:

Households and similar computerized databases of nonsensitive information indicates that, by contrast, our common notion of privacy is not thus limited. The power of computers and networks to gather and synthesize information exposes individuals to the scrutiny of others in unprecedented ways. Although guarding the intimate realm against unwarranted invasion is an important aspect of protecting privacy, information technology indicates a need for a more inclusive theory. Neglecting the broader sphere will rob from people the ease and comfort of anonymity as they stroll through actual town squares as well as electronic town squares, conduct trade, socialize, and engage in political and recreational activity both on and off line. It will deprive them of privacy in public.

Acknowledgments

I acknowledge the perceptive comments of Jonathan Schonsheck and members of the audience. Thanks also to Grayson Barber and Julian Gorelli for legal insights and for drawing attention to recent important and relevant New Jersey cases.

References

Culnan, M. J., & Smith, H. J. (1995). Lotus Marketplace: Households . . . Managing information privacy concerns. In D. G. Johnson & H. Nissenbaum (Eds.), *Computers, ethics and social values* (pp. 269–278). Englewood Cliffs, NJ: Prentice Hall.

DeCew, J. W. (1986). The scope of privacy in law and ethics. *Law and Philosophy, 5,* 145–173.

Doe v. Poritz, 142 N.J. 1 (1995).

Dyson, E. (1990, April 30). Data is dandy. *Forbes,* p. 180.

Fried, C. (1984). Privacy. In F. Schoeman (Ed.), *Philosophical dimensions of privacy: An anthology* (pp. 203–222). Cambridge, England: Cambridge University Press.

Friedrichs, C. (1971). Secrecy versus privacy: The democratic dilemma. In J. R. Pennock & J. W. Chapman (Eds.), *Privacy: Nomos XIIII* (pp. 105–120). New York: Atherton.

Gerety, T. (1977). Redefining privacy. *Harvard Civil Rights-Civil Liberties Law Review, 12*(12), 233–293.

Gerstein, R. (1984). Intimacy and privacy. *Philosophical dimensions of privacy: An anthology.* Cambridge, England: Cambridge University Press.

Higg-A-Rella, Inc. v. County of Essex. 141 N.J. 35 (1985).

Hunter, L. (1985, January). Public image. *Whole Earth Review,* 32–37.

Parent, W. (1983). Privacy, morality, and the law. *Philosophy & Public Affairs, 12*(5), 269–288.

Rachels, J. (1984). Why privacy is important. In F. Schoeman (Ed.), *Philosophical dimensions of privacy* (pp. 290–299). Cambridge, England: Cambridge University Press.

Regan, P. (1995). *Legislating privacy: Technology, social values, and public policy.* Chapel Hill: University of North Carolina Press.

Reiman, J. (1984). Privacy, intimacy and personhood. In F. Schoeman (Ed.), *Philosophical dimensions of privacy: An anthology* (pp. 300–316). Cambridge, England: Cambridge University Press.

Schoeman, F. (Ed.). (1984). Privacy and intimate information. *Philosophical dimensions of privacy: An anthology.* Cambridge, England: Cambridge University Press.

Schoeman, F. (1994). Gossip and privacy. In R. F. Goodman & A. B. Ze'ev (Eds.), *Good gossip* (pp. 72–84). Lawrence: University Press of Kansas.

Stephen, J. F. (1873). *Liberty, equality and fraternity.* New York: Holt.

Waks, R. (1989). *Personal information: Privacy and the law.* Oxford, England: Clarendon.

Ware, W. H. (1991, August). *Contemporary privacy issues.* Address given at the National Convention on Computing and Values, New Haven, CT.

KDD, Privacy, Individuality, and Fairness

Anton H. Vedder

Introduction

Knowledge discovery in databases (KDD) has been described as the nontrivial extraction of implicit, previously unknown, and potentially useful information from data (Frawley, Piatetsky-Shapiro, and Matheus, 1991). The KDD process is usually divided into three phases: the data warehousing phase, the data mining phase, and the interpretation phase. In the data warehousing phase, data is collected, enriched, checked, and coded. The data is analyzed in the data mining phase. Finally, the results are interpreted. During these phases, a search hypothesis is used to guide the process. Confusingly, the whole process of KDD, i.e., all three phases together, are often referred to also as "data mining." It may be better to use the latter notion only for the middle phase of KDD. KDD is important because it enables us to analyze and discover all kinds of, until now, unforeseen patterns in enormously large databases that, until recently, seemed unassailable because of their extent. KDD offers great opportunities regarding the description and prediction of behavior of groups (Fayyad, Piatetsky-Shapiro, and Smyth, 1996). KDD has already been acknowledged as an important set of techniques in analyzing data for purposes such as direct marketing and credit scoring. Other applications include checking for patterns in criminal behavior for forensic and judicial purposes and analyzing medical data and data about medical drug consumption in combination with demographic data to predict potential risk groups. It is exactly the production of group profiles with the help of KDD on which I will focus in this contribution. Group profiling with the help of KDD offers undoubtedly many great opportunities that can be applied for the benefit of people. There are nevertheless also disadvantages attached to it from a moral and a social point of view. This paper focuses on the negative social impact of group profiling through KDD.

It should be noted that, throughout this paper, I will treat KDD only insofar as it involves the use of personal data. I include KDD insofar as it involves the use of personal data *in combination with* other data. But I will not address KDD involving no personal data at all. For instance, KDD focusing on production processes exclusively with the help of data about machines and materials will not be of my concern, here. Group profiling through KDD involves the use of personal data in the sense of data immediately relating to individually identifiable persons as a part of the source-material, i.e., the complete set of data to which the KDD techniques are applied. Once this source-material is processed with the help of KDD techniques they are gradually anonymized. At some stage of aggregation or processing, the data is disconnected from identifiers of individuals and is combined with an identifier of a group. A group identifier can be a group or class characteristic such as a certain age, the ownership of a certain type of car, the residency in a certain area with a certain postal code, a certain position to characteristics indicating the use of a certain medicine, or a combination of some such characteristics.

In this paper, I will first point out that the current privacy law and non-legal privacy norms are based on a narrow definition of personal data. For this reason, problems associated with group profiles do not fall within their scope. I will draw attention to the serious social problems that may arise from the production and application of group profiles. I will introduce the notion of "categorial privacy" as a starting point for a possible remedy. I will close with discussing some of the ways in which we could try to solve the problems relating to group profiling.

Personal Data, Law, and Ethics

Personal data is often considered to be the exclusive kind of data eligible for protection by privacy law and privacy norms. Personal data is commonly defined as data and information relating to an identified or identifiable person. A clear illustration of this rather narrow starting point can be found in the highly influential European Directive 95/46/EC of the European Parliament and of the European Council of 24 October 1995, "on the protection of individuals with regard to the processing of personal data and on the free movement of such data." Because a European Directive must be implemented in the national law and regulation of European Union countries, the definitions and principles formulated in the Directive are mirrored in the national privacy laws and regulations throughout the European Union. With regard to the processing of personal data, the Directive poses some basic principles. For the purposes of this paper, I will highlight some of these. It is important to notice that—as may be expected from the definition of personal data—most of these principles lean heavily on the idea that there is some kind of direct connection between a designate person and his or her data.

First, there are some principles regarding data quality. Personal data should only be collected for specified, explicit, legitimate purposes and should not be further processed in a way incompatible with these purposes. No excessive amounts of data should be collected, relative to the purpose for which the data is collected. Moreover, the data should be accurate and, if applicable, kept up to date. Every reasonable step must be taken to ensure that inaccurate or incomplete data is either rectified or erased. Also, personal data should be kept in a form that permits identification of data subjects for no longer than is necessary for the purpose for which the data were collected.

Secondly, some principles apply for legitimizing personal data processing. If an individual has unambiguously given his or her consent, data processing is legitimate. Without such consent, there are only a few situations in which data processing is legitimate. For instance, personal data processing is legitimate if it is needed for the performance of a contract to which the data subject is a party, for compliance with a legal obligation, to protect a vital interest of the data subject, for the performance of a task that is carried out in the public interest, or for the purposes of the legitimate interests pursued by the controller or by third parties to whom the data is disclosed.

Thirdly, the data subject has some specific rights with regard to "his or her" personal data. Among these rights are the right of access (knowing what data is being stored and whether the data relating to the data subject are being processed), the right of rectification, the right to know to whom the data has been disclosed, and the right to object to the processing of data relating to the data subject.

The Directive's definitions and principles themselves certainly reflect ideas about informational privacy currently held amongst legal and ethical theorists. Sometimes, these theoretical views on informational privacy are not much more than implicit assumptions. However, things are different and more articulate where theorists define informational privacy as being in control over (the accessibility of) personal information, or where they indicate some kind of personal freedom, such as the preference-freedom in the vein of John Stuart Mill's individuality, as the ultimate point and key value behind privacy (see, for instance Parent, 1983 and Johnson, 1989). These theorists consider privacy to be mainly concerned with information relating to designating individuals. They also tend to advocate protective measures in terms of safeguarding an individual's control and consent regarding disclosure of personal information.

Applying the narrow definition of personal data and the protective measures connected to that definition to the KDD process is not without difficulties. Of course, as long as the process involves personal data in the strict sense of data relating to an identified or identifiable individual, the principles apply without reservation. However, as soon as the data has ceased to be personal data in the strict sense, it is not at all clear how the principles should be applied. For instance, the right of rectification applies to the personal data in the strict sense itself; it does not apply to information derived from this data. The same goes for the requirement of consent. Once the data has become anonymous, or has been processed and generalized, an individual cannot exert any influence on the processing of the data at all. The rights and requirements make no sense regarding anonymous data and group profiles.

Social Consequences

The data used and the profiles created do not always qualify as personal data. Nevertheless, the ways in which the profiles are applied may have a serious impact on the persons from whom the data was originally taken or, even more for that matter, to whom the profiles are eventually applied. In fact, since these profiles are often used *as if they were* personal data while in fact they are not, the impact on individual persons is sometimes even stronger than with the use of "real" personal data.

Where profiles are used as a basis for formulating policies of public and private organizations, or where they just slip into the body of public knowledge, individuals are affected indirectly. Persons are judged and treated more and more as *members of a group*, i.e., of the reference group that makes up the data or information subject, rather than as individuals with their own characteristics and merits. This consequence of KDD using or producing personal data in the broad sense may, at first sight, seem rather innocent. It loses, however, much of its innocent appearance where the information contained in the profile is of a sensitive nature because it is typically susceptible to prejudice and taboo or because it can be used for selections in allocation procedures. So, for instance, information about persons having a certain probability of manifesting certain diseases, of lifestyles, or of having been involved in crime, etc. may easily give rise to stigmatization and discrimination. The information may also be used for giving or denying access to provisions, like insurance, loans, or jobs.

Increasing use and production of group profiles may even result in growing unfairness in social interaction in other ways. This is poignantly clear in the case of what I will call nondistributive profiles, as opposed to distributive profiles. Distributive profiles assign certain properties to a group of persons in such a way that these properties are actually and unconditionally manifested by all the members of that group. Distributive profiles are put in the form of down-to-earth, matter-of-fact statements. Nondistributive profiles, however, are framed in terms of probabilities and averages and medians, or significant deviance from other groups. They are based on comparisons of members of the group with each other and/or on comparisons of one particular group with other groups. Nondistributive profiles are, therefore, significantly different from distributive profiles. The properties in nondistributive profiles apply to individuals as members of the reference group, whereas these individuals taken as such need not, in reality, exhibit these properties. For instance, in a credit-scoring application, a loan can be refused on the basis of the fact that an applicant belongs to a reference group, e.g., having a certain kind of job, which has the nondistributive profile of a bad debtor, whereas the applicant himself is in fact an extremely trustworthy person who has not missed an installment on a loan in his whole life. Or an applicant may be refused life insurance on the basis of a nondistributive profile about certain health risks of the group (e.g., defined by a postal code) to which he happens to belong, whereas he or she is a clear exception to the average risks of his or her group. In all such cases, the individual is judged and treated on the basis of his, coincidentally, belonging to the "wrong" category of persons.

Of course, these problematic consequences are not unique to KDD. As a matter of fact, they are inherent to many forms of matching and profiling, and even to certain forms of noncomputerized generalizations of personal data (Vedder, 1995, 6–11, 105–114; 1997). What is new with KDD, however, is the enormous scale on which data can be processed and profiles can be produced. Relatively new, also, are the ever-growing possibilities of discovering hitherto unnoticed relationships between characteristics and features of persons, created by KDD. This also creates ample opportunities of covering up or hiding the use of certain delicate pieces of information. On the basis of a statistical correlation between the ownership of a certain kind of car and belonging to a high-risk group for a certain disease, an insurance company could, for instance, allocate its health insurance according to the type of car owned by a candidate. The company would then be able to select candidates without asking or checking for their health condition and prospects; it would not arouse the suspicion of selecting on the basis of health criteria. This possibility may be used in countries where selection on the basis of health is forbidden for health insurance (Vedder, 1997).

However this may be, one can be sure that the profiles will be used more and more as a basis for policy-making by public and private organizations. Although many uses of the products of KDD are morally acceptable, and even desirable, many other possible applications are at odds with commonly held values regarding the individuality of human persons.

Categorial Privacy

Most conceptions of individual privacy currently put forward in law and ethical debate have one feature in common: Not only do they assume that the personal data with which privacy is concerned *originally* contains statements about states of affairs or aspects accompanied by indicators of individual natural persons, but they also assume that the data as a result of processing *continues* to contain statements about states of affairs or aspects accompanied by identifiers of individual natural persons. This feature of current privacy conceptions has two important consequences: It makes it difficult to label the problematic aspects of using data abstracted from personal data and producing and applying group profiles; it also makes it difficult to fathom the seriousness of these problems in practice.

It should be observed that group profiles may occasionally be incompatible with respect to individual privacy and laws and regulations regarding the protection of personal data, as it is commonly conceived of. For instance, distributive profiles may sometimes be rightfully thought of as infringements of (individual) privacy when the individuals involved can easily be identified through a combination with other information available to the recipient or through spontaneous recognition. In the case of nondistributive profiles, however, the information remains attached to an information subject constituted by a group. It cannot be traced back to individual persons in any straightforward sense. The groups that are the information subjects of nondistributive profiles can often only be identified by those who defined them for a special purpose. From the perspectives of others than the producers and certain users of the profiles, the definition of the information subject will remain hidden because they do not know the specific purposes of the definition. When coincidentally found out by the latter, they will probably think of the definition as being arbitrarily chosen. Most importantly, however, the information contained in the profile envisages individuals as members of groups; it does not envisage the individuals as such. Supposing for the sake of argument that the profile has been produced in a methodically sound and reliable way, it only tells us some truth about individual members of those groups in a very qualified, conditional manner.

Therefore, privacy rules and conventions, as they are traditionally conceived of, do not apply.

Regarding the privacy of the information subject, i.e., the reference group as a whole, one might think that perhaps we could be saved by a notion of collective privacy. However, collective privacy will not do the job properly. The notion of collective privacy is too easily associated with the concept of collective rights. The subjects of collective rights are groups or communities. In order to make sense of the idea of collective rights, these subjects are often treated as beings analogous to persons or moral agents, or at least as conglomerates having certain characteristics that cannot ultimately and exhaustively be explained by the input of the individual members. Furthermore, they are often thought to be structured or organized in some way so as to be able to exercise their rights or let their rights be advocated by vicarious agents (Hartney, 1991). All of these properties are out of the question as regards to the reference groups of the profiles we are considering. From the perspective of their members, these groups are mostly randomly defined. Their members do not have any special ties of loyalty among one another. They do not have organizational structures either. Therefore, they are not capable of taking decisions or acting in their quality of collectivities.

The analytical and distinctive evaluative potential of our privacy vocabulary can perhaps be improved by introducing the notion of "categorial privacy." The "categorial" in this neologism should not be associated with the Kantian categorical imperative, but rather with the verb categorize in the sense of assigning to a group. I suggest that we conceive of categorial privacy as a value, in many respects similar to individual privacy, except that it relates to data or information to which two conditions do apply: (1) the information was originally taken from the personal sphere of individuals, and—after aggregation and processing according to statistical methods—is no longer accompanied by identifiers of individual natural persons, but, instead, by identifiers of groups of persons; and (2) when attached to identifiers of groups and when disclosed, the information is apt to carry with it the same kind of negative consequences for the members of those groups as it would for an individual natural person if the information were accompanied by identifiers of that individual.

Categorial privacy is strongly connected with individual privacy. The values that oppose infringements of individual privacy, such as personal autonomy, individuality, and certain social interests, equally oppose infringements of categorial privacy. Unlike collective privacy, however, categorial privacy has its points in respecting and protecting the individual rather than in respecting and protecting the group to which the individual belongs. Furthermore, the conception of categorial privacy presented here—just like many current conceptions of individual privacy—builds on a conventionally predefined conception of (information concerning) the personal sphere (Johnson, 1992). Categorial privacy, however, is different from its individual counterpart in that it draws attention to the attribution of generalized properties to members of groups, which, however, may result in the same effects as the attribution of particularized properties to individuals as such. In this respect, categorial privacy resembles stereotyping and wrongful discrimination on the basis of stereotypes (Harvey, 1991). Normative claims on the basis of categorial privacy, therefore, could also be stated in terms of justice, fairness, and respect for the individuality of persons.

Solutions

Infringements of categorial privacy cannot be dealt with in ways similar to those in which individuals are protected against possible infringements of individual informational privacy. The application of principles and rights of, for instance, rectification and consent to potential infringements on categorial privacy is, to a large extent, impossible. Even if it were possible, it would nevertheless be unacceptable for obvious reasons. First, as has been explained above, the reference group of the profile will only rarely be able to reach and enact collective decisions because of its lack of organizational structure and personal or social ties. Secondly, if one were to turn from the group as such to the individual members of the group, then an individual's possibility of refusal or opting out could be harmful to other members of the reference group as well as to the very person refusing to allow personal information to be used in producing the profile. Actual refusal will reduce the reliability of the profile, while, nevertheless, all members of the reference group, including the individual who opted out, are at risk of being judged and treated on the basis of just this profile with reduced reliability. Of course, the possibility of opting out may also, in some respects, benefit the members of the reference group. If, in the case of profiles intended for application in selection procedures, only people with bad risks actually refuse the use of their information, this may turn out to be rather advantageous for the healthy and well-to-do. This, however, does not diminish the wrongfulness of, for instance, judging and treating persons on the basis of properties that they do not, if only with a decreased probability, instantiate.

The only way to protect individuals against the possible negative consequences of the use of group profiles based on personal information in the broad sense lies in a careful assessment of the ways in which the profiles are in fact used and can be used. By meticulously investigating and evaluating these applications, one may hope to find starting points for restrictions of the purposes for which these data and profiles may be produced and applied. An elaborate proposal concerning such acceptable and unacceptable purposes cannot be provided here. It is important, however, to keep in mind that solutions will not be found only in forbidding the production and application of profiles for certain purposes. In many cases, it may be more appropriate to reconsider those purposes themselves. Sometimes it may be easier or even morally more desirable to do something about social and economic arrangements that induce wrongful applications of information technologies, like the ones used for KDD, than abolishing those applications. This is the case especially where, for instance, profiles can be used for desirable purposes and for undesirable purposes at the same time. Also, in such situations where there is a possibility of good use and bad use of the same newly produced information, doubtlessly some help is to be expected from cryptologists. Sometime in the future, it must be possible to make the information in certain profiles accessible to some people and not to others, for some purposes and not for others, and to protect databases against the possibility of applying certain types of queries.

Closing Remarks

I have tried to draw attention to the problems of KDD using personal data in terms of categorial privacy, and I have indicated the shortcomings of traditional privacy conceptions. My main concern was to specify some important problematic consequences that KDD may have for the ways in which individuals are judged and treated, so that they may not be overlooked, but be critically assessed. I have tried, in a sense, to extend the notion of privacy and the traditional privacy norms. The notion of privacy is still overwhelmingly dominant in the legal and moral conceptual frameworks of those working in the fields of information technology and the law and information technology and public policy. The notion of categorial privacy could make it easier to introduce normative elements like those of social justice, fairness, and respect for the individuality of persons in the debate on information technologies. At least, it could save us from some serious blind spots in the assessment of modern information technology.

Acknowledgements
I am grateful to Robert van Kralingen and Eric Schreuders, Tilburg University, for their suggestions and contributions to an earlier version of this paper relating to my reading of the European Directive 95/46/EC. I presented this earlier version of the paper at the CEPE Conference, December 1998 at the London School of Economics. I also want to thank Herman Tavani, Rivier College, Nashua, for his inspiring comments on that occasion. Another version of that paper appeared as Anton Vedder, "KDD: the challenge to individualism," in Ethics and Information Technology 1999; 1: 4: 275–281. The research that lies at the basis of this paper was in part funded by the Netherlands' Organization for Scientific Research PIONEER-program "Ideals in law, morality and politics."

References
Fayyad, U., Piatetsky-Shapiro, G., and Smyth, P. Knowledge discovery and data mining: towards a unifying framework, in: E. Simoudis, J. Hian and U. Fayyad, eds., *Proceedings of the second international conference on knowledge discovery & data mining*, Menlo Park, CA: AAAI Press/MIT Press, 1996.

Frawley, W. J., Piatetsky-Shapiro, G. and Matheus, C. J. Knowledge discovery in databases: An overview, in: G. Piatetsky-Shapiro and W.J. Frawley, eds., *Knowledge discovery in databases*, Menlo Park, CA/Cambridge, MA/London: AAAI Press/MIT press, 1991.

Hartney, M. Some confusions concerning collective rights. *Canadian journal of law and jurisprudence* 1991; 4: 293–314.

Harvey, J. Stereotypes and group-claims: Epistemological and moral issues and their implications for multiculturalism in education. *Journal of philosophy and education* 1991; 24: 39–50.

Johnson, J. Privacy, Liberty and Integrity. *Public affairs quarterly* 1989; 3: 15–34.

Johnson, J. A theory of the nature and value of privacy. *Public affairs quarterly* 1992; 6: 271–288.

Parent, W. A., Recent Work on the Concept of Privacy. *American philosophical quarterly* 1983; 20: 341–356.

Vedder, A. H. The values of freedom. Utrecht: Thesis Utrecht University, 1995.

Vedder, A. H. Privatization, information technology and privacy: reconsidering the social responsibilities of organizations, in Geoff Moore, ed., *Business ethics: principles and practice*. Sunderland: Business Education publishers, 1997, 215–226.

Data Mining and Privacy

Joseph S. Fulda

I. Knowledge Discovery and Data Mining

Traditional information retrieval from databases returns database records—or tuples derived from fields of records—in response to a query. Hence what is returned is explicit in the database. Knowledge discovery using data mining techniques differs from ordinary information retrieval in that what is sought and extracted—mined—from the data is not explicit in the database. Rather, objects that "typically will not exist a priori,"[1] patterns that are implicit in the data and can be used for either descriptive or predictive purposes, are discovered. The process of discovering such patterns, which is termed *data mining* when considered apart from the necessary concomitant parts of the knowledge discovery process (work preparing the data so that it can be searched for patterns, and work done on the patterns to make them useful after they are found), may:

(a) *classify* data into preexisting categories;
(b) *cluster* data by mapping them into categories created during data analysis and determined by the data;
(c) provide a *summary* of the data, which is useful in a sense that the raw data are not;
(d) describe *dependencies* between variables;
(e) find *links* between data fields;
(f) use *regression* to predict future values of data; and
(g) *model sequential patterns* in the data that may indicate revealing trends.[2]

Data mining is most easily accomplished when the data are highly structured and available in many different forms at many different levels in what are known as *data warehouses*. The data warehouse contains:

(a)   *integrated data,* which by allowing data to be compared and contrasted in different form(at)s, does away with much of the need for "data cleansing;

(b)   both *detailed* and *summarized* data—the former is important because certain patterns can be detected only by examining "data in its most granular form," and the latter is important because some patterns are apparent only on higher-order data;

(c)   *historical data,* which if mined can yield cyclic and seasonal activity as well as long-term trends; and

(d)   *metadata,* which provide the context of the data.[3]

II. The Issue

Much of the current concern about privacy arises because of data mining and, more generally, knowledge discovery. In traditional computer-science terms, data is uninterpreted, while knowledge has a semantics that gives it meaning. While the data stored in databases are not truly uninterpreted, the old legal rule that anything put by a person in the public domain (e.g., by purchasing an item in a public place of business) is not legally protected served well when the data was not mined so as to produce classifications, clustering, summaries and profiles, dependencies and links, and other patterns.

It is unnerving, however, when a database of film garnered from a bank video camera at an ATM shows a pregnant woman and her ATM card (which is linked in the database to her address) and triggers an avalanche of circulars, advertisements, and e-mail spam for products for newborns sold by another subsidiary of the bank's corporate holding company. Yet it is not truly the *pregnancy* that is private, much less her address; it is the *linkage* that disturbs. This example brings into relief the difficult philosophical question that data mining and knowledge discovery have created: Is it possible for data that do not in themselves deserve legal protection to contain implicit knowledge that does deserve legal protection, and, if so, what balance must be struck between the freedom to use whatever knowledge one has at one's disposal to further one's own ends and—to put it in Kantian terms—the freedom not to have one's *personal* data mined into knowledge that will be used as a means to someone else's ends?

III. Analysis

We propose to answer this question through an analysis based on our previous work in developing a theory of privacy rights based generally on tort law—updated for the information age[4]—in which data need not any longer be encapsulated in property and so protection of information through (at least ordinary) property rights is inadequate.

(The standard we developed there is that *privacy is invaded when any means are used that bypass the subject's consent as manifested by the subject's observable (i.e., objective) behavior, reasonably interpreted.*[5] This rule, which might be termed an anti-circumvention rule, mirrors that recently passed by Congress for intellectual property, the Digital Millennium Copyright Act. But while the restrictions of that Act on technological progress—as opposed to its specific use to take property—is in my view misguided, the thrust of the law protecting abstract property from circumvention measures is philosophically well-motivated. Such circumvention in the realm of privacy constitutes the tort of appropriation refigured for the information age and, in the case of a government actor acting without a search warrant (or in some cases merely probable cause), a violation of the Fourth Amendment. Indeed, we regard reputation—i.e., that which privacy protects—as property, a fundamental part of what a person owns in himself, and we have elsewhere given a full account of this.[6] The process we will use to perform this analysis—education—is to find examples where two (conventional) data about an individual, each innocuous, are combined, but together produce new (conventional) knowledge about the individual. This is akin to data mining. We then formulate the rule that emerges from the cases and apply it, in turn, to (technological) data mining.

When I have a guest over, often a request of the form "Can I read this?" is made. The answer is always, "Well, it is published; nothing published can be considered private." But although that is a good rule of thumb, it is certainly not without its exceptions. Suppose I have a stack of magazines in my living room and buried within them is a "men's magazine." Wouldn't it be wrong for someone to go through the stack, even though it is readily apparent that it contains only published material? I think it would, for although the magazine is not private and the stack showing that I keep magazines is not private, the fact that the former is in the latter—the association— is private.

Consider a second case: I have an archives, a small archives, with everything I have had published. Can someone—a guest, that is—simply take the liberty of browsing through my archives? It would seem so, based on the rule of thumb, until one learns that twice I have authored articles pseudonymously. It is not that the articles themselves are private—I wanted them published for reasons that I thought were good. But for equally good reasons, I did not want my name associated with the articles. In isolation, the guest could read the articles, as they were openly published, but yet he could not examine the particular copies of the articles found in the archives. If I had the periodicals in which they appeared on my stack of magazines (see above), no problem would present itself. It is only the association with my authorship by their presence in my archives that presents a privacy issue.

Consider a third case: Suppose, contrary to fact, people generally considered their home addresses matters of public record. The mailman comes by and drops off a stack of letters. Is it all right for a guest to go through the stack without opening any of the letters? Certainly not, for although the return addresses are, *arguendo*, not private, their association with my address and home is private: I may not want my guest to know with whom I correspond, even though the correspondents' addresses in isolation are no more private than the fact that I received correspondence. The association between the two data—both attached in some way to me—is private, however.

None of these cases involve technology, but sifting through a stack of magazines, an archives, or a stack of letters to find associations between two data and an individual are all pre-technological forms of data mining, and they are all improper. Technology cannot make right what is otherwise wrong, so such data mining is, indeed, a violation of privacy; if data about an individual is mined and implicit knowledge about him is discovered, an appropriation has occurred, and further disclosure should not be permitted.

Unfortunately, that is not what the case law says. The governing case is *Smith v. Maryland*, 442 U.S. 735 (1979), in which it was held that the Fourth Amendment provides no protection against the use of pen registers, devices that record the telephone numbers dialed from a telephone line, without recording the conversation. Clearly, neither the calling line nor the numbers called are private—but the association between them and the party in question is. Pen registers were, at the time of the ruling, still a new technology: A case two years earlier[7] (in which it was assumed by the lower court that Fourth Amendment protections *did* apply and in which the Court expressly withheld judgment on that issue) revolved around whether a telephone company could be compelled "to furnish the FBI all information, facilities and technical assistance necessary to employ the devices...."[8]—in other words, the technology was new enough that the FBI needed outside technical expertise. This may perhaps explain why the Court reached what we would consider the wrong result: There was at the time no intuition about pen registers, and the Court failed to make the comparisons that we have made here regarding print materials, a very old technology.

If the courts will not protect private data from being associated with each other and forming new information about an individual, there is a long-standing set of methodologies, based on cryptographic protocols, which can provide such protection. Devised by computer scientist David Chaum,[9] these techniques prevent the "dossier society, in which computers could be used to infer individuals' life-styles, habits, whereabouts, and associations from data collected in ordinary consumer transactions [and which] can have a "chilling effect," causing people to alter their observable activities..."[10] while answering the need "for organizations to devise more pervasive, efficient, and interlinked computerized record-keeping systems"[11] so that everything from consumer credit to social services is not abused. Unfortunately, there is no real incentive for organizations to implement these rather simple methodologies, despite consumer concern with data collection and mining. Thus, as long as the law is silent on the subject, it appears that existing nonintrusive technological means of solving this problem will remain merely a unit in various advanced courses in the computer science curriculum.

Notes

1. Tomasz Imilienski and Heikki Mannila, "A Database Perspective on Knowledge Discovery," *Communications of the ACM* 39 (November 1996): (11)58–64, at 60.

2. *See* Usama Fayad, Gregory Piatetsky-Shapiro, and Padhraic Smyth, "The KDD Process for Extracting Useful Knowledge From Volumes of Data," *Communications of the ACM* 39(November 1996): (11)27–34 *and* Usama Fayad, Gregory Piatetsky-Shapiro, and Padhraic Smyth, "From Data Mining to Knowledge Discovery in Databases," *AI Magazine* 17(Fall 1996): (3)37–53.

3. W. H. Inmon, "The Data Warehouse and Data Mining," *Communications of the ACM* 39(November 1996): (11)49–50.

4. Joseph S. Fulda, "A New Standard for Appropriation, with Some Remarks on Aggregation," *University of New Brunswick Law Journal* 48(1999): 313–323.

5. *Ibid.*, at 316.

6. Joseph S. Fulda, "Reputation As Property," *The St. Croix Review* 33(April 2000): (2)30–31.

7. *United States v. New York Telephone Co.*, 434 U.S.159 (1977).

8. *Ibid.*, Syllabus, internal quotation omitted.

9. David Chaum, "Security without Identification: Transaction Systems to Make Big Brother Obsolete," *Communications of the ACM* 28(October 1985):1030–1044.

10. *Ibid.*, at 1030.

11. *Ibid.*

Workplace Surveillance, Privacy, and Distributive Justice

Lucas D. Introna

Introduction

Surveillance has become a central issue in our late modern society. The surveillance of public spaces by closed circuit television, the surveillance of consumers through consumer surveys and point of sale technology, and workplace surveillance, to name but a few. As surveillance increases, more and more questions are being raised about its legitimacy. In this paper I want to focus on one of the more problematic areas of surveillance, namely workplace surveillance. There is no doubt that the extensive use of information technology in all organisational processes has created enormous potential for cheap, implicit, and diffused surveillance, surveillance that is even more 'close' and continuous than any human supervisor could be. The extent of current surveillance practices are reflected in the following indicators:

- Forty-five percent of major U.S. firms record and review employee communications and activities on the job, including their phone calls, e-mail, and computer files. Additional forms of monitoring and surveillance, such as review of phone logs or videotaping for security purposes, bring the overall figure on electronic oversight to 67.3% (American Management Association 1999).
- Piller (1993) reported in a *MacWorld* survey of 301 business that 22% of the businesses have searched employee computer files, voice mail, e-mail, or other networking communications. The percentage jumped to 30% for businesses with 1000 or more employees.

This essay originally appeared in *Computers and Society,* Vol. 30, No. 4 (December) 2000: 33–39. Copyright © 2000 by Lucas D. Introna. Reprinted by permission.

- The International Labour Office (1993) estimates that some 20 million Americans may be subject to electronic monitoring on the job, *not including telephone monitoring.*

- In 1990 it was reported that up to one million jobs in Britain are subject to security checks (Lyon 1994, p. 131).

It would be reasonable to say that these formal surveys do not reflect the actual practice. It would also be reasonable to assume that organisations would not tend to publicise the degree to which they engage in systematic monitoring. Surveillance often functions as a resource for the execution of power, and power is most effective when it hides itself. One can imagine that the vast majority of organisations engage in anything from isolated incidents of specific monitoring to large-scale systematic monitoring.

The purpose of this paper is not to bemoan surveillance as such. I believe it is rather more important to understand the context and logic of surveillance in the workplace. In this paper I will argue that the real issue of workplace surveillance is justice as fairness. I will argue that it is the inherent political possibilities of surveillance that concerns employees, that they simply do not trust the interested gaze of management, and they have very good reason for such mistrust. Finally I will discuss the possibility of using Rawls' theory of justice to establish a framework for distributing the rights of privacy and transparency between the individual (employee) and the institution (the employer).

Resisting Workplace Surveillance

In the second half of the twentieth century, two major trends seem to create the background for our contemporary discussion of workplace surveillance. The first of these are the increasing challenges by the employees of their conditions of work, especially the normalising practices of discipline. The social revolution of Marxism and later of liberal democracy trickled into the production floor. Initially as labour became increasingly unionised, the debate about surveillance became articulated as a conflict between labour and capital in the Marxist idiom. Later workers demanded rights in the workplace they were already accorded elsewhere. Modern management increasingly needed to justify its surveillance practices. A second trend that intensified the debate was the rapid development of surveillance technology that created unprecedented possibilities for comprehensive surveillance. With the new technology, surveillance became less overt and more diffused. In fact, it became built into the very machinery and processes of production (workflow systems, keystroke monitoring, telephone accounting, etc.). This increasingly 'silent' and diffused potential of surveillance technology also started to concern policy makers, unions, social activists, and the like. However, in spite of their best efforts, and considerable progress in the establishment of liberal democracy in Western society, the balance of power is still firmly in the hands of the employer. The United States Congress'

Office of Technology Assessment report (U.S. Congress 1987) into employee monitoring concludes that *"employers have considerable latitude in making use of new monitoring technologies; they have generally been considered merely extensions of traditional management prerogatives"* (p. 6). Even today there exists very little enacted legislation in Western democracies that articulate the fair use of workplace monitoring[1] (U.S. Congress 1987, Appendix A). I would argue that that one of the reasons for this lack of adequate protection may be the inappropriate way in which the workplace monitoring debate has developed (I will address this in detail in the next section).

In the United States, the right of the employer to conduct workplace surveillance as a means to protect the employer's interest to organise work, select technology, set production standards, and manage the use of facilities and other resources is recognised by the law. This means that there is no legal obligation on employees to ensure that "monitoring be 'fair', that jobs be well designed or that employees be consulted about work standards, except insofar as these points are addressed in union contracts..." (U.S. Congress 1987, p. 2). As less than 20% of office work in the U.S. is unionised, it seems that decisions about work monitoring are made solely at the discretion of employers.

Recent legal developments seem to confirm this asymmetry power. For example, in the area of e-mail monitoring, the right to use surveillance of communications technology supplied for business purposes has been confirmed in the Electronic Communications Privacy Act of 1986 ("ECPA"). Essentially the ECPA expanded preexisting prohibitions on the unauthorised interception of wire and oral communications to encompass other forms of electronic communications. However, the ECPA does not guarantee a right to e-mail privacy in the workplace because of three very important exceptions. I will just focus on two here. The first is the *business extension* or ordinary course of business exception. This exception allows the employer to monitor any communications that use communications technology supplied to the employee in the ordinary course of business for use in conducting the ordinary course of business. This means that the telephone or the e-mail account supplied to an employee to conduct their work can legally be monitored as long as the monitoring can be justified as having a valid business purpose (Dichter and Burkhardt 1996, p. 14). The second is the *consent exception*. This exception allows monitoring in those cases where prior consent has been obtained. It is important to note that implied consent is also recognised by the law. Employers who notify employees that their telephone conversations or e-mail is likely to be monitored will have the implied consent of their employees (Santarelli 1997). It also seems as if common law does not provide any correction in the balance of power. In common law the decision of permissibility hinges on the notion of a "reasonable expectation of privacy." This may mean, for example, that if an employee is provided with a space to store personal belongings, or a particular phone line for personal calls, it would be reasonable for them to expect it not to be monitored. Johnson (1995) and others have remarked that this expectation of privacy can easily be removed by an explicit pol-

---

[1] Sweden is the exception here. The Swedish Codetermination Act of 1976 requires employers and employees to participate in decisions about electronic monitoring (U.S. Congress 1987, Appendix A).

icy that all communication using company equipment can and will be subjected to monitoring.

From this brief discussion it is clear that it would be fairly easy for employers to monitor all aspects of work and communications (on equipment made available for ordinary business use) as long as the employer explicitly communicates policy that monitoring can take place, and that the employer can justify it for a valid business purpose. It is hard to image what sort of monitoring—excluding some extreme cases—can not be defended as being for a valid business purpose (productivity, company moral, safety, etc). It is also hard to image what sort of resources an individual employee can use to generate a 'reasonable expectation of privacy' in a context where accepting an employment contract also means accepting the policies of the organisation and thereby relinquishing the right to a "reasonable expectation of privacy"—assuming there is an explicit monitoring policy. In the context of the typical asymmetry of power present in such employment situations, it is hardly a matter of choice. It is clear, and acknowledged by many, that the current U.S. climate is heavily biased in favour of the employer.[2] The lack of legislation in other countries would also indicate that it would be reasonable to conclude that workplace monitoring is still largely viewed as a right of employers with the burden of proof on the employee to show that it is invasive, unfair, or stressful. It would seem that a legal correction in the imbalance of power is not likely to be forthcoming in the near future.

In spite of this imbalance of power, surveillance has not become a widespread practice, as one would assume (U.S. Congress 1987, p. 31). In addition, it seems that where surveillance is operating, it is not always challenged to the degree that one would assume (U.S. Congress 1987, p. 31). Why is this so? It seems that there is not sufficient evidence to suggest surveillance *of individuals* would lead to *long term* productivity improvements. To use Denning's well known quality dictum (revised accordingly): productivity is not merely a matter of surveillance, but is rather an emerging element of a system designed for productivity as a whole. There is also accumulating evidence that surveillance *of individuals* leads to stress, a lost sense of dignity, and a general environment of mistrust. In this environment of mistrust employees tend to act out their employer's expectations of them—thereby eradicating any benefit that the surveillance may have had (Marx 1986; U.S. Congress 1987). Furthermore, I believe surveillance is not always challenged because we all at times benefit from its fruits. For example, the use of surveillance data for performance assessment can result in a more equitable treatment of employees. Such data can provide evidence to prevent unfair allocation of blame. It would be possible to think of many ways in which employees may use surveillance for their own benefit, such as "the boss can see on the CCTV that I do actually work many hours overtime," and the like.

Like power, surveillance "passes through the hands of the mastered no less than through the hands of the masters" (Foucault 1977). It does not only bear down upon us as a burden but also produces possibilities and resources for action that can serve

---

[2] There has been an attempt to change this in the unsuccessful Privacy of Consumers and Workers Act (PCWA) of 1993.

multiple interests. Surveillance is no longer an unambiguous tool for control and social certainty, nor is it merely a weight that weighs down on the employee—rather its logic and its effects have become increasingly difficult to see clearly and distinctly. Surveillance, with modernity, has lost its shine.

In the next section, I want to consider the relationship between surveillance and autonomy and indicate its link with justice. This will provide the background for the following section where I will develop a framework for distributing the rights of privacy and transparency between the individual and the collective.

Privacy as a Matter of Justice

Privacy is by no means an uncontroversial issue. Some, like Posner (1978), tend to see the need for privacy as a way of hiding or covering up what ought to be exposed for scrutiny. He argues that exposure through surveillance would provide a more solid basis for social interaction because the participants will be able to discern all the facts of the matter for themselves. Privacy, for him, creates opportunities for hiding information that could render many social interactions "fraudulent." To interact with someone without providing that person with all information would be to socially defraud that person, or so he argues. This is a very compelling argument, which has made Posner's paper one of the canons in the privacy literature. As such, it provides a good starting point for our discussion.

At the root of Posner's argument—and the argument for surveillance in general—is the fundamental flaw of the modernity's belief in surveillance as a neutral gaze, as a sound basis for certainty—for knowing that we know. Surveillance can only fulfill its role as guarantor of certainty if it is complete and comprehensive—in short, omnipresent—and if it can be done from a vantage point where all things are of equal or no value—which is impossible. If these conditions can be fulfilled, then Posner's argument will be valid. However, once surveillance looses its omnipresent and value free status—which it never had in the first place—it no longer deals with facts but rather with values and interests. Science becomes politics—as it has been from the beginning (Latour 1987; Latour and Woolgar 1986 {1979}). Knowing is replaced by choosing. We have to select what to survey, and most importantly, we have to select how to value what we find in our surveillance.

Employees do not fear the transparency of surveillance, as such, in the way argued by Posner. It is rather the choices, both explicit and implicit, that the employers will by necessity be making that employees mistrust. They are concerned that these choices may only reflect the interests of the employer. They are rightly concerned that the employer will only have 'part of the picture,' and that they may be reduced, in subsequent judgements, to that 'part of the picture' alone. They are also concerned that employers will apply inappropriate values when judging this 'part of the picture.' More than this, they will also be concerned by the fact that employers may implicitly and unbeknowingly bring into play a whole lot of other 'parts' of pictures that ought not be considered in that *particular context*—for example, judging a particular employee candidate for promotion or not because it is also known that the employee is a Muslim. They are concerned because we can not, contrary to the modern mind, separate out what 'pictures' we take into account or not when making judgements, *in the act of judging itself* (Merleau-Ponty 1962).

We are entangled and immersed in our values and beliefs to the point that they are merely there, available for use, part of the background that we do not explicitly attend to in making actual judgements (Heidegger 1962 {1937}). It is part of our thrownness (*Befindlichkeit*). It is therefore fruitless to posit that we should or should not apply particular data or particular values in making a particular judgement. We can simply not say to what degree we did or did not allow our judgement to become influenced by certain facts and certain value dispositions in making a particular judgement. The facts and values are not like fruits in a basket before us from which we can select, by rational choice, to take some and not others. We are immersed, engrossed, and entangled in our world in ways that would not normally make us explicitly attend to the particular facts, values, and interests that we draw upon in making particular judgements. We can of course attempt to make them explicit as bureaucracies and scientific management tried to do. However, Dreyfus (1992; 1986) has shown that skilled actors do not normally draw upon these explicit representations *in action*. Foucault (Foucault 1977) has also shown that these explicit representations are more important as resources for the play of power than resources for 'objective' judgements, which is exactly why employees mistrust them.

To conclude: It is the very political possibilities of surveillance, in the data selected, the values applied, the interest served, and the implicit and entangled nature of the judgement process, which makes employees—and persons in general—have a default position of mistrust rather than trust in 'exposing' themselves. It is this untrustworthy nature of judgements—of the products of surveillance—that moved Johnson (Johnson 1989) to define privacy as the right to the "freedom from the judgement of others." It is also this untrustworthy nature of judgements that made the OTA report argue that they view the issue of fairness as the most central issue of workplace monitoring. Fairness, as the levelling of the playing field, as serving all interests, not only the few.

Thus, the issue of workplace privacy is not merely a matter of 'bad' employees wanting to hide their unscrupulous behaviour behind a call for privacy (undoubtedly this is the case in some instances); it is rather a legitimate concern for justice in a context in which the employees are, for the most part, in a relationship of severe power asymmetry. I would therefore argue that the development of the workplace privacy debate will be best served if it is developed along the lines of *fairness and organisational justice* rather than along the lines of a general notion of privacy as a matter of some personal space. The personal dignity and autonomy argument can so easily be seen as personal lifestyle choices that have no place in the public workplace as expressed by Cozzetto and Pedeliski (1999) in their paper on workplace monitoring: "*Autonomy embraces areas of central life choice and lifestyle that are important in terms of individual expression, but irrelevant to an employer and of no public concern.*" I believe many employers and authors in the field find the concept of workplace privacy problematic because they link it to the general debates on privacy that are often cast exclusively in the mould of personal dignity and autonomy. This leads to claims of irrelevance. As one employer expressed it in the Canadian Information and Privacy Commissioner's (IPC) report (1993) on workplace privacy: *"The paper over-states this issue as a problem of pressing concern for employees and employers and the general public... the IPC is making more of an issue out of this, and looking for problems where none need exist"* (p. 9).

If we accept the general idea that workplace privacy and surveillance is a matter of justice, how should one go about structuring the debate? In the next section I will discuss the distribution of privacy and transparency as an issue of distributive justice using the work of Rawls (1972).

Privacy, Surveillance, and Distributive Justice

For the individual, privacy secures autonomy, creates social capital for intimacy, and forms the basis of structuring many diverse social relations (Introna 1997; Westin 1967). It is generally accepted that it is in the interest of the individual to have maximum control over her privacy—here taken to be the *freedom from the inappropriate judgement of others*. For the collective or institution, transparency secures control and thereby efficiency of resource allocation and utilisation, as well as creating mechanisms for disciplinary intervention (Foucault and Sheridan 1979). It is generally accepted that it is in the interest of the collective or institution to have maximum control over surveillance—here taken to mean *subjecting all individuals in the institution to reasonable scrutiny and judgement*. If the individuals are given an absolute right to privacy, they may act only in their own interest and may thereby defraud the institution. If the institution is given a complete right to transparency, it may strip the individual of autonomy and self-determination by making inappropriate judgements that only serve its own interest.

Thus, from a justice perspective we need a framework that would distribute the rights to privacy—of the individual (the employee in this case)—and right of transparency—of the collective (the employer in this case)—in a way that would be seen to be fair to all concerned. I would argue that wherever individuals and institutions face each other, the distribution of privacy and transparency rights will become an issue to be resolved. In this regard the institution can be as diverse as the family, the workplace, the community, the state, and so forth. At this stage I will exclude from my discussion the conflict of privacy and transparency rights between different institutions such as between the corporation and the state. Given this conflict between the individual employee and the institutionalised workplace, how can we decide on a fair distribution of privacy and transparency rights? I will propose that we may use the Rawlsian theory of justice as a starting point. Obviously one could use other frameworks. I am not arguing that Rawls is the only or even vastly superior perspective. Nevertheless, it does seem as if the Rawlsian framework is useful in this regard.

Rawls (in his seminal work *A Theory of Justice* of 1972) proposes a framework of justice as fairness in opposition to the leading theory of the day, viz. utilitarianism. For Rawls, utilitarianism puts no restrictions upon the subordination of some people's interests to those of others, except that the net outcome should be good. This would allow for any degree of subordination, provided the benefit to those advantaged was great enough. Rawls argues that a theory of justice cannot allow disadvantages to some to be justified by advantages to others. In our case this would imply a view that may posit the limited cost of the loss of individual privacy against the enormous economic benefit to the collective of securing effective control over productive resources. Such utilitarian arguments can easily make the individual's claim to privacy look trivial in the face of the economic prosperity of the whole. I would claim that it is exactly this utilitarian type of logic that continues to limit the legitimacy of the individual employee's claim to privacy in the workplace.

If this is so, how can we establish a set of rules that would ensure a fair distribution of privacy and transparency rights? Rawls (1972) argues that this can only happen behind a 'veil of ignorance' in the so-called original position. According to this formulation, a fair set of rules for this distribution would be a set of rules that *self-interested* participants would choose if they were completely ignorant about their own status in the subsequent contexts where these rules will be applied. What would be the rules for distributing privacy and transparency rights that may be selected from behind such a veil of ignorance?

As a starting point we need to outline the facts—about interests and positions— which we may assume to be available to those in the original position. This information will provide the force that may shape their choices. Obviously these need to be debated, but I would propose the following facts are known—first from the perspective of the individual, then from the perspective of the collective.

From the individual perspective:

- That there are no such things as neutral or objective judgements. Every judgement implies interests. Once data is recorded, it can in principle become incorporated into a judgement process that may not serve the individual's interests. It would therefore seem reasonable that the self-interested individual would try to limit all forms of capturing of data about themselves and their activities.

- In the context of typical organisational settings, the employee is normally in a disadvantaged position—in a relation of severe power asymmetry. Thus, it is not possible for the individual, as an individual, to bargain for and ensure the fair use of data once it is captured. It would therefore be in the interest of the individual to limit all forms of capturing of data about themselves and their activities.

- If data about themselves and their activities are captured, it is in their interest to have maximum control over it—what is captured, who sees it, for what purposes, and so forth.

From the perspective of the collective:

- Without the capturing of complete and comprehensive information about the relevant activities of the individual, resources can not be efficiently and effectively allocated and control over the use of these resources can not be maintained.

Without such control the collective would suffer. It would therefore seem reasonable to monitor all relevant activities of the individual. Relevant here would be understood to be those activities that imply the allocation and utilisation of collective resources.

- Self-interested individuals would not always tend to use resources—allocated by the collective—for the sole purposes of furthering the aims and objectives of the collective. In fact they may use it completely for their own purposes. It would therefore seem reasonable to monitor all individual activities that allocate and utilise collective resources.

- The collective needs to use data collected to coordinate and control the activities of the individuals for the good of the collective. It would be in the interest of the collective to have maximum control over the capturing and utilisation of relevant data about the individuals.

Given these facts—and other similar ones we may enumerate—what rules would those behind the veil of ignorance choose in distributing individual privacy and collective transparency rights? Before attempting to suggest some rules, it may be important to highlight Rawls' 'difference principle'—which he argues those behind the veil of ignorance would tend to choose. This principle states that an inequality is unjust except insofar as it is a necessary means to improving the position of the worst-off members of society. Without this principle it would be difficult for those behind the veil of ignorance to establish rules for distributing privacy and transparency rights, as its seems equally reasonable to grant and limit these rights both to the individual and the collective. However, we know, as indicated above, that in the context of the modern organisation the individual is in a position of severe power asymmetry. In the prevailing climate it would be difficult to argue that the individual employee is not 'the worst-off' with respect to securing a fair and reasonable level of privacy rights in the workplace. This would seem to indicate that most individuals behind the veil of ignorance would tend to want to argue for some bias toward securing the rights of the individual over and against that of the institution. With this in mind I will suggest—mostly for illustrative purposes—a set of fair 'rules' or guidelines that may be put forward by those behind the veil of ignorance. I would contend that they would acknowledge the following:

- That the collective (employer) does indeed have a right to monitor individuals' activities with respect to the allocation and utilisation of collective resources. The collective also has a right to use the data collected in a fair and reasonable way for the overall good of the collective as a whole.

- That the individual (employee) does have a legitimate claim to limit the surveillance of their activities in the workplace. The individual also has a right to secure a regime of control that will justify all monitoring and that will ensure that the data collected will be used in a fair and reasonable way.

- Based on the 'difference principle,' it will be up to the collective (employer) to justify the collection of particular data in particular contexts. Furthermore, the regimes for controlling the collected data should be biased toward the individual.

Obviously one could develop these rules in much more detail. However, even this very limited, initial reflection would seem to suggest that the prevailing organisational practices that favour the collective (both in capturing and control) would seem to be unfair.

Obviously this analysis is still too crude and unsophisticated. However, it does illustrate that one may arrive at very different conclusions if one takes the issue of workplace privacy to be one of fairness rather than as a matter of working out the private/public distinction in the workplace—since it will always be relatively easy to argue that the workplace is a de facto public space, devoid of almost any privacy rights.

Conclusion and Some Implications

The potential for workplace surveillance is rapidly increasing. Surveillance technology is becoming cheap, silent, and diffused. Surveillance technology has created the potential to build surveillance into the very fabric of organisational processes. How should we concern ourselves with these facts? Clearly each workplace will be different. Some will be more bureaucratic, some more democratic. Nevertheless, the conflict between the individual right to privacy and the institutional right to transparency will always be there. In each individual case, different tactics will be used by the different parties to secure their interests.

In the case of workplace privacy, the prevailing legal and institutional infrastructure makes it difficult for the individuals to secure their interests, leaving them power-less, but by no means powerless. One of the major reasons for the unsuccessful challenge of modern workplace surveillance is the inappropriate manner in which the workplace privacy debate has evolved. In my opinion it incorrectly attached itself to the public/private distinction, which leaves the employee in a position of severe power asymmetry. In opposition to this debate I have argued that if one articulates the issue of workplace surveillance along the lines of competing, but equally legitimate claims (for privacy and transparency), needs to fairly distribute the possibilities for the individual to resist inappropriate workplace surveillance increases dramatically. Using the Rawlsian theory of justice I argued that those behind the veil of ignorance would tend to adopt a position that biases the right of the employee—the worst off—over that of the employer. This would suggest that a fair regime of workplace surveillance would tend to avoid monitoring unless explicitly justified by the employer. It will also provide mechanisms for the employee to have maximum control over the use of monitoring data. Both of these rules seem to suggest that most of the prevailing organisational surveillance practices are unfair. This, I believe, is the challenge to us: To set up the intellectual and organisational resources to ensure that workplace surveillance becomes and stays fair.

References

Association, American Management. 1999. *Workplace monitoring and surveillance:* American Management Association.

Commissioner/Ontario, Information and Privacy. 1993. *Workplace Privacy: The need for a Safety-Net,* http://www.ipc.on.ca/web_site.ups/matters/sum_pap/papers/safnet-e.htm: Information and Privacy Commissioner/Ontario.

Cozzetto, D and T. B. Pedeliski. 1999. *Privacy and the Workplace: Technology and Public Employement,* http://www.ipma-hr.org/pubs/cozzfull.html: International Personnel Association.

Dichter, M. S. and M. S. Burkhardt. 1996. Electronic Interaction in the Workplace: Monitoring, Retrieving, and Storing Employee Communications in the Internet Age. In *The American Employment Law Council: Fourth Annual Conference.* Asheville, North Carolina.

Dreyfus, Hubert L. 1992. *What computers still can't do: A critique of artificial reason.* Cambridge, MA: The MIT Press.

Dreyfus, Hubert L. and Stuart E. Dreyfus. 1986. *Mind over machine: The power of human intuition and expertise in the era of the computer.* New York: The Free Press.

Foucault, M. 1977. Truth and Power. In *Power/Knowledge: Selected Interviews & Other Writings 1972–1977,* ed. C. Gordon. New York: Pantheon Books.

Foucault, Michel and Alan Sheridan. 1979. *Discipline and punish: the birth of the prison.* Harmondsworth: Penguin.

Heidegger, Martin. 1962 {1937}. *Being and time.* Translated by John Macquarrie.

(ILO), International Labour Organisation. 1993. *Conditions of work digest: Monitoring and surveillance in the workplace.* Geneva: International Labour Office.

Introna, L. D. 1997. Privacy and the Computer: Why We Need Privacy in the Information Society. *Metaphilosophy* 28, no. 3: 259–275.

Johnson, B. T. 1995. *Technological Surveillance in the Workplace,* http://www.fwlaw.com/techserv.html: Fairfield and Woods P.C.

Johnson, J. L. 1989. Privacy and the Judgement of Others. *The Journal of Value Inquiry* 23: 157–168.

Latour, Bruno. 1987. *Science in action: How to follow scientists and engineers through society.* Cambridge, MA: Harvard University Press.

Latour, Bruno and Steve Woolgar. 1986 {1979}. *Laboratory life: The construction of scientific facts.* Princeton: Princeton University Press.

Lyon, David. 1994. *The Electronic Eye: the rise of the surveillance society.* Cambridge: Polity Press.

Marx, G. T. 1986. Monitoring on the Job: How to Protect Privacy as well as Property. *Technology Review.*

Merleau-Ponty, M. 1962. *Phenomenology of Perception.* Translated by Colin Smith. London: Routledge.

Piller. 1993. Bosses with x-ray eyes. *MacWorld,* July: 118–123.

Posner, R. 1978. The Right to Privacy. *Georgia Law Review* 12: 383–422.

Rawls, J. 1972. *A Theory of Justice.* Cambridge, Mass: Harvard University Press.

Robinson, Edward. Oxford: Basil Blackwell.

Santarelli, N. 1997. *E-mail Monitoring in the Work Place: Preventing Employer Liability,* http://wings.buffalo.edu/complaw/complawpapers/santarelli/html: Computers and Law Internet site.

U.S. Congress, Office of Technology Assessment (OTA Report). 1987. *The Electronic Supervisor: New Technology, New Tensions.* Washington DC: U.S. Congress.

Westin, A. 1967. *Privacy and Freedom.* New York: Atheneum.

Privacy and the Varieties of Informational Wrongdoing

Jeroen van den Hoven

1. Introduction

The privacy issue lies at the heart of an ongoing debate in nearly all Western democracies between liberalists and communitarians over the question of how to balance individual rights and collective goods. The privacy issue is concerned more specifically with the question of how to balance the claims of those who want to limit the availability of personal information in order to protect individuals and the claims of those who want to make information about individuals available in order to benefit the community. This essential tension emerges in many privacy discussions, e.g., undercover actions by the police on the internet, use of Closed Circuit Television in public places, making medical files available for health insurance purposes or epidemiological research, linking and matching of databases to detect fraud in social security, or soliciting information about on-line behavior of internet users from access providers in criminal justice cases.

Communitarians typically argue that the community benefits significantly from having knowledge about its members available. According to communitarians, modern Western democracies are in a deplorable condition and our unquenchable thirst for privacy serves as its epitome. Who could object to having his or her data accessed if honorable community causes are served? Communitarians also point out that modern societies exhibit high degrees of mobility, complexity, and anonymity. As they are quick to point out, crime, free riding, and the erosion of trust are rampant under these conditions. Political philosopher Michael Walzer observes that "Liberalism is plagued by free-rider problems, by people who continue to enjoy the benefits of membership and identity while no longer participating in the activities

This essay originally appeared in *Computers and Society*, Vol. 27, No. 3 (September) 1997: 33–37. Copyright © 1997 by Jeroen van den Hoven. Reprinted by permission.

that produce these benefits. Communitarianism, by contrast, is the dream of a perfect free-riderlessness."[1]

The modern Nation States with their complex public administrations need a steady input of personal information to function well or to function at all. In post-industrial societies 'participation in producing the benefits' often takes the form of making information about oneself available. Those who are responsible for managing the public goods therefore insist on removing constraints on access to personal information and tend to relativize the importance of privacy of the individual.

2. Panoptic Technologies and the Public Good

Information technology's applications—panoptic technologies as Oscar Gandy and Jeffrey Reiman call them[2]—ranging from active badges, Intelligent Vehicle Highway Systems (IVHS), Closed Circuit Television (CCTV) and data-base mining techniques, encourage government agencies, public administrators, and business firms to pursue the communitarian dream of perfect free-riderlessness. It is the logic of the public goods problem that contributes to the initial plausibility of their aspirations.

Many public administration problems can be characterized as free-rider problems: law enforcement, tax collection, implementation of environmental policy. The general description of a free-rider problem is that it is a situation where a number of persons contribute to the production and maintenance of a public good, where each person individually has an incentive to profit from the public good without making the necessary contribution to its production or maintenance. When too many persons ride free, i.e., benefit without contributing, the means fall below the minimum required and the public good can no longer be produced or sustained, so it disappears altogether. For example, all citizens in a country have to contribute to the budget for the protection of the environment in order to sustain particular environmental programs, but if too many persons profit from a healthier environment without paying their eco-tax, the basis for a sustained environmental policy will eventually crumble.

The free-rider problem manifests itself in many areas and has the structure of the Prisoners' Dilemma. The Prisoners' Dilemma is a strategic choice situation, where the optimal result is individually inaccessible, and the only equilibrium is suboptimal. In the free-rider problem, as in the Prisoners' Dilemma, we need some way of constraining the egoistic motives, which are individually rational but do not lead to Pareto optimal results. One way for optimal results to ensue is to see to it that cooperation is in itself so highly valued by the parties involved so as to affect

---

[1] Michael Walzer, "The Communitarian Critique of Liberalism." In A. Etzioni (ed.), *New Communitarian Thinking.* Charlottesville/London: University of Virginia Press, 1995. See p. 63.

[2] Oscar H. Gandy, *The Panoptic Sort: A Political Economy of Personal Information.* Boulder, Colo.: Westview Press, 1993. Jeffrey Reiman, "Driving to the Panopticon: A Philosophical Exploration of the Risks to Privacy Posed by the Information Technology of the Future," in: *Critical Moral Liberalism. Lanham, Boulder,* New York, London: Rowman & Littlefield. pp. 169–188.

the pay-off matrix in the right direction. This is sometimes referred to as the 'internal solution' to the dilemma. Philosophers and game theorists have proposed ways to avoid the worst outcome by following strategies of constrained maximization.[3] Public administration however, has to deal with free-riders without assuming unrealistic levels of self-constraint in the population. Therefore government agencies try to discourage free-riders by *excluding* non-contributors or by tracking them down and punishing them, that is, by affecting the pay-off matrix by external solutions. But as De Jasay observes:

> (...) *it is not non-exclusion that makes retaliation impossible (for there may be other ways of punishing the free-rider than by excluding him), but anonymity of the free-rider. Clearly in a small group it is easier to spot the free rider and sanction him in one of many possible ways once he is identified than in a large group, where he can hide in the crowd"* (cursivation JVDH).[4]

Free-rider problems can only take on socially unacceptable forms if the provider of the public good does not know who rides free and can not determine who the free-riders are. An increase in relevant identifying information increases chances of retaliation by alleviating the problem of anonymity. Information technology is ideally suited to uncover identities of free-riders. Mobile computing, ID-chip cards, and palm-top computers allow street-level bureaucrats to verify information on site so as to increase the effectiveness of public administration and law enforcement procedures. Often millions of dollars of community money can be saved by simple and cheap database applications. IT provides the cost efficient means to affect the pay-off matrix of free-riders and thereby establish results that are superior in terms of social utility.

In the market sector, the logic of the situation is the same in principle. In a society of strangers trust and the means to establish normative status and moral reputation are of paramount importance. By means of 'credentials' (on-line searchable databases, front-end verification) and 'ordeals' (polygraphs, log-in procedures, and biometrical identification) we try to compensate for our ignorance about those with whom we have encounters and dealings.[5] Information Technology is expected to give us techniques of perfect information by reducing transactions and information cost dramatically and by reducing the risks of commerce among strangers, so as to approximate levels of trust associated with smaller, traditional, and less volatile communities.

Both in the private as well as in the public sector, IT is seen as the ultimate technology to resolve the problem of anonymity. Information and communication technology therefore presents itself as the technology of the logistics of exclusion and access-management to public goods and goods involved in private contracts. Whether

---

[3] D. Gauthier, *Morals by Agreement,* Oxford: Oxford University Press, 1986.

[4] A. De Jasay, *Social Contract, Free Ride. A Study of the Public Goods.* Oxford: Clarendon Press. See p. 149, n. 9.

[5] See for the distinction between 'credentials' and 'ordeals' Steven L. Nock, *The Costs of Privacy, surveillance and reputation in America.* Aldine de Gruyter, New York, 1993.

IT really delivers the goods is not important for understanding the dynamics of the use of personal data. The fact that it is widely believed to be effective in this respect is, I think, sufficient to explain its widespread use for these purposes. The game-theoretical structure and the calculability of community gains make the arguments in favor of overriding privacy seem clear, straightforward, and convincing.

But the communitarian interpretation of our modern moral predicament goes deeper than just pointing to crime, fraud, and free-riding in a liberal individualis-tic society. It questions the very viability of the liberal conception of the self on behalf of which privacy is claimed and which is central to much of modern ethical theo-ry and political philosophy. The liberal self is—as Michael Sandel calls it—an "un-encumbered self": a self that makes its choices, including choices about its own goals and identity, in isolation and far removed from a community. But individuation does not precede association. The liberal conception of the self does not account for the constitutive attachments that precede the formation of identities. The liberal con-ception of the self is unrealistically voluntaristic, disengaged, and radically unsit-uated, as Charles Taylor and Seyla Benhabib have argued. The liberal self is an autonomous bricoleur of identities and symbolic personal information, which claims for itself the elbow room to shape itself in a splendid isolation from a pre-existing community of speech and action, while reducing the risk of being unmasked, exposed, and caught in inconsistencies by others.

From a communitarian point of view, the idea of a moral right to privacy there-fore seems doubly wrong. First of all, the autonomous subject of the moral right is a figment of Enlightenment Philosophy and it does not exist strictly speaking. Secondly, the protection it offers is not worth wanting.

In the final section I will provide a characterisation of some of the main features of the liberal self on which defenses of a moral right to privacy seem to be based. In the first part of the paper (Sections 2–6) I shall argue that we can and should *decon-struct* the privacy notion and that we must distinguish at least three types of moral wrongdoing on the basis of personal information that have nothing to do with pri-vacy,[6] but nevertheless justify data protection. I thus suggest a broad and revi-sionary conception according to which claims to data-protection or to constraints on access to personal information can be identified on the basis of the types of moral reasons for such claims.

I think the following types of moral reasons for data-protection can be distin-guished: 1) information-based harm, 2) informational inequality, 3) informational injustice, and 4) encroachment on moral autonomy. In many cases where we want epistemic or cognitive access to ourselves and our data restricted, we do not want to be 'left alone' or to be 'private,' but we want to prevent others from wronging us by making use of knowledge about us. We want fair treatment, equality of oppor-tunity, and do not want to be harmed or discriminated against.

Only the fourth type of moral reason can be identified with a privacy violation in a strict sense. It is important to note that not all cases where data-protection is

---

[6] I have first proposed this in a seminar at the University of Virginia in the summer of 1996. I thank Judi DeCew, Jim Childress, Joe Kupfer for their comments.

justified are privacy cases, although in all cases where privacy (in a narrow sense) is at stake, data-protection is justified. On this broader conception of informational wrongdoing and data-protection, privacy interests are identified with interests in moral autonomy, i.e., the capacity to shape our own moral biographies, to reflect on our moral careers, to evaluate and identify with our own moral choices, without the critical gaze and interference of others. Where moral reasons of this type can be used appropriately we can say that privacy is at issue. I will deal with this type of moral reason in the final section.

Data protection regimes (like that of the European Community) and their application to specific types of situations and sectors can thus be justified on the basis of the values of preventing harm, achieving equality of opportunity, realising justice, and safeguarding moral autonomy. In practice we may find that some of them apply to the same cases and that data-protection in these cases is morally overdetermined. I think it is still important to be able to analytically distinguish between these different types of moral reasons for the protection of personal information and to have a fine-grained account of moral reasons for data protection, because it enables us to weigh competing claims more carefully.

Both liberals and communitarians can acknowledge the validity of the moral reasons to justify data protection concerned with harm, equality, and justice, although they would disagree about the validity of justifications for restricting access to personal data that are premised on appeals to moral autonomy and the disputed liberal conception of the self associated with it. In practice we will find both liberals and communitarians agreeing on data protection laws, since—as this account from informational wrongdoing shows—the essentially contested concept of the self need not always be involved.

3. Information-Based Harm

The first type of moral reason for data protection is concerned with the prevention of harm, more specifically harm done to persons by making use of personal information about them. The fact that personal information is used to inflict harm or cause serious disadvantages to individuals does not necessarily make such uses violations of a moral right to *privacy*. Cybercriminals and malevolent hackers are known to have used computerized databases and the Internet to get information on their victims in order to prepare and stage their crimes. The most important moral problem with 'identity theft' for example is the risk of financial and physical damages. One's bank account may get plundered and one's credit reports may be irreversibly tainted so as to exclude one from future financial benefits and services. Stalkers and rapists have used the Net and on-line databases to track down their victims, and they could not have done what they did without tapping into these resources. In an information society there is a new vulnerability to information-based harm. The prevention of information-based harm provides government with the strongest possible justification for limiting the freedom of individual citizens. Policies that encourage rigorous security measures must be put in place to protect citizens against information-based harm. This seems to be a matter of security and not of privacy. No other moral principle than John Stuart Mill's Harm Principle is needed to justify limitations of the freedom of persons who cause, threaten to cause, or are likely to cause information-based harms to people. Protecting personal information, instead of leaving it in the open, diminishes the likelihood that people will come to harm, analogous to the way in which restricting the access to firearms diminishes the likelihood that people will get shot in the street. We know that if we do not establish a legal regime that constrains citizens' access to weapons, the likelihood that innocent people will get shot increases. In information societies, information is comparable to guns and ammunition.

4. Informational Inequality

The second type of moral reason to justify data-protection is concerned with equality and fairness. Several authors have pointed out that privacy may be disappearing as a foundational moral value in the West. According to Calvin Gottlieb, the laws safeguarding privacy don't work because "people don't want them to work in far too many situations."[7] One reason for this development is that people welcome the benefits (convenience, discounts, knowledge) that information technology can give them in exchange for the use of their personal data. More and more people are keenly aware of the benefits a market for personal data can provide. If a consumer buys coffee at the shopping mall, information about that transaction can be generated and stored. Many consumers realize that every time they come to the counter to buy something, they can also sell something, namely, information about their purchase or transaction, the so-called transactional data. Likewise, sharing information about ourselves on the Net with web sites, browsers, or autonomous agents may pay off in terms of more and more adequate information (or discounts and convenience) later. Many privacy concerns have been and will be resolved in *quid pro quo* practices and private contracts about the use and secondary use of personal data. But although a market mechanism for trading personal data seems to be kicking in on a global scale, not all individual consumers are aware of this economic opportunity, and if they do, they are not always trading their data in a transparent and fair market environment. Moreover they do not always know what the implications are of what they are consenting to when they sign a contract. We simply cannot assume that the conditions of the developing market for personal data guarantee fair transactions by independent standards. Data protection laws should be put in place in order to guarantee equality and a fair market for personal data. Data protection laws in these types of cases typically protect individual citizens by requiring openness, transparency, participation, and notification on the part of business firms and direct marketeers to secure fair contracts.

5. Informational Injustice

A third and important moral reason to justify the protection of personal data is concerned with justice in a sense that is associated with the work of the political philosopher Michael Walzer.

---

[7] Calvin Gottlieb, "Privacy: a concept whose time has come and gone." In: Lyon and Zureik (eds.). *Computer, Surveillance and Privacy.* Minneapolis: University of Minnesota Press, 1996. See p. 156.

Michael Walzer has objected to the simplicity of Rawls' conception of primary goods and universal rules of distributive justice by pointing out that "there is no set of basic goods across all moral and material worlds, or they would have to be so abstract that they would be of little use in thinking about particular distributions."[8] Goods have no natural meaning; their meaning is the result of socio-cultural construction and interpretation. In order to determine what is a just distribution of the good, we have to determine what it means to those for whom it is a good. In the medical, the political, the commercial sphere, there are different goods (medical treatment, political office, money) that are allocated by means of different allocative or distributive practices: medical treatment on the basis of need, political office on the basis of desert and money on the basis of free exchange. What ought to be prevented, and often is prevented as a matter of fact, is dominance of particular goods. Walzer calls a good *dominant* if the individuals that have it, because they have it, can command a wide range of other goods. A monopoly is a way of controlling certain social goods in order to exploit their dominance. In that case, advantages in one sphere can be converted as a matter of course in advantages in other spheres. This happens when money (commercial sphere) could buy you a vote (political sphere) and would give you preferential treatment in healthcare (medical), would get you a university degree (educational), etc. We resist the dominance of money—and other social goods for that matter (land, physical strength)—and think that political arrangements allowing for it are unjust. No social good X should be distributed to men and women who possess some other good Y merely because they possess Y and without regard to the meaning of X.

What is especially offensive to our sense of justice, Walzer argues, is the allocation of goods internal to sphere A on the basis of the distributive logic or the allocation scheme associated with sphere B, second, the transfer of goods across the boundaries of separate spheres, and thirdly, the dominance and tyranny of some goods over others. In order to prevent this, the 'art of separation' of spheres has to be practiced and 'blocked exchanges' between them have to be put in place. If the art of separation is effectively practiced and the autonomy of the spheres of justice is guaranteed, then 'complex equality' is established. One's status in terms of the holdings and properties in one sphere are irrelevant—ceteris paribus—to the distribution of the goods internal to another sphere.

Walzer's analysis also applies to information, I claim. The meaning and value of information is local, and allocative schemes and local practices that distribute access to information should accommodate local meaning and should therefore be associated with specific spheres. Many people do not object to the use of their personal medical data for *medical* purposes, whether these are directly related to their own personal health affairs, to those of their family, perhaps even to their community or the world population at large, as long as they can be absolutely certain that the only use that is made of it is to cure people from diseases. They do object, however, to their medical data being used to disadvantage them socio-economically, to discriminate against them in the workplace, refuse them commercial services, deny

---

[8] M. Walzer, *Spheres of Justice.* Oxford: Basil Blackwell, 1983. See p. 8.

them social benefits, or turn them down for mortgages or political office on the basis of their medical records. They do not mind if their library search data are used to provide them with better *library* services, but they do mind if these data are used to criticize their tastes, and character. They would also object to these informational cross-contaminations when they would benefit from them, as when the librarian would advise them a book on low-fat meals on the basis of knowledge of their medical record and cholesterol values, or a doctor who poses questions on the basis of the information that one has borrowed a book from the public library about AIDS.

We may thus distinguish another form of informational wrongdoing: "informational injustice," that is, disrespect for the boundaries of what we may refer to, following Michael Walzer, as 'spheres of justice' or 'spheres of access.' I think that what is often seen as a violation of privacy is oftentimes more adequately construed as the morally inappropriate transfer of data across the boundaries of what we intuitively think of as separate "spheres of justice" or "spheres of access."

6. Spheres of Access

This construal of constraints on access to personal information in terms of spheres[9] captures an important aspect of what people find threatening and problematic about information technology: the fact that it facilitates the violation, blurring, or annihilation of boundaries between separate social realms or provinces of meaning. Several moral philosophers and sociologists have written about social differentiation using the intuitively plausible but somewhat nondescript notion of social "spheres," "domains," or "fields." The massive literature on social differentiation may provide us with useful insights into how social reality is carved up and how information management is practiced in order to maintain the integrity and functional unity of what Walzer refers to as spheres of justice. Although there are differences in vocabularies, sociologists and philosophers from Erving Goffman, Bourdieu and Luhman and Walzer have made very much the same point about the separateness, segregation, autonomy, and integrity of audiences, fields and systems, domains and spheres.

According to Pierre Bourdieu, in highly differentiated societies the social cosmos is made up of a number of such relatively 'autonomous social microcosms' or 'fields,' such as the artistic field, the religious field, or the economic field, which all

---

[9] Ferdinand Schoeman (*Privacy and Social Freedom,* Cambridge, 1992) introduced the notion of a "spheres of access" or "spheres of life" in the privacy literature. He contends that different domains of life deserve protection from various kinds of intrusion (p. 157): "We can begin to think about a sphere of life by identifying a sphere as defined by an associational tie. One important function of privacy is to help maintain both the integrity of intimate spheres as against more public spheres and the integrity of various public spheres in relation to one another." Geoffrey Brown (*The Information Game. Ethics in a Microchip World,* New York, 1989) has proposed along these lines that access to particular information about person P should be systematically related in the appropriate way to the network of social relationships in which P stands to others, by virtue of their places in the role structure. An invasion of privacy can be said to have occurred wherever the flow of information becomes divorced from the social role structure, what Brown labels a "Short Circuit Effect." According to Brown, privacy is important because it allows one to manage one's role identity. If someone accepts a particular social role (P acts as a doctor, P gives a lecture, P borrows a book in the public library), this person thereby assents to the appropriateness of an associated pattern of information exchange.

follow specific logics and are irreducible to each other. A field is a network of objective relations between agents or institutions (positions), which are defined by their present/potential situation (situs) in the structure of distribution of species of power (or capital). One's place in this relational space determines one's access to the specific profits that are at stake in the field. The question of the delineation of the boundaries of the field is a very difficult one, if only because it is always at stake in the field itself. Boundaries can only be determined by an empirical investigation. It is only by studying them that you can assess how concretely they are constituted, where they stop, who gets in and who does not, and whether at all they form a field.

Michael Philips, following Walzer, proposes a moral theory on the basis of the distinction between different social domains and the articulation of domain specific standards:

> "Domain-specific standards regulate activities and relationships in specific domains of social life. Individuating by roles, examples of domains include the family, the educational system, the scientific community, the criminal justice system, the medical system, the economic system, the political system, and so forth."[10]

There are also core standards, which regulate a single category of action across all domains. Philips takes the prohibition against lying as an example. The single category of action involved here is 'information exchange.' But there is no general standard 'do not lie.' Information exchange is regulated differently in different domains; there is a cluster of regulations governing information exchanges in various domains.

Seyla Benhabib has made a distinction between two types of communitarian thinking, integrationist and participatory.[11] According to the former, only the recovery of a coherent value scheme can solve the problems of individualism, anomie, egotism, and alienation in modern societies. Participationists see the problems of modernity not in fragmentation or a loss of belonging and solidarity but in a loss of political agency and efficacy. This loss may be a consequence, she surmises, of certain contradictions between the various spheres, which diminishes one's possibilities for agency in one sphere on the basis of one's position in another sphere (as, for example, when the right to vote is made dependent upon income). Social differentiation is not the problem that participationist communitarianism attempts to overcome; it is the reduction of contradictions and tensions between spheres and the articulation of nonexclusive principles of membership among the spheres.[12]

Data protection, as a set of normative constraints on information exchange, is an instrument of the art of separation and the design of blocked exchanges and it

---

[10] Michael Philips, *Between Universalism and Skepticism, Ethics as Social Artifact.* Oxford: Oxford University Press, 1994. See p. 95 ff.

[11] Seyla Benhabib, *Situating the Self.* New York: Routledge, 1992. See pp. 77 ff.

[12] Benhabib 1992, 77–78.

can be regarded as a means of establishing an interesting level of social justice, political agency, and efficacy by diminishing the tensions among spheres.

7. Encroachment on Moral Autonomy

Information-based harm, informational inequality, and informational injustice are the three types of moral reasons to protect personal data acceptable to both liberalists and communitarians. They are framed in moral terms that should be acceptable to both liberalists and communitarians. One other reason for protecting personal data is what I think is the privacy concern in a strict sense.

I think that philosophical theories of privacy that account for its importance in terms of the *moral* autonomy,[13] i.e., the capacity to shape our own moral biographies, to reflect on our moral careers, to evaluate and identify with our own moral choices, without the critical gaze and interference of others and a pressure to conform to the 'normal' or socially desired identities, provide us with a bridging concept between the privacy notion and a liberalist conception of the self. Such a construal of privacy's importance, or core value, will limit the range of application of the privacy concept, but may invigorate its value, if the underlying conception of the self should be vindicated. Privacy, conceived along these lines, would only provide protection to the individual in his quality of a *moral* person engaged in self-definition and self-improvement against the normative pressures that public opinions and moral judgements exert on the person to conform to a socially desired identity. Information about Bill, whether fully accurate or not, facilitates the formation of judgements about Bill. Judgements about Bill, when he learns about them, suspects that they are made, fears that they are made, may bring about a change in his view of himself, may induce him to behave differently than he would have done without. There are several mechanisms of what Von Wright referred to as 'normative pressure'[14] operative here.

To modern contingent individuals, who have cast aside the ideas of historical and religious necessity, living in a highly volatile socio-economic environment, and a great diversity of audiences and settings before which they make their appearance, the *fixation* of one's moral identity by means of the judgements of others is felt as an obstacle to 'experiments in living' as Mill called them. The modern liberal individual wants to be able to determine himself morally or to undo his previous determinations, on the basis of more profuse experiences in life, or additional factual information.[15] Data protection laws can provide the leeway to do just that.

---

[13] Joe Kupfer has made a similar proposal in his "Privacy, Autonomy and Self-concept," *American Philosophical Quarterly,* 24 no. 1 (1987) 81–89. Privacy, according to Kupfer enables " (...) self-knowledge, self-criticism, and self-evaluation. This sort of control over self-concept and self is a second-order autonomy."

[14] Judith DeCew has also identified the prevention of 'pressure to conform' as one of the important rationales of privacy protection. See her *In Pursuit of Privacy.* Cornell University Press, 1997.

[15] Kierkegaard identified 'irony' as the originating concept of the modern individual, it is the "liberty of the subject to refuse any determination proposed to him or projected onto him. It is absolute freedom: the capacity to say No without limit and without qualification." See L. Mackey, *Points of View, Readings of Kierkegaard. Tallahassee: University Presses of Florida,* 1986. See p. 133.

This conception of the person as being morally autonomous, as being the author and experimentator of his or her own moral career, provides a justification for protecting his personal data. Data-protection laws thus provide protection against the fixation of one's moral identity by others than one's self and have the symbolic utility[16] of conveying to citizens that they are morally autonomous.

A further explanation for the importance of respect for moral autonomy may be provided along the following lines. Factual knowledge of another person is always knowledge by description. The person himself however, does not only know the facts of his biography, but is the only person who is *acquainted* with the associated thoughts, desires, and aspirations. However detailed and elaborate our files and profiles on Bill may be, we are never able to refer to the data-subject as he himself is able to do. We may only approximate his knowledge and self-understanding. Bernard Williams has pointed out that respecting a person involves 'identification' in a very special sense, which I refer to as 'moral identification,' which has a *static* and a *dynamic* dimension:

> " (...) in professional relations and the world of work, a man operates, and his activities come up for criticism, under a variety of professional or technical titles, such as 'miner' or 'agricultural labourer' or 'junior executive.' The technical or professional attitude is that which regards the man solely under that title, the human approach that which regards him as a man who has that title (among others), willingly, unwillingly, through lack of alternatives, with pride, etc. (...) each man is owed an effort at identification: that he should not be regarded as the surface to which a certain label can be applied, but one should try to see the world (including the label) from his point of view."[17]

Moral identification thus presupposes knowledge of the point of view of the data-subject and a concern with what it is for a person to live that life. Persons have aspirations, higher order evaluations, and attitudes and they see the things they do in a certain light. Representation of this aspect of persons seems exactly what is missing when personal data are piled up in our databases and persons are represented in administrative procedures.[18] The identifications made on the basis of our data fall short of respecting the individual person, because they will never match the identity as it is experienced by the data-subject. It fails because it does not conceive of the other on his own terms. Respect for privacy of persons can thus be seen to have a distinctly epistemic dimension. It represents an acknowledgement that

---

[16] See for the notion of 'symbolic utility,' Robert Nozick, *The Nature of Rationality,* Princeton: Princeton University Press, 1993.

[17] Bernard Williams, *Problems of the Self.* Cambridge: Cambridge University Press, 1973. See p. 236.

[18] See Protection of personal data used for employment purposes, Council of Europe, Recommendation No. R (89) 2, adopted by the Committee of Ministers on 18 January 1989, article 2: "(...) respect for human dignity relates to the need to avoid statistical dehumanisation by undermining the identity of employees through data-processing techniques which allow for profiling of employees or the taking of decisions based on automatic processing which concern them" (Explanatory Memorandum, para. 25). Quoted by B. W. Napier, "The Future of Information Technology Law," *Cambridge Law Journal,* 51, no. 1, 1992, p. 64.

it is impossible to really know other persons as they know and experience themselves. Even if we could get it right about moral persons at any given point in time, by exhibit of extraordinary empathy and attention, then it is highly questionable whether the data-subject's experience of himself, as far as the *dynamics* of the moral person is concerned, can be captured and adequately represented. The person conceives of himself as trying to improve himself morally. The person can not be identified, not even in the sense articulated by Bernard Williams, with something limited, definite, and unchanging. This point was made by the French Existentialist Gabriel Marcel:

> *"(...) il faudra dire que la personne ne saurait etre assimilee en aucune maniere a un objet dont nous pouvons dire qu'il est la, c'est-a-dire qu'il est donne, present devant nous, qu'il fait partie d'une collection par essence denombrable, ou encore qu'il est un element statistique (...)."*[19]

The person always sees itself as becoming, as something that has to be overcome, not as a fixed reality, but as something in the making, something that has to be improved upon:

> *"Elle se saisit bien moins comme etre que comme volonte de depasser ce que tout ensemble elle est et elle n'est pas, un actualite dans laquelle elle se sent a vrai dire engagee ou implique, mais qui ne la satisfait pas: qui n'est pas a la mesure de l'aspiration avec laquelle elle s'identifie."*[20]

As Marcel puts it, the individual's motto is not *sum* (I am) but *sursum* (higher). The human person has a tendency not to be satisfied, but he or she is always aspiring to improve him or herself. Always on his or her way, *Homo Viator*.[21]

It is clear that this construal of privacy implies a disengaged, unsituated, and 'punctual' self. At the end of his very perceptive paper on Privacy and Intelligent Vehicle Highway Systems[22] Jeffrey Reiman observes that there is a profound link between liberalism, privacy, and conceptions of the self: "The liberal vision is guided by the ideal of the autonomous individual, the one who acts on principles that she has accepted after critical review, rather than simply absorbing them unquestioned from outside. Moreover, the liberal stresses the importance of people making sense of their own lives (...) and has an implicit trust in the transformational and ameliorative possibilities of private inner life."

---

[19] Gabriel Marcel, *Homo Viator.* Paris: Aubier, Editions Montaigne, 1944. See p. 31. This neatly accommodates the fact that in French criminal law, statistical evidence relating to persons is not allowed in court. I thank Daniele Bourcier for pointing this out to me.

[20] *Op. cit.,* p. 32

[21] This is only part of Marcel's diagnosis of the modern subject. His work is in part a way of remedying its deficiencies.

[22] Jeffrey Reiman, "Driving to the Panopticon." In *Critical Moral Liberalism.* Lanham: Rowman & Littlefield, 1997. See p. 182–183.

Communitarians have always felt themselves comfortably supported by Aristotle in their critique of this liberalist conception of the individual and its relation to the community. He has traditionally been interpreted as exalting the community and public realm over the private and the individual. Judith Swanson persuasively argues however, that privacy plays an important role in Aristotle's political philosophy.[23] The rationale of privacy for Aristotle is to enable one to turn away in order to achieve moral excellence. Insofar as private activity requires pulling away from the drag of common opinion, the public should foster privacy, that is, not sites but activities that cultivate virtue without accommodating or conforming to common opinion.[24]

Protecting privacy here is proposed as a way of acknowledging our systematic inability to identify the data subject as being the same as the moral self with which the data subject identifies itself. Justifying data protection by an appeal to privacy is to ask for a 'moral time out,' that is, not a time out from the moral point of view, but a time out from prevailing social morality. It can be granted only if and insofar as it is used to moral reflection and self-improvement. Communitarians should decide what the best way is to pursue their dream of perfect free-riderlessness by granting privacy or by refusing it.

---

[23] Judith A. Swanson, *The Public and the Private in Aristotle's Political Philosophy.* Ithaca/London: Cornell University Press, 1992.

[24] Swanson notes: "(...) in Aristotle's view, every human being has a right to privacy insofar as everyone—from children to the slavish to the philosophical—should be granted (...) opportunities to cultivate the most virtue of which they are capable. But this right may sometimes require denying some persons (for example, children, law breakers) freedom to make choices, or it may circumscribe their choices; and it does not grant the eligible merely the freedom to choose, but also the resources and thus the encouragement or direction to choose virtuously." Op. cit., p. 7, n. 17.

Introduction to Chapter 5:
Security and Crime in Cyberspace

In this chapter we examine a wide range of security- and crime-related issues involving cybertechnology. In the context of cyberethics, issues of security and crime are closely related, and in some cases they intersect. However, some useful distinctions can be drawn between cybersecurity and cybercrime. Consider that while virtually all cyber-related security violations are also criminal acts, not all instances of cybercrime necessarily involve breaches of computer security. For example, crimes involving Internet pornography, cyberstalking, and digital piracy are not necessarily the result of insecure computer systems. On the other hand, activities involving unauthorized access to data in a computer system, as well as activities aimed at damaging or disrupting computer systems and their resources, are examples of cybersecurity issues that are also criminal in nature. So while issues involving cybersecurity and cybercrime may overlap in certain instances, there are other cases where they are distinct. For purposes of this textbook, however, we include readings that address cybersecurity and cybercrime issues in one chapter.

Three Distinct Aspects of Computer Security

The term "security" in the context of computers and cybertechnology is often ambiguous. It can refer to at least three distinct kinds of concerns, which involve: (i) the integrity of the data that resides in a computer system or that is communicated between two or more computer systems, (ii) the vulnerability of computers and their system resources to attacks by malicious programs, and (iii) the vulnerability of computer networks, including the Internet itself (which serves as a "backbone" for much our current network-dependent infrastructure), to attack. The first type of cyber-related security issues involve *data security*. The second category of concerns fall under the heading *system security*, and the third can be understood as *network/ Internet security*. We briefly describe each category of computer security in this introduction. Specific issues involving each category are discussed in detail in the first four readings of this chapter.

Data security is concerned with unauthorized access to data that either (a) resides in one or more computer systems or computer databases, or (b) is exchanged between two or more computer systems. For example, data security issues can include concerns about the integrity of data affecting student grades stored in a university's database, or they can include concerns about the integrity of information contained in email messages being communicated between computers. Concerns involving data security sometimes overlap with privacy issues in cyberspace.[1] As we saw in Chapter 4, privacy concerns often arise when users worry that organizations (especially businesses and government agencies) claim to have some legitimate need for and right to personal information in order to make important decisions. Concerns involving data security, on the other hand, sometimes arise because personal and proprietary information can be (and has been) accessed and manipulated by individuals (and occasionally by organizations as well) who have no legitimate need for, or right to, such information. So we can distinguish security issues involving data integrity[2] from concerns involving online privacy.

System security, unlike data security, is concerned with a cluster of vulnerabilities involving computer systems themselves. These vulnerabilities include attacks directed at a computer system's resources, such as its operating system software, applications programs, disk drives, and so forth. Specifically, system security focuses on a computer system's vulnerability to the kinds of damage and destruction caused by malicious programs such as viruses and worms, which Ann Branscomb (1990) generically refers to as "rogue computer programs." By installing security countermeasures such as anti-virus software and firewall technology, owners and operators of individual computers, as well as system managers and administrators try to defend against these kinds of attacks.

Network/Internet security is concerned with securing an entire computer network—from one or more privately owned computer networks (such as LANs and WANs) to the Internet itself—against cyber-attacks designed to disrupt the flow of information across computer networks. The Internet's infrastructure, which includes the set of protocols allowing communication across individual computer networks, has been the victim of several cyber-attacks. By launching viruses and worms, malicious hackers and cyber-vandals have severely disrupted activities on the Internet and, in certain instances, have rendered the Internet inoperable. In 1988, many ordinary users (and perhaps even some security experts) realized for the first time

---

[1] For a discussion of some similarities and differences between issues involving data security and on line privacy, see Tavani (2000).

[2] Issues involving data security have also been discussed under the category "information integrity." See, for example, Spinello (2000).

just how vulnerable the Internet was to these kinds of attacks. That year, a Cornell University student named Robert Morris unleashed a program, later described as the "Internet worm," or "Cornell virus," that brought activity on the Internet to a virtual standstill. The Michaelangelo, Melissa, ILOVEYOU, and Blaster viruses have since followed, each wreaking havoc in varying degrees for the Internet and its users.

Crime, "Hacktivism," and Terrorism in Cyberspace

Stories about criminal activities involving computers have been highly publicized, and much has been written about the "hacker culture."[3] In the early days of computing, many seemed to be indifferent (and some even seemed to be sympathetic) to hackers who broke into computer systems of large organizations. In fact, some questioned whether computer hacking should even be classified as a criminal activity. Others have advocated for a distinction between hacking and "cracking," arguing that only the latter behavior actually violated the law (because cracking involves malicious intent on the part of the perpetrator). Many have since argued that our traditional understanding of "hacking" should be further analyzed to delineate conceptual distinctions. For instance, Deborah Johnson (1994) suggests that a distinction can be drawn between "hacking for fun" and "hacking for profit."

In the past, some defenders of "hacker's rights," such as Mitch Kapor (1991), have worried that the civil rights of hackers were being violated. Today, however, there seems to be far less sympathy for hackers of any sort. Growing concerns about the fragility of the Internet have caused many people to be suspicious of hackers of any stripe.

The first three readings in this chapter examine issues involving crime, hacktivism, and terrorism in cyberspace. In the opening essay, Herman Tavani asks whether coherent criteria can be established to determine which crimes involving computer technology should count as instances of computer crime. He considers incidents involving cyber-attacks (in the form of "distributed denial-of-service" attacks) on commercial web sites, the unleashing of viruses and worms (such as the ILOVEYOU virus), and the unauthorized sharing of proprietary information on the Internet (such as proprietary MP3 files, originating with the Napster controversy). Contrasting this set of criminal activities involving cybertechnology with three types of criminal acts in which: (i) pedophiles use the Internet to lure young children, (ii) stalkers use the Internet to track individuals and possibly cause harm to them, and (iii) pornographers use the Internet to distribute child pornography, Tavani asks us to compare these two sets of

---

[3] See, for example, Levy (1984) and Himanen (2002).

criminal activities. Following a critique of some traditional definitions of computer crime, he proposes an alternative definition. Tavani concludes that genuine computer crimes, unlike computer-enhanced and computer-assisted crimes, will fall into one or more of three general categories.

Mark Manion and Abby Goodrum, in a paper entitled "Terrorism or Civil Disobedience: Toward a Hacktivist Ethic," question whether some cyber-attacks directed at commercial or business interests on the Internet could be best understood as acts of *hacktivism,* which they suggest can be viewed as "electronic political activism." Specifically, the authors ask us to consider whether the "denial-of-service" attacks directed at major e-commerce sites in February 2000 (which are also examined in the preceding reading in Chapter 5) should be viewed as: (a) mere nuisance attacks perpetrated by malicious teenagers, (b) more serious attacks of cyberterrorism, or (c) evidence of a growing outrage over an increasingly "commodified Internet." Manion and Goodrum speculate that at least some of these cyber-attacks might also suggest a new form of "civil disobedience," integrating the talent of traditional computer hackers with the interests and social consciousness of political activists. Manion and Goodrum point out that while the media tends to portray hackers as vandals, terrorists, and saboteurs, it has yet to consider the possibility that some of these individuals might be politically motivated hacktivists. The authors also believe that important questions surrounding the possible rise of an "ethic of hacktivism" have not been sufficiently examined in the popular press or in the computer ethics literature.

Can a meaningful distinction be drawn between acts of hacktivism and cyberterrorism? Computer security expert Dorothy Denning (1999) suggests that one can. Denning defines hacktivism as the "convergence of activism and computer hacking." Noting that activism (in the context of cyberspace) can be viewed as normal, non-disruptive use of the Internet to support a cause, she points out that an activist can use the Internet to discuss issues, form coalitions, and plan and coordinate activities. As such, activists could engage in a range of activities from browsing the Web to sending email, posting material to a web site, constructing a web site dedicated to their political cause, and so forth. Hacktivists, according to Denning, intend to disrupt, but not serously harm, a larger web site by using hacking techniques. These disruptions could be caused by "email bombs" and "low grade" viruses that cause only "minimal disruption," and do not result in severe economic damage or loss of life. She argues that *cyberterorism,* on the other hand, consists of operations that are intended to cause great harm such as loss of life or severe economic damage, or both.

In the third reading of Chapter 6, Denning provides a careful analysis of cyberterrorism, which she defines as "the convergence of terrorism and cyberspace," where a cyberterrorist attack results in violence or generates fear. According to Denning, cyberterrorism is generally understood to mean "unlawful attacks and threats of attack against computers, networks, and the information stored therein when done to intimidate or coerce a government or its people in furtherance of political or social objectives." In Denning's scheme, cyber-related attacks that lead to death or bodily injury, explosions, plane crashes, water contamination, or severe economic loss would be examples of cyberterrorism. Serious attacks against critical infrastructures also could be acts of cyberterrorism, depending on their impact. For example, a cyberterrorist might attempt to bring down the US stock market or take control of a transportation unit to cause a train crash. She admits, however, that it can be difficult to separate acts of cyberterrorism from other forms of unwelcome behavior in cyberspace, such as cybervandalism and hacktivism.

Although Denning believes that activism, hacktivism, and cyberterrorism are conceptually distinct, she also notes that as we progress from activism to cyberterrorism, the boundaries become "fuzzy." For example, should an "email bomb" sent by a hacker who is also a political activist be classified as a form of hacktivism or as an act of cyberterrorism? We should note, however, that these distinctions tend to be of little interest to those in the law enforcement sector. Law enforcement agencies are more concerned with deterring and catching individuals who engage in any form of unauthorized and illegal activities in cyberspace than with understanding their particular goals, objectives, and ideological beliefs.

Data Encryption, Internet Anonymity, and Cyberstalking

The next three readings in Chapter 5 examine issues involving encrypted communication, anonymous behavior, and stalking in cyberspace. Some controversies pertaining to data encryption and anonymity were identified in our introduction to Chapter 4, in conjunction with our discussion of privacy-enhancing technologies (or PETs)[4]. In that discussion, we briefly considered roles that PETs can play in protecting privacy. Some PETs have been designed to protect the identity of individuals who are engaged in online activities (via the use of online anonymity tools), where others have been developed to protect the integrity of data in messages communicated in computer networks. As tools developed in response to requests by online users to protect their identity and their communications in cyberspace, PETs have subsequently raised concerns about both anonymity and data encryption.

---

[4] The article in Chapter 4 by Tavani and Moor, which critically analyzes PETs, can be read in conjunction with readings four through six in Chapter 5.

Why exactly are issues involving Internet anonymity and data encryption relevant to discussions of cybersecurity? First consider some controversies over tools that enable users to roam the Web either anonymously or pseudonymously. Many users who are interested in protecting their online privacy believe that Internet anonymity is a positive feature. Others, including those in the law-enforcement sector, however, fear that criminals and terrorists will abuse anonymity and exploit this feature of the Internet for their own sinister ends.

Next, consider some controversies generated by data encryption. Internet users can communicate with each other via electronic messages that are encrypted. And like concerns with anonymity, many worry that users with malicious intent can abuse this feature of Internet communication. Those in the law-enforcement sector also worry that criminals, terrorists, and others will use strong-encrypted communications for illegal and subversive activities. They note, quite correctly, that it would be extremely difficult for governments and law-enforcement agencies to monitor the communications of terrorists and criminals if strong encryption programs are used to encrypt those messages.

Members of the e-commerce community are also interested in Internet-security features made possible by data encryption. Because many online entrepreneurs believe that strong encryption is essential for realizing the full potential of e-commerce, they have looked to encryption-based technologies to resolve some of their security-related worries. One solution verifies authentication between online consumers and merchants through the use of strong-encryption tools. While the e-commerce community might favor a solution to its security problems that is based on the use of strong encryption programs, this kind of solution could cause problems for law-enforcement agencies.

In the fourth reading in this chapter, Jean Camp describes some specific features of private- and public-key encryption. How exactly are these two forms of data encryption different? First, we should note that data encryption, or cryptography, is a technique that involves encrypting ordinary ("plain text") communication by translating it into "ciphertext." The party receiving an encrypted communication then uses a "key" to decrypt the ciphertext by converting it back into plain text. As long as both parties have the appropriate key, they can successfully encode and decode messages. One challenge in ensuring the integrity of encrypted communications is to make sure that the key is communicated while it remains private. Thus, an encrypted communication will be only as secure and private as its key. The cryptographic technique described thus far is called private-key encryption; both parties use the same encryption algorithm and the same private key.

A relatively recent encryption technology, called public-key cryptography, uses two keys: one public and the other private. If A wishes to communicate with B, A uses B's public key to encode the message. That message can then only be decoded with B's private key, which is secret. Similarly when B responds to A, B uses A's public key to encrypt the message. That message can be decrypted only by using A's private key. The strength here lies in the system of keys used. Although information about an individual's public key is accessible to others, that individual's ability to communicate encrypted information is not compromised. Governmental agencies responsible for protecting national security and military intelligence, preventing terrorism, and enforcing laws, are particularly interested in public-key encryption.

In the chapter's fourth reading, Camp also considers how the use of pseudonyms in online transactions enables researchers to engage in extensive demographic studies without violating the privacy of individuals.[5] For example, Camp's article, like Nissenbaum's paper in Chapter 4 on protecting privacy in public, considers whether those who browse the Web (a "public space," according to Camp) can expect to protect their privacy while doing so. Camp's answer to this question, however, appeals to a "right to privacy" that she believes can be found in the American legal tradition (rather than one based on a need for a principle such as "data protection," as Elgesem suggests in his article included in Chapter 4).

In the next reading in Chapter 5, Helen Nissenbaum critically examines the meaning of "anonymity" in an information age. She considers the question whether anonymity should always be protected in cyberspace. Nissenbaum begins her essay by asking what is meant by the term "anonymity." She believes that before we advocate for anonymity in cyberspace, we should be able to articulate precisely what it is that we are so interested in protecting. This question is important because, as Nissenbaum so aptly puts the matter: "after all is said and done, we would not want to discover that the thing we have fought so hard to protect was not worth protecting after all."

Frances Grodzinsky and Herman Tavani, in the sixth reading, examine cyberstalking behavior and the role that anonymity plays in stalking activities on the Internet. They consider whether an individual's ability to operate anonymously in cyberspace correlates to the rise of morally objectionable behavior on the Internet. For example, they question whether anonymity tempts individuals who never would have considered stalking

---

[5] Camp's paper, entitled "Web Security and Privacy: An American Perspective," can also be read in conjunction with the privacy articles by Dag Elgesem and Helen Nissenbaum in Chapter 4.

a person in physcial space to engage in cyberstalking activities. The authors also consider what responsibility Internet Service Providers (ISPs) might have for stalking activities that are carried out in their online forums; and they consider an ordinary user's responsibility, if any, to assist others who become the target of one or more cyberstalkers. For example, they ask whether users who discovered that Amy Boyer was being stalked on the Internet by Liam Youens were morally obligated to notify Boyer. (They also point out that doing so in this particular incident of cyberstalking could have saved Boyer's life.) These and other questions are considered in the reading on cyberstalking included in Chapter 6.

Biometric Technologies

In the chapter's final two readings, Irma van der Ploeg and Philip Brey consider security issues having to do with biometric technologies.[6] What exactly is biometric technology? Richard Power (2002) defines biometrics as the biological identification of a person, including eyes, voice, hand prints, fingerprints, retina patterns, and handwritten signatures. Many computer security experts consider biometrics to be one of the most reliable forms of authentication. But does the use of biometric technologies raise any ethical concerns?

In the seventh reading, "Written on the Body: Biometrics and Identity," Irma van der Ploeg notes that, at first glance, biometric technology might appear to be similar to older existing techniques used to verify personal identity. For example, consider that computer-matching techniques (predating biometrics) have been used to identify criminals, income-tax cheats, deadbeat parents, etc. So, why should the use of biometric technology to identify people suspected of criminal activities raise any special moral concerns? However, van der Ploeg argues that there are some significant differences worth noting, when we consider ethical implications of using biometric vs. earlier technologies to identify individuals. Elsewhere, van der Ploeg (1999) examines some proposals that have generated considerable controversy for using biometric identifiers in European Union (EU) nations. For example, she has carefully analyzed issues surrounding the controversial *Eurodac* Project, an EU proposal to use biometrics in controlling illegal immigration and border crossing by asylum seekers in European countries. In 2002, a proposal was made to implement Eurodac, despite the controversies surrounding that project.

---

[6] Because both papers also address privacy-related aspects of biometrics, they can be read in conjunction with the articles included in Chapter 4.

Chapter 5 closes with Philip Brey's article, "Ethical Aspects of Facial Recognition Systems in Public Places," which examines the use of face-recognition systems or "facecams" in public places such as large sports stadiums and airports. Brey outlines some of the arguments used by proponents and opponents of facecams, and he is particularly interested in identifying the underlying values and assumptions in these arguments. He describes how this technology was used at SuperBowl XXXV in Tampa, Florida (in early 2001) and why it caused considerable controversy at the time. Brey's paper critically discusses three problems with the use of facecams: (i) the problem of error, (ii) "function creep," and (iii) privacy. Brey notes that matches resulting from biometrics technology can contain errors, especially when the threshold for what can count as a legitimate match is expanded. He also notes that the uses for which biometric technologies were originally authorized can be expanded significantly, leading to possible abuses of this technology.

An interesting question to consider is how attitudes regarding the use of biometric technologies such as facecams may have changed, especially in the United States, in the period following the tragic events of September 11, 2001. When facial-recognition technology was used to match faces at the Super Bowl XXXV in January 2001, it drew scathing criticism from both civil liberties groups and privacy advocates. In the post-September 11 world, however, Americans overwhelmingly support practices that employ biometric technologies in public places. In one sense, issues surrounding the use of facial-recognition technology cause us to ask how much privacy we are willing to sacrifice for security. A Harris Interactive poll conducted in October 2001 indicated that more than 86% of Americans approved of the use of biometric technologies such as facial recognition devices in sports stadiums and airports.

Discussion Questions

1. What exactly is *computer crime*? Can a coherent definition of computer crime be framed? If so, which features can be used to distinguish "genuine" computer crimes from ordinary crimes that also involve either the use or presence of one or more computers?

2. Should political activists be permitted to engage in cyber-attacks on commercial web sites because they believe that the Internet has become too "commodified"? Can a legitimate distinction be drawn between a hacktivism and cybervandalism?

3. What does Dorothy Denning mean by the expression *cyberterrorism*? How can cyberterrorism be distinguished from activism (on the Internet) and hacktivism? Contrast Denning's definition of hacktivism with the one used by Manion and Goodrum, in conjunction with their question about how to classify the denial-of-service attacks directed at major e-commerce sites in February 2000.

4. What are some of the controversies surrounding the use of data encryption, especially the use of strong encryption, to communicate messages over computer networks, including the Internet? How does Jean Camp distinquish between public-key and private-key encryption?

5. What exactly is anonymity, and what problems does Internet anonymity pose? Why does Helen Nissenbaum believe that we must understand what exactly is at stake in Internet anonymity before we frame appropriate policies? Are current policies that allow users to navigate the Web anonymously or pseudonymously policies worth protecting?

6. What exactly is cyberstalking and what kinds of ethical issues does it raise? Do Internet Service Providers (ISPs) have any responsibilities for protecting individuals in their online forums from stalkers? Do ordinary Internet users have a duty to assist fellow users when they find out that these individual are being targeted on-line by stalkers?

7. What is biometric technology, and what kinds of ethical issues do certain uses of that technology raise? According to Irma van der Ploeg, what kinds of ethical concerns does the use of biometric technology raise, and how are they different from concerns raised by earlier techniques used by law enforcement to identify criminals?

8. What are facial-recognition systems, also known as "facecams"? Identify the three kinds of ethical concerns that Brey believes that the use of facecams in public places raises? Can the use of face-cam technology and related schemes involving biometrics be ethically justified in the post-September 11 Era?

References

Branscomb, Ann (1990). "Rogue Computer Programs and Computer Rogues: Tailoring the Punishment to Fit the Crime," *Rutgers Computer and Technology Law Journal,* Vol. 16, pp. 1–6.

Denning, Dorothy E. (1999). "Activism, Hacktivism, and Cyberterrorism: The Internet as a Tool For Influencing Foreign Policy." Paper presented to the World Affairs Council (Dec. 10). Available at: http://www.nautilus.org/info-policy/workshop/papers/denning.html.

Johnson, Deborah G. (1994). *Computer Ethics.* 2nd ed. Englewood Cliffs, New Jersey: Prentice Hall.

Himanen, Pekka (2001). *The Hacker Ethic: A Radical Approach to the Philosophy of Business.* New York: Random House.

Kapor, Mitch (1991). "Civil Liberties in *Cyberspace.*" *Scientific American,* Vol. 265, No. 3, pp. 23–32.

Levy, Steven (1984). *Hackers: Heroes of the Computer Revolution.* New York: Anchor Doubleday.

Power, Richard (2000). *Tangled Web: Tales of Digital Crime from the Shadows of Cyberspace.* Que Corp.

Spinello, Richard A. (2000). "Information Integrity." In D. Langford, ed. *Internet Ethics.* London, UK: Macmillan Publishers, pp. 158–180.

Tavani, Herman T. (2000). "Privacy and Security." In D. Langford, ed. *Internet Ethics.* New York: St. Martin's Press, pp. 65–95.

van der Ploeg, Irma (1999). "The Illegal Body: 'Eurodac' and the Politics of Biometric Identification," *Ethics and Information Technology,* Vol. 1, No. 4, pp. 295–302.

Suggestions for Further Readings: Computer Security

Arquilla, John. (1999). "Can Information Warfare Ever Be Just?" *Ethics and Information Technology,* Vol. 1, No. 3, pp. 203–212.

Baase, Sara (2003). "Encryption and Interception of Communications." Chapter 3 in *A Gift of Fire: Social, Legal, and Ethical Issues in Computing.* 2nd ed. Upper Saddle River, NJ: Prentice Hall.

Camp, L. Jean (2000). *Trust and Risk in Internet Commerce.* Cambridge, MA: MIT Press.

Denning, Dorothy E. (1998). *Information Warfare and Security.* Reading, MA: Addison-Wesley.

Diffie, Whitield and Susan Landau (1998). *Privacy on the Line. The Politics of Wiretapping and Encryption.* Cambridge, MA: MIT Press.

Garfinkel, Simson and Eugene Sapfford (1996). *Practical UNIX and Internet Security.* 2nd ed. Cambridge, MA: O'Reilly & Associates, Inc.

Goodrum, Abby and Mark Manion (2000). "The Ethics of Hacktivism," *Journal of Information Ethics,* Vol. 9, No. 2, pp. 51–59.

Levy, Steve (1995). "The Battle Over the Clipper Chip." In D. G. Johnson and H. Nissenbaum, eds. *Computing, Ethics & Social Values,* Englewood Cliffs, NJ: Prentice Hall, pp. 651–663.

Marx, Gary (2001). "Identity and Anonymity: Some Conceptual Distinctions and Issues for Research." In J. Caplani and J. Topley, eds. *Documenting Individual Identity.* Princeton, NJ: Princeton University Press.

Neuman, Peter. "Inside Risks." A column that appears regularly in *Communications of the ACM.*

Schneier, Bruce. (2000). *Secrets and Lies: Digital Security in a Networked World.* New York: John Wiley and Sons.

Spafford, Eugene H. (1992). "Are Computer Hacker Break-Ins Ethical?" *Journal of Systems Software,* Vol. 17, pp. 41–47.

Spafford, Eugene H., Kathleen A. Heaphy, and David J. Ferbrache (1989). *Computer Viruses: Dealing With Electronic Vandalism and Programmed Threats.* Arlington, VA: ADAPSO Press.

Spinello, Richard A. (2003). "Securing the Electronic Frontier." Chapter 6 in *CyberEthics: Morality and Law in Cyberspace.* 2nd ed. Sudbury, MA: Jones and Bartlett Publishers.

Tavani, Herman T. (2004). "Security in Cyberspace." Chapter 6 in *Ethics and Technology: Ethical Issues in an Age of Information and Communication Technology.* Hoboken, NJ: John Wiley and Sons.

Thompson, Paul B. (2001). "Privacy, Secrecy, and Security." *Ethics and Information Technology,* Vol. 3, No. 1, pp. 13–19.

Vlug, Albert and Johan van der Lei (2001). "Double Encryption of Anonymized Electronic Interchange." In R. A. Spinello and H. T. Tavani, eds. *Readings in Cyberethics.* 1st ed. Sudbury, MA: Jones and Bartlett Publishers, pp. 493–500.

Wallace, Kathleen (1999). "Anonymity." *Ethics and Information Technology,* Vol. 1, No. 1, pp. 22–35.

Suggested Further Readings: Computer Crime

Baase, Sara (2003). "Computer Crime." Chapter 7 in *A Gift of Fire: Social, Legal, and Ethical Issues in Computing.* 2nd ed. Upper Saddle River, NJ: Prentice Hall.

Denning, Dorothy E. and Peter J. Denning, eds. (1998) *Internet Besieged: Countering Cyberspace Scofflaws.* New York: ACM Press.

Edgar, Stacey L. (2003). "Computer Crime." Chap. 5 in *Morality and Machines: Perspectives on Computer Ethics.* 2nd ed. Sudbury, MA: Jones and Bartlett

Forester, Tom and Perry Morrison (1994). "Computer Crime." Chap. 2 in *Computer Ethics: Cautionary Tales and Ethical Dilemmas in Computing.* 2nd ed. Cambridge, MA: MIT Pres.

Girasa, Roy J. (2002). *Cyberlaw: National and International Perspectives.* Upper Saddle River, NJ: Prentice Hall.

Grodzinsky, Frances S. and Herman T. Tavani. (2001). "Is Cyberstalking a Special Type of Computer Crime?" In T. W. Bynum, et al., eds. *Proceedings of the Fifth International Conference on the Social and Ethical Impacts of Information and Communications Technologies: Ethicomp 2001.* Vol. 2. Gdansk, Poland: Mikom Publishers, pp. 73–85.

Hafner, Katie and John Markoff (1995). *Cyberpunk: Outlaws and Hackers on the Electronic Frontier.* New York: Touchstone Books.

Johnson, Deborah G. (2001). "Hacking and Hacker Ethics." In *Computer Ethics.* 3rd ed. Upper Saddle River, NJ: Prentice Hall, pp. 97–102.

Johnson, Deborah G. and Helen Nissenbaum (1995). "Crime, Abuse, and Hacker Ethics." In D. G. Johnson and H. Nissenbaum, eds. *Computing, Ethics and Social Values.* Englewood Cliffs, NJ: Prentice Hall, pp. 57–60.

Ludlow, Peter, ed. (2001). *Crypto Anarchy, Cyberstates, and Pirate Utopia.* Cambridge, MA: MIT Press

Parker, Donn B. (1998). *Fighting Computer Crime: A Framework for Protecting Information.* New York: John Wiley and Sons.

Rotenberg, Marc (1995). "Computer Virus Legislation." In D. G. Johnson and H. Nissenbaum, eds. *Computing, Ethics and Social Values.* Englewood Cliffs, NJ: Prentice Hall, pp. 135–147.

Sinnott-Armstrong, Walter (1999). "Entrapment in the Net?" *Ethics and Information Technology,* Vol. 2, No. 1, pp. 95–104.

Tavani, Herman T. (2004). "Cybercrime and Cyber-related Crime." Chapter 7 in *Ethics and Technology: Ethical Issues in an Age of Information and Communication Technology.* Hoboken, NJ: John Wiley and Sons.

Thomas, Douglas (2002). *Hacker Culture.* Minneapolis: University of Minnesota Press.

Wall, David S. (1997). "Policing the Virtual Community: The Internet, Cybercrimes, and the Policing of Cyberspace." In P. Francis, P. Davies, and V. Jupp, eds. *Policing Futures.* London: Macmillan, pp. 208–236.

Wall, David S. (1998). "Catching Cybercriminals: Policing the Internet." *International Review of Law, Computers & Technology.* Vol. 12, No. 2, pp. 201–218.

Defining the Boundaries of Computer Crime: Piracy, Trespass, and Vandalism in Cyberspace

Herman T. Tavani

Recent criminal, or at least questionable, activities involving the use of computer technology have received considerable media attention. Reports of these activities have recently appeared as cover stories in reputable periodicals, as headlines in major newspapers, and as lead stories on television news programs in the U.S. and around the globe. Consider three recent incidents, each of which illustrates a different type of criminal activity involving computer technology. In May 2000, the ILOVEYOU computer virus, also referred to as the *Love Bug*, infected computer systems in the U.S., Europe, and Asia, disrupting e-commerce activities as well as the operations of many governmental agencies. In February 2000, a series of cyber-attacks on major commercial Web sites, owned and operated by Amazon, eBay, CNN, Yahoo, and others, resulted in "denial of service" to users who wished to access those sites for legitimate purposes. And in December 1999, the owners and operators of the Napster Web site were sued by the Recording Industry Association of America for "illegally" distributing copyrighted music (in the form of MP3 files) on the Internet.

Each of the incidents described in the preceding paragraph would seem to be a genuine instance of computer crime or cybercrime. Other recently reported criminal activities that also involve the use of computer technology, and which might initially appear to be instances of computer crime, arguably are not. For example, there have been reports about pedophiles using the Internet to lure unsuspecting young children. There have also been reported cases of cyberstalking, one of which resulted in the death of the stalking victim. And there have been reports of individuals using the Internet to distribute child pornography. Should these three examples of criminal activities also be viewed as instances of computer crime? Or are these cases different, in certain important respects, from the three examples that we considered in the preceding paragraph? It would seem that having a clear and coherent definition of computer crime would be useful in helping us to sort out which criminal acts involving computer technology fit and which do not fit into the category of computer crime.

In this essay, an attempt is made to establish clear and coherent criteria for determining which criminal activities involving the use of computer technology should

This essay, which is revised slightly for the second edition of *Readings in CyberEthics,* originally appeared in *Computers and Society,* Vol. 30, No. 3 (September) 2000: 3–9. Copyright © 2000 by Herman T. Tavani. Reprinted by permission.

and should not count as genuine instances of computer crime. First, we consider whether having a distinct category of crime called "computer crime" is either necessary or useful. In doing so, we differentiate legal, moral, and descriptive categories of computer crime. Following a defense of the view that having a descriptive category is indeed worthwhile, some recent definitions of computer crime are considered and rejected. A new definition of computer crime is then proposed and defended. Finally, it is argued that the application of such a definition can help to eliminate at least some of the confusion currently associated with criminal activities involving computer technology.[1]

Do We Need a Category of Computer Crime?

Before attempting to answer the question of whether having a distinct category of computer crime is necessary or even useful, it is important to consider briefly some background issues and discussions involving crime and computer technology that can inform the current debate. For while the recent flurry of criminal activities involving computer technology has been the subject of much media attention, the association of certain kinds of crimes with computers is hardly new. In the 1970s and 1980s, for example, we read about disgruntled employees who altered files in computer databases or who sabotaged computer systems in the act of seeking revenge against employers. Other highly publicized news stories described computer hackers breaking into computer systems—especially those systems thought to be highly secure—either as a prank or as a malicious attempt to subvert data or disrupt its flow. There were also reports, frequently sensationalized and occasionally glamorized by some members of the press, involving hackers who used computers to transfer monetary funds from wealthy individuals and corporations to poorer individuals and organizations. Some earlier reports in the popular media went so far as to portray young computer hackers as "countercultural heroes."[2] Today, however, the attitude of many of those in the media—which itself has been a victim of recent cyber-attacks (e.g., attacks on the New York Times and the CNN Web sites)—as well as the sentiment of the public in general has shifted considerably. Fewer and fewer individuals and organizations are now sympathetic to the causes of computer hackers, perhaps because of our increased dependence on the Internet. There is a growing concern among those in both the private and public

---

[1] By "computer technology" I mean the range of computing technologies that include stand-alone personal computers, privately owned computer systems and networks (e.g., LANs and WANs), and the Intenet itself.

[2] In a separate paper (Tavani, 1999), I describe specific examples of some of these earlier computer crimes. For an in-depth discussion of some of these earlier computer crimes, including an account of the "hacker culture," see Levy (1984) and Wessles (1990).

sectors that cyberspace must become a more secure[3] place and that hacking of any type should not be tolerated.

Even though concerns about crimes involving the use of computer technology have received considerable attention in the popular press as well as in certain scholarly publications, the criteria used by news reporters, computer ethicists, and legal analysts for determining what exactly constitutes a computer crime has been neither clear nor consistent. For example, there has been some disagreement as to whether crimes involving the presence of one or more computers should necessarily be classified as computer crimes. On the one hand, some news reporters and journalists have seemed, at times, to suggest that any crime involving the presence of a computer is *ipso facto* a computer crime. On the other hand, there are those who have argued that there is nothing special about crimes that involve computers. Gotterbarn (1991), who has criticized much of the earlier media hype surrounding computer-related crimes, could be interpreted as supporting the view that crimes involving computers are not necessarily in need of a special category. He asks, for example, whether we would consider a crime in which an individual uses a surgeon's scalpel in committing a murder to be an issue in medical ethics, simply because a medical instrument was used in the criminal act.[4] And Johnson (1985), in her early writing in computer ethics, defended the view that crime is crime—whether it is committed with or without the use of a computer—suggesting that crimes involving computers are not qualitatively different from crimes in which no computer is present (compare Johnson, 1994).[5]

Based on concerns raised by Gotterbarn and other critics, we can reasonably ask whether having a separate category of computer crime is necessary or even useful. It is perhaps also worth noting that some critics have pointed out that crimes of diverse types are committed in many different sectors, but we don't have separate categories for crimes committed in each of those areas. So it would certainly seem reasonable for these critics to ask why we need a separate category of crime for criminal acts involving computer technology.

---

[3]Recently, much of the discussion about online activities involving electronic break-in as well as the discussion about sabotage or disruption to computer system resources (in the form of computer viruses) has been categorized under the label of computer security rather than under the heading of computer crime. Unfortunately, this shift in categorization has lead to certain confusions involving computer security. I have argued elsewhere (Tavani, 2000) that "computer security" is an ambiguous expression and one that is often used equivocally. In one sense, "security" in the context of computer technology has come to be identified with the set of concerns involving a computer system's vulnerability to "attacks" from viruses or worms or what Branscomb (1990) describes more generally as "rogue computer programs." There is another sense of "security," which intersects with issues related to privacy, which is concerned with the protection of personal and proprietary information from unauthorized access—i.e., the protection of information that resides in databases as well as information that is communicated over the Internet (e.g., e-mail). These two senses of "security" are sometimes confused in the current literature on computer security.

[4]It must be noted that Gotterbarn never explicitly asserts that there is no need for a category of computer crime; instead, he argues that crimes involving computers are not necessarily issues in computer ethics. In holding that position, however, he seems to have supported the view that such crimes are not essentially "computer crimes" but are simply instances of ordinary crimes, which also happen to involve the use or presence of one or more computers.

[5]In the second edition of *Computer Ethics* (1994), Johnson modifies her earlier position on computer crime and devotes an entire chapter to that topic.

To support the position of those critical of the need for a separate category of computer crime, consider three hypothetical scenarios, each of which illustrates a criminal activity involving a computer lab but none of which convincingly demonstrates the need for a distinct category of computer crime. Scenario one: An individual steals a computer device (e.g., a printer). Scenario 2: An individual breaks into the computer lab and then snoops around. Scenario 3: An individual enters a lab that he or she is authorized to use and then places an explosive device, which is set to detonate a short time later, on a computer mainframe or server. Clearly, each of the above acts would be considered criminal in nature. But should any of these criminal acts necessarily be viewed as a computer crime? On the one hand, it would not have been possible to commit any of these three crimes in precisely the same manner if computer technology had never existed. This factor might initially influence some to believe that these three criminal acts are somehow unique, or perhaps special, to computer technology. Yet the three criminal acts in question can easily be understood and prosecuted as specific examples of ordinary crimes involving theft, breaking and entering, and vandalism, even though each criminal act coincidentally happens to involve the presence of computer technology.

Considering our analysis thus far, one might be inclined to infer that there are no legitimate grounds for having a separate category of computer crime. But would such an inference be justified at this point? Putting aside that question for the moment, one still might ask what practical purpose would be served in our framing such a category of crime. For example, would having a category of computer crime help us to understand better certain nuances of illegal or immoral activities involving computer technology? Or might having such a category of crime be helpful in prosecuting certain criminal activities involving the use of this technology that otherwise would be more difficult to prosecute under conventional legal statutes? Let us briefly consider some possible reasons for framing one or more categories of computer crime.

Legal, Moral, and Informational/Descriptive Categories of Computer Crime

Arguments for having a category of computer crime can be advanced from at least three different perspectives: legal, moral, and informational or descriptive. We consider arguments for each, beginning with a look at computer crime as a separate *legal* category. From a legal perspective, computer crime might be viewed as a useful category for prosecuting certain kinds of crimes. For example, in some states in the U.S., crimes involving handguns can be prosecuted under the legal category of handgun crime. That is, in certain states criminal legislation has been proposed and enacted into law, based on the notion that crimes involving handguns are worth distinguishing, for relevant purposes, from similar crimes in which no handguns are present. So even though a critic like Gotterbarn is correct in pointing out that a murder committed with a surgeon's scalpel would not be treated as a separate category of murder, and even though, in one sense, murder is murder whether it involves the use of a scalpel, an ice pick, or a handgun, current criminal laws in certain states nonetheless distinguish between crimes committed with and without the use, or even the presence, of a handgun. Perhaps, then, the same kind of reasoning could be applied to crimes involving computer technology.

We can, of course, inquire into the value of having a separate legal category of handgun crime and we can ask whether that particular category of crime is always clear in its implementation. For example, if X assaults Y by striking a blow to Y's head with a handgun, should that crime be prosecuted as a handgun crime simply because a handgun is used? Also, if Z uses a fake (or toy) handgun to rob a convenience store, should that crime be prosecuted as a handgun crime? In the first scenario, a handgun was used in, but was not essential to carrying out, the crime since many different kinds of devices or objects (e.g., a hammer, a rock, or even a computer hardware device) could have been used by X to assault Y. And in the second situation, no genuine handgun was used in the crime. However, legislation concerning handgun crime has been written in such a way that, in a criminal act, either the mere presence of a handgun or the use of a device that might give the impression of being an authentic handgun is sufficient for that criminal act to be prosecuted as an instance of handgun crime.

How do the two scenarios in the preceding paragraph, both of which involve crimes that can be prosecuted under the category of handgun crime, affect our question of whether crimes involving computer technology should also be treated as a separate legal category of crime? For one thing, both scenarios illustrate some of the problems inherent in attempts to draft clear and coherent legislation involving a special *category* of crime. In deciding whether to frame a distinct category for crimes involving handguns, it might initially seem that drafting appropriate legislation would be a relatively straightforward and unproblematic process. However, we have seen some of the confusions that can result in prosecuting all criminal acts involving the presence of one or more handguns under a general category of crime. This can help us to anticipate some of the challenges we might face in deciding whether to prosecute all crimes involving the use or presence of computer technology under a specific legal category of computer crime.[6]

Independent of arguments for whether it is useful to have a distinct legal category of computer crime, questions can be raised about the usefulness of computer crime as a *moral* category. Johnson and Nissenbaum (1995) note that because computer crime is a "territory" that is not so well defined, a number of ethical questions both "precede and follow from" declaring certain computer-related activities illegal. They note, for example, that we can still reasonably ask questions such as: Which forms of online behavior should we criminalize? Are current illegal forms

---

[6]Perhaps a more practical problem involved in prosecuting computer crimes, at least those involving the Internet as well as some privately owned Wide Area Networks (WANs), has to do with jurisdictional issues. For example, can someone who resides in one state (e.g., New York) and who operates a Web site whose content is perfectly legal in that state, but illegal in certain states where that content can also be viewed online, be prosecuted by law enforcement personnel from the state in which that content is illegal (e.g., Texas)? Not only are there interstate problems associated with prosecuting crimes involving the Internet, but there are also problems of international law to be considered. The Council of Europe is currently considering some of these issues, and on April 27, 2000 it released a first draft of an international convention of "Crime in Cyberspace" (see http://conventions.coe.in/treaty/en/projects/cybercrime.htm). Although issues pertaining to jurisdictional concerns are important for criminal activities involving computer networks, such issues are not considered in the present study.

of online behavior inherently immoral or are they considered immoral only because they are declared illegal? Are current forms of punishment for online criminal acts fair? An additional problem in determining whether crimes involving computer technology justify the need for a separate moral category is that many of the ethical issues associated with computer crime also border on distinct, but related, issues involving intellectual property, personal privacy, and free speech in cyberspace.

In addition to the legal and the moral rationales, a third rationale for having a category of computer crime is one that can be viewed as *descriptive* or *informational* in nature. That is, one virtue of having a category of computer crime as a purely descriptive rubric is that it could help us gain a certain level of clarity and precision in analyzing crimes involving the use of computer technology. On pragmatic grounds, having such a category might better enable us to determine which characteristics currently used to link together crimes associated with computers are relevant and which are not. In our effort to provide an adequate definition of computer crime, our primary interest in the present study will be with computer crime as a descriptive, rather than as either a legal or moral, category of crime.

Computer Crime as a Descriptive Category of Crime

At the outset, one might reasonably ask what the value would be in pursuing questions about computer crime from the point of view of a descriptive category. One argument to support the view that having a descriptive category of computer crime is worthwhile can be advanced by appealing to an insight of James Moor's with respect to certain conceptual confusions that have arisen because of the development and use of computer technology. Moor (1985, 1998) points out that computers create "new possibilities" for action which, in turn, give rise to ethical and social issues that are not easily anticipated and that are not always able to be subsumed under existing policies and laws. As a result, we are left with what Moor calls "policy vacuums." Initially, it might seem that we can simply either extend our existing policies or frame new policies to fill these vacuums. But this move will not always work, Moor claims, because computer technology also presents us with certain conceptual vacuums or what he calls "conceptual muddles." Consider, for example, the concept of computer software. Before we can determine whether to have a policy that would grant legal protection to software as a form of property, we must first answer the question: "What exactly is computer software?"

We can apply Moor's model regarding the process of identifying conceptual vacuums that arise because of the use of computer technology in general to identify some of the specific confusions that emerge because of criminal activities made possible by computer technology. So in showing why a separate category of computer crime as a descriptive category is justifiable on pragmatic grounds, we can begin by noting that computers make possible certain kinds of criminal activities that otherwise would not have been possible in the pre-computer era. We can next see why, because of certain conceptual confusions or muddles surrounding computer technology itself, the exact nature of some of the criminal activities involving computer technology is not always clearly understood. We can also see, then, why our existing laws and policies are not always able to be extended to cover adequately at least certain kinds of crimes involving computers. Thus it would seem that having a descriptive category of computer crime might enable us to resolve some of the conceptual confusions and muddles underlying crimes involving computers, which could also eventually help us to frame some coherent normative (legal and ethical) policies regarding computer crime.

Establishing Clear and Coherent Criteria

We next consider which specific criteria would be essential for framing a plausible definition of computer crime. Perhaps a computer crime could, as Forester and Morrison (1994) suggest, be defined as a criminal act in which a computer is used as the "principal tool." On that definition, the theft of a computer hardware device—e.g., the theft of a printer as we considered in an earlier scenario—or, for that matter, the theft of an automobile or a television that also happened to contain a computer component (e.g., a microprocessor), would not count as an instance of computer crime, since a computer is not the principal tool for carrying out the crime. Even though such cases of theft can involve computer technology in some sense—i.e., the presence of one or more computers or computing devices—a computer is not the principal tool used to carry out the criminal act. The same line of reasoning could also be applied to the cases we considered previously involving the breaking and entering into the computer lab as well as vandalizing a computer system in the lab. Forester and Morrison's definition, then, correctly rules out the three examples of crimes involving activities in a computer lab that we considered before.

At first glance, Forester and Morrison's definition of computer crime might seem plausible. But is such a definition satisfactory? Consider the case of someone who uses a personal computer to process his federal income tax returns. Let us call him Bill. In the act of completing his income-tax forms, Bill decides to cheat the government by filling in false information on the forms of his online tax-return program package in his personal computer. In this case, a computer is arguably the principal tool used by Bill to carry out the criminal act. But should this particular criminal act be considered a computer crime? Surely, Bill could have committed the same crime by manually filling out a standard (hardcopy) version of the income-tax forms by using a pencil or pen. That Bill happened to use a computer rather than a pen or pencil in the act of committing the crime is coincident with, but by no means essential to, this particular criminal act. So it would seem that Forester and Morrison's definition of computer crime is not adequate.

Taking into account Moor's point that computer technology creates new possibilities for action—and by extension, new possibilities for criminal acts—as well as Forester and Morrison's point that computer technology provides a tool that can be used to carry out certain kinds of criminal acts, perhaps we can put forth a definition of computer crime that incorporates both insights. It is argued that for a criminal act to count as a genuine instance of computer crime, the act must be one that *can be carried out only through the use of computer technology*. Limiting genuine computer crimes to ones that can be carried out "only through the use of computer technology" would incorporate Moor's insight that new opportunities (including new possibilities for crime) are made possible because of the existence of computer technology. And including in our definition the fact that computer technology provides the means for carrying out certain criminal activities also incorporates Forester and Morrison's insight regarding computer technology as a tool that can be used in certain crimes, while at the same time restricting the range of crimes that will count as genuine computer crimes. For example, our proposed definition would rule out as a genuine instance of computer crime an act in which an individual uses a computer to cheat on his income tax return. It would also preclude as a genuine computer crime a criminal act in which a computer device was used in the act of assaulting someone. That is, neither the criminal act of cheating on one's income-tax return nor the act of assaulting an individual depends on the existence of computer technology to carry out that particular criminal act.

Applying Our Definition to Some Specific Cases

In the introductory section of this essay, we considered three examples of criminal activities involving computers which, intuitively, appeared to be genuine computer crimes and three examples that seemed possibly to border on being genuine computer crimes but were also questionable cases. Because criminal acts such as issuing denial-of-service attacks on commercial Websites, unleashing of the ILOVEYOU virus, and distributing proprietary MP3 files via the Napster Web site each satisfy our newly proposed definition of computer crime, we can now see why each of those activities can be classified as genuine instances of computer crime.

We can also see why those borderline or "questionable" cases also considered in the introductory section—viz., criminal activities involving pedophiles, child pornographers, and (cyber) stalkers using the the Internet to commit their criminal acts—are not, strictly speaking, computer crimes. First, consider the specific case involving pedophile activities on the Internet. Admittedly, a criminal act in which a pedophile uses the Internet to lure young children might initially be thought of as an instance of computer crime. However, pedophiles have engaged in the practice of luring unsuspecting children long before the introduction of computers and the Internet. And although computer technology can be used as a tool—and perhaps even the principal tool—to carry out pedophile-related criminal acts, such crimes can be (and have been) carried out in ways that do not involve computer technology. Pedophiles can, for example, use telephone directories or lists that contain the names of children attending a certain elementary school or day-care facility to assist them in their criminal activities. So, based on the proposed definition of computer crime put forth in this study, cases involving the use of computer technology by pedophiles to lure children would clearly not count as instances of computer crime.

The same reasoning process used in the pedophile example, of course, would apply to the two other questionable examples of criminal acts involving the Internet that were also briefly mentioned in the introductory section of this essay. So we can now see why the examples of distributing child pornography and stalking an ex-lover, each of which also happened to involve the use of computer technology as a tool in carrying out particular criminal acts, are also not genuine instances of computer crimes.

Three Types of Computer Crime: Piracy, Trespass, and Vandalism in Cyberspace

Which specific types of criminal activities will count as genuine instances of computer crime, and how could we catalogue those crimes? Using the criteria suggested previously, one type would include the set of activities involving the use of computer technology to make one or more unauthorized copies of (i.e., "pirating") proprietary digitized information, including software. Another type would include the range of activities involving the use of computer technology by one or more individuals to gain unauthorized access to (i.e., break into) another party's computer system, whether for amusement or for personal gain. And a third type would include those activities in which one or more individuals use computer technology to unleash software programs designed to vandalize a computer system or a computer network by disrupting system activities on a privately owned computer system or on the Internet, or by damaging or destroying either data or system resources. In each of these three types of criminal acts, the crime can be carried out *only* through the use of computer technology. Crimes that fit our definition would fall into one of three distinct categories:

1. *Cyberpiracy*—using computer technology to (a) make one or more unauthorized copies of proprietary information in digital form, including computer software, or (b) download, upload, or exhange unauthorized proprietary information (in digital format) over a computer network.

2. *Cybertrespass*—using computer technology to gain unauthorized access either to (a) an individual's or an organization's computer system, or (b) to a password-protected Web site.

3. *Cybervandalism*—using computer technology to unleash one or more programs that (a) disrupt the flow of electronic information across one or more computer networks, including the Internet, or (b) destroy data resident in a computer or damage a computer system's resources, or both.

Let us briefly consider how each of the three crimes discussed in the introductory section of this study fit into one of these three categories. Recall the three examples: (i) exchanging proprietary MP3 files (containing copyrighted material) on the Internet via the Napster Web site, (ii) unleashing the "ILOVEYOU" computer virus, and (iii) "attacking" commercial Web sites so that they would result in "denial of service" to users. On the model of computer crime advanced in this study, each of these recent incidents falls into one or more of the three distinct types of computer crime articulated. For example, the exchange of MP3 files involved in the Napster case falls under the category of cyberpiracy (category 1), while the unleashing of the ILOVEYOU virus clearly falls under cybervandalism (category 3). Because cyberattacks directed at the targeted commercial Web sites involved the unauthorized use of (i.e., the breaking into) third party computer systems (in universities and other organizations) to send "spurious requests" to the Web sites in question, these attacks would fall into our second category of computer crime—viz., cybertrespass. However, because the attacks on these Web sites also disrupted activities on the Internet by resulting in service being denied to users who attempted to access those particular sites for legitimate purposes, these cyber-attacks would also fall into our third category: cybervandalism. So, it would seem that this particular criminal activity would cut across two of our three categories of computer crime.

Concluding Remarks

The main purpose of this study has been to determine whether a coherent definition of computer crime can be framed. We began by considering whether having a distinct category of computer crime is necessary or even useful. We then noted that arguments for having such a category of crime could be advanced from legal, moral, and descriptive/informational perspectives. Appealing to Moor's insight regarding certain "conceptual muddles" that arise from computer technology, we saw that having a descriptive category of computer crime could help to eliminate some of the conceptual confusions with respect to criminal activities associated with computer technology. Showing that Forester and Morrison's definition was inadequate, we argued that for any criminal act to count as an instance of computer crime, it must be such that it can be carried out *only* through the use of computer technology. In applying that definition, we saw that any genuine instance of a computer crime would typically fall into one of three general categories: cyberpriracy, cybertrespass, and cybervandalism.

We have also noted that computer technology, especially the Internet, has provided a new forum for certain illegal activities which, at first glance, might seem like instances of computer crime. On closer inspection, however, some of these criminal acts turned out not to be computer crimes at all—at least not in the strict sense of the category of criminal activity that we have defended in this essay. We can now see why some of those crimes—e.g., certain crimes involving pedophiles, child pornographers, and cyberstalkers that we briefly described in the introductory section of this essay—are not, strictly speaking, computer crimes, despite the fact that computer technology was a means used for carrying out those criminal acts.

Future cases of criminal activity involving computer technology may cause us to reexamine the tripartite scheme of computer crime advanced in this essay. One recent form of criminal activity that seems potentially to border on computer crime is a criminal act involving the use of digital telephony. Baase (1997) points out that in the use of cellular phones, a popular technique for avoiding charges is "cloning"—i.e., reprogramming one's cellular phone to transmit another customer's number. When true "computer telephony" (the merging of computers and telephones, also known as Internet phones or I-phones) arrives, we may need to reexamine our proposed definition of computer crime and we may discover the need to modify, or possibly even expand on, the three broad categories of activities that we have defended as genuine instances of computer crime. For the time being, however, one virtue of having a working model of computer crime in place is that we can appeal to a consistent set of criteria in determining which illegal activities that involve existing computer technology should and should not count as genuine instances of computer crime.

A principal goal of this essay has been to establish criteria for computer crime as a *descriptive category*. It may turn out that for reasons beyond those considered in this study, lawmakers will decide to frame a definition of computer crime or cyber-crime as a legal category that makes any criminal activity on the Internet a form of cybercrime. In the same way that certain lawmakers and law-enforcement rep-resentatives have supported a legal category of handgun crime in which the mere presence of a handgun in a criminal act would be sufficient for that act to be pros-ecuted as a handgun crime, lawmakers may decide to frame an Internet crime law in such a way that the mere use of Internet technology to carry out a criminal act would be sufficient to have that criminal act prosecuted as an instance of Internet crime or cybercrime.[7] However, our purpose in considering computer crime as a descriptive category, rather than as a legal or as a moral category, has been to gain a clearer understanding of those conditions that separate genuine computer crimes from those criminal activities in which computer technology is: (a) merely pres-ent in some form, or (b) used in a way simply to assist in carrying out a type of crim-inal activity that otherwise could have been committed without the presence or use of computer technology. Such a definition can, I believe, help to eliminate cer-tain confusions we might have with regard to the range of criminal activities involv-ing computer technology.

Acknowledgments

I am grateful to Lloyd Carr, Chuck Huff, Deborah Johnson, and Jim Moor for their helpful comments on an earlier draft of this essay.

References

Baase, Sara (1997). *A Gift of Fire: Social, Legal, and Ethical Issues in Computing*, Upper Saddle River, NJ: Prentice Hall.

Branscomb, Anne W. (1990). "Rogue Computer Programs and Computer Rogues: Tailoring the Punishment to Fit the Crime," *Rutgers Computer and Technology Law Journal*, Vol. 16, pp. 1–6.

Forester, Tom and Perry Morrison (1994). *Computer Ethics: Cautionary Tales and Ethical Dilemmas in Computing*. 2nd ed. Cambridge, MA: MIT Press.

Gotterbarn, Don. (1991). "Computer Ethics: Responsibility Regained," *National Forum: The Phi Kappa Phi Journal*. Reprinted in *Computing, Ethics and Social Values*. Edited by D. G. Johnson and H. Nissenbaum (1995). Englewood Cliffs, NJ: Prentice Hall, pp. 18–24.

Johnson, Deborah G. (1985). *Computer Ethics*. Englewood Cliffs, NJ: Prentice Hall.

---

[7] Also, lawmakers might wish to frame a cybercrime law in which a subset of crimes assisted by computer technology would also be included. For example, lawmakers might elect to group certain crimes involving the use of computer technology, such as those involving pedophilia, cyber-stalking, drug trafficking, and child pornography, into crimes that can be prosecuted as cybercrimes. Even though these four crimes, each of which is enhanced by computer technology, do not fit our definition of a pure computer crime, it could be argued that each crime involves the use of computer technology in ways that certain crimes that involve comput-er technology only incidentally—e.g., crimes involving theft, break-ins, or vandalism in a computer lab—do not. That is, computer technology can assist pedophiles, drug traffickers, pornographers, and stalkers in significant ways that enhance the committing of those crimes, especially in terms of both ease and scale. However, in the case of other crimes that happen to involve the mere presence of computer technology—e.g., the examples of crime involving the computer lab—the role of computer technology in car-rying out the particular criminal act would seem to be merely accidental or incidental to crimes involving theft, breaking and enter-ing, or vandalism.

Johnson, Deborah G. (1994). *Computer Ethics*. 2nd ed. Englewood Cliffs, NJ: Prentice Hall.

Johnson, Deborah G. and Helen Nissenbaum, editors (1995). *Computing, Ethics and Social Values*, Englewood Cliffs, NJ: Prentice Hall.

Levy, Steven (1984). *Hackers: Heroes of the Computer Revolution*. Garden City, NY: Doubleday.

Moor, James H. (1985). "What is Computer Ethics?" *Metaphilosophy*, Vol. 16, October, pp. 266–275.

Moor, James H. (1998). "Reason, Relativity, and Responsibility in Computer Ethics," *Computers and Society*, Vol. 28, No. 1, pp. 14–21.

Tavani, Herman T. (1999). "Social and Ethical Aspects of Information Technology," *Encyclopedia of Electrical and Electronics Engineering* (Vol. 19). Edited by J. G. Webster. New York: John Wiley and Sons Publishers, pp. 413–425.

Tavani, Herman T. (2000). "Privacy and Security." Chap. 4 in *Internet Ethics*. Edited by D. Langford. New York: St. Martin's Press.

Wessells, Michael G. (1990). *Computer, Self, and Society*. Englewood Cliffs, NJ: Prentice Hall.

Terrorism or Civil Disobedience: Toward a Hacktivist Ethic

Mark Manion and Abby A. Goodrum

Introduction

In this era of global commerce via the Internet, strikes against the hegemony of bureaucratic capitalism and the commercialization of the Internet will inevitably be carried out on the World Wide Web. In fact, recent proliferation of hacking activity has shocked the commercial Internet world. On February 8, 2000, hackers attacked Yahoo, Amazon, eBay, CNN and Buy.com, closing them for several hours. Through "denial of service" attacks originating from dozens of independent computers, the sites were flooded with millions of simultaneous requests. This increase in fake service requests effectively blocked legitimate users from accessing the sites.

These hacks have led to widespread speculation regarding the motivation of the perpetrators. Are they mere nuisance attacks perpetrated by malicious teenagers, more serious acts of cyberterrorism, or evidence of growing outrage over an increasingly commodified Internet? Although at present no individuals or groups have officially claimed responsibility, MSNBC reported receipt of an 18-page letter claiming responsibility by an individual who angrily criticized the sites for their "capitalization of the Internet" (Kirby, 2000). Numerous reports in the popular press have portrayed the hackers as vandals, terrorists, and saboteurs, yet no one seems to have considered the possibility that this might be the work of electronic political activists or "hacktivists."

Perhaps these attacks are evidence of a new form of civil disobedience, which unites the talents of the computer hacker with the social consciousness of the political activist. Adapting a variation of civil disobedience, with its practices of "trespass" and "blockade" to the electronic age, participants in what has been called electronic civil disobedience, or hacktivism, can attack the Web sites of any individual, corporation, or nation that is deemed responsible for oppressing the ethical, social, or political rights of others. Through an investigation of hacktivism, this essay seeks to make clear the growing tensions between the cooperative and liberal ideology of the originators of the "electronic frontier," speaking in the name of social justice, political decentralization, and freedom of information, and the more powerful counteracting moves to reduce the Internet to one grand global "electronic marketplace."

Hacktivism has the potential to play an active and constructive role in the overcoming of political injustice, to educate, inform, and be a genuine agent of positive political and social change. However, there is the fear that cyber-activism could reduce to more radical and violent forms of cyber-terrorism (Arquilla & Ronfeldt, 1993). How governments and societies react to this new form of social activism has not been sufficiently addressed in the computer ethics literature. Researchers concerned with ethical issues in computing, policy makers, and computer professionals must come to terms with the complex set of issues surrounding the potential power of hacktivism.

Background

Hacktivism is defined as the (sometimes) clandestine use of computer hacking to help advance political causes. Hacktivist groups such as the Electronic Disturbance Theater, the Cult of the Dead Cow, and the Hong Kong Blondes have used electronic civil disobedience to help advance the Zapatista rebellion in Mexico, protest nuclear testing at India's Bhabba Atomic Research Center, attack Indonesian Government Web sites over the occupation of East Timor, as well as protest anti-democratic crackdowns in China. In addition, hacktivism has been used to inveigh against the corporate domination of telecommunications and mass media, the rapid expansion of dataveillance, and the hegemonic intrusion of the "consumer culture" into the private lives of average citizens.

These concerns give rise to two institutional forces that hacktivist protests aim to confront: the commodification of the Internet at the hands of corporate profiteers and violations of human rights at the hands of oppressive governments. Hacktivism thus poses a potential threat at two levels: the private industry/intellectual property level and the national government/national security level. Both of these issues will be discussed in this paper.

Electronic Civil Disobedience

Civil disobedience entails the peaceful breaking of unjust laws. It does not condone violent or destructive acts against its enemies, focusing instead on nonviolent means to expose wrongs, raise awareness, and prohibit the implementation of perceived unethical laws by individuals, organizations, corporations, or governments. In a civil society, it is the responsibility of all ethical individuals to take a stand against oppression, inequality, and injustice (Honderich, 1997). Civil disobedience is a technique of resistance and protest whose purpose is to achieve social or political change by drawing attention to problems and influencing public opinion. Breaking specific laws, which are unjust, constitutes *direct* acts of civil disobedience. *Symbolic* acts of civil disobedience are accomplished by drawing attention to a problem indirectly. Sit-ins and other forms of blockade and trespass are examples of *symbolic* acts of civil disobedience.

The Internet has created a brave new world of digital activism by providing forums for organizing, communicating, publishing, and taking direct action. The use of the computer as a tool of civil disobedience has been termed Electronic Civil Disobedience (ECD) (Wray, 1998). Electronic civil disobedience comes in many forms, ranging from conservative acts such as sending email and publishing Web sites, to breaking into computer systems. A distinction must be made between the use of computers to *support* ECD and the use of computers as an *act* of ECD. If a U.S. citizen wishes to speak out against the government's actions in Kosovo, it is legal to publish a Web site or host mailing lists or chat rooms for this purpose. This activity does not constitute an act of civil disobedience, electronic or otherwise. These types of activity are usually referred to as "electronic activism," which uses the Internet in fully legitimate ways to publish information, to coordinate effective action, and to directly lobby policy makers. Running a computer program such as FloodNet, however, that posts the reload command to a Web site hundreds of times a minute constitutes an act of symbolic ECD since the intended aim of such programs is to create an electronic disturbance akin to a sit-in or blockade.

The effect of hundreds of persons reloading a targeted page on the Internet thousands of times effectively blocks entrance by outsiders and may even shut down the server, as occurred in the attacks on the commercial Web sites of Yahoo, Amazon, etc. In 1998, pro-Zapatista activists took this kind of action against Mexican government Web sites (Cleaver, 1999). This is easily seen as a symbolic act of ECD because it tries to draw attention to a perceived violation of rights, rather than attacking the suspected violator(s) directly. The purpose of most ECD is to disrupt the flow of information into and out of institutional computer systems. The point is not to destroy information or systems but to block access temporarily. This results in virtual sit-ins and virtual blockades. Since institutions today are no longer localized in physical structures but exist in the decentralized zones of cyberspace, electronic blockades can cause financial stress that physical blockades cannot (Critical Art Ensemble, 1994).

The changing nature of authoritative and repressive power has necessitated qualitative changes in resistance to this power. Power/Capital, having constituted itself in a new electronic form in cyberspace, requires that opposition movements have to invent new strategies and tactics that counter this new "nomadic" power of capital. This entails that certain old ways of trespass and blockade—such as street demonstrations—are being modified through electronic civil disobedience, or hacktivism, to meet the new conditions (Critical Art Ensemble, 1996).

Hacktivism and Electronic Civil Disobedience

Nothing has fired debate about ECD so heatedly as the issue of hacktivism. The central question is whether hacking can reasonably be defined as an act of civil disobedience. Now the refusal to obey governmental commands, even if it entails breaking the law, is often morally sanctioned if certain preconditions are met. Even though philosophers often disagree as to when the breaking of a law actually constitutes an act of civil disobedience, most would agree on the following set of core principles as forming the necessary conditions, and hence ethical justification, for acts considered civilly disobedient. They are:

- No damage done to persons or property
- Non-violent
- Not for personal profit
- Ethical motivation—i.e., the strong conviction that a law is unjust, unfair, or to the extreme detriment of the common good
- Willingness to accept personal responsibility for outcome of actions

Are acts of hacktivism consistent with the philosophy of civil disobedience? In order for hacking to qualify as an act of civil disobedience, hackers must be clearly motivated by ethical concerns, be non-violent, and be ready to accept the repercussions of their actions. Examined in this light, the hack by Eugene Kashpureff clearly constitutes an act of ECD. Kashpureff usurped traffic from InterNIC to protest domain name policy. He did this non-anonymously and went to jail as a result. Further evidence of ethical motivation for hacktivism can also be seen in the messages left behind at hacked sites (Harmon, 1998):

- "China's people have no rights at all, never mind human rights..."
- "Save Kashmir" overlaid with the words "massacre" and "extra-judicial execution."
- "Free East Timor" with hypertext links to Web sites describing Indonesian human rights abuses in the former Portuguese colony.

In order to justify hacktivism's direct action praxis and to legitimate its theoretical foundations, two things must be demonstrated. First, it must be shown that hacktivism is *not* the work of curious teenagers with advanced technical expertise and a curiosity for infiltrating large computer networks for mere intellectual challenge or sophomoric bravado. Moreover, the justification of hacktivism entails demonstrating that its practitioners are neither "crackers"—those who break into systems for profit or vandalism (Anonymous, 1998), nor are they cyberterrorists—those who use computer technology with the intention of causing grave harm such as loss of life, severe economic losses, or destruction of critical infrastructure (Denning, 1999). Hacktivism must be shown to be ethically motivated. Second, politicized hacking must be shown to be some form of civil disobedience—a form of civil disobedience that is morally justified. In order to determine the motivations of hacktivists, one place to look is what hacktivists *themselves* say is their motivation.

On October 12, 1998, the Web site of Mexican president Erenesto Zedillo was attacked. From all accounts, the Zedillo hack was not the work of bored teens. It was a political act, according to the Electronic Disturbance Theatre, to "demonstrate continued resistance to centuries of colonization, genocide, and racism in the western hemisphere and throughout the world" (Harmon, 1998). Earlier, in August of the same year, the hacktivist group "X-Ploit" hacked the Web site of Mexico's finance ministry, defacing it by replacing the contents with the face of the revolutionary hero Emiliano Zapata, in sympathy with the Zapatista rebellion in the Chiapas region of southern Mexico. These acts are political protests, which draw attention to what is perceived to be grave social injustice. The reason for these actions is clear: They are motivated by a socio-economic system that perpetuates discrimination, racism, and economic inequality, not the mere thrill and challenge of breaking into computer networks for fun.

In June of 1998, the hacktivist group "MilwOrm" hacked India's Bhabba Atomic Research Centre to protest against recent nuclear tests. Later, in July of that year, "MilwOrm" and the group "Astray Lumberjacks" orchestrated an unprecedented mass hack of more than 300 sites around the world, replacing web pages with antinuclear statements and images of mushroom clouds. Not surprisingly, the published slogan of MilwOrm reads: "Putting the power back in the hands of the people" (Hesseldahl, 1999). These examples seem to be motivated by belief in the positive forces of democracy and freedom rather than the mere thrill of vandalism or the nihilism of "cyberterrorism."

Mail-bombs were delivered and several Chinese government Web sites were hacked to protest the targeting of Chinese and Indonesian citizens for torture, rape, and looting during the anti-Suharto riot in May of 1998 (Hesseldhal, 1999). On August 1, the Portuguese group "Kaotik Team" hacked 45 Indonesian government Web sites, altering web pages to include calling for full autonomy of East Timor and the cessation of the harsh military crackdown on dissidents (Hesseldhal, 1999). Again, fighting for social justice and human rights is motivated by ethics, not anarchy. Many other hacktivist activities can be sited to demonstrate the ethical motivation behind this new form of political activism.

These messages, and many others like them, demonstrate a striking change from hacker messages of the past. Prior hacks have had little if any socio-political content and bear a closer resemblance to "tagging" and other forms of boasting graffiti. There has been a certain juvenile style to messages left by hackers in the past. The hacks listed above, however, represent a new breed of hacker, one who is clearly motivated by the advancement of ethical concerns and who believes such actions should be considered a legitimate form of (electronic) civil disobedience.

Hacktivism and Cyberterrorism

If hacktivism can be defined as an act of electronic civil disobedience, then the punitive outcomes must be brought into alignment with other forms of civil disobedience. Traditional penalties for civil disobedience are mild compared to penalties for hacking. Penalties for hacktivism are meted out with the same degree of force as for hacking in general, regardless of the motivation for the hack or the political content of messages left at hacked sites. Most governments do not recognize hacking as a political activity, and the penalties for breaking into computers can be extreme (Jaconi, 1999). For example, the hack of China's "Human Rights" Web site by the Hong Kong Blondes, attacks on Indonesian Government Web sites regarding policy in Kashmir, attacks on India's nuclear weapons research center Web sites to protest nuclear testing, as well as the hacks on the commercial Web sites of Yahoo, CNN, etc. are all subject to felony prosecution if apprehended. All of these examples provide convincing evidence in support of our thesis that hacktivism should be considered a legitimate form of civil disobedience, and not the work of "cybervandals" or "cyberterrorists." Under U.S. law, terrorism is defined as an act of violence for the purpose of intimidating or coercing a government or civilian population. Hacktivism clearly does not fall into this category, as it is fundamentally non-violent.

Since many acts of hacktivism have been perpetuated against government Web sites, however, hacktivism is increasingly being equated with acts of information warfare and cyberterrorism (Kovacich 1997, Furnell & Warren 1999). In August of 1998, the Center for Intrusion Control was established by a coalition of various government agencies to respond to these "cyber-warfare threats" (Glave 1998b). Similarly, organizations such as RAND and the National Security Agency (NSA) have categorically denied the existence of hacktivism as an act of civil disobedience and repeatedly refer to all acts of hacking as cyberwar or cyberterrorism in an attempt to push for stronger penalties for hacking, regardless of ethical motivations (Bowers 1998, Gompert 1998).

In order to determine the kinds and range of threats to its critical infrastructures posed by possible cyberterrorists, the U.S. government established the President's Commission on Critical Infrastructure Protection (PCCIP) in 1996. The PCCIP findings have led to the development of the National Infrastructure Protection Center (NIPC), the Critical Infrastructure Assurance Office (CIA), the National Infrastructure Assurance Council (NIAC), and the Joint Task-Force Computer Network Defense (JTF-CND), established by the Department of Defense. The development and findings of these research centers imply that the threat posed by cyberterrorism is very real. That much is clear. However, it is a mistake to identify hacktivism with cyberterrorism. As we have established above, acts of hacktivism are more akin to acts of civil disobedience than to acts of terrorism, and it is important to keep this distinction clear.

In fact, potential acts of cyberterrorism are explicitly condemned by hacktivists. During a December 1998 press conference, one member of a hacktivist group, which calls itself the Legion of the Underground (LoU), declared "cyberwar" on the information infrastructures of China and Iraq. This declaration of war prompted a coalition of hacktivist groups to condemn the "declaration of war" as "irresponsible." In a "Joint Statement by 2600, The Chaos Computer Club, The Cult of the Dead Cow, !Hispahack, L0pht Heavy Industries, Phrack and Pulhas," the leaders of the hacktivist community denounced the LoU declaration of war, saying

> We strongly oppose any attempt to use the power of hacking to threaten or destroy the information infrastructure of any country, for any reason. Declaring 'war' against anyone, any group of people, or any nation is a most deplorable act...this has nothing to do with hacktivism or the hacker ethic and is nothing a hacker can be proud of (Hackernews, 12/29/98).

This immediately prompted a quick response from the leaders of LoU who issued a statement saying that the declaration of war did not represent the position of the group. The letter states:

> The LoU does not support the damaging of other nations' computers, network or systems in any way, nor will the LoU use their skills, abilities or connections to take any actions against the systems, network or computers in China or Iraq which may damage or hinder in any way their operations. (Hackernews, 01/7/99).

Why is it, then, that a growing number of experts refuse to make this distinction, and insist on conflating hacktivism and cyberterrorism? It may be that describing hacktivists as criminals helps entrench a certain conception of, and control over, intellectual property, and obscures the larger critique about the ownership of information, and the legal system's need to protect the powerful economic interests of corporations attempting to dominate and completely commercialize the Internet. Moreover, labeling the hacktivist as a national security threat provides further legitimation for the erasure of individual privacy at the hands of the national security state, which compiles and stores vast databases on hundreds of thousands of citizens each year. The demonization of the hacker may also be an attempt to obscure the violation of our privacy at the hands of corporations. As one critic put it,

> Through the routine gathering of information about transactions, consumer preferences, and creditworthiness, a harvest of information about an individual's whereabouts and movements, tastes, desires, contacts, friends, associates, and patterns of work and recreation become available in the form of dossiers sold on the tradable information market, or is endlessly convertible into other forms of intelligence through computer matching. Advanced pattern recognition technologies facilitate the process of surveillance, while data encryption protects it from public accountability (Ross, 1998).

Hence, one rationalization for the vilification of hacktivism is the need for the power elite to rewrite property law in order to contain the effects of the new information technologies. As a result of the newly evolving intellectual property laws, information and knowledge can now be held as capital. Since new information technology supports easy reproduction of information, the existence of these laws effectively curtails the widest possible spread of this new form of wealth. In addition, unlike material objects, information can be shared widely without running out. As two experts put it

> Intellectual property is not a tangible, material entity. It is nothing more than a volatile pattern of electrons arrayed in patterns of open and closed gates to

form intelligible numerical or textual symbols. Information, documents, and data reside inside computers in a form that can be 'stolen' without ever being removed, indeed without ever being touched by a would-be thief, or depriving the 'owner' from still using and profiting off of the 'property' (Michalowski and Pfuhl, 1991).

Although the information inside of computers is clearly of value, the form of this value is both intangible and novel. According to Michalowski and Pfuhl, its character as "property" remained legally ambiguous until a rapid proliferation of computer crime laws took place in order to create the legal environment that helped define and delimit the debate over the nature of intellectual property. These laws and rulings ultimately served to protect the immediate financial interests of the corporate techno-elite and directed the state to protect the profit potential of telecommunications industries, financial investors, and entrepreneurs capitalizing on the Internet.

Ironically, the rapid proliferation of computer laws during the 1980s, which saw 47 states enact computer crime laws, as well as two Congressional pieces of computer crime legislation, which entered the legal system at the same time, resulted in relatively few arrests or prosecutions. For example, "Operation Sundial," the largest Secret Service sting on suspected hackers, which took place during the first week of May, 1990, led to no serious charges. A few hackers pled guilty and paid a total of $233, 000 in fines, and spent 14 months in jail (Halbert, 1997). This rapid criminalization of computer abuse represents, moreover, an exception to the gradual and reformist nature of typical law formation in common law jurisdiction (Hollinger and Lanza-Kaduce, 1998). Michalowski and Pfuhl conclude from this that "the violations of computer security posed a broad challenge to the hegemonic construction of property and authority relations, and it was this challenge, more than the concrete losses resulting from unauthorized computer access, that created a climate of fear about computer crime that led to the swift and non-controversial passage of computer crime laws" (Michalowski and Pfuhl, 1991).

The power elite, often synergistically intertwined with the design and operation of information technologies, will always come to the aid and defense of technologies of control, making revolt difficult and reform hard. Intellectual property laws attest to this, as do the excessively stringent laws against hacktivism. Nevertheless, if we say we support civil disobedience as a legitimate form of social protest, then we must support the computerization of these efforts as well. This means bringing penalties for hacktivism, or electronic civil disobedience, in line with penalties for traditional mechanisms used for the breaking of what are perceived to be unjust laws.

Toward a Hacktivist Ethic

Every technology affords opposing possibilities toward emancipation or domination, and information technology is no different. The new information technologies are often portrayed as the utopian promise of total human emancipation and freedom. However, the promise of freedom from work, e-democracy, and global community, once hailed as the hallmarks of the computer revolution, are nowhere to be found. As critics are quick to point out, the only entities that seem to largely benefit from the Internet are large transnational business corporations.

For such critics, advanced information technology threatens to turn into an Orwellian nightmare of totalitarian domination and control, a dystopia of complete repression of free thought. They remind us that the Internet is quickly becoming subordinated to the pecuniary interests of the techno-elite, which merely pays lip service to the growth of electronic communities and participatory democracy. In reality, these interests are devoted to shutting down the anarchy of the Net in favor of virtualized commercial exchange. Hence, the power elite must destroy the public cyber-sphere for its own survival. This may account for the vilification of hacktivists, as well as why the charges against hacktivism are so high.

As is well known, however, the lifeblood of the hacker ethic has always been the freedom of information and the full democratization of the public sphere. The core principles of the hacker ethic were spelled out in Steven Levy's book, *Hackers: Heroes of the Computer Revolution* (Levy, 1984). Three of these principles are relevant here. They are:

1. Access to computers—and anything that might teach you something about the way the world works—should be unlimited and total. Always yield to the Hands-On Imperative!
2. All information should be free
3. Mistrust Authority—Promote Decentralization

Hacktivists prioritize freedom of information and are suspicious of centralized control over, or private ownership of, information. Hackers question why a few corporations can own and sell huge databases of information about others, as well as control information helpful to the public at large. Hackers are frustrated to discover that their coveted "electronic agora," a true marketplace for the free-play of ideas, which was the original ideal behind the formation of the Internet, has been invaded and taken over by avaricious and enterprising entrepreneurs who prefer dollars to the free-flow of information and knowledge. In sum, this ethic puts hackers in direct confrontation with the commercial-industrial complex who wish to own and control the Internet.

One of the most powerful positions against the panoptical intentions of the "Captains of Technology" is demonstrating that their system does not work. Every successful hack in some way reinforces the popular perception that the rise of the total panoptic surveillance society is not inevitable. Hence, the hacker ethic, libertarian and anarchist in its right-to-know principles and its advocacy of decentralized technology, is a principled attempt to challenge the tendency to use technology to form information elites.

The debate over the control of intellectual property demands that we address issues of social justice, such as wealth distribution and equality of opportunity. Politically, the resistance to corporate domination of the Internet must force not only the question of privacy and property, but it must also place the critique of the technological society itself into the center of pubic consciousness and debate. Hacktivist activities put these issues of techno-control on the political agenda by performing acts of electronic civil disobedience.

Furthermore, resistance to political oppression and corporate manipulation must be embedded in a well-articulated theory, one that is morally informed and widely shared. Movements acting out of outrage often dissipate. They need to be durable and sustain a commitment, lasting through adversities of repression. This leads to the necessity of creating a form of technocultural activism that can bring to reality the ideals of human emancipation. Activism today is no longer a case of putting bodies on the picket line; it requires putting minds and virtual bodies "on-line." This is the promise of hacktivism, the fusion of the political consciousness of the activist with the technical expertise of the computer "hacker."

Conclusion

Hacktivism is in its infancy, but, given the ubiquity and democratizing possibility of the Internet, we will certainly bear witness to the movement's growing pains and increasing maturity. One thing is sure, however. Incidents of cyberactivism are on the rise and will continue to be on the rise in the near future.

Never in the long and storied history of political and social activism have dissidents had at their disposal a tool as far-reaching and potentially effective as the Internet. Sadly, this inherently civil strategy of ECD is being deliberately and officially misconstrued through mis-information as cyberterrorism, which it is clearly not. Steps must be taken to separate political direct action in cyberspace from organized criminality or cyberterrorism.

When is it legitimate to practice direct action protest on the Internet? Some will inevitably argue that electronic civil disobedience is never justifiable, while others will argue that it is always justified. What are the limits of political protest in cyberspace? How far can activists go without infringing on the legitimate rights of the people and institutions against whom they are protesting? These questions demand a more extensive argument that extends beyond the scope of this essay. One thing is clear, however. In order for hacktivism to become a legitimate form of social protest, it must be provided sound ethical foundations. This, in turn, means expanding the ethical justification of civil disobedience to include acts of hacktivism.

References

Anonymous, (1998). "The language of hacking," *Management Review* 87 (9), pp. 18–21.

Arquilla, J. and Ronfeldt, D. (1993). "Cyberwar is coming," *Comparative Strategy*, Volume 12, no. 2, 141–165.

Bowers, S. (1998). "Information warfare: the computer revolution is altering how future wars will be conducted," *Armed Forces Journal International*, August, pp. 38–49.

Cleaver, H. (1998). "The Zapatistas and the electronic fabric of struggle," www.eco.utexas.edu/faculty/Cleaver/zaps.htm (accessed 5/18/99)

Critical Art Ensemble (1996*). Electronic civil disobedience and other unpopular ideas*. Brooklyn, NY: Autonomedia.

Critical Art Ensemble (1994). *The electronic disturbance*. Brooklyn, NY: Autonomedia.

Denning, Dorothy (1999). "Activism, Hacktivism, and Cyberterrorism: The Internet as a Tool for Influencing Foreign Policy," paper presented at the Internet and International Systems: Information Technology and American Foreign Policy Decisionmaking Workshop, Georgetown University, Washington, D.C.

Furnell, S. and Warren, M. (1999). "Computer hacking and cyberterrorism: The real threats in the new millennium," *Computers & Security*, 18, 28–34.

Glave, J. (1998). "Hacker raises stakes in DOD attacks," *Wired News,* available at: http://www.wired-news.com

Gompert, D. (1998). "National security in the information age," *Naval War College Review*, 51 (4), pp. 22–41.

Hackernews, available at http://www.hackernews. com/archive.html

Halbert, D. (1997). "Discourses of danger and the computer hacker," *The Information Society*, 13, 361–374.

Harmon, A. (1998). "Hacktivists of all persuasions take their struggle to the web," *The New York Times*, October 31, 1998, page 1 column 5.

Hesseldhal, Arik (1999). "Hacking for Human Rights?," *Wired News,* 21 May. Available at: http://www.wirednews.com/news/news/politics/story/13693.html.

Hollinger, R. and Lanza-Kaduce, L. (1988). "The process of criminalization: The case of computer crime laws," *Criminology* 26 (1), pp. 101–26.

Honderich, T. (1997). "Hierarchic democracy and the necessity of mass civil disobedience," in Bontekoe, R. ed. *Justice and democracy: cross-cultural perspectives*. University of Hawaii Press: Honolulu.

Jaconi, J. (1999). Federal cybercrime law, Section 1030 "Computer Fraud & Abuse Act," www.antion-line.com (accessed 6/17/99)

Kirby, Carie (2000). "Net hackers strike again," *The San Francisco Chronicle*, February 9, p. A1.

Kovacich, G. (1997). "Information warfare and the information systems security professional," *Computers & Security*, 16, 14–24.

Levy, Stephen (1984). *Hackers: computer heroes of the computer revolution*, New York: Delta Trade Paperbacks.

Michalowski, R. and Pfuhl, E. (1991). "Technology, property and law: The case of computer crime," *Crime Law and Social Change* 15 (3), pp. 255–275.

Ross, Andrew (1998). "Hacking away at the counterculture," in *Technoculture*, Penley and Ross. Eds. Minneapolis: University of Minnesota Press.

Wray, S. (1998). "Electronic civil disobedience and the word wide web of hacktivism: a mapping of extraparliamentarian direct action net politics," available at: http://www.nyu.edu/projects/wray/wwwhack.html

Cyberterrorism

Dorothy E. Denning

Cyberterrorism is the convergence of terrorism and cyberspace. It is generally understood to mean unlawful attacks and threats of attack against computers, networks, and the information stored therein when done to intimidate or coerce a government or its people in furtherance of political or social objectives. Further, to qualify as cyberterrorism, an attack should result in violence against persons or property, or at least cause enough harm to generate fear. Attacks that lead to death or bodily injury, explosions, plane crashes, water contamination, or severe economic loss would be examples. Serious attacks against critical infrastructures could be acts of cyberterrorism, depending on their impact. Attacks that disrupt nonessential services or that are mainly a costly nuisance would not.

Cyberspace is constantly under assault. Cyber spies, thieves, saboteurs, and thrill seekers break into computer systems, steal personal data and trade secrets, vandalize Web sites, disrupt service, sabotage data and systems, launch computer viruses and worms, conduct fraudulent transactions, and harass individuals and companies. These attacks are facilitated with increasingly powerful and easy-to-use software tools, which are readily available for free from thousands of Web sites on the Internet.

Many of the attacks are serious and costly. The recent ILOVEYOU virus and variants, for example, was estimated to have hit tens of millions of users and cost billions of dollars in damage. The February 2000 denial-of-service attacks against Yahoo, CNN, eBay, and other e-commerce Web sites was estimated to have caused over a billion in losses. It also shook the confidence of business and individuals in e-commerce.

Some attacks are conducted in furtherance of political and social objectives, as the following examples illustrate:

- In 1996, a computer hacker allegedly associated with the White Supremacist movement temporarily disabled a Massachusetts ISP and damaged part of the ISP's record keeping system. The ISP had attempted to stop the hacker from sending out worldwide racist messages under the ISP's name. The hacker signed off with the threat, "you have yet to see true electronic terrorism. This is a promise."

This essay was originally presented as testimony before the Special Oversight Panel on Terrorism, Committee on Armed Services, United States House of Representatives, May 23, 2000. Copyright © 2000 by Dorothy E. Denning. Reprinted by permission.

- In 1998, Spanish protestors bombarded the Institute for Global Communications (IGC) with thousands of bogus e-mail messages. E-mail was tied up and undeliverable to the ISP's users, and support lines were tied up with people who couldn't get their mail. The protestors also spammed IGC staff and member accounts, clogged their Web page with bogus credit card orders, and threatened to employ the same tactics against organizations using IGC services. They demanded that IGC stop hosting the Web site for the Euskal Herria Journal, a New York-based publication supporting Basque independence. Protestors said IGC supported terrorism because a section on the Web pages contained materials on the terrorist group ETA, which claimed responsibility for assassinations of Spanish political and security officials, and attacks on military installations. IGC finally relented and pulled the site because of the "mail bombings."

- In 1998, ethnic Tamil guerrillas swamped Sri Lankan embassies with 800 e-mails a day over a two-week period. The messages read "We are the Internet Black Tigers and we're doing this to disrupt your communications." Intelligence authorities characterized it as the first known attack by terrorists against a country's computer systems.

- During the Kosovo conflict in 1999, NATO computers were blasted with e-mail bombs and hit with denial-of-service attacks by hacktivists protesting the NATO bombings. In addition, businesses, public organizations, and academic institutes received highly politicized virus-laden e-mails from a range of Eastern European countries, according to reports. Web defacements were also common. After the Chinese Embassy was accidentally bombed in Belgrade, Chinese hacktivists posted messages such as "We won't stop attacking until the war stops!" on U.S. government Web sites.

- Since December 1997, the Electronic Disturbance Theater (EDT) has been conducting Web sit-ins against various sites in support of the Mexican Zapatistas. At a designated time, thousands of protestors point their browsers to a target site using software that floods the target with rapid and repeated download requests. EDT's software has also been used by animal rights groups against organizations said to abuse animals. Electrohippies, another group of hacktivists, conducted Web sit-ins against the WTO when they met in Seattle in late 1999. These sit-ins all require mass participation to have much effect, and thus are more suited to use by activists than by terrorists.

While the above incidents were motivated by political and social reasons, whether they were sufficiently harmful or frightening to be classified as cyberterrorism is a judgement call. To the best of my knowledge, no attack so far has led to violence or injury to persons, although some may have intimidated their victims. Both EDT and the Electrohippies view their operations as acts of civil disobedience, analogous to street protests and physical sit-ins, not as acts of violence or terrorism. This is an important distinction. Most activists, whether participating in the Million Mom's March or a Web sit-in, are not terrorists. My personal view is that the threat of cyberterrorism has been mainly theoretical, but it is something to watch and take reasonable precautions against.

To understand the potential threat of cyberterrorism, two factors must be considered: first, whether there are targets that are vulnerable to attack that could lead to violence or severe harm, and second, whether there are actors with the capability and motivation to carry them out.

Looking first at vulnerabilities, several studies have shown that critical infrastructures are potentially vulnerable to cyberterrorist attack. Eligible Receiver, a "no notice" exercise conducted by the Department of Defense in 1997 with support from NSA red teams, found the power grid and emergency 911 systems had weaknesses that could be exploited by an adversary using only publicly available tools on the Internet. Although neither of these systems were actually attacked, study members concluded that service on these systems could be disrupted. Also in 1997, the President's Commission on Critical Infrastructure Protection issued its report warning that through mutual dependencies and interconnectedness, critical infrastructures could be vulnerable in new ways, and that vulnerabilities were steadily increasing, while the costs of attack were decreasing.

Although many of the weaknesses in computerized systems can be corrected, it is effectively impossible to eliminate all of them. Even if the technology itself offers good security, it is frequently configured or used in ways that make it open to attack. In addition, there is always the possibility of insiders, acting alone or in concert with other terrorists, misusing their access capabilities. According to Russia's Interior Ministry Col. Konstantin Machabeli, the state-run gas monopoly, Gazprom, was hit by hackers who collaborated with a Gazprom insider. The hackers were said to have used a Trojan horse to gain control of the central switchboard that controls gas flows in pipelines, although Gazprom, the world's largest natural gas producer and the largest gas supplier to Western Europe, refuted the report.

Consultants and contractors are frequently in a position where they could cause grave harm. This past March, Japan's Metropolitan Police Department reported that a software system they had procured to track 150 police vehicles, including unmarked cars, had been developed by the Aum Shinryko cult, the same group that gassed the Tokyo subway in 1995, killing 12 people and injuring 6,000 more. At the time of the discovery, the cult had received classified tracking data on 115 vehicles. Further, the cult had developed software for at least 80 Japanese firms and 10 government agencies. They had worked as subcontractors to other firms, making it almost impossible for the organizations to know who was developing the software. As subcontractors, the cult could have installed Trojan horses to launch or facilitate cyberterrorist attacks at a later date. Fearing a Trojan horse of their own, last February, the State Department sent an urgent cable to about 170 embassies asking them to remove software, which they belatedly realized had been written by citizens of the former Soviet Union.

If we take as given that critical infrastructures are vulnerable to a cyberterrorist attack, then the question becomes whether there are actors with the capability and motivation to carry out such an operation. While many hackers have the knowledge, skills, and tools to attack computer systems, they generally lack the motivation to cause violence or severe economic or social harm. Conversely, terrorists who are motivated to cause violence seem to lack the capability or motivation to cause that degree of damage in cyberspace.

Terrorists do use cyberspace to facilitate traditional forms of terrorism such as bombings. They put up Web sites to spread their messages and recruit supporters, and they use the Internet to communicate and coordinate action. However, there are few indications that they are pursuing cyberterrorism, either alone or in conjunction with acts of physical violence. In February 1998, Clark Staten, executive director of the Emergency Response & Research Institute in Chicago, testified before the Senate Judiciary Committee Subcommittee on Technology, Terrorism, and Government Information that it was believed that "members of some Islamic extremist organizations have been attempting to develop a 'hacker network' to support their computer activities and even engage in offensive information warfare attacks in the future." And in November, the Detroit News reported that a member of the militant Indian separatist group Harkat-ul-Ansar had tried to buy military software from hackers who had stolen it from Department of Defense computers they had penetrated. The Provisional Irish Republican Army employed the services of contract hackers to penetrate computers in order to acquire home addresses of law enforcement and intelligence officers, but the data was used to draw up plans to kill the officers in a single "night of the long knives" if the British government did not meet terms for a new cease-fire. As this case illustrates, terrorists may use hacking as a way of acquiring intelligence in support of physical violence, even if they do not use it to wreak havoc in cyberspace.

In August 1999, the Center for the Study of Terrorism and Irregular Warfare at the Naval Postgraduate School in Monterey, California, issued a report titled "Cyberterror: Prospects and Implications." Their objective was to articulate the demand side of terrorism. Specifically, they assessed the prospects of terrorist organizations pursuing cyberterrorism. They concluded that the barrier to entry for anything beyond annoying hacks is quite high, and that terrorists generally lack the wherewithal and human capital needed to mount a meaningful operation. Cyberterrorism, they argued, was a thing of the future, although it might be pursued as an ancillary tool.

The Monterey group defined three levels of cyberterror capability

- Simple-Unstructured: The capability to conduct basic hacks against individual systems using tools created by someone else. The organization possesses little target analysis, command and control, or learning capability.
- Advanced-Structured: The capability to conduct more sophisticated attacks against multiple systems or networks and possibly, to modify or create basic hacking tools. The organization possesses an elementary target analysis, command and control, and learning capability.
- Complex-Coordinated: The capability for coordinated attacks capable of causing mass-disruption against integrated, heterogeneous defenses (including cryptography). Ability to create sophisticated hacking tools. Highly capable target analysis, command and control, and organization learning capability.

They estimated that it would take a group starting from scratch 2-4 years to reach the advanced-structured level and 6-10 years to reach the complex-coordinated level, although some groups might get there in just a few years or turn to outsourcing or sponsorship to extend their capability.

The study examined five terrorist group types: religious, New Age, ethno-nationalist separatist, revolutionary, and far-right extremists. They determined that only the religious groups are likely to seek the most damaging capability level, as it is consistent with their indiscriminate application of violence. New Age or single issue terrorists, such as the Animal Liberation Front, pose the most immediate threat, however, such groups are likely to accept disruption as a substitute for destruction. Both the revolutionary and ethno-nationalist separatists are likely to seek an advanced-structured capability. The far-right extremists are likely to settle for a simple-unstructured capability, as cyberterror offers neither the intimacy nor cathartic effects that are central to the psychology of far-right terror. The study also determined that hacker groups are psychologically and organizationally ill-suited to cyberterrorism, and that it would be against their interests to cause mass disruption of the information infrastructure.

Thus, at this time, cyberterrorism does not seem to pose an imminent threat. This could change. For a terrorist, it would have some advantages over physical methods. It could be conducted remotely and anonymously, and it would not require the handling of explosives or a suicide mission. It would likely garner extensive media coverage, as journalists and the public alike are fascinated by practically any kind of computer attack. Indeed cyberterrorism could be immensely appealing precisely because of the tremendous attention given to it by the government and media.

Cyberterrorism also has its drawbacks. Systems are complex, so it may be harder to control an attack and achieve a desired level of damage than using physical weapons. Unless people are injured, there is also less drama and emotional appeal. Further, terrorists may be disinclined to try new methods unless they see their old ones as inadequate, particularly when the new methods require considerable knowledge and skill to use effectively. Terrorists generally stick with tired and true methods. Novelty and sophistication of attack may be much less important than assurance that a mission will be operationally successful. Indeed, the risk of operational failure could be a deterrent to terrorists. For now, the truck bomb poses a much greater threat than the logic bomb.

The next generation of terrorists will grow up in a digital world, with ever more powerful and easy-to-use hacking tools at their disposal. They might see greater potential for cyberterrorism than the terrorists of today, and their level of knowledge and skill relating to hacking will be greater. Hackers and insiders might be recruited by terrorists or become self-recruiting cyberterrorists, the Timothy McVeigh's of cyberspace. Some might be moved to action by cyber policy issues, making cyberspace an attractive venue for carrying out an attack. Cyberterrorism could also become more attractive as the real and virtual worlds become more closely coupled, with a greater number of physical devices attached to the Internet. Some of these may be remotely controlled. Terrorists, for example, might target robots used in telesurgery. Unless these systems are carefully secured, conducting an operation that physically harms someone may be as easy as penetrating a Web site is today.

In conclusion, the violent pursuit of political goals using exclusively electronic methods is likely to be at least a few years into the future. However, the more general threat of cybercrime is very much a part of the digital landscape today. In addition to cyberattacks against digital data and systems, many people are being terrorized on the Internet today with threats of physical violence. On-line stalking, death threats, and hate messages are abundant. The Florida teen who threatened violence at Columbine High School in an electronic chat room is but one example. These crimes are serious and must be addressed. In so doing, we will be in a better position to prevent and respond to cyberterrorism if and when the threat becomes more serious.

Web Security and Privacy:
An American Perspective

L. Jean Camp

1. Introduction

Browsing the Web gives one the heady feeling of walking without footprints in cyber-space. Yet data surveillance can be both ubiquitous and transparent to the user. Can those who browse the Web protect their privacy? And does it matter if they cannot? I offer answers to these questions from the American legal tradition. The American legal tradition focuses on a right to privacy, rather than a need for data protection. Yet illuminating Web privacy from this particular perspective throws a broader light on how the fundamental rights of speech, assembly, and freedom of religious inquiry may depend upon electronic privacy in the information age.

What technological threats to privacy exist for a person who is browsing on the Web? Why do these threats matter?

To answer these questions I must first delineate the differences between pri-vacy, security, and anonymity. I then discuss what information is transferred dur-ing Web browsing and its implications. I describe some of the available technology for privacy protection, including cryptography and Web proxies.

I then turn to legal considerations. I describe the American tradition of privacy in common, statutory, and constitutional law. American common law was origi-nally based upon case law from the United Kingdom. In fact, the original defini-tion of a right to privacy by Warren & Brandeis (Warren & Brandeis, 1890) drew upon that English tradition. However, in this information age, European and American law have diverged, as the right to privacy remains the dominant issue in the United States while the European focus is upon data protection.

With the support of the American tradition of a right to privacy, I close by argu-ing that although Web privacy has no current legal protection in the United States, the right to privacy in the analog equivalents to Web-based actions has been rec-ognized in the American legal tradition. By identifying the types of threats to pri-vacy that exist on the Web, I hope to also contribute to the European debates as to what data should be protected, and why.

2. Definitions

In a seminal work on computer security, Prof. Denning (Denning, 1982) declared, "Security is privacy." The confusion between privacy and security remains with many in the computer security community. Privacy requires security, because without the ability to control access and distribution of information, privacy cannot be protected. But security is not privacy.

Information is secure if the *owner* of information can control that information. Information is private if the *subject* of information can control that information. Anonymous information has no subject, and thus ensures that information is private. Anonymity requires security and guarantees privacy, but is neither.

Security is often confused with privacy because security is concerned with confidentiality. Confidential information is not disclosed to unauthorized parties. Contrast this with private information, which is not disclosed without consent of the subject. Security can be used to limit privacy by preventing the subject of information from knowing about a compilation of information, or to violate privacy by using data in ways that do not coincide to the subject's wishes.

Security has three goals: integrity, authentication, and confidentiality. Availability or survivability is also frequently a security goal, although in some systems shutting down is an appropriate response to an attack.

Integrity means that information is not altered. Information has integrity during transmission if the recipient can be certain that the information was not altered in transit. Integrity means that what is received is exactly what was sent.

Integrity also means that information is not altered during storage. A stored file that has integrity can be altered only by authorized users.

Authentication is establishing user identity or other attributes of interest. Authentication is necessary for access control. For example, on the Web the attribute may be the user's right to spend an electronic dollar or access a file.

Authentication enables access control. With access control individual files or data fields can have different levels of access. The following table offers an example of access control for a hypothetical medical record. Note that access control can protect privacy as well as integrity by limiting both read and write access.

Table 1   Access Control List

Data Party	AIDS Status	History of Drug Use	Medication Prescribed	Medication Administered
Patient	Read	Read/Write	Read	Read
Doctor	Read	Read/Write	Read/Write	Write
Nurse	None	None	Read	Write
Laboratory	Write	None	Read	Read

Access control creates privacy conflicts. Access control can protect privacy by keeping records of who used the data about a specific individual. This could increase patient control of the data, and therefore has the potential to increase patient privacy. Conversely, access control can limit privacy by keeping track of data use by a specific individual. For example, if every record written by a nurse was authenticated by that nurse, then it would be trivial to track the nurse's behavior in detail. Thus patient privacy would increase but the nurse's workplace would become a place of constant surveillance, reducing the nurse's privacy.

Availability is also an issue in access control. If an attacker can change the access control list, that attacker can deny access to critical data. For example, an attacker could replace a password field with random data, thereby denying access to all.

A system that maintains availability while under attack exhibits survivability. Systems with survivability exhibit graceful degradation in the face of attacks. An example of an incident that illustrates survivability is the Morris worm incident, where the Internet slowly lost the ability to provide service but was never completely destroyed. Compare this to an incident involving the power grid on the West Coast on July 2. On that day, a tree hit a power line—an isolated incident that cascaded to cause a widespread blackout. The outage resulted in loss of power for over four million people (Western Systems Coordinating Council, 1996).

Security has a set of tools that can be used to meet these goals. These tools are not goals in themselves nor does their use assure security. Cryptography in particular is a tool of computer security that is often itself confused with computer security.

A brief sketch of three types of cryptographic tools is necessary for discussion of Web privacy and security: hash values, public key cryptography, and private key cryptography.

Hash functions compress information. Cryptographically secure, collision-free hash functions provide the ability to verify information without exposing it. Cryptographically secure hash functions compress information into unpredictable values. Collision free hash functions compress data into unique hash values.

There are two fundamentally different types of cryptography for general purpose encryption: private key and public key. With private key there is one key shared between various parties. With public key there is a set of keys, one secret and held only by the owner, and the other widely publicized. Physical analogs are shown in Figure 1.

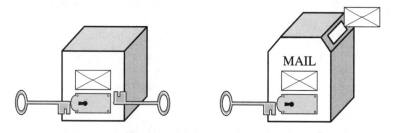

Figure 1 Private & Public Key Systems

In private key encryption there is one mathematical key that both encrypts and decrypts. Thus private key cryptography is also called *symmetric* cryptography.

Private key systems can be used for authentication between parties who share a key. Thus if Alice, Bob, and Carol share a key, Alice can present the key to Bob and verify her claim to be Alice. However, if Alice, Bob, and Carol all share a key, Bob can also present the key to Carol and claim to be Alice. Thus private key systems create the opportunity for *replay attacks*. In replay attacks information used for authentication is literally replayed, enabling the person who replays the data to masquerade as another (see Figure 2).

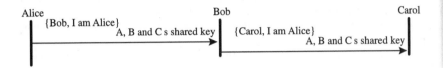

Figure 2   A Replay Attack

In public key cryptography there are two keys. Anything encrypted with one key can only be decrypted with the other key. One key is held secret, shared with no one. The other key is widely publicized. Public key cryptography is sometimes called *asymmetric* cryptography.

Public key systems have an advantage in providing authentication: replay attacks are more difficult with public key systems. The publication of one key provides no information about the other key.

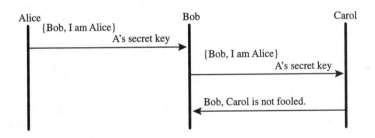

Figure 3   Simple Replay Attacks Fail with Public Key Cryptography

Simple replay attacks do not work with public key systems, as shown in Figure 3.

Public key systems can provide authentication, access control, and integrity. Public key systems provide integrity through the use of *digital signatures*. A digital signature is simply an encryption with the secret key. It can be decrypted with the publicized key, so anyone can verify that the message has not been changed. Anyone who alters the document cannot then sign it with the secret key, so integrity and authentication of the initiator are assured.

3. Browsing Information

Thus there exist security tools and security goals. Is any of this used on the Web? What is the state of Web privacy?

Consider the information transferred in the process of browsing on the Web. Browsing information depends on the policies, practices, and physical configuration of the user's Internet Service Provider (ISP). The configuration of the browser's system and other technical and business services provided by the ISP affect what information is made available when the person browsing connects to the Web.

Technical services provided by the ISP may include fingerID and .plan generation. The finger daemon provides information about a specific user by displaying the user's .plan or profile. For example, finger bsy@cs.ucsd.edu and you will find the name, professional affiliation, contact information and the URLs of the Web pages that bsy has authored.

An ISP business service that can affect user privacy is the provision of aggregate profiles of customers. An ISP may sell financial profiles, history of use profiles, or customized analyses of their customer database. The existence of these services affects the information that is shared when a person browsing accesses a Web server.

When a browser client connects with a server, the server can determine the *Internet protocol* (IP) address of the person browsing. An IP address appears on the right hand side of the @ sign in an email address. This is the electronic equivalent of physical location information, and like a physical street address, the IP address can imply other information.

With an IP address a server can obtain the customer's hostname using the Domain Name System (DNS), which provides a mapping between domain names (ex., miami.epp.cmu.edu) and the corresponding network addresses (ex., 128.2.58.26).

If the user's ISP requires a unique name for each user's machine, then the IP address can correspond exactly to the user's identity. For example, the IP address of Professor Tygar at Carnegie Mellon University is tygar.trust.cmu.edu, because the university required this naming convention. Thus this IP address uniquely identifies an individual. However, someone connecting through AT&T's access services would provide only att.com as an IP address, thus providing very limited information.

An observer can also detect that there is traffic between machines. If browsing information is unencrypted, a well placed observer can watch a person's browsing habits.

Information availability depends upon the type and version of the customer's browser. Every browser sends its type and version to the server. Browsers also send information about the machine on which they reside—the operating system, computer type, and helper applications.

For more effective communications, browser software can send information on available helper applications to servers. Helper applications offer probabilistic information about the consumer's machine and even interests. For example, the number and variety of helper applications, presence of shareware or freeware applications, and the presence of advanced helper applications together imply a level of user technical sophistication.

After sending a request command to the Web server, the customer's client will send an accept command. This command can include information on: monitor quality, including size and identification of color monitors, helper applications available, and the quality of the connection. Alternatively, the accept command may just request "send what you have," and let the client machine sort the data.

When using anonymous file transfer protocol (ftp) it has been the polite tradition for the client to log in as anonymous and then offer her email address as the password. This tradition is incorporated into most browsers as a preference. However, this means that any anonymous ftp request may include the email address of the user. Any server can initiate an ftp request without the knowledge of the client simply by preceding the images to be shown in the page with ftp instead of http. For example, the anchors A Href = http://www.cs.cmu.edu/afs/cs/user/jeanc/www/Addie_Walter.gif and A Href = ftp://www.cs.cmu.edu/afs/cs/user/jeanc/www/Addie_Walter.gif would both result in the same lovely image being sent to the browser—however, the latter would send the browser's email address to the server.

Browsers have capabilities beyond the requests and responses described above. These capabilities include cookies, javascript, applets, common gateway interface scripts, and ActiveX. These are dual-edged technologies: they can protect or subvert privacy.

Cookies are effectively commands initiated by the server and accepted by the browser that return text back to the server. A cookie can be used to store browser preferences, or even to make the Web less annoying by assuring that no site sends the same advertisement to the browser twice. Cookies can also provide tracking of Web use. Text sent to the initiator can include previous pages visited (from the cache) or bookmarks. Cookies can stay resident and send updates to the server, at subsequent visits, of all a browser's selected sites.

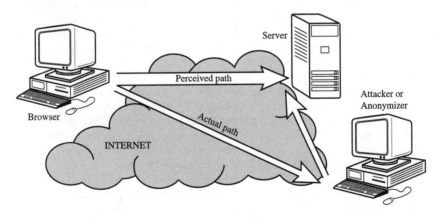

Figure 4   A Web Proxy

For a person browsing to effectively hide identity, the browser must use an anonymity-providing proxy to prevent browser-based network information from providing identity information. For an illustration, visit http://anonymizer.cs.cmu.edu/.

Javascript, CGI, Java, and ActiveX enable proxy attacks. In a proxy attack, the browser thinks it is visiting a server directly, but in fact all commands are sent through a third machine. This third machine is invisible to the person browsing, and can make the browser's machine invisible to the server. Thus proxies can be security and privacy problems, or a proxy can serve to protect user information. Figure 4 illustrates the use of a friendly, anonymizing proxy as found at http://www.anonymizer.com, and a proxy attack, an example of which can be found at http://ww.cs.cmu.edu/~alma.

4.   Legal Issues & Societal Implications

Americans have long been concerned with privacy, yet privacy concerns trail the introduction of new technologies. By definition the law must respond to what technology defines as possible.

The American tradition of concern for privacy varies from the European approach. Whereas the European Community and Canada have principles of data protection, the American tradition is based on privacy.

The American right to privacy is actually two sets of rights: rights of autonomy and rights of seclusion.

The right of seclusion can be seen in the original definition of the right to privacy by Warren and Brandeis as "the right to be let alone" (Warren & Brandeis, 1890). This right to be let alone has been defined into four kinds of privacy rights cases since Prosser's (Prosser, 1941) treatise on torts: intrusion upon seclusion, appropriation of name and likeness, false light, and public disclosure of private facts.

An intrusion upon seclusion is clearly a violation of rights to seclusion. The original definition of privacy clearly singled out the press for intruding into private affairs: "Gossip is no longer the resource of the idle and of the vicious, but has become a trade which is pursued with industry as well as effrontery." (Warren and Brandeis, 1890). But what is electronic seclusion? Is it one's own electronic mailbox where particular messages are unwelcome? Is it one's cache, which can be read and passed back through cookies? The law has not answered these questions, and users may have widely varying perceptions.

Appropriation of name and likeness is the use of a person's name, reputation, or image without his or her consent. An early and well-known case is that of a young woman who found her image distributed throughout the city on bags of flour. She had given no consent and received no compensation. The makers of the flour had thought her face would be commercially useful and that she was owed no compensation for the luck of having such a countenance. The New York courts agreed. Despite her failure in seeking restitution, appropriation of name and likeness is now recognized across America when there is commercial gain, although limits remain in different states on the ability to seek restitution if there is no commercial gain.

False light is the publication of information that is misleading, and thus shows an individual in a false light. This is similar to libel. The ability to charge another with false light depends on the standing of the victim and the role of the privacy violator. Private persons (as opposed to public figures) need show only falsehood in a case of false light; however, concerns over speech rights hinder the pursuit of restitution. False light is recognized as an offense in all fifty states under one rubric or another, but not necessarily as a privacy violation.

Public disclosure of private facts is self-explanatory. Information deemed as "newsworthy" can be printed even if it is a violation of privacy. Currently public disclosure of private facts is treated seriously in some jurisdictions, including New York and South Carolina. However, in some jurisdictions, notably North Carolina and Texas, one cannot bring action under this tort (Alderman & Kennedy, 1995).

The Constitutional right to privacy is based on rights of autonomy. In 1969 the Supreme Court made the right to privacy explicit in Griswold v Connecticut. The Court found the right to privacy implied in the Constitution in the First, Third, Fourth, Fifth, Ninth, and Fourteenth Amendments (Compaine, 1988; Trublow, 1991).

The First Amendment states:

> "Congress shall make no law respecting an establishment of religion, or prohibiting the free exercise thereof; or abridging the freedom of speech, or of the press; or the right of the people peaceably to assemble, and to petition the government for a redress of grievances."

The privacy implications are that people under surveillance are not likely to express views, or go to assemblies or religious meetings with which the agencies of surveillance are likely to disagree. The freedom to read is actually the freedom to read without fear of surveillance. The Court has ruled that the right to privacy covers the right to read—unobserved—material that the Federal Government finds objectionable. The Court has ruled that the right to privacy covers memberships and personal associations (NAACP v Alabama, 1958), confirming the "right of members to pursue their lawful private interests privately and to associate freely with others."

The Third Amendment states:

> "No soldier shall, in time of peace be quartered in any house, without the consent of the owner, nor in time of war, but in a manner to be prescribed by law."

The Fourth Amendment states:

> "The right of the people to be secure in their persons, houses, papers, and effects, against unreasonable searches and seizures, shall not be violated, and no warrants shall issue, but upon probable cause, supported by oath or affirmation, and particularly describing the place to be searched, and the persons or things to be seized."

Together the Third and Fourth Amendments create a region of privacy, a space inviolate by the government except in constrained circumstances. These Amendments suggest that what one does in one's own home is not the business of the government. Note that members of the NAACP were found to have not only the First Amendment right to associate, but also the right to "pursue private interest privately," as one might in one's own home.

The Fifth Amendment states:

> "No person shall be held to answer for a capital, or otherwise infamous crime, unless on a presentment or indictment of a grand jury, except in cases arising in the land or naval forces, or in the militia, when in actual service in time of war or public danger; nor shall any person be subject for the same offense to be twice put in jeopardy of life or limb; nor shall be compelled in any criminal case to be a witness against himself, nor be deprived of life, liberty, or property, without due process of law; nor shall private property be taken for public use, without just compensation."

The government cannot imprison people without charge, nor require that they speak. The implication is that the government has no right to hear all that you might say, thereby intruding into your thoughts. Just as the government has no right to search your papers by the Fourth Amendment, the government has no right to search your thoughts by the Fifth. Nor does the government have the right to arbitrarily limit your movements.

The Ninth Amendment states:

> "The enumeration in the Constitution, of certain rights, shall not be construed to deny or disparage others retained by the people."

Without the Ninth Amendment, the right to privacy could not be found in the Constitution. The right to privacy is nowhere specifically identified in the Constitution. Thus, without the Ninth Amendment's specific identification of the list of rights mentioned as not being exclusive, the right to privacy as implied by the other Amendments could not exist.

Section 1 of the Fourteenth Amendment states:

> "All persons born or naturalized in the United States, and subject to the jurisdiction thereof, are citizens of the United States and of the state wherein they reside. No state shall make or enforce any law which shall abridge the privileges or immunities of citizens of the United States; nor shall any state deprive any person of life, liberty, or property, without due process of law; nor deny to any person within its jurisdiction the equal protection of the laws."

Sections 2-5 of the Fourteenth Amendment addresses apportionment of representatives and Civil War disqualification and debt, and thus are not of interest here.

None of the rights set forth in the Constitution can be abridged by the States. If the Federal Government has no right to your home, speech, or papers, neither do the state governments. The rights, which together provide privacy from the Federal Government, provide privacy from state and local governments as well.

The Constitutional right to privacy allows individuals to take certain actions without fear of retribution, rather than preventing the publication of information as with tort law. In some cases rights of seclusion and rights of autonomy can be in conflict. In cases where speech rights conflict with the right to be let alone, the speaker's First Amendment shield is often stronger than the subject's civil sword.

At the state and federal level, protections are topical and highly variable. For example, commercial transactions are covered under the Right to Financial Privacy Act, unless the purchase is a rental of a video tape. Then the records are covered by the so-called Bork Bill, the Video Privacy Protection Act, which extends greater protection. Of course, if the purchase is a credit purchase, then the credit records are protected by the Fair Credit Reporting Act. In contrast, if one purchases medical services with any currency, there is no federal privacy protection of the medical records. Thus there is no coherent principle that underlies all statutory protections of privacy.

5. What Are You Doing on the Web?

In this section I argue that browsing on the Web actually consists of many different actions. Many of the analog equivalents of these actions have found privacy protection in the United States, but when done electronically they fall under the general rubric of browsing.

When on the Web, a person is likely to be obtaining free information, purchasing information, making friends and contacts, and will certainly be communicating electronically.

The analog practice of obtaining free information is often done through the mails, or through libraries. The American tradition has maintained not only the right to print and speak freely, but also the right to read anonymously (Cohen, 1996). Thus obtaining free information has been found to have the highest level of protection, as free access to information is a fundamental democratic right.

One most famous case of the right to read anonymously is Lamont v Postmaster General. In this case the Congress had instructed the Postmaster General to remove from the general mail all information pertaining to communism. The recipient of any such mail then had to request the mail and sign his or her name declaring that the information was wanted. The Supreme Court found this to be unreasonable, stating that, "any addressee is likely to feel some inhibition in sending for literature which Federal officials have condemned."

Web browsers may also purchase information. In the United States the Right to Financial Privacy Act limits government access to financial information. The Right to Financial Privacy Act was a response to the United States v Miller, 1976, in which the court determined that a financial transaction is inherently a public act. The Right to Financial Privacy Act limits government access to financial records, thereby applying the Fourth Amendment to financial records in the wake of Miller.

However, there is no expectation of privacy from the provider of financial services or the merchant. United States v Miller determined that all financial records are owned by the financial services institution, and that the customer has no privacy interests in these records. Thus, other than limitations on supplying information to the government, financial data have no protection. This is in contrast to what one might reasonably assume—that in payment for information some contractual rights, such as data protection, are created.

Many people browse the Web to finds groups and people with whom they sympathize. So while browsing, many people are making friends and contacts, joining chat rooms, finding mailing lists, and in general, associating and assembling electronically.

Like reading, the rights of association extends to the right to associate without surveillance. A case that illustrates this is NAACP (National Association for the Advancement of Colored People) v Alabama, 1958. Nineteen fifty-eight was some six years before the murder of activists in Freedom Summer that required Federal intervention. At that time the senior official of the NAACP in neighboring Mississippi, Medgar Evers, was under constant threat of death for activities. (He was eventually shot at his home in 1963, and the self-confessed murderer remained free until 1994). It was in this environment of fear that the state of Alabama requested the membership list of the NAACP. The NAACP appealed to the Supreme Court, which stated that the First Amendment right to associate is also the right to "pursue private interest privately," as one might in one's own home.

Today the Web is the meeting place of both marginal groups and mainstream groups who are sometimes the target of violent attacks. Gay rights advocates, feminists, and advocates of reproductive rights have all been subject to violent attacks in physical space. All of these groups have found safe places to associate on the Web, and coexist in cyberspace with even their most extreme opponents. However, due to the lack of authentication and encryption, the identities and associations of members of any and all of these groups can be tracked by invisible observers.

Electronic communications are subject to the protection of the Electronic Communications Privacy Act (ECPA). The Electronic Communications Privacy Act protects from observers, but not participants or employers. There is an assumption of equal bargaining power in one to one communications that does not hold in client/server relationships as on the Web.

The failure of the Electronic Communications Privacy Act to protect Web browsing is because it is based on a telephony model, with one to one communication, rather than the publishing model of the Web.

6. Conclusions

There are privacy promises of information technology. Many of the conflicts between data availability and privacy can be resolved. For example, the use of pseudonyms enables extensive demographic or longitudinal studies without violating privacy. The use of access control lists allow tighter constraints on the sharing of information. The example shown here illustrates that access to information can be protected at a higher level of granularity. Using cryptography, alterations can be detected and tracked. Thus the need for data availability does not justify the amount of information that can be captured on the Web today. Data availability and privacy can be resolved in some cases using anonymous updates to aggregates and verifiable pseudonyms.

Yet the market has failed to protect privacy, there is limited legal protection, and technological protections available but unused.

Often a delay extends between the introduction of new technologies and the extension of privacy rights to the users of that technology. Consider the case of telephony. In 1928 the Supreme Court determined that no person has a right to privacy in telephone conversations (Olmstead v United States, 1928). The Supreme Court ruled that recording telephone conversations was not a search under the Fourth Amendment because the conversation left the defendant's home on lines that could not be secured. The Court stated that since the technology was inherently without security, people knowingly sacrificed privacy when they communicated using the telephone. The Supreme Court reasoned that telephone correspondents knew that the signals went outside their homes and only the most naive would expect privacy. Olmstead reads: "There was no searching. There was no seizure. The evidence was secured by the use of the sense of hearing and that only. There was no entry of the houses or offices of the defendants. . . . The language of the amendment cannot be extended and expanded to include telephone wires, reaching to the whole world from the defendant's home or office. The intervening wires are not part of his house or office, any more than are the highways along which they are stretched."

The reasoning in Olmstead applies to the Internet today. Of course, this reasoning remains true for the telephone network as well. For the decades between Olmstead v United States and Katz v United States (Katz v United States, 1967), the law of access to telephone conversations essentially stated that because the system was open, privacy was not to be expected. Although there were great technological advances in telephony between 1928 and 1967, the change in the law arguably reflected changes in social rather than technical practices. The Court has not determined which judgment applies to the Internet today.

Why is this? Does this prove that Americans have no concern for privacy? I argue that an examination of American legal tradition shows that Americans do have concern for privacy. Yet privacy threats are invisible, while privacy protections are not. Use of privacy-protecting technology requires time and skills that many users of the Web do not have. Lack of technical savvy and legal protections limit privacy, and therefore personal and political autonomy, in the information age.

References

12 USC §552 Privacy Act

12 USC §1829 Bank Secrecy Act

12 USC §1829 Money Laundering Act

12 USC §3403 Financial Privacy Act

12 USC §202 Home Mortgage Act

15 USC §1691 Equal Credit Opportunity Act

115 USC §1694 Electronic Funds Transfer Act

18 USC §1029 Computer Fraud and Abuse Act

335 USC §3401 Right to Financial Privacy Act

42 USCS §3608, 15 USC §1681, 12 USCS §1708 Fair Credit Reporting Act

Alderman, E. and Kennedy, C. (1995) *The Right to Privacy,* Alfred A Knopf, New York, NY.

Cohen, J. (1996) "The Right to Read Anonymously: A Closer Look at Copyright Management in Cyberspace," *Connecticut Law Review,* Vol. 28, 981.

Compaine B. J. (1988) *Issues in New Information Technology,* Ablex Publishing; Norwood, NJ.

Denning, D. (1982) *Cryptography and Data Security,* Addison-Wesley Publishing; Reading, MA.

Katz v United States (1967) 389 US 351, 369 F2d 130 (9th Cir).

Lamont v Postmaster General (1965) 381 U.S. 301, 301.

NAACP (National Association for the Advancement of Colored People) v Alabama (1958) 357 US. 449.

Olmstead v United States (1928) 277 US 438, 48 SCt 564, 72 LEd2d 944.

Prosser, W.L. (1941) *Handbook of the Law of Torts,* West Publishing Co., St. Paul, MN.

Trublow, G. et al (1991) *Privacy Law and Practice,* Times Mirror Books, New York, NY.

Warren S. and Brandeis L. (1890) "The right to privacy," *Harvard Law Review,* Vol. 4, 193–220.

Western Systems Coordinating Council (1996) "WSCC technical experts discover the cause of western U.S. electrical outage," Press Release, July 21, available at http://www.spectrum.ieee.org/publicaccess/9608teaser/whatsn56.html; April 7, 1997.

The Meaning of Anonymity in an Information Age

Helen Nissenbaum

Should anonymity be protected in electronic interactions and communications? Would this be a good thing for community, responsibility, free expression, political participation, and personal fulfillment? If so, when and why? These key normative questions probe the value of anonymity in our computerized society and political order. In this brief discussion, I do not directly address these important questions but address questions that undergird them about the meaning of anonymity in a contemporary, computerized society: What is anonymity? And what are we seeking to protect when we propose to protect it? Although answers to these foundational questions will not immediately yield answers to the key normative questions just mentioned, they are essential to understanding what is at stake in the answers to these questions. For, after all is said and done, we would not want to discover that the thing we have fought so hard to protect was not worth protecting after all.

The natural meaning of anonymity, as may be reflected in ordinary usage or a dictionary definition, is of remaining nameless, that is to say, conducting oneself without revealing one's name. A poem or pamphlet is anonymous when unattributable to a named person; a donation is anonymous when the name of the donor is withheld; people strolling through a foreign city are anonymous because no one knows who they are. Extending this understanding into the electronic sphere, one might suppose that conducting one's affairs, communicating, or engaging in transactions anonymously in the electronic sphere is to do so without one's name being known. Specific cases that are regularly discussed include:

- Sending electronic mail to an individual, or bulletin board, without one's given name appearing in any part of the header.
- Participating in a "chat" group, electronic forum, or game without one's given name being known by other participants.
- Buying something with the digital equivalent of cash.
- Being able to visit any Web site without having to divulge one's identity.

The concern I wish to raise here is that in a computerized world concealing or withholding names is no longer adequate, because although it preserves a traditional understanding of anonymity, it fails to preserve what is at stake in protecting anonymity. Why?

Information technology has made it possible to trace people in historically unprecedented ways. We are targets of surveillance at just about every turn of our lives. In transactions with retailers, mail-order companies, medical caregivers, day-care providers, and even beauty parlors, information about us is collected, stored, analyzed, and sometimes shared. Our presence on the planet, our notable features and momentous milestones, are dutifully recorded by agencies of federal, state, and local government, including birth, marriage, divorce, property ownership, driver's licenses, vehicle registration, moving violations, passage through computerized toll roads and bridges, parenthood, and, finally, our demise. In the great store of information we are identified through name, street address, e-mail address, phone number, credit-card numbers, social security number, passport number, level of education, and more; we are described by age, hair color, eye color, height, quality of vision, purchases, credit-card activity, travel, employment and rental history, real-estate transactions, change of address, ages and numbers of children, and magazine subscriptions. The dimensions are endless (Nissenbaum 1997).

From these bits of information, public identities may be formed that are not only elaborate, but permanently accessible in an active electronic form for those who may need or want them. Even when these identities are not complete, and may in fact be quite fragmentary, inferential tools and network capabilities enable linking, matching, mining, and all the other activities that for one purpose or another transform bits of a person into a more complete, recognizable, possibly identifiable (virtual) person. Critically important to the question of anonymity is that these techniques allow linking of pieces and fragments of information; from a variety of pieces of information, or fragments of information, that are not each uniquely identifying, we may infer or link to those that are. For example, in most states, we can identify the owner's name and home address from the number on a car license plate; from a phone number we may reach a person or household; from an electronic mail address, or from an electronic pseudonym, we may be able to pinpoint a person's geographic whereabouts and physical identity.

Even where fragments of information do not lead to information that is uniquely identifying, people may be identified with a high degree of probability when various properties are compounded to include a smaller and smaller set of individuals who satisfy them all. If an unnamed individual, who regularly contributes to America Online discussion groups for Corvette owners and stamp collectors, reveals that he shops at Safeway, was born on 4 May 1965, graduated from Stanford in 1992, lives in Palo Alto in a three-bedroom house appraised at $525,000, and is divorced with two children in local public schools, we easily may be able to identify him without knowing his name. Although in the past the most direct and effective way of "getting at" a person was through his or her name, the electronic medium now offers many points of entry, some of which may be even more effective than a name.

[Latanya Sweeney has carefully demonstrated this phenomenon in, for example, Sweeney (1997). Also, note close parallels to two of Gary Marx's categories of identification, namely, identification through distinctive appearance or behavior patterns, and identification through social categories (Marx, 1999).] Marketers use these techniques to track suitable targets to their home addresses by mining databases containing a diverse range of transactional information about them.

The power of information technology to extract or infer identity from nonidentifying signs and information has been inventively applied by literary scholars to settling disputes and unraveling mysteries of authorship—say, to discover whether it was Shakespeare who wrote a given sonnet. These scholars infer authorship by comparing the stylistic and lexical features of anonymous text with the known style of authors whose texts have been analyzed along these same dimensions. In a recently publicized case, Donald Foster, a professor of dramatic literature at Vassar College, identified Joe Klein as the author of the controversial political novel *Primary Colors* (Pristin, 1997), published anonymously. Foster also helps law-enforcement officials identify extortionists and kidnappers by analyzing what they have written.

Why does this matter? For situations in which we judge anonymity acceptable, or even necessary, we do so because anonymity offers a safe way for people to act, transact, and participate without accountability, without others "getting at" them, tracking them down, or even punishing them. This includes a range of possibilities. Anonymity may encourage freedom of thought and expression by promising people a possibility to express opinions and develop arguments about positions that, for fear of reprisal or ridicule, they would not or dare not take otherwise. Anonymity may enable people to reach out for help, especially for socially stigmatized problems like domestic violence, HIV or other sexually transmitted infection, emotional problems, or suicidal thoughts. It offers the possibility of a protective cloak for children, enabling them to engage in Internet communication without fear of social predation or—perhaps less ominous but nevertheless unwanted—overtures from commercial marketers. Anonymity may also provide respite to adults from commercial and other solicitations. It supports socially valuable institutions like peer review, whistle-blowing, and voting.

In all these cases, the value of anonymity lies not in the capacity to be unnamed, but in the possibility of acting or participating while remaining out of reach, remaining unreachable. Being unreachable means that no one will come knocking on your door demanding explanations, apologies, answerability, punishment, or payment. Where society places high value on the types of expression and transaction that anonymity protects (alluded to in the previous paragraph), it must necessarily enable unreachability. In other words, this unreachability is precisely what is at stake in anonymity. If, in previous eras, namelessness—that is, choosing not to reveal one's name—was the best means of achieving unreachability, it makes sense that namelessness would be protected. However, remaining unnamed should be understood for what it is: not as the end in itself of anonymity, but rather, the traditional means by which unreachability has been achieved. It has been the most effective way to keep others at bay, avoid ridicule, prevent undeserved revenge, harm, embarrassment, and so forth.

In the computerized world, with the systems of information that we currently have in place, namelessness by itself is no longer sufficient for protecting what is at stake in anonymity. If it is true, as I have suggested, that one can gain access to a person through bits, or constellations of bits, of information, then protecting anonymity today amounts to more than merely withholding a name. It means withholding the information or constellation of information it now takes to get at, or get to, a person. When we think of protecting anonymity we must think about this broader range of possibilities; we must think not only of how a person can prevent his or her name from being divulged, but how a person can prevent all the crucial bits of information from being divulged, especially the bits of information that when divulged would enable access to him or her.

Deepening our understanding of the issue of anonymity in an information age, and reaching wise decisions about it, will, in other words, require not only resolving the key normative questions stated at the beginning (to achieve a balance among potentially conflicting interests), but requires an appreciation of what it takes to be "unreachable" or "out of grasp" in a world where technologies of knowledge and information are increasingly efficacious at reaching, grasping, and identifying: This is a moving target.

To secure the possibility of being unreachable, we need both to promote understanding and also pursue advocacy. Understanding may be achieved partly through a priori reasoning (figuring things out) and partly through increased knowledge about networks of information. People may figure out, either on their own or through the insights of others, how various pieces of information may link to their identities and whereabouts and therefore defy the efficacy of traditional anonymity. Thus, a person may suddenly become aware that bar codes link to her identity when she pays for purchases with a credit card, figures out that electronic mail sent pseudonymously (under a fictitious name, frequently devised specifically for electronic communications) or anonymously may nevertheless yield identifying information about her via her computer's IP address, or realizes that she becomes more easily identifiable through an electronic mail address that includes information about her geographic location (for example, by identifying her place of work).

Beyond what we can figure out, there is a great deal we can learn empirically about the linkages that exist that may potentially undermine the possibility of anonymity (and pseudonymity). In general, these linkages establish a correspondence between the sign under which people attempt to act and transact anonymously (or pseudonymously) and information about them that either itself makes people reachable, or links to other signs and information that ultimately link to information that makes them reachable. These revelations of identity may occur by various means. One is by linking the sign under which an anonymous person is acting into a network of information that ultimately leads to the person him- or herself. As discussed earlier, those whose business it is to watch, record, match, infer, and identify may manage to converge on individuals only with some degree of certainty, or they may manage to do so by linking ultimately to that one crucial piece of information—the work address, the IP address, the street address, the motor vehicle registration—that places the unnamed person within their reach.

Another way of defying anonymity, not yet discussed, is by breaking systems of "opaque" identifiers. What I mean by an opaque identifier is a sign linking reliably to a person—chosen, assigned, or arising naturally—that, on the face of it, carries no information about the person. That is, the opaque identifier holds no clue, by itself, as to the real identity of the person or how to reach that person. The chosen screen names (or pseudonyms) of Internet service subscribers may serve in this way as opaque identifiers. The Social Security number is an instance of an assigned identifier, and biometrics, such as fingerprints, retinal images, and DNA profiles, are instances of naturally occurring ones. As well as serving important societal needs, such as law and order, secure entry, and financial transaction, these systems of identification offer the means of dealing reliably but anonymously with individuals. For example, a professor wishing to announce course grades anonymously may list grades alongside Social Security numbers. People may interact with a stable cohort knowing only screen names and not real identities, and so forth.

Problems arise when the key to a system of opaque identifiers is compromised, as, for example, critics say has occurred with Social Security numbers. They charge that the mapping between these numbers and information that allows people to be reached has seeped slowly but surely into the public domain. The Social Security number has become a sure-fire way not only to "get at" a person but to extract an enormous array of other information that has been keyed to it. In other cases, a key to the mapping can be less inadvertently and more directly betrayed, such as occurred in a controversial case involving Timothy McVeigh, a member of the U.S. Navy. Navy personnel, investigating his alleged homosexuality, managed to elicit McVeigh's real identity from America Online on submitting his screen name, "boysrch" (*McVeigh v. Cohen*, 1998). It is of great importance that people at least have an accurate grasp of the existing level of integrity for each of these systems of opaque identification.

My purpose here is not to suggest that anonymity in an information age is impossible. I am mainly arguing that achieving it is a more demanding business than merely allowing people to withhold their names. Although I do not mean to imply that contemporary networks of information, and the compromise of opaque identifiers, are the result of insidious conspiracy and subterfuge, I recognize, at the same time, that all interests are not equally served by promoting a sufficient public understanding. It is this level of understanding that would make people more cautious, more guarded, more mindful of the information they divulge to others in various transactions and, as a result, more capable of protecting the possibility of anonymity. The understanding may also lead them to realize that anonymity and pseudonymity are not all-or-nothing qualities but can be achieved in degrees and through layers of cloaking. But public understanding is not, in my opinion, enough. Knowing where landmines are buried can help people avoid them, but clearing the landmines is a more robust and lasting solution.

Beyond the effort it would take to educate toward a more comprehensive understanding, we will need to pursue lines of advocacy. If, as a society, we agree that what is importantly at stake in anonymity is the capacity to be unreachable in certain situations, then we must secure the means to achieve this. This will include a dramatic reversal of current trends in surveillance, as well as a relentless monitoring of the integrity of systems of opaque identifiers. Without at least these measures, even if we nominally secure a right to anonymity through norms and regulations, we will not have secured what is at stake in anonymity in a computerized world.

References

McVeigh v. Cohen Decision. 1998. U.S. District Court, District of Columbia.

Marx, Gary. 1999. What's in a name? Some reflections on the sociology of anonymity. *The Information Society* 15(2):1–15.

Nissenbaum, Helen. 1997. Toward an approach to privacy in public: Challenges of information technology. *Ethics & Behavior* 7(3):207–219.

Pristin, T. 1997. From sonnets to ransom notes. *The New York Times,* 19 November:Bl.

Sweeney, Latanya. 1997. Weaving Technology and Policy Together to Maintain Confidentiality. *Journal of Law, Medicine and Ethics* 25:98–110.

Ethical Reflections on Cyberstalking

Frances S. Grodzinsky and Herman T. Tavani

This essay examines some ethical aspects of stalking behavior in cyberspace. We have argued elsewhere that recent online stalking incidents raise a wide range of ethical concerns, including issues affecting gender (Grodzinsky and Tavani, 2001), personal privacy (Tavani and Grodzinsky, 2002), and physical vs. virtual harm (Grodzinsky and Tavani, 2002). The primary axis of discussion in this essay has to do with implications that cyberstalking has for our notion of *moral responsibility,* both at the collective (or group) and individual levels. For example, do collectivities and organizations such as Internet service providers (ISPs) have any moral obligations to cyberstalking victims, which go beyond legal obligations covered in strict liability law? And do ordinary Internet users have a moral obligation to inform (and possibly also to assist) persons whom they discover to be the targets of online stalkers? In our analysis of these questions, particular attention is paid to a cyberstalking incident involving Amy Boyer.

1. Introduction: Stalking Incidents in Cyberspace

What is cyberstalking? And how do stalking incidents in cyberspace raise ethical concerns? In answering these questions, we begin with a definition of stalking in general. According to *Webster's New World Dictionary of the American Language,* to engage in stalking is "to pursue or approach game, an enemy, etc. stealthily, as from cover." In the context of criminal activities involving human beings, a stalking crime is generally considered to be one in which an individual ("the stalker") clandestinely tracks the movements of another individual or individuals ("the stalkee[s]"). Cyberstalking can be understood as a form of behavior in which certain types of stalking-related activities, which in the past have occurred in physical space, are extended to the online world. We should note, however, that criteria used in determining which kinds of behavior should count as stalking crimes in the physical realm has been neither consistent nor clear. Hence, it also has been more difficult to determine what the criteria should be for a determining a stalking crime in the cyber-realm.

One difficulty in understanding some of the essential features of cyberstalking crimes is that they sometimes border on, and thus become confused with, broader forms of "harassment crimes" in cyberspace. Consider a recent incident involving twenty-year old Christian Hunold, who was charged with terrorizing Timothy McGillicuddy, a high school principal in the state of Massachusetts. Hunold constructed a Web site that included "hit lists" of teachers and students at that Massachusetts school, on which he also included a picture of the school that was displayed through "the cross hairs of a rifle." Using various pseudonyms, Hunold corresponded with several eighth graders in the school. He then made specific threats to these Massachusetts students, who had no idea that they were communicating with a person who lived in Missouri ("The Web's Dark Side," 2000). Should this particular criminal incident be viewed as a case of cyberstalking? Or is it better understood under a different description such as "cyber-harassment?"

A criminal incident involving Randi Barber and Gary Dellapenta is sometimes also included under the category of cyberstalking. In 1996, Barber met Dellapenta, a security guard, through a friend. Although Dellapenta wanted a relationship with Barber, she spurned his advances. A few months later, Barber began to receive telephone solicitations from men; and in one instance, a "solicitor" actually appeared at the door of her residence. Barber seemed to be unaware of how potentially dangerous her situation had become. For example, she had no idea that Dellapenta had assumed her identity in various Internet chat rooms, when soliciting "kinky sex." Anonymity and pseudonymity tools, available to any Internet user, allowed Dellapenta to represent himself as Barber, via screen names such as a "playfulkitty4U" and "kinkygal30." Barber became aware of what was going on only after she asked one caller why he was phoning her (Foote, 1999). Note that in this alleged case of *cyber*stalking, Dellapenta engaged others to stalk his intended victim in physical space. So once again, we can ask whether the Barber/Dellapenta incident is a genuine case of cyberstalking or whether it can be more appropriately described as an instance of a harassment involving the use of Internet technology.

Thus far we have briefly described two different criminal incidents that some authors have referred to as examples of cyberstalking. It is perhaps worth noting that no physical harm resulted to victims in either incident; and in both cases, it was difficult to separate certain harassment activities (in general) from stalking behavior in particular. Also, in the Barbar/Dellapenta case, the stalking-related activities involved both physical space and cyberspace. We next examine a stalking incident involving Amy Boyer, which we believe is a clearer case of cyberstalking.

2. The Amy Boyer Cyberstalking Case

On October 15, 1999, Amy Boyer, a twenty-year-old resident of Nashua, NH, was murdered by a young man who had stalked her via the Internet. Her stalker, Liam Youens, was able to carry out most of the stalking activities that eventually led to Boyer's death by using a variety of online tools available to any Internet user. Through the use of online search facilities, for example, Youens was able to find out where Boyer lived, where she worked, what kind of vehicle she drove, and so forth. Youens was also able to use other kinds of online tools, typically provided by Internet service providers (ISPs), to construct two Web sites. On one site, he posted personal information about Boyer, including a picture of her; and on another site, Youens described, in explicit detail, his plans to murder Boyer.

The Amy Boyer case raises several ethical and social questions, independent of the important fact that the stalking behavior in this incident eventually led to Boyer's death. For example, some have argued that Boyer's privacy was violated. We could ask whether Boyer was a victim of online defamation. We could also ask whether Youens had a right to post information about Boyer on his Web site, and whether such a "right" is one that ought to be protected by free speech. Or should such "speech" be controlled in cyberspace? Also, we could ask whether issues raised in the Boyer case are more ethically significant than those in other online stalking incidents because of the physical harm caused to Boyer, resulting in her death. Although the Amy Boyer case raises several ethical issues, we can ask whether there is anything unique or even special about these issues from a moral point of view.

3. What, if Anything, Is Ethically Significant About Cyberstalking Crimes?

From an ethical perspective, an interesting question is whether there is anything unique or even special about the Amy Boyer case in particular, or cyberstalking in general. On the one hand, we do not claim that cyberstalking is a new kind of crime; nor, for that matter, do we argue that cyberstalking is a "genuine" computer crime (Tavani, 2000). Yet can we reasonably ask whether Internet technology has made a relevant difference in the stalking case involving Amy Boyer? Perhaps the more important question, however, is: Has cybertechnology made a moral difference? One might be inclined to answer *no*. For example, one could argue that "murder is murder," and that whether a murderer uses a computing device that included Internet tools to assist in carrying out a particular murder is irrelevant from an ethical point of view. One could further argue that there is nothing special about cyberstalking incidents in general—irrespective of whether or not those incidents result in the death of the victims—since stalking activities have had a long history of occurrence in the "off-line" world. According to this line of reasoning, the use of Internet technology could be seen as simply the latest in a series of tools or techniques that have become available to stalkers to assist them in carrying out their criminal activities.

However, it could also be argued that the Internet has made a relevant difference with respect to stalking-related crimes because of the ways in which stalking activities can now be carried out. For example, Internet stalkers can operate anonymously or pseudononymously while online. Also consider that a cyberstalker can stalk one or more individuals from the comfort of his or her home, and thus does not have to venture out into the physical world to stalk someone. So Internet technology has provided stalkers with a certain mode of stalking that was not possible in the pre-Internet era.

It could also be argued that cyberstalking has made possible certain kinds of behavior that challenge our conventional moral and legal frameworks. These challenges have to do primarily with issues of *scale* and *scope*. For example, a cyberstalker can stalk multiple victims simultaneously through the use of multiple "windows" on his or her computer. The stalker can also stalk victims who happen to live in states and countries that are geographically distant from the stalker. So, potentially both the number of stalking incidents and the range of stalking activities can increase dramatically because of the Internet (Tavani, 2002). However, we leave open the question whether any of these matters make a moral difference.

In the remainder of this essay, we focus on two questions involving issues of moral responsibility in the Boyer case: (1) Should the two ISPs that permitted Youens to post information about Amy Boyer on Web sites that reside in their Internet "space" be held morally accountable? (2) Do ordinary users who happen to come across a Web site that contains a posting of a death threat directed at an individual (or group of individuals) have a moral responsibility to inform those individuals whose lives are threatened?

4. Moral Responsibility and Internet Service Providers (ISPs)

As noted above, Youens set up two Web sites about Amy Boyer: one containing descriptive information about Boyer, as well as a photograph of her, and another on which he described in detail his plans to murder Boyer. To what extent, if any—either legally or morally, or both—should the ISPs that hosted the Web sites created by Youens be held responsible? Because this question is very complex, it would be beneficial to break it down into several shorter questions. For example, we first need to understand what is meant by "responsibility" in both its legal and moral senses. We also have to consider whether we can attribute moral blame (or praise) to an organization or collectivity (i.e., a group of individuals), such as an ISP. We begin by briefly examining some recent laws and court challenges that either directly or indirectly pertain to questions involving responsibility and liability for ISPs.

In *Stratton Oakmont* v. *Prodigy Services Company* (1995), the court determined that Prodigy could be held legally liable since it had advertised that it had "editorial control" over the content in the computer bulletin board system (BBS) it hosted. In the eyes of the court, Prodigy's claim to have editorial control over its BBS made that ISP seem similar to a newspaper, in which case the standard of strict legal liability used for original publishers could be applied. In response to the decision in the Prodigy case, many ISPs have since argued that they should not be understood as "original publishers," but rather as "common carriers," similar in relevant respects to telephone companies. Their argument for this view rested in part on the notion that ISPs provide the "conduits for communication but not the content." This view of ISPs would be used in later court decisions (such as *Zeran* v. *America Online Inc.* 1997).

In Section 230 of the Communications Decency Act (CDA), the function of ISPs was interpreted in such a way that would appear to protect them from lawsuits similar to the one filed against Prodigy. Here the court specifically stated, "No provider or user of an interactive computer service shall be treated as the publisher or speaker of any information provided by another information content provider." Although the U.S. Supreme Court eventually struck down CDA, Section 230 of that Act has remained intact. While ISPs are not legally liable for the content of their Web sites or for the content of other electronic forums that they also might host— e.g., forums such as bulletin boards, chat rooms, and list servers—they have nonetheless been encouraged to monitor and filter, to the extent that they can, the content of these electronic forums. But this has presented ISPs with a thorny legal problem. Consider, for example, that the more an ISP edits content, the more it becomes like a publisher (such as a newspaper). And the more it becomes like a publisher, with editorial control, the more liable an ISP becomes from a legal perspective. So, effectively, there could be some disincentive for ISPs to monitor and filter content. This, in turn, raises a moral dilemma for ISPs.

Should Internet Service Providers be held morally accountable for objectionable behavior that occurs in their forums? Deborah Johnson (2001) notes that while it might be easier to make a utilitarian case for holding ISPs legally liable in certain instances, it would be much more difficult to make the case that ISPs should be morally responsible for the behavior of their customers. Recently, however, Richard Spinello (2001) and Anton Vedder (2001) have tried to show, via very different kinds of arguments, why ISPs also should be held morally accountable to some extent. Neither Spinello nor Vedder address the issue of cyberstalking per se; however, we believe that Spinello's remarks regarding "on-line defamation" and Vedders's comments regarding on-line "harm," both of which are associated with ISPs, can help shed some light on the question before us. We briefly examine both arguments.

4.1 ISP Accountability: The Spinello View

Arguing that ISPs should be held morally accountable in cases involving defamation, Spinello first distinguishes between "moral responsibility" and "moral accountability." In making this distinction, he uses a model advanced by Helen Nissenbaum (1994). According to Nissenbaum's scheme, accountability, unlike responsibility, does not require *causality* or a causal connection. Spinello points out that because ISPs do not *cause* defamation, they cannot be held responsible in the strict or narrow arrow sense of the term. However, he argues that they could, nonetheless, be held accountable—i.e., "answerable"—in the sense that they "provide an occasion or forum" for defamation. Spinello is careful to point out that simply because an ISP presents an "occasion for defamation," it does not necessarily follow that an ISP is accountable. Rather, for an ISP to be accountable, two further conditions are required: (a) the ISP must also have some *capability* to do something about the defamation, and (b) the ISP failed to take action once it had been informed. Spinello believes that this standard of accountability takes into consideration what ISPs can reasonably do—i.e., what they are *capable* of doing—to prevent defamation or at least to limit its damage. So the fact that an ISP might not have caused the defamation does not rule out the possibility that the ISP can be held accountable in some sense for defamatory remarks.

Spinello concedes that technical and economic factors make it virtually impossible for ISPs to take preventative, or what he calls "pre-screening," measures that would detect or filter out defamatory messages. Thus we cannot hold ISPs responsible in a causal sense for defamation. Assuming that Spinello's overall argument is correct, however, we might hold ISPs accountable if they fail to take certain actions once they are informed that a victim has been defamed. For Spinello, these steps would include three actions: (i) prompt removal of the defamatory remarks; (ii) the issuance of a retraction on behalf of the victim; and (iii) the initiation of a good faith effort to track down the originator so that the defamation does not reoccur.

Does this threefold requirement provide us with a standard of accountability that is a "reasonable middle ground," as Spinello suggests? Or is it an unreasonable expectation for ISPs? Spinello notes that in the current system, a victim of defamation has no legal recourse because of the absolute immunity given to ISPs. On the other hand, the strict legal liability that was applied in the Prodigy case seems unduly harsh for ISPs. So Spinello believes that his alternative scheme provides the appropriate middle ground needed, because it grants some protection to victims of defamation without burdening the ISP. So even if the law does not require ISPs to take any action, Spinello believes that "post-screening" in a "diligent fashion" for content along the lines of the threefold criteria described above is the morally right thing to do. He concedes, however, that ISPs do not have the capability to "pre-screen" content for defamation.

4.2 ISP: Accountability: The Vedder Argument

Anton Vedder (2001) has recently advanced a very different kind of argument for why we should consider holding ISPs morally responsible for harm caused to individuals. Vedder suggests that we begin by drawing an important distinction between two senses of moral responsibility: *prospective* and *retrospective* responsibility. Whereas retrospective responsibility tends to be "backward looking," prospective responsibility is "forward looking." Vedder believes that in the past, arguments that have been used to ascribe legal liability to ISPs have tended to be *prospective* in nature. This is because the primary objective of liability laws has been to deter future on-line abuses rather than punish past offenses.

Vedder also notes that even though ISPs are not legally liable for their content under current U.S. law, the mere threat of legal liability can be used to deter ISPs from becoming lax about "policing" their electronic forums to some reasonable extent. So underlying the reasoning for arguments for applying strict legal liability to ISPs is the utilitarian principle that having liability laws in place will deter harm to ISP users in the future. And this legal argument, in turn, is based on a notion of moral responsibility that is essentially *prospective* in nature. Vedder also points out that we are hesitant to attribute a retrospective sense of responsibility to ISPs because this sense of moral responsibility:

(A) is usually applied to individuals (as opposed to organizations or what he calls "collectivities"), and

(B) it also often implies guilt.

And as Vedder correctly notes, the notion of guilt is typically attributed to individuals and not to organizations or collectivities. He suggests, however, that in some cases it also makes sense to attribute the notion of guilt to a collectivity such as an ISP.

Attributing some moral accountability to ISPs makes sense, in Vedder's scheme, because of the connection that exists between retrospective and prospective responsibility. Vedder argues that it makes no sense to hold an agent (i.e., either an individual or a collectivity) responsible for an act in a prospective sense if that agent could not also be held responsible for the act in a retrospective sense as well. So Vedder concludes that if we assume that collectivities such as ISPs can be held responsible in a prospective sense— a rationale that has been used as the basis for utilitarian arguments in attributing legal liability for ISPs—then we can also ascribe retrospective responsibility to ISPs. So, as in the case of Spinello, Vedder believes that ISPs can be held morally accountable to some extent for speech that is communicated in their electronic forums.

4.3 Some Implications for ISP Accountability in the Amy Boyer Case

We can now apply Vedder's and Spinello's arguments to the Amy Boyer cyberstalking case. Should Tripod and Geocities, the two ISPs that enabled Liam Youens to set up his Web sites about Boyer, be held morally accountable for the harm caused to Boyer and to her family? And should those two ISPs be held morally accountable, even if they were not responsible (in the narrow sense) for causing harm to Boyer and even if they can be exonerated from charges of strict legal liability? If the arguments by Vedder and Spinello succeed, then it is reasonable to hold these ISPs morally accountable if it also could be shown that Tripod and Geocities were capable of limiting the harm that resulted to Boyer. (Tim Remsberg, Amy Boyer's stepfather, has recently filed a wrongful death suit against both ISPs.)

Of course, one might ask what the purpose would be in attributing moral responsibility to ISPs if no legal action could be taken against them. At least two different replies are possible to this question, both of which might also cause us to be more careful in our thinking about moral issues involving cyberspace. First, an analysis of moral issues in this light could help us to distinguish further between moral and legal aspects of controversial cyberspace issues. Second, such an analysis can also help to consider some ways in which moral responsibility can be applied at the collective, as well as at the individual, level.

5. Moral Responsibility and Ordinary Internet Users

We next examine questions of moral responsibility that apply at the individual level, i.e., at the level of individual users in online communities. For example, do ordinary Internet users have a moral responsibility to inform "would-be victims" of their imminent danger to online stalkers? If an Internet user had been aware of Boyer's situation, should that user have notified Boyer that she was being stalked? In other words, should that user be morally obligated to do so?

Various proposals for controlling individual behavior in online communities have resulted in a conflict between those who wish to regulate strictly by law and those who wish to preserve the practice of self-regulation. Of course, this dispute is sometimes also at the base of arguments involving claims having to do with a "safe" social space vs. a "restrictive" one. In the case of cyberstalking, should we assist others based strictly on formal legal regulations, or should we assist them because it is the morally right thing to do?

5.1 A Minimalist Sense of Moral Obligation vs. an "Ethic of Care"

Some have argued that while morality can demand of an agent that he or she "do no harm" to others, it cannot *require* that an agent actively "prevent harm," or "do good." In one sense, to do no harm is to act in accordance with the rules of a moral system. But is doing so always sufficient for complying with what is required of us as moral agents? In other words, if it is in our power to prevent harm and to do good, should we do so? Some theoretical frameworks suggest that individuals should prevent harm (and otherwise do good), whenever it is in their power to do so. For example, if one believes, as some natural law theorists assert, that the purpose of morality is to alleviate human suffering and to promote human flourishing, whenever possible, then clearly we would seem obligated to prevent harm in cyberspace. An interesting account of this view has been advanced by Louis Pojman (2001). Unfortunately, we are not able to present Pojman's argument here in the detail that it deserves, since doing so would take us beyond the scope of this paper. But we can see how, based on a model like Pojman's, one might develop a fuller theory in which individuals have an obligation to "assist" others in the act of preventing harm from coming to those persons.

We recognize the difficulties of defending a natural law theory; and we are not prepared to do so here. However, we also believe that the kind of limited or moderate natural law theories that can be found in Pojman, and to some extent in James Moor (1998), can be very useful in making the case for an extended sense of moral obligation at the level of individuals.

Another moral framework that implies an expanded sense of moral responsibility on the part of individuals is the "ethic of care," introduced in a seminal work by Carol Gilligan (1982). Complying with a "care ethic," individuals would assist one another whenever it is in their power to do so. As such, an ethic based on care is more robust than a mere "non-interference" notion of ethics that simply involves "doing no harm to others"—i.e., it is concerned with a sense of commitment to others that Virginia Held (1995) describes as "above and beyond the floor of duty."

Gilligan's ethic of care has been contrasted with traditional ethical systems, such as utilitarian and Kantian theories. Alison Adam (2000) points out that traditional ethical theories are often based simply on following formal rules and that they tend to engender a sense of individualism (as opposed to community). Adam (2001, 2002) has also argued that an ethic of care, in particular, and feminist ethical theory in general, can help us to understand more clearly some of the social and ethical implications of cyberstalking behavior in ways that traditional ethical theories cannot.

Adopting an "ethic of care" in cyberspace would mean that individuals, i.e., ordinary Internet users, would be prone to assist others whenever they can help to prevent harm from coming to them. From this perspective, individuals would assist one another, even though there may be no specific laws or rules that require them to do so. In what sense would such an expectation on the part of individuals expand our conventional notion of moral obligation?

5.2 Expanding the Sphere of Moral Responsibility: A *Duty to Assist*

Questions concerning whether individuals have a "duty to assist" others often arise in the aftermath of highly publicized crimes such as the one involving the Kitty Genovese case in 1964. Genovese, a young woman, was murdered on the street outside her apartment building in Queens, New York, as thirty-eight of her neighbors watched. None of her neighbors called the police during the 35-minute period of repeated stabbings. Some have since referred to this refusal to assist a neighbor in critical need as "the Genovese Syndrome." Several police officers interviewed in the aftermath of the Genovese incident believed that Genovese's neighbors who witnessed the attack were morally obligated to notify the police, even though there may have been no formal law or specific statute requiring them to do so.

Drawing an analogy between the Genovese and Boyer cases, we can ask whether users who might have been able to assist Boyer should have done so (i.e., whether they were morally obligated to assist her). We can also ask what kind of community cyberspace will become, if people refuse to assist users who may be at risk to predators and murderers. First, we need to consider the potential harm that could come to members of the online community if we fail to act to prevent harm from coming to those individuals, when it is in our power to help and when doing so would neither cause us any great inconvenience nor put our safety at risk. What would have happened to Randi Barber if no one had intervened in her behalf? In the cyberstalking case involving Barber and Dellapenta, Barber's father, with the cooperation of the men who were soliciting her, provided evidence that led to Dellapenta's arrest. In the case of Amy Boyer, however, the same sense of individual moral responsibility and concern was not apparent. Consider that some Internet users had, in fact, viewed the Youens' Web site but did not inform Boyer that she was being stalked and that her life was in imminent danger. Like Kitty Genovese who received no assistance from members of her physical community, Amy Boyer received no assistance from members of the online community.

Because of what happened to Amy Boyer, and because of what could happen to future victims of online stalking, we argue that ordinary users, as members of an online community, should adopt a notion of moral responsibility that involves assisting fellow users. Doing so would help to keep cyberspace a safer place for everyone, but especially for women and children who are particularly vulnerable to stalking activities. Failing to embrace such a notion of moral responsibility, on the other hand, could result in users disconnecting themselves from their responsibilities toward fellow human beings.

6. Conclusion

We have examined some ethical concerns involving cyberstalking in general, and the Amy Boyer case in particular. We saw that stalking activities in cyberspace raise questions about the sphere of moral responsibility, both for ISPs and ordinary Internet users. We argued that ISPs and individual users, each in different ways, should assume some moral responsibility for helping to prevent harm from coming to individuals targeted by cyberstalkers.

Acknowledgments

We are grateful to Anton Vedder for some very helpful comments on an earlier version of this paper. We also wish to thank Detective Sergeant Frank Paison of the Nashua, NH Police Department, who was the chief investigator in the Amy Boyer cyberstalking case, for some helpful information that he provided during an interview with him.

Portions of this essay are extracted from Tavani (2004). We are grateful to John Wiley and Sons, Publishers for permission to reprint that material.

References

Adam, Alison (2000). "Gender and Computer Ethics," *Computers and Society,* Vol. 30, No. 4, pp. 17–24.

Adam, Alison (2001). "Cyberstalking: Gender and Computer Ethics," In Eileen Green and Alison Adam, eds. *Virtual Gender: Technology, Consumption, and Identity.* London: Routledge, pp. 209–234.

Adam, Alison (2002). "Cyberstalking and Internet Pornography: Gender and the Gaze." *Ethics and Information Technology,* Vol. 4, No. 2, pp. 133–142.

Foote, D. (1999). "You Could Get Raped," *Newsweek,* Vol. 133, No. 6, Feb. 8, pp. 64–65.

Gilligan, Carol (1982). *In a Different Voice.* Cambridge: Harvard University Press.

Grodzinsky, Frances S. and Herman T. Tavani (2001). "Is Cyberstalking a Special Type of Computer Crime?" In Terrell Ward Bynum, et al., eds, *Proceedings of ETHICPMP 2001: The Fifth International Conference on the Social and Ethical Impacts of Information and Communication Technology.* Vol. 2. Gdansk, Poland: Wydawnicktwo Mikom Publishers, pp.72–81.

Grodzinsky, Frances S. and Herman T. Tavani (2002). "Cyberstalking, Moral Responsibility, and Legal Liability Issues for Internet Service Providers." In Joseph Herkert, ed. *Proceedings of ISTAS 2002: The International Symposium on Technology and Society.* Los Alamitos, CA: IEEE Computer Society Press, pp. 331–339.

Held, Virginia (1995). "The Meshing of Care and Justice," *Hypatia,* University of Indiana Press, Spring.

Johnson, Deborah G. (2001). *Computer Ethics.* 3rd. ed. Upper Saddle River, NJ: Prentice Hall.

Moor, James H. (1998). "Reason, Relativity, and Responsibility in Computer Ethics," *Computers and Society,* Vol. 28, No. 1, 1998, pp. 14–21.

Nissenbaum, Helen (1994). "Computing and Accountability," *Communications of the ACM,* Vol. 37, No. 1, pp. 73–80.

Pojman, Louis P. (2001). *Ethics: Discovering Right and Wrong.* 4th ed. Belmont, CA: Wadsworth.

Spinello, Richard A. (2001). "Internet Service Providers and Defamation: New Standards of Liability." In R. A. Spinello and H. T. Tavani, eds. *Readings in CyberEthics.* Sudbury, MA: Jones and Bartlett, pp. 198–209.

Tavani, Herman T. (2000). "Defining the Boundaries of Computer Crime: Piracy, Break–ins and Sabotage in Cyberspace," *Computers and Society,* Vol. 30, No. 4, 2000, pp. 3–9.

Tavani, Herman T. (2002). "The Uniqueness Debate in Computer Ethics: What Exactly Is at Issue, and Why Does it Matter?" *Ethics and Information Technology,* Vol. 4, No. 1, pp. 37–54.

Tavani, Herman T. (2004). *Ethics and Technology: Ethical Issues in an Age of Information and Communication Technology.* Hoboken, NJ: John Wiley and Sons.

Tavani, Herman T. and Frances S. Grodzinsky (2002). "Cyberstalking, Personal Privacy, and Moral Responsibility," *Ethics and Information Technology,* Vol. 4, No. 2, pp. 123–132.

"The Web's Dark Side: In the Shadow's of Cyberspace, an Ordinary Week is a Frightening Time," *U.S. News & World Report,* Vol. 129, No. 8, Aug. 28, 2000.

Vedder, Anton H. (2001). "Accountability of Internet Access and Service Providers: Strict Liability Entering Ethics." *Ethics and Information Technology,* Vol. 3, No. 1, pp. 67–74.

Written on the Body:
Biometrics and Identity[1]

Irma van der Ploeg

1. Introduction

In May 1996, the Department of Public Aid of Illinois launched a project called I-SCAN. After buying software and equipment from a company named EyeDentify, the department invited all eligible welfare clients for interviews, at the end of which they were asked to look into an eyepiece, and to focus on a lighted target. A camera scanning the retina registered the highly individual pattern of blood vessels, and the image thus obtained was stored in the central computer system. The clients were told that compliance was conditional for receiving further benefits, and people who refused or did not show up for the interview were disqualified, or subjected to other forms of administrative sanctions.[2]

In December 1997, a New Jersey company demonstrated a new client identification system for ATMs (automatic teller machines) to an audience at the Banking Administration Institute's Conference in New Orleans. Instead of checking and matching pin numbers or passwords, the ATM would be equiped with a stereo camera. On introduction of an ATM card, this camera would be able to locate the face, find the eye, and take a digital picture of the iris at a distance of up to three feet. This image would then be compared with the one the customer supplied initially. To operationalize the system for existing ATM clients, the bank could take pictures during eight to ten ATM transactions, the best of which would then be used for the record copy.[3]

At the same occasion, another ATM security system was demonstrated displaying a completely "hands off" authentication method, based on face recognition and voice verification. The software, 'FaceIT', detects, locates, tracks, and

This essay originally appeared in Computers and Society, Vol. 29, No. 1 (March) 1999: 37–44. Copyright © 1999 by Irma van der Ploeg. Reprinted by permission.

identifies the face, after which the user is to speak his or her password into a microphone. The system then matches the voice against a previously recorded 'voice-print,' and, if all goes well, the user is granted access to their account.[4]

In the autumn of 1997, the face recognition system of the Sentri automated inspection commuter lane for low-risk vehicular traffic on the Otay Mesa crossing of the US/Mexican border was turned on. Dr. Atick, CEO of Visionics, Inc, indicated that the system uses FaceIt technology to automatically capture faces of drivers as they drive through the border, and performs facial verification against the enroll-ment record of the authorized driver. "Sentri has provided biometrics with one of the most difficult scenarios to date—it requires acquisition in an outdoors envi-ronment (while enrollment is indoors). It also involves totally uncontrolled condi-tions, lighting variability, uncontrolled pose and distance, car height, and all that has to be done in real time with moving subjects."[5]

Biometrics is often described as 'the next big thing in information technology.' Since the revolution in IT, with all its new forms of communication, surveillance, transaction, data generating, gathering, and commodification has changed so many aspects of social and economic life in western countries, the new levels of complexity call forth a need for new ways of maintaining order and providing secu-rity. Although some feel that biometrics are much overhyped, all major IT devel-opers and many smaller companies are rushing to put their biometric products, with names like UareU, FaceIT, TrueFace, SpeakEZ Voice Print, HourTrack, Veincheck, I-Scan, Viisage Gallery, Cybertouch, or NRIdentity, on the market.

Generally speaking, biometric technology involves the collection with a sensor-ing device of digital representations of physical features unique to an individual, like a fingerprint, pattern of the iris, the retina, the veins of the hand, physiognomic fea-tures, shape of the hand, or voicepatterns; it may also include typical behavioral pat-terns like typing or writing a signature. This digital representation of biometric data is then usually transformed via some algorithm to produce a so-called 'template.' This algorithmic transformation is said to be irreversible, meaning that from the template one cannot deduce the biometric data themselves. These templates are stored in a centralized database that is accessed when on following occasions the finger, hand, face, eye, or voice is presented to the system. After a similar algorithmic transformation of this second biometric image, a comparison can be executed. If a matching tem-plate is found, the person presenting themselves is 'recognized' and counts as 'known' to the system. It may also be the case that templates are not stored centrally, but on a chipcard instead. The user then has to present both chipcard and requested body part to 'prove' they are the legitimate user of the card, quite like pincodes now—the difference being, obviously, that pins can be forgotten or told to a friend in order to authorize them to use the card. In this form, biometric data in principle need not be stored by the organization, but given the opacity of information systems to common users, it may be worthwhile to observe that the biometric signal will always be avail-able for a moment during each interaction of the user with the system.

At first glance, biometrics appears not so different from older and existing forms of establishing and verifying personal identity in the deliverance of all kinds of social services and securing economic exchanges. The practices of requesting birth certificates, passports, identity cards, or drivers licenses, providing signatures, pictures, and data like place of birth, current address, have been around for a long time, and similarly serve the purpose of proving that one is who one claims to be—that is, a person entitled to the services, benefits, or privileges applied for. Such identification practices are based on certified documents issued by certifying agencies and institutions, and subsequent chains of such documents that serve their purpose by virtue of their referring to each other.[6] For example, a birth certificate is needed to get a passport; a passport, in turn, is requested when applying for a university student card, which then must be presented to get the university library card, and so on. Thus, the right to walk into the library, to make use of its computers, catalogues, attendants' time and expertise, and to take valuable books home, is premised on a set of identity markers that together, and by internal reference, establish that one is a student so and so, who payed their university tuition, paid previous fines on late returns, and thus is a deserving member of the population the library is there to serve. Such chains or webs of referencing documents are perceived as cumbersome and have often been proven sensitive to fraud and forgery. The issue of 'seed documents' is usually not accompanied by extensive checking of the identity of the requesting person; once issued, a false seed document can be used to obtain several other identity-documents that, in accumulation, are supposed to present reliable evidence of a person's identity. This is what Roger Clarke (1994) calls 'the entry-point paradox': the problem of low integrity being propagated from seed documents onward to derivative documents, or, phrased differently, the perception of high integrity identity produced by accumulating a collection of low integrity evidence.[7]

This general problem of so-called 'token-based' identification schemes, that is, identification based on possesion of a 'thing,' usually a document—alternative schemes are name, code, or knowledge-based schemes, which each suffer from particular weaknesses with regard to security and efficiency—is hoped to be solved by the much more reliable and efficient ways of establishing identity that biometrics can provide: A mere glance in a camera or a touch of some special table pad might do away with all the bureaucratic paperwork and the carrying around of endlessly multiplying identity papers, smart cards, and pins that always seem to get lost or forgotten when one needs them. Instead the inalienable features of one's own body will suffice to establish 'real' or 'positive' identification, so it is promised. "Biometrics are turning the human body into the universal ID card of the future."[8]

Major buyers of biometric technology can be found in the private sector, particularly among corporations with high security interests and/or limited access areas like banks and nuclear plants, but an important impetus comes from governments and government-related departments and services catering to client populations of thousands, often millions of people. Public institutions concerned with, e.g., the distribution of welfare and child benefits, immigration and applications for political asylum, or the issue of passports and car licenses are increasingly looking toward biometrics in order to improve what are perceived as system-threatening levels of fraud. Also, employers interested in keeping track of the whereabouts and activities of their employees, hospitals, and insurance companies in the process of introducing electronic patient records are among the many interested parties.

Finally, access to PCs and information systems themselves, instead of being controlled by passwords, codes, and login names, can be regulated by biometrics.

In April 1998, a couple of major IT corporations, including IBM, Microsoft, Novell, and Compaq, took the initiative to found "The BioApI™ Consortium," dedicated to the development of a so-called 'generic application programming interface' or 'API.' This involves the development of a specification for a global standard for existing and new biometric systems that will allow for their easy implementation in operating systems and application software already in use. To enhance its chances for succes, The Consortium invites as many other actors from industry and (US) government involved in biometrics and security technology as possible to participate in shaping the API. Recently, Siemens, Unisys, IriScan, Recognition Systems, The National Registry, The National Security Agency, and the Information Technology Laboratory of the National Institute of Standards and Technology have joined in.[9]

Although as of yet biometrics still represents a small portion of the total activity in IT, it is expected to grow significantly in years to come. Moreover, with so many forces joining in a coordinated effort to *make* it succeed, biometrics can be expected to become one of the dominant ways for bodies and information systems to connect. In the process, the very notion of identity is being reconstructed in ways that are highly relevant for the contemporary philosophical debate on the relations between the body, identity, and information technology.

This paper tries to contribute to this debate by exploring the types of questions that can be raised in relation to biometrics as a new type of technology affecting how we perceive identity. It seeks to articulate the significance of the fact that biometrics puts the body center-stage in matters of identification and information technology. To this task, it reviews some of the literature about IT and identity as it has developed during roughly the past decade, and asks whether this literature can help to make sense of biometrics, or whether this new technology perhaps poses genuinely new challenges. I argue, first, that biometrics requires a theory of identity that, unlike much of the available literature, takes the body and the embodied nature of subjectivity fully into account; and, second, that we need to investigate what *kind* of body the biometric body is, by researching the practices and informational configurations of which the 'readable' biometric body becomes a part.

2. Identifying Biometric Identity

The main question arising is in what sense 'identity' is at stake in biometric identification techniques. There are some indications that these techniques actually involve a very narrow concept of identity, which may not be very significant from a social, theoretical, or philosophical perspective.

In one of the few significant Dutch studies on legal aspects of biometrics, for instance, Van Kralingen et al. (1997) make a distinction between *determination* of identity and *verification* of identity. Whereas determination of identity, or 'real' identification, refers to a process involving investigation into a range of personal data, a right reserved to just a few agencies like the police and public services, verification is said to involve merely the comparison of two data, in order to determine whether they belong to the same person. Technically, the difference can be expressed as follows: identification refers to a search for a 'one to many' match, whereas verification refers to a search for a 'one to one' match. According to Van Kralingen et al., it is mainly the latter that is involved in biometric identification. Generally, the authors claim, verification can never provide certainty about the 'true identity' of a person.[10]

In the philosophical literature, some efforts can be discerned to make a comparable distinction. Schechtman (1990) for instance, claims that most of the analytical philosophical literature on identity is concerned with answering the question of *reidentification* as opposed to the question of *self-knowledge*. According to her, in a formulation typical of analytical philosophy, the question of reidentification involves spelling out "the necessary and sufficient conditions for saying that a person at t1 is the same person as a person at t2," resulting in criteria of personal identity over time. The question of identity as self-knowledge is said to involve something quite different, for it refers to the beliefs, values, and desires that are "expressive of who one really is."[11] Thus, whereas the first concept is said to refer to an answer to the question 'what makes a person the same as herself through time and space,' the second answers 'what makes a person unique and different from others.'

Although Schechtman is not in any way concerned with biometrics, one can see how her concept of 'reidentification' and that of 'verification' of Van Kralingen et al. both serve to distinguish a more narrow concept of identification from a broader one. Only the former may be at stake in biometrics, while the latter is taken to refer to something both authors perceive as "true" identity. The 'sameness of body' as mentioned by Schechtman as a primary criterion of sameness of the person—next to sameness of mind, or psychological identity, which traditionally has received far more philosophical attention—is obviously the one that biometric verfication is concerned with.

In view of comments and distinctions like these, the question must be raised in what sense, then, biometrics is about identity. Is it really just about verification of identity, as Van Kralingen et al. claim? If not, is it then perhaps merely about reidentification in the sense of Schechtman's continuity of the person, having nothing to do with one's personal identity understood as that which makes a person unique and different from others?

With respect to the first question, it should be made clear that there is indeed more at stake in biometrics than Van Kralingen's 'verification' practices. A quick look at available biometric products soon reveals that there are many systems being introduced, for example, by government social services interested in combatting fraud, which do not just involve the search for a 'one to one' match, but indeed a 'one to many,' as Van Kralingen defined the difference between the two technically. Whereas the first suffices for, say, biometrically secured ATMs where the client simultaneously presents the requested body part and a smart card on which biometric data are stored for comparison, it will not do for systems that are used for detection of "double dippers." Many biometric systems in social services are introduced precisely to prevent or catch people using fake identities in order to receive more benefits or welfare payments. These systems are designed to check an applicant's identity against an already enrolled client population, which necessitates the identity check of the 'one to many' kind. The crucial difference is whether the biometric feature is compared to a database containing a collection of centrally stored biometric data or not. In the case of personalized smart cards it is indeed possible to have the biometric data, once processed and stored on the card, destroyed. But even for ATMs and comparable applications, the technology tends toward replacement of token-based identification altogether, and promises to do away with not just the pincodes but the smart cards themselves. This means that the biometric data will have to be stored in the system—and, one might add, it also means that control over the data shifts from the card holder to the system controller. But apart from the promises of the imminent advent of the "completely hands-off ATM" (see introduction), it should be noted, as George Tomko (1998) explains, that at the basis of every verification procedure—he calls it 'authentication,' as many others do—lies an identification procedure, so that even 'just' verification always implies that an identification procedure has taken place at some time.[12] Verification of identity as sufficient for establishing whether or not the requesting person is entitled to the service or benefit applied for only makes sense if eligibility has been established before. In order to establish eligibility, identity (and usually many other personal data as well) is checked. Verification then serves to confirm that the requesting person is indeed the person whose eligibility was demonstrated before. Moreover, if biometrically personalized tokens are to become as ubiquitous in the future as is being planned for today, Tomko quite plausibly conjectures, then 'efficiency' and 'cost reduction' of replacement of lost, stolen, or damaged cards will probably become the justification to have biometric data stored centrally by many organizations.

Thus, biometrics is not just about as narrow an identity check as some authors maintain. It does involve the generation and storage of digital representations of unique physical features for the purpose of identifying that person within an information system. And although it may differ from system to system to whom or what exactly (which authority, which social servant, which machine, or database) the system "reports back" its findings and to what effect, or whether this effect requires other people to intervene or triggers automated action ("no, you have not been recognized, you may not enter this building," "yes, you have been recognized, you will be prosecuted for "double dipping"), the general potential of biometric representation and recognition schemes is exactly that they differentiate between one human individual and another. They recognize *both* sameness and difference.

This latter point is pertinent to Schechtman's philosophical distinction between different kinds of identification, or better, different concepts of identity, too. It may appear quite plausible to argue—as it is often done—that biometrics is merely about establishing *sameness* of the person rather than affecting the issue of what makes this person unique and different from others. At first glance there seems to be a fundamental difference here that renders biometrics an innocent technological practice that only in a rather trivial sense is concerned with personal identity. However, here too, several reasons exist not to accept such an account too readily.

First, the traditional stress in philosophical accounts of identity (in both senses) on psychology (character, beliefs, desires) rather than the body, is unwarranted, and reflects the longstanding denial of the relevance of embodiment to subjectivity within western philosophy. Whereas in accounts like Schechtman's, the body is recognized when talking about criteria for identity as sameness of the person—albeit short and as a mere aside to the extensive treatment of the psychological criterion—in the matter of identity as unicity of the person the body has disappeared completely, and only a disembodied kind of self-reflexivity and subjectivity remains. However, if we would consider the body for just one moment in the matter of what makes a person unique and different from others, it would become immediately clear that it is, of course, highly relevant. There are obviously no two bodies the same, and it is actually quite a tour de force to ignore the body in how we differentiate one person from another (a fact of which biometricists, unlike some philosophers, are obviously quite aware). It seems almost too banal, but it appears quite plausible that the mind-body split in modern Western discourses is accountable for the fact that it is apparently still hard to acknowledge that, even in talking individual psychology, the kind of body one has, the fact of embodiment, is quite relevant. Perhaps the Cartesian relegation of the body to the domain of objects and matter has made philosophers equate the body too much with the standardized, normalized, generalized medical textbook version of the body to remain sensitive to the unicity of each body. And while the 'mind' has been associated with immateriality and subjectivity, psychology as a discipline itself is the most obvious example of treating 'the mind' as an object of study amenable to lawlike generalizations and normalization.

A second indication that relativizes the philosophical distinction between the two concepts of identity can be found in the way Schechtman characterizes the difference between the concept of identity as sameness of the person, and identity as the object of self-knowledge about one's "true values, beliefs, and desires."[13]

Another way to express this difference would be to characterize the former as involving a third person perspective, and the latter as requiring a first person perspective. Schechtman speaks of 'objectification' and 'subjectification' here. There are, however, several problems with absolutizing the distinction between third person and first person perspectives in matters of identity, and hence with the assumption that biometrics is only concerned with third person establishment of sameness of the person.

First, absolutizing the difference implies the assumption that there is something like an authentic, true self to which the subject has an exclusive, epistemologically privileged access. This ignores the social and cultural dimension in identity formation of even the most 'private' self. For a long time now, theories on the constitution of the subject from many different hues, ranging from psychoanalysis, symbolic interactionism, to poststructuralism, feminist theory, and communitarian ethics, have converged toward a consensus on the fact that the notion of a centered, authentic core self existing prior to the social and cultural is a fiction—however valuable and "real in its consequences" this fiction may be. Rather, this centered self is a contingent achievement, that is constantly, and often only partly, or temporarily succesfully, *performed*.

Second, this performance, which involves the simultaneous co-construction of 'the other,' 'the object' etc., occurs in a cultural, social, and material world of which technology forms an increasingly significant, constitutive element. In view of this as well, the assumption that biometrics merely involves establishing identity in the sense of sameness of the person becomes questionable. Rather than assuming that technology expresses or registers a pregiven identity, we may want to look into the possibility and the ways in which technology is *actively involved* in practices of defining who we are. The growing contemporary interest in theorizing the issue of identity in relation to rapidly developing and changing technological practices—among which medical and information technologies in particular attract much attention—signals the importance of this issue.[14]

For instance, on the issue of identity in relation to information technology, a growing literature is developing that doubtless is concerned with identity in the "broader" sense: It deals with personal identity as self-conception that is performed in computer mediated social interaction and informed by cultural narratives. This mostly interdisciplinary literature builds upon the theoretical traditions mentioned and often involves empirical research. It seeks to answer the question *how* information technology is involved in shaping and changing our identities. The next section reviews some exemplary work on this question in order to evaluate its usefulness in making sense of biometrics.

3. Virtual Identities

One of the first examples that springs to mind in this context is, of course, the seminal work of Sherry Turkle. A relatively early, and by now almost classical work on the question of identity in relation to information technology is her 1984 *The Second Self; Computers and the Human Spirit,* followed in 1995 by *Life on the Screen; Identity in the Age of Internet.* Turkle observed and interviewed a large number of different computer users, varying from school children to members of the early 'hacker culture' at MIT. Extending her research into the developments surrounding the Internet during the early 1990s, she consistently finds people redefining themselves through their interactions with computers.[15]

A perspective combining psychoanalysis and critical theory is represented by Raymond Barglow's *The Crisis of the Self in the Age of Information* (1994). Barglow bases his analysis of human-computer interaction and the constitution of subjectivity and identity on empirical data in the form of dreams of (professional) computer users and their own interpretations of these. He finds that while mechanical technologies such as the car support the modernist conception of the autonomous, well defined, separate subject, information technology undermines it, or rather, engenders a form of 'hyperindividualism' and isolation, while simultaneously endorsing experiences of fragmented, decentered selves, and dissolution of the boundary between self and machine.[16]

Rooted in a more monodisciplinary philosophical tradition is the work of Robyn Brothers, who, in *Cyborg Identities and the Relational Web* (1997), argues that IT and virtual reality give us cause to rethink our ethical concepts of personhood and identity more thoroughly, since computer mediated communication and interaction give rise to forms of agency and social interaction that challenge traditional notions of community. Arguing from a conception of identity as found in the hermeneutics of Ricoeur, or in the work of communitarians and narrativists like Macintyre, Nussbaum, Rorty, and Taylor, Brothers finds their accounts of narrative identity based on too restricted a form of narrative to accommodate the effects of new forms of fictional interaction on personal identity formation that information technology engenders. She argues that what is needed is a reinterpretation of both individualism and the underlying assumptions of communitarianism, since the electronic revolution is changing the very ontological underpinnings of these accounts of self and identity.[17]

From a different perspective, Mark Poster (1990, 1995) presents arguments amounting to a position comparable to that of Brothers. He too sees the new information and communication technologies as entailing a fundamental change in culture, which encourages a different type of subject, and changes the very way identities are structured.[18] "Discussions of these [ICT] technologies tend often to miss precisely this level of analysis," he claims, "treating them as enhancements for already formed individuals to deploy to their advantage or disadvantage." [19]

This selection, although inevitably somewhat idiosyncratic, can nevertheless be viewed as representative of the kind of positions taken on the issue of IT and identity. In this literature, IT is seen as a fundamental challenge to traditional concepts of the self and personal identity. Usually, the concepts of subjectivity and identity at stake are described as the paradigmatic modernist, autonomous, centered self as the one being either threatened, falsified, or merely historically overtaken, whereas the kind of subjectivity fostered by IT is described as the paradigmatic postmodernist view on the subject: decentered, with uncertain boundaries, fragmented and multiple.

However, what most of this literature has in common—and the four authors discussed are no exception—is an emphasis on what is perceived as the most distinguishing characteristic of IT mediated interaction, and the identities it affords, the *absence of bodies*. Relying much on the metaphor of cyberspace as a virtual space in which identities are performed or narratives are being developed, it is above all the disembodied nature of subjectivity in relation to IT that takes on significance in these accounts. It is perhaps no coincidence that the primary example of IT use in the context of debates on identity concerns that of cyberspace and virtual reality, or specifically, the electronic 'spaces' exemplified by discussion lists, MUDs, MOOs, and other games. What captures the imagination of many authors is the way such games afford opportunities for role-playing with multiple invented or fictional characters referred to as 'virtual selves' or 'avatars.' Thus it is claimed that IT allows for the extension and multiplication of personal identities, which, in many cases, is likened to the postmodernist idea of the fragmented or multiple self. Characterized by the absence of bodies and other identity clues, these 'playgrounds' are perceived as a realm of social freedom, where the restraints of ordinary life are left behind and the imagination is set free.

There are obvious questions to be raised against such views—for instance, about the significance of the fact that most of these accounts tend to overemphasize the importance of interactive games, to the utter neglect of, e.g., administrative uses of IT, or the overoptimistic views on what setting peoples' fantasies free will accomplish in terms of social freedom. But it is, first, the assumption that the body / embodiment *could* be irrelevant to identity, and, second, the assumption that in electronic interaction the body is 'left behind' that are most problematic.

With regard to the first assumption, it appears that these very contemporary and even 'postmodernist' accounts of identity are still haunted by a 'modernist' mind-body dualism, despite the fact that situatedness, embodiment, and 'difference' are highly thematized within postmodernist theories on subjectivity and identity. Indeed, concepts like these were at the core of the deconstruction of modern, universalist accounts of the rational subject in the first place. Whereas the literature discussed does subscribe, in general, to the insight that identity is performative, intersubjectively and socially constituted within culturally defined parameters, it manages to ignore the material and physical dimensions implied in this process. In this respect, ironically enough, it risks ending up in the corner of those believing that 'consciousness' is so independent of materiality and embodiment that they actually phantasize about 'downloading' consciousness into an electronic network, leaving the cumbersome physical body, the "wet platform," behind for good.[20]

The second assumption is also dubious, especially in the context of biometrics. Today already, one is repeatedly warned about the ease with which one's name, location, and movements on the Internet can be traced by anyone so interested. An abundant privacy literature, accompanied by actual activism, legislation efforts, and policy regulations, testifies to the identifying and tracking potential of many IT practices. The concept of the 'digital persona,' coined by Clarke (1994) to capture the enormous amount of personal data existing dispersed through databases and electronic networks, amounts to a kind of shadow identity of which the subject in question may be unaware, but which can be assembled into an extensive biography.[21] While Clarke remained somewhat vague about the relationship between the 'digital persona' and the subject whose identity is concerned, it may be that biometrics will become the 'missing link,' unequivocally tying the digital biography to one particular body.

Moreover, one of the fastest growing applications of biometrics is in access control and security of PCs and electronic networks themselves. As Oscar Pieper, president of Identicator Technology, a large company specializing in fingerprint recognition, and supplier to the US Ministry of Defense, put it: "The world is wired. The world is online. And so one of the greatest applications for biometric technology is access to that wired PC world. Biometrics is a method of being sure that the person who is gaining access, who is a faceless person, to whatever it is, a financial transaction, a data access type of transaction, a brokerage account or something like that, is who he really claims to be."[22] Thus, rather than IT rendering the body irrelevant to identity—a mistaken idea to begin with—the coupling of biometrics with IT unequivocally puts the body center stage.

4. Questioning the Biometric Body

The question to be raised about biometrics is what the ramifications are of the fact that, quite contrary to what has been written on the subject of IT and identity thus far, bodies will become important to identity. One is tempted to add "once again," for despite philosophical theories to the contrary, it is not particularly new for bodies to be taken as a crucial clue to identity. Far from it: For the larger part of history, and often to extreme extents, the kind of body one has has been perceived as determining one's identity. Though the attributed importance and significance may have varied over time, and the particular characteristics deemed significant (skin, eye, and hair color, size and shape of various body parts, age, gender, sexual inclination, language use, etc.) as well as, *who* one is perceived to be, what one essentially is like, capable of, or allowed to do, has, at one time or another, depended largely on whether one had blond hair and blue eyes, a small skull and thick, connecting eyebrows, or a high pitched voice and an elegant gait—and it still often does. Challenged as 'biological determinism,' these ways of tying identity to the body took the biomedical body as a signifier of identity. Historical research has shown how the modern, biomedical body was not the result of objective scientific method, as the standard view on the developments of 18th and 19th century science would have it, but was in fact demonstrably shaped in relation and response to political challenges of the time. Claims to equality from women and people of color from the colonies during the period in which the 'universal rights of man' were proclaimed made anatomical and physiological scientists focus on sexual and racial bodily traits that could justify exclusion of certain groups from citizenship.[23] The contemporary emphasis on historical specificity, situatedness, and embodiment is in large part a reaction to double-tongued discourses that on the one hand proclaimed the universal equality of man, while simultaneously taking only one small category of humans as exemplary, defining everyone else as deviant by nature. The abstractions that proclaimed one form of human subjectivity to be generic have been brought back down to earth to show their hidden specificity and rootedness in particular forms of human embodiment. So, paradoxically, fighting the spectre of biological determinism necessitates taking issue with views on (rational) subjectivity and identity that disregard embodiment and situatedness.

How does the biometric body and its determination of identity relate to all this? What is the significance of the fact that it is the *body* that is used as an identifier? Is the identifying biometric body somehow biological determinism in a new guise? To attempt answering these questions, we will need theories of identity that take the body and the embodied nature of subjectivity fully into account. And, first of all, we need to investigate what *kind* of body the biometric body is.

To approach this latter question, let me first quote once more from the congressional hearing on biometrics, held by the Committee on Banking and Financial Services in May 1998. One of the representatives present tried to express what he found disturbing about biometrics, saying: "what we are gathering is medical information. It is not just biometrics and fascinating technology, which it absolutely is; biometrics: bio, as in having to study biology; biometrics, this is specific fingerprinting of each human individual."[24] Despite the somewhat clumsy formulation, we can clearly sense that the biometric body is likened here to the biomedical body; comparable to it with regard to its personal nature and its close 'belonging' to the individual. Biometric data are therefore perceived as very sensitive information. In contrast, J.L. Wayman, director of the National Biometric Test Centre at San Jose State University, argued: "We must note that with almost all biometric devices, there is virtually no personal information contained therein. From my fingerprint, you cannot tell my gender; you cannot tell my height; my age, or my weight. There is far less personal information exposed by giving you my fingerprint than by showing you my driver's license."[25]

At first glance, the representative seems to be mistaken, and Wayman getting it right; it is of course not *medical* information that is gathered and stored through biometric technology; it is not about the functioning of the body, nor about its history of pathologies and diseases. Biometrics is not a branch of medicine, but instead a special form of mathematical and statistical science. But if the body that biometrics is concerned with is not a biomedical body, what kind of body is it? Mr. Wayman seems to have a point in saying that from a fingerprint, or any other biometric alone, we, in general, will not be able to tell anything about another person. Nevertheless, the recently proposed Californian 'Consumer Biometric Privacy Act' includes the provision that "collection of a biometric identifier must not conflict with race, gender, or other anti-discrimination laws," which suggest that there are at least some people perceiving dangers in this respect.[26]

So we are stuck with a riddle: How can a biometric identifier be both identifying and not saying anything particular about you? I think the key to this riddle may be found in the idea that meaning is not something intrinsic, but, following Wittgenstein, determined by *use*. Following this kind of reasoning, we should perhaps not expect to be able to determine any intrinsic meaning of biometric data, or the biometric body in general, but investigate quite specifically what uses and practices biometrics will become part of. That way, we can see how the biometric body might differ from the biological body of biological determinism: The whole idea of biological determinism derived its force (and its threat) from the concept of the biological body as existing and being knowable independently from culture, history, and society (even though this has repeatedly been shown to be a myth). This body functioned in political arguments by virtue of the proclaimed objectivity and ahistoricity of the qualities and characteristics attributed to it.

Unlike the body of biological determinism, the biometric body is quite clearly and undeniably a body that does not exist apart from technology and its concomitant cultural practices, but is inseparable from the technology that produces it. Unlike the body rendered *knowable* in the biomedical sciences, biometrics generates a *readible* body: It transforms the body's surfaces into digital codes and ciphers to be read by a machine. "Your iris is read, in the same way that your voice can be printed, and your fingerprint can be read," [27] by computers that, in turn, have become "touch-sensitive," and endowed with seeing and hearing capacities. Thus transformed into readible "text," the meaning and significance of the biometric body will be contingent upon "context" and the relations established with other "texts." Building on these discursive metaphors, we might say that the contexts giving meaning to biometrics are constituted by the practices it is part of, while its meaning in an intertextual sense will be brought about by the data to which it is going to be linked electronically.

This opens up ways to investigate the different meanings that will become attached to the biometric body and the ways in which it will be tied to identity. Anticipating the empirical work this will require, we may hypothesize some plausible outcomes. Judging from the uses to which biometrics are being put today, and the forces motivating its rapid development, testing, and implementation, biometrics seem to be about maintaining social order by regulating in- and exclusion from socio-economic goods, geographic spaces, and liberties. The groups targeted for (obligatory) biometric identification disproportionately include criminals, recipients of welfare, medicaid or other benefits, workers, asylants, and immigrants. There are indications that most of the applications involving "one to many" searches will be found in social services, where fears of "double dipping" are the motivation behind implementing the new systems. Conversely, biometric identification may exemplify privilege as well, as for example in airports and border control, where "members of the club," after being assessed as 'low-risk travelers' (who will be seen as high risk travelers?), are given the privilege to jump the queue and avoid thorough controls. Other examples of privilege regulated by biometrics might include granting access to secured geographical spaces, particular parts of IT systems and types of information, or authorizations for executing remote financial transactions.

If these intuitions would be confirmed, we could conclude that it is not a form of biological determinism we are encountering in biometrics. Instead, biometrics would become one of the clearest examples of the way technology renders the nature-culture distinction (biological and social identity) obsolete, since the difference between natural bodies and social structures has become meaningless. Just like our culture of biotechnology transforms innate bodily characteristics, rendering 'nature' more and more an object of design, with biometrics bodies may become inscribed with identities shaped by longstanding social and political inequalities.

References

1. This project was carried out within the framework of the Incentive Programme Ethics and Policy, which is supported by the Netherlands Organization for Scientific Research. I wish to thank Jeroen van den Hoven, Jos de Mul, and Deborah Johnson and the participants of CEPE 98, London School of Economics, 14-15 December 1998, for their encouragements and useful suggestions. This paper is reprinted from *Computers and Society* Vol.29, No.1, pp. 37–44.

2. *Biometrics in Human Services,* Vol.1, No.4, 1997, p. 3.

3. *Biometrics in Human Services,* Vol.2, No1, 1998, p. 10.

4. Ibidem, p. 12.

5. *Biometrics in Human Services,* Vol.1, No.6, p. 2.

6. Roger Clarke (1994). Human Identification in Information Systems: Management Challenges and Public Policy Issues. *Information Technology and People*, Vol.7, No.4, pp. 6–37.

7. Ibidem, p. 16.

8. ABC News, Jan 15, 1998, quoted in *Biometrics in Human Services*, Vol.2, No.1, p. 14.

9. *Biometrics in Human Services* Vol.2, No.5, p. 15.

10. Robert Van Kralingen, Corien Prins, Jan Grijpink (1997). *Het lichaam als sleutel. Juridische beschouwingen over biometrie* [The body as key. Legal aspects of biometrics], Samsom Bedrijfsinformatie, Alphen aan den Rijn/Diegem. pp. 3–66, specifically p. 9 (see for a version in English http:\\ www.consortium.org).

11. Marya Schechtman (1990). Personhood and Personal Identity. *The Journal of Philosophy*, Vol 87, No.2, pp. 71–92.

12. George Tomko (1998). *Biometrics as a Privacy-Enhancing Technology: Friend or Foe of Privacy?* Paper presented at the Privacy Laws & Business 9th Privacy Commissioners' / Data Protection Authorities Workshop, Santiago de Compostela, Spain.

13. Schechtman (1990). p. 71.

14. Important work in this area, though not discussed in this paper, is done by Donna Haraway and by Katherine Hayles.

15. Sherry Turkle (1984). *The Second Self. Computers and the Human Spirit* Simon and Schuster, New York; (1995) *Life on the Screen. Identity in the Age of Internet.* Simon and Schuster, New York.

16. Raymond Barglow (1994). *The Crisis of the Self in the Age of Information. Computers, Dolphins and Dreams.* Routledge, London / New York, p. 73–4.

17. Robyn Brothers (1997). Cyborg Identities and the Relational Web: Recasting 'Narrative Identity' in Moral and Political Theory. *Metaphilosophy* Vol.28, No.3, pp. 249–258; specifically p. 255–6.

18. Mark Poster (1990). *The Mode of Information. Poststructuralism and Social Context* Polity Press, Cambridge, UK.; (1995) Postmodern Virtualities. In: Mike Featherstone and Roger Burrows (eds.) *Cyberspace, Cyberbodies, Cyberpunk. Cultures of Technological Embodiment.* Sage, London, pp. 79–95, specifically p. 79.

19. Ibidem, p. 80.

20. This refers to the ideas of "transhumanists" like Marvin Minsky, Hans Moravec, and their followers.

21. Roger Clarke (1994). The Digital Persona and Its Application to Data Surveillance. *The Information Society*, Vol.10, pp. 77–92.

22. Michael N. Castle (Chair) (1998). *Hearing on Biometrics and the Future of Money*, Committee on Banking and Financial Services, Washington, May 20, p. 104.

23. Two excellent studies on this subject are: Londa Schiebinger (1993). *Nature's Body. Gender in the Making of Modern Science.* Beacon Press, Boston; and Thomas Lacqueur (1990). *Making Sex. Body and Gender from the Greeks to Freud.* Harvard U.P., Cambridge Mass./ London.

24. Michael N. Castle (Chair) (1998). *Hearing on Biometrics and the Future of Money*, Committee on Banking and Financial Services, Washington, May 20, p. 47.

25. Ibidem, p. 49.

26. *Biometrics in Human Services*, Vol.2, No.2, May 1998, p. 11.

27. Michael N. Castle (Chair) (1998). *Hearing on Biometrics and the Future of Money*, Committee on Banking and Financial Services, Washington, May 20, p. 80.

Ethical Aspects of Facial Recognition Systems in Public Places

Philip Brey

1. Introduction

After Super Bowl XXXV in Tampa, Florida in June 2001, a major controversy ensued. It became public that police had used video cameras equipped with facial recognition technology ("facecams") to scan the faces of the 100,000 visitors to the Bowl in search of wanted criminals. Many people were outraged, and this Super Bowl has since been dubbed the "Snooper Bowl." Although not well known to the general public, facial recognition technology is nowadays used in many places across the world. It is used for a variety of purposes, one of them being surveillance in public areas, as in the Super Bowl.[1] Even at the time of Super Bowl XXXV, facecams were already in use in several cities, including cities in the U.S. and the U.K, for routine surveillance of public areas.

Since the September 11 terrorist attacks, just months after the Super Bowl event, federal governments and airports have taken an interest in the technology as an instrument in the fight against international terrorism. It is currently in trial use in several international, airports, including Boston's Logan, Dallas-Fort Worth International and Palm Beach International.[2] Moreover, the Enhanced Visa Entry Reform Act of 2002 will require all Americans and all non-U.S. citizens visiting the U.S. to have a passport with a biometric chip that contains their encoded facial features by October, 2004. This data would then be checked with a database of suspected criminals and terrorists upon arrival in the U.S. This measure follows the recommendations of the International Civil Aviation Organization (ICAO), which earlier ruled that facial recognition technology should be the the method used to identify travelers worldwide and who is proposing a global database that encodes passport information and facial features of all passport holders worldwide.[3] The European Union is also working on new passports with facial biometrics.

This essay originally appeared in the *Proceedings of the Fourth Conference on Computer Ethics–Philosophical Enquiry* (CEPE 2001), Lancaster University, UK, pp. 14–25. Copyright © 2001 by Philip Brey. Reprinted by permission.

[1] "Critics Blast U.S. Ties to 'Snooper Bowl' Technology," Jay Lyman, *NewsFactor Network,* August 2, 2001

[2] "Face the Facts - Facial recognition technology's troubled past–and troubling future;" David Kopel and Michael Krause, *ReasonOnline,* October 2002. (http://www.reason.com/0210/fe.dk.face.shtml)

[3] "Next level in passport technology may not be ready," Brian Bergstein, *Associated Press,* August 24, 2003; "Your ID Going Digital," *Cnews Canada,* June 11, 2003.

In this paper, I will examine ethical aspects of the use of facial recognition technology for surveillance purposes, focusing particularly on the balance between security and privacy and other civil liberties. My ethical analysis will be based on a careful analysis of current facial recognition technology, of its use in video surveillance (CCTV) systems, and of the arguments of proponents and opponents of such "smart" CCTV systems. From an ethical point of view, Smart CCTV is interesting because it involves two contested technologies: video surveillance technology and biometrics. I will examine how ethical objections to Smart CCTV (or facecams) refer to objections to these two broader types of technology.[4]

To focus my discussion, I will be discussing a particular facial recognition technology, the FaceIt engine that has been developed by Identix, a leading developer of identification technologies and systems. In the next section, I will carefully analyze the technology behind the FaceIt engine and consider the types of applications for which the engine is used. In Section 3, I will consider the use of the FaceIt engine in Smart CCTV systems in public places, focusing specifically on their use in the Ybor City district of Tampa, Florida. I will describe the particular system that is used, as well its users, the setting in which it is used, and the purposes for which it is used. In Section 4, I will turn to the debate on Smart CCTV, focusing again on Ybor City as a case. I will outline the arguments used by proponents and opponents of the system, and identify the values and assumptions that underly these arguments. This will then lead me to a straight-on discussion of the ethical aspects of facecams in Section 5, where I will critically discuss three problems with the use of facecams: problems or error, function creep, and privacy. In Section 6, I conclude with a policy discussion of the use of facecams in public places.

2. Facial Recognition Technology: the FaceIt Engine and Its Applications

There are now several firms that market facial recognition technology. Some of these specialize in the development of facial recognition software, whereas others specialize in the implementation of complete systems consisting of both hardware and software. The core of a facial recognition system, however, is its software, and specifically the software that is capable of analyzing digital images and recognizing faces in them. I will here consider one such program, or "software engine," the FaceIt® software engine of Identix Corporation. The FaceIt engine is currently the most widely used facial recognition technology and is also one of the most advanced systems on the market. The FaceIt engine was originally developed by Visionics Corporation, which merged in 2002 to become Identix. Identix is a U.S. corporation based in Minnetonka, Minnesota, with over 500 employees worldwide, and is the current worldwide leader in identification technologies and systems, including fingerprint identification and facial recognition technology.

---

[4] All information on Identix and the FaceIt system in this section has been taken from Identix' website, www.identix.com, in 2003, and from its predecessor's website, www.visionics.com, in 2001, unless indicated otherwise. The views expressed and conclusions drawn in this and other sections are my own and not those of Identix Corp. FaceIt® is a registered trademark.

FaceIt is a software engine that is run on a computer to detect and recognize human faces. It takes as its input digitally encoded images, which are either digitally coded photographs or still images obtained from streaming video, and "scans" them for faces. The engine can be used for mere *face finding*, which is locating one or more faces in an image. However, its more customary use is that of *face recognition*: comparing a face found in an image against a database of facial images in order to find a match. Such face recognition can be organized in two ways. In *one to one matching*, also called *verification or authentication*, the system is used to determine if a face matches an entry in the database. In *one to many searching*, or *identification*, a list of matches is generated for those entries in the database that are above a certain threshold similarity to the input face. Next to face finding and face recognition, the engine is also capable of *tracking*: following the face of a person in a video field of view as the person moves around.

The FaceIt engine works by analyzing up to eighty facial points around the nose, cheekbones, and eyes in a facial image. It can do this by means of a specially developed mathematical technique called Local Feature Analysis (LFA). This technique is based on the assumption that a facial image is built up out of a finite number of facial building elements, or features, that vary in each face and that may moreover have different positions relative to one another. Such building elements and their relative positions are detected using a complex algorithm, and are then encoded into a complex mathematical formula called a *faceprint*. A faceprint is a mathematical formula that is unique to a person's face. It is moreover resistant to changes in lighting, skin tone, eyeglasses, hairstyle, and facial hair, and is also indifferent to the angle at which a face is observed, as long as the eyes are clearly visible. Faceprints come in two sizes: a light version of just 88 bytes and a detailed version of 3.5 Kilobytes.

Faceprints have several advantages over mere digitized facial images for the purpose of facial recognition. First, they specify features that are unique to an individual's face and distinguish it from millions of others, without including information that may be different in different circumstances, such as lighting, facial angle, facial expression, and eyeglasses. Second, they can be processed at a much greater speed than facial images. Using a 733 MHz Pentium III CPU, for example, a FaceIt engine can search up to 1 million faceprints per second. Third, they allow for very precise and reliable estimates of the degree to which two facial images match each other. According to Identix, the error rate for matches of facial images of good quality is less than one percent.

The FaceIt engine is a software engine, not a complete hardware system. It can be combined with various types of hardware and software to create different kinds of face recognition systems. Moreover, the engine itself can be configured in different ways, to accommodate for specific contexts and purposes of use. This means that the FaceIt engine is extremely flexible, and allows for a very broad range of applications. Currently, the engine is used in four broad types of applications: authentication systems, identification systems, criminal justice database systems, and surveillance systems.

When used as an *authentication system*, the FaceIt engine is used to secure transactions and to clearly associate each action with the identity of the person who is conducting it. In this modality, it may serve as a replacement of a password or PIN, and may be used for access control, border control, computer and network security, and banking transactions. Currently, FaceIt is used in all these capacities, ranging from its use as a biometric screensaver in SONY laptops to its use in a border crossing system by the Israeli Ministry of Defense to manage the flow of individuals entering and exiting the Gaza Strip.

When used as an *identification system,* the engine is used to compare the picture on ID documents (such as passports, driver's licenses, etc.) with a database in order to detect identity fraud, which may occur in the form of identity theft, duplicate aliases, and fictitious identities. The engine has been used, for example, in the July 2000 election in Mexico to search for possible duplicates in voter registration records, and is also used in many driver licensing and social service benefits systems. Used in *criminal justice database systems,* the engine allows law enforcement agencies to compare photographs (usually, mug shots) of suspects with the images in its databases. In 2001, the engine was used in this capacity by law enforcement agencies in eight U.S. states.

The use of the engine as a *surveillance system* is the use that I will be concerned with in the remainder of this paper. In this type of application, the engine is used to recognize faces at a distance, often in a crowd or in an otherwise complex scene, or to follow the presence or position of persons in a video field of view. Such surveillance is performed with the use of one or more video cameras. Often, the system is a stationary CCTV system, which is then sometimes called "Smart CCTV;" the cameras that are used are sometimes referred to as "facecams." Surveillance using face recognition technology can have various purposes, such as identifying criminals or terrorists, identifying missing persons, identifying VIP guests or customers, and tracking suspicious characters. In this capacity, the FaceIt engine is currently used in town centers, airports, casinos, construction job sites, and various other places.[5]

3. Using Facecams: Video Surveillance in Public Places with "Smart CCTV"

In discussing "smart" video surveillance, I will focus on its use in public city areas. I will not discuss its use in the private sector, in which it is not used very often anyway (e.g., it is used as a time and attendance system by a British civil construction firm).[6] I will also pay little attention to places that are privately run but nevertheless publicly accessible (e.g., airports,[7] casinos, and stores[8]); I will only briefly consider its use in airports.

---

[5] Sources: www.visionics.com and "Facial ID Systems Raising Concerns About Privacy," Robert O'Harrow Jr., *Washington Post,* August 1, 2001; and: "Matching Faces With Mug Shots," Robert O'Harrow Jr., *Washington Post,* July 31, 2001. Also on Technews.com.

[6] Press release by Visionics Co., "O'Rourke Group, Major Civil Construction Firm, Deploys Visionics' FaceIt Technology at Main UK Concrete Production Site," *SMN Newswire,* March 22, 2001.

[7] According to a Visionics/Identix press release, Keflavik airport in Iceland has been the first airport to use the technology. Others that have followed include Boston's Logan, Dallas-Fort Worth International, and Palm Beach International. See also Kopel and Krause, *ibid.*

[8] The use of Smart CCTV in stores is relatively rare. The U.K. bookstore chain Big Borders was piloting its use in its stores to catch shoplifters, but the pilot was ended after protests by human rights organizations. See "Big Borders bookshop is watching you," *Sunday Herald,* August 26, 2001

Smart CCTV is only used in a small number of public city areas worldwide. In 2001, the FaceIt engine was used in three public city areas worldwide, one in the U.S. and two in the United Kingdom. Only a few have followed since. The first city to adopt the FaceIt system for surveillance purposes was London, which started using it in October 1998 in the neighborhood of Newham. In 2001, the system was tied to 300 CCTV cameras in this neighborhood, which are linked to a central CCTV control room operated by London Metropolitan Police Service. In April 2001, the FaceIt system was deployed in Birmingham, U.K., where it was integrated in the CCTV system already in place in the city centre. In June 2001, Tampa, Florida became the first American city to start using Smart CCTV. The Tampa police department started using FaceIt in its CCTV system that was already in place in the Ybor City entertainment district.[9]

In all three cities, the system is used in a busy neighborhood, and involves a CCTV system with a large number of video cameras. In all three cities, also, the system is operated by the city police department, and is used for routine surveillance, meaning that people in the area will be routinely scanned and have their faces searched in a database. In all three cities, also, the main purpose of the system is to identify known criminals or criminal suspects with an arrest warrant, so that they can be monitored or stopped and arrested. In 2002, the police department of the American city Virginia Beach started using a Smart CCTV system with the FaceIt engine at the beachfront, thus becoming the second U.S. city to use a Smart CCTV system. This system gained a somewhat broader use: not only to identify criminals, but also to help locate lost children and missing persons.[10]

My focus in the remainder of this paper will be on the Tampa system, and the controversy it has sparked. The system used in Tampa came into operation on June 29, 2001, and was added to an existing CCTV system that had already been in use since 1998. The system, run by the Tampa police department, included 36 cameras in the historic Ybor City entertainment district, a popular district in the centre of Tampa that is frequented by tens of thousands of locals and tourists every day. The cameras, that have the ability to tilt and pan, were linked to a central command post that includes ten video screens and computers running the FaceIt software. The cameras were concentrated in the Centro Ybor entertainment complex and along E. Seventh Avenue. Pedestrians were informed about the cameras by curbside warning signs reading "Area under video monitoring" and "Smart CCTV is in use."

The system was linked to a database consisting of known felons on active warrants (the most important category), people convicted of past sexual offenses in the state of Florida, and missing children and runaway teens. In 2001, the database consisted of 30,000 images of individuals in these categories, with plans to further enlarge the database.[11] The system engages in constant, automated monitoring of pedestrians. If there is a resemblance during a matching process, the computer will rate it from 1 to 10, sounding an alarm for matches of 8.5 and above. The officer

---

[9] See www.identix.com and "Ybor police cameras go spy-tech," *St.-Petersburg Times,* June 30, 2001.

[10] See www.identix.com and "Surveillance Cameras Incite Protest," *New York Times,* July 16th 2001.

[11] "Tampa Face-Recognition Vote Rattles Privacy Group—Update," *Washington Post,* August 3, 2001.

doing the monitoring will then alert others on the street by radio, who will stop the person and determine their identity. If they are wanted, they will be arrested. If they are not, the situation will be explained to them, and they are free to go.

The police department became interested in the software after it had been approached by Visionics Corp., the developer of the software, which later merged to become Identix. Use of the software required approval of the city council, which was granted in May 2001, a month before the system was put in use, in a meeting that did not include a public hearing. Since then, some public protests have ensued and some council members voiced concern about the technology and claimed they did not realize what they had voted for in their earlier vote. A second vote was held on June 19, after a public hearing, that resulted in a 3-3 split vote in the council, with the mayor casting the deciding vote. He voted to give the Tampa police permission to install the system, which was subsequently installed on June 29. A motion was brought to the floor in August 2001 by two council members to terminate the contract with Visionics Corp. The motion was rejected on a 4-2 vote.

4. The Debate on Facial Recognition Technology: Privacy Versus Security

The Tampa Smart CCTV system has generated a lot of debate, as has Smart CCTV and facial recognition technology in general. In this section, I will identify participants in the debate on Smart CCTV, with special emphasis on Tampa-based participants, and consider the main arguments used by both proponents and opponents of the technology. All references are to 2001, which is the year in which the system was installed. I will show that, perhaps predictably, the debate on Smart CCTV was strongly centered around the notions of privacy and security, with proponents arguing for the security benefits of the technology, and opponents emphasizing its threat to privacy. I will also attempt to show that certain types of arguments are repeated over and over in this debate.

In the Tampa debate on facecams, nearly all vocal participants are either proponents or opponents of the technology. The proponents include, of course, the manufacterers, i.e., Identix' predecessor Visionics Corp. along with its industrial partners. They also include members of the Tampa police department, which has adopted the technology, supportive local government officials, and citizens who support the technology. Opponents include city council members and citizens who oppose the technology, as well as privacy and human rights groups, and media critics who have chosen to participate in the debate. The privacy and human rights groups that have been involved with the Tampa case include the Tampa Electronic Privacy Information Center (EPIC) and the American Civil Liberties Union of Florida.[12] Also involved has been the Law Enforcement Alliance of America (LEAA). The backdrop of the Tampa debate is a wider media debate on facial recognition technology that was picking up steam in 2001.

The security vs. privacy dimension is very visible in the Tampa debate, as well as in the wider media debate. Proponents typically argue that the technology has

---

[12] "TV Cameras Seek Criminals in Tampa's Crowds," *New York Times,* July 4, 2001.

significant security benefits and minimal privacy losses, and that any privacy losses are in any case offset by the great security benefits. Opponents typically argue that the security benefits are overestimated and the privacy losses are underestimated by the proponents, and that the costs to privacy of the technology are greater than the gains in security. Importantly, not all arguments used by opponents refer to privacy as an eroded right; some refer instead to the erosion of individual freedom. Some, for example, claim that an arrest of an innocent citizen based on an incorrect match is a violation of personal freedom, and not of privacy.

Let us first consider statements in the debate that address the *security value* of the technology. Proponents argue that the technology is highly valuable as a means to reducing crime and enhancing security and the quality of life in neighborhoods, because it is an effective and accurate technology. Detective Bill Todd of the Tampa police department, who is in charge of the operation in Ybor City, has called the technology a "powerful tool to assist in maximizing public safety."[13] City councilman Robert Buckhorn calls it a "public safety tool."[14] The belief in safety is echoed by citizens in favor of the system, like Gil Rizzo, a 42-year old account representative in Tampa, who claims "I'm in favor of it because of the security. A lot of nights, there has been shoplifting, women got mugged and robbed. It's safer because of the cameras."[15]

Indeed, proponents make frequent reference to the alleged value the technology has in stopping crime, and arresting criminals like murderers, drug traffickers and sexual offenders. They also refer to the added feeling of security that the technology may bring. For instance, John Woodward, author of a 2001 RAND report in favor of facial recognition technology, writes: "Many parents would most likely feel safer knowing their children's elementary school had a facial recognition system to ensure that convicted child molesters were not granted access to school grounds."[16] Several proponents also point out another societal value of the technology, which is the location of missing persons and runaways. Opponents do not usually deny the importance of stopping crime and locating missing persons, but often question if the technology is sufficiently reliable and effective as a means for stopping crime—or simply deny that it is. For example, Kate Rears of EPIC has pointed out that the technology is not proven and that similar technology did not help to make any arrests when used in the XXXVth Super Bowl.[17]

Let us now turn to statements that address implications of the technology for privacy and freedom. Opponents of the technology emphasize that it poses a real threat to privacy and freedom. Randall Marshall, of the American Civil Liberties Union of Florida, emphasized the "Big Brother feel" of the technology, and claimed that using the technology amounts to subjecting the public to a digital lineup. ACLU Associate Director Gregory Nojeim made the same comparison, claiming: "If

---

[13] Visionics Co. press release, June 29, 2001 and "Tampa Scans the Faces in Its Crowds for Criminals," Dana Canedy, *New York Times*, July 4, 2001.

[14] Canedy, *ibid.*

[15] Canedy, *ibid.*

[16] Woodward, John D., *Super Bowl Surveillance: Facing Up to Biometrics*, Santa Monica, CA: RAND, IP-209, 2001.

[17] "Anger over face-scanning cameras," *BBC News*, August 20, 2001.

this isn't Big Brother, I don't know what is."[18] Jason Skinner, a security guard in Ybor, said "It's invading people's privacy. They're all over the place." [19] Ryan Rovelto, a clerk in Ybor City, said "It's kind of like a police state. Whether I have a warrant or not, it makes me uncomfortable they can pick me out of a crowd and run my image."[20] There have also been public protests to the technology used in Ybor City in which privacy was the issue. Just before the introduction of the technology, a hundred people protested in Ybor City, wearing signs like "We're under house arrest in the land of the free" and shouting slogans like "Big Bro, hell no."[21] Some opponents also questioned the accuracy of the system and voiced their fear that the system would result in matches that wrongly identified innocent citizens as criminals, thus violating their civil liberties.

A different form of opposition has come from the Law Enforcement Alliance of America (LEAA), a coalition of law enforcement professionals, crime victims, and concerned citizens with over 65,000 members. The LEAA issued a statement on 3 July 2001 calling for the immediate removal of the Tampa system because it represents a violation of people's 4th Amendment right to privacy. The argument of the LEAA was not, however, that surveillance with Smart CCTV is not compatible with privacy rights. Rather, their argument was that the system in Tampa violates the privacy policies that the manufacturer, Visionics, had subscribed to as a member of the International Biometric Industry Association (IBIA). As the LEAA pointed out, the IBIA policy claims that "clear legal standards should be developed to carefully define and limit the conditions under which agencies of national security and law enforcement may acquire, access, store, and use biometric data." The LEAA claimed that since no such legal standards were in place, the system was in violation of the manufacturer's privacy policy and should therefore be removed.[22]

Proponents of the system addressed the privacy issue in various ways. Some simply denied that there is a privacy issue. City Councilman Robert Buckhorn claimed that in the public streets of a crowded neighborhood like Ybor City, "your expectation of privacy is somewhat diminished, anyway."[23] This sentiment was echoed by law professor Erwin Chemerinsky of the University of Southern California, who claimed in relation to face recognition technology: "We have no reasonable expectation of privacy in a public place—that we're not going to be seen, or that our picture won't be taken."[24] Detective Bill Todd of the Tampa police called the privacy issue overblown because he claimed that the cameras do not record images of people when they are not recognized to match an image in the database; when there is no match, people's facial images are immediately discarded. Some citizens also felt that the privacy issue is overblown, because they did not find the technology to be invading their privacy. Said Jill Wax, owner of a clothing store in Ybor: "I don't find it an inva-

---

[18] "Big Brother cameras on watch for criminals," Martin Kasindorf, *USA Today,* August 2, 2001.

[19] Canedy, *ibid.*

[20] "Ybor Police Cameras go Spy-Tech," Amy Herdy, *St. Petersburg Times,* June 30, 2001.

[21] Kasindorf, *ibid.*

[22] LEAA statement, *US Newswire,* July 3, 2001. (See http://www.notbored.org/leaa.html)

[23] Canedy, *ibid.*

[24] Kasindorf, *ibid.*

sion of my privacy, and my customers don't either."[25] Some proponents made the argument that the technology merely automates a procedure that has not previously been seen to violate privacy. City Coucilman Robert Buckhorn claimed that the technology is "no different than having a cop walk around with a mug shot;"[26] this is, incidentally, the exact same argument that had been made by Police Chief A.M. Jacocks of Virginia Beach, who had lobbied to get the technology accepted in that city.[27]

Next to those proponents of the technology who either deny or downplay the threat to privacy, there are others who do recognize it as a potential problem. Visionics, for one, acknowledged, along with RAND, that Smart CCTV can lead to violations of privacy. However, Visionics and RAND both claimed that such violations can be minimized when the proper safeguards are put into place. Visionics, now Identix, has argued, along with others in the biometrics industry, for legislation regulating the use of facial recognition technology, and has proposed a set of "industry-established" privacy guidelines, that include the rules that "Clear signage has been posted throughout the area indicating that "Smart CCTV" is in use; The images in the database are those of known offenders; Non-matching images are discarded from the system once the comparison has been conducted."[28]

Proponents who recognized that facecams can negatively affect personal privacy still favored the system because they believed that in the trade-off between privacy and security, the security gains are much greater than the losses in privacy and liberty. Both Visionics and Tampa police claimed, for example, that the chance of a false arrest is an acceptable trade-off for the possibility of arresting a criminal who might otherwise remain at large. And Woodward claimed in his RAND report: "We should not let the fear of potential but inchoate threats to privacy, such as super surveillance, deter us from using facial recognition where it can produce positive benefits."[29]

Opponents make different trade-offs. Philip Hudok, a concerned citizen commenting on plans to install Smart CCTV in Virginia Beach, stated: "I wouldn't even go near the vicinity of a place that condones this. There's no benefit great enough to sacrifice this much personal privacy."[30] Thomas Greene, an author commenting on the RAND report in favor of facecams, complained that the author of the report "reckons that the natural rights of the majority of ordinary, law-abiding citizens should be sacrificed for the sacred mission of identifying and prosecuting a mere handful of sexually perverted or homicidal lunatics." He went on to claim: "Surely, the suffocating, risk-free environments our governments are trying so desperately to sell us to extend their powers of observation and control are far more grotesque and soul-destroying than anything a terrorist or a pedophile might ever hope to produce."[31]

---

[25] Canedy, *ibid.*

[26] Canedy, *ibid.*

[27] "Beach may scan Oceanfront faces," Agnes Blum, *The Virginian-Pilot*, July 6, 2001.
The Rand report even makes the argument that Smart CCTV can benefit privacy because it is not physically invasive like some other forms of surveillance. See also Woodward, 2001.

[28] Visionics Co. press release, June 29, 2001.

[29] Woodward, *ibid.*

[30] "Va. Beach mayor opposes plan to scan faces," Agnes Blum, *The Virginian-Pilot*, July 10, 2001.

[31] "Think tank urges face-scanning for the masses," Thomas Greene, *The Register*, August 13, 2001.
(http://www.theregister.co.uk/content/6/20966.html)

5. Ethical Considerations for the Use of Facecams

The privacy versus security debate on Smart CCTV is about a genuine issue, since security and privacy may easily come to stand in opposition to each other. And just like opponents of facecams cannot easily discard their potential security benefits, proponents cannot easily sidestep the threats they pose to civil liberties. Trade-offs will therefore have to be made between security and civil liberties in deciding whether and how to use facecams. What is needed, most of all, is a better understanding of how trade-offs can be made: how much infringement of civil liberties can be justified by reference to security concerns?   The debate on this question has, unfortunately, been shallow so far. What has been lacking is a good understanding of what is at stake with facial recognition technology, and what consequences its use can bring. A better understanding is needed of both the importance of civil liberties and the importance of security, of the power and reliability of the technology, and of its potential uses and abuses. In helping to clarify some of these issues, I will now analyze three particular problems that have been associated with Smart CCTV, and address their moral implications. These are the problem of error, the problem of function creep, and the problem of privacy.

Error

The *problem of error* is mentioned repeatedly by opponents of facecams. This is the problem that with face recognition technology, incorrect matches can occur that cause innocent citizens to become subjected to harassment by police. Problems of error are not unique to facial recognition technology, but may occur with any database system that stores personal information: the database may contain erroneous personal information that may lead to cases of mistaken identity, it may be used incorrectly, with the same consequences, or its matches are based on probability estimates and therefore have a margin of error. That errors may occur was already demonstrated in the first few weeks in which the Tampa system was used: the system yielded several false positives. Moreover, a feature article in a newspaper on the systems, accompanied by still images of several scanned faces, led to an attempted arrest of one of the men in the pictures because a reader falsely believed that he was her ex-husband, who had a warrant for child neglect charges.[32]

However, if the problem of error is kept distinct from the problem of privacy and privacy rights, which I will discuss later, then it must be concluded that the occurrence of errors does not, in itself, present a strong case against facecams. It would only do so if the error rate is so great, and the success rate of the technology in reducing crime so low, that the apprehension of one felon would require the stopping and questioning of dozens of innocent citizens. The question is, therefore, if a good ratio can be attained between false and true positives, and if the questioning of individuals who may be false positives can be done in a way that is not too obtrusive. If so, then from a purely pragmatic point of view, the trade-off may well be acceptable. After all, the public tends to accept the idea that it has to suffer minor inconveniences so that criminals can be apprehended. It accepts, for example, that it is questioned or even searched when boarding a plane, or visiting a rock concert, or football match.

---

[32] Kopel and Krause, *ibid.*

So the problem of error, when considered separately from the more profound problem of privacy, may not in itself present a strong argument against facecams. It does suggest, however, that there are problems with installing and using a system that is inaccurate, because it yields many false positives for each true positive. In that case, the harm done to innocent citizens that turn up as false positives may begin to outweigh the benefits of a few additional arrests of wanted criminals.

Function creep

A second, and more pressing, problem with facecams is the problem of *"function creep,"* an expression that I borrow from RAND report author John Woodward. Function creep is the phenomenon by which a technology designed for a limited purpose may gain additional, unanticipated purposes or functions. This may occur either through institutionalized expansions of its purposes or through systematic abuse. In relation to Smart CCTV, it is the problem that, because of the flexibility of the technology, the purposes for which the system is used may be easily extended from recognizing criminals and missing persons to include other purposes.

There are, I claim, four basic ways in which Smart CCTV can become the subject of function creep. The first is by *widening of the database*. The databases used in London, Birmingham, Tampa, and Virginia Beach only included felons on a warrant, past sexual offenders, and missing persons. Such databases can be easily expanded with the use of already existing databases such as those of the departments of motor vehicles (DMVs) in the U.S., which include digitized photographs of licensed drivers. It is relatively easy, then to include new categories of people that are to be monitored, like people with misdemeanors, political activists, or people with a certain ethnic background. Needless to say, some of these expansions, if they were to occur, would be morally highly problematic.

The second way in which function creep may occur is by *purpose widening*. This is the widening of the purpose for which the technology is used. For example, a police force using Smart CCTV may start using it not only to identify wanted individuals in crowds, but for example to do routine analysis of the composition of crowds in public places, or to do statistical analysis of faceprints for the purpose of predicting criminal activity, or to track individuals over longer distances. Smart CCTV has the potential to do these things, and police departments may be tempted to use the technology for such additional purposes in their efforts to fight crime and improve the quality of life in neighborhoods.

A third way for function creep to occur is by *user shifts*. Systems, once developed, may come to be used by new types of users. For instance, the FBI or CIA may require access to a system used by a police department in a search for terrorists. Or a city government or commercial organization may ask a police department to use the system for its demographic research. Also, individual operators may be using the system for their own personal reasons. As Reuters journalist Richard Meares reports, there have been several occurrences of CCTV operators being sacked because of their repeated abuse of the system, for example by tracking and zooming in on attractive women.[33]

---

[33] "Nowhere to hide, Video Eyes are Watching," Richard Meares, *Reuters,* May 24, 2001.

A fourth and final occurrence of function creep lies in *domain shifts*: changes in the type of area of situation in which the system is used, such as changes from city neighborhoods to small villages or nature parks, or from public to private areas, or from domestic areas to war zones. Function creep in Smart CCTV may hence occur in several ways, which may add up to result in new uses of the technology for new purposes by new users in new domains. Studies of technology use have shown that function creep almost invariably occurs when a new technology is used, and should therefore be taken into account.[34] Function creep can be limited by strict regulation of the technology (which is not currently in place), but cannot be wholly avoided. This imposes an obligation on the developers and users of the technology, therefore, to anticipate function creep and to take steps to prevent undesirable forms of function creep from occurring.

Privacy

The problems of error and function creep do not really address the problem with facial recognition technology that many of its opponents hold to be central to it: its alleged violation of personal privacy. Regardless of whether error or function creep occur, the question is whether the very use of Smart CCTV surveillance in public places violates a basic right to privacy. Some of the proponents cited above argue that it does not, because people in public places do not have a strong expectation of privacy anyway. In an important essay, Helen Nissenbaum has argued that even if the expectation of privacy is diminished in public places, people still have justifiable privacy expectations even when they are in public.[35] She argues that surveillance in public places that involves the electronic collection, storage, and analysis of information on a large scale often amounts to a violation of personal privacy.

Nissenbaum's argument for privacy in public rests on two premises. First, citing empirical data, she claims that many people are dismayed when they learn that personal information is collected about them without their consent, even when they are in public places. This negative response shows that many people do indeed have some privacy expectations even when they are in public spaces. Second, she argues that these popular sentiments can be justified by analyzing characteristics of public data harvesting through electronic means that make it quite different from the everyday observation of people in public places. She argues that electronics harvesting involves two types of practices that raise privacy concerns. The first is the practice of *shifting information* from one context to another. The second is the combination or *aggregation* of various sources of personal information to yield new information.

The first practice described by Nissenbaum, of shifting information, is the use of electronically collected information in a different context than the one in which it is collected. For example, information about people's supermarket purchases may be sold to a list service for magazine subscriptions, or information collected for scientific purposes may be used in a political context. Nissenbaum argues that when people divulge personal information, they tailor the amount and type of informa-

---

[34] "Big Brother Logs On;" Ivan Amato, *Technology Review,* September 2001 (http://www.technologyreview.com/articles/amato0901.asp) and: "Stop the webcams, we want to get off!" Katharine Mieszkowski, www.salon.com, 28 August 2001.

[35] Nissenbaum, Helen, "Protecting Privacy in an information age: The problem of privacy in public," *Law and Philosophy,* 17: 559–596, 1998.

tion they disclose to the context in which they disclose it. People provide doctors with details of their physical condition, discuss their children's problems with their children's teachers, and divulge financial information to loan officers at banks. She argues that there are norms—both explicit and implicit—that govern how much information and what type of information is fitting for what context.

Nissenbaum next introduces the notion of *contextual integrity*. When information-governing norms are respected, Nissenbaum claims, contextual integrity is maintained, whereas a violation of information-governing norms violates contextual integrity. Nissenbaum's point is that the practice of shifting information often violates contextual integrity: it often violates the trust that people have that information appropriate to one context will not be used in a context for which it was intended and in which it is not deemed appropriate. Yet, the practice of shifting information is very common in public data harvesting, and relatively few limitations have been imposed, by law or by custom, to prevent data collectors from using personal information in different contexts. Public data harvesting is therefore a practice that cannot be trusted to maintain contextual integrity. Nissenbaum claims that contextual integrity is one of the conditions of privacy, and that therefore, the practice of shifting information in public data harvesting poses a privacy problem.

Next to information shifting, Nissenbaum identifies aggregation as another practice in the collection and use of public data that violates privacy expectations. Aggregation is known variously as "profiling," "matching," "data aggregation" and "data mining," and is the practice in which different sources of information about people are aggregated to produce databases that include complex personal records. For instance, there are bureaus that combine publicly available personal information such as drivers' license and motor vehicle records, voter registration lists, Social Security number lists, birth records, and information from credit bureaus, to devise comprehensive profiles of individuals that indicate such things as their purchase power and purchasing activity. This is just one example: many organizations in both the private and public sector engage in some form of data aggregation. Nissenbaum argues that the main objection to data aggregation is that its profiles are capable of exposing people in ways that the isolated bits of information out of which aggregates are composed are not capable of. They may reveal personal information that people could never dream would be revealed about them on the basis of isolated public bits of personal information that are much less privacy-sensitive. Hence, Nissenbaum argues, aggregation is a practice that frequently violates reasonable expectations of privacy.

Shifting information and aggregation can both be seen as instances of function creep. Shifting information corresponds, particularly, to what I have called purpose widening and user shifts, and aggregation can be seen as an instance of purpose widening. This shows that the problems of function creep and of privacy are linked: when function creep occurs, privacy is often violated as a result. However, it does *not* follow that privacy violations resulting from the use of Smart CCTV are always the result of function creep. Privacy may also be an issue when no function creep occurs. Let us suppose, for example, that very strict regulation and norms are to govern the use of Smart CCTV so that the occurrence of function creep is minimal: images of people in public places are only matched against a database of known offenders and images are discarded immediately if no match is found. Is there no privacy issue involved in this case?

Nissenbaum's analysis supports the notion that privacy may then still be an issue. This is the case because the very practice of matching faces of people in public places against faces in a database of wanted criminals appears to violate contextual integrity according to norms held by many. Many people who willingly show their face in a public place would not willingly participate in lineup at a police station, especially not if they had been picked for the lineup because they resembled a composition sketch of a suspect. Yet, the presence of Smart CCTV in public places leaves them with no choice: they cannot choose not to divulge personal information about their facial features that will be used in a context in which they may not want it to be used. Nissenbaum argues that at the heart of our concept of privacy is the idea that privacy protects a "safe haven," a sphere where we people are free from the scrutiny of others, and within which they are able to control the terms under which they live their lives. Different people draw this sphere differently. Yet, many seem to hold that Smart CCTV takes away too much of this control, by subjecting them to routine large-scale scrutiny when they frequent public places.

Next to this privacy objection derived from Nissenbaum's analysis, another privacy objection against Smart CCTV may be made. Smart CCTV is a form of biometric technology, and this type of technology has been claimed to involve special privacy issues.[36] The main issue is that biometric technologies digitally encode a highly personal aspect of one's body, like a thumb print, iris pattern, or face. Two things happen because of this. First, this aspect of one's body acquires a new meaning or function: it is now enrolled in a larger functional, rationalized system of identification or authentication in which it plays a specific functional role that is comparable to that of other identifiers like passwords, PIN numbers, and bar codes. In the context of this functional system, one's body part is nothing more than an information structure. For example, the unique features of one's face, by which others recognize you and which helps to define your uniqueness, can be encoded into a computer file of only 88 bytes. This functional reduction of body parts to information structures is one that many people find dehumanizing.

Second, this process of functional reduction involves the creation of informational equivalents of body parts that exist outside their owner and are used and controlled by others. There is hence not just a process of reduction occurring, but also one of alienation: the faceprint that uniquely characterizes your face is not "yours," but "theirs:" it is not owned by you and even if it were, it would not be understood by you because you do not understand the technology. In this way, people may come to feel that some of their body parts are no longer completely "theirs," because they have acquired meanings that their owner does not understand, and uses that are partially realized outside their own body.

Facecams hence pose a dual privacy problem: they face the same privacy problems that apply to surveillance cameras and public data harvesting more generally, and they also face the privacy problems that apply to biometric technologies. Moreover, a case can be made that these problems are intensified in facecams: the privacy problems with surveillance cameras are enhanced in facecams because of the additional tracking and monitoring functions afforded by such cameras, and

---

[36] Hes, Hooghiemstra, and Borking, At Face Value – On Biometrical Identification and Privacy. *Registratiekamer,* September 1999. (http://www.cbpweb.nl/downloads_av/AV15.pdf)

the privacy objections raised to biometric technology can be expected to apply especially to facial recognition technology, because the human face has always been regarded as the most unique and distinguishing aspect of the human body. For these reasons, then, the debate on facecams is not likely to go away very soon.

6. Policy Issues

It follows from my discussion that before Smart CCTV can be used in an ethically responsible way, three ethically charged issues first have to be dealt with in a satisfactory way. They are the problems of error, function creep, and privacy. I will now briefly discuss, for each, the conditions that must be realized for them to be handled satisfactorily, the requirements this imposes on the technology, and the policies that must result that regulate its use. I will also briefly assess the prospects that these conditions and their resulting requirements are indeed met.

To effectively deal with function creep, it seems clear that legal standards must be developed for the use of facial recognition technology that specify which uses are authorized and which ones are not, and specify the conditions under which users may share or aggregate information. The need for such legal standards also recognized by the industry itself, as remarked in Section 4. The industry's organization for this, IBIA, has developed its own good use guidelines and called for legislation to specifically address the use of biometric technologies. Identix, which is a member of IBIA, also emphasizes the importance of legislation, and has developed additional ethical policies for the proper use of its products. So function creep is currently an issue for visual recognition technology, largely because of the absence of clear legislation for its use. However, if detailed legal standards were to be adopted in the future and strictly adhered to, then the problem of function creep may become less significant.

The problem of privacy is more profound than the problem of function creep, because it is not a problem that may be "solved" through regulation or through a redesign of the technology. It could even be argued that privacy is an absolute right and that therefore the use of Smart CCTV in public areas cannot be warranted under any circumstances. Such an absolutist position would, however, automatically entail that privacy is more important than security. Yet, security entails protection from harm, which corresponds with very basic rights such as the right to life, liberty, and property. So it will not do if opponents of the use of Smart CCTV claim that it violates privacy and that privacy is an absolute right. It would have to be shown, rather, that its violation of privacy trumps the added security, if any, that Smart CCTV offers.

Three questions seem relevant in this privacy vs. security debate: How much added security results from the use of Smart CCTV? How invasive to privacy is the technology, as can be judged from both public response and scholarly arguments? Are there reasonable alternatives to the technology that may yield similar security results without the privacy concerns? I will not try to answer all of these questions, but I will address the first one, which also relates to the problem of error.

Smart CCTV in public areas is successful, by the standards of both police and manufacturers, when it results in the arrest of a significant number of wanted offenders without at the same time producing large numbers of false positives ("errors") that result in the stopping and questioning of innocent citizens. While

Smart CCTV has performed very well in controlled circumstances, it seems that the current technology has not been successful in actual use. In August 2003, the Tampa police force decided to suspend using the system, two years after it was installed, because it had yielded not one arrest or positive identification. "It's just proven not to have any benefit to us," said Capt. Bob Guidara, a department spokesman. The system in use at Virginia Beach has, likewise, not resulted in any arrests so far.[37] Yet, as mentioned before, the system in Tampa had already yielded several false positives during its first few weeks in usage.

An article by investigators Kopel and Krause of the Independence Institute suggests that the reason for its failure may be that the technology is not yet up to being used in real-life circumstances: a trial at a security checkpoint at Palm Beach Airport resulted in 1,081 false alarms in a four-week period while people in the database were only stopped 47% of the time.[38] The problem of error hence still seems to loom large for Smart CCTV. I conclude that the use of Smart CCTV in public places still faces major problems. The problem of function creep is still unresolved, largely because of the absence of clear legislation. The problem of error is also unresolved, because the current technology seems to yield many false positives and few, if any, true positives. And privacy concerns with the technology cannot be sidestepped by reference to the importance of the technology in providing security, because the technology appears to be unreliable as of yet, nor has it been demonstrated that there are no alternatives available.

7. Concluding Remarks

This paper discussed the use of Smart CCTV in public places, with special attention to the FaceIt system of Identix Corp. and on its use in the city of Tampa, Florida. After discussing facial recognition technology and its possible applications, I considered its use in public (city) areas, with special attention to its use in Tampa. I then discussed how public and political debates on Smart CCTV proponents tend to emphasize the security benefits of Smart CCTV while downplaying their threats to privacy and other civil liberties, whereas opponents of the technology make the opposite argument. Following up on this debate, I then went on to discuss ethical considerations for the use of facecams, arguing that there are three distinct moral problems that the use of facecams may incur: the problem of error, the problem of function creep, and the problem of privacy. I ended with a discussion of policies for the use of facecams, focusing on the question whether the use of current Smart CCTV really results in significant security benefits that trump its negative implications for privacy and civil liberties. I concluded that so far, the security benefits of the technology have not yet been demonstrated and that the problems of function creep, error, and privacy have not been addressed well, so that the current use of Smart CCTV in public places is difficult to defend.

---

[37] Kopel and Krause, *ibid.*

[38] Kopel and Krause, *ibid.*

Introduction to Chapter 6: Professional Ethics, Codes of Conduct, and Computer/Information Professionals

The readings included in this chapter consider ethical issues that directly impact professionals working in the field of computing and information technology (IT). Ethical issues in computing and IT span two distinct areas of applied ethics.[1] On the one hand, issues in applied ethics arise because of controversies surrounding certain policies and practices affecting the general public. Policy debates associated with computing and IT involve issues such as speech, property, privacy, security, and so forth—i.e., the issues discussed in readings included in Chapters 2 through 5 in this textbook. On the other hand, concerns about special responsibilities that the members of a profession have *as professionals* in a certain field raise a different set of applied ethics issues. For example, professionals in various fields sometimes face moral dilemmas because of decisions they must make professionally. An engineer might be asked to design a controversial product, and a medical doctor may be forced to decide whether to use a particular technology either to sustain or terminate a human life. Consider that a computer programmer might find herself in a situation where she has to determine whether to participate in developing software that has some controversial, unreliable, or unsafe features, or that could very easily be used for undesirable ends.

Ethical issues for computer professionals, then, include concerns about responsibility and accountability for the design, development, implementation, and maintenance of computer hardware and software systems, and especially for the reliability of "safety-critical" and "life-critical" systems. The range of professionals affected by these kinds of ethical issues can include, but need not be limited to, those employed as software and hardware engineers, applications programmers, technical writers, computer science instructors, and so forth.

---

[1] Applied ethics, unlike ethical theory (see Chapter 1), focuses on describing and analyzing specific moral problems rather than on analyzing conceptual aspects of the various ethical theories themselves. Essentially, applied ethics is concerned with identifying moral problems in a topical area (such as law, medicine, the environment, etc.) and then analyzing those problems through the application of one or more ethical theories.

Applied ethics issues involving the conduct of professionals working in a particular field, such as law, medicine, or computing, are often considered under the label *professional ethics*. Such issues, as they relate specifically to professionals in computing and IT, are the primary focus of the readings included in Chapter 6.

The Computer/Information Profession and Professional Codes of Conduct

In the chapter's first reading, "Ethical Considerations for the Information Professions," Elizabeth Buchanan provides an overview of the field of information ethics. Buchanan describes this field as one that bridges many disciplines, including library and information science, computer science, records management, informatics, educational media technologies, ect. While providing a broad conceptual overview of information ethics, Buchanan's essay also addresses important ethical considerations for the information worker. Furthermore, it provides an excellent introduction to several important issues comprising the field of professional ethics.

Buchanan additionally provides a brief discussion of professional codes of ethics and explains why they are important. Do professionals working in the field of computing and IT need a formal code of conduct? Some argue that because computer professionals, and particularly software engineers, have special moral obligations—e.g., responsibilities to develop computer systems that are reliable, safe, secure, etc.—a specific code of conduct for the computer profession is necessary. Large computer organizations such as the Association for Computing Machinery (ACM) and the Institute for Electrical and Electronics Engineers (IEEE) have developed and adopted professional codes of ethics. The complete text of the ACM Code of Ethics and Professional Conduct is included as the chapter's second reading. This code of ethics contains twenty-four imperatives, each formulated as a statement of personal responsibility. It also includes general statements about what is expected to be an ACM member in good standing.

The IEEE's Computer Society (IEEE-CS) and the ACM have approved a joint code of ethics, which was developed by the IEEE-CS/ACM Joint Task Force on Software Engineering Code of Ethics and Professional Practices. The code that resulted from this task force, the Software Engineering Code of Ethics and Professional Practices (SECEPP), is included as the chapter's third reading. Intended to educate and inspire software engineers, SECEPP documents the ethical and professional responsibilities and obligations of software engineers and engineering teams. (Software engineering teams include technical writers, managers, instructors, students, and others who work with software engineers in the process of designing, developing, testing, implementing, and maintaining software systems and products.) SECEPP emphasizes the profession's obligation to the public at large, including concerns for the public's health, safety, and welfare, which are paramount. It also includes specific language about the importance of ethical behavior during the maintenance phase of software development, as well as in the design and implementation stages.

It would seem that few, if any, persons would oppose a code of conduct for computer professionals in general, or specifically for software engineers. However, professional codes have, at times, been criticized on various grounds. One criticism is that professional codes of ethics tend to be incomplete and thus do not include an exhaustive list of guidelines for computer professionals. Another criticism is that professional codes contain principles that are much more like legal (than moral) directives and that professional codes provide no mechanism for determining which directive to choose when two or more conflict. We briefly examine each criticism.

N. Ben Fairweather (1998) believes that some of the computer profession's codes of conduct are incomplete because of a conception of computer and information ethics that is limited to four principal areas of concern: privacy, accuracy, property, and accessibility. He argues that such a narrow foundation of the computing profession cannot support an adequate ethical code and that is also could conceivably result in harm. For example, such a code could provide an organization with various loopholes and thus offer that organization an easy way out of having to address certain ethical issues, such as its responsibilities to disabled workers that it may employ. Fairweather also points out that many ethical issues facing computing professionals, such as concerns about the implications of computer use involving weapons, environmental injustice, and telework and telecommuting, would not be covered in a code that was based on concerns exclusively (or even primarily) related to privacy, accuracy, property, and access. He also worries that authors of incomplete codes might, by virtue of what they leave out of a specific code, be indirectly responsible for sanctioning behavior on the part of some employees that, in the final analysis, turns out to be immoral.

John Ladd (1995) is also suspicious of professional codes of ethics, which he believes rest on a set of confusions that are both intellectual and moral in nature. At the intellectual level, Ladd argues that confusion occurs because professional codes are not really ethical codes at all; instead they are more like formal legal directives in that they have sanctions and they threaten punishment. At the moral level, Ladd claims that confusion arises because ethics is ultimately about deliberation, not blindly following directives; furthermore, confusion occurs when two or more directives in a professional code conflict, because professional codes of conduct fail to provide us with a mechanism for nonarbitrarily deciding which directive to choose.

Don Gotterbarn, Keith Miller, and Simon Rogerson (1999), the primary authors of the SECEPP Code (described previously), argue that SECEPP can avoid many of the charges brought by critics of professional codes. Regarding Fairweather's criticism of incompleteness, the authors concede that the eight main Principles that comprise SECEPP are not exhaustive; in fact, they point out that no professional code can anticipate every possible case of moral controversy. However, they believe that SECEPP provides "general guidance for ethical decision making." And with respect to Ladd's criticism that professional codes do not provide a decisive directive when two or more conflict, Gotterbarn et al. point out that SECEPP has a "hierarchy of principles" and that with this hierarchy, software engineers can prioritize their individual responsibilities. The ordering of the Eight Principles that make up SECEPP offers guidance in determining which rules are overriding in cases where two or more conflict. At the top of the hierarchy, for example, are principles that have to do with service and well being. SECEPP's hierarchy of principles states that concern for the health, safety, and welfare of the public is primary in all ethical judgments.[2] Gotterbarn, Miller, and Rogerson point out that ethical tensions that arise can best be addressed by "thoughtful consideration of fundamental principles, rather than blind reliance on detailed regulations."

You can examine the contents of both the ACM and the SECEPP Codes to determine whether they are sufficiently robust, both in terms of their breadth and depth, to withstand the attacks of critics. Clearly, well developed codes of conduct, such as the ACM and SECEPP Codes, play a vital role for professionals in the fields of computing and IT in general, and software engineering, in particular. On the other hand, critics such as Fairweather and Ladd seem to be correct in stating that an ethical code of conduct can never substitute for careful moral deliberation. We conclude our brief discussion of professional ethical codes by noting that well developed codes of conduct provide computer professionals with an important first step in the ethical deliberation process.

Strategies for Raising Ethical Awareness for Computer Professionals

Readings four through six describe some strategies for raising the level of ethical awareness among computer professionals. Don Gotterbarn, in

---

[2] Elsewhere, Gotterbarn (1999) provides arguments to show how SECEPP can respond to some of the kinds of traditional attacks that critics have leveled against professional codes of ethics.

the chapter's fourth reading, discusses the "life cycle" of cyber and computer ethics. He argues that ethical issues involving the computing profession can be understood as passing through three stages: (i) naïve innocence and technological wonder, (ii) power and control, and (iii) understanding the essential relationships between technology and values. Gotterbarn believes that this mini cycle models the "ethical awakening" process in professional practice and education. The "Age of Innocence" is characterized by computer *hubris* in which it is assumed that the computer will provide us with solutions to all social problems. (In fact, we are so taken by the new "toy" that we don't stop to think about its social impact.) We feel a sense of "power" (personal *hubris* as controller of the computing device) when we commit to large untested software projects believing that we can do something simply because we think we can. At this stage, the social impact of these projects is not considered until after a product has been developed. At the final stage of responsible awareness, however, we assess the social impact *before* we develop the product. Gotterbarn claims that we need to understand this cycle and recognize where we are in it, at any given point, to understand and address specific computer ethics issues. Gotterbarn concludes that computer professionals must understand this cycle of cyber and computer ethics issues to raise their level of ethical awareness *as professionals*.

In the fifth reading, "Unintentional Power in the Design of Computing Systems," Chuck Huff focuses on the concept of *power*—a notion that also plays an important role in Gotterbarn's life cycle of computer ethics. Huff believes that software designers have the power to affect others in ways that often are *unintended*; he notes that this "unintentional power" carries a concomitant responsibility to be aware, as reasonably as possible, of the consequences of our actions. To illustrate the force of Huff's insight, consider the example of the digital divide—the gap between technology "haves" and "have-nots"—that currently exists at the global level. Initially, one might be tempted to say that the digital divide is not the concern of computer professionals per se but rather is a problem for politicians and policy makers to resolve. If Huff is correct, however, computer professionals who design software applications have the power to address some of the issues underlying the digital divide.[3]

Computer professionals may be disposed to feel a sense of powerlessness when it comes to making a difference regarding broad social and ethical issues involving technology, especially those issues that affect people in developing countries. Huff points out that the designers of computer

---

[3] See Tavani (2003) for a discussion of how Huff's model can be applied to issues affecting the digital divide.

systems sometimes fail to realize the power that they have because often they are far removed, geographically, from the situations in which their power has its effect. He notes, for instance, that because software designed in Chicago might be used in Calcutta, the person or persons with the power (i.e., those in Chicago who design the software) are physically removed from those who are affected. Thus, it is often difficult for those who have the power to foresee the possible consequences of their work.

Huff suggests that computer professionals must carefully consider social consequences for society when designing software and hardware systems. On the one hand, a significant burden of responsibility has been placed on computer professionals because their products can have unintended consequences. On the other hand, as computer professionals gain a greater awareness of the potential for these kinds of consequences, they will also see why they need to develop products that responsibly address social and ethical concerns. (In this case, they would move from the second to the third stage of ethical awareness in Gotterbarn's "cycle" described previously.)

Richard Epstein, in the chapter's sixth reading, is concerned that computer science undergraduate students who are preparing to become computer professionals may not receive the appropriate level of instruction in ethics. As a result, he fears that these students will not be aware of many of their ethical responsibilities when they become employed as computer professionals. Epstein also believes that the computer science curriculum does not do enough to help students to see their ethical and social responsibilities as computer professionals. This creates a challenge for computer science instructors who, like Epstein, believe that in addition to teaching students the basic skills required to be competent programmers—i.e., giving them instruction in C++, Java, data structures, algorithms, etc.—students need direction on how to be socially and ethically responsible professionals. The moral challenge for Epstein is whether he can allow himself to be part of the "process that produces software developers who live for the paycheck" and who escape their professional ethical responsibilities.

Epstein proposes a strategy for getting students (and some instructors as well) to see the importance of ethics and professionalism. He begins with a story about "the Wheel," which sets the context for his analysis of the full meaning of work. He then provides computer science instructors and students with some specific guidelines and strategies for understanding the breadth of their roles as computer professionals, which requires them to consider certain ethical and social implications of their work.

The ACM and IEEE-CS have recently issued a combined report, recommending the inclusion of 16 hours of instruction on ethical, social, and professional issues (designated as SP Units) in the undergraduate computer science curriculum. A joint IEEE-CS/ACM Computing Curriculum 2001 report, entitled *Computing Curricula 2001 (CC 2001)*, describes the various SP Units. However, many who support the newly revised curriculum remain concerned that, despite the efforts of CC 2001, some undergraduate computer science students will not receive instruction in ethical and professional issues. Instructors who share this concern will no doubt find Richard Epstein's strategies in his reading ("The Wheel") useful in helping their students to recognize and appreciate some of their ethical responsibilities as future computer professionals.

Risk Analysis and the Problem of Unreliable Computer Systems

Computer professionals face the ethical challenge to develop computer systems that are both reliable and safe. To reduce the risks associated with software failures and computer malfunctions, some argue that we must first develop adequate models of risk analysis and risk assessment. Don Gotterbarn addresses this concern in the chapter's seventh reading, entitled "Reducing Software Failures: Address Ethical Risks with Software Development Impact Statements (SoDIS™)." He believes that ethical risks associated with the entire software development life cycle must be taken into consideration. In Gotterbarn's scheme, the life cycle of software includes the maintenance phase, in addition to the design and development stages.

Gotterbarn worries that while cost-effectiveness issues have been addressed, the models of risks used in software development have paid very little attention to ethical considerations. He shows that in these models, the concept of risk has typically been understood in terms of three conditions, where software is either: (1) behind schedule, (2) over budget, or (3) fails to meet a system's specified requirements. Gotterbarn argues that software can still fail to meet an acceptable standard of risk assessment while satisfying all three conditions. To see how this is possible, Gotterbarn considers a case involving the Aegis Radar System, which was developed by the US Navy to allow ships to monitor space around them.

In July 1988, the USS Vincennes, a US Navy ship equipped with the Aegis system, accidentally shot down an Iranian passenger aircraft, killing 230 people. Many believe that a contributing element to—and arguably the key reason for—the accident was the poor design of the system's user interface. In response to the Vincennes incident, some computer ethicists have argued that system designers need to better understand the importance of having features that affect "human abilities and limitations" built into the interfaces of safety-critical systems. Gotterbarn believes that if an

adequate model of risk analysis were used, accidents like the one involving the Aegis system on the Vincennes could be better understood. Consider
that the Aegis Radar System met all of the requirements that the developer and the customer had set for it; in fact, it satisfied the three conditions previously specified. Yet the use of the Aegis system resulted in the
deaths of more than 200 airline passengers.

Are risks involving accidents of this magnitude acceptable in schemes
for software development? Gotterbarn believes that the evidence suggests that software failures like the one involving the Aegis system result
from two defects in current models of risk assessment: (a) an overly narrow conception of risk, which is limited to quantitative issues; and (b) a
limited notion of "system stakeholders." With respect to (a), Gotterbarn
argues that a model of risk assessment based solely on cost effectiveness,
in terms of criteria such as budget and schedule, is not adequate. Instead,
the notion of risk analysis must be enlarged to include social, political,
and ethical issues. Regarding (b), Gotterbarn notes that the stakeholders
who are typically given consideration in risk assessment models for software development are limited to the software developers and the customers. He argues that this limited notion of "system stakeholders" leads
to developing systems that have unanticipated negative effects. (Recall
Chuck Huff's notion of "unintended consequences" described previously.) Gotterbarn concludes that unless an adequate risk model for software
development is framed, we may be doomed to experience future computer
malfunctions similar in scale to the one involving the Aegis Radar System.

Nanocomputing and Future Developments in IT

In the final reading, entitled "Lilliputian Computer Ethics," John Weckert
examines some controversies surrounding research and development in
nanotechnology and nanocomputing. *Nanotechnology,* a term coined by K.
Eric Drexler in the 1980s, is a branch of engineering dedicated to the development of extremely small electronic circuits and mechanical devices built
at the molecular level of matter. Current microelectricomechanical systems (or MEMS), tiny devices such as sensors embedded in conductor
chips used in airbag systems to detect collisions, are one step away from
the molecular machines envisioned in nanotechnology. Drexler (1991)
believes that developments in this field will lead to computers at the
nano-scale, no bigger in size than bacteria, called *nanocomputers.* To appreciate the scale of future nanocomputers, imagine a mechanical or electronic device whose dimensions are measured in nanometers (billionths
of a meter, or units of 10^{-9} meter). Ralph Merkle (1997) envisions nanocomputers having "mass storage devices that can store more than 100 billion

bytes in a volume the size of a sugar cube." He also predicts that these nano-scale computers will be able to "deliver a billion billion instructions per second—a billion times faster than today's desktop computers."

Should research and development in nanotechnology and nanocomputing continue? Nanotechnology's advocates are quick to point out many of the advantages that would likely result for both the medical field and the environment. For example, nano-particles inserted into bodies could diagnose diseases and directly treat diseased cells. Doctors could use nanomachines (or *nanites*) to make microscopic repairs on areas of the body that are difficult to operate on with conventional surgical tools. And using nanotechnology tools, the life signs of a patient could be better monitored. In the environment, nanites could be used to clean toxic spills, as well as to eliminate other kinds of environmental hazards. Nanites could also dismantle or "disassemble" garbage at the molecular level and recycle it again at the molecular level via "nanite assemblers." On the other hand, opponents of research and development in nanotechnology and nanocomputing see things quite differently. Since all matter (inanimate objects and organisms) could theoretically be disassembled and reassembled by nanites, some worry that if nanomachines were created to be self-replicating and if there was a problem with their limiting mechanisms, they could multiply endlessly like viruses. Some also worry that nanite assemblers and disassemblers could be used to create weapons; and because guns, explosives, and electronic components of weapons could all be miniaturized, some critics (see, for example, Chen, 2002) worry that nanites themselves could be used as weapons.

Many of the claims and predictions regarding nanotechnology seem quite plausible; reputable scientists and researchers tend to agree with the projection that nanocomputers of some sort will be available sometime around the middle of the 21st century. Weckert suggests that because the evidence is so credible, ethical implications should be considered now rather than later. He also responds to some points raised in a controversial article by Bill Joy (2000), who has suggested that because developments in nanotechnology are threatening to make us an "endangered species," the only realistic alternative is to limit the development of that technology. Weckert believes that we must seriously consider the implications of nanotechnology research, given Joy's predictions. Furthermore, if computer scientists elect to carry out research and development in this area, Weckert (2001) believes that we must determine whether they should be held morally responsible for outcomes involving nanotechnology.

Should computer professionals who currently work on projects related to nanocomputers be asked to discontinue their work? And should aspiring computer scientists who plan to enter that field of research be discouraged, or perhaps even prevented, from doing so? Weckert offers a strategy for deliberating over this question. Weckert's paper, which strongly recommends that we proactively examine the ethical implications of future developments in nanocomputing for computer professionals rather than waiting to respond in a reactive manner, concludes this chapter as well as the second edition of *Readings in CyberEthics*.

Discussion Questions

1. Who exactly are computer professionals? Do computer professionals have any special moral responsibilities in addition to those that apply to ordinary computer users? If so, what are some of those responsibilities? What does Elizabeth Buchanan mean by the expression "the information professions," and what are some of the "ethical considerations" she outlines for the members of those professions?

2. What are some benefits of having one or more professional codes of ethics for computer and information professionals? Are there any disadvantages? On balance, do the advantages outweigh the disadvantages? Assess some of the strengths and weaknesses of the ACM Code of Ethics and Professional Conduct.

3. Describe some challenges involved in framing a coherent code of professional conduct for professions such as computing and IT in general, and for software engineering in particular. Does the SECEPP Code meet those challenges?

4. According to Don Gotterbarn, what is the "life cycle" of cyber and computer ethics issues, as seen from the perspective of computer professionals? How can understanding this cycle help computer professionals to raise their level of ethical awareness?

5. What does Chuck Huff mean by "unintentional power," and how can that kind of "power," on the part of software designers, have social consequences that are often unforeseen and unintended?

6. Why is Richard Epstein concerned that undergraduate computer science students might not get the appropriate level of instruction on aspects of their professional responsibilities that are ethical and social in nature? Is his concern justified? Should major computer organizations such as the ACM and IEEE mandate that a certain number of hours of instruction on ethical, social, and professional issues be required of all undergraduate CS students?

7. According to Don Gotterbarn, what criteria must be included in an adequate model of risk analysis in the development of software? How would such a model help to reduce failures in computer systems, especially for safety-critical computer systems such as the Aegis Radar System?

8. Assess some of the arguments for and against continued research and development in the field of nanocomputing, as presented by John Weckert. What kinds of ethical guidelines, if any, should be established before research and development in this field continues?

References

Chen, Andrew (2002). "The Ethics of Nanotechnology." Available at http://www.actionbioscience.org/newfrontiers/chen.html.

Drexler, K. Eric (1991). *Unbounding the Future.* New York: Quill.

Fairweather, N. Ben (1998). "No, PAPA: Why Incomplete Codes of Ethics Are Worse Than None at All." In G. Collste, ed. *Ethics in an Age of Information Technology.* Delhi: New Academic

Publishers. Reprinted in R. A. Spinello and H. T. Tavani, eds. 2001. Readings in *CyberEthics*. 1st ed. Sudbury, MA: Jones and Bartlett, pp. 545–556.

Gotterbarn, Don (1999). "How the New Software Engineering Code of Ethics Affects You." *IEEE Software,* November/December, pp. 58–64.

Gotterbarn, Don, Keith Miller, and Simon Rogerson (1999). "Software Engineering Code of Ethics: Approved!" *Communications of the ACM,* Vol. 42, No. 10, pp. 102–107. Reprinted in R. A. Spinello and H. T. Tavani, eds. (2001). Readings in *CyberEthics*. 1st ed. Sudbury, MA: Jones and Bartlett, pp. 535–544.

Joy, Bill (2000). "Why the Future Doesn't Need Us." *Wired,* Vol. 8, No. 4.

Ladd, John (1995). "The Quest for a Code of Professional Ethics: An Intellectual and Moral Confusion." In D. G. Johnson and H. Nissenbaum eds., *Computers, Ethics and Social Values*. Englewood Cliffs, NJ: Prentice Hall, pp. 580–585.

Merkle, Ralph (1997). "It's a Small, Small, Small World." *Technology Review,* Vol. 25, February/March.

Tavani, Herman T. (2003). "Ethical Reflections on the Digital Divide," *Journal of Information, Communication, and Ethics in Society,* Vol. 1, No. 2, pp. 99–108.

Weckert, John (2001). "The Control of Scientific Research: The Case of Nanotechnology," *Australian Journal of Professional and Applied Ethics,* Vol. 3, No. 2, pp. 29–44.

Suggestions for Further Readings

Baase, Sara (2003). "Professional Ethics and Responsibilities." Chap. 10 in *A Gift of Fire: Social, Legal, and Ethical Issues in Computing*. 2nd ed. Upper Saddle River, NJ: Prentice Hall.

Buchanan, Elizabeth A. (1999). "An Overview of Information Ethics in a World-Wide Context." *Ethics and Information Technology,* Vol. 1, No. 3, pp. 193–201.

Bynum, Terrell Ward and Simon Rogerson, eds. (2004). *Computer Ethics and Professional Responsibility: Introductory Text and Readings*. Oxford: Blackwell.

Gotterbarn, Don (1991). "Computer Ethics: Responsibility Regained." *National Forum: The Phi Kappa Phi Journal,* Vol. 71, No. 3, pp. 26–31.

Gotterbarn, Don (2000). "Computer Professionals and YOUR Responsibilities." In D. Langford, ed. *Internet Ethics*. New York: St. Martin's Press, pp. 200–219.

Gunn, Alastair S. and P. Aarne Vesiland (2003). *Hold Paramount: The Engineer's Responsibility to Society*. Brooks/Cole-Thompson Learning.

Harris, C. Ed, Michael Pritchard, and Mike Rabins, eds. (2000). *Engineering Ethics: Concepts and Cases*. 2nd ed. Belmont, CA: Wadsworth.

Johnson, Deborah G., ed. (1991). *Ethical Issues in Engineering*. Englewood Cliffs, NJ: Prentice Hall.

Johnson, Deborah G. (2001). "Professional Ethics," Chap. 3 in *Computer Ethics*. 3rd ed. Upper Saddle River, NJ: Prentice Hall.

Langford, Duncan (1999). *Business Computer Ethics*. Reading, MA: Addison-Wesley.

Merkle, Ralph (2001). "Nanotechnology: What Will it Mean?" *IEEE Spectrum,* January.

Moor, James H. (1998). "If Aristotle Were a Computing Professional," *Computers and Society,* Vol. 28, No. 3, September, pp. 13–16.

Nissenbaum, Helen (1994). "Computing and Accountability," *Communications of the ACM,* Vol. 37, No. 1, pp. 73–80.

Tavani, Herman T. (2004). "Professional Ethics, Codes of Conduct, and Moral Responsibility." Chap. 4 in *Ethics and Technology: Ethical Issues in an Age of Information and Communication Technology.* Hoboken, NJ: John Wiley and Sons.

Weckert, John (2001). "Computer Ethics: Future Directions." *Ethics and Information Technology,* Vol. 3, No. 2, pp. 93–96.

Ethical Considerations for the Information Professions

Elizabeth A. Buchanan

Introduction

The field of information ethics is relatively new, with the term coined as recently as the late 1980s by Robert Hauptman in the United States and Rafael Cappuru in Germany. The issues specific to information ethics, however, have certainly been with us for a longer time, yet continue to gain prominence and complexity in public discourse with the popularization of information and computer technologies. Information ethics bridges many disciplines, including library and information science, computer science, archival science, records management, informatics, educational media technologies, and more. Weckert and Adeney (1997, p. ix) contend "the domain of information ethics comprises all of the ethical issues related to the production, storage, access and dissemination of information." Similar to the term "computer ethics," first articulated by Walter Maner in 1976, "information ethics" reflects the meeting of the social, the technological, and the philosophical.

Recognizing the importance of the ethical issues surrounding "information" assumes a critical role for information workers, librarians, or computer scientists alike. Certainly, we are all becoming "information workers" in some form or another, and yet, few of us receive any formal education on the ethics of information or ethics in general. Pemberton (1998, p. 76) notes an existing distinction between ethical understandings and technical knowledge of a profession: "professional communities . . . have many responsibilities for ethical behavior that transcend the lower-order technical concerns of their work. Ethics . . . lies in the domain of morality rather than in the more ordinary sphere of technical competence." Such sentiments promote noteworthy considerations for the education of information professionals, advocating *both* technical as well as ethical training.

Today's social obsession with technologies, especially information technologies, raises many serious concerns and considerations, while we continue to explore and exploit the seemingly unlimited potential of technology and its powers, serious reflection on the social, ethical, and legal ramifications of technologies remains minimal. Moreover, many existing moral principles and frameworks are being stretched and contorted to fit newfound situations and issues, as technologies create heretofore unheard of ethical dilemmas. As Stichler and Hauptman aptly state, "modern technology is not a simple tool but a complex interdependent network that behaves like an ecosystem that no single individual or group can control. Just when it seems that we have solved one technical problem here, an unintended consequence springs up over there" (1998, p. 1). These unintended consequences have been explored in Tenner (1996), who describes in great detail the many unintended consequences of medical, informational, and biotechnological tools and technologies.

This chapter includes a brief introduction to the philosophical foundations of ethics and morality and an overview of basic principles of information ethics, describes particular issues and areas of particular concern to information professionals, and discusses codes of ethics for the information professions. An abbreviated resource list is included for additional information and sources.

Philosophical Foundations

Ethics is generally defined as the philosophical study of moral behavior, of moral decision-making, or of how to lead a "good life." Brincat and Wilke (1999) distinguish between ethics and morality:

> Ethics is the study of morality; the study of what we do. Morality could exist without ethics (if no one investigated how morality is done) but there cannot be ethics without morality (we cannot study morality unless there is morality).... Morality is like eating; it is an inevitable part of everyone's life. Ethics, on the other hand, is like nutrition. It is crucial to living a good life but it is not an inevitable part of living or an activity engaged in by all.

Too, Serverson (1997, p. 7–8) differentiates between ethics and morality on the basis that "morality refers to the sense of conscience and right and wrong that we derive from our upbringing. Morality is highly personal and often functions instinctively.... Ethics, on the other hand is more structured and deliberative; it is a kind of critical thinking about the moral life."

Three major realms of ethics can be identified: Descriptive—focusing on existing situations or conditions; normative—focusing on what ought to be; and thirdly, metaethics, the logical analysis of moral language and the aim to make precise the meaning of moral terms and clarify the moral arguments that are at stake. Overarching theories of ethics include universalism or objectivism and relativism. Distinct versions of universalism and relativism are aptly described by Weckert and Adeney, while Oz (1994) provides a succinct discussion of particular ethical theories.

Major Issues

In "An Overview of Information Ethics Issues in a World-Wide Context," I differentiate between qualitative and quantitatively grounded ethical issues, noting that the ethics surrounding the information professions span many areas in terms of quantity—such as the paucity of third world scientists and their countries in such significant information resources as the *Science Citation Index*—in addition to the quality of culturally relevant information, entertainment, and education produced in, of, and from the North or developed countries such as the US and infused into Southern or developing countries with little regard or sensitivity to cultural relevance or appropriateness.

The foundations of global inequities in regard to information first addressed by Masmoudi (1979) deserve recognition and continue to plague information professionals, both on local as well as global dimensions. Despite the twenty-some years of change, global development, and "shrinking" of the world due to such technologies as the Internet, there remains:

1. A flagrant quantitative imbalance between the North and the South (which is situationally replicated in the US in terms of our digital divide among urban, suburban, and rural populations);
2. An inequality in information resources;
3. A de facto hegemony and a will to dominate;
4. A lack of information on, about, and for developing countries;
5. Survival of the colonial era;
6. An alienating influence in the economic, social, and cultural spheres; and,
7. Messages ill-suited to the areas in which they are disseminated.

In addition to the areas Masmoudi identified, further ethical issues challenge information professionals. Librarians, for instance, have historically been charged with providing free and unfettered access to information in all forms and types. Libraries, much like other cultural institutions as museums and archives, are facing dire changes as they attempt to keep up with technological changes, competing interests in the forms of information brokers and fee-based information provision, and accessible formats for all of their clientele. As information delivery mechanisms change to DVD and online availability only, patrons without the comforts of home theatre systems and computers need the public institutions more than ever, while libraries attempt to serve all individuals; librarians must make collection development decisions, for instance, and these decisions possess strong ethical challenges. Librarians and information providers alike must weigh the pros and cons of adopting newfound formats and delivery and whether they are contributing to inequitable access. Further, many information professionals forego the once esteemed roles of public service in the name of profits and commercial endeavors. The free versus fee debate rages on in the profession, albeit with new dimensions. The ethics of information provision become startling when we realize that a large majority of our societies face information poverty or "second-class" information, as buying information—better information—from brokers or online services becomes commonplace, if of course one can afford it.

This idea of a two-tiered system of information access reaches into formal channels of education as well. Students who can afford to pay for online journals and/or immediate delivery of scholarly and research materials hold an advantage over those who can not afford such conveniences and luxuries. Is it the ethical responsibility of librarians and information workers in educational settings to avoid this disparity? To disallow its occurrence? Or, are libraries, as many sadly predict, obsolete anyway? The scenario surrounding distance education offered by McManus offers a sad commentary of the evolving state of free access: "Unless we are cautious in how we define and program [library] services . . . students will sit at their home PCs and electronically debit $20 per course to the university and $400 to Time-Warner" (McManus, 1998, p. 432). The information age, in all of its glory, reveals a vigorous consumerism,[1] one that is badly altering the ethics of information provision and access through the creation and perpetuation of an information elite. (An aside to this elitism is the elitism surrounding the ability to buy protection of one's quickly diminishing personal privacy: "Privacy will be available for a price, but only a few will pay to protect it" (Costello, et al, 2000, p. 67)).

Given this state of information access, one of the most prominent ethical issues and that which has garnered significant attention is the digital divide, and information professionals have an ethical responsibility to consider how they may be contributing to this divide. The National Telecommunications and Information Administration (NTIA) has been tracking the digital divide for a number of years and has released three subsequent studies focusing on race, ethnicity, geographical location, level of education, and the relationship of these variables to access to computers, Internet, and other "Information Age tools" (NTIA, 1999). Not surprisingly, Whites are more likely to be connected to these tools than African-American, Hispanic, or Native American peoples. Further disparities arise in terms of income levels and geographical location. Rural Americans find themselves left considerably behind, as do individuals with disabilities[2] and those with minimal education. While the statistics the NTIA offers will certainly not shock anyone, they confirm Masmoudi's findings of more than twenty years ago. What should shock us as we read these statistics is the vast disparity of wealth—informational wealth—

---

[1] Consumerism and commercialism are affecting the information professions in multiple ways, as the patrons of such public entities as museums and archives now think twice before donating their family's memorabilia or treasures to the public good. Years ago, many would display their namesakes in public museums through donations. Now, these treasures and their owners sit awaiting the *Antique Roadshow* to roll into town, to see what dollar amount can be made.

[2] Information professionals charged with world wide web design, for instance, have the ethical and legal responsibility to adhere to the World Wide Web Consortium's (W3C) *Web Content Accessibility Guidelines* for Americans with Disabilities Act compliance. Despite the fact that the ADA celebrated its tenth anniversary this year, accessibility issues for online materials are only now emerging as a major consideration for information professionals—despite the fact that the center for Applied Special Technology (CAST), the creator of Bobby, was founded in 1984. The overwhelming minority of web pages can bear the "Bobby" logo, indicating that the page conforms to such accessibility standards as text equivalents for all non–text elements, provides summaries of all graphs and charts, and presents alternative information without color.

right here in our own back yards. We need not look to poor, developing countries to see the inequities of information access, but look only to our neighbors.

As we do look to the disconnected—technologically, economically, and educationally disconnected—information professionals must ask what other factors contribute to the marginalization. While the plethora of available information seemingly saturates us, what is the quality of that information? To whom does it speak? From what vantage point or cultural perspective is this information constructed and delivered? Can we truly say the information industry is a democratic industry, in which many viewpoints and subjectivities are reflected? Sclove's work (1995) on democratic and democratizing technologies holds great potential for information professionals, as he criticizes the ways in which technologies and the many significant decisions surrounding them are often out of our control. The idea of social upheaval caused by information and technologies, as well as the infusion of inappropriate technologies and use, can be combated, or at least minimized, by participatory design and development. Information professionals must be charged with a responsibility to provide resources and services that do not negatively disrupt cultural traditions or specificity. Information provision should follow theories of cultural relativism to avoid overt colonialism; the imperialism of American or Northern perspectives is reflected in English language domination,[3] as well as American cultural icons and ideals. However, this challenge of providing alternatives may prove too difficult, or simply impossible, in the age of mergers and conglomeration.

Robert McChesney's review (1999) of the three major media producers reveals the realities of diminishing choice. Information professionals need to seek alternative outlets from which to obtain information, lest they will be reading, viewing, and hearing the same mainstream news story from NewsCorp's Fox, Harper Collins, and *New York Post*, all of which it owns, in addition to major stakes in European radio, telecommunications companies, and TV and satellite delivery, among numerous other media outlets and ventures (McChesney, pp. 96–97). The paucity of choice is indeed an ethical dilemma, as information continues to be increasingly centralized: The creators of information are also the owners of the means of transmission, thereby narrowing any chance of alternative or contrarian perspectives. Furthermore, McChesney presents the realities of such conglomeration and its impact on cultural erosion: "One thinks of Disney CEO Michael Eisner's delight when someone presented him with a photograph of a woman from Timbuktu wearing a cap for Disney's Anaheim Mighty Ducks hockey team. 'Now that's the definition of global reach!' Eisner enthused" (p. 101).

A further pessimistic outcome of this paucity of choice may also result in an erasure or adaptation of history and historical record. While seemingly science fiction-like or perhaps communist-like, our collective memories are shrinking with the reliance on electronic information, coupled with questionable agendas of the major media conglomerates. From an ethical perspective, serious concerns abound.

---

[3] Shorris (2000, pp. 35–36) presents an insightful look into the world's languages, noting that ". . . as many as 3000 languages, comprising half of all the words on earth, are doomed to silence in the next century. . . . English dominates the world. It is the lingua franca of science, the Internet, the movies, rock and roll, television, and even sports."

Information professionals must be teaching about the responsible and critical use, understanding, evaluation, and preservation of all information. The questionable revisions that occur throughout Orwell's *Animal Farm* seem all too real in our age of 'here today, gone tomorrow' web sites, electronic journals, and digital resources. Thus, the practicality of preservation and archival measures must meet the ethical in our professional training and education of information specialists.

Intellectual property and constitutional issues comprise a major area of information ethics. Individual's intellectual property must be protected for individual and social reasons. The protection of the intangible efforts in the forms of books, musical scores, computer programs, and the like deserve protection to encourage innovation, valuation of intellectual endeavors, and the continued production of such individual efforts for the benefits of society as a whole. Under the guise of copyright and patents, intellectual property is protected from undue copy and use. And yet, the evolution of technologies pose new trials to this legal protection. As the currently ongoing Napster suit is revealing, technologies enable illegal and unethical behaviors. Many rationalize the debate with such sentiments as "Bill Gates is not going to be hurt by my borrowing a friend's version of MS Office," and "Metallica has made plenty of money off their records and CDs that my downloading a few songs won't hurt." Such rationalization reveals the ambiguous relationships that exist among people and technology: The technology allows us to do something and it is not "hurting" anyone, so how can it be unethical?

While legality and morality are not always in sync,[4] information professionals must understand intellectual property laws and the ethical underpinnings of them in order to teach others of these responsibilities. Copyright, patent, privacy, libel, pornography, and censorship are areas in which every information professional should be versed. (For detailed discussion on these areas, see Baase, Oz, Weckert and Adeney, Severson, and Hauptman.) Technology changes the relationships of intellectual property in the ease with which manipulation, copying, distortion, and removal can occur. The Computer Ethics Institute's *Ten Commandments of Computer Ethics* should be posted in every school, every office, library, and so on.

Further, implementing ethical education into schools when children begin keyboarding is imperative, so that a natural respect of and adherence to principles of social responsibility in regard to technologies ensues seamlessly. Information professionals face educating the public about ethics on a number of additional levels, including those surrounding the loss of reflective abilities, which are critical to ethical decision making. Computing in general facilitates instantaneous action and a sense of immediacy. Such immediacy denies the opportunity for reflection and conscious thinking. The phases of ethical decision-making are often overlooked and in their stead, knee-jerk or uncritical decisions made.

Finally, intellectual property and hacking are strange bed-fellows. The long standing adage "information wants to be free" is a rallying call for hackers the world over. Interesting perspectives on the ethics of computer hacking are discussed in

---

[4] Ethics is distinct from law in that the law provides a structured context to which we look for "reasonable" decisions; the law does not necessarily tell us what is inherently good or bad. It does not prescribe behavior for the purpose of morality but for the purpose of satisfying a societal requirement or rule; rules are dictated by authority, not necessarily morality.

Goodrum and Manion (2000), who describe the "ethics of hacktivism," noting that computer attacks on unjust governments and their web sites should not be considered unethical, but seen as a form of Emersonian civil disobedience.

Another area of ethical import to information professionals is the growing reliance and anthropomorphizing of technologies. Seely Brown and Duguid (2000) describe the shrinking division between the human and the digital in the shape of "bots," "personal assistants," or "agents." Do we ascribe more power, autonomy, or indeed—humanness—to these bots than we should, and if so, what is this tendency to trust and rely on automated programs doing to our social relations and interpersonal interactions? The increasing reliance on bots, whose capabilities are growing exponentially, raises questions and concerns in terms of the digital divide as well. Consider: Less-skilled and less-educated individuals have found work in the information professions in data entry and the like. While these professions may not be considered highly valuable, they often afford an opportunity in the information age and its industries, with the chance for individuals to further educate themselves as they work in those tedious positions. A light at the end of the digital tunnel exists for some. This is not to discredit the accurate portrayal Kester (1998) offers:

> What is more clearly happening . . . is a growing division of labor between the low-paid insecure and often unsafe jobs in the service sector, assembly and manufacturing, and a minority of highly privileged managerial, technical, and professional positions. This is a division that is reiterated in both the local and the global level, with the expansion of 'informal' economies in major American cities, fueled by immigrant labor . . . what can be described as 'the revival of nineteenth century seated trades in the richest cities on earth.' (p. 225)

However, with bots or other automated labor, which some now say have "decision-making powers, social abilities, learning capabilities, and autonomy" (Seely Brown and Duguid, p. 39), this light may quickly dim. As a society, we have difficult decisions to make, as Seely Brown and Duguid assert; ". . . we will all have to confront [these complex social issues], asking to what extent agents should or can be woven into the fabric of human life in all its complexities. These are issues that everyone must face" (p. 40).

Information professionals can be better equipped to recognize, understand, and react to such complex ethical dilemmas through formal and informal education, as well as through professional codes of ethics. To these we now turn.

Codes of Ethics

Codes of ethics in general can be understood as sets of "best practices." Some professional or organizational codes, such as the ACM, contain extremely detailed guidelines, while others present conceptual ideas with little specificity, such as the ALA's. Such major organizations of the information professions include the American Library Association, the American Society for Information Science, Association of

American Archivists, and the International Council on Museums, with many others embodying records management and information processing. Oz and Baase provide thorough reviews of professional organizations and codes of ethics.

It is generally accepted that professional ethics is differentiated from general ethics in that professionals are experts in a field, which provides them an advantage over the lay person and that professionals' work has the potential to impact—either positively or negatively—the general public at large. Thus, as information professionals, we have the potential to adversely affect our increasingly large and diverse clientele by failing to act responsibly, fairly, timely, and appropriately in the aforementioned areas of information ethics concerns.

Professional ethics seek to identify and discuss "the most serious problems of professional conduct, the resolution of problems arising from conflicts of interest, and the guarantee that the special expertise of the members of a profession will be used in the public interest" (SAA, 1992). Codes must provide guidelines for "justice, beneficence, nonmalefience, independence, objectivity, and professionalism" (Mason, p. 152). Further, a code mustn't be a list of do's and don'ts—it mustn't be prescriptive—but must demonstrate the guiding ethical principles and why they are so. The efficacy of a code of ethics depends on how thoroughly it articulates the socio-professional ideals of any profession or organization. "The development and adaptation of a professional code of ethics is predicated on the normative purpose of the profession. It is the professional purpose that provides the filter through which principles are strained. . . . The purpose of a profession does not change. The purpose is itself a normative filter, the basic ethical conduit through which a profession's contribution to the welfare of society takes on additional importance and new responsibility" (Palmiter, 1996, p. 230).

Johnson (1985) identified four channels through which professional codes of ethics should be judged: obligations to society, obligations to employer, obligations to clients, and obligations to colleagues and organizations. In terms of information ethics, these four areas remain highly significant. As information professionals, we have the ethical responsibility to uphold principles of social, personal, and organizational responsibility. Such organizations as Computer Professionals for Social Responsibility—which includes librarians, archivists, computer programmers, and philosophers alike—and in particular, its Ethics Working Group, provide useful resources for understanding and adhering to ethical principles related to information and computer work.

Many professionals enter the field with little or no ethical preparation or training. Many have never encountered the ALA's Code or ICOM's code. Thus, it is highly important for professional schools and programs to begin to teach ethical responsibilities and allow students to "practice" ethics before they are faced with thorny situations in the workplace. In the ethics class I teach, each student works through various case scenarios after they have been armed with philosophical theories of ethics and evaluation procedures. Acting out ethical dilemmas encourages the processual thinking requisite to understanding the impact of each decision and action. An apt policy for the information professions includes training staff on ethical issues and appropriate responsibilities through cases and role playing. New hires should be made familiar with the appropriate code of ethics and how professional ethics are a part of the organization; likewise, stressing the currency of professional education for all members holds value. Ethical training and decision-making must become systemically and systematically integrated into all aspects of the profession, so when the "hot" cases strike, every member of the team is ready and able to make sound decisions.

Ethical codes of conduct provide guidelines and frameworks, but may more often than not fail to give us "answers." Thus, a series of questions can be used in evaluating and justifying decisions and behaviors. I have divided such deliberations into two phases (Buchanan, 2000).

Phase 1: Issue Definition and Evaluation:

- Define the issue or situation as objectively as possible. Then, define it with your own biases.
- Are you confident of your competence in the issue?
- Who are the stakeholders or affected parties?
- How would you describe the situation to an outsider and an insider?
- How did the situation or issue arise? What variables played into the issue?
- Separate the trivial from the significant in the situation—are we understanding the situation fully? What is really important?
- Where do your loyalties fall? Is there any conflict of interest? Can you differentiate your decisions as a member of society and as a member of an organization?
- Do you understand all aspects and perspectives of the issue?
- Can you discuss the issue with the stakeholders before moving to Phase 2 of the decision-making evaluation?

Phase 2: Action/Inaction Evaluation and Implementation

- Consider the boundaries of the actions and inactions. What is the intention behind an action or inaction?
- Evaluate alternatives and their repercussions. Try to establish believable alternatives and credible repercussions—do you really believe your decision will result in X? Or, is X a far shot that most likely won't happen, but you are trying to convince yourself it will?
- Determine a course of action with which you are comfortable and can face yourself and those involved with or affected by your decision. Are you really considering how your decision will impact others? Can you live with your decision? Will you be confident disclosing your decision publicly?
- Under what, if any, conditions would you allow exceptions to your decision? Evaluate those exceptions closely.
- Decision making is cumulative: one decision often builds on previous. How does your decision fit in with the previous decisions? Also, your decision affects other decisions you will make—are you satisfied with the course of actions you are taking? How will this decision impact how you proceed?

- Can you universalize the decision? If not, why?
- Before decisions are made, refer to codes of professional ethics. Is there consistency or conflict in regard to the codes and your plans?

To complement these series of questions, a strategy I suggest to organizations as well as individuals is to "journal" the responses to these questions and have a "cooling off" period before actions are taken. After a day or two, revisit the journal and reflect upon the answers. Has a change in perspective or evaluation of the issue changed? If so, why? What factors contribute to that change? This strategy therefore encourages the processual thinking requisite to ethical decision-making.

Finally, Edson (1997, p. 11) offers a valid comment concerning ethical decision-making: "The important measure of all decision making is that the seriousness of the risk is never to be out of proportion to the worthiness of the cause or the means of circumvention." By weighing and evaluating such proportions, individuals and organizations can take confidence in their decisions to act in a particular manner.

Conclusion

Information ethics, much like the technologies that continue to contribute to its complexity, will thrive and present new challenges to all of us. Ethics will continue to be put through new tests as technologies race ahead of many social and cultural conventions and norms.

As a professor in a school of library and information science, I have had the opportunity to teach information ethics to both graduate library and information science students and undergraduate information resources management students. My experiences in the academy tell me that there is still a major divide between the theory surrounding information ethics and its application in the fields of information work. Students repeatedly tell me that information ethics is unrealistic and nice to discuss in the confines of the university, but in the "real world" of information technologies, "ethics" serve little purpose, that IS/IT professionals will use any appropriate tool to complete a task, with little reflection on the ethics surrounding the tool, the task, or the outcome. My students, for instance, often praise the monopolistic and anti-competitive behaviors of Microsoft. What, many ask, is unethical about their success or how they became what they have?

Part of the problem with such attitudes is the lack of ethics education to complement the major push toward technology literacy in K-16 education. Instilling a sense of civic responsibility surrounding technologies from the earliest ages must occur. As students learn how to transfer files, they must also understand the concepts of copyright, ownership of information, and the rights and privileges of using other individuals' intellectual property.

In closing, information ethics must be understood as impacting each and every member of the "information society." As such, each member must accept certain responsibilities and act accordingly. Information ethics, as with information literacy, must become integral to formal and informal education. The Kantian Categorical Imperative reveals promise, yet once again, as a guiding principle for the information age and as a critical tenet of information ethics.

Selected Resources

American Library Association Code of Ethics: http://www.ala.org/alaorg/oif/ethics.html

American Library Association Office of Intellectual Freedom: http://www.ala.org/alaorg/oif/

American Society for Information Science Professional Guidelines:
    http://www.asis.org/AboutASIS/professional–guidelines.html

Association for Computing Machinery (ACM) Code of Ethics:
    http://www.acm.org/constitution/code.html

Canadian Library Association Code of Ethics: http://www.cla.ca/about/ethics.htm

Center for Applied Special Technology (Bobby): http://www.cast.org/bobby

Center for the Responsible Use of Information Technologies: http://ces.uoregon.edu/responsibleuse/default.html

Computer Ethics Institute, Ten Commandments of Computer Ethics:
    http://www.cpsr.org/program/ethics/cei.html

Computer Professionals for Social Responsibility: http://www.cpsr.org

Electronic Privacy Information Center: http://www.epic.org

International Council of Museums Code of Professional Ethics: http://www.icom.org/ethics.html

Society of American Archivists Code of Ethics:
    http://www.archivists.org/governance/handbook/app_ethics.html

The Electronic Frontier Foundation: http://www.eff.org/

The Loka Institute: http://www.loka.org

The Tavani Bibliography of Computing, Ethics, and Social Responsibility:
    http://cyberethics.cbi.msstate.edu/biblio/index.html

W3C Accessibility Guidelines. http://www.w3.org

References

Brincat, and Wilke, T. *Morality and the Professional Life: Values at Work*. New York: Prentice Hall.

Buchanan, E. (1999). An Overview of Information Ethics in a World–Wide Context. *Ethics and Information Technology, 1* (3), 193–201.

——. (2000). Organizing Ethics in Archives, Museums, and Libraries: Challenges and Strategies for Meeting Ethical Responsibilities. Presented at the Institute on Legal and Ethical Issues in the Information Age. Milwaukee, WI. May.

Costello, M., Moynihan, M., Sege, R., Westin, A., and Harrison, C. (2000). The Searchable Soul: Privacy in the age of information technology. *Harpers, 300* (1796), 57–68.

Edson, G. (ED.) (1997). *Museum ethics*. New York: Routledge.

Goodrum, A. and Manion, M. (2000). The ethics of hacktivism. *Journal of Information Ethics*, Fall.

Johnson, D. (1985; 1994). *Computer Ethics.* Englewood Cliffs: Prentice Hall.

Kester, G. (1998). Access Denied: Information policy and the limits of liberalism. In *Ethics, Information, and Technology: Readings*. Edited by R Stichler and R. Hauptman. Jefferson: McFarland.

Masmoudi, M. (1979). The new world information order. *Journal of Communications* (Spring), 172–185.

Mason, F. (1996). Ethics and the electronic society. In *Professional Ethics in Librarianship: A Real Life Casebook* (Ed. Fay Zipkowitz), pp. 148–152. Jefferson: McFarland.

McChesney, R. (1999). *Rich media, poor democracy: Communication politics in dubious times.* Urbana: University of Illinois Press.

McManus, M. (1998). Neither Pandora nor Cassandra: Library services and distance education in the next decade. *C&RL News,* 432–435.

National Telecommunications and Information Administration. (1999). Falling through the net: Defining the digital divide. Available: http://www.ntia.doc.gov/ntiahome/fttn99/ contents.html

Oz, E. (1994). *Ethics for the information age.* B&E Tech.

Palmiter, C. W. (1996). Personal and sociological ethical amid technological change. In *Social and Ethical Effects of the Computer Revolution* (Ed. Joseph Kizza), pp. 230–247. Jefferson: McFarland.

Pemberton, J. M. (1998). 'Through a glass darkly': Ethics and information technology. *Records Management Quarterly, 32* (1), 76–84.

Sclove, R. (1995). *Democracy and technology.* New York: Guilford.

Seely Brown, J. (2000). *The Social life of information.* Boston: Harvard Business School Press.

Severson, R. (1997). *The Principles of information ethics.* Armonk: ME Sharp.

Shorris, E. (2000). The last word. Can the world's languages be saved? *Harpers, 301* (180)3, 35–43.

Stichler, R. and Hauptman, R., Eds. (1998). *Ethics, information and technology: Readings.* Jefferson: McFarland.

Tenner, E. (1996). *Why things bite back: Technology and the revenge of unintended consequences.* New York: Vintage.

Weckert, J. and Adeney, D. (1997). *Computer and information ethics.* Westport: Greenwood Press.

ACM Code of Ethics and Professional Conduct

Adopted by ACM Council 10/16/92

Preamble

Commitment to ethical professional conduct is expected of every member (voting members, associate members, and student members) of the Association for Computing Machinery (ACM).

This Code, consisting of 24 imperatives formulated as statements of personal responsibility, identifies the elements of such a commitment. It contains many, but not all, issues professionals are likely to face. Section 1 outlines fundamental ethical considerations, while Section 2 addresses additional, more specific considerations of professional conduct. Statements in Section 3 pertain more specifically to individuals who have a leadership role, whether in the workplace or in a volunteer capacity such as with organizations like ACM. Principles involving compliance with this Code are given in Section 4.

The Code shall be supplemented by a set of Guidelines, which provide explanation to assist members in dealing with the various issues contained in the Code. It is expected that the Guidelines will be changed more frequently than the Code.

The Code and its supplemented Guidelines are intended to serve as a basis for ethical decision making in the conduct of professional work. Secondarily, they may serve as a basis for judging the merit of a formal complaint pertaining to violation of professional ethical standards.

It should be noted that although computing is not mentioned in the imperatives of Section 1, the Code is concerned with how these fundamental imperatives apply to one's conduct as a computing professional. These imperatives are expressed in a general form to emphasize that ethical principles that apply to computer ethics are derived from more general ethical principles.

It is understood that some words and phrases in a code of ethics are subject to varying interpretations, and that any ethical principle may conflict with other ethical principles in specific situations. Questions related to ethical conflicts can best be answered by thoughtful consideration of fundamental principles, rather than reliance on detailed regulations.

Contents & Guidelines

1 General Moral Imperatives

As an ACM member I will ...

1.1 Contribute to society and human well-being.

This principle concerning the quality of life of all people affirms an obligation to protect fundamental human rights and to respect the diversity of all cultures. An essential aim of computing professionals is to minimize negative consequences of computing systems, including threats to health and safety. When designing or implementing systems, computing professionals must attempt to ensure that the products of their efforts will be used in socially responsible ways, will meet social needs, and will avoid harmful effects to health and welfare.

In addition to a safe social environment, human well-being includes a safe natural environment. Therefore, computing professionals who design and develop systems must be alert to, and make others aware of, any potential damage to the local or global environment.

1.2 Avoid harm to others.

"Harm" means injury or negative consequences, such as undesirable loss of information, loss of property, property damage, or unwanted environmental impacts. This principle prohibits use of computing technology in ways that result in harm to any of the following: users, the general public, employees, employers. Harmful actions include intentional destruction or modification of files and programs leading to serious loss of resources or unnecessary expenditure of human resources such as the time and effort required to purge systems of "computer viruses."

Well-intended actions, including those that accomplish assigned duties, may lead to harm unexpectedly. In such an event the responsible person or persons are obligated to undo or mitigate the negative consequences as much as possible. One way to avoid unintentional harm is to carefully consider potential impacts on all those affected by decisions made during design and implementation.

To minimize the possibility of indirectly harming others, computing professionals must minimize malfunctions by following generally accepted standards for system design and testing. Furthermore, it is often necessary to assess the social consequences of systems to project the likelihood of any serious harm to others. If system features are misrepresented to users, coworkers, or supervisors, the individual computing professional is responsible for any resulting injury.

In the work environment the computing professional has the additional obligation to report any signs of system dangers that might result in serious personal or social damage. If one's superiors do not act to curtail or mitigate such dangers, it may be necessary to "blow the whistle" to help correct the problem or reduce the risk. However, capricious or misguided reporting of violations can, itself, be harmful. Before reporting violations, all relevant aspects of the incident must be thoroughly assessed. In particular, the assessment of risk and responsibility must be credible. It is suggested that advice be sought from other computing professionals. See principle 2.5 regarding thorough evaluations.

1.3 Be honest and trustworthy.
Honesty is an essential component of trust. Without trust an organization cannot function effectively. The honest computing professional will not make deliberately false or deceptive claims about a system or system design, but will instead provide full disclosure of all pertinent system limitations and problems.

A computer professional has a duty to be honest about his or her own qualifications, and about any circumstances that might lead to conflicts of interest.

Membership in volunteer organizations such as ACM may at times place individuals in situations where their statements or actions could be interpreted as carrying the "weight" of a larger group of professionals. An ACM member will exercise care to not misrepresent ACM or positions and policies of ACM or any ACM units.

1.4 Be fair and take action not to discriminate.
The values of equality, tolerance, respect for others, and the principles of equal justice govern this imperative. Discrimination on the basis of race, sex, religion, age, disability, national origin, or other such factors is an explicit violation of ACM policy and will not be tolerated.

Inequities between different groups of people may result from the use or misuse of information and technology. In a fair society, all individuals would have equal opportunity to participate in, or benefit from, the use of computer resources regardless of race, sex, religion, age, disability, national origin, or other such similar factors. However, these ideals do not justify unauthorized use of computer resources nor do they provide an adequate basis for violation of any other ethical imperatives of this code.

1.5 Honor property rights including copyrights and patents.
Violation of copyrights, patents, trade secrets, and the terms of license agreements is prohibited by law in most circumstances. Even when software is not so protected, such violations are contrary to professional behavior. Copies of software should be made only with proper authorization. Unauthorized duplication of materials must not be condoned.

1.6 Give proper credit for intellectual property.
Computing professionals are obligated to protect the integrity of intellectual property. Specifically, one must not take credit for other's ideas or work, even in cases where the work has not been explicitly protected by copyright, patent, etc.

1.7 Respect the privacy of others.

Computing and communication technology enables the collection and exchange of personal information on a scale unprecedented in the history of civilization. Thus there is increased potential for violating the privacy of individuals and groups. It is the responsibility of professionals to maintain the privacy and integrity of data describing individuals. This includes taking precautions to ensure the accuracy of data, as well as protecting it from unauthorized access or accidental disclosure to inappropriate individuals. Furthermore, procedures must be established to allow individuals to review their records and correct inaccuracies.

This imperative implies that only the necessary amount of personal information be collected in a system, that retention and disposal periods for that information be clearly defined and enforced, and that personal information gathered for a specific purpose not be used for other purposes without consent of the individual(s). These principles apply to electronic communications, including electronic mail, and prohibit procedures that capture or monitor electronic user data, including messages, without the permission of users or bona fide authorization related to system operation and maintenance. User data observed during the normal duties of system operation and maintenance must be treated with strictest confidentiality, except in cases where it is evidence for the violation of law, organizational regulations, or this Code. In these cases, the nature or contents of that information must be disclosed only to proper authorities.

1.8 Honor confidentiality.

The principle of honesty extends to issues of confidentiality of information whenever one has made an explicit promise to honor confidentiality or, implicitly, when private information not directly related to the performance of one's duties becomes available. The ethical concern is to respect all obligations of confidentiality to employers, clients, and users unless discharged from such obligations by requirements of the law or other principles of this Code.

2 More Specific Professional Responsibilities.

As an ACM computing professional I will ...

2.1 Strive to achieve the highest quality, effectiveness, and dignity in both the process and products of professional work.

Excellence is perhaps the most important obligation of a professional. The computing professional must strive to achieve quality and to be cognizant of the serious negative consequences that may result from poor quality in a system.

2.2 Acquire and maintain professional competence.

Excellence depends on individuals who take responsibility for acquiring and maintaining professional competence. A professional must participate in setting standards for appropriate levels of competence, and strive to achieve those standards. Upgrading technical knowledge and competence can be achieved in several ways:

doing independent study; attending seminars, conferences, or courses; and being involved in professional organizations.

2.3 Know and respect existing laws pertaining to professional work.

ACM members must obey existing local, state, province, national, and international laws unless there is a compelling ethical basis not to do so. Policies and procedures of the organizations in which one participates must also be obeyed. But compliance must be balanced with the recognition that sometimes existing laws and rules may be immoral or inappropriate and, therefore, must be challenged. Violation of a law or regulation may be ethical when that law or rule has inadequate moral basis or when it conflicts with another law judged to be more important. If one decides to violate a law or rule because it is viewed as unethical, or for any other reason, one must fully accept responsibility for one's actions and for the consequences.

2.4 Accept and provide appropriate professional review.

Quality professional work, especially in the computing profession, depends on professional reviewing and critiquing. Whenever appropriate, individual members should seek and utilize peer review as well as provide critical review of the work of others.

2.5 Give comprehensive and thorough evaluations of computer systems and their impacts, including analysis of possible risks.

Computer professionals must strive to be perceptive, thorough, and objective when evaluating, recommending, and presenting system descriptions and alternatives. Computer professionals are in a position of special trust, and therefore have a special responsibility to provide objective, credible evaluations to employers, clients, users, and the public. When providing evaluations the professional must also identify any relevant conflicts of interest, as stated in imperative 1.3.

As noted in the discussion of principle 1.2 on avoiding harm, any signs of danger from systems must be reported to those who have opportunity and/or responsibility to resolve them. See the guidelines for imperative 1.2 for more details concerning harm, including the reporting of professional violations.

2.6 Honor contracts, agreements, and assigned responsibilities.

Honoring one's commitments is a matter of integrity and honesty. For the computer professional this includes ensuring that system elements perform as intended. Also, when one contracts for work with another party, one has an obligation to keep that party properly informed about progress toward completing that work.

A computing professional has a responsibility to request a change in any assignment that he or she feels cannot be completed as defined. Only after serious consideration and with full disclosure of risks and concerns to the employer or client, should one accept the assignment. The major underlying principle here is the obligation to accept personal accountability for professional work. On some occasions other ethical principles may take greater priority.

A judgment that a specific assignment should not be performed may not be accepted. Having clearly identified one's concerns and reasons for that judgment, but failing to procure a change in that assignment, one may yet be obligated, by contract or by law, to proceed as directed. The computing professional's ethical judgment should be the final guide in deciding whether or not to proceed. Regardless of the decision, one must accept the responsibility for the consequences.

However, performing assignments "against one's own judgment" does not relieve the professional of responsibility for any negative consequences.

2.7 Improve public understanding of computing and its consequences.

Computing professionals have a responsibility to share technical knowledge with the public by encouraging understanding of computing, including the impacts of computer systems and their limitations. This imperative implies an obligation to counter any false views related to computing.

2.8 Access computing and communication resources only when authorized to do so.

Theft or destruction of tangible and electronic property is prohibited by imperative 1.2—"Avoid harm to others." Trespassing and unauthorized use of a computer or communication system is addressed by this imperative. Trespassing includes accessing communication networks and computer systems, or accounts and/or files associated with those systems, without explicit authorization to do so. Individuals and organizations have the right to restrict access to their systems so long as they do not violate the discrimination principle (see 1.4). No one should enter or use another's computer system, software, or data files without permission. One must always have appropriate approval before using system resources, including communication ports, file space, other system peripherals, and computer time.

3 Organizational Leadership Imperatives

As an ACM member and an organizational leader, I will ...

BACKGROUND NOTE: This section draws extensively from the draft IFIP Code of Ethics, especially its sections on organizational ethics and international concerns. The ethical obligations of organizations tend to be neglected in most codes of professional conduct, perhaps because these codes are written from the perspective of the individual member. This dilemma is addressed by stating these imperatives from the perspective of the organizational leader. In this context "leader" is viewed as any organizational member who has leadership or educational responsibilities. These imperatives generally may apply to organizations as well as their leaders. In this context "organizations" are corporations, government agencies, and other "employers," as well as volunteer professional organizations.

3.1 Articulate social responsibilities of members of an organizational unit and encourage full acceptance of those responsibilities.

Because organizations of all kinds have impacts on the public, they must accept responsibilities to society. Organizational procedures and attitudes oriented toward quality and the welfare of society will reduce harm to members of the public, thereby serving public interest and fulfilling social responsibility. Therefore, organizational leaders must encourage full participation in meeting social responsibilities as well as quality performance.

3.2 Manage personnel and resources to design and build information systems that enhance the quality of working life.

Organizational leaders are responsible for ensuring that computer systems enhance, not degrade, the quality of working life. When implementing a computer system, organizations must consider the personal and professional development, physical safety, and human dignity of all workers. Appropriate human-computer ergonomic standards should be considered in system design and in the workplace.

3.3 Acknowledge and support proper and authorized uses of an organization's computing and communication resources.

Because computer systems can become tools to harm as well as to benefit an organization, the leadership has the responsibility to clearly define appropriate and inappropriate uses of organizational computing resources. While the number and scope of such rules should be minimal, they should be fully enforced when established.

3.4 Ensure that users and those who will be affected by a system have their needs clearly articulated during the assessment and design of requirements; later the system must be validated to meet requirements.

Current system users, potential users, and other persons whose lives may be affected by a system must have their needs assessed and incorporated in the statement of requirements. System validation should ensure compliance with those requirements.

3.5 Articulate and support policies that protect the dignity of users and others affected by a computing system.

Designing or implementing systems that deliberately or inadvertently demean individuals or groups is ethically unacceptable. Computer professionals who are in decision making positions should verify that systems are designed and implemented to protect personal privacy and enhance personal dignity.

3.6 Create opportunities for members of the organization to learn the principles and limitations of computer systems.

This complements the imperative on public understanding (2.7). Educational opportunities are essential to facilitate optimal participation of all organizational members. Opportunities must be available to all members to help them improve their knowledge and skills in computing, including courses that familiarize them with the consequences and limitations of particular types of systems. In particular, professionals must be made aware of the dangers of building systems around oversimplified models, the improbability of anticipating and designing for every possible operating condition, and other issues related to the complexity of this profession.

4 Compliance with the Code

As an ACM member I will ...

4.1 Uphold and promote the principles of this Code.

The future of the computing profession depends on both technical and ethical excellence. Not only is it important for ACM computing professionals to adhere to the principles expressed in this Code, each member should encourage and support adherence by other members.

4.2 Treat violations of this code as inconsistent with membership in the ACM.

Adherence of professionals to a code of ethics is largely a voluntary matter. However, if a member does not follow this code by engaging in gross misconduct, membership in ACM may be terminated.

This Code and the supplemental Guidelines were developed by the Task Force for the Revision of the ACM Code of Ethics and Professional Conduct: Ronald E. Anderson, Chair, Gerald Engel, Donald Gotterbarn, Grace C. Hertlein, Alex Hoffman, Bruce Jawer, Deborah G. Johnson, Doris K. Lidtke, Joyce Currie Little, Dianne Martin, Donn B. Parker, Judith A. Perrolle, and Richard S. Rosenberg. The Task Force was organized by ACM/SIGCAS and funding was provided by the ACM SIG Discretionary Fund.

IEEE-CS/ACM Software Engineering Code of Ethics and Professional Practice

(Version 5.2) as recommended by the

IEEE-CS/ACM Joint Task Force on Software Engineering Ethics and Professional Practices

Short Version

PREAMBLE

The short version of the code summarizes aspirations at a high level of abstraction. The clauses that are included in the full version give examples and details of how these aspirations change the way we act as software engineering professionals. Without the aspirations, the details can become legalistic and tedious; without the details, the aspirations can become high sounding but empty; together, the aspirations and the details form a cohesive code.

Software engineers shall commit themselves to making the analysis, specification, design, development, testing, and maintenance of software a beneficial and respected profession. In accordance with their commitment to the health, safety, and welfare of the public, software engineers shall adhere to the following Eight Principles:

1 PUBLIC - Software engineers shall act consistently with the public interest.
2 CLIENT AND EMPLOYER - Software engineers shall act in a manner that is in the best interests of their client and employer, consistent with the public interest.
3 PRODUCT - Software engineers shall ensure that their products and related modifications meet the highest professional standards possible.

4 JUDGMENT - Software engineers shall maintain integrity and independence in their professional judgment.

5 MANAGEMENT - Software engineering managers and leaders shall subscribe to and promote an ethical approach to the management of software development and maintenance.

6 PROFESSION - Software engineers shall advance the integrity and reputation of the profession consistent with the public interest.

7 COLLEAGUES - Software engineers shall be fair to and supportive of their colleagues.

8 SELF - Software engineers shall participate in lifelong learning regarding the practice of their profession and shall promote an ethical approach to the practice of the profession.

SOFTWARE ENGINEERING CODE OF ETHICS AND PROFESSIONAL PRACTICE

IEEE-CS/ACM Joint Task Force on Software Engineering Ethics and Professional Practices

Full Version

PREAMBLE

Computers have a central and growing role in commerce, industry, government, medicine, education, entertainment, and society at large. Software engineers are those who contribute by direct participation or by teaching, to the analysis, specification, design, development, certification, maintenance, and testing of software systems. Because of their roles in developing software systems, software engineers have significant opportunities to do good or cause harm, to enable others to do good or cause harm, or to influence others to do good or cause harm. To ensure, as much as possible, that their efforts will be used for good, software engineers must commit themselves to making software engineering a beneficial and respected profession. In accordance with that commitment, software engineers shall adhere to the following Code of Ethics and Professional Practice.

The Code contains eight Principles related to the behavior of and decisions made by professional software engineers, including practitioners, educators, managers, supervisors, and policy makers, as well as trainees and students of the profession. The Principles identify the ethically responsible relationships in which individuals, groups, and organizations participate and the primary obligations within these relationships. The Clauses of each Principle are illustrations of some of the obligations included in these relationships. These obligations are founded in the software engineer's humanity, in special care owed to people affected by the work of software engineers, and in the unique elements of the practice of software engineering. The Code prescribes these as obligations of anyone claiming to be or aspiring to be a software engineer. It is not intended that the individual parts of the Code be used in isolation to justify errors of omission or commission. The list of Principles and Clauses is not exhaustive. The Clauses should not be read as separating the acceptable from the unacceptable in professional conduct in all practical situations. The Code is not a simple ethical algorithm that generates ethical decisions. In some situations, standards may be in tension with each other or with standards from other sources. These situations require the software engineer to use ethical judgment to act in a manner that is most consistent with the spirit of the Code of Ethics and Professional Practice, given the circumstances.

Ethical tensions can best be addressed by thoughtful consideration of fundamental principles, rather than blind reliance on detailed regulations. These Principles should influence software engineers to consider broadly who is affected by their work; to examine if they and their colleagues are treating other human beings with due respect; to consider how the public, if reasonably well informed, would view their decisions; to analyze how the least empowered will be affected by their decisions; and to consider whether their acts would be judged worthy of the ideal professional working as a software engineer. In all these judgments concern for the health, safety, and welfare of the public is primary; that is, the "Public Interest" is central to this Code.

The dynamic and demanding context of software engineering requires a code that is adaptable and relevant to new situations as they occur. However, even in this generality, the Code provides support for software engineers and managers of software engineers who need to take positive action in a specific case by documenting the ethical stance of the profession. The Code provides an ethical foundation to which individuals within teams and the team as a whole can appeal. The Code helps to define those actions that are ethically improper to request of a software engineer or teams of software engineers.

The Code is not simply for adjudicating the nature of questionable acts; it also has an important educational function. As this Code expresses the consensus of the profession on ethical issues, it is a means to educate both the public and aspiring professionals about the ethical obligations of all software engineers.

PRINCIPLES

Principle 1 PUBLIC Software engineers shall act consistently with the public interest. In particular, software engineers shall, as appropriate:

1.01. Accept full responsibility for their own work.
1.02. Moderate the interests of the software engineer, the employer, the client and the users with the public good.

1.03. Approve software only if they have a well-founded belief that it is safe, meets specifications, passes appropriate tests, and does not diminish quality of life, diminish privacy, or harm the environment. The ultimate effect of the work should be to the public good.

1.04. Disclose to appropriate persons or authorities any actual or potential danger to the user, the public, or the environment, that they reasonably believe to be associated with software or related documents.

1.05. Cooperate in efforts to address matters of grave public concern caused by software, its installation, maintenance, support, or documentation.

1.06. Be fair and avoid deception in all statements, particularly public ones, concerning software or related documents, methods, and tools.

1.07. Consider issues of physical disabilities, allocation of resources, economic disadvantage, and other factors that can diminish access to the benefits of software.

1.08. Be encouraged to volunteer professional skills to good causes and to contribute to public education concerning the discipline.

Principle 2 CLIENT AND EMPLOYER Software engineers shall act in a manner that is in the best interests of their client and employer, consistent with the public interest. In particular, software engineers shall, as appropriate:

2.01. Provide service in their areas of competence, being honest and forthright about any limitations of their experience and education.

2.02. Not knowingly use software that is obtained or retained either illegally or unethically.

2.03. Use the property of a client or employer only in ways properly authorized, and with the client's or employer's knowledge and consent.

2.04. Ensure that any document upon which they rely has been approved, when required, by someone authorized to approve it.

2.05. Keep private any confidential information gained in their professional work, where such confidentiality is consistent with the public interest and consistent with the law.

2.06. Identify, document, collect evidence, and report to the client or the employer promptly if, in their opinion, a project is likely to fail, to prove too expensive, to violate intellectual property law, or otherwise to be problematic.

2.07. Identify, document, and report significant issues of social concern, of which they are aware, in software or related documents, to the employer or the client.

2.08. Accept no outside work detrimental to the work they perform for their primary employer.

2.09. Promote no interest adverse to their employer or client, unless a higher ethical concern is being compromised; in that case, inform the employer or another appropriate authority of the ethical concern.

Principle 3 PRODUCT Software engineers shall ensure that their products and related modifications meet the highest professional standards possible. In particular, software engineers shall, as appropriate:

3.01. Strive for high quality, acceptable cost, and a reasonable schedule, ensuring significant tradeoffs are clear to and accepted by the employer and the client, and are available for consideration by the user and the public.

3.02. Ensure proper and achievable goals and objectives for any project on which they work or propose.

3.03. Identify, define, and address ethical, economic, cultural, legal, and environmental issues related to work projects.

3.04. Ensure that they are qualified for any project on which they work or propose to work, by an appropriate combination of education, training, and experience,.

3.05. Ensure that an appropriate method is used for any project on which they work or propose to work.

3.06. Work to follow professional standards, when available, that are most appropriate for the task at hand, departing from these only when ethically or technically justified.

3.07. Strive to fully understand the specifications for software on which they work.

3.08. Ensure that specifications for software on which they work have been well documented, satisfy the users' requirements, and have the appropriate approvals.

3.09. Ensure realistic quantitative estimates of cost, scheduling, personnel, quality, and outcomes on any project on which they work or propose to work and provide an uncertainty assessment of these estimates.

3.10. Ensure adequate testing, debugging, and review of software and related documents on which they work.

3.11. Ensure adequate documentation, including significant problems discovered and solutions adopted, for any project on which they work.

3.12. Work to develop software and related documents that respect the privacy of those who will be affected by that software.

3.13. Be careful to use only accurate data derived by ethical and lawful means, and use it only in ways properly authorized.

3.14. Maintain the integrity of data, being sensitive to outdated or flawed occurrences.

3.15 Treat all forms of software maintenance with the same professionalism as new development.

Principle 4 JUDGMENT Software engineers shall maintain integrity and independence in their professional judgment. In particular, software engineers shall, as appropriate:

4.01. Temper all technical judgments by the need to support and maintain human values.

4.02 Only endorse documents either prepared under their supervision or within their areas of competence and with which they are in agreement.

4.03. Maintain professional objectivity with respect to any software or related documents they are asked to evaluate.

4.04. Not engage in deceptive financial practices such as bribery, double billing, or other improper financial practices.

4.05. Disclose to all concerned parties those conflicts of interest that cannot reasonably be avoided or escaped.

4.06. Refuse to participate, as members or advisors, in a private, governmental, or professional body concerned with software related issues, in which they, their employers or their clients have undisclosed potential conflicts of interest.

Principle 5 MANAGEMENT Software engineering managers and leaders shall subscribe to and promote an ethical approach to the management of software development and maintenance. In particular, those managing or leading software engineers shall, as appropriate:

5.01 Ensure good management for any project on which they work, including effective procedures for promotion of quality and reduction of risk.

5.02. Ensure that software engineers are informed of standards before being held to them.

5.03. Ensure that software engineers know the employer's policies and procedures for protecting passwords, files, and information that is confidential to the employer or confidential to others.

5.04. Assign work only after taking into account appropriate contributions of education and experience tempered with a desire to further that education and experience.

5.05. Ensure realistic quantitative estimates of cost, scheduling, personnel, quality, and outcomes on any project on which they work or propose to work, and provide an uncertainty assessment of these estimates.

5.06. Attract potential software engineers only by full and accurate description of the conditions of employment.

5.07. Offer fair and just remuneration.

5.08. Not unjustly prevent someone from taking a position for which that person is suitably qualified.

5.09. Ensure that there is a fair agreement concerning ownership of any software, processes, research, writing, or other intellectual property to which a software engineer has contributed.

5.10. Provide for due process in hearing charges of violation of an employer's policy or of this Code.

5.11. Not ask a software engineer to do anything inconsistent with this Code.

5.12. Not punish anyone for expressing ethical concerns about a project.

Principle 6 PROFESSION Software engineers shall advance the integrity and reputation of the profession consistent with the public interest. In particular, software engineers shall, as appropriate:

6.01. Help develop an organizational environment favorable to acting ethically.

6.02. Promote public knowledge of software engineering.

6.03. Extend software engineering knowledge by appropriate participation in professional organizations, meetings, and publications.

6.04. Support, as members of a profession, other software engineers striving to follow this Code.

6.05. Not promote their own interest at the expense of the profession, client, or employer.

6.06. Obey all laws governing their work, unless, in exceptional circumstances, such compliance is inconsistent with the public interest.

6.07. Be accurate in stating the characteristics of software on which they work, avoiding not only false claims but also claims that might reasonably be supposed to be speculative, vacuous, deceptive, misleading, or doubtful.

6.08. Take responsibility for detecting, correcting, and reporting errors in software and associated documents on which they work.

6.09. Ensure that clients, employers, and supervisors know of the software engineer's commitment to this Code of ethics, and the subsequent ramifications of such commitment.

6.10. Avoid associations with businesses and organizations that are in conflict with this code.

6.11. Recognize that violations of this Code are inconsistent with being a professional software engineer.

6.12. Express concerns to the people involved when significant violations of this Code are detected unless this is impossible, counter-productive, or dangerous.

6.13. Report significant violations of this Code to appropriate authorities when it is clear that consultation with people involved in these significant violations is impossible, counter-productive, or dangerous.

Principle 7 COLLEAGUES Software engineers shall be fair to and supportive of their colleagues. In particular, software engineers shall, as appropriate:

7.01. Encourage colleagues to adhere to this Code.

7.02. Assist colleagues in professional development.

7.03. Credit fully the work of others and refrain from taking undue credit.

7.04. Review the work of others in an objective, candid, and properly-documented way.

7.05. Give a fair hearing to the opinions, concerns, or complaints of a colleague.

7.06. Assist colleagues in being fully aware of current standard work practices including policies and procedures for protecting passwords, files, and other confidential information, and security measures in general.

7.07. Not unfairly intervene in the career of any colleague; however, concern for the employer, the client, or public interest may compel software engineers, in good faith, to question the competence of a colleague.

7.08. In situations outside of their own areas of competence, call upon the opinions of other professionals who have competence in that area.

Principle 8 SELF Software engineers shall participate in lifelong learning regarding the practice of their profession and shall promote an ethical approach to the practice of the profession. In particular, software engineers shall continually endeavor to:

8.01. Further their knowledge of developments in the analysis, specification, design, development, maintenance, and testing of software and related documents, together with the management of the development process.

8.02. Improve their ability to create safe, reliable, and useful quality software at reasonable cost and within a reasonable time.

8.03. Improve their ability to produce accurate, informative, and well-written documentation.

8.04. Improve their understanding of the software and related documents on which they work and of the environment in which they will be used.

8.05. Improve their knowledge of relevant standards and the law governing the software and related documents on which they work.

8.06 Improve their knowledge of this Code, its interpretation, and its application to their work.

8.07 Not give unfair treatment to anyone because of any irrelevant prejudices.

8.08 Not influence others to undertake any action that involves a breach of this Code.

8.09. Recognize that personal violations of this Code are inconsistent with being a professional software engineer.

This Code was developed by the IEEE-CS/ACM joint task force on Software Engineering Ethics and Professional Practices (SEEPP):

Executive Committee: Donald Gotterbarn (Chair),Keith Miller and Simon Rogerson; Members: Steve Barber, Peter Barnes, Ilene Burnstein, Michael Davis, Amr El-Kadi, N. Ben Fairweather, Milton Fulghum, N. Jayaram, Tom Jewett, Mark Kanko, Ernie Kallman, Duncan Langford, Joyce Currie Little, Ed Mechler, Manuel J. Norman, Douglas Phillips, Peter Ron Prinzivalli, Patrick Sullivan, John Weckert, Vivian Weil, S. Weisband and Laurie Honour Werth.

The Life Cycle of Cyber and Computing Ethics[1]

Don Gotterbarn

I. Introduction

In many respects Cyber Ethics as a discipline is derivative from Computer Ethics. Individuals working in cyberspace get caught in what I call "the life cycle of computer ethics." Understanding this life cycle and what drives it will help to mitigate many of the ethical issues addressed in this text. There has been significant discussion about what constitutes computer ethics. Moor [1985] argued that computer ethics addresses the policy vacuums that occur as computing technology creates situations that have not been addressed before. Is it acceptable for you to use the SubSeven[2] Trojan horse virus to track users who download things from your web site? Johnson [1985] argued that computer ethics has the same types of questions as traditional ethics but that computing gives these issues a different twist—computer ethics is a new species of traditional ethics. Is it acceptable to spy on others by using the SubSeven virus to track users who download things from someone else's web site? Does this violate the downloader's privacy? Gotterbarn [1991] claimed that computer ethics is merely a subset of professional ethics and is primarily about the responsibilities of the computing professionals. What are the professional responsibilities of the developer of the SubSeven virus? Maner [1996] and Frans Birrer [2001], on the other hand, emphasize the uniqueness of computer and cyber ethics and minimize its relation to the traditional models of ethics. With only slight modification these theories could also apply to cyber ethics. Is it acceptable to 'violate privacy' and surreptitiously place the SubSeven virus on a child pornography web site and then use the result of this virus to catch people who download child pornography images? Both cyber and computer ethics have problems with traditional concepts of intellectual property, privacy, and security. Instead of addressing the finer

---

This essay originally appeared in the *Proceedings of the Sixth Annual Ethics and Technology Conference,* Boston College, Chestnut Hill, MA, 2003, pp. 98–105. Copyright © 2003 by Don Gotterbarn. Reprinted with permission.

[1] A version of this paper was the "Making a Difference Award" acceptance address presented at the 2002 ISTAS Conference Raleigh, North Carolina.

[2] The SubSeven virus can capture key stokes and sites visits and email this undetected to a hacker. See recent decision on its use by a law enforcement agency in US vs. Jarrett. No. CR.A. 3:02CR11. Nov. 1, 2002.
http://www.uea.ac.uk/~n029076/pub/cylaw/doc/ jarrett.html

point of the definitions of cyber and computer ethics, I will just refer to the total sets of issues in computer and cyber ethics as C-ethics.

Whichever of these diverse theories is adopted, there is a common experience faced by those who are actively involved in cyberspace. It is important to understand the nature of this experience and how it affects our attempts to identify, understand, and address these C-ethics issues. No matter which interpretation is taken of C-ethics, the individual decision-maker[3] generally interprets the situation from one of three stages of ethical awareness: 1) naïve innocence and technological wonder, 2) power and control, and 3) finally, sometimes because of disasters during the second stage, an understanding of the essential relationship between technology and values. Their understanding and reaction to the problem is conditioned by the stage they are in. The failure to recognize the distinction between these stages contributes to computer ethics problems and causes new ones. An appreciation of these stages or viewpoints is critical to those who have to deal with C-ethics issues as a matter of policy or in their personal lives.

We can develop a model of these stages of ethical awareness. I will show how this model of ethical development applies to one area of C-ethics—ethics issues for the practicing computer professional including designer, developers, and managers of cyberspace—and then show how it applies to the other areas of C-ethics.

II. Socio-Cultural C-ethics

At a recent software engineering conference Ed Yourdon, a leading software engineer, used Margaret Meade's significant work "Coming of Age in Samoa" [Meade 1928][4] to model some current changes in the development of software. Meade's work is remembered for its thesis that our behavior is primarily based on cultural influences rather than biological influences. Some of Meade's theories apply directly to C-ethics.

Stages of Development and Acculturation

Margaret Meade studied many aspects of primitive culture. Her theory about the stages of socio-cultural development is a useful model of an individual's ethical awakening and helps us identify unique elements of computer ethics. Understanding these processes will help us when we teach, manage, or exercise our judgment in computer ethics and understanding these learning patterns will help us address computer ethics issues as educators and as citizens of society.

Stages of Socio-cultural Development

Margaret Meade spoke of three stages in our adaptation to the culture from the age of innocence through a coming of age into the age of family (tribal) values. We regularly traverse similar stages when addressing the impacts of new technologies.

---

[3] This same issue is easily extendable to groups.

[4] Although this work has been criticized for the accuracy of its description of life in Samoa, the categories Meade uses to organize her account are still useful.

These stages model our learning of society's mores. They describe the stages of ethical awakening. Mead's stages of socio-cultural development are

- Age of Innocence
- Coming of Age
- Age of Family (tribal values).

We can map Meade's three stages of socio-cultural development to the ethical awakening of computer professionals.

The Age of Innocence maps to the *age of innocence* for computer practitioners who view the computer as a benign but positive tool. They are unaware of any major ethical issues. Values are not even considered.

Coming of Age maps to the *Age of Power and Control* where practitioners recognize both their power over the computer and the control that using that power gives them. Their practice is no longer completely neutral and there is the beginning of some questioning about their responsibility in the way they develop and use the technology. Their power over the machine predominates. The power of the tool and the power it gives the developers of the technology are recognized. This progresses toward the *age of awareness*

The Age of Family maps to the *Age of Awarenes*—an awareness that all technological decisions have impacts on others and consequently involve value decisions. This involves an awareness of the essential connectedness of technology and values. There is internal pressure from the practitioners themselves to improve. There is also an external pressure, from those affected by the technology, for the developers to improve. In response to these internal and external pressures, work is done to develop codes of ethics and standards of practice. The latest gadgets—blue tooth, WiFi, Face Recognition software, remote RFI Internet technology—are enthusiastically adopted for one use, but then we start to realize that it gives us power for another use. And then there is the inevitable realization that we have overlooked the way it impacts other people, giving rise to professional and ethical issues. Giving attention to these broader impacts of the development and application of technology is doing ethics.

Progress through these stages is not strictly linear. There will be some backsliding and revisiting some stages. Progress through these sorts of stages can be seen—writ large—in the development of computing over the past 50 years in the United States.

Age of Innocence (1950s–60s)

When computers initially made their way into the work place, they were large mysterious machines controlled by scientists and mathematicians. Companies placed computer professionals in white lab coats, separated from other employees by glass walls.

Computing was only done by a select group of people who were highly regarded because of their special knowledge and skills.

The computer's role was (for most of us) benign. Computers helped big business. They printed bills, calculated accounting documents, and were useful tools for the corporations that owned them.

Computers had little to do with our daily lives. The big computer applications made airplane reservations, calculated interest on bank accounts, and printed bills on punched cards. In this environment, the ethical issues where not obvious. At Yale in 1972, Alan Perlis told his computer class, "All you need is to be a good person." There are no ethical issues in computing. The qualifications for a computer professional are an ability to do logic and mathematics. There was no mandatory curriculum and no accreditation procedures. Until the mid 1970s, only a few colleges had computer science departments that were separate from math departments. The quality of computer software was determined by how efficiently the program worked.

Ethical issues were not a major concern. Must computer professionals were honest people. The discovery of a dishonest professional was rare enough to be newsworthy. It was only the badly intentioned software developer who committed fraud. People were not aware of problems such as the way the SABRE reservation system favored American Airlines flights over other airlines.

As a practitioner during this period, I thought I was a good person with a good work ethic. Ethics was involved only if one tried to do bad things. I understood we had to be professional. It was my job to be a problem solver using a computer. Jim Moore's 1978 American Philosophical Association conference paper entitled "Are their decisions computers should not make?" seemed like an abstract 'academic' discussion. At that point, no one envisioned a USA Predator drone that could be programmed to kill tall people wearing turbans in Afghanistan.

Computer practitioners would put "backdoors" into programs to make it easier to fix them when a customer wanted changes. People wrote auditing programs to prevent fraud. One such program was a Medicare fraud detection program. It accuses doctors of fraud if they submit "suspicious bills." A suspicious bill might be one for two amputations of the same arm or a bill for a hysterectomy for a male patient. No attention was given to the impact this program would have on people seeking hospital admission or the impact it would have on the patient's income if Medicare did not cover their bills. The hospital patient who was suffering through multiple amputations of a gangrene-infected limb—foot, below knee, above knee—would not have their hospital bill paid and their doctors would be accused of fraud. The developer's lack of "domain knowledge" contributed to this problem. Domain knowledge was not a requirement for the well-intentioned computer professional. The important part of their work was to get the computer to do the job. Developing the skill to program computers to do difficult jobs leads to the next stage.

Age of Power and Control (1960s...)

In this stage the practitioners were impressed and misled by their power over the computer and a need to control the way in which their computer programs were used. This was often accompanied by a feeling of superiority over those who are mere users of computer products. 'USER' was considered a four letter word. At this stage developers often refer to themselves as "wizards."

The developer was better than anyone else because of the things he could make the machine do. "Tell me what you want and I can make the machine do it!!" At this stage there was a tendency to write powerful but incomprehensible programs as a sign of the programmer's power. The scientist in the lab coat came out from behind the glass wall. The programs they wrote were now proof of their mastery of the machine

Computing's movement beyond data processing to controlling processes in everyday life contributed to this sense of power. The wizard had a private domain of knowledge with only a vaguely defined discipline. The new realization of this power leads to overconfidence in one's skills.

Paternalism is the most common professional model at this stage. Wizards didn't intend to harm anyone. The practitioner was a good person whose computing/technical acts were ethically neutral. At this stage programmer optimism was focused on the technical task at hand. Little attention was paid to the impact of the task. They just worked with the machines. The model was still—"If I intend nothing wrong then I don't have to think about ethics."

Wizards wrote simple programs that controlled the movement of control rods in nuclear reactors. At this stage programmer optimism was focused on the technical task at hand. There was little attention paid to the impact of the task. Everything was fine as long as you were a good person and a Cracker Jack software developer. Ethics was no problem. Moreover you could develop ethically significant programs that would save lives. For example, the US Navy tracks the explosive powder that goes into shells. If a particular batch of powder becomes unstable, they would want to recall all shells containing that powder so that no one would be hurt by unplanned explosions of the shell. To a wizard, this might have looked like a simple spreadsheet program.

Transition to the Age of Awareness

Many things affect the way we move from one stage to another. The transition to the *age of awareness* was effected by several social changes. One such change was the commercialization and release of the IBM personal computer on August 13, 1981. With the availability of computers, many thought they could be wizards. Everyone now had the opportunity to be a powerful wizard. Now everyone could control and understand a computer and had the opportunity to be a wizard or be a bad guy. On the negative side, word-processing facilitated plagiarism and software theft became an option for everyone.

Another significant event occurred when, in November 1983, President Reagan announced plans for a computerized shield of the United States. Amongst the numerous reactions to this plan was the claim by reputable computer professionals that this **should not** be done. Reasons for this claim varied from "it was technologically impossible at the time" to "even if we put such a system in place there was no way to test it." The important thing to notice is that this was a moral reaction to a technological decision—a moral reaction to limit and not expand the applications of computing. The important thing here is the very public stance taken by computer professionals and the formation of organizations such as Computer

Professionals for Social Responsibility, which based moral decisions on their understanding of technical issues.

Developers begin to ask questions about the impacts of their decisions. Many other people can access backdoors put into programs during the *age of innocence*. Is the customer put at risk by installing a backdoor for the developer's convenience? Is the integrity of our missile defense system at risk when placing a remotely accessible backdoor into missile control software? The phrase 'computer ethics' is no longer treated as an oxymoron.

The impacts of some software decisions can be very significant. The shells of Iowa class battle ships contain 1200 lbs. of powder per shell. In 1987 the powder exploded in a gun turret of a recommissioned Iowa class battle ship blowing up two sailors. Among the many questions about the cause of this explosion "Was it caused by a program that failed to track projectiles containing unstable powder?" —a program created by a macho programmer. Incidents like this make it easier to see that all our technical decisions are mitigated by values.

The awareness that values and technology are necessarily connected emerges at this stage and constitutes an ethical awakening. There is a belief that technological training is incomplete unless it includes a discussion of the professional, ethical, and social impacts of the technology. The software professional is no longer an individual Macho developer, but a developer of software technology for a technology-based society. In the early 1990s several computer professional societies rewrote their codes of ethics to emphasize the connection between the development and use of computer artifacts and their impacts on society. They specified their obligation to society.

Historically the inclusion of ethics and social issues into the curriculum mark this stage. Broader social issues become the concern of professional organizations. For example, Computer Professionals for Social Responsibility, whose primary mission was addressing SDI, now addresses issues such as vote-counting technology problems, the misuse of technology, and loss of privacy. Computer ethics books began to appear. Articles attempting to define computer ethics appear. Corporations set up ethics offices. The National Science Foundation supports a major ethics conference and then supported multiple workshops to train faculty to teach computer ethics.

Finally the need to develop ethical models to help those moral software developers be socially responsible as they practice their craft is recognized. This was mirrored in the development of professional codes of ethics and articles about how these codes could be used in making decisions [Anderson 1993].

This stage is marked by the development of technical standards guided by a consideration of who will be affected by the development of this software. This is a model of the movement through Meade-like stages in the ethical awakening of software developers. If this were the end of the story it might merely be an interesting historical tale. We need to bring in one other element, the way the speed of technology affects learning.

Acculturation

Meade also studied how people learn the mores or standards of that culture—the acculturation process. She claims that how we learn is defined by specific elements of our culture. I believe that her theory does, at least, apply to the way we learn C-ethics. The way we progress through these stages is affected by the rate of technological development. The speed at which we go through stages is similar to the way we learn about our culture based on who was learning from whom

1. In cultures where there is little cultural change, children can learn from parents, elders, or others in authority. When progress is slow children can learn from parents.
2. When progress is of moderate speed, children and parents learn from their peers.
3. In some cultures, when progress is very rapid, parents learn from children.

When progress is very rapid the authorities have to prepare children for things those authorities have never experienced.

This distinction is reminiscent of the changes in the rate of technological change. In the Iron Age technological change was slow—we learned from craftsman or from our parents, or from cultural icons. In the industrial age change was more rapid and we learned from our peers. The rate of change in the computer age is characterized by Moore's law—which has been interpreted as the doubling of knowledge (actually Moore said "processor speed") every 18 months. How does Meade's model apply to the development of technology?

4. In cultures where progress is slow children can learn from parents, Aristotle was the source of scientific knowledge for many centuries.
5. In cultures where progress is of moderate speed, children and parents learn from their peers. In the early 1950s and 1960s computer specialists were both learning from each other and developing new concepts.
6. In cultures where progress is very rapid parents learn from children. Parents have no experience with what is currently happening and children often reject the old standards.

Parents/citizens have no experience with what is currently happening in computing. When progress is very rapid, the authorities have to prepare children for things those authorities have never experienced. It seems like there is no position of authority to talk from. How do we teach mores and standards for that which has not yet been developed? The technology moves so fast that every day we are faced with something we have no model for.

This problem leads quickly to the position that all of the previous knowledge is out of date—wrong or irrelevant—and it all ought to be rejected. This response is one of the risks in maintaining a position like Manner's [1996] that all computer ethics issues are absolutely unique. The rate of technological change—the way in which you learn—is used to justify ignoring value judgments.

III. The Computer Ethics Mini Life Cycle

The stages of ethical awakening have been described in terms of a particular technical–cultural environment (1950–2000 in the USA), an environment where the rate of technological development was slow. Meade's model of acculturation is relevant to C-ethics in two ways. First as the speed and degree of technological change increases, we must go through this ethical life cycle again and again. Second, the first two stages are very dangerous and lead to problems of professionalism and C-ethics issues. We cannot totally avoid going through these two stages but we need to be aware of how dangerous they are and as we move through them keep an eye on and try to mitigate the potential problems raised by each new technology. We need to move quickly through the first two stages before significant ethical harm is done by our fascination with using our power and the power of each new technology. Otherwise significant ethical harm is done by our fascination with using our power and the power of the technology.

The changes in technology change who is affected and how they are affected. With each major technological change we are faced with events we did not anticipate and have never experienced. We get caught-up in the cycle again with each new technology. It no longer takes 30 years to develop significant new technologies. Because of the speed of the learning process we work in each new technology from the perspective of the age of innocence.

A decade ago when the Internet started, it was generally thought to be a wonderful thing that was going to promote democracy and knowledge world wide. It was only a beneficial thing. It did not take ten years to realize many of the problems.

We view each new technology from the perspective of the age-of-innocence.

Consider some of the new technologies and where they are on an ethical awakening mini-life cycle.

- Age of Innocence—naïve innocence
  - The web is a wonderful thing and will allow us all to share information (1994)
  - What are the qualifications for Web designers, e-commerce specialists
  - Face recognition software will enhance security. (All 2001 Super Bowl attendees were biometrically scanned by the police and compared to a criminal database.)
- Power and control—taking technology to its limits because we can
  - We can capture your files over the web, even without your permission
  - Nano-technology enables us to implant computer chips with GPS chips into individuals. These chips can also contain identification information. These chips are currently being sold to law enforcement agencies around the world.
  - Radio Frequency Identification chips can broadcast information. These chips are being used in identity cards. With an RFI reader I can gather information from a card in someone's wallet as they walk by.
  - No one could object to the biometric scanning because they were not informed that it was happening.
  - Internet filtering allows parents, libraries, and oppressive governments to limit access to information.
- Relation between technology and values
  - We can share music files without the composer's copyright permission.

- Many government agencies have stopped using face recognition software because it has limited application to controlled environments, "Nevertheless, officials at Logan Airport in Boston and T.F. Green airport in Providence, Rhode Island, have announced that they will be installing the technology." http://archive.aclu.org/features/f110101a.html
- Who are the stakeholders in each new technology?
- How should we modify the technology and public policy to minimize this impact?
- What guides can we develop to help make decisions regarding this technology

These are the stages of ethical awakening for acting professionals. It is also the same development cycle IT students go through. As new students they work on interesting and challenging projects, and then they begin to think of themselves as better than those who are not computer specialists and are thrilled by the exercise of their own power. For both student and practitioner, we need to clearly indicate how values and technology are bound to each other.

We need to make sure that thinking about the impact of computing is understood as an integral part of the way a quality system is developed and implemented.

IV. Conclusion

We have delineated a computer ethics life cycle from the perspective of professional C-ethics. This mini cycle models ethical awakening in professional practice and education. It also applies beyond professional C-ethics. The Age of Innocence is modeled when society views changes in technology *a priori* as "advances" and as such should be employed. The age of innocence is also characterized by computer *hubris* in which the computer or the Internet is always right and will provide us with the solution to all social problems. The sense of power occurs when we commit to large untested software projects with the belief that we can do something simply because we think we can.

There is nothing astonishing about the stages of ethical awakening in C-ethics. It is critical to recognize that we need to traverse these stages for each new technology. We need to know this cycle and recognize where we are in it when making a decision—where we are in it when we address C-ethics issues as enlightened citizens of society.

Computer Professionals for Professional Responsibility distribute a poster that gives us guidance for every trip through a mini cycle. The poster says,

"Technology and Values Interact.
Make sure the interaction is not haphazard."

These stages of ethical awakening for acting professionals are also psychological views of one's profession. It is the same development cycle that students of cyberspace go through. As new students, they work on interesting and challenging projects, and then they begin to think of themselves as better than those who are not computer specialists, better than those who don't know XHTML. They are thrilled by the exercise of their own power. It is important that thinking about the impact of computing is understood as an integral part of the way a quality system is developed and implemented.

The iterative nature of these stages for each new technology requires a professional attitude at the early stages to mitigate ethical issues and to build a more reliable and ethically sensitive product. For each new technology we must work to avoid or mitigate its negative impacts of the technology. The result will be a more ethically sensitive Internet.

Acknowledgments

This work was made possible by a non-instructional assignment from East Tennessee State University

References:

Anderson, R., et.al. "Using the ACM Code of Ethics in Decision Making," *Communications of the ACM,* October 1993.

Birrer, F. "Applying Ethical and Moral Concepts and Theories to IT Contexts: Some Key Problems and Challenges." In R. A. Spinello and H. T. Tavani, eds. *Readings in CyberEthics.* 1st ed. Sudbury MA: Jones and Bartlett, 2001.

Gotterbarn, D. "Computer Ethics: Responsibility Regained," *National Forum,* Spring 1991.

Johnson, D. *Computer Ethics.* Prentice Hall 1985.

Jurvetson, S. "Transcending Moore's Law" http://news.com.com/2010-1075-281576.html?legacy=cnet (Discusses Gordon Moore's 1985 claim that transistor density doubles every 18 months.)

Maner, W. "Unique Ethical Problems in Ethical Technology," *Science and Engineering Ethics,* Vol. 2, 1996.

Meade, M. *Coming of Age in Samoa: A Psychological Study of Primitive Youth for Western Civilization,* 1928.

Meade, M. *Growing Up in New Guinea: A Comparative Study of Primitive Education,* 1932.

Moor, J. "What is Computer Ethics?" *Metaphilosophy* Vol. 16, no. 4, 1985.

Unintentional Power in the Design of Computing Systems

Chuck Huff

Abstract

Unintentional power is the ability to affect others even though one does not intend, or even foresee, the likely effect. Software designers and other computer professionals have this kind of power because computers instrument human action, and thus control it, or at the least guide it. Examples of this power are provided from accidents with medical technology and in the case of gender bias embedded within educational software. I also make some suggestions about what computer professionals can do, and ought to do, about the power their role gives them.

Unintentional Power in the Design of Computing Systems

> For in much wisdom is much grief: and he that increaseth knowledge
> increaseth sorrow. Ecclesiastes 1:18
>   ...computing professionals who design and develop systems must
> be alert to, and make others aware of, any potential damage... ACM
> Code of Ethics, 1992

Why was the Hebrew scholar and author of Ecclesiastes so skeptical about the worth of knowledge? At least in our time, we find the rapid increase in knowledge to be both exhilarating and hopeful. As knowledge increases, we cure more diseases, connect more people, ease much poverty. Increases in knowledge certainly drive the technology industry and make faster, better, more almost a mantra of progress.

So it can be surprising to read words like those above. They smack of obscurantism, obstruction, willful ignorance. Surely attitudes like this can only come

This essay originally appeared in *Computer Ethics and Professional Responsibility: Introductory Text and Readings.* (Eds. Terrell Ward Bynum and Simon Rogerson) Blackwell Publishers, 2004. pp. 76–81 Copyright © 2003 by Charles W. Huff. Reprinted by permission.

from unreconstructed technophobes. The implied advice is to avoid sorrow by avoiding knowledge—to retreat into ignorance. By the time you are done with this article, I hope to have convinced you that knowledge brings with it increased responsibility. If I succeed, you may have some sympathy for the weariness of the ancient scholar. You may still reject the implied advice.

What sort of knowledge increases sorrow? At least for our purposes, it is the sort of knowledge that allows us to predict possible effects of the products we design. The sort of knowledge that makes us, at least in part, responsible for either producing or avoiding those effects. This knowledge makes our lives more complicated because it brings with it the sorts of "trouble" that involve more responsibility. Those who know about dangers or difficulties have a responsibility to take them into account. The ACM code recognizes this in the second quote listed at the beginning of this article. Computer professionals have a responsibility to design products that are safe and that perform well the functions for which they were designed.

For instance, the designers of the Therac-25 Radiation Therapy machine (Jacky, 1991; Leveson & Turner, 1992) knew the radiation their product used could be delivered in dangerous dosages. Yet they produced a machine that, when used under the standard conditions in busy hospitals, could and did result in serious mistakes in dosage. Most analyses of the design process in this case agree that the designers were negligent in both the initial design and in following up on reports of malfunction. As a result several people died, and many were injured.

The great advance of the Therac-25 was that all of its controls had been moved into software. The operator now interacted with the machine solely through the computer terminal. Safety interlocks that might prevent lethal dosage levels were also included in the software, and eliminated from the hardware of the machine. This allowed easy reprogramability of the dosage levels, and easy maintenance and upgrading of the machine. It meant that the operator had more time to actually interact with the patient and made treatment a more humane experience. It also meant that the safety interlocks depended upon the correctness of the software.

And not only the software, but also the software as it was used by the technician. It turned out that, if the technician set the machine for one type of dosage (low level electron beam) and then changed the setting to another type (high level electron beam with a metal target interposed to alter the beam to low level X-rays), the machine would switch to the high electron beam but not interpose the target—thus directly irradiating the patient with lethal levels of the electron beam. When this happened, the computer screen would simply indicate "malfunction 54" for incorrect dosage. But since "malfunction 54" occurred up to 40 times a day for entirely innocuous reasons (e.g., the beam was slightly "out of tune"), technicians learned to ignore it. When a malfunction occurs this regularly in a busy medical facility, it is no wonder the technicians ignored it rather than stopping for the day to recalibrate (and thereby making patients wait).

Had the designers thought carefully about the conditions under which their product would be used, they could have made a better attempt to avoid the delivery of lethal or harmful dosages. Had they considered how widespread use of their product could become, they might have designed a feedback process that could have sent "fixes" to these widespread sites. They did not do these things. And in part they neglected to do them because they had construed their job narrowly as technically proficient design (Leveson & Turner, 1992).

Levels of Constraint in Software Engineering

But isn't the job of the software engineer simply to be technically proficient and to make the best technical decisions he or she can, on time and within budget? Certainly technical proficiency is crucial. And because technical proficiency is so difficult to achieve and to maintain, we often think it should be the only criterion by which work is measured. At least life would be simpler if this were so.

But there are very few technical decisions that are entirely constrained by math and physics. Those that are (like some issues in queuing theory) are still likely to be only portions of a larger project that has additional constraints. What are these additional constraints? Table 1 lists some of them.

Table 1   Constraints on the Design of Systems

Level 1:   Technical systems design issues, standards, tradeoffs in design and performance

Level 2:   Company policies, specifications, budgets, project timelines

Level 3:   Anticipated uses & effects; interactions with other technologies & systems

Level 4:   Larger "impact on society" issues (e.g., privacy, property, power, equity)

These constraints on design range from thoroughly tested design standards to concerns about the "worth" of computing to society. Many are clearly in the domain of "engineering" popularly conceived. Some are clearly far from engineering. Level 1 constraints are commonly covered in training programs that serve as gateways into the field. But even at this level, value judgments abound: which standards? how to resolve tradeoffs? Often these decisions are not based on mathematical proofs or on physical constraints. They are based instead on criteria whose applicability is at least a matter for debate. And these debates are based on disagreements about what things we should value more. Thus, value judgments.

For example, the decision to implement all the safety interlocks on the Therac-25 in the software—and none in the hardware—was based (at least in part) on the value associated with having reprogrammable drivers for the machine. Easy reprogramability is of value because it reduces costs on upgrades. It did not *have* to be done this way, but if you value flexibility and easy upgrading, you *should* design this way. In this instance, the designers mistakenly underestimated other, equally important values such as those associated with causing injury to patients.

In this instance the designers underestimated the difficulty of controlling the dosage levels in a busy hospital radiation therapy room. Their neglect of this difficulty was based on their ignorance of the hurried and hectic conditions that occur in these settings. In a very important sense these designers had it "within their power" to design a safe product if they had inquired about the conditions under which their product would be used. Subsequent designs now take into account these difficulties (Jacky, 1991).

Another, less catastrophic example may help. There is widespread concern about the gender imbalance in computer science in the United States (Martin & Murchie-Beyma, 1992, Camp, 1997). The large majority of graduate students in computing (and even larger majorities of professors) are men. Fewer undergraduate women are enrolling in computer science courses today, so it seems as though this imbalance is likely to continue. There is some consensus among researchers that a major reason women do not pursue careers in computer science or in related fields is that, from early adolescence onward, computing is defined as a male field and most uses of computing are portrayed as interesting only to males (Martin & Murchie-Beyma, 1992).

We were interested in this claim, and designed a study to determine the extent to which this portrayal of computing as a male domain infiltrated itself into the software that students might use in school. We had teachers design educational software for either boys, girls, or (gender unspecified) "children" (Huff & Cooper, 1987). We then had the designers and independent raters rate those programs in terms of characteristics like time pressure, verbal interaction required, control given the user, etc. We found that programs designed for boys looked like games (with time pressure, eye-hand coordination, and competition most important), while programs for girls looked like "tools" for learning (with conversation and goal-based learning). So far, this is unremarkable. However, programs designed for "children" looked just like those designed for boys. Thus, programs designed for "students in general" were really programs designed for boys. Interestingly, 80% of the designers of our programs were female, many of whom expressed concern that educational software was male-biased. Thus, the portrayal of computing as a male domain can be subtly and strongly woven into software itself, even by well-meaning, female educators (see Friedman & Nissenbaum (1996) for a detailed exposition of how bias is incorporated in computer systems).

This statement bears repeating on a more general level. The design of the software itself was affected by the social expectations of the designers. This is as true for this more subtle effect of gender bias in design as it is for the clearly mistaken (and clearly deadly) effects of the expectations of the designers of Therac-25.

However, even if value judgments show up in the lower levels of system engineering, perhaps it is still possible to limit the work of the software designer to only those relatively simple value judgments that occur when choosing among algorithms or standards. Unfortunately, even a little knowledge about how computing systems are used will increase the sorrow of those who hope this. Look again at the two examples we have covered. In both cases issues from higher levels in the table of constraints worked their way down to the system design level. Choices about where to implement safety checks should have been made based upon better knowledge of the hectic work environment of radiation therapy. Choices about basic program characteristics should have been made based upon a broader assumption about who the users of the software would be. Thus, though it might be desirable to cleanly delineate the work of the software engineer, it is clearly impossible. Good engineering at the level of basic system design requires attention to many levels of constraint.

So, if you limit yourself only to considering constraints that are clearly at the "engineering" level, you can have an effect on the world that you would clearly prefer to have avoided. This is true, to a greater or lesser extent for both the examples we have seen here. And thus, to a greater or lesser extent, the designers of these products had power over the users of their products. They were unaware of the effect their design might have had. They certainly did not intend any negative effects from their design. But they occurred nonetheless.

Unintentional Power

I call this power to harm[1] others in ways that are difficult to predict *unintentional power*. Obviously, the design decisions that software engineers make will affect the performance of a product, and they thereby affect the users of that product. They have these effects because computing systems instrument human action, in much the same way that hammers instrument human action (Johnson, 1998). There are some things one can do with a hammer, and other things best not attempted. Thus designers of tools structure the way the user of the tool can behave, and thus effect the user, and possibly others.

Many of these effects are intentional: the product works faster, is easier to maintain, has increased capability. Some are unintentional: the product is more difficult to maintain, it confuses or frustrates users, it kills users. In the same way that a large man may unintentionally thrust people aside as he carries an awkward package down a street, a software designer may unintentionally harm users of a product that she has designed for a good purpose. Both are exercising power. Both the software designer and the package carrier are affecting others intentionally and unintentionally. One cannot conveniently claim credit for the positive effects and deny responsibility for the negative ones.

To understand the issue of unintentional power, we must first get the most useful definition of this sort of power firmly in hand. To begin with, it is similar to both the physical science definition of power (the potential to do work) and our usual social definition of power (the ability to influence others). At this level, both definitions make it clear that intention is not important. In the one case it is simply irrelevant, and in the other, we recognize that one can have both intentional and unintentional influence on others (remember the package courier?).

Thus, we all have unintentional power associated with our actions whenever those actions have unintentional consequences. The issue then becomes, should we have been aware of the likelihood that those consequences would occur? Could we have foreseen them? Might we have been more careful? Here is an important principle about unintentional power: it carries with it a concomitant responsibility to be as aware as reasonably possible of the consequences of our actions.

The Problems of Unintentional Power

One difficulty with unintentional power in computing systems is that the designers are often far removed from the situations in which their power (now carried by the

---

[1] In this paper, I am only looking at the negative effects of unintentional power. Obviously, positive effects are possible. One of the claims of the Open Source movement is that positive but unintentional effects can come from the decision to make source code publicly available (Raymond, 2000).

software they have designed) has its effect. Software designed in Chicago might be used in Calcutta. Software, or bits of software, might be reused for purposes other than ones its original designer envisioned. Software might be used in environments that are more complex or more dangerous than those for which it was initially designed. Thus, the person or persons with the power are removed from those who are affected. This makes it difficult for the designer to foresee possible consequences.

This distancing also makes it difficult for the user to recognize that it was, in fact, the designer who affected them. People are likely to blame themselves for the difficulties the software produces rather than to see it as an issue of bad design (Huff, Fleming & Cooper, 1991). After all, they are the ones closest to the harm, and it often doesn't occur to them that their software was designed by someone. Responsibility for harm, then, becomes difficult to assign and easy to avoid.

Another effect of distancing is that the response to the problem cannot be standardized for any particular domain of applications. The effects change too much from implementation to implementation. In response to a similar problem, computer professionals in human computer interaction have taken to field testing, iterative reviews, user testing, and other methods to improve the odds that their products will fit in the particular domains for which they are designed (Landauer, 1995; Shneiderman, 1992; Borenstein, 1991). There are simply far too many possible consequences to catch them all (on time and within budget).

Coping with Unintentional Power

Here, then, comes the rub: what is a "reasonable" attempt on the part of a designer to avoid the negative consequences of unintentional power? Clearly, anyone who now designs software for radiation therapy should take into account the conditions under which their product will be used. We now know this because several people have died. I would submit, and hope you agree, that this sort of "user-testing" is to be avoided. A general lesson we might draw from this is that designers of "safety-critical" systems need to take more constraints into account than simply low-level design constraints. But surely we cannot expect a wide ranging inquiry, looking at all the levels of constraint listed in Table 1, before we decide to build any system?

Still, there are some things we can do, and that we should be expected to do. Research on the broader effects of computing has advanced enough to have some clear things to say about the dangers of ignoring the constraints listed earlier in this article. Software design is no longer in its infancy and should be expected to develop methods to deal with these constraints without bankrupting designers or their employers. Here are some beginning suggestions as to how we might go about addressing these issues:

Recognize the problem and attempt to limit its domain. Clearly we cannot address a problem we prefer to ignore. Some designers prefer to inflate the costs of looking at these issues (e.g., you mean we have to look at every possible implementation?), declare the problem too large and frightening to approach, and then to ignore it. Ignoring it will not make it go away. A better approach is to recognize the parameters of the problem, attempt to limit the domains where it can cause a problem, and to then address the problem within those limited domains.

Developing standards (for safety critical computing, for computing interfaces, for data exchange, etc.) is one way to limit the domain.

Use developing methods to inform yourself of those effects worth predicting. Methods for quality-based (TQM) software design are now becoming available (Dunn, 1994; Arthur, 1992). In addition to these methods, the use of a social impact statement, or SIS (Huff, 1996; Shneiderman, 1990; Shneiderman & Rose, 1996) can help you both to determine what sorts of effects you should care about and to investigate the constraints that will guide your solution. Rogerson & Gotterbarn (2001) make credible claims that doing this is not an additional burden on the software design process, it is simply part of the process and results in good software design and financial savings to clients. They have designed a method called SoDIS (for Software Development Impact Statement) to investigate the sort of questions we are concerned with and supporting software to help instrument this method. But even with all this help, TQM methods or SIS approaches will not make the decisions for you. Making these decisions depends upon the computing professionals' judgment for a particular project in a particular setting. This is what professionalism is about.

Make provisions in the life-cycle of software to look for the effects. You simply cannot identify all the possible effects of a computing system ahead of release. For this reason, you should be ready to identify them after release, and as soon as possible after release. Software design methods currently incorporate a life-cycle design philosophy, and it is relatively easy to incorporate some of the methods from social impact statements or SoDIS into this life-cycle model.

Conclusion

The approaches I recommend are not a sea of change in software engineering standards, but an evolutionary step. The standards are already designed to take account of late occurring effects, and to make designers aware of interactions between the software and some environmental issues. Quality design requires that we broaden our vision about the constraints we should consider in our designs.

You cannot make all designs safe under all conditions, but you can make them more safe, or more usable, or more equitable, under more conditions. Software engineers should take responsibility where emerging methods allow them to, and should be humble about their ability to guarantee perfect functioning where they cannot measure or test performance in real conditions. By increasing knowledge about the social effects of software, and by adopting methods that allow us to anticipate these effects, we may be able to decrease sorrow, and thus confound the prophet's prediction. But we will do so at the expense of our own more simplistic approaches to software design.

References

Arthur, L. J. (1992). *Improving Software Quality: An Insider's Guide to TQM.* New York: John Wiley and Sons.

Borenstein, N. S. (1991). *Programming as if people mattered: Friendly program, software engineering, and other noble delusions.* Princeton, NJ: Princeton Univ. Press.

Camp, Tracy (1997). "The Incredible Shrinking Pipeline," *Communications of the ACM,* 40, 2, pp. 103–110.

Dunn, R. H. (1994). *TQM for Computer Software.* New York: McGraw-Hill.

Friedman, B. & Nissenbaum, H. (1996). Bias in computer systems. *ACM Transactions on Information Systems.* 14, 3.

Huff, C. W. & Cooper, J. (1987). Sex bias in educational software: The effects of designers' stereotypes on the software they design. *Journal of Applied Social Psychology,* 17, pp. 519–532.

Huff, C. W. (Feb. 1996). Practical Guidance for Teaching the Social Impact Statement (SIS). in C. Huff (Ed.) *Computers and the Quality of Life: The proceedings of the Symposium on Computers and the Quality of Life.* pp. 86–89, New York: ACM Press.

Huff. C. W., Fleming, J. F., & Cooper, J. (1991). The social basis of gender differences in human-computer interaction. In C.D. Martin & E. Murchie–Beyma (Eds.). *In search of Gender-free paradigms for computer science education.* (pp. 19–32). Eugene OR: ISTE Research Monographs.

Jacky, J. (1991). Safety Critical Computing: Hazards, Practices, Standards, and Regulation. in C. Dunlop & R. Kling (Eds.) *Computerization and Controversy,* (pp. 612–631), New York: Academic Press.

Johnson, D. (2000). The future of computer ethics. In G. Colllste (Ed.) *Ethics in the age of information technology.* (pp. 17–31), Linköping Sweden, Linköping University Press.

Landauer, T. K. (1995). *The trouble with computers: Usefulness, usability, and productivity.* Cambridge, Mass: MIT Press.

Leveson, N. G., & Turner, C. S. (1992). *An investigation of the Therac-25 accidents.* Technical Report #92-108. Department of Information and Computer Science, University of California, Irvine.

Martin, C. D., & Murchie-Beyma, E. (Eds.) (1992). *In search of gender free paradigms for computer science education.* Eugene, Oregon: International Society for Technology in Education.

Raymond, E. S. (2001). *The Cathedral and the Bazaar: Musings on Linux and Open Source by an Accidental Revolutionary.* New York: O'Reilly & Associates.

Rogerson, S., & Gotterbarn, D., (2001). *The Ethics of Software Project Management,* In G. Colllste (Ed.) Ethics in the age of information technology. (pp. 278–300), Linköping Sweden, Linköping University Press.

Shneiderman, B. (1990). *Human Values and the Future of Technology: A Declaration of Empowerment.* Computers and Society, 20(3):1–6.

Shneiderman, B. (1992). *Designing the user interface: Strategies for effective human-computer interaction.* New York: Addison Wesley.

Shneiderman, B., & Rose, A. (1996). Social Impact Statements: Engaging Public Participation in Information Technology Design. In C. Huff (Ed.) *Computers and the Quality of Life: The proceedings of the Symposium on Computers and the Quality of Life.* pp. 90-96, New York: ACM Press.

The Wheel

Richard G. Epstein

"We are in need of spirit in order to know what to do with science."
- *Abraham Joshua Heschel*

Introduction

The weighty social importance of what we are doing is beginning to dawn upon those of us who work in the computer profession, whether in academia or in industry. Perhaps we have begun to realize the awesome power that fate has placed in our hands, the unleashing of a new form of intelligence that was implicit in the nature of things from the very start. In recent years, computer science educators have paid more and more attention to issues of professionalism, social responsibility, social implications, and computer ethics. I would now like to propose a strategy for getting students to see the importance of ethics and professionalism. This approach involves getting students to see their careers in the broadest possible terms. In particular, I am proposing that we get students to see their careers as being important for their own spiritual growth and evolution.

The major part of this essay follows the outline of a lecture that I gave to my undergraduate course on professionalism and software engineering this spring semester. I gave this lecture about half way through the semester. The students received an earlier draft of this essay as a handout.

On the very first day of class I told the students the story of "the wheel", which I shall soon share with you. I told the students this story before introducing myself, before giving out the syllabus, before saying anything to anybody. (I guess you have to be somewhat of a ham to pull this off.) I intended the story of the wheel to be a warning and a point of departure for the entire course. Here is the story of the wheel as I related it to my students on that first day of class:

The Original Story of the Wheel

A man was sentenced to thirty years in prison. During his years in prison he was forced to turn a gigantic wheel, day after day. Day after day he turned this wheel and

This essay originally appeared in *Computers and Society,* Vol. 27, No. 2 (June) 1997: 8–13. Copyright © 1997 by Richard G. Epstein. Reprinted by permission.

he had no idea what the ultimate purpose of the wheel was. Was he grinding wheat? Was he milling corn? What was he actually doing? All he knew about the wheel was that it was on the outside wall of the prison. When he was finally released, after thirty years, the first thing he did was to run to see what the wheel was connected to, so that he would finally know what he had been doing for those many arduous years. Much to his chagrin he discovered that the wheel was not connected to anything. He had spent thirty years of his life turning the wheel with no apparent purpose or benefit to anybody. Upon realizing this, he shouted a great shout and he died.

This story seems to be an outstanding device for getting students to see their unstated attitudes toward their careers and toward their professional lives as computer scientists. I started the course with this story, with these words. I did not know at that point in time where I would be going with this wheel stuff, but I was attempting to address an ethical dilemma in my own work. That ethical dilemma has to do with the quality of the graduates that we are producing and, more importantly, the quality of the lives that they will be leading. At a school like my own, where most of our students are first generation college students from working class families, many students view their careers simply in terms of earning money. They do not see, nor does the computer science curriculum help them to see, their true potential and the true spiritual rewards that work can offer. The ethical dilemma is whether it is ethical for me to be part of a process that produces software developers who will live for the paycheck, who will look longingly at their watches for the end of the work week, and who will inevitably engage in all kinds of escapist activities in order to escape from the emptiness of their work. In other words, is it ethical for me to prepare students for a life at that wheel, the wheel of drudgery, the wheel of meaningless, life-destroying work?

I think it is important for all computer science educators to consider this ethical dilemma. I think it is important for us to not only teach our students about C++, Java, data structures, algorithms, programming language paradigms, but also about the liberating potential of work.

The bottom line is this: I assert that the key to teaching ethics and professionalism *so that students will take it to heart* is to get the students to see their careers in the broadest possible perspective, as a means of realizing their full human potential, as a means of spiritual enlightenment and liberation. I do not see how a work force that views work as drudgery, that views work merely as a means of earning a livelihood, can be an ethical work force. I do not see how a work force that views work as drudgery can produce a technology that is life-enhancing.

A work force that sees its work in spiritual terms, in terms of spiritual growth and in terms of serving and cooperating, in terms of growing self-awareness and perfection, will be a more ethical work force, because ethics and integrity are a part of a larger package, the package of human spiritual evolution. Furthermore, such a work force will be more likely to produce forms of technology that make a positive contribution to the quality of human life.

After I gave this lecture, one of my students came up to me and said that this is an effective way to get students to see the value and relevance of ethics. This lecture came after about six weeks of discussing computer ethics, team work, organizational cultures, professional responsibilities, and so forth, but apparently for this student, nothing tied these topics together as effectively as this one, unified vision, this vision of work as a spiritual journey, as a tool for spiritual evolution. Thus, I offer this essay to my colleagues in the hope that they might consider this approach to the teaching of ethics in the computer science curriculum.

The rest of this essay closely follows the original lecture notes that I distributed to my students. The first part presents the "redeemed" story of the wheel, a version of the wheel story that brings out the liberating potential of our work. The second part presents a list of twenty-six ways in which our work can help us to grow and evolve spiritually. A new section has been added that applies some of these concepts to the teaching profession. I close with a quote from a book entitled *Zen Lessons: The Art of Leadership* that summarizes very effectively what we need to communicate to our students, that the path of integrity is not a new path, it is not something that comes from the speculation of philosophers, it is something that can be seen directly in the heart, it is the timeless truth about the nature of reality.

The Lecture

During the first half of this course the emphasis has been on professional issues in computing. These included issues of professional responsibilities, risks and liabilities, computer ethics, teams and team dynamics, the ethics of speech, organizational issues, and corporate cultures.

Part of my agenda has been to do some "consciousness raising" concerning our careers and the role that they play in our lives. I started the course with the story of the wheel, which I encountered in a book about traditional Jewish spirituality. The author of that book failed to explore the liberating potential of work. Indeed, the intention of the story of the wheel was to criticize people who devote too much energy to their work, and in this day and age, when workaholism is a problem, this is a valid point to make. However, I would like to explore the spiritual growth and the liberation that is possible within work, because while work is only part of our lives, it is an important part. If we cannot find meaning in the mundane, then any attempt at spirituality is just escapism. The purpose of spirituality is not to escape, but rather to imbue life with goodness, excellence, beauty, and meaning. I hope that this lecture will help you to see why work is so important for one's spiritual growth. I also hope you will come to realize that the wheel can be viewed as a metaphor for the Cosmos itself.

In this lecture I draw upon many of the spiritual traditions that I studied, including my own Jewish tradition. Insofar as I can tell, no tradition is more true than any other. What matters is that we, as human beings, develop hearts of goodness. A good heart can turn a tradition that has deteriorated into intolerance and meaningless rituals into a vehicle for enlightenment and truth. An evil heart can turn the beautiful teachings of the Christ or of Mohammed or of Moses into something truly evil and despicable. So, the particular rituals and traditions are not as important as the goodness that we develop in our own hearts. Spiritual traditions have no objective reality. They exist in hearts and minds of the followers. It is our responsibility to imbue our respective traditions with goodness and to redeem our traditions from the forces of darkness and intolerance that abound everywhere.

I would like to start with a conjecture that the Book of Exodus in the Bible is fundamentally about our relationship to work. I am bringing this out in order to help you to see that the idea of acknowledging the spiritual value and significance of work is not new. This has been a central preoccupation of religious thinkers since the dawn of the Judeo-Christian heritage over three thousand years ago. In this regard, I should mention the saying of the Prophet Mohammed to the effect that "a man without a profession is a man without a religion."

Here is a brief outline of the Book of Exodus from the point of view of the meaning of work:

a. the Israelites are enslaved by the Pharaoh, representing the ego, in Egypt, which in Hebrew means a narrow place. *The ego keeps us enslaved in a narrow place.*

b. liberation from slavery, which involves a transit through a narrow and dangerous passageway.

c. revelation of the Divine Law (i.e., the Ten Commandments which provide the general principles behind an intricate ethical system).

d. application of the Divine Law (the general principles given in the Ten Commandments) to developing a system of ethics, including business ethics and social justice, with special attention to the rights of the stranger, the widow, and the orphan.

e. the sanctification of work through the building of the Tabernacle, its vessels and utensils, and through the creation of the priestly vestments. Bezalel, the builder of the Tabernacle, is given Divine inspiration for his task that even exceeds the Wisdom of Moses in some dimensions.

f. the perversion of work as symbolized by the Golden Calf (not only do the Israelites devote their craftsmanship to building an idol, it is an idol of gold, symbolizing work for the sake of money, the worship of money).

g. reaffirming the sacred nature of work—the narrative returns to a description of the Tabernacle, thus reaffirming the sacred nature of work even if the true purpose of work is sometimes perverted or loss sight of.

Thus, *the liberation from slavery in this primordial human saga did not mean the liberation from work.* It involved the sanctification of work that could only occur after the Israelites were exposed to a new ethical code, which included ethical and moral obligations to the "other." Sanctification implies holiness, but what is holiness? The root meaning of holiness in Hebrew is to separate (and of course, the Christian notion of holiness derives from the Hebrew Bible). I interpret this to mean that we can use our work to separate ourselves from the illusions of the world. Actually, the illusions of the world are our own delusions. Thus, I see work as providing a means by which we can attain self-understanding and enlightenment, freedom, and true creativity.

I also associate holiness with laughter. When we see the foolishness of the world and when we develop a little bit of wisdom, we can have ourselves a good belly laugh, or perhaps we will cry because of all of the terrible suffering that human stupidity has caused. Is there anything more holy than deeply-felt laughter shared between people who love and respect one another? So, even though the rest of this essay is fairly serious, let us not lose sight of the value of humor, especially in an age when there is so much anger, intolerance, frustration, and violence.

This lecture presents a list of ways in which we can use our careers to grow spiritually. Spiritual growth, in part, or perhaps even in large measure, has to do with ridding oneself of delusory notions (this is wisdom) and ridding oneself of harmful behaviors (this is an aspect of wisdom that is called virtue). I feel quite qualified to write about human defects since God gave me so many of them. There is not a single human defect that I have ever written about here or in the killer robot or in anything else that I have ever written that is not my own defect. Thus, I have been studying wisdom for quite some time, and as a teacher, I would like to share what I have learned with you, my students. I realize that our defects are, in part, the price that we pay for this human birth. Wisdom arises because we are forced, by our own true natures, to examine the faults that we have inherited from our parents and that we have acquired from our environment, and to remove those faults with strenuous spiritual efforts. Consequently, you should understand everything that I have said or written about ethics and spiritual struggle as a reflection of my own spiritual struggle. Consequently, I do not feel that I am preaching at you. I am sharing with you and I am preaching to myself.

This course began with the story of the wheel. *[I repeated the story of the wheel at this point for the students.]* Now, I would like to present a revised story of the wheel, what I would like to call...

The Redeemed Story of the Wheel

A man was sentenced to thirty years in prison. During his years in prison he was forced to turn a gigantic wheel, day after day. At first his whole being rebelled against his predicament, but then he learned to surrender to the reality of his situation. In that surrender, he learned to recognize a part of himself that was beyond his body and his mind, a quiet, peaceful, and radiant presence. This was not only a presence, but an awareness, and that awareness was his own innate awareness, and in that awareness he could see himself more clearly. In seeing himself more clearly he got to understand how he wound up in prison in the first place, the secret of his birth, the story of the human race, the story of his ancestors, his family, his parents, and his siblings. He realized that they were all prisoners as much as he. He began to see his personal demons, and he confronted them, and with each confrontation, the peaceful radiance became more powerful and more clear. He identified less and less with the fluctuating energies of the body-mind complex and more and more with that inner radiance. Within that inner radiance he discovered timeless Wisdom, and then he discovered the Source of that Wisdom, the Source of Everything. He became aware of the other prisoners, who were suffering a fate just like his, and with the help of that inner Wisdom, he was able to help them to discover the inner treasures that he had discovered. After many years in prison, he discovered innumerable points of Wisdom within himself, and he realized that his own heart contained endless and inexhaustible wealth. He began to see the Wisdom in his work and in all of his prison-bound relationships. The radiance grew and grew, and he became more peaceful, loving, and compassionate. His fellow prisoners improved as well and he realized that they were a part of him, and he was a part of them. His spiritual strivings affected them, and their spiritual strivings affected him. As his radiance grew, his laughter grew, and deepened, and he learned and could tell more wheel jokes than just about anybody. And the other prisoners, many of whom had a wheel of their own to turn, loved his wheel jokes and his sense of humor lightened everyone's burden. He became a source of peace and light for those around him, and each day he saw his fellow prisoners as being more and more beautiful, and they began to amaze him with their wisdom. Each day, as he turned the wheel, he dove deeper and deeper into himself, and each new insight and discovery brought more peace and more happiness, more self-acceptance and more love for his fellow prisoners and even for the prison guards, who didn't seem to have much Wisdom, but who in the end, were nonetheless the agents of the Eternal Wisdom of the Source of Everything. Finally, the day came for his release, and he was curious about the wheel. What had he been doing all of those years? Was he grinding wheat? Was he milling corn? He walked outside the prison and saw the wheel he had been turning outside the prison wall. The wheel was not connected to anything. For thirty years, he had been turning a wheel that was not connected to anything. With this realization, he found some wild flowers and placed them in front of the wheel and he made a gesture of reverence toward it, for he realized that the wheel had been an instrument of his liberation. He realized that the wheel was holy and that the prison was a sacred place.

26 Ways in Which Our Careers Can Help Us to Grow

The following list contains 26 ways in which our careers can help us to grow. I have included annotations (in italics) that expand upon these points. These annotations are based on some of the insights that I have gained from the various teachers that I have studied with. I am taking an eclectic approach to spirituality in this lecture for the following reason. Some of you may want to commit yourselves to this idea that your career is not just about making money. Some of you may want to commit yourselves to the idea that your career can be a tool for your own personal growth and liberation, for the realization of your full human potential. This commitment will require that you do a lot of studying on your own. I know from personal experience that this kind of venture cannot succeed if one goes off by oneself. You need to be part of a community of people who share your interest in excellence and in developing human potential to the fullest extent. Your community will have its own spiritual language, different from my eclectic language. My eclectic language is intended for an audience that consists of people from diverse backgrounds. Hopefully, your community will be one of tolerance, embracing all of humanity with love and appreciation. From within the social interactions and understandings generated within that community, in the language of your own faith, you should be able to develop your own list of ways in which your career can help your soul and spirit to evolve.

So, here is my list.

In our work we can learn ...

1. **Self-Awareness.** We can learn how to become more aware, both of our strengths and of our weaknesses. Other people can become a mirror in which we can see our own positive qualities as well as our defects. Becoming aware of our faults, we can remove them. Becoming aware of our strengths and talents, we can nurture them. We can study the way we react to circumstances, and we can continually refine ourselves until we become "virtuosos." It takes a lot of strenuous effort to become a virtuoso, but just imagine the joy that a virtuoso feels as she pours out her being through her music. In the same manner, imagine the joy that you will feel when you can pour out your talents, your compassion, and your humanity using the mysterious and miraculous bag of skin that God gave to you as your primary vehicle of expression.

2. **Transforming weaknesses into strengths.** We can learn how to overcome our deficiencies and personality flaws, replacing them with strengths. *[Many traditions view weaknesses, even sins, as potentialities that can be transformed into strengths. One metaphor that is often used is that a garden cannot grow to its full potential without a lot of manure. When we look at the circumstances of our birth, at our families, and at the world around us, we will see a lot of manure. Manure isn't all bad. It contains the possibility of transformation. In a garden, the foul-smelling manure eventually becomes the perfume of a rose. On a farm, the same foul-smelling manure becomes life-giving grain.]*

3. **Overcoming adversity.** We can learn how to meet and to overcome challenges and adversity. We can realize fully that life is an inner struggle and a spiritual adventure, and not just a situation comedy. We can learn how to deal with failure as well as success. Although we may not be able to ward off failure and adversity, we can choose the manner in which we react to circumstances and the manner in which we interpret the meaning of life. If we can attain to mindfulness of the body-mind complex, then we will see that the way we react to failure is not inevitable. It is a choice. We can choose to view all difficulties as important life lessons. We can transcend the idea that we are victims. *[I think it is useful to contemplate the role of the hero in mythology, religion, and literature. In my mind, a hero is a person who can change the very parameters of what people believe to be an objective reality. Christ was clearly a hero-figure of this nature. God wants us to be heroes and to change the parameters of reality, so that our future will not be like the past, because the past is more than just grim, it is a tragedy of enormous proportions.]*

4. **Setting and achieving goals.** We can learn to set goals for ourselves. It is important to constantly set goals and to challenge ourselves, so that we are never dormant or static. One needs to be in a state of constant learning and constant growth.

5. **Learning the value of cooperation and teamwork.** We can learn the intricacies of teamwork and all that this involves. We can learn to learn from others and to share our knowledge with them. We can learn the value of conflict that is conducted with mutual respect and with the intention of promoting knowledge and excellence. We can learn how to deal with difficult people and how to deal with ourselves when we become angry and upset. We can learn to see how human cooperation and interdependence are an essential fact of life that needs to be acknowledge and celebrated. Outside of work, we can learn to appreciate the value of community, our responsibilities to our community, and our community's responsibilities to us.

6. **Developing a sense of competence.** We can learn how to develop a sense of competence, of "adequate means" or "skillful means." Competence, in part, comes from setting personal goals and achieving them. It also comes from the flow of work that is performed artfully and expertly from day to day. *[The part of ourselves of which we are aware may be very tiny compared to*

the totality. A feeling of competence ("flow") is really something beyond the rational mind. Our lives become more meaningful when we realize that the universe is using us for some worthwhile purpose (certainly, parents should have this feeling when they bring children into the world). The point is that skillful means comes from acknowledging that the entire universe is cooperating in the work that we do.]

7. **Attaining to more global perspectives.** We can learn to see things from a more global, less self-centered perspective. *[The idea of the killer robot was to focus on the programmer and then slowly to draw a more and more complete picture of the context in which the programmer works. Clearly, in any system, each of us is just one tiny part of a much more complicated picture. One Zen master says that we must become ABC–"a bigger container." We must be able to contain more and more, and to exclude less and less, from our compassion and from our concern.]*

8. **Influencing things in a positive manner.** We can learn how to manipulate things so as to direct things into a more positive direction. Our words and actions have consequences. We can influence a project in a positive direction, or we can watch the whole thing go down in flames. It takes knowledge and wisdom to influence things in a positive direction–and constant vigilance.

9. **Learning to work with causality.** We can learn how to anticipate the consequences of our actions and we can learn to accept responsibility for those consequences. We need to learn the qualities of the people that we interact with. If we try to help a snake, he will probably bite us and fill us with his poison. If we try to help a bear, he will grab us and hold on to us, and he will never let go. It takes great subtlety to learn how to deal with difficult people, people who may be filled with self-doubts, insecurity, anger, and resentment. We need to accept the consequences of our actions. We need to understand that no one can claim exemption from the law of causality–the law that good begets good and evil begets evil. On the street this law is stated as "What goes around, comes around." No one can claim that the law of causality does not apply to him or to her despite the fact that God is compassionate and forgiving. I am not concerned here with the hereafter, but rather, the way that this lawful universe operates. The person who claims an exemption from the law of causality simply cannot grow, simply cannot refine his or her character, simply cannot become a true Human Being who accepts the awesome responsibility of freedom. The law of causality is important for achieving a sense of responsibility and of autonomy. The law of causality becomes a powerful tool that can help us to refine and to perfect our character. Working with the law of causality and accepting the Wisdom behind it, we can attain to higher and higher states of refinement, awareness, sensitivity, and perfection.

10. **Appreciating differences and diversity.** We can learn how to work with people of different cultural, spiritual, and ethnic backgrounds. We can free ourselves from the poisonous illusion that we were lucky enough to belong to the one group that has a monopoly on the truth) or a monopoly on beauty or virtue. We can appreciate the beauty and value of each person and of each ethnic group and of each spiritual tradition. We can also learn to appreciate different viewpoints concerning the way things should get done at work. We can learn from people with opposing perspectives, and by treating them with respect, we can share our own perspectives with them. Communication can become communion, and eventually, synergistic action.

11. **Developing humility and true self-confidence.** We can learn to appreciate the beauty and splendor of humility while at the same time not losing touch with our inner sense of self-worth and value. On occasion I believe that I have had a foretaste of what genuine humility might actually be like. It is not a behavior (self-effacement and all of that stuff that is often just a defense mechanism of the ego). It is a glorious feeling of appreciation that comes from a great depth of silent listening and

observation. How rare it is that we really appreciate and admire the genius of another human being: the skilled craftsman or artisan, the composer, the artist, the mathematician, the doctor, the so-called "common person" we meet every day—just the wonder of this human body and its marvels. We should revere those who are truly talented, and those who are wise, and those who are making a positive contribution to life. Not recognizing the worth of others is a form of arrogance. Arrogance is the ego's desperate attempt to obscure the essential equality and unity of all human beings. Arrogance is the ego's attempt to fill emptiness of heart with worldly accomplishment, intellectual brilliance, fame, and money. "If I can impress people with my brilliance, then I must really be somebody. If I can impress people with my money and fame, then I must really be somebody." While some of these things potentially has value, the person who pursues them for their own sake will never escape from that gaping void—which will ultimately manifest as fear of the most intense kind. The ego that desperately needs to acquire these things cannot possibly appreciate the simple beauty of another person, the silent and heartfelt appreciation of the "other." It is just too threatening. I should know. I am an expert on all of these subjects.

12. **Defending our "Divine Status."** We can learn to appreciate the Buddhist saying, "I alone am the Honored One between heaven and earth!" or the Jewish and Christian idea that each human being is created in the Image of God, or the utter humility of the Sufi martyr Al Hallaj when he declared, "I am the Creative Truth!" We need to develop this kind of confidence that we are embodiments of something timeless, holy, great, and awesome. We need to do this while confronting life with complete and total humility. In part, humility is related to the realization that the "other" is the Honored One as well. Each human being represents an awesome miracle. *[It is a grave error to consider another as greater than oneself just because that person has a title or lots of money or because that person attended a prestigious university. It is important to develop your warrior spirit and your sense of self-worth. This is why spiritual investigation is so important. The world of Truth is a great leveler. For example, in Islam there is the teaching that all believers are equal, like the teeth of a comb. The Torah teaches that God does not take bribes and early Christianity placed a strong emphasis on communal living, brotherhood, charity, and equality. Regardless of what the world would have you believe, each of you is fully capable of tremendous accomplishments if you would just commit yourselves to the kind of struggle that I am writing about. You must see and learn how to avoid the millions upon millions of pitfalls that await you, that will try to demoralize you, to ensnare you, to disfigure your Divine Face (as one of my favorite writers, Professor S. H. Nasr of the George Washington University puts it). Just as it is a grave error to demean one's own Divine Status, so it is also a grave error to think that one is greater than another, that is, to demean the Divine Status of the "other." In the end, the "Honored One" is just that—the One. Realizing your own inner worth and potential greatness, you must make an inviolate inner commitment to your own self worth and you must learn how to defend your Divine Status against people who might consider themselves more privileged and important than you, people who might try to demoralize you in order to inflate their own egos at your expense. These people are vampires who live off the blood of others. Indeed, the vampires you see in the movies are merely metaphors for these real-life vampires. When you meet a person like this, you naturally feel depleted.]*

13. **Bringing balance into one's life.** We can learn how to see things in perspective, bringing balance into our lives, balancing our work with other interests and obligations and activities. We can devote ourselves to activities that are conducive to happiness and well-being on all levels, including family-centered activities, fun-filled vacations and relaxation, music, cultural and intel-

lectual enrichment, hobbies, etc. We can learn how to manage stress and how to use stress to our advantage. We can avoid the self-sabotage that drugs, alcohol abuse, smoking, overeating, and other unhealthy habits represent.

14. **Developing the attitude of the "eternal student."** We can learn the importance of never being a teacher and always being a student. In order to see life clearly we need to be able to listen to others from a place of great silence and depth. People who talk a lot often do not know how to listen. I cannot imagine anyone in this world ever coming to a state in which they think that their learning is complete, or that they have attained a state of perfection. The best attitude is one of humility and of being a student of wisdom *forever and ever.* With this attitude, even when death comes, the warrior spirit, this love of learning and of truth, survives and acts. Every spirit, whether good or evil, creates its own new circumstances.

15. **Appreciating the value of the particular work that we do, and the work that others do.** We can learn the specific values embodied in the work that we do, whether it is to help a company to run efficiently, or whether it is to provide high quality information that people need and can benefit from. That is, we can see our work from the point of view of the manner in which we are providing something that society needs. We can also learn to appreciate the work that other people do, regardless of economic status. We can develop the wisdom to avoid work that degrades human life, that harms human beings, that harms the environment, and causes needless suffering to other creatures. We can become free to choose the form of work that best expresses our values and our commitments, our talents, and our true natures. *[Each profession has a profound spiritual meaning and reflects the multitudinous personalities, attributes, and activities of the Ultimate Source of Everything. For that Ultimate Source of Everything is truly Doctor, Teacher, Nurse, Tailor, Architect, Poet, Composer, Singer, Comedian, Actor, Athlete, Plumber, Carpenter, Farmer, Chemist, Biologist, Physicist, Geologist, Cosmologist, Truck Driver, Soldier, Engineer, and so on. That Ultimate Source of Everything is also the ultimate Database Administrator, Systems Analyst, Systems Designer, Network Designer, Virtual Reality Creator, and Applications Programmer.]*

16. **Developing integrity and a personal sense of ethics.** We can learn how to assert our personal integrity and values even if that is difficult and even if the environment may not support us at first. We can learn the basic ethical and legal principles that apply to our profession, and we can strive to embody integrity, honesty, competence, respect for others, and excellence in our work.

17. **Developing compassion, tolerance, and patience.** We can learn how to develop positive qualities of compassion and patience and tolerance, while at the same time learning how to handle anger, resentment, and other negative emotions. We can become more adept at transforming negative emotions into positive feelings and actions. We can learn to be conscious of the "body-mind complex" rather than identifying completely with the body-mind complex. We can use our work to become conscious of who we are and how we react to things. We can learn how to channel aggressiveness and anger into positive activities and achievements. We can learn to stand our ground and to represent something positive.

18. **Developing empathy and justice.** We can learn the essential art of judging other people favorably without compromising on necessary professional standards. When problems arise, we can focus on fixing the problem, not on fixing the blame. We need wisdom in order to judge the quality of the information that we receive, and in order to make competent professional judgments on the basis of that information. In terms of judging others, we need tolerance and compassion. How can anyone of us pretend to understand what it is like to be in the other person's shoes? We know hardly anything about the other, their suffering, the challenges that they have

overcome. Certainly, "Judge not and you will not be judged" is good guidance, even as we use our wisdom to promote excellence and quality in our work.

19. **Acquiring and utilizing wealth and power.** We can learn how to acquire wealth and to use that wealth in a manner that is socially compassionate and responsible. We can learn how to acquire wealth and how to use that wealth in a manner that is truly beneficial for ourselves, our families, our friends, and our communities.

20. **Developing one's personality and talents to the ultimate extent.** Learning about oneself, learning about one's personal demons and deficits, learning about one's strengths and talents, learning about how the world operates—all of these forms of learning can help us to develop our potential and our skills to the fullest extent possible. We can realize and develop the potential that we have, not only in the work sphere, but in other spheres of our lives. One can develop a commitment to excellence, quality, and integrity. *[One Zen master said that the purpose of life is to develop one's personality to a feverish pitch (i.e., to the utmost). I would assert that all true spiritual traditions have this as the ultimate goal. For example, in Sufism, the emphasis is on Insan Kamil—Arabic for "the Perfect Man." Some Christian mystics have written about the birth of Christ in the soul. These concepts are related to the strength of spirit that one can develop in one's life. This is rightfully called the warrior spirit, for the inner life is a battle for sure. A human being who denies that life is a meaningful spiritual struggle has lost the war right from the start.]*

21. **Realizing the nature of the soul and one's purpose in life.** We can learn how to acknowledge the nature of reality, the psychological suffering that people endure. We can learn to acknowledge the enormity of the human catastrophe on our planet. We can acknowledge the reality of the soul and the fact that the world is a hostile environment for the soul. We can realize that the essence of the soul is its ability to filter out impurities, extracting the pure gold that the soul relishes, the gold of wisdom, goodness, virtue, beauty, and love. *[The Sufi teacher that I studied with said that the world is a hostile environment for the soul. This is consistent with traditional Jewish and Christian thought. Once we realize that the world is a hostile environment for the soul, and once we realize that every human being is in the same boat, then we can develop tolerance, compassion, and patience. Everyone would like to be perfect, if they could be, but this realm is a hostile environment for those qualities that the soul most earnestly wishes to express—the qualities of goodness, love, beauty, wisdom, and virtue. Once we realize that this is the truth—that this realm is a hostile environment for the soul, then we can become more accepting of others, especially when they hurt us or do not act the way we would like, and then we can become more accepting of ourselves. This is perhaps the most important spiritual teaching of all—because it helps us to understand our own imperfections and the imperfections that we observe in others. This insight (it seems to me) is essential for the development of compassion and love and appreciation for other people. This same Sufi teacher called this world "the upside-down world." This is clearly consistent with Jewish mysticism and the original teachings of Christianity. This world is upside-down, but the educational system (for the most part) cannot acknowledge that, because the educational system is an upside-down system taught by many people who are upside-down people[1]. The soul needs to experi-*

---

[1] How can one distinguish between an upside-down person and an upside-up person? We cannot judge other people ultimately. But, we need to know whether WE are upside-up or upside-down. I would say that an upside-down person is a person who loses all or most of his wealth when he dies and an upside-up person loses only an insignificant fraction of his wealth when he dies. In the language of the Gospels, the upside-up person stores his treasure in heaven (in terms of gracious qualities and good deeds) and the upside-down person stores his treasure here on earth (in terms of money, prestige, and fame).

ence this period of suffering in the upside-down world in order to realize its own true nature. The truth can only be revealed in juxtaposition to the false, in the same way that light cannot be seen without the presence of darkness. Consequently, the work of the soul in this world is the work of developing wisdom, of seeing the sense in which the world is upside-down. The work of the soul is to extract true wisdom from the false wisdom that is contained in the world. In is important to see that the world is offering millions upon millions of forms of false wisdom that ultimately lead to human degradation and unhappiness. This work of extracting wisdom from this hostile environment is a dangerous undertaking, not something to be taken lightly. This work is the essence of what it means to be a Human Being.]

22. **Creating work, wealth, and prosperity.** Some of you may learn how to become entrepreneurs, starting your own businesses, thus providing a livelihood for dozens, maybe even hundreds or thousands of employees. According to Jewish tradition, this is one of the greatest of human virtues—providing work for another (or even, to teach someone how to earn a good livelihood) so that they might provide food, shelter, and clothing for themselves and for their families. Yet, being an employer brings with it special obligations in terms of fairness, justice, honesty, and ethics. It is imperative that the entrepreneur respect the dignity of his or her employees and the dignity of the work that they do. The spiritual heights that a business person can achieve are exalted indeed, for an entrepreneur of this nature can exercise great leadership skills, can mentor others into positions of leadership, and can help his or her employees to make progress on all of the twenty-six points that we have been discussing. In addition, he or she can be a great benefactor for the larger community.

23. **Creating new worlds and new knowledge.** We can learn how to build new knowledge within ourselves. In the workplace this means developing new skills, both technical skills, social skills, and organizational skills. Outside the workplace this means to learn new things (turn off that television!), to express ourselves through art, craft, music, social action, and other activities that have enduring value. We can develop our talents and personalities to a feverish pitch, as that Zen master said. Ultimately, we can become truly creative, inspiring others, teaching others, while retaining the attitude of a student. We can create a new reality, freeing ourselves from social convention and the stultifying limitations that others believe in. We can do this from a wise and profound assessment of our own abilities and limitations.

24. **Mastering the ethics of speech.** We can learn how to control that thing between the teeth, perhaps our most difficult human challenge. We can realize that life is not a situation comedy and that our words have real consequences. Words can heal and words can create. Words can destroy and words can kill. *[Prophet Mohammed said, "If you can control the thing between your teeth and the thing between your legs, then I can guarantee you paradise!"]*

25. **Mentoring others with respect and love.** We can learn how to mentor those who come along, those who may be younger than us, or those who may be less experienced. We can do this without losing the essential attitude of being a student. *[The spiritual path is not about becoming better than others. The spiritual path is about becoming better than we have been in the past and this transformation requires that we develop wisdom, an insight into our own delusions and errors, an insight into our own strengths and talents. The spiritual path is about realizing that the ultimate nature of reality is not what is seen or what is heard. One aspect of this formless reality is a plenitude—a plenitude of goodness and blessing. Perhaps one can describe the highly developed individual as someone who lives passionately and completely in each moment from the depths of this plenitude, from the depths of this inexhaustible source of*

goodness, from the depths of the heart of goodness. Thus, realizing the nature of reality is certainly important for the development of ethical and caring human beings.]

26. **Becoming a wise human being.** We can learn how to develop wisdom. This is perhaps the most important point of all, because it is all-encompassing. Wisdom is the ability to distinguish between truth and falsehood. This world is a mixture of good and evil, light and darkness, truth and falsehood. The soul has the ability to extract the light from the darkness, the truth from the false, the good from the evil, and the gold from the dross. The soul is in a hostile environment. The situation is very much like a miner that has to go into a dark and dangerous mine in order to extract gold or some other precious material. The soul has come to this hostile environment in order to extract wisdom, goodness, and truth. This is the paramount functioning of the soul. The soul cannot function properly unless it understands the true situation, that the world is a hostile environment for the soul and that the world's values are upside-down values. Day after day, in the workplace, one can extract new wisdom and knowledge, and one can apply that wisdom to one's behavior, in order to evolve spiritually. Thus, by using our career as a tool for developing wisdom in a comprehensive way, in an ambitious way, we can escape from the Wheel of Suffering and we can lead lives that are filled with challenge, purpose, meaning, wonder, achievement, compassion, goodness, and peace.

In conclusion, in our work we can develop the warrior spirit, a total commitment to our own Divine Status, even as we learn the profound humility, gentleness, and openness that this Divine Status actually entails. We can develop our personalities to a feverish pitch and we can develop wisdom and virtue. When death comes, our souls will be rich beyond measure, and even as we leave behind our possessions in this world, we will be at peace and we will not feel the deep regret of the man who died when he realized that his thirty years of work turning the wheel had all been in vain.

— end of lecture —

This lecture is just a bunch of meaningless words unless we commit ourselves to devoting our energies, with love and compassion, to our work, to helping others and improving the quality of life through the work that we do. For those of us in the teaching profession, it means continually renewing our energies and continually reminding ourselves what it is all about.

In the above lecture I stated that the world is a hostile environment for the soul. The hostile environment is the creation of many billions of people over many thousands of years. The hostile environment is the residue of countless acts and thoughts born out of ignorance. We contribute to the perpetuation of the hostile environment by accepting a limited, false, and incomplete description of reality. We become the prisoners of our own delusions. This is what is called the Cosmic Mountain in the spiritual traditions. All human beings that are born into this world inherit this huge mountain of ignorance and evil. It is the history of brutality and genocide that we read about in books and it is the reality of our own negative qualities and ignorance.

I believe that you and I are like explorers or astronauts. We have come from that Original Source of Everything into this hostile environment, this hostile environment that was created by many thousands of years of human evil. Our purpose in coming here is to investigate the nature of a barbaric world such as this, to realize the truth concerning our true natures and our true origins, and then by our commitment to truth and integrity, to civilize this barbaric world, to utterly transform it into an environment in which the soul can thrive and find peace and happiness. We civilize this barbaric world by working on ourselves, completely eradicating the barbarian within our own hearts, certainly not by becoming barbarians and murderers ourselves. Thus, I suppose there are various levels of success on a dangerous mission such as ours. Failure would be to fall into a state of confusion, to become a barbarian oneself, to lose touch with the Plenitude, the Outflow of Goodness and Blessing, the Effulgence, accepting conventional materialistic perspectives, losing touch with the true nature of reality. Better than a failure, but not quite a success, would be to understand the nature of the problem, to decontaminate oneself, to civilize oneself, to save oneself, while not accomplishing much in terms of civilizing the barbaric world. Total success would be to civilize the barbaric world, through the work of the Spirit, by peaceful means, which is the shared religious dream of establishing the Kingdom of God. This is the truth concerning this human birth insofar as I have been able to ascertain up until this point in my life.

The great mystics and sages of generations past were the explorers and astronauts of their day. Surrounded by human evil on all sides, they established islands of sanity and integrity and truth. The following quote from an ancient Zen master helps us to see that the issue of achieving integrity in our lives is not something that arises from speculative philosophy, but comes from a direct perception into the spiritual truth, into the ultimate nature of reality.

ONE DAY AT A TIME

From Zen Lessons: The Art of Leadership[2],
translated by Thomas Cleary, Shambhala Press, Boston, MA.

> "When you cut and polish a stone, as you grind and rub you do not see it decreasing, yet with time it will be worn away. When you plant a tree and take care of it, you do not see it increase, but in time it gets large.
>
> "When you accumulate virtue with continued practice, you do not see the good of it, but in time it will function. If you abandon right and go against truth, you do not see the evil of it, but in time you will perish.
>
> "When students finally think this through and put it into practice, they will develop great capacity and emanate a fine reputation. This is the way that has not changed, now or ever."

---

[2] This is a compilation of sayings by Zen masters from the early centuries of Zen Buddhism in China.

Acknowledgments

I am indebted to many people who helped me to appreciate different spiritual traditions. Professor Herbert Jehle, in whose memory I dedicated my book, *The Case of the Killer Robot,* Professor of Physics at the George Washington University, introduced me to the study of the world's religions from the perspective of finding the primordial truth that they all contain (perennial philosophy). As I wrote in the introduction to my book, Professor Jehle was a pacifist and a member of the German Christian resistance to Nazism. M. R. Bawa Muhaiyadeen, the Sufi master, had a great influence on my religious thinking as did the Islamic scholar, S. H. Nasr (whom I mentioned in the essay), whose books gave me a deeper insight into perennial philosophy from an Islamic perspective. I also spent some time with the Zen teacher, Eido Shimano Roshi, and it seemed that almost every gesture of his taught some aspect of the truth. In addition, I greatly benefitted from the writings of numerous authors, including Annemarie Shimmel, and Tarthang Tulku, whose book *Skillful Means* is about the subject of this essay—seeing one's work as a vehicle for spiritual growth. I am also indebted to numerous Jewish authors who have helped me to find the spiritual gold in the Jewish tradition. Finally, I am indebted to Rabbi David Glansberg-Krainin, who taught me how to chant from the Torah scrolls and whose open heart has helped to create a thriving Jewish community here in West Chester, PA, a community that shares my own values and love of God.

Reducing Software Failures: Address Ethical Risks with Software Development Impact Statements (SoDIS™)

Don Gotterbarn

Introduction

Software developers and software engineers have been evolving and refining techniques to mediate risks of developing software products that meet the needs of their clients. The risks focused on include: missed schedule, over budget, and failing to meet the system's specified requirements. In spite of this attention to risks, a high percentage of software is being delivered late, over budget, and not meeting all requirements, leading to software development being characterized as a "software crisis."

A narrow approach to risk analysis and understanding the scope of a software project has contributed to significant software failures. A process is presented that expands the concept of software risk to include social, professional, and ethical risks that lead to software failure. Using an expanded risk analysis will enlarge the project scope considered by software developers. This process is incorporated into a software development life cycle. A tool to develop Software Development Impact Statements is also discussed.

Software Risk

The Problem

Working with the typical concept of "software project failure" as either over-budget, behind schedule, or delivered with limited functionality has contributed to significant software disasters and the production of harmful web sites and software cyber products. We need to correct the meaning of "Software Failure," or more precisely, focus attention on some overlooked meaning of "Software Failure," Software fails even when it is produced on schedule, within budget, and meets the customer's specified software requirements. Software has been developed which, although meeting stated requirements, has significant negative social and ethical impacts.

This essay originally appeared in *The Australian Information Systems Journal,* Vol. 9, No. 2 (May) 2002. Copyright © 2001 by Don Gotterbarn. Reprinted with permission.

By ethical impact I mean those impacts of software that positively or negatively impact the circumstances, experiences, behavior, livelihood, or daily routine of others. The ethical stakeholders in developed software are those who are so affected by it. The dyslexic who is harmed by viewing a web site with an abundance of sans serif characters and a brilliant white background is a stakeholder in the development of that site.

The Aegis radar system, for example, met all requirements that the developer and the customer had set for it. The system designer's did not take into account the users of the software nor the conditions in which it would be used. The system was a success in terms of budget, schedule, and requirements satisfaction; even so, the limitations of the user interface to the system was a primary factor in the Vincennes shooting down an Iranian commercial airliner killing 263 innocent civilians. The user interface that met specifications had a significant impact on the lives of others.

Examples of this kind of system failure are not always so obvious. The ethical stakeholders in developed software are those who are so affected by it. The dyslexic who is harmed by viewing a web site with an abundance of sans serif characters and a brilliant white background is a stakeholder in the development of that site. The web site that is delivered on time, within budget, and meeting all required functionality may, nevertheless, be a failure

There are two factors that contribute to these professional and ethical failures; both related to those who have something to gain or lose as a result of the software project-system stakeholders. First, there is significant evidence that many of these failures are caused by limiting the consideration of system stakeholders to just the software developer and the customer. This limited scope of consideration leads to developing systems that have surprising negative affects because the needs of relevant system stakeholders were not considered. In the case of the Aegis radar system the messages were not clear to the users of the system who were operating in a hostile environment. Second, these types of failures also arise from the developers limiting the scope of software risk analysis to just technical and cost issues. A complete software development process requires (1) the identification of all relevant stakeholders and (2) enlarging risk analysis to include social, political, and ethical issues. I propose to add a process to a standard life cycle model that will help identify the relevant stakeholders and broaden the scope of risks anticipated.

Software Quality and its Risks

The typical goal of software developers is the production of quality systems that meet the needs of the user. "Software quality" is defined in terms of customer satisfaction. "Risk" is understood as any potential threat to the delivery of a quality product. To meet the goal of quality software, developers focus on particular risks including: project and schedule slips, cost increases, technical and quality risks, the timeliness of the product, and risks that the final product will not fit the business for which it was designed.

Projects are managed by focusing on these risks. Tools used to help identify and manage these risks include: risk tables, and checklists of risks categorized by type, probability, and impact. The checklist process is reminiscent of the process pilots go through before take off. As airline passenger, we are made more comfortable by the fact that they go through this procedure. But unlike pilots, developers choose to ignore some risks. Risks levels are determined based on the anticipated impact of the risk and its probability of occurring. Only risks above limited specified levels are addressed. The use of web-safe colors or the implementation of effective security may be ignored in an effort to get a product out in time.

Software Development Life Cycles (SDLC) and Risk

There are several models for developing software that reduce planning risks. All of these models contain similar phases: develop a statement of the customer's desires —the requirements phase; design how to achieve those desires—the design phase; code and test what was designed—the implementation phase; and determine that the requirements are satisfied by the system developed—system testing phase. The ordering and content of the steps through these phases is called the system development life cycles (SDLC). Many SDLCs are linear and require the documented completion of one phase before going on to the next phase and are directed at the satisfaction of the customer's explicit requirements. Only a few SDLCs include any risk analysis or expand the number and type of system stakeholders considered.

Spiral Lifecycle and Risk

Barry Boehm's "spiral lifecycle" is one of the few SDLCs that specifically addresses risk. Although Boehm's model was designed for the development of large software systems, it applies equally well to web development projects. Following his model, software is developed in a series of incremental releases. Each iteration through the spiral includes tasks related to: Customer communication, Planning, Risk Analysis, Engineering the development of the next level, Construction and Release and, Customer evaluation and assent. Each incremental element of the product that passes through these phases has undergone risk analysis and evaluation by the customer. Although this model introduces a focus on risks, those risks are limited to the risks identified above.

Lifecycle Measurement (LIME) and Stakeholders

LIME [Buglione, 1999] introduces a multidimensional analysis of quality and performance during software development. This model defines quality in terms of an economic dimension from the managers' viewpoint with particular attention to cost and schedule drivers; a social dimension from the user's viewpoint, and a technical dimension from the developer's viewpoint, with particular attention to technical quality that has a different impact during each SDLC phase. This model examines the role of a stakeholder in all phases of the project development. Although this method includes a consideration of a stakeholder in all phases of project development, the stakeholder is limited to the user for whom quality is achieved by the satisfaction of the specified requirements.

The Real Problem

Limitations of LIME and the Spiral SDLC

Both the Spiral and LIME models are improvements over earlier SDLCs that either had no risk analysis or had a very limited view of system stakeholders. The Spiral model incorporates risk analysis and LIME incorporates a consideration of an additional stakeholder throughout the development process. The risks considered by the Spiral model are limited to the technical risks identified earlier and LIME expands the risk analysis to include risks to one stakeholder in terms of requirements specification.

All of these methods attempt to anticipate and avoid all potential threats to a software project. The negative possibilities are those that would delay the delivery of the software that performs the desired functions in a timely and cost effective manner. However, none of these methods consider the ethical issues that need to be identified and addressed during the planning stages and re-considered throughout the development process.

Failure Research

Recent research has confirmed that inadequate identification of project stakeholders and how they are affected by a project is a significant contributor to the project's failure. Establishing the right project scope is essential in defining project goals. The stakeholders determine the scope of consideration. Normally, the stated needs of the customer are the primary items of concern in defining the project objectives. Investigating 16 organizational IS-related projects led [Farbey et al, 1993] to conclude that, "... the perception of what needed to be considered was disappointingly narrow, whether it concerned the possible scope and level of use of the system, [or] the range of people who could or should have been involved...." They discovered, with the exception of vendors, all stakeholders involved in evaluation were internal to the organizations. The reason for this restricted involvement is that these are the only stakeholders originally identified in the traditional project goals or system requirements. We should not limit our consideration of stakeholders to those who are financing the project or politically influential. Stakeholders are individuals or groups who may be directly or indirectly affected by the project and thus have a stake in the development activities. Those stakeholders who are negatively affected are particularly important.

Negative effects include both overt harm and the denial or reduction of goods. So obviously the development of medical software that delivers erroneous dosages of medicine that killed patients would have a negative effect; but we would also include as having negative effect software that limited people's freedom of expression. Limitations on positive ethical values and rights are negative effects. The way a web filter is designed has significant impacts that need to be considered in its development.

Many companies have gone out of business because they have only emphasized short-term efficiency and productivity. The quantity and cost of major product recalls in terms of dollars and company reputation is evidence of this mistaken emphasis on short-term goals. When considering software development we need to consider the impact of the system as a whole. In the past, the developers have restricted their involvement in the development of a product to the technical elements of a piece of software. This self-imposed limitation has contributed to the development of software that has been inferior and has had negative consequences for others: software that is not socially sensitive. The systems we develop perform tasks that affect other people in significant ways. The production of quality software that meets the needs of our clients and others requires both the carefully planned application of technical skills and a detailed understanding of the social, professional, and ethical aspects of the product and its impact on others. The risk analysis is incomplete if it only includes the technical elements.

Frequently the failure to consider social, ethical, and other risks has led to the delivery of unacceptable software that should be recalled and modified. Because the process of recall and modification is too expensive for the developer, the product remains on the market. The scope of a project needs to be identified in terms of its real stakeholders.

The expansion of the scope of a project to include all relevant stakeholders will also broaden the types of risks considered. Many companies have gone out-of-business because they have only emphasized short-term efficiency and productivity. The quantity and cost of major product recalls in terms of dollars and company reputation is evidence of this mistaken emphasis on short-term goals. When considering software development we need to consider the impact of the system as a whole. In the past, the developers have restricted their involvement in the development of a product to its technical elements. This self-imposed limitation has contributed to the development of software that has been inferior and has had negative consequences for others. The systems we develop perform tasks that affect other people in significant ways. The production of quality software that meets the needs of our clients and others requires both the carefully planned application of technical skills and a detailed understanding of the social, professional, and ethical aspects of the product and its impact on others.

Stakeholder Identification

Some of these software development methods distinguish between direct system stakeholders—[those who] "receive services from the system and send control information to the system"—and indirect stakeholders—[those who] "have an interest in some of the services that are delivered by the system but do not interact directly with it." These would include the passengers on the Iranian airliner or the driver of an automobile whose brakes are controlled by a computer program. Unfortunately (1) these methods do not provide an ethical or philosophical foundation for this distinction to reach beyond identifying those who have a business relation to the customer. They would not have identified as indirect stakeholders the 47 people killed by falling debris from a Patriot missile. These methods also fail to (2) provide a method of identifying the social and ethical impacts on the indirect stakeholders.

We need to extend the traditional software project stakeholder list from customers and corporations or shareholders to include all those who will be affected by the software and by its production. This enlargement of the domain of stakeholders has been implicitly endorsed by professional societies in the paramouncy clause—"Protect public health, safety, and welfare" in their codes of ethics. This extension has been explicitly adopted in several legal decisions in the

United States. This extended domain of stakeholders includes: users of the software, families of the users, social institutions that may be radically altered by the introduction of the software, the natural environment, social communities, software professionals, employees of the development organization, and the development organization itself. Given such a range of stakeholders, how is one ever to learn how to identify the relevant and significant stakeholders?

Software Development Impact Statement

Funded research has been done on the development of a risk management process employing software development impact statements. The Software Development Impact Statement (SoDIS), a modification of an environmental impact statement, is a way of addressing the need to modify project tasks in a formal way. A SoDIS, like an environmental impact statement, is used to identify potential negative impacts of a proposed project and specify actions that will mediate those impacts. A SoDIS is intended to reflect both the software development process and the more general obligations to various stakeholders.

We can generically divide software project development into three distinct phases. They are: the Feasibility Phase that includes considerations of preparedness to start a project and managing action items needed to start the project; the Requirements Phase that defines the specifications of a system and identifies and manages potential risks with each requirement; and the Detailed Phase that uses a detailed software project management plan to manage each task on system development. Each of these phases has its own peculiar risks. The purpose of the SoDIS is to identify these risks in a pre-audit of each phase.

In the Requirements Phase, we can develop a high-level analysis of the expected impacts of a project. A detailed SoDIS is developed from a preliminary software development plan. The goal of the SoDIS process is to identify significant ways in which the completion of individual tasks may negatively affect stakeholders and to identify additional project tasks needed to prevent any anticipated problems.

A detailed SoDIS is developed from a preliminary Gantt chart. The process of developing a SoDIS encourages the developer to think of people, groups, or organizations related to the project (stakeholders in the project) and how they are related to each of the individual tasks that collectively constitute the project. The goal of the SoDIS process is to identify significant ways in which the completion of individual tasks may negatively affect stakeholders and to identify additional project tasks needed to prevent any anticipated problems. Although all software projects have some unique elements, there are significant similarities between projects so that a generic practical approach can be taken to refocus the goal of a project to include a consideration of all ethically relevant stakeholders as well as all technically relevant stakeholders.

Figure 1 SoDIS Project Auditor

To aid with the major clerical task of completing this process for every task and for every stakeholder, a tool—the SoDIS Project Auditor—was developed. The SoDIS Project Auditor keeps track of all decisions made about the impact of project tasks on the relevant project stakeholders and it enables a proactive way to address the problems identified. A review of the tool will help explain and demonstrate the SoDIS process.

SoDIS Stakeholder Identification

A preliminary identification of software project stakeholders is accomplished by examining the system plan and goals to see who is affected and how they may be affected. When determining stakeholders, an analyst should ask: Whose behavior, daily routine, and work process will be affected by the development and delivery of this project; Whose circumstances, job, livelihood, and community will be affected by the development and delivery of this project, and Whose experiences will be affected by the development and delivery of this product. All those pointed to by these questions are stakeholders in the project.

Stakeholders are also those to whom the developer owes an obligation. The imperatives of the Software Engineering Code of Ethics and Professional Practice and similar codes define the rights of the developer and other stakeholders. These imperatives can be used to guide the stakeholder search. The process of identifying stakeholders also identifies their rights and the developers' obligations to the stakeholders. Many of the computing codes have similar imperatives. These have been reduced and categorized under five general principles in the SoDIS process and incorporated into the SoDIS Project Auditor.

On a high level, the SoDIS process can be reduced to four basic steps: (1) the identification of the immediate and extended stakeholders in a project, (2) the identification of the tasks or work breakdown packages in a project, (3) for every task, the identification and recording of potential ethical issues violated by the completion of that task for each stakeholder, and (4) the recording of the details and solutions of significant ethical issues that may be related to individual tasks and an examination of whether the current task needs to be modified or a new task created in order to address the identified concern.

The SoDIS process also includes a consideration of other phases of an SDLC. Some risks can be identified when a project is first conceived or can be identified at an intermediate stage when the customer's desires are being specified in the requirements phase. The SoDIS Project Auditor also provides a pre-audit for these two project phases.

A complete SoDIS process (1) broadens the types of risks considered in software development by (2) more accurately identifying relevant project stakeholders. The utilization of the SoDIS process will reduce the probability of the types of errors identified by Farbey. The SoDIS should be part of a SDLC.

Identification of Stakeholders

The identification of stakeholders must strike a balance between a list of stakeholders that includes people or communities that are ethically remote from the project, and a list of stakeholders that only includes a small portion of the ethically relevant stakeholders.

The SoDIS process provides a standard list of stakeholders that are related to most projects. This standard list of stakeholder roles changes with each change of project type. For example, a business project will include corporate stockholders, while a military project will not have stockholders as a standard stakeholder role. The system also enables the SoDIS analyst to add new stakeholder roles.

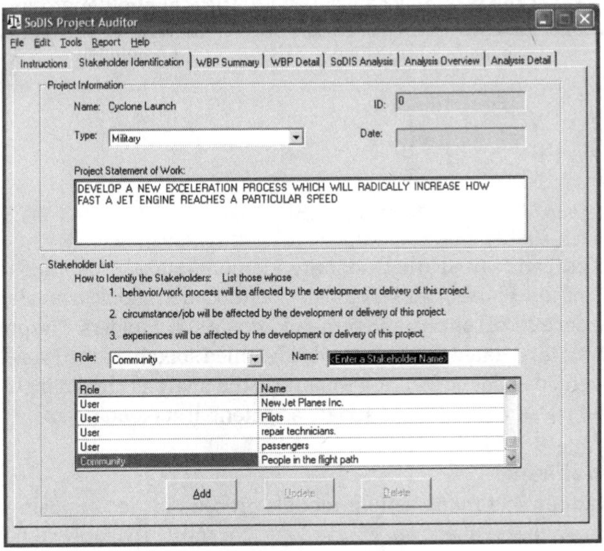

Figure 2 Stakeholder Identification

The stakeholder identification form (Figure 2) contains a Statement of Work that helps remind the analyst of the project goals and facilitates the identification of relevant stakeholders. The stakeholder form and the SoDIS analysis form are dynamic and enable the iterative process. If, while doing an ethical analysis, one thinks of an additional stakeholder he/she can shift to the stakeholder identification form, add the stakeholder, and then return to the SoDIS analysis that will now include the new stakeholder.

Rogerson & Gotterbarn [1997] proposed a method to help identify stakeholders based on Gert's moral rules [Gert 1988]. Gert gives 10 basic moral rules [Gotterbarn 1991]. These rules include: Don't kill, Don't cause pain, Don't disable, Don't deprive of freedom, Don't deprive of pleasure, Don't deceive, Don't cheat, Keep your promises, Obey the law, and Do your duty. These rules carry with them a corresponding set of rights such as the right to liberty, physical security, personal liberty, free speech, and property. How can these rules be used to identify stakeholders?

A matrix can be set up for each ethical rule such as "Don't cause harm." The column headers of the "Don't cause harm matrix" are the stakeholders, such as the "developer" and the "customer," and there is a row for each major requirement. The SoDIS analysts then visits each cell in the matrix asking, for each requirement, whether meeting this requirement violates that obligation to the stakeholder. Because the analysis as described is organized by particular software requirements, it will be easy to identify those requirements that generate a high level of ethical concern. Thus, the list will also be used to determine if particular requirements have to be modified to avoid significant ethical problems. This method can be used at this stage to give a composite picture of the ethical impact of the entire project from the point of view of these stakeholders.

Might the completion of this requirement cause harm to the stakeholder? ('Y' indicates that the task may cause harm to the stakeholder group.)

Req\ Stakeholder	Customer	Developer	User	Community	Additional Stakeholders...
Requirement 1	N	N	N	N	
Requirement 2	N	N	N	Y	
Requirement 3	Y	N	Y	Y	

This process can be used to both identify additional stakeholders and to determine their rights. The first phase of the stakeholder identification should have identified some areas of broader ethical concern and some additional stakeholders. The primary stakeholder analysis is repeated for these newly identified stakeholders. Even if there were no new stakeholders identified, at a minimum the analysis should include software users, related cultural groups, and society as potential stakeholders.

Identification of Tasks

Most software project management models proceed by decomposing the project into component tasks called "work breakdown packages" that only address the technical issues. These individual task descriptions are used in the reviewing and monitoring of the project. All of these tasks are ordered in a hierarchy of dependency on one another.

Each of these individual tasks may have a significant ethical impact. The specific SoDIS is used to help the developer responsibly address the ethically loaded potential of each work breakdown package. This is accomplished by including a SoDIS analysis in the standard descriptive elements of a work breakdown package (Figure 3).

Figure 3 WBP Detail Screen

The SoDIS analysis process also facilitates the identification of new tasks or modifications to existing tasks that can be used as a means to mediate or avoid identified concerns. The identified tasks need to be incorporated into the software project management plan. The early identification of these software modifications saves the developer time and money and leads to a more coherent and ethically sensitive software product.   This phase of the SoDIS process is a pre-audit of a detailed project plan that is developed late in a software development life cycle.

Identify Potential Ethical Issues

This stakeholder identification process has been modified in the SoDIS Project Auditor. Gert's ethical principles have been combined with ethical imperatives from several computing codes of ethics to reflect the professional positive responsibility of software developers. These principles have been framed as a set of 32 questions related to stakeholders in a software project, and to generalized responsibility as a software professional. These questions are placed in the bottom frame of the SoDIS Analysis screen (Figure 4).

There may be some special circumstances that are not covered by these 32 questions, so the system enables the SoDIS analyst to add questions to the analysis list. When the analysis is complete there are several usage statistics reports that give various snapshots of the major ethical issues with the project.

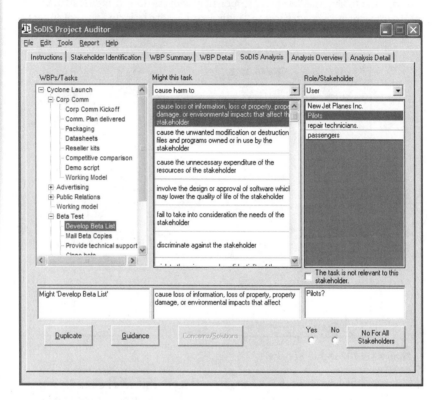

Figure 4 SoDIS Analysis screen

When an ethical concern has been identified, the analyst gets an ethical concern form (Figure 5) that asks the analyst to record their concern with the task and record a potential solution. The most critical part of this process is on this form, where the analyst is asked to assess the significance of their concern with the work breakdown package being analyzed. If the problem is significant then they have to determine whether the problem requires a modification of the task, deletion of the task from the project, or the addition of a task to overcome the anticipated problem. It is these adjustments to the software requirements or management project plan that complete risk analysis.

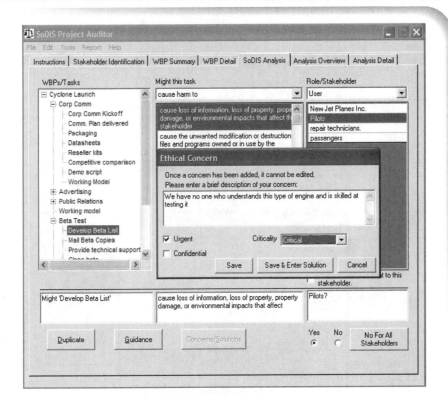

Figure 5 Concern Screen

The process of developing a SoDIS requires the consideration of ethical development and the ethical impacts of a product—the ethical dimensions of software development. The SoDIS analysis process also facilitates the identification of new requirements or work breakdown packages that can be used as a means to address the ethical issues. Figure 6 shows the proposed solution—two added tasks to the original project plan that identify the need to start to identify people who are competent to test the proposed new software.

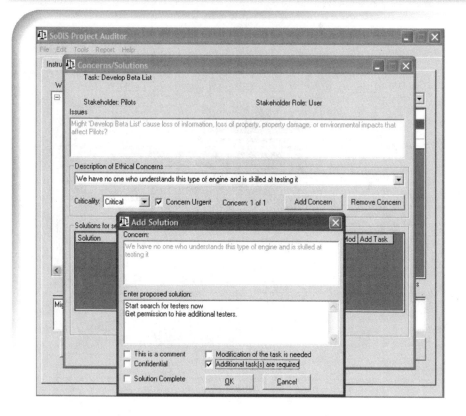

Figure 6 Proposed Solution Screen

The identified things to do need to be incorporated into the software project management plan. The early identification of these software modifications saves the developer time and money, and leads to a more coherent and ethically sensitive software product. When the developer arrives at the point of testing the jet engine they will have experienced testers.

The SoDIS analysis process also facilitates the identification of new tasks or modifications to existing tasks that can be used as a means to mediate or avoid identified concerns. The identified tasks need to be incorporated into the software project management plan. The early identification of these software modifications saves the developer time and money and leads to a more coherent and ethically sensitive software product. This phase of the SoDIS process is a pre-audit of a detailed project plan that is developed late in an SDLC.

The SoDIS process also includes a consideration of other phases of an SDLC. Some risks can be identified when a project is first conceived or can be identified at an intermediate stage when the customer's desires are being specified in the requirements phase. The SoDIS Project Auditor also provides a pre-audit for these two project phases.

A complete SoDIS process (1) broadens the types of risks considered in software development by (2) more accurately identifying relevant project stakeholders. The utilization of the SoDIS process will reduce the probability of the types of errors identified by Farbey. The SoDIS should be part of an SDLC.

Integration of the SoDIS and an SDLC

Barry Boehm's modified spiral model—the Win-Win Model (WW)—comes close to meeting (1) the stakeholder identification problem and (2) the risk limitation problem. His Win-Win spiral software development technique is used to elicit project requirements for all stakeholders. At each phase of a project's development the analyst identifies the stakeholders for that stage, determines the win conditions for each new stakeholder, and then negotiates to have these new win condition requirements fit into a set of Win-Win conditions that have already been established for all concerned. There is a set of win conditions for the Aegis radar customer. These conditions would be identified and a process developed to meet those conditions. Then new stakeholders would be identified, for example the sailors using the system on the Vincennes, and their win conditions would be identified. They would consider it important to be able to clearly determine if an approaching aircraft were hostile. This win-condition would be incorporated, via negotiation, into the existing process plan.

Although this approach is similar to Rawl's wide reflective equilibrium in deriving a coherent set of requirements through negotiation, the ethical element is missing from Boehm's method. There is no methodology to identify ethically relevant stakeholders nor is there an ethical foundation for the negotiation process.

The method is also limited in that it assumes all stakeholders are equal and that they will equally be aware of and able to describe their own win conditions. The negotiation amongst stakeholders will be unjust and will likely lead to failed systems, unless, contrary to fact, each stakeholder has such an equal identification and descriptive skill of their own win conditions. There is also an implicit assumption that all requirements are negotiable. As the method is constructed, all requirements have equal status—none are rejected because they are morally impermissible or required because they are morally mandatory.

This model has two strengths. First it comes closer to properly expanding stakeholder identification than other software engineering methodologies. Unlike all of the other approaches that presume the impact analysis is done as a single process, the Win-Win model is iterative requiring a re-identification of system stakeholders at each stage of the development process.

The negotiation activities include:

1. Identification of system stakeholders—defined as "anyone that has a direct business interest in the system or product to be built and will be rewarded for a successful outcome or criticized if the effort fails."
2. Determinations of the stakeholder's win conditions.

3. Negotiation of the stakeholder's win conditions to reconcile them into a set of win-win conditions for all concerned.

Although risks and stakeholders are incorporated into the model, negotiations Activity 1 does not identify a broad base of stakeholders. The sailors using the Aegis radar system and the passengers who lost their lives would not be stakeholders as would the dyslexics viewing a poorly designed web site

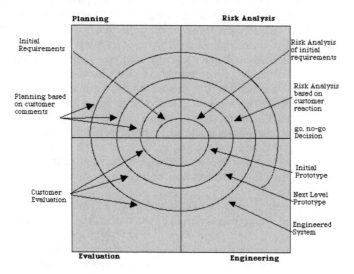

Figure 7   Spiral Model adopted from Pressman _Software Engineering:_
A Practitioner's Approach

The types of risks are also limited. The Project Risks include: difficulties associated with budget, schedule, personnel (staffing and organization), resources, and customer. Technical Risks include technical uncertainty, technical obsolescence, and difficulties in interfacing, maintenance, design, and implementation. The Business Risks include: market risk (the product no one wants), product line skew (product does not match product line), and management risk (change in physical management or focus). These risks do not include risks to the users of the Aegis radar system.

In a further modification to his model, Boehm adds three process milestones to help mark the completion of one spiral. These three "anchor points"—life cycle objectives, life cycle architecture, and initial operational capacity—provide technical information used to make decisions about whether and how the project might proceed.

The Win-Win model has the ability to analyze risk and incorporate stakeholders. The inclusion of a SoDIS analysis as a starting point for the project and as the fourth anchor point of the Win-Win model would be an effective SDLC which addressed the technical and ethical risks of software development.

The SoDIS process completes the process of risk analysis and can be included as a pre-audit process in most software development methodologies. It facilitates the expansion of software risk analysis beyond the technical issues. Using this pre-audit process in tests in the UK and the USA facilitated the early identification of project risks. Using a SoDIS process will make producing software of high quality and producing software that is ethically sensitive second nature to the software developer.

Acknowledgments:
This research was partially funded by NSF Grant 9874684 and was made possible by a non-instructional assignment from East Tennessee State University. An earlier version of this paper appeared in *The Australian Journal of Information Systems* Vol. 9 No 2.

References:
Boehm, B,"Using the WINWIN Spiral Model: A Case Study," *Computer* July 1998.

Buglione, L and Abran, A, LIME: A Three-Dimensional Measurement Model for Life Cycle Project Management," *Proceedings of the International Workshop on Software Measurement* September 1999.

Farbey B, Land F and Targett D, *How to assess your IT investment,* Butterworth Heinemann, 1993.

Gert B, *Morality,* Oxford University Press, 1998.

Gotterbarn D, *Computer Ethics: Responsibility Regained,* National Forum, The Phi Kappa Phi Journal, Vol 71 No 3., 1991.

Gotterbarn D, "Promoting Ethical responsibility in Software Development," *Proceedings of the AICE Computer Ethics Conference,* 1999.

Gotterbarn D and Miller K and Rogerson S, *Software Engineering Code of Ethics,* Communications of the ACM, 1998.

http://computer.org/computer/code-of-ethics.pdf.

Green R M, *The Ethical Manager,* Macmillan Publishing, 1994.

McCarthy J, *Dynamics of Software Development,* Microsoft Press, 1996.

Rogerson S and Gotterbarn D, *"The Ethics of Software Project Management," in Ethics and Information Technology,* ed. Göran Collste, New Academic Publisher, Delhi, 1998.

Lilliputian Computer Ethics

John Weckert

1 Introduction

Nanotechnology and quantum computing have the potential to radically change information technology. If these technologies are successful, and there are signs that they will be, computers will become very, very small, very, very fast, and have an enormous amount of memory relative to computers of today. This is creating excitement in some quarters, but anxiety in others. Speaking of nanotechnology, in a recent and much publicised article, Bill Joy wrote that

> It is most of all the power of destructive self-replication in genetics, nanotechnology, and robotics (GNR) that should give us pause. ...The only realistic alternative I see is relinquishment: to limit development of the technologies that are too dangerous by limiting our pursuit of certain kinds of knowledge." [Bill Joy, Wired, 8.04, 2000]

Given the variety of benefits promised by nanotechnology in medicine, the environment, and information technology, to pick out just a few, Joy's claim seems a little strong. This paper will discuss a few potential developments to see what the appropriate reaction to this technology is. Are the worries enough to give his call for a halt to research any plausibility?

Before proceeding to examine the claim that some research in computing should not take place, we need to look at nanotechnology and quantum computing, to see what dangers there might be.

2 Nanotechnology and Quantum Computing

Nanotechnology is relatively new, although it was first mooted in by Richard Feynman in a lecture entitled "There's plenty of room at the bottom," in 1959. Nanotechnology involves the manipulation of individual atoms and molecules in order to build

This essay originally appeared in *Metaphilosophy,* Vol. 33, No. 3, 2002: 366-375. Copyright © 2002 by Blackwell Publishers. Reprinted with permission.

structures. One nanometre is one billionth of a metre (three to five atoms across), and "nanoscience and nanotechnology generally refer to the world as it works on the nanometer scale, say, from one nanometer to several hundred nanometers" [NSTC, 1999]. This technology is important because it enables very small things to be built, and gives great control over the properties of the materials constructed. This technology is claimed to have enormous benefits in a variety of fields. Nanoparticles inserted into the body could diagnose and cure diseases, building materials could adapt to the weather conditions, cheap and clean energy could be produced, sensoring devices could become much more sensitive, and computers much faster and have more memory. While these benefits have not yet accrued, they are not mere speculation. The theories underlying the proposed applications are, it is argued, scientifically based. The technology for manipulating atoms individually is available, and in 1989 IBM physicists produced the IBM logo by manipulating atoms.

The main interest in this paper is the relationship of nanotechnology with computing. Quantum computers will be much more powerful. According to one researcher, it is expected that a quantum computer would be able to perform some computations that could not be performed by all the current computers on the planet linked together, before the end of the universe [Simmons, 2000]. Computers will also become very small. For example, at one end of the spectrum there would be devices that incorporate "nanoscale computers and several binding sites that are shaped to fit specific molecules, [that] would circulate freely throughout the body ..." [Merkle, 1997]. At the other end "we should be able to build mass storage devices that can store more than 100 billion billion bytes in a volume the size of a sugar cube, and massively parallel computers of the same size that can deliver a billion billion instructions per second—a billion times more than today's desktop computers" [Merkle, 1997]. Smalley is a little more cautious, but still estimates that the efficiency of computers will be increased by a factor of millions [1999]. In addition there could be "detecting devices so sensitive that they could pick up the equivalent of the drop of a pin on the other side of the world" [Davies, 1996].

This technology, if it develops in the predicted matter, will facilitate some interesting developments. Monitoring and surveillance will become very easy, particularly when the new computer and communication technologies are linked. People with microscopic implants will be able to be tracked using Geographic Positioning Systems (GPSs) just as cars can be now, only more efficiently. One need never be lost again! Other implants could increase our memory, reasoning ability, sight, hearing, and so on. Some argue that the distinction between humans and machine may no longer be useful [Kurzweil, 1999]. And virtual reality will be indistinguishable from reality itself.

Before considering some of the ethical issues raised by these possible developments, it is worth asking just how credible are the claims. Many of the claims are quite credible, it seems. Many are being made by researchers with impressive records in computer science and in other sciences, and research is being supported by reputable universities and governments. More importantly, some progress has been made. It is already possible to manipulate individual atoms, as stated earlier, nanotubes have been developed, and some progress has been made on building simple quantum computers. Theoretically it can work, and progress has been made on building some applications. There is enough evidence to suggest that nanotechnology and quantum computing are possible, probably sometime around the middle of this century, and so it is worth looking at any ethical questions that they might raise.

3 Ethical Questions

While nanotechnology has potential benefits and dangers in a wide variety of areas, for example in health and in the environment as previously mentioned, we will consider here just some potential dangers in the computing area. That there are also benefits in this area is not being questioned.

There are at least two sets of issues. One set concerns existing problems that will be exacerbated by the miniaturisation of computers. This miniaturisation will involve the development of smaller, much more powerful machines (much faster and with much more memory), and with much more sensitive input devices. The second set concerns potentially new problems, problems that as yet have not arisen, at least not in any significant way.

3.1 Exacerbated problems

It is likely that most existing ethical problems in computing will be exacerbated. Easier and faster copying onto ever smaller devices will make protecting intellectual property more difficult. There will be more worries about Internet content as that content becomes more realistic and more difficult to control. It is likely however that one of the greatest impacts will be on privacy.

Privacy

Privacy problems will be enormously increased. Vast databases that can be accessed at very high speeds will enable governments, businesses, and so on to collect, store, and access much more information about individuals than is possible today. In addition, the capacity for data mining, the exploration and analysis of very large amounts of data for the purpose of discovering meaningful and useful rules and patterns, will increase dramatically. And perhaps most importantly, the monitoring and surveillance of workers, prisoners, and in fact, the population in general, will be greatly enhanced with the use of small, powerful computers and new sensoring devices for input. GPSs will be able to specify the location of individuals, cameras with artificial neural nets (or other learning technologies), will be able to pick out unusual behaviour in crowds, or just on the streets, and notify authorities.

While all of these possibilities have benefits, for example for safety and efficiency, the possibility is also opened for large scale control of individuals, either by governments, employers, or others with authority. There will be a need for the reassessment of privacy legislation, the use of personal information by governments and corporations, and guidelines and legislation for the use of monitoring devices.

3.2 New problems

The problems in this category are new in the sense that they have not needed to be faced in any important way yet. Just three will be mentioned here.

Artificial intelligence

If machines are developed that behave in much the same way as humans do, in a wide variety of contexts, the issue will arise of whether or not they are things with moral rights and responsibilities. Consideration would need to be given as how they should be treated. If they behaved like us, would we be justified in treating them differently?

Bionic humans

Chip implants in humans that enhance various of the senses, memory and perhaps even other capacities such a reasoning ability and creativity, may blur the distinction between human and machine. We already have spectacles, hearing aids, cochlear implants, hair implants, skin grafts, tooth implants, pace makers, transplants, and so on, so why should these more advanced implants matter? Perhaps there is a difference between helping people to be "normal," that is, correcting a deficiency, and making a normal person a "super human." But it would need to be spelt out just why this is the case.

Virtual Reality

Virtual reality systems will improve to the point where it may become difficult to tell the difference between "real" and "virtual" reality. There may be no apparent difference between really hang gliding and doing so virtually.

4 Should the Research Be Controlled?

If Joy is right about the dangers of this new technology, then there is some research that computer scientists ought not do, and if they do, they can be held morally responsible for the consequences of that research. Or so it would seem. There are however a number of issues that need to be sorted out before we can be confident in affirming this. One concerns the differences between pure research, technological development, and the use to which that development is put. The first question here is whether there is any pure research that should not be undertaken. This issue is often discussed under the heading of "forbidden knowledge;" is there any knowledge that we should not attempt to discover? A related question is whether there is any technology that should not be developed, and the further one of limits to the uses of that technology.

Earlier a distinction was made between knowledge, the technology developed from that knowledge, and the uses to which the knowledge is put. Certain uses of knowledge (or the technology based on the knowledge) ought to be avoided if those uses cause harm. The emphasis for the moment is on the knowledge itself. The knowledge must also be distinguished from the method of gaining that knowledge. Clearly certain methods for gaining knowledge are wrong, for example those that cause harm. (In particular situations it might be that there is some greater good that makes some degree of harm, both in the gaining of knowledge and in its use, permissible.) The question of whether the knowledge itself ought to be forbidden is, or seems to be, quite a different matter. The knowledge is neither morally good nor bad in the way that the methods or uses might be.

It is difficult to make sense of the claim that there is some knowledge that is morally bad in itself regardless of any consequences. It is certainly difficult to find any
examples. It is easy to find examples of knowledge that have harmful consequences.
Joy himself seems to acknowledge this when he says that knowledge of nanotechnology should be limited in order to limit the technologies that would be developed
from that knowledge. If knowledge has harmful consequences should it be forbidden? Not always, because many types of knowledge can be put to both beneficial
and harmful uses, and we do not want to automatically rule out the beneficial.

At this point it is worth looking briefly at Somerville's argument in *The Ethical Canary,*
because perhaps the discussion should not be couched just in consequentialist
terms. Her two basic principles are these:

> ... we have a profound respect for life, in particular human life ... and
> we must act to protect the human spirit—the intangible, invisible,
> immeasurable reality that we need to find meaning in life and to make
> life worth living—that deeply intuitive sense of relatedness or connect-
> edness to the world and the universe in which we live. [2000, xi – xii]

She suggests that if scientific research violates either one of these principles,
then it ought to be avoided even if it has some beneficial consequences. Her second principle has particular relevance for nanotechnology and quantum computing, although she does not discuss these fields. We will return to this later, and now
consider some more consequentialist arguments.

To help to clarify matters, the consequences of knowledge can be divided into
two groups, physical and mental. Physical consequences are always uses to which
the knowledge is put. The knowledge that is of most concern is that which will almost
certainly be used in harmful ways. There may be no way to prevent the harm without preventing the knowledge in the first place. A case could be made that that
knowledge is not the fit subject of research and ought to be forbidden. Mental consequences do not necessarily involve uses. Some knowledge is such that simply
knowing it has negative consequences on life. Nicholas Rescher puts it this way:

> There are various things we simply ought not to know. If we did not
> have to live our lives amidst a fog of uncertainty about a whole range
> of matters that are actually of fundamental interest and importance
> to us, it would no longer be a human mode of existence that we would
> live. Instead, we would become a being of another sort, perhaps
> angelic, perhaps machine-like, but certainly not human. [1978, 9]

Suppose that as a result of research in IT, it became known how to build machines
that in behaviour were indistinguishable from humans, and moreover, that it was
obvious that these machines were purely deterministic and without freewill. If we
knew this, we would obviously have to see ourselves in a new light. Would we, in our
present stage of evolution, be able to cope? If the GNR technology discussed by Joy
develops in the manner that he fears, would we be able to continue to live happy and

satisfying lives? If some knowledge has profound effects on the way we see ourselves, should it be forbidden? It seems that here, just as in the case of knowledge that almost inevitably leads to harm, a plausible argument can be made for forbidding it.

It has just been suggested that a case can be made in certain circumstances to restrict or prohibit research, but who should do this restricting or prohibiting? Does the State have a role?

A strong statement for the freedom of science from political control is supplied by David Baltimore:

> First, the criteria determining what areas to restrain inevitably express certain sociopolitical attitudes that reflect a dominant ideology. ... Second, attempts to restrain directions of scientific inquiry are more likely to be generally disruptive of science than to provide the desired specific restraints. [1979, 41]

A number of arguments are offered to support these claims. First, is what Baltimore calls the "Error of Futurism," that is the supposition that we can predict the consequences of any research accurately enough to make any sensible decisions. The second argument is a version of one of John Stuart Mill's. Freedom of speech and expression allows the development of new ideas, increases the choices in life, and generally renews and vitalises life and makes it richer. A third argument is that repression in scientific research is likely to lead to repression in other areas and so will increase fear rather than strength in society. A fourth argument is based on the unpredictability of science. Even if some research is not allowed, the knowledge to which it may have led might emerge from other research quite unexpectedly.

This argument is aimed at pure or basic research, and Baltimore admits that the further one moves toward applications of research, the weaker these arguments become. If these arguments hold for pure research, then all of the responsibility for undertaking worthwhile research rests on the scientists themselves, which is where, according to Baltimore and others, it ought to rest. It must be noted here that it does not necessarily follow that the scientists' responsibilities extend to the uses to which the knowledge is put. They create or generate the knowledge from their research but others decide how it is to be used. Whether this separation of responsibilities is ultimately sustainable is another matter, but for the moment we will accept it.

We now return to Baltimore's arguments that research should not be externally controlled. His first argument, the "Error of Futurism" is that prediction is too unreliable to provide the basis for any restrictions on research. Consider for example Weizenbaum's prediction that research into speech recognition could have no useful consequences [1984, 271]. It now appears to be an important tool in Human Computer Interface design for users with certain disabilities. Prediction is certainly fraught with danger, however we often must base our actions on predictions, on what we believe may happen, and it is not clear why the case of research should be any different. The second argument is that freedom of speech and expression allows the development of new ideas, thereby increasing life's choices and generally making it richer. This is true, and this form of freedom is undoubtedly an important good, but it is not the only one, and can be in conflict with others. In general we are restricted in the performance of actions that will, or are likely to, harm others. Again it is unclear why research should be treated differently. The third argument is that repression in scientific research is likely to lead to repression in other areas and so will increase fear rather than strengthen society. While we can agree that repression is not good, many things are restricted, or repressed in a civilised society, for example, certain research using human subjects and driving under the influence of alcohol, but these restrictions would surely reduce rather than increase fear. If probable harm is as closely associated with knowledge as suggested earlier, there is no reason why pure research should be treated differently from other aspects of life. The final argument was that, because of the unpredictability of science, the undesired knowledge might emerge unexpectedly from research other than that which was disallowed. This is true but not to the point. While it may not be possible to ensure that some undesirable knowledge will be discovered, it is almost certainly possible to reduce that probability.

It is then, permissible or even obligatory on occasions to restrict or forbid research on the ground that mental or physical harm is likely to result from it. However, this should not be done lightly, because freedom in this area is important, not only for the good of science but also for the good of society. There should be a presumption in favour of freedom of research. If research is to be restricted the burden of proof should be on those who want to restrict it. However, there seems to be a conflicting intuition here. If a prima facie case can be made that some particular research will most likely cause harm, either mentally or physically, then the burden of proof should be on those who want the research carried out to demonstrate that it is safe. The situation then appears to be this. There is a presumption in favour of freedom until such time as a prima facie case is made that the research is dangerous. The burden of proof then shifts from those opposing the research to those supporting it. At that stage the research should not begin or be continued until a good case has been made that it is safe.

The conclusion to this point then is that the case against the state having a role in the control of scientific research has not been made, but that such control has dangers and it should not be embraced lightly. The argument so far has focused primarily on pure research, because that is where it is most difficult to make a case for control. However, it is not obviously much different in the case of technological development, one of the fruits of pure research. Just as a scientist can say that he or she is just adding to knowledge and therefore has no responsibility for the use to which that knowledge is put, so technologists can say that they are just developing tools, and it not up to them how those tools are used.

5 Nanotechnology and Quantum Computing Research

It has been argued in this paper that nanotechnology and quantum computing do raise some worrying ethical questions. While there seems to be potential for great benefit, it is not benefit unalloyed, and some of the potential problems were outlined earlier. It has also been argued that there are cases in which it could be justified to halt certain types of research. The question here is whether research into nanotechnology and quantum computing is in this category.

Given the quite fundamental changes that these technologies could facilitate, it is not enough to merely consider the potential benefits and harms as they might apply to life as we know it now. The issue is more one of the kind of life that we want. Can we, and do we want to, live with artificial *intelligences?* We can happily live with fish that swim better than we do, with dogs that hear better, hawks that see and fly better, and so on, but things that can reason better seem to be in a different and altogether more worrying category. Do we want to be "super human" relative to our current abilities, with implants that enhance our senses, our memory, and our reasoning ability? What would such implants do to our view of what it is to be human? Does it matter if our experiences are "real" or not, that is, if they are had in a virtual world or in the real one? Would there be any sense in that distinction? These are all big questions that cannot be answered here, but the suggestion is that they are the important ones when considering the future of research into nanotechnology and quantum computing. These questions seem related to Somerville's second principle, that of protecting the human spirit. Perhaps research into nanotechnology and quantum computing do not violate that principle, but much more examination of the issues is warranted.

References
Baltimore, David, (1979), Limiting science: a biologist's perspective, in G. Holton and R.S. Morrison (eds.) *Limits of Scientific Inquiry,* W.W. Norton, 37–45.

Davies, Paul, (1996), Foreword in Milburn, Gerard, *Quantum Technology,* Allen and Unwin.

Feynman, Richard, (1959), There's Plenty of Room at the Bottom: An Invitation to Enter a New Field of Physics, talk given on December 29th at the annual meeting of the American Physical Society at the California Institute of Technology Online at http://www.zyvex.com/nanotech/feynman.html accessed 27/03/01

Joy, Bill, (2000), Why the future doesn't need us, *Wired* magazine, 8.04.

Kurzweil, Ray, (1999), *The Age of Spiritual Machines: When Computers Exceed Human Intelligence,* Allen and Unwin.

Merkle, Ralph, (1997), It's a small, small, small world, MIT Technology Review, Feb/Mar. 25. Online at http://www.techreview.com/articles/fm97/merkle.html accessed 02/11/00.

NSTC, (1999), Nanotechnology: Shaping the World Atom by Atom, report of National Science and Technology Council (NSTC), Committee on Technology, The Interagency Working Group on Nanoscience, Engineering and Technology, online at http://itri.loyola.edu/nano/IWGN.Public.Brochure/ accessed 27/03/01

Rescher, Nicholas, (1987), *Forbidden Knowledge and Other Essays on the Philosophy of Cognition,* D. Reidel.

Simmons, Michelle, (2000), Faster, smaller, smarter, talk at Small Things, Big Science: Nanotechnology, Horizons of Science forum, University of Technology, 23 November.

Smalley, R. E., (1999), Nanotechnology, Prepared Written Statement and Supplemental Material of R. E. Smalley, Rice University, June 22, online at http://www.house.gov/science/smalley_062299.htm accessed 27/03/01.

Somerville, Margaret, (2000), *The Ethical Canary: Science, Society and the Human Spirit,* Viking.

Weizenbaum, Joseph, (1984), *Computer Power and Human Reason: From Judgement to Calculation,* Penguin Books, (originally published San Francisco, W.H. Freeman, 1976).

Outstanding New Titles:

Computer Science Illuminated, Second Edition
Nell Dale and John Lewis
ISBN: 0-7637-0799-6
©2004

Programming and Problem Solving with C++, Fourth Edition
Nell Dale and Chip Weems
ISBN: 0-7637-0798-8
©2004

Programming and Problem Solving with Java
Nell Dale, Chip Weems, and Mark R. Headington
ISBN: 0-7637-0490-3
©2003

C++ Plus Data Structures, Third Edition
Nell Dale
ISBN: 0-7637-0481-4
©2003

Databases Illuminated
Catherine Ricardo
ISBN: 0-7637-3314-8
©2004

Applied Data Structures with C++
Peter Smith
ISBN: 0-7637-2562-5
©2004

Foundations of Algorithms Using Java Pseudocode
Richard Neapolitan
and Kumarss Naimipour
ISBN: 0-7637-2129-8
©2004

Foundations of Algorithms Using C++ Pseudocode, Third Edition
Richard Neapolitan
and Kumarss Naimipour
ISBN: 0-7637-2387-8
©2004

Artificial Intelligence Illuminated
Ben Coppin
ISBN: 0-7637-3230-3
©2004

Managing Software Projects
Frank Tsui
ISBN: 0-7637-2546-3
©2004

The Essentials of Computer Organization and Architecture
Linda Null and Julia Lobur
ISBN: 0-7637-0444-X
©2003

Readings in CyberEthics, Second Edition
Richard Spinello
and Herman Tavani
ISBN: 0-7637-2410-6
©2004

A Complete Guide to C#
David Bishop
ISBN: 0-7637-2249-9
©2004

C#.NET Illuminated
Art Gittleman
ISBN: 0-7637-2593-5
©2004

A First Course in Complex Analysis with Applications
Dennis G. Zill
and Patrick Shanahan
ISBN: 0-7637-1437-2
©2003

Discrete Mathematics, Second Edition
James L. Hein
ISBN: 0-7637-2210-3
©2003

Take Your Courses to the Next Level

Turn the page to preview new and forthcoming titles in Computer Science and Math from Jones and Bartlett...

Providing solutions for students and educators in the following disciplines:

- Introductory Computer Science
- Java
- C++
- Databases
- C#
- Data Structures

- Algorithms
- Network Security
- Software Engineering
- Discrete Mathematics
- Engineering Mathematics
- Complex Analysis

Please visit http://computerscience.jbpub.com/ and http://math.jbpub.com/ to learn more about our exciting publishing programs in these disciplines.